KT-473-837

WOMEN IN AMERICAN THEATRE

WINCHESTER

KA 0366553 4

WOMEN IN AMERICAN THEATRE

REVISED AND EXPANDED
THIRD EDITION

EDITED BY
HELEN KRICH CHINOY
AND
LINDA WALSH JENKINS

THEATRE COMMUNICATIONS GROUP   NEW YORK   2006

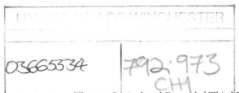

03665534   792.973
           CH4

Women in American Theatre: Revised and Expanded Third Edition is
copyright © 1981, 1987, 2006 by Helen Krich Chinoy and Linda Walsh Jenkins

Women in American Theatre: Revised and Expanded Third Edition is published by
Theatre Communications Group, Inc., 520 Eighth Ave., 24th Floor, New York, NY 10018-4156.

All rights reserved. Except for brief passages quoted in newspaper, magazine, radio or television reviews, no part of this book may be reproduced in any form or by any means, electronic or mechanical, including photocopying or recording, or by an information storage and retrieval system, without permission in writing from the publisher.

Professionals and amateurs are hereby warned that this material, being fully protected under the Copyright Laws of the United States of America and all other countries of the Berne and Universal Copyright Conventions, is subject to a royalty. All rights including, but not limited to, professional, amateur, recording, motion picture, recitation, lecturing, public reading, radio and television broadcasting, and the rights of translation into foreign languages are expressly reserved. Particular emphasis is placed on the question of readings and all uses of the contents of this book by educational institutions, permission for which must be secured from the publisher.

Please refer to Endnotes and Biographies at the back of the book for all credit information and details about the contributors.

Originally published in 1981 by Crown Publishers, Inc.

This publication is made possible in part with public funds from
the New York State Council on the Arts, a State Agency.

TCG books are exclusively distributed to the book trade by
Consortium Book Sales and Distribution, 1045 Westgate Dr., St. Paul, MN 55114.

LIBRARY OF CONGRESS CATALOGING-IN-PUBLICATION DATA
Women in American Theatre / edited by Helen Krich Chinoy and Linda Walsh Jenkins.—
Rev. ed.
p. cm.
Includes bibliographic references.
ISBN-13: 978-1-55936-263-4
ISBN-10: 1-55936-263-4 (pbk. : alk. paper)
1. Women in the theatre—United States. I. Chinoy, Helen Krich. II. Jenkins, Linda Walsh.

PN2286.8 .W66 2000
792'.082'0973—dc21   00-037753

Cover design by Susan Mitchell
Book design and composition by Lisa Govan

First Printing, February 2006

To Our Children
Claire Nicole, Michael, Robert and Martha

CONTENTS

UNIVERSITY OF WINCHESTER
LIBRARY

INTERROGATING THE PAST, OR WOMEN IN THEATRE— THEN AND NOW

As we enter this new millennium, it is both very rewarding and very challenging to be preparing the third edition of *Women in American Theatre*. Our book has become an ongoing stocktaking of the wide-ranging and ever-changing participation of women in the complex life of the American theatre. Because this project has been part of our lives for more than twenty-five years, Linda Jenkins and I want to share some personal stocktaking. Hence we offer two prefaces that suggest the interaction of the personal and the political in our work.

I want to take you with me on a nonlinear, sort of postmodern hopscotch in and out of several different decades of my life. Let me start with "then"— suggesting briefly how women fared in two contrasting theatres of the 1930s.

In 1935 my mother took me across the Hudson River from my home town of Newark to New York City for a very special treat. To please the stage-struck thirteen-year-old, she had gotten tickets to see our first Broadway show. It was *Victoria Regina*, the starring vehicle in which Helen Hayes, whose career started before the 1920s, transformed herself from the sprightly young queen in 1837 through her more than fifty-year reign, to the time when she had become a dowdy old lady. I still remember the great expedition and the virtuosity of the actress. But I realized even then, I think, that the performance had little to do with me or my immigrant mother or the life we were living in the midst of the Great Depression a half-hour away in Newark. I discovered years later that, in a way, it also had little to do with Hayes herself. Reminiscing in 1958, shortly after a Broadway theatre had been named in her honor, she recalled that all that was needed for the theatre of her youth were some "personal gifts" and some "technique for communicating through her instrument." But in preparing her roles, Hayes revealed, "I gazed outward toward the world—not inward to myself . . . I learned that there was never going to be any chance for me to use my real self or remembered experience of my own." Only very late in her career, when playing in Eugene O'Neill's *A Touch of the Poet*, did she feel that "something happened inside that made it possible to communicate using every part of me." She called it "my great divestiture."

Most of her career she no doubt molded herself to the accepted image of woman onstage and off. According to a study of Pulitzer Prize plays up to the 1940s, a woman was conceived as someone whose sole motivation in life is the search for romantic love; she is emotional rather than rational in her deliberations, rarely works at a job, almost never becomes a successful career person, is physically passive and is either totally selfless or sinfully selfish. Not only her creations but the playwright herself was defined by those widely held values. Even at the end of the 1930s, a decade in which the Pulitzer Prize was won by Susan Glaspell for *Alison's House* and Zoe Akins for *The Old Maid*—the second and third of these coveted prizes awarded to women—critical opinion was still busily cataloguing the intellectual and creative limitations to be found "When Ladies Write Plays."

This was the view of the critical mainstream in 1939 when I started college at New York University. During that first academic year, the big attractions on Broadway were *Life with Father*, *The Man Who Came to Dinner* and *The Male Animal*. Except as necessary actresses, women were scarcely visible. They were certainly absent from the texts we studied in our classes and from our drama-club productions. I don't recall anything by women in the summer stock company with which I acted.

Most of us didn't question this established order because we weren't sure how to think about ourselves as women. Of course the authority figures around us did. When I was awarded a graduate fellowship, the professor in charge warned me not to get married. The department did not want all the money they were investing in me to be wasted. My father was concerned about wasting money, too, but he was worried that no one would marry me if I had another degree. To succeed, we felt we had to imitate "the boys," though for them marriage was not a career impediment. I guess I played the role well enough to earn my Master of Arts degree and a teaching assistantship, and in 1946 I was recommended for my first regular teaching position. The English department at the Newark College of Rutgers University needed someone to teach veterans on the GI Bill in an accelerated program. The chairman interviewed me again and again; he wasn't sure I could manage male students. The college had never had a woman teaching, and even though I had the proper credentials all they could see was a "girl" in her early twenties with all the limitations that implied. But World War II had created a shortage of teachers. I was hired, and to their surprise I managed very well. The guys had fun whistling when I came to class, but I succeeded in convincing most of these highly critical and demanding young men who had lost part of their youth fighting in the war that there was some value in learning to write well, study poems and novels, and even act in plays.

After two years, during which I spent a summer in England studying Elizabethan drama and started to work toward a Ph.D. degree at Columbia and on a book about actors, I did what a woman academic was not supposed to do: I fell in love, left my job to get married and joined my husband in Toronto, where he had just started his academic career. I eagerly applied to the university's English department for an opening to teach freshman English, but at the interview I was told that despite my good preparation, the university did not hire people with outside interests like a husband and a home.

Devastated and furious, I took various odd jobs to supplement our very meager income. Despite academic isolation, I worked away on the book I had begun in Newark with Toby Cole, my sister-in-law. It would be published in 1949 as *Actors and Acting* and has been continuously in print. We were amazed that no one had ever thought to gather the wisdom of actors about their craft. But actors were perceived from Plato on much as women were— emotional, irrational, childlike creatures who really didn't know what they were doing. It was our reading of Konstantin Stanislavsky, whose theories and theatre elevated the artistic and social status of performers, that encouraged us to believe that actors would have much to tell us. We both had studied Stanislavsky's system in acting classes in Newark's lively left-wing theatre groups, where I recall acting at picket lines and in union halls. We staged anti-war, anti-Nazi agitprop plays whose dramatic formula, we used to quip, was, "In the first act, we suffer; in the second act, we give out leaflets; in the third act, we go on strike." Participation in the burgeoning workers' theatre movement exposed us to ideas of theatre as well as society that differed totally from those of Broadway, the academic world and our families. In the research and writing of a book that valorized actors I felt valorized myself, and the idea of an engaged theatre for the people would greatly influence my life's work.

It may seem odd to credit the 1930s as having a positive outcome for women, in or out of theatre. Confronted with the worst economic disaster in history, the nation turned away from the issues of women's rights, so lively in the 1920s. "Don't steal a job from a man," women were admonished as they were dismissed from factories, banks and schools. But the 1930s were paradoxical years. The depression drastically reduced the operations of show business, from about 240 shows on Broadway at the end of the 1920s to about eighty shows in 1939. As options for careers dimmed, however, a new generation of theatre artists turned their despair into the struggle for change in theatre and in society. Even Burns Mantle, a Broadway critic, sensed that "shaken by the economic element," the theatre "might be finding its soul." The "lean" years of the depression became "full" years for many women.

It was Hallie Flanagan, then teaching drama at Vassar College, who in a prophetic article in 1931 proclaimed that "[a] new theatre is being born," one that would "create a national culture by and for the working classes of America" and would undertake the "reorganization for our social order." She coauthored a widely performed agitprop play about the suffering caused by the devastating drought of the 1930s in which two young women propose most of the activism of the drama. As a schoolgirl I saw the play performed, and the piercing cry with which it ends, "Can you hear their voices?"—still rings in my ears and my conscience.

In 1935, Flanagan became head of the new Federal Theatre Project, which she transformed from a relief measure for unemployed workers into a daring, innovative network of theatres across the country. Her idea of a "free, adult, uncensored" theatre was part of what she identified as "a tremendous re-thinking, re-building and re-dreaming of America," "a new frontier against disease, dirt, poverty, illiteracy, unemployment and despair, and against self-ishness, special privilege and social apathy." It was her own struggle as a woman artist, a young widow with children, that in part inspired her large vision of our only national theatre. I feel honored to have taught most of my career in the theatre that she created at Smith College and to have written her biography for the *Notable American Women* series.

The theatres on the left were by no means feminist. Sexism was as rampant in the old left of the 1930s as it would be in the new left of the 1960s. Yet since Marxist rhetoric included the "woman question," we thought we belonged in the struggle for the ignored and exploited masses. The experience of some talented actresses in the idealistic collectivist Group Theatre exemplifies the contradictions we felt in the 1930s. Ruth Nelson confessed that as far as her career as a performer was concerned, her ten years in the Group Theatre were a disaster, but "working together with a group of like-minded people, working for a common goal outside of ourselves . . . suffering and having joy together; it was a life experience that was very deep and enriching. Nothing can compare with it, nothing." Phoebe Brand told me that the women were overlooked, not consulted, but then she sadly noted, "Nobody treated women properly in those days." Frances Farmer, the beautiful and talented Hollywood star (Jessica Lange played her in the movie *Frances*), joined the Group. She was terribly disappointed when directors Harold Clurman or Lee Strasberg ignored the needs of the women in the company. "Why don't you ask me what I want to do?" she complained and put the name of the great suffragette orator Lucy Stone on her dressing-room door. In retrospect she has been called a "premature feminist"—an apt label for many of us in the late 1930s.

Let me jump ahead to the late 1960s on our way to now. It's an easy leap to make. The postwar years and the 1950s were a bad time for theatre, which was sliding downhill as both an art and a business, despite Arthur Miller and Tennessee Williams, and it was a terrible time for women. Although we were in the "age of affluence," supposedly happily living out the American dream, we were all suffering from the "disease without a name." It was there that my old friend Betty Friedan found us and changed our lives by writing *The Feminine Mystique*. That book inspired the second feminist awakening.

By the late 1960s, in response to this "raising of our consciousness" during the era of great social turmoil, many of us were caught up in the extraordinary grassroots feminist theatres that had suddenly sprung up across the country. Let me take you back to 1969. I had completed my doctoral dissertation on a grant from the American Association of University Women, had published *Directors on Directing* with Toby Cole, and after a number of indignities, had achieved a tenured position at Smith College. My husband holds a chair in sociology, and we have a son and a daughter who love to hang around Mama's theatre. For my course in American drama, which I introduced to the college, I have arranged for a performance in our Hallie Flanagan Theatre of *How to Make a Woman* by Bobbie Ausubel's Caravan Theatre. I want you to experience with me and my students what a theatre "by, for and about women" felt like. We see two young women enter a dress shop run by men, who seduce them into certain garments the men have designed. In a dream sequence, the women are put through the rituals that will make them into acceptable women—little girls learning how to walk with ladylike steps, how to carry a purse, how to type, and so on, through rape, marriage, family and old age. Choreographed in an acting style influenced by the experiments in abstract movement of the Living Theatre and the Open Theater, the play presented what were clearly the rites of passage that every "girl" in the audience recognized. We responded to this parable of the patriarchal construction of a woman with wild applause, but then, with new "feminist energy," we broke up into small consciousness-raising groups to explore the personal facts of our own lives in relation to the political implications of what we had seen. Like the workers' theatres of the 1930s, about which I was writing at this time as part of my research for articles, books and a television documentary on the Group Theatre, the feminist theatres were a "response to a strongly felt and shared need" that "radically" changed the perceptions of those who participated. The immediacy of live theatre was the perfect medium for these "rhetorical" projects intended to transform an oppressive society and each individual in it. With such odd names as Medusa's Revenge, Woman's Patrol, and It's All Right to Be Woman, they dramatized women's anger and reinforced emerging positive self-images, evolving a collective, supportive, nonhierarchical production process that involved audiences directly in the performance event. These groups' work became part of a major redefinition of theatre.

The spring of 1975 brought tragedy to our family. My fifty-four-year-old husband was killed in a one-car accident. In the fall of that year my son took off for Asia, where he would make his career as a distinguished foreign correspondent, eventually working for CNN. My daughter, still an undergraduate at Harvard, was preparing herself for what would become a career as a wonderfully creative artist, specializing in flamenco and Gypsy culture. They and my work sustained me during difficult times.

By the late 1970s and 1980s, this vital stirring of female creativity encouraged women scholars to revise the whole story of American theatre. Paralleling the compensatory history already undertaken in other fields, we uncovered an unknown past. Since the enterprise of theatre has been mainly run by men, women in both the business and the art of theatre have usually been seen only in terms of male definitions of success. A shift of focus shed light on their obscured accomplishments. Linda Jenkins and I looked to the many different places where women's work could be found—the art theatres and little theatres of an earlier day, community theatres, educational theatres, feminist theatres and regional theatres, in addition to Broadway—to document this lost history in our anthology, *Women in American Theatre*, first published in 1981. We collected the work of many scholars, mostly women, who had researched the life of women in forgotten times and ignored venues. For all of us, it was thrilling to uncover experimental forms, organizational innovations and remarkable roles that would become a much-needed legacy for the new women's theatre of the 1980s.

Out of the renewed feminism came not only the feminist theatres but also major new awards for women, such as the Susan Smith Blackburn Prize. Major older awards, such as the Pulitzer Prize, which hadn't been given to a woman since 1958, were awarded in 1981 to Beth Henley for *Crimes of the Heart*, in 1983 to Marsha Norman for *'night, Mother*, and in 1989 to Wendy Wasserstein for *The Heidi Chronicles*. In 1982, Ellen Burstyn was installed as the first woman president of Actors' Equity in its sixty-three-year history and Colleen Dewhurst followed her in this important position in 1985. Although Broadway remained largely inhospitable, more work by women was seen in the emergent Off-Broadway and Off-Off-Broadway theatres and in the regional theatres. A few anthologies of scripts and several important theoretical, critical and historical studies were published. It looked like the 1980s would finally be the decade of women in theatre.

But just as it began to seem that women would overcome the obstacles to gaining that full equality and self-recognition that the feminist movement fought for, a vicious backlash during the Reagan years tried to derail their accomplishments and aspirations. One tactic was to blame feminism for evident malaise among women. But what was troubling women in theatre as elsewhere was that there was still a long way to go to achieve their dreams. The feminist theatres that had been a transforming experience for so many of us did not survive the cutbacks in support for the arts and were also defeated by those internal tensions analyzed by Charlotte Canning in the new coda to our original section on feminist theatre. When some theatres tried to embrace lesbian and multicultural participation, what was originally conceived as a theatre for a "universalized sisterhood" found itself fragmented and eventually destroyed by the emerging "identity politics." The "dream of a common language" gave way to "fractured discourses," and the interest shifted to "looking at theatre" through theory.

Two volumes published in 1988—*Feminism and Theatre* by Sue-Ellen Case and *The Feminist Spectator as Critic* by Jill Dolan—have become standard introductions to the burgeoning theoretical feminist literature. Adding a sampling made by Linda Jenkins from the many important articles and books analyzing feminist theory and performance to our section on Feminist Theatres was one of the motivations for this revised and enlarged third edition. This addition required elimination of some valuable earlier material, but we can all be proud to note that the explosion of new resources makes up for this change. (Keep your copy of the second edition when you buy the third!) The varied new selections on theory distinguish among different feminist positions and evolve new paradigms. This work has given theatre studies new status in the academy, where many of the writers have established a strong beachhead.

Important as it has been, the emphasis on theory has not been enthusiastically welcomed by all feminists. Some considered it elitist, removed from theatre practice and the needs of political action. It's not an unusual complaint. In my studies of the 1930s I found similar conflicts between Marxist theoreticians and theatre practice. But today there is ongoing rethinking of the dynamic interaction between theory and practice. Jill Dolan, serving as president of the American Association for Theatre in Higher Education, put it this way: "The world is changing and rather than be nostalgic for the old days when universality—or radicalism, for that matter—seemed possible in life as well as art, we need to change the terms of our work in order to connect ourselves more directly with a diverse public sphere." I was heartened to find her urging us never to forget that "theatre remains a site to which people travel to view and/or experience something together."

"Voices at the Millennium," the concluding section of our third edition, brings us back to the making of this unique theatre experience by women playwrights, directors, actors, designers, performance artists, teachers, company managers and producers from across the country. They have much to tell us in the brief selections from interviews, articles, plays, published and unpublished texts about the challenges, failures and accomplishments, the hopes and aspirations of women's work in theatre at the end of the 1990s.

Set in the context of the long history of women's experience and the varied theories captured in our book, including our original Introduction, their words inspire us each in our own way to continue to work toward those large visions of theatre that have been our heritage.

I am happy to make this my final contribution to what may be ongoing revisions and updates as women move forward. Linda and I remain close friends after our long, rewarding collaboration, and I warmly thank all those who, over a quarter of a century, have shared this adventure with us.

Helen Krich Chinoy
December 2003

THEATRE, ACTIVISM AND PERSONAL CHANGE

I left a tenured position at Northwestern University in 1989 to try different ways of writing and being in the world. And although theatre has nourished my imagination, spirit and quests for many years, it is no longer the fabric through which I filter questions. Unlike my coeditor, Helen Krich Chinoy, I have stepped out of the field. I offer a version of my journey as an example of how theatre provides a way for the human spirit to grow and a nexus for political and spiritual interests, as well as occasional employment. If theatre can provide a happy medium for me to articulate my current passions, I may dip into its waters once again.

Helen and I first met at a theatre convention in Minneapolis in 1974. I was completing a dissertation on the performances of Native Americans as American theatre, and she was one of the most admired scholars in the field. Our concern that women's stories be included in a proposed multivolume history of American theatre, designed to honor this country's bicentennial, led to our creating a volume by and about women. Although there are differences between the two of us in ethnicity, age and other such seemingly significant aspects of what is often called identity, the two of us have enjoyed a mutually enlightening and heartfelt affinity for more than thirty-five years.

How did I get into women's studies from Native American studies? Or was it vice versa? How did I get to Minnesota from Texas, from an undergraduate degree in English to theatre studies, from the segregated construction of Southern Lady to a loudmouthed hippie? Although I have been involved in the theatre since the age of four, when I played a Mop and Mow in *The Tempest* with Fort Worth's Reeder School of the Arts, it may be that the journey truly began with desegregation. I entered activism for girls in 1957–58, at about the same time that I began playing my small role in the great project of unraveling segregation. After organizing a Y-Teens club in my semirural Texas junior high school in the late 1950s, I made monthly bus trips into downtown Fort Worth to meet with other teenagers at the whites-only YWCA. Since white adults never talked about segregation, much less explained it, I thought like many white kids that racial separation was something black people and white people had agreed on mutually. When the white women at the Y explained segregation to me and other girl leaders at these monthly sessions, our world spun.

I was invited to participate in the merging of the black and white Y's, and this activity took me into black schools and to leadership retreats with black and white girls. Black and white women taught us nonviolent civil-rights strategies and invited us to imagine solutions for changing our own communities. I realized that segregation had cheated me of the opportunity to grow up singing and learning with these girls, and I had been denied the concept of "Woman" now being presented to me by the black female leaders. From this project, which continued throughout my years in high school, I went to Rice University at a time when that Southern institution was combating in court its whites-only founding charter. I participated in play readings and discussions with black and white teenagers conducted by the Houston Council on Human Relations. Desegregation soon became thought of as integration.

Although my college years were marked by the assassination of John F. Kennedy and the escalation of the Vietnam War after the Gulf of Tonkin "incident," one of the brightest moments was Barbara Jordan's election to Congress, for which I served as a poll watcher. In a parallel but separate track, I continued activism for women's rights by leading challenges to my university's restrictive curfew and dress codes and by sharing administrative responsibilities with peers for Rice's student-run women's colleges. Meanwhile, I focused on dramatic literature and the New Criticism, preparing to become a professor of English through a Ford Foundation–funded program. I also performed in extracurricular plays and took productions such as Ionesco's *The Lesson* into unconventional campus spaces. At the end of my senior year, I hid an unexpected pregnancy and moved to Minneapolis, where I had planned to begin theatre graduate studies, acknowledging that my love for dramatic literature and theatre arts was far greater than my devotion to English. My daughter, born in September and adopted in the "blind" process of that era, found me as she was turning thirty in 1996, and we have begun to build a relationship. There was no women's movement to turn to when I went through that pregnancy alone.

Minnesota appealed to me for graduate work in the mid-1960s because of its quasi-socialist community values and strong per-capita commitment to the arts, as well as the exciting non-Broadway theatre produced at the then new Guthrie. Overnight I went from the steamy Gulf to the frozen Great Lakes and from deeply ingrained racism to a more tolerant culture. Here I played out the domestic antiwar drama with The AnyPlace Theatre, a multiracial collective that performed in streets and schools. Funded by the Rockefeller Foundation, we did not charge admission, thus embodying the American irony of political freedom paid for by capitalist "pirates," caught up in the Marxist slogans of Mao and Che.

Excited by the plays and poetry emerging from Prague in the mid-1960s and curious about the situation of the artist in a socialist democracy, I made plans to go to Czechoslovakia. Even though Soviet tanks bludgeoned Czech spirits in the spring of 1968, I traveled that fall with my new actor-director husband into Slovenia, then part of Yugoslavia, intending to continue into Prague and possibly remain in socialist Europe. However, in a few brief months that included a week at a Belgrade student performing-arts conference, as well as a quick tour through Hungary, I observed Marxist pragmatics and witnessed the impoverishment of the arts under even the most liberal socialist system. I deduced then that Marxist principles do not grasp the primitive and fundamental roles of initiative, incentive and imagination in human behavior. Furthermore, implementation of Marxism requires coercion and massive bureaucracy. It seems to me inevitable that artists will suffer under any centrally organized system that is driven by any ideology.

Returning from Yugoslavia, I performed and served as literary editor with the Children's Theatre Company of the Minneapolis Institute for the Arts in the 1970s while I resumed my coursework toward a Ph.D. degree. My son was born in 1970. Introduced to Native American studies by activism with the Twin Cities–based American Indian Movement (AIM), I happened upon John G. Neihardt's book, *Black Elk Speaks*, and was profoundly moved by Black Elk's account of how his Lakota tribe performed a vision he had when he was very ill. The idea that a society would see performance events as healthy for the whole community and would commit to performing people's visions because everyone's lives truly depended on such an activity caught my imagination. This tribal impulse to create theatrically seems inseparable from spiritual expression, and these performances' symbolic, earth-based poetry is breathtakingly bold.

Researching Native American performance introduced me to an enormous range of social sciences as well as to thorny problems of historical reconstruction and culturally specific vocabularies. To attempt to describe a Lakota performance two hundred years ago requires examining sources as diverse as medical journals, trappers' diaries, Lakota mythology, congressional documents, military records, geography, anthropological field notes and Lakota oral histories, among others. These require sensitivity to bias and the imperfections of human interpretations and memory, aided by reading deeply in historical logic, comparative religions and methodologies for oral cultures. The stimulating multidisciplinary breadth of Indian studies not only has benefited my work in women's studies, it also has enriched my life immeasurably.

Awarded a Danforth Graduate Fellowship for Women in 1973, I was freed from having to work while I completed my dissertation. I felt compelled to contribute my time to the new women's movement of that era, as well as to AIM, combining my earlier activism for women and girls with theatricality and theatre studies. Toting my toddler son, I campaigned Yippie style for the presidency of the University of Minnesota on the Child Care Coalition ticket,

UNIVERSITY OF WINCHESTER
LIBRARY

using my one press conference to argue for child care facilities at the university. Then, I soaked up everything in print and in the air about women's issues while helping Professor Toni McNaron, who taught Shakespeare, begin the discipline of women's studies through a series of bag-lunch seminars with women scholars and staff. Intellectually and spiritually, I was still very much engrossed in Native American studies, while politically I was working for women's rights. And I worked dramaturgically with both the Children's Theatre and the Guthrie Theatre's second stage, eventually assembling, editing and publishing two volumes of original children's plays.

When Helen and I met at the American Theatre Association (ATA) 1974 conference, I generated a women's caucus in that organization with my very pregnant and very capable colleague, Mary Saboe. At the same time, I was arguing for a presence for Native American theatre artists and for a more multicultural view in the field in general. Multicultural linkages and mutual support developed among numerous people in ATA during the late 1970s, as the formal Women's Program got off the ground. ATA mutated into the Association for Theatre in Higher Education (ATHE), but the Women's Program rode through that storm.

My psychic distancing from the Women and Theatre Program, however, began in 1981, after that organization decided to hold its first preconference meeting in New York City. Since the Black Theatre Program had already announced its intention to do the same, I believed that the Women's Program should wait and not force black women to choose between the two groups for which some of them had worked very hard and creatively. When the Women's Program went ahead with its plans, I attended the Black Theatre Program Pre-Conference that year, enabling me to hear black women discuss their interests, needs, discoveries, dreams and theories among male and female peers. Following that conference, I felt like an interested but marginal observer in the Women's Program, which seemed de facto "white" and somewhat oblivious to the practices and vocabulary that made it so. When women become separated racially by the focus on gender, I am not so interested in the construct of "Woman" that seems to necessitate division.

I began teaching at Northwestern in 1976, and for years I juggled course assignments in Greek and European theatre with scholarship in Native American performance and the work on this book. Divorced in 1978, I also experienced the challenges of being a single mother. Parallel to chairing the Ph.D. program and producing an annual student playwriting festival, I helped women faculty organize and develop a women's studies program. My greatest joys came from teaching classical drama and guiding student playwrights. It wasn't until the 1980s that the theatre department permitted me to offer a course in American theatre, and not until the late 1980s was I able to introduce women's theatre to the department. I also served dramaturgically in Chicago's Wisdom Bridge Theatre and Victory Gardens Theatre, and as the Goodman Theatre's Resident Humanist, I taught writing in Stateville Prison.

During my last two years at Northwestern, Women's Center director June Terpstra, Chicago artist Marlene Zuccaro and I created a project on sexism and racism. In this program, students performed true stories they evolved dramaturgically about faculty, staff and student experiences at NU. Marlene brought to us directorial skills she had developed at Zebra Crossing, an inner-city-based theatre committed to color-and-gender-blind casting that tackled issues such as homophobia and racism. We took the performance into dormitories and other university spaces, then followed its very effective scenes with audience discussions led by social workers. With the Campus Climate Project, I finally brought together disparate threads that had fed my passions since childhood, finding a way to work politically and theatrically for women without isolating gender from the larger community and related issues of identity.

By the time feminist theatre scholars were marrying psychosemiotics with Marxism, I had removed myself both from the ATHE program and from theorizing to create the Climate project, to try to reclaim the enthusiasm I had felt for Native American performance, and to begin my own creative writing. The self-containment of academic culture felt awkward for me. Unable to focus my scholarship, creativity and activism at Northwestern or within the Women's Program, I felt oddly homeless as an intellectual. In the late 1980s, my dean told me that he did not believe in women's studies because "with women, there's the problem of complicity." Even as Helen and I prepared the second edition of *Women in American Theatre* in the mid-1980s, I was contemplating leaving academe. Should I stay and devote my life to fighting the academic machine? I had no heart for that course. Theatre had taught me that life is dynamic, choices are before us, and change is possible.

Suspecting that my self-knowledge and therefore evolution were constrained by the artificial security tenure both offers and imposes, I quit academia in 1989. What may come of this new path I can't predict, but I haven't had one moment of regret. Academic "freedom" didn't buy me the liberation I feel now, and theatre isn't offering me the communal experiences I desire as I age and struggle for survival without a net, somehow closer to what I sense is the human condition. I sincerely hope that in this new century theatre will enjoy a new vitality, perhaps led by women, as it addresses the age-old challenge of performing visions to heal community and bridge divides.

Linda Walsh Jenkins
December 2003

ART VERSUS BUSINESS: THE CHALLENGE OF WOMEN IN AMERICAN THEATRE

As we had hoped, the introduction to the first edition (published in 1981) stirred considerable discussion, ranging from attacks on its "binary" thinking to praise for valorizing women's work in venues far from show business. We reprint it without revision because, despite its limitations, it suggests a perspective that may challenge and perhaps inspire as women carry on their theatre work in the new millennium.

In the decade or more since the women's movement began, a number of books on the female experience in literature, in art and architecture, in film, and in dance have been published, but no comparable attempts have been made to identify a women's tradition in the complex art of theatre. Some excellent volumes of plays by women and some about women, some interesting articles on individuals and on the new feminist theatres, a symposium or an interview here or there have appeared. With the exception of the reissue of Rosamond Gilder's classic *Enter the Actress*, however, no overall study has tried to see how women have used and have been used in theatre.

Yet questions about women's participation in all aspects of theatre have become more insistent. As women with new self-awareness and enthusiasm try to use theatre to explore what it means to be a woman, they also look back in the hope of locating themselves in some female tradition that will help them understand their problems in the present as well as plan for the future. Despite the public life of theatre, we know very little about the role that women have played. It has not been easy to see a female network in the composite art of theatre or to find a sense of "we-consciousness," as Simone de Beauvoir calls it, among actresses, playwrights, designers, directors and producers.

In this anthology we have juxtaposed in a single volume some of the many different things we are only now beginning to learn about women in all aspects of theatre. When viewed together in this way, the studies in this collection, varied as they are and gathered as they were without any single preconception or ideological thrust, do highlight some continuities in women's experience in theatre. The recurrent patterns that appear in these pages and in the body of research out of which this volume grew suggest that women's role in theatre has been special. From female rites to Broadway shows to sisterhood sessions, women seem to have found the sharing, collective, creative, community aspects of theatre especially congenial. They have tended to commit their energies to the nurturing art rather than to the competitive business of theatre. A brief overview of women's role based on this insight, which only a formal history could fully document, is sketched here. It is offered as an introduction to the selections that follow in the hope that it will raise questions for discussion and stimulate much-needed further research.

As a starting point, there is the striking evidence of women's continued and extensive participation in theatre. Acting, of course, has been the obvious career for women. If you were pretty but poor, or wellborn but hard-up, with no useful skills but your feminine attractions to offer, the stage was always a possible way to earn a living. In *Aria da Capo*, Edna St. Vincent Millay neatly satirizes the easy link of women and acting. When Columbine complains that she can't act, Pierrot answers: "Can't act? Can't act? La, listen to the woman! . . . You're blond, are you not?—you have no education, have you? can't act! you underrate yourself, my dear!" In addition to their obvious but crucial function as actresses, women—often starting as actresses—have been involved in greater numbers and in a greater variety of jobs than are indicated in the theatre history books, which usually mention only the big names who made it on Broadway.

Many of these unsung women were born into theatrical families where they learned to do all that was necessary. Some added management to acting on the death of their fathers or their husbands; others started their own theatres, often the first in an outlying area, out of the need to earn a living for themselves or their children or a desire to enrich the life of a community. There were those who were the power behind the scene, managing actress-daughters, or those who enriched or almost ghostwrote the plays of their husbands. Various strong, independent women served theatre on their own terms, whether that meant playing male roles to satisfy their own sense of power and authority or alternatively exploiting their female sexuality in defiance of the "flabby, sanctimoniousness" of good women who, they chided, dwindled into "nonentities" on marriage.

Liberated by their work in the very public, often vulgar world of theatre, they wrote plays for themselves or for others to star in, courted commercial success, or struggled for personal expression. They organized companies, trained young performers in their troupes and later in notable studios and schools. They experimented with chemical and physical laws to devise new scenic effects and directed the plays they wrote to ensure that they were staged properly. They have been casting and dramatic agents, producers, financiers and lawyers for theatre. Especially since the turn of the twentieth century, women have made their way into all the specialized positions in theatre, where they can be found if you have a mind to look for them and some sense of where they are most likely to be located.

For although many women have made their mark in theatre, it hasn't been easy for them to do so on Broadway or in the mainstream of theatre. Their accomplishments are celebrated in this volume, but at the same time the limitations and constraints they faced are also clearly indicated. In show business as in other businesses and professions, women have not easily or regularly come into positions of importance or power in the major institutions. They have been restricted by the blatant prejudice against letting women have any say where big money and decision making have been involved, as well as by their socialization into a passive but emotional self-image.

To the usual limits on female career aspirations—marriage, family, appropriate submissive behavior and acceptable feminine appearance—theatre has imposed further restrictions by being socially and morally suspect in puritanical, middle-class America. In a country where theatre was thought of as Satan's haunt and actresses often equated with harlots whose "lascivious smiles, wanton glances and indelicate attitudes" threatened the ideal of "womanhood," the women who worked in theatre had a difficult time. Defined in this way by society, they could exploit their erotic attractions before an often largely male audience and make a rather free and easy life for themselves outside the limits of correct society. Or anxious to get on, they could fit themselves to the stereotypes acceptable to the popular audience—the innocent ingenue, the noble wife, the fallen woman. From the beginning, however, some women challenged the debased image of theatre and of women in it. Attracted by the stage, they tried to reform it and to raise the moral and aesthetic level of the profession. Although they were sometimes snobbish, prudish, even priggish, reflecting what was thought appropriate when a "lady" turned to theatre, these women through their efforts over the years and in response to changing values eventually transformed their defensive attitudes into a dynamic idea of theatre in America.

Uncomfortable in the commercial theatre or barred from full participation there, important creative women have insisted that their theatre must be more than "amusement . . . prostituted to the purpose of vice," to quote Mercy Otis Warren, our first woman dramatist, or "more than an amusement" to catch an echo in a Sunday *New York Times* headline about Zelda Fichandler's Arena Stage. In an earlier day women dramatists and actresses spoke of themselves as "reformers" who would grace the theatre with "their own pure and blameless lives" or with the "benign influence of a noble womanly spirit," to quote Anna Cora Mowatt, the lady who wrote *Fashion*.

Olive Logan, actress, writer, bluestocking, suggested that theatre could become "a worthy channel for gifted, intelligent and virtuous young women to gain a livelihood through" if producers would only get rid of the "leg business" made popular in hits like Adah Isaacs Menken's "nude" *Mazeppa* or *The*

Black Crook. In her fascinating series of essays, *Apropos of Women and Theatre,* written in 1869, Olive Logan argued that a career on the decent, serious stage was one of the few in which women could earn equally with men and was therefore worthy of an aspiring, independent woman. Julia Marlowe, we can suggest, was such a young woman who deliberately prepared herself by hard work and careful study of Shakespeare to be a "moral force" in acting his plays. She conceded that what impelled her as an actress was "the dramatic attraction of the woman who stays pure." Her contemporary, Mary Shaw, equally ideal- istic, was impelled by the possibility of using the stage for a feminist vision. "Women exert a tremendous and virtually irresistible influence over the stage," she insisted. "Aristocrat of the arts and child of religion," she told the International Congress of Women in London in 1899, the drama "is a field for women." With Jessie Bonstelle, actress, director-manager of important stock companies, Mary Shaw projected a Woman's National Theatre devoted to communicating "distinctive feminine feeling or opinions," one of several such theatres planned in the early years of the twentieth century.

By 1931, Eva Le Gallienne, actress-director of the Civic Repertory Theatre, could look back on this heritage of high-minded activism when ana- lyzing "Women's Role in the Theatre" in the *Alumnae Quarterly* of Smith College, which had just given her an honorary degree. Her point of departure was an attack on women by Gordon Craig, who had written that "to achieve the reform of the theatre, to bring it into the condition necessary for it to become a fine art, women must have first left the boards." Miss Le Gallienne's defense began in an apologetic, familiar vein, noting the absence of women in ancient theatre and the use of only "lower types of women" in "orgies of licen- tiousness" during the "degenerate days of Rome and the Renaissance." The modern movement in theatre, however, disavowing sexism and show business, was created by both men and women. Indeed, Le Gallienne suggested, at first somewhat hesitantly and then in stronger terms by the end of her comments, the modern theatre was in many ways the accomplishment of women. Looking at the achievements of, among others, Miss Horniman in Manchester, Lady Gregory in Ireland, Irene and Alice Lewisohn, Mary Shaw and Minnie Maddern Fiske in New York, she pointed out that, as she saw it, women were really the "doers" in the development of the modern art theatre.

Looking today for what seems especially to distinguish the contributions of notable women, for a female network or feminine consciousness in American theatre, we find ourselves reinforcing Miss Le Gallienne's sugges- tion that, counter to Craig's perverse admonition, serving the art of theatre has in many ways been the special function of women. The women who have made major contributions to American theatre have tended to identify them- selves—whether they were actresses, playwrights, directors, or producers— with an idea of the theatre larger than that of Broadway. In the 1920s Edith Isaacs, editor of *Theatre Arts Monthly,* the journal of the art theatre movement, dubbed this alternative theatre "the tributary theatre." In her important essay, she rejected commercial New York theatre as "not an artist's goal" and urged Americans to go to "the four corners of the country and begin again, training playwrights to create in their own idiom, in their own theatres." In declaring that theatre must have a "relation, human or aesthetic, to the life of the people," she sounded a call to which women have responded with unusual dedication.

The association of women with regional, institutional, little, art and alternative theatres is striking. Think of Susan Glaspell, who became an innovative playwright after founding the Provincetown Players with her husband, George Cram Cook; of Theresa Helburn, executive director for many years of the famed Theatre Guild; of Edith Isaacs, for more than twenty-five years reviewer, editor and manager of *Theatre Arts Monthly*; of Rosamond Gilder, her disciple and associate, critic, historian, activist in the National Theatre Conference, ANTA, and voice of America through the International Theatre Institute; of Cheryl Crawford, cofounder with Harold Clurman and Lee Strasberg of the Group Theatre, and later collaborator with Eva Le Gallienne and Margaret Webster in the American Repertory Theatre; of Hallie Flanagan Davis, creator of the Vassar Experimental Theatre and the Smith College theatre department and head of the great Federal Theatre Project; of Margo Jones, director-producer in Dallas, "high priestess" of the post–World War II regional theatre movement; of Nina Vance of the Alley Theatre in Houston, of Zelda Fichandler of the Arena Stage; of Judith Malina, guru of the Living Theatre; of Ellen Stewart, La Mama of the whole Off-Off-Broadway theatre movement.

Most of these women turned their backs on making it on Broadway. They rejected what sociologists consider the male preoccupation with power and climbing the ladder in the "cash-nexus world." Their concerns have tended to be with the values of what has been called the "status world," in which love, duty, tenderness, individuality and expressiveness are central. Their activities belong to the tradition of female rites in which, as Linda Jenkins has pointed out, performance events are used primarily for family and social bonding rather than largely for entertainment and profit.

Eva Le Gallienne, to stick with her instructive experience, turned against what she felt was the "stultifying effect of a successful engagement" as a leading lady to try her hand at special matinees of "better" plays. Her determination to stage Ibsen, Hauptmann and Chekhov led to the founding of the Civic Repertory Theatre, where the satisfactions of ensemble playing, repertory scheduling, low prices and free training for performers replaced the triumphs she could have easily had as a star. Other leading actresses also freed themselves from being "commodities" in the hands of producers to head their own companies or join institutional theatres or even just tour an individual production that would allow them to perform personally and culturally meaningful plays. Think of the great Minnie Maddern Fiske, who was called the "most civilizing force" of the stage of her day, of Katharine Cornell, of Lynn Fontanne, of Helen Hayes, of Julie Harris and Irene Worth, among many others.

Many of these women tend to look on their companies as family units within a larger community group, sharing, supporting, learning and teaching. They reject the "atmosphere of hysteria, crisis, fragmentation, one-shotness and mammon-mindedness" of the Broadway system as inappropriate for the "collective and cumulative" art of theatre. They tend to turn away from the "nameless faces and the anonymity" of New York to places where they have a "feeling of roots." They tend to work for a theatre "which is part of everybody's life . . . where there is a theatre in every town providing entertainment and enlightenment for the audience and a decent livelihood along with high artistic goals for the theatre worker." This sampling of quotations, it should be noted, like most of the illustrations here, antedates the new feminist theatres where these nurturant, supportive, cooperative, community values have become the basis for a new kind of theatre that can even call itself, as one feminist troupe does, "It's All Right to Be Woman."

Perhaps because they were not locked into the show business aesthetic, women won the major prizes offered early in this century with plays that aimed at being more than just hits. Josephine Preston Peabody, for example, won the competition for a play to inaugurate the new Shakespeare Memorial Theatre in 1910 with her poetic drama, *The Piper*, and Alice Brown won the $10,000 prize offered by Winthrop Ames for her *Children of Earth*, chosen over seventeen hundred other manuscripts. Although not a stage success, the play has been praised for the "note of repressed and insurgent desire for participation in life" its heroine expressed.

It was out of this kind of need to tell what Megan Terry was later to call "the psychic news" that women early on in the century began the experiment with dramatic form and staging techniques that now characterize the *New Women's Theatre*, as Honor Moore calls it in her fine collection of plays. Rachel Crothers, in exploring the conflicts of the "New Woman" as artist and wife-mother, extended the range of the social-problem drama of the day. She thought women's evolution the most "important thing in modern life" and felt herself very avant-garde when among other innovations she made her heroines over thirty years old. "No more is it necessary to confine heroines to ingenues, stage age seventeen," she declared in the early years of this century.

While Crothers in her almost fifty years of acting, writing and directing represents the older ladylike tradition of "ethical concern" brought to the theatre, the new bohemian artists, the Greenwich Village feminists, probed the psyche of their characters in new forms that seemed invented especially to express the troubled spirit of modern woman.

Alice Gerstenberg's *Overtones*, for example, produced by the Washington Square Players with a set by Lee Simonson, used the then novel Freudian concepts of ego and id to project the divided selves of her two characters. Each woman is shadowed by a veiled alter ego who speaks her innermost feelings in this one-acter that is thought to be the first American play "to depart from realism to show the unconscious."

In Susan Glaspell's *The Verge* (1921), done by her Provincetown Players, the struggles of the heroine to enlarge the boundaries of her life, to be "stabbed to awareness," are paralleled in some ways by the playwright's struggle to extend the boundaries of her dramatic form. She calls for striking expressionistic lighting and scenic effects, provided originally by Cleon Throckmorton, to image forth the search for "otherness" and "apartness" that makes her heroine reject home, husband and child in a mad vision of passion and self-realization. In Glaspell's more realistic plays, the anguished heroine often does not appear, but the discovery of her "suppressed desires" is the device for dramatic action and tension.

In Sophie Treadwell's *Machinal* (1928), designed by Robert Edmond Jones, the playwright uses stream-of-consciousness passages and expressionistic sounds, rhythms and images to suggest the "mechanical, nerve-nagging" environment that drives her young woman to illicit love and to the murder of her husband, once her boss. When the young woman cries out "I won't submit" as she is led to the electric chair, Treadwell thrusts a powerful image of women's anguish and revolt at audiences.

An interest in the downtrodden, the unfulfilled and the defeated is often found in women's plays. In addition to the few just mentioned, there are many in which the trials of Indians, workers, farmers, blacks, lesbians and antiwar activists are dramatized. Rachel France's important anthology, *A Century of Plays by American Women*, is the place to find some of these usually unavailable plays. Despite great difficulties black women playwrights from Angelina Grimke to Lorraine Hansberry, Alice Childress and Adrienne Kennedy have, along with actresses and directors like Rose McClendon, Ruby Dee and Vinnette Carroll, raised their voices to document and celebrate the "life, experience and humor" of black people. Women have also pioneered in other neglected areas, providing children's creative dramatics, settlement-house culture and prison entertainment.

Even some of the scholarly studies written by women have been devoted to ignored subjects. Long before the black movement and women's liberation, Edith Isaacs's *The Negro in the American Theatre* showed the significance of black art as one of our few native resources, and Rosamond Gilder's *Enter the Actress* told of women who were pioneers in theatre rather than queens of the stage. Even Marilyn Stasio's recent *Broadway's Beautiful Losers*, full of plays that have "failed as commercial products" despite the fact that they had "merit as theatre art," supports the view that, for all the varied reasons suggested here, women have generally been for art rather than business in American theatre.

This brief overview with its selective illustrations may seem an overstatement made to isolate a female tradition. Certainly when the history of women in theatre is written, it will detail with more than the few suggestions possible here those many talented women who made it in the man's world of theatre because, as Anita Loos once put it, "I was just a girl writer who liked money" in a field where girls, she felt, were mostly smarter than men. They were "doers," not just "dreamers," to recall Le Gallienne's observations. But in reviewing the wide range of activities represented in the pages of this collection and in related research, one learns again and again that much of what women did was dedicated to realizing a dream of a different kind of theatre. Perhaps this concluding sketch of the career of one woman will capture the essence of the special spirit that seems to have animated many of the women in American theatre.

During the "full, lean years" of the Depression, a tiny woman in a fedora hat cast a huge shadow which covered the whole land with the vision of a different kind of theatre. Hallie Flanagan Davis, during the few short years of the Federal Theatre Project, made the tributary the mainstream. The educational, regional, experimental art theatre became our national people's theatre. When she was appointed national director of the Federal Theatre Project in August 1935, the *New York Times* wrote that "the boys—the local gentry for whom the theatre does not exist outside Manhattan—did not quite know what to make of that." To them the appointment "represented 'art' . . . There was headshaking. What this project needed, they said, was an old-line Broadway manager who knew the commercial theatre's devious ways."

There were many reasons why Harry L. Hopkins, with President Franklin Roosevelt and, we might add, Mrs. Eleanor Roosevelt supporting him, wanted someone outside the commercial theatre, but here we only want to ask what were some of the qualities that Hallie Flanagan Davis brought to the job.

Born in South Dakota and brought up in Grinnell, Iowa, she belonged to the vast reaches of America that Broadway thought of as a "dumping ground" for some of its products. Although she eventually became part of the Eastern scene, she always recalled, in often lyrical prose, the great quiet prairies and the "long summer days and long winter evenings" of a "serene childhood" and youth spent in the spacious West.

At Grinnell College she, like the rest of her group, was "imbued with the Grinnell conception of public service," and she developed a strong sense of the importance of being "part of an institution." She wrote of herself, "I can't imagine just being a floating rib someplace." She could not imagine theatre apart from the life of a group.

She started her first work experience like a latter-day Nora trying to earn money in secret for her ailing young husband by giving drama lessons, one of the few skills this young wife had. When her husband died, she thrust herself into teaching to earn money for herself and her two children. Her first notice came as a playwright when she won a prize offered by the Des Moines Little Theatre Society in a regional contest open only to Iowans. This success, plus her effective productions at Grinnell College, led her to Professor George Pierce Baker's Workshop 47 at Harvard, where she earned a master's degree. With her small son Frederick, this indomitable little woman went east to learn the art of theatre after suffering the death of both her husband and her seven-year-old son Jack. Professor Baker, she recalled, "believed that I should give up everything and write plays. But I couldn't—I had a family to support!" All her active life she was concerned to support herself and her family; her work was for her no fanciful creative outlet but a serious economic commitment. But the work was also more than just a job.

She went back to Grinnell, where she used all she learned at Harvard. A production at her Grinnell Experimental Theatre of *Romeo and Juliet*, into which she confessed that she "secretly" poured her remembrances of her young husband, won the attention that led to the award of a Guggenheim

Fellowship, one of the first given to a woman. It also won her a position at Vassar College, where President Henry MacCracken asked her to set up another experimental theatre.

With her Guggenheim Fellowship she traveled to Europe to see the *Shifting Scenes*, as she would call her book about the journey. Her exposure to the innovations of Craig, Reinhardt, Stanislavski and especially Meyerhold sharpened her awareness of and commitment to theatre as a dynamic instrument to serve the people as they change the world around them.

In the next few years at Vassar, she and her Experimental Theatre became the "dynamo," to use another word that would become a title of one of her books, that "releases youth's burning energy . . . into the power of creative change." She foreshadowed the later Living Newspapers in her Depression documentary and call to action, *Can You Hear Their Voices?*, and she found ways of transforming classic dramas into contemporary actions. Her innovations attracted the attention of educators, artists and critics, as well as government officials, and led eventually to her appointment as the national director of the Federal Theatre Project.

When this "soft-spoken slave driver," as she was admiringly called, took on the Federal Theatre Project to employ out-of-work performers, she tried to realize for the nation the values of the kind of theatre in which she had worked. With her associates she tried to create a regional, popular, educational art theatre in which, as Harry Hopkins told her in urging her to take the appointment, "the profits won't be money profits."

Without arguing the success or failure of the Federal Theatre or the mistakes or limitations of Hallie Flanagan Davis, we can observe that she brought us closest to the realization for the nation of the dream widely shared by the other women discussed here. In her Federal Theatre, the profits were human. Papa, who might have been an actor, a playwright, a designer, or a technician, had a job even if the salary was only twenty-five dollars a week. The roots were regional. The theatre tried to "explore sources of Native American life." The accomplishments were national. Theatre became for a new audience of millions an artistic medium "of free expression," an "access to the arts and tools of civilization," and a "bulwark of the democratic form of government."

From the female shaman with whom our volume opens to the Broadway star and on to the feminist activists with whom it closes, this large vision has shaped the role of women in American theatre. Liberated, mostly by circumstance and sometimes by desire, from male pressure to "make a mark in the world" and "develop the ego," women have served the art and the people.

HKC
From the 1987 edition

THE ROLES
WE PLAYED

1 FEMALE RITES

A section on female rites opens our collection on women in American theatre because these performance events, interesting and important in
themselves, also can help us understand how women have functioned in our
theatre. Indeed, exact definitions of "ritual" and "theatre" continue to elude
theorists, since these two activities share so many features. Often it is context,
not content, that determines whether a performance event is one or the other.
It is widely accepted now that no event is clearly one or the other. Rather, ritual and theatre belong to the same family of human behavior in which the
major variables are whether or not an event is purely aesthetic or is believed to
be socially or spiritually efficacious.

If we look to the end of the ritual-theatre continuum, where performance
is solely for fun—and profit—emphasizing the here and now, making no
attempt at social bonding, we find some women but few relative to the number of men. If, however, we look at family and public performance events, in
which social and religious bondings are established, we find women. They are
decorating and embellishing the parade floats, church interiors, schools and
homes; they are managing the feasting and preparations; they are singing in
the choirs, if not on the stage; they are lighting candles and playing the organ;
they are guarding order and dignity.

These roles in performance have been women's rights. It would help us
greatly to understand why, for example, there have been few women directing
on Broadway if we look to the broader "theatre" of American life to see what
society has not only allowed but expected. Traditionally, women have not
been encouraged to create anything "for fun," but rather to create for others,
for community, for social and religious good and for the maintenance of
order. Often woman is herself a social decoration; even her self-adornment is

done for the pleasure of others and might be understood as her way of being a visual artist within sex-role demands.

When we look for women in the ritual and ceremonial aspects of American life, we see great diversity and contribution. Shakers, possessed by the spirit of Mother Ann, created events that combined pantomime, singing and clowning. Psychologist Rev. Audrey Bronson and her jazz-pianist sister have led her congregation through spiritual experiences in the Sanctuary Church of the Open Door in Philadelphia. Storyteller Laura Simms advertised her performances as a ritual theatre art. Sculptor Suzanne Benton used masks to create performance happenings she called rituals. Composer Pauline Oliveros combined meditative techniques and figurative theatrical elements in her *Crow Two, A Ceremonial Opera*.

As women in contemporary society challenge old ways, they can look to rites for reform and reconsideration. Jewish feminists, for example, are revising the traditional seder and Haggadah to give themselves a more active role and to make the language more inclusive of Jewish women past and present. Even the consciousness-raising groups that were such an important part of the women's liberation movement of the early 1970s became events with gestures, stories, interactions and patterns that began to have the aura of ritual about them.

Material in this chapter is arranged to suggest what Richard Schechner has called the ritual-theatre continuum. The first essay surveys Native American women's sex-role expectations and observes their place in the range of events in their tribes. In considering these events and women's participation, we may reflect on ways in which sex-role expectations with regard to contemporary theatre may be a relic of other tribal pasts. We can see parallels between the ways in which Native women have been "overlooked" by fieldworkers and historians and the ways in which other American women have been overlooked.

In the events of the Woman's Crusade of 1873–74, Women's Trade Union League and National Woman's Party we see women who performed according to role expectation—prayer, song, saving the home, friendship, bonding, decoration and pageantry—but took their performance into a context in which it made a political statement.

By contrast, and ironically, in American beauty pageants women perform in ways that have not been appropriate for modest homemakers and home-savers—showing off their bodies, calling attention to themselves by singing, dancing, acting. Yet they are seen as bolstering, not challenging, the given order. It might be noted that beauty pageants by minority groups, such as Miss Black America and Indian Princesses, have not existed merely to ape the Miss America pageant; they have challenged white America's ideal of beauty. Through public events like Miss America and homecoming parades, American society judges the premarital (virgin?) female on the basis of her physical beauty, bearing and other potential (talent) for embellishing her future family (primarily her husband?). But the postmarital female, Mrs. America, is then judged on her ability to bake pies and sew. Perhaps TV commercials form an ongoing Mrs. America pageant, as we see our contestants tested on dirty collars, coffee making and floor waxing.

Starhawk's account of the ritual event grounding a "Take Back the Night" march reminds us of the unbroken, though always threatened, tradition of witchcraft and ancient goddess religions. Barbara Ann Teer's ritual work with the National Black Theatre and the ritual drama created by At the Foot of the Mountain might be said to straddle the ritual-theatre continuum. Teer looked to ritual sources as an alternative to Anglo-European theatre, while At the Foot of the Mountain created *The Story of a Mother* both to display a mother's life through imitation-enactment and to engage the audience in an actual ritualistic summoning of individual mothers.

Finally, Adrienne Kennedy has made female rites of passage part of the dramatic core of her plays. In them we encounter social rituals that form woman's identity with resultant agony. As a playwright, Kennedy is at the other end of the continuum from the traditional female performance role, and yet her work connects us with the female shaman introduced in the first essay. Kennedy, like a shaman, understands and reveals balance and imbalance in the rites that create a female.

LWJ

SEX ROLES AND SHAMANS

Linda Walsh Jenkins

The first "theatre" on the North American continent was the performance activity of hundreds, perhaps even thousands, of Native cultures. Some of these performance traditions continue into the present day, and new events have been and continue to be created. When theatre texts select photos or drawings of Native events for chapters on "primitive ritual" and "beginnings of theatre," they tend to select exotic and romantic images such as George Catlin's paintings of Mandan buffalo dancers (male) or photos of ceremonies in which live snakes are handled by men. When thinking of Indian performances the most common images are probably those of a male Plains warrior dancing in full regalia, men sacrificing their flesh in the Sun Dance, or some of the Southwest Indian events that appear in magazines like *National Geographic*. Hollywood films and mythology of the Old West have helped place the Indian male activity at the forefront of the popular imagination. What of the roles and contributions of Native women in these performances, particularly in the time prior to the reservation experience at the end of the nineteenth century?

When historians or ethnographers describe performance events in Native American cultures, they rarely refer to the participation of Indian women, so even finding the women in the available evidence from past centuries is a job requiring a patient sifting of elements. The temptation for scholars, it seems, has been to assume that if women aren't mentioned, they aren't important and their activity is not a topic to be pursued. However, there is enough evidence to assume that women were involved in performance and that their story has not been fully recorded or told.

Many problems in the very nature of fieldwork keep knowledge of women's activities invisible to the outsider. Most researchers were and are people whose knowledge of theatre/performance is very slight and who saw/see Indian performance solely as a part of the culture's social/religious complex, not as theatre. Even the most thorough and valuable recorders do not give us much evidence for rehearsal process, methods of teaching and transmitting performance techniques, or aspects of an event other than the actual performing. For example, recorders were not noting that even when only males are dancing they are wearing costumes, and in many instances those costumes were made by women, so the women have not only participated in the event, but the dance is an exhibition of their art, their visions in kinetic sculptures. Usually the informants to field-workers were male (Arctic surveyor Knud Rasmussen noted that men had greater periods of idleness and women always had work to do, so men had time to talk with field-workers.[1]) As men and women in most tribes often had very separate activities such that they almost had two separate cultures (in some instances they even had separate languages, with the women understanding both languages but the men not understanding the women's), most male informants could not speak knowledgeably about women's deeds or thoughts. Within tribal traditions there may be biases that obscure women's work. For example, according to Black Elk, all of the seven sacred rites of the Oglala Sioux were the results of male visions, even the menstrual rites.[2] The author does not investigate for us if it was traditional for the Oglala to credit men with such contributions. In oral traditions it is tradition, not the "hard fact" of Western science, that determines how history is recorded.

Some of this lack of visibility is desired by the women themselves. Minnie Two Shoes, an activist with the American Indian Movement, explained in a meeting at the University of Minnesota in 1971 that it was to the Indian women's advantage to keep men like AIM leaders Russell Means and Dennis Banks in the spotlight. That permitted the women to behave as a true underground, traveling freely under the noses of the FBI, teaching the children, carrying on the work. She criticized non-Indian women for failing to understand the strategy of anonymity, for believing every woman should strive to emulate male leaders and want their fame.

Taking her cue and looking for American Indian women in historical materials with an eye to finding them between the cracks, I find women present in (and significant in their contributions to) performance at almost every age, every stage of life, sometimes out in the thick of the dancing and singing, sometimes on the "fringes," making it all happen. Most Native American tribes recognize and celebrate through performance the paradoxical nature of life: life can be known and life cannot be known, life is explicable and mysterious at one and the same time. That which can be known—the ordered relationships among people, between people and the natural world, within the natural world, the stars and cycles of living, and so forth—is honored and symbolically expressed through performances. Performances also celebrate, dramatize that which cannot be known directly, that which is sacred and can only be dramatized symbolically. In each tribe the symbols used, the conventions followed, are particular to the collective consciousness and memory of that tribe. Although some of these performances follow patterns that were established long ago in tribal history, they may be altered as individuals bring new visions to them.[3]

In most cases, what the men and women did in traditional Native theatre was determined by sex role, based on division of labor in the tribe. Women's primary performance responsibilities, like larger tribal responsibilities, were to celebrate ordered relationships, decorate, provide for the group welfare (feasting), maintain the group's dignity. But there is evidence that sex-role division is not always strict and that in some cases women perform in the same ways as men, often while retaining their gender identity as women.

The following information and descriptions should not be considered a composite portrait of the Native woman in performance, as tribal variances make any such composite impossible. But generally, when participating according to sex role, women were involved in performance as young girls (premenstrual, pure, not yet possessing women's "power"), in menstruation rites, as postmenstrual women of childbearing age and as old women (past childbearing). As young girls they often participated in the performances of male societies—they were the virgins, carrying the major symbols of the tribe's purity and honor, even leading processions and dancing between the males and the rest of the tribe (this was particularly prevalent in Northern Plains cultures). John Neihardt recorded from the Oglala Sioux holy man, Black Elk, this description of girls in his elk ceremony:

> The four virgins represented the nation's hoop, which has four quarters . . . The four virgins wore scarlet dresses, and each had a single eagle feather in her braided hair; for out of the woman the people grows, and the eagle feather again was for the people as in the bison ceremony. The faces of the virgins were painted yellow, the color of the south, the source of life. One had a daybreak star in red upon her forehead. One had a crescent moon in blue, for the power of the woman grows with the moon and comes and goes with it. One had the sun upon her forehead; and around the mouth and eyebrows of the fourth a big blue circle was painted to mean the nation's hoop . . . One of the virgins also carried the flowering stick, another carried the pipe which gives peace, a third bore the herb of healing and the fourth held the sacred hoop; for all these powers together are women's power.[4]

The young girls also danced with young boys in children's events (as in certain Southwest dances today in which children perform as clouds). Their menstrual time was handled variously—for some tribes only the women and a male holy man had contact with the girl, while in others there were (and are) elaborate private and public aspects to this rite of passage that took days and involved the whole tribe.[5]

Once a girl began menstruation she entered women's society in a new way. Women of childbearing age were charged with the domestic responsibilities of the people—theirs was the daily round of cooking, sewing, gathering, making the home and camp tidy and harmonious. In some tribes they fished or did some small-game hunting or farmed. It has been assumed by most scholars who have mentioned them that these women were not permitted to dance because their "bleeding" made them taboo or that the constant domestic chores kept them from having time to make dance preparations. Women who were menstruating probably were kept in isolation from the tribe, but otherwise these women performed and aided performance to a surprisingly great extent. There were songs, dances and ceremonies to celebrate the birth of a child and there were women's social dances of all sorts (basket dances, friendship dances, special dances traditional to or made up for the various women's social groups, performances of women's societies formed as a result of female shamans' visions). Women created parades and honoring dances (the Scalp Dance) for war leaders. In a great many tribes they danced, imitated, narrated and sang together with the men, participating in bawdy sketches or enacting tribal legends.

Ample illustrations of almost every aspect of the range that women's performing and performance participation took may be found in one complex of events, the Winter Ceremonial of the Kwakiutl of what is now British Columbia. Franz Boas observed women beating skin drums (it is often thought Native women do not drum) and noted that in one society's dances one woman's duty was to sing all the sacred songs.[6] He recounts numerous instances in which women were involved in comic sketches, including a take-off on white society which involved an old woman and Indians dressed as policemen and a judge. Four men dressed as policemen came into the lodge where everyone was gathered, wanting to know if all were there and determining that one person was missing. They went out and returned with an old woman, who was handcuffed. They then held a mock trial to punish her for her absence. The judge pored over his law book and fined her seventy dollars; she offered seventy blankets instead, claiming she was poor and had no money. The judge accepted the exchange. Then her friends protested, "That is always your way, policemen. As soon as you see anyone who has money, you arrest and fine him." The old woman was released and then seventy blankets were brought out by her relatives and distributed to the group, so the whole skit was a prelude to a giveaway. This sketch, which he witnessed in 1895, while obviously something made up after contact with white society, nevertheless suggests that for the Kwakiutl it was conventional to create such satirical sketches and that they were quite at ease with having women involved.

For a radical shift in tone and style, Boas gives a long description of a woman who was chosen to "throw" the supernatural power into the people because she had performed that role more than anyone else. A male leader threw the power into the group of people, and she was told to try to catch it and do the same.

> When she caught the spirit, the sound of whistles which she had hidden in her mouth was heard. Four times she ran backward and forward, then she threw the supernatural power among the people, who stopped . . . Then they began to laugh and to utter their cries.

And so she went through the various houses, singing the sacred song of the power thrower.

Thus by looking at the Kwakiutl alone we can begin to see the mature Native woman as a much livelier person and more complete participant than popular conceptions by non-Indians suggest. Further reading into other tribes of very different cultures than that of the Kwakiutl, such as the Cherokee and the Cahuilla, confirms that the Kwakiutl women were not alone in being active in this realm of performance activity separate from sex-role demands.

However, in keeping with the labor assigned to them as women, there were performance roles that they carried out either alone or sometimes in concert with the men. Women bore much of the responsibility for the over-all event arrangements. If men in their family were performing, women might help gather properties and other performers needed and do some of the sewing. In tribes that used tipis the women (who usually owned the tipis) took down the regular encampment, moved to the performance site and pitched the tipis in whatever special manner was appropriate for the event. They cooked the food, which sometimes had to feed many visitors for many days. They were responsible for the overall harmony and dignity of the occasion. The observance of proper order and procedure in all these aspects of the tribe's life was part of keeping the whole life of the people balanced.

In addition to helping with the feasting and arrangements, older women sometimes guarded the periphery of a performance event, offering songs, prayers and ceremonies to keep evil influences out of the occasion. Similarly, they often made songs at times of death. An old woman might actually be the major personage in an event—in the Blackfoot Sun Dance, for example, Sun Dance Woman performs a pivotal role, beginning and ending the event as well as providing focus for many observances within the event.

Allied to this presence of an old woman as Sun Dance Woman is the frequent practice of having a female or feminine presence as the spirit that bonds a performance. In the Pawnee Hako a series of events occur that are male-performed, but the whole Hako complex is dedicated to and overseen by the mystery of Corn Mother. Sometimes the feminine presence (such as Mother Earth or Female Rain) is represented by a masked person (often, but not always, male), and at other times She is invoked through prayer (the Hako). Nevertheless, She is there as a spiritual presence and Her feminine nature pervades the male activity—again, a way of creating and celebrating balance.

UNIVERSITY OF WINCHESTER LIBRARY

To the non-Indian some of these roles and responsibilities may seem trivial, and indeed have been treated as such in most scholarship. Although to the theatre specialist every aspect of stage and "house" management is considered significant, these elements in Native performance have been ignored. But there is nothing trivial to Native peoples about any gesture or contribution to those events that honor and express ordered relationships; they make life whole and keep it whole.

Performing as a shaman was not part of a woman's sex-role expectation. In some tribes, it seems that role was expressly forbidden to women, or at least that is what field-workers were told.[7] The shaman, who lives to understand the sacred, performs variously depending on the culture. It is generally agreed that the shaman bridges and reveals the realms of paradox—what can be known and what cannot be known. First the shaman makes and keeps contact with mystery through dreams and visions, then performs an event either by taking the participants into the edges of the realm of mystery or by going into that realm as participants observe. In the latter case, the observers are at least touched by the presence of mystery. An individual is chosen for this task by virtue of the power of his or her visions, and the people's recognition of that power. The shaman has received a great deal of attention in Western psycho-analytic and theatre theory in the past decade or more as the "technician of the sacred" whose technique is "to cure by means of ecstasy."[8] Typically, the performance consists of the shaman's singing/dancing/drumming, with or without helpers, over a person who is ill, in the presence of family and other tribal members. The shaman experiences (or appears to experience) an ecstatic state and often takes the ill person and the others into the same state. Often the shaman sucks a stone or object out of the sick body or performs some other such astonishing and "impossible" feat—this aspect of the event has most fascinated Westerners, who seem more anxious to cry "fraud" than to pay attention to the shaman's imitation of paradox. The shaman "cures" through creating ecstasy or some other liminal experience, bridging the known and unknown, restoring the balance between the two for the person who is ill and the tribe. The "fraudulent" feat need not be believed any more than a contemporary audience believes Peter Pan actually flies; in the success of the illusion the shaman confirms the power to contact the world of mystery.

Some contemporary women are shamans, and while their visions, chanting and performance may be somewhat influenced by contact with Christianity and non-Indian ways, we can see in them the tradition of female shamans. Flora Jones, a Wintu shaman, uses trance performances to heal. In these her spirit helpers arrive (trickster suckerfisher, black wolf, star, moon, mountain spirits) and speak through her voice, sometimes arguing or joking with one another, and with their presence she discovers a patient's ills. When a person is close to death, Flora may perform the Soul Dance, a ritual dance at midnight, performed to the beating of sticks.[9]

Mesoamerican (Mazatec) shaman María Sabina discovered her powers with the teo-nanácatl (psilocybin mushroom) when she was eight. She cured with herbs until she married and began having children, which she says left her no time for the teo-nanácatl. One of her night vigils, in which she chants and calls forth her visions, is recorded by R. G. Wasson and others.[10] Joan Halifax's abbreviation of that text leads us into the woman's performance, into the realm of her spirit. Following is a fragment of her vision chant:

> Woman who thunders am I, woman who sounds am I,
> Spider woman am I, hummingbird woman am I,
> Eagle woman am I, important eagle woman am I,
> Whirling woman of the whirlwind am I, woman of a sacred,
>   enchanted place am I,
> Woman of the shooting stars am I, yes Jesus Christ says,
> Clock woman am I, yes Jesus Christ says . . .
>
> Jesus oh Mary, holy child, the arm and the hand of the lord of
>   the world.
> Dangerous things are being done, tragedies are being worked
>   out.
> We are left only perplexed, we mamas.[11]

María Sabina's statement that her children left her no time for the teo-nanácatl is a clue to one of the reasons why there were far fewer female shamans than male—with the strict division of labor, a woman was usually restricted during her childbearing years. She found it difficult to maintain the sometimes several days' long vigils and concentration required of a shaman and at the same time fulfill her first role. However, there were often other women around to help. Perhaps in this hesitancy to permit women to be both female and shaman there is some fear that women would have too much power (more than males) if they can bear children, bleed, be the source of the people and simultaneously have access to mystery as shamans.[12] To further discover the female shaman we will have to search carefully between the lines of tribes' performance histories; and as none of those have been written, she is even more elusive. But she and her sisters were essential to the first theatre in America and carry those ancient traditions into the present.

TRAMPLING OUT THE VINTAGE

Susan Dye Lee

There are many ways of understanding the Woman's Crusade of 1873–74. It can be seen as an evangelical temperance revival, as a female protest against the saloon, as the feminization of a male-dominated reform movement and as a militant extension of home-centered values into the community.

Without neglecting these themes, this article also considers the Crusade as a kind of pentecostal melodrama, a spectacular nineteenth-century version of street theatre in which pious, retiring housewives publicly presented themselves as victims of male drinking habits and collectively dramatized their demands for an end to the liquor traffic. As a result, thousands of wives, mothers and sisters not only managed to bring their grievance to the attention of a nationwide audience, but learned to accept themselves in a new role—that of social reformer.

During the winter of 1873–74, anyone traveling through the towns of Ohio or of its neighboring states saw a novel sight indeed. Bands of praying women were on the march. Their destination? Any place in the community that sold intoxicating spirits. Their mission? With peace, prayer and persuasion to convince rum-sellers that salvation lay in forsaking the traffic in liquor.

The Woman's Crusade, as it came to be called, was the most remarkable confluence of women, evangelism and temperance witnessed in the nineteenth century. Whatever animated these crusaders—an addicted relative, abused wives, broken families, righteous indignation—their motives were translated into a female insurrection whose outlines were shaped by the necessities of evangelical piety. The Crusade resembled a gospel temperance revival, featuring prayer, exhortation and soul-saving. Even militant tactics of direct confrontation and civil disobedience were rationalized by a belief in the moral superiority of women and their mission to act as God's instrument in restoring communities to sobriety. As a result, the movement combined the fervor of a revival with the dramatic spectacle of pious housewives invading male territory to plead for a redress of their grievances. A newspaper correspondent in Newark, Ohio, reported that he would never forget

> the touching and imposing spectacle that burst upon my view as I beheld walking calmly, solemnly and deliberately, over two hundred ladies, representing our best society, enshrined with silence and beautified by tears. The streets were crowded by thousands as they moved, and many a head was uncovered as the ladies passed, as if they had a special power from God.[1]

The Crusade began on Christmas Eve of 1873 in the quiet town of Hillsboro, in southwestern Ohio. Prompted by a temperance lecture on "The Power of Woman's Prayer in Grog Shops," a group of seventy-five ladies dedicated themselves to a campaign against intemperance and began going to saloons to pray for the conversion of liquor dealers.[2] This revolutionary idea—of a prayer meeting "with the locale changed"—soon spread to hundreds of cities throughout Ohio, Indiana, Michigan, Illinois, western Pennsylvania and upstate New York. From town to town, women "who had never even tried to speak or pray outside their own homes were moving rough men to tears with words of tender eloquence."[3]

The most common, definitive feature of the Crusade was saloon visitation. Because this tactic contained the dramatic element of contrast—of the physically weaker sex pleading with the stronger—of morally superior women appealing to spiritually inferior men—the Crusade commanded a widespread audience, from throngs of street spectators to newspaper readers as far away as Europe. No approach to the problem of intemperance had ever so effectively captured the imagination of press and public alike as did the saloon prayer meeting of the "woman's whiskey war." A reporter in Waynesville, Ohio, described a typical visitation:

> I dropped my pencil a moment to an afternoon meeting, held, by permission of Mr. Bowman, at his saloon. It was the most remarkable and impressive scene I have yet witnessed . . . The ladies sang some beautiful hymns, then the leader called on a very nice-looking old lady to pray . . . Men that had probably not heard half a dozen prayers in as many years were deeply touched; and as the ladies rose from their knees, there were tears on almost every face. Not a man seemed to have stirred during the prayer, but at its close the band sang with great force and beauty:
>
> "Tell me the old, old story,"
>
> and one by one, reverently and in silence, the men dropped from the room. The very genius of primitive Christianity seems to have descended upon some of these praying women.[4]

The crusaders frequently alluded to Christ's atonement when they thought of "going into the low part of town and entering one of those vile dens which respectable people abhorred at a distance . . ."[5] If Christ died to cleanse his children of their sins, he surely expected them to undertake soul-saving in a spirit of loving sacrifice. "We knew the blessedness of being reviled and persecuted for Christ's sake," said one woman, ". . . and we all felt it was sweet not only to work, but to suffer for His sake."[6] In this respect, the temperance protest became a means of experiencing Christ. "Never have we felt ourselves nearer heaven," said one crusader, "than when kneeling on the floor of a drinking house, praying for the keeper and for the success of the Woman's Crusade."[7] Many hymns the ladies sang during their visitations reflected this desire for redemption through suffering:

> I am coming to the cross;
> I am poor and weak and blind;
> I am counting all things dross,
> I shall full salvation find.[8]

Another popular hymn, which the women often sang when their entreaties met with failure, affirmed their identification with Christ:

> Must Jesus bear the cross alone?
> No there's a cross for me.[9]

Identification with suffering not only had its sources in the evangelical quest for holiness, but in the women's personal feelings of oppression as well. Woman as victim in need of rescue was often the message that praying bands conveyed in their visitations. In Springfield, Ohio, a teacher who brought her entire class of young ladies to a saloon to sing "Say, Mr. Barkeeper, has father been here?" asked in prayer:

> How long! oh, Lord, how long! must we suffer on and on, while we have left the power to suffer? Oh, God, consider the tears of the oppressed, for on the side of the oppressor is power, which Thou alone can crush.[10]

Correspondents on the scene presented a similar image in their descriptions. An observer in Jeffersonville, Indiana, wrote:

> In their solemn march, they have been compared to a funeral procession; and well they may, for there are mothers there who mourn their first-born slain, and there are mothers, wives and sisters who are pleading for the lives of those dearer to them than life itself.[11]

Underlying this appearance of passivity, however, lay feelings of militant determination. The crusaders saw their visitations as contests with sin, and placed their experience in the tradition of familiar Biblical stories of good battling evil. In their accounts, they likened themselves to Hebrew children passing unscathed through the fiery furnace or to Daniel in the lion's den. In this sense, the Crusade was a sexual confrontation in which women, compelled by the moral urgencies of evangelicalism, attempted to impose their values on men. Crusade minutes were laced throughout with belligerent war imagery. The ladies "enlisted in the ranks," sought out the "fortress of the enemy," engaged in "hand-to-hand combat with the rum power," and demanded a saloon keeper's "unconditional surrender."[12]

Some saloon keepers were not won over by tearful professions of love from the praying ladies. At Savegaut's Saloon in Wheeling, West Virginia, a fist fight broke out and the "police rushed in and cleared the way with their clubs, and delivered the ladies." In New Vienna, Ohio, the proprietor of the Dead Fall Saloon "baptised the crusaders with buckets of dirty water," and in another town a saloon keeper's angry wife drenched the band in beer. In a cock-fighting saloon in Cleveland, the group leader was set upon by dogs, and in Carthage, Missouri, the praying women were pelted with rotten eggs. Such abuse made stirring newspaper copy. On May 5, 1874, "Black Tuesday" in Bucyrus, Ohio:

> Women were thrown down, were dragged and wrenched by brute force from posts and rails to which they clung; were seized by ruffians who were intoxicated, and carried several rods from their companions.[12]

Opposition only spurred the crusaders' determination. When locked from a saloon, they moved their theatre of operation into the street. Since they conducted street work despite the severe weather conditions, the women presented a heartrending sight. At Ripley, Ohio, for example, the ladies were not permitted to hold a prayer meeting in Reinert's Saloon, and so:

> Down on their knees the ladies fell upon the pavement, in snow and sleet, ith a most pitiless wind blowing. Men stood with uncovered heads, and the crowd wept . . . Close against the pane a mother bowed in prayer, and a moment later the door was opened, and Mr. Reinert said, "Ladies, I will quit the business . . ."[12]

Much as they suffered from the weather, the crusaders were delighted with the sympathy that such scenes roused. "I saw that instead of being a disaster," said Mother Eliza Stewart of Springfield, "it was often an advantage, as we had so many more auditors on the street than we could have in the saloon. It excited the sympathy of the throng for the women, and their indignation against the saloon-keeper.[13] "It was a sight calculated to melt the stoutest heart," admitted a reporter in Hillsboro, when the ladies were locked from Dunn's Drugstore and conducted their prayer meeting on the cold flagstones instead.[14]

Exhortation through prayer was not the only tactic used by the crusaders in their campaign to eliminate the liquor traffic. They soon devised other, quite ingenious means of applying social pressure to strip drinking of its respectability. Pledge-collecting, a favorite antebellum practice, resurfaced during the Crusade. In Delaware, Ohio, for example, the young ladies of Ohio Wesleyan University refused to associate with any young man who had not signed the pledge.[15] In Waynesville, Ohio, "books were kept in which the name of every man entering either saloon was registered; the result was a large falling off in the patronage."

Few temperance men questioned this novel reversal of leadership roles. Faith in the redemptive power of women was a shared assumption. "We men must take back seats and be ready to do whatever the women command," said a Cincinnati partisan.[16] The women agreed. They were in charge. "We deem it important," said one committee of crusaders, "to keep this work in the hands of the women of our city."[17]

Nowhere was the truth of this development more visible than at mass temperance meetings, where the full force of community opinion was brought to bear on nonconformists. At these public gatherings, the evangelical belief in the right of "the female brethren" to self-expression reached full flower. Crusaders, along with ministers, offered prayers for the deliverance of their communities. Moses T. Handy, a reporter for the *New-York Daily Tribune* described the scene he found in Mount Vernon, Ohio:

> The meeting, to use a homey Western expression, run itself. Nobody presided. The meeting progressed with the greatest religious fervor till a young man made his appearance and crowded his way to the

pulpit, where, facing the audience, with an excited gesture he called their attention. "Ladies," he said, "I have come to tell you that I can't hold out any longer; I, too, give in. I shall not sell any more liquor, and I want to sign the pledge."[18]

Like a protracted revival meeting, the confrontation gripped communities all over the Western states in a fever pitch of suspense.[19] Praying bands grew in number. Stories of whole towns gone dry were widely circulated in the press. "The world has seen nothing like this woman's temperance movement," said one of its zealous advocates. "It is sweeping over this country like a magnificent prairie fire."[20]

The surrender of a saloon keeper, particularly when he was the final hold-out, prompted a mass celebration in communities where it occurred. In Xenia, Ohio, for example, the "siege" of an intransigent rum-seller ended on February 19, 1874:

> Mr. Steve Phillips, proprietor of the "Shades of Death," invited the ladies to enter, and announced that he would never sell anything intoxicating in Xenia again. Then the ladies, joined by the spectators, sang:
>
> > "Praise God, from whom all blessings flow,"
>
> while the liquors were rolled into the street. A half-barrel of blackberry brandy, the same of high wines, a few kegs of beer and some bottles of ale and whiskey, were soon emptied into the street, amid the shouts of an enthusiastic multitude . . . On every side nothing was witnessed but smiles, laughter, tears, prayers, handshakings and congratulations.[21]

At Hillsboro, the crusaders knocked bungs from barrels and cheered as their contents spilled into the gutter. "I didn't know I was so strong," said one woman, "but I lifted that axe like a woodman and brought it down with such force that the first blow stove in the head of a barrel and splashed the whiskey in every direction."[22] Millennial feelings of great joy permeated all these community celebrations. Typical was the one at South Charlestown, Ohio, where the citizens formed a triumphal procession, marched to the saloon of the last man to surrender, and to the accompaniment of a brass band, serenaded the owner. Christ's kingdom on earth had arrived. Said one: "Who will blame us for feeling unspeakably happy? for we saw the light gleaming over the hill tops."[23]

The millennium was short-lived. By the end of summer, the Crusade had worn itself out. Gradually, bands of temperance agitators ceased their visitations and saloons opened for business as usual. Clearly, the Crusade had not succeeded in abolishing the traffic in liquor.

By other standards, however, the Crusade was not a failure. Intended as a mission to save the souls of liquor dealers, the Crusade instead became a transforming experience for the participants. It brought thousands of women out of their homes and into the community. It gave many their first opportunity to speak publicly, to lead groups, to formulate plans and to execute goals. Uniting in a cause women could identify with gave the crusaders a chance to express shared feelings of sisterhood. And, having learned the power of association, they began to organize beyond the local level. In November 1874, more than one hundred delegates at a convention in Cleveland formed the National Woman's Christian Temperance Union, an organization that was to command the largest following of American women in the nineteenth century.[24] The Crusade not only broke down sectarian boundaries, but also showed women how to liberate themselves from second-class status in the temperance movement.

The crusaders had made an irreversible debut into public life, and they were aware of it. It "startled me into an active thinking life," said one. It gave me "broader views of woman's sphere and responsibility," said another.[25] For many participants, then, the Crusade was a watershed experience, one they celebrated whenever and wherever they gathered for the rest of their lives. By significantly altering their self-concept, the Crusade changed women's ideas about themselves and their relationship to the larger society. As Frances Willard asserted, "Going out on the street brought women face to face with the world's misery and sin," and for the crusaders home would never be quite the same again.[26]

FRIENDSHIP AND RITUAL IN THE WTUL

Elizabeth Payne Moore

Since the publication of Carroll Smith-Rosenberg's "The Female World of Love and Ritual: Relations Between Women in Nineteenth-Century America," scholars interested in women's history have become increasingly concerned with the nature of female ritualized behavior and with what has been labeled "woman-bonding."[1] Female rites such as visiting, gift-giving and parties served to refresh ongoing relationships, to intensify women's identification with each other and to create a "female world." These women, of course, were from a fairly homogeneous background and were not "public" women involved in a career or reform activities.

One sees, however, some of the same phenomena among a group of women who associated together as the Women's Trade Union League (WTUL) more than fifty years later. Founded in 1903 during the annual convention of the American Federation of Labor, the League worked to organize unskilled, mostly immigrant, working women into trade unions and to educate the public on the needs of working women. Few organizations could claim a more sociologically diverse membership. Jewish seamstresses, Italian finishers and Swedish bootworkers came together with middle-class "allies" to work for the improvement of conditions of women workers. Membership included Margaret Dreier Robins and her sister, Mary Dreier, former debutantes from Brooklyn Heights society, as well as Rose Schneiderman, a Polish immigrant seamstress and Elizabeth Maloney, a Chicago waitress.

Members organized women into union locals and provided support for strikers during most of the nation's major labor upheavals of the period. It was they who conceived and then secured the passage of federal legislation providing for the nineteen-volume pioneering survey which paved the way for much of the legislation of the Progressive Era. These women were purposeful, serious about themselves, and passionately committed to changing the social and economic structure in important ways.

But this is the "official" side of their lives and their organization. Underlying their public endeavors, the fabric of their personal relationships and their social life together provided an encouraging context for accomplishing goals that they had set for themselves in the broader society. Female rites like birthday and anniversary parties, open houses and choral groups as well as pageants, festivals and celebrations of strike victories gave women immediate, face-to-face contact across class and ethnic barriers. Such communal experiences did not obliterate the personal hostilities nor mute the cultural differences that such a diverse membership inevitably brought to the organization, but they did give form to the women's quest for fellowship and "solidarity."

A close look at the organization reveals that both workers and allies expressed a yearning for what they called "a larger life" or as the Lawrence picket sign demanded, "Roses as well as bread."[2] David Dubinsky, president of the International Ladies Garment Workers' Union, readily acknowledged that a union "could not hold working women just by a dollar more in their pocket and a short work day. You had to give them something more."[3] Indeed, much of the ritualized social behavior observed in the League was later institutionalized in the Amalgamated Clothing Workers' Union and the International Ladies Garment Workers' Union, predominantly female organizations.[4]

That the women's voices and the particular content of their protest arose precisely when they did was no accident. Female garment workers at the time were America's lowest-paid industrial workers, but that does not in itself explain the intensity of the women's protest since women seamstresses had been among the poorest-paid workers throughout the nineteenth century. Several important segments of American industry had mechanized and subdivided work during the 1880s and 1890s, but the garment industry was the first large one which employed a majority of women to divide work intensively. The large Chicago manufacturer of men's clothing, Hart, Schaffner and Marx, for example, moved "inside"—a term used to denote the assemblying of all work processes under one roof—the same year the League was organized, 1903. The speeding-up system typical of the highly competitive garment factories, especially of the newly emerging women's ready-to-wear industry, and the seasonal nature of the trade resulted in fourteen- to sixteen-hour days, six-day weeks and three- to five-dollar weekly wages—a way of life which made one feel "so dead that one never sees anything," according to a young Russian-

Jewish seamstress.[5] Constant tiredness and fatigue were the ultimate threats to natural growth and to the development of one's potentiality, not the least of which was one's potential motherhood, a fact always in the back of the women's minds. In essence, factory time was being substituted for human rhythm.

In addition to offering avenues for cultivating friendship and expressing sociability, then, the League's social gatherings provided space for experiencing what these women saw as a more natural rhythm. As such, their activities helped members confront discontinuities they faced in the broader society by providing emotional sustenance—what one sociologist calls emotional "nutrition"[6] to women who often found their social environment enervating. Seen negatively, their choral singings, parties and pageants presented a mere countervailing force to the monotony and fatigue of factory life.[7] Seen more positively, however, they were oriented to stimulate, to arouse and deliberately to play with the emotions in order to elicit creativity and hence evoke new self-perceptions. Although they did not necessarily do so, at times the female rites practiced by League women led to "an awakening"—the libidinally loaded euphemism they used to describe a young woman's budding interest in the labor movement. The Chicago WTUL, for example, sponsored Sunday afternoon poetry readings as one of its first activities, and through reading poetry, Margaret Dreier Robins felt, young women became alive to the fact that each had her own story and message to tell. "And so," she later recalled, "one of the first demands in the old days when we were simply reading poetry was for classes in public speaking."[8] Robins obviously felt that reading poetry together had inspired women to develop skills—mastering parliamentary law, English grammar and public speaking, for example—which would enable them to enlarge their scope within the broader society. In 1915 at their biennial convention, for example, one member thought that the League had "grown in surety and strength of purpose to somewhat the proportions of a women's labor parliament," but in tone and atmosphere the convention seemed more like a "jolly family gathering."[9]

Their parties ranged from small, intimate occasions at a member's home to large banquets celebrating a significant event in the history of the League or perhaps a recent strike victory. Life-cycle events like birthdays and anniversaries were the focus of special attention. Often women composed songs or poems for the occasion, detailing events from the life of the one whose birthday was being celebrated. Historians of women working in documents of the Progressive period are frequently amused at the extent to which the female reform community celebrated September 6, Jane Addams's birthday. Yet birthday celebrations were common among all women's organizations, clubs and friendship circles. Birthdays evoked a feeling of basic human *prima materia*—everybody had birthdays—at the same time they focused on the biography of a particular and "special" person.[10]

Not merely preliminary to "serious" work, neither were their social gatherings and celebrations peripheral to the League's identity as a group. In 1924 Samuel Gompers, with whom the women had had a constant tug-of-war, began a drive to assimilate the WTUL under the auspices of a Women's Department in the AFL. Most members energetically fought the move, rejecting male unionists' criticism that they had been ineffectual in their work. Agnes Nestor, a Chicago glove worker and the first woman to head an international union, wrote Robins that year describing a recent party sponsored by the League. She wished, she wrote, that Gompers and other proponents of the absorption plan could have attended "our Girls' dinner," since it was exactly the kind of activity that Illinois Federation of Labor President John Walker and other critics had warned against the League's sponsoring. "We had 111 at the dinner and fully one hundred were trade union women and most of the program was singing . . . We had so much singing that it really was everybody's party. It was a great success. I tried to picture the men getting it up or arranging it."[11]

Drama especially appealed to League women. They read and acted out parts of plays, sometimes writing the plays or pageants themselves. "The festival of life" or "the pageant of life" were metaphors frequently used to describe the richness and diversity which they felt lay beyond the horizon of most working women but which could nevertheless be tapped and experienced via drama. Robins had a highly developed sense of the dramatic, had directed her younger siblings in plays as a child and enjoyed "the something which happens to each of us when for the moment we are caught up in a spirit of exaltation."[12] The League's plays and pageants frequently dealt with themes in the history of women or labor, but the purpose of their dramatic undertakings was less to inform than to encourage creativity. Through writing plays, staging pageants and acting parts, it was hoped that women would discover their own hidden potentiality. Although sometimes didactic, their plays and pageants were essentially celebrations of the powers and capacities of womanhood, allowing women to experiment with roles or ways of being not otherwise encouraged.

League members enjoyed giving each other gifts. Although complex, the ritual of giving gifts seems to have functioned largely for these women as what sociologist Barry Schwartz calls a "generator of identity."[13] As in other rites observed in the League, gifts gave women a freedom to experiment and even to "play" with their self-perceptions. The gift of copies of Ibsen's plays to Rose Schneiderman from a group of women whom Schneiderman had just organized into a union local conveyed how those women saw her as well as what she had evoked in them.[14] The giving of gifts furthermore helped create a system of "gratitude imperatives" without which any group, especially one with women from such diverse backgrounds, could not have long sustained itself. Accepting gifts bonded the recipient to the giver and helped transcend incipient hostilities.

Historians have frequently interpreted the social and leisure-time activities of the League as deflecting time and energy away from the serious task of economic reform, and on occasion—but very rarely—some of the activities were criticized by working women as the charitable concerns of the middle-class allies.[15] One could, however, more appropriately invert this critique: for many of the League women there would have been little energy or vision to tackle economic reform without the intimate, ritualized social contact that the women had with each other. Clearly their social activities were not mere epiphenomena, but neither was there a straight line of evolution from, say, celebrating one's birthday or writing a poem to organizing a new union. The relationship between their social life together and their reform efforts was more subtle and circuitous than that. It was ultimately a matter of being energized and of taking courage—literally of being *encouraged*—or as Leonora O'Reilly had written in her diary, a matter of women saying to other women at crucial times, "go ahead . . . we believe in you."[16]

RITES AND RIGHTS

Cynthia Patterson and Bari J. Watkins

At first glance, the relationship between pageants and the modern women's movement reveals a curious historical irony. In September 1968 members of various radical women's organizations demonstrated against the Miss America Pageant in Atlantic City, New Jersey, for the oppressive image of women the competition perpetuated. The radical women's street-theatre tactics captivated the mass media and provided the American public with its first front-page exposure to the emerging women's liberation movement. More than fifty years earlier, however, the radical women of the National Woman's Party had staged rather than disrupted pageants to protest the same legal and cultural subordination of women in American society. In both instances, women activists acted from a recognition of the power of pageants to create a public image of women. The crucial difference between the radical women of the 1920s and the 1960s lies not in their objectives but in their tactical alternatives. In the 1920s, the Woman's Party organized pageants to depict women in the positive imagery of equality, while in the 1960s, beauty pageants presented an image of women against which women activists rebelled.

Since the early nineteenth century, pageants have held a special place in the development of "female rites." First used by women reformers, by church groups and by schoolteachers to present dramatically social ideals and female solidarity, the female rites of pageantry as an organizational style unique to women's groups and clubs developed naturally into a part of the organized women's movement. Since the Seneca Falls Convention of 1848, women's organizations have frequently utilized the theatrical *rite* of pageantry to promote and publicize their political commitment toward the attainment of various *rights* for women in American society. In this context, the Woman's Party's "Equal Rights Pageants" represent a significant and highly innovative expression of the idea of "female rites" in the history of women in American theatre.

In 1923, the Woman's Party proposed the first Equal Rights Amendment to the U.S. Constitution. By that time, the mass organization supporting the drive for suffrage had disbanded, leaving the Woman's Party as the sole representative of radical feminism in the United States. Viewed as outsiders, the Woman's Party faced a long and disappointing struggle to preserve the earlier spirit of the women's movement.

The Woman's Party's equal rights program aimed at replacing legal inequalities and cultural beliefs in women's innate inferiority and natural domesticity with the ideals of equality, liberty and justice. To secure these goals, the Woman's Party adopted a strategy of legal reform and education designed to eliminate the institutional and cultural barriers underlying the subjugation of women in American society. While the passage of the ERA formed the core of their legal program, the Woman's Party viewed the process of education as the essential prerequisite for transforming cultural attitudes toward women and employed a wide variety of techniques to diffuse their ideas throughout society. The most interesting and creative of their tactics, however, were the Equal Rights Pageants.

From 1923 through 1925, the Woman's Party sponsored three national pageants and a series of state and regional pageants. The basic theme in each pageant was the historical evolution of the women's rights movement. The first major pageant, held in Seneca Falls, New York, July 1923, marked the seventy-fifth anniversary of the Seneca Falls Convention of 1848, when the women's rights movement in the U.S. was officially initiated. As the prototype of the Woman's Party style of pageantry, the Seneca Falls celebration demands careful consideration. The event, worked out in sumptuous detail, involved an opening processional, musical productions and a series of tableaux. At nightfall, a processional of one hundred women dressed in purple flowing gowns, singing the "March of the Woman," paraded from the local Episcopal church to the lake area where a bi-level platform stage stood. Following the processional, approximately five hundred banner girls arrived on barges from across the lake. The banner bearers, dressed in white and carrying the purple, white and gold banners of the Woman's Party, were joined by women representing various professions and together the ensemble encircled the stage and the audience. Then, after a brief silent interlude, Madame Vander Ver, a professional opera singer, performed Handel's *Largo* with lyrics written by Hazel Mackaye, the pageant's director.

When the entire processional had been completed, the lights revealed a higher platform upon which the entire delegation to the 1848 Seneca Falls Convention was represented, complete with hooped skirts and high beaver hats. The climax of the ensuing tableaux occurred when Lucretia Mott followed by Elizabeth Cady Stanton stepped forward and Stanton recited the "Declaration of Sentiments" adopted at the 1848 Convention. As Stanton read the list of principles, trumpets sounded and her words were flashed in light against the darkened sky. Lavinia Egan captured the spirit and format of the pageant in her description of this moment, which appeared in the Woman's Party's weekly journal:

From the darkness below the stage came a solitary figure, frail, grey-clad, Quaker garbed, fearless Lucretia Mott . . . The picture of the intrepid woman who seventy-five years ago dared to emerge from the darkness of ignorance and prejudice and age-old traditions and stand forth against the whole world for a principle was strikingly manifest . . . Elizabeth Cady Stanton and Lucretia Mott clasped hands in the pad of comradeship and co-operation in the great work of freeing one-half of the human race. The symbolism of the thing was superb; the dramatic impact on the mind of the spectator was tremendous.[1]

The closing recessional preserved the idealistic and dramatic quality of the performance as the entire cast sang "Onward Christian Soldiers" and disappeared behind the stage.

The rhetorical flair and idealism conveyed in both the pageant and Ms. Egan's description of the event prevailed in all of the Woman's Party's pageants. The major pageants in Colorado (September 1923) and Westport, New York (August 1924), repeated the basic scheme of their predecessor. The Colorado pageant added the story of the Western pioneer women and their contributions to women's advancement and to the historical drama of the women's movement. At Westport, the historical scope of the pageant was extended even further as women's struggle for equality was re-created on the stage from ancient Greece through the contemporary equal rights campaign of the Woman's Party. In each case, the artistic imagination and ingenuity of the Woman's Party conveyed to thousands of Americans a vision of a better society in which women had finally triumphed in their battle against inequality and subjugation.

The Woman's Party's motives for staging pageants involved much more than a simple desire to entertain. As an instrument of education, the pageant was uniquely suited to overcome the obstacles the Woman's Party confronted among women and throughout the culture. The Woman's Party regarded women as the worst victims of the cultural indoctrination and perpetuation of Victorian notions of womanhood which remained as the major restrictions upon women throughout the 1920s. Blinded by blissful ignorance and false consciousness, content in her subjugation and traditional roles, the American woman of the 1920s stood out as the primary target for the Woman's Party's educational arsenal. Further, the political apathy, materialism, frivolity and conspicuous consumption which seemed to dominate the cultural mainstream presented a related, added source of frustration to the Woman's Party in their educational endeavors. With the Equal Rights Pageants, the Woman's Party believed that it had created an educational medium powerful enough to convert men and especially women to their cause of equality and to transform cultural attitudes toward women.

In 1923, Hazel Mackaye, the Woman's Party's pageant director, explained the educational purpose and methodology underlying these colorful events. "The one consuming passion of the American people," she initially posited, "is to make money . . . The next most absorbing passion is the search for an outlet for the sensuous emotions which have been repressed by the grind of the business world." According to Mackaye, these emotional needs were manifested in the popularity of recreational indulgences such as jazz, car racing, melodramatic sentimental movies and bootlegging. Given this set of priorities, she continued, everything, whether merchandise, ideas, or even religion, must be "sold to the public." Thus, the Woman's Party believed it had to find some medium through which they could educate and inspire an anti-intellectual, apathetic and self-deceiving public. The Woman's Party's solution appears as a variation of the "do as the Romans do" approach: "To get into the game . . . and 'sell' our program to the public." Since the Woman's Party could not bestow monetary profit or social prestige upon individuals, it must reach the public through its other main interest—having a good time.

The pageants, Mackaye pointed out, provided individuals with "a chance to take part in a 'big show,' done on a large scale, with color and beauty—a chance in short to have a good time." Once a public audience was attracted to the event, the success of the educational process was ensured as the nonbelievers were converted to the righteousness and urgency of the Woman's Party's program. With rhetorical flair and conviction, Mackaye described the impact of the pageants on both the cast and the audience:

> The realization came to them that these women today were going on with the noble traditions of the past; that they were forging ahead to win the goal so grandly and so uncompromisingly demanded by those intrepid women seventy-five long years ago. Not one of those women or girls who participated in the pageant could ever again feel indifference toward the cause of Equal Rights. And the same was true of the ten and twenty thousands in the audience. Their imaginations had been touched, illuminated. They were, for the moment, lifted to an unaccustomed but none the less pleasurably thrilling plane of idealism—where all the sordid, petty matters of the ordinary lives ceased to exist.

Once the flame of idealism, the desire for equality, liberty and justice, had begun to burn in the hearts of men and women, the Women's Party felt assured that it could never be extinguished. "Through the pageant therefore," Mackaye concluded, "we found that friends were made for Equal Rights who could never have been gained by any other method, at once so winning and so disarming."[2]

Yet the meaning of female rites as rituals in relation to the Woman's Party goes even deeper than the party's commitment to theatrical rites as a medium for social expression by women. Like all cultural rituals, theatre possesses an internal structure of meanings revealing as much about the artist's perception of him/herself as about the relationship between certain artistic forms and corresponding social and cultural conditions.

In this context, the "Equal Rights Pageants"[3] were also an important symbolic manifestation of the Woman's Party's self-image as a vanguard of idealists whose thoughts and actions were carrying forward the historical struggle of women to achieve equality. The Woman's Party's conviction that their ideals were righteous, their sense of mission and their belief that victory was inevitable emanated from their reflections regarding their own historical importance. For example, the Seneca Falls pageant of 1923, celebrating the seventy-fifth anniversary of the beginning of the women's rights movement, explicitly expressed their self-perception as "torchbearers." During the pageant the symbolic torch of women's emancipation was passed on from the pioneers, Lucretia Mott, Elizabeth Cady Stanton and Susan B. Anthony, to the Woman's Party. The Woman's Party thus created their own past. By drawing a direct historical linkage from themselves back to the early feminist pioneers, the Woman's Party engaged in a search for a continuity of opposition and for historical antecedents to their ideological beliefs.

The Woman's Party's creation of a usable past signified a crucially important aspect of their collective identity and ideological system. Their ability to find themselves in their selective past allowed them to justify their contemporary position as an unsuccessful, criticized and often ignored extremist group while simultaneously providing them with "proof" that they were the end point rather than the beginning in the evolution of a historical movement. Thus, the pageants were as important and meaningful as rituals for the Woman's Party as the Woman's Party hoped they would be for their audience.

Finally, we are left with yet another historical irony. The Woman's Party lost their battle in the 1920s to liberate women and create an egalitarian society. Perhaps, if their pageants had been the effective tool of cultural education the Woman's Party intended them to be, there might never have been an antipageant protest some fifty years later in Atlantic City.

CROWNING MISS CALIFORNIA, AGAIN

James H. Bierman

The *San Francisco Chronicle* had already gone to press with its Sunday paper when Deanna Rae Fogarty was crowned Miss California on Saturday night, June 23, 1979, and the coronation was not considered of sufficient importance to bother holding a space for it. Monday's paper devoted half its front page to the eighth annual Gay Freedom Day Parade, but contained no coverage of the Miss California Pageant. Ten years ago, the paper would not have missed the event. It was not negligible, however, to the sponsors who paid $114,500 to broadcast the event live on seven West Coast network television stations or to the audience which filled the two-thousand-seat Santa Cruz Civic Auditorium to capacity for three nights in a row at a cost of six dollars per seat for the two preliminary showings and twelve dollars for the final pageant. Despite the ups and downs of public opinion the Miss California Pageant has managed to hold its own over fifty-six years.

Being Miss California or possibly Miss America, with the crown and scepter which accompany the office, is the closest thing to obtaining royalty possible for young women in a democratic society, short of marrying a prince of Monaco, and the image of success which comes with it is still very much a piece of the American Dream. More than one hundred thousand women annually apply to compete in local pageants. Seventy thousand enter the competition and their numbers are reduced through local pageants, state pageants and finally the Miss America Pageant to one queen. This program is supported by 250,000 volunteer workers who labor with astonishing civic zeal for the cause. Their cooperative efforts contribute to the mammoth structure of the Miss America Pageant, a nonprofit organization which franchises subsidiary state pageants, which in turn sell franchises to local pageants.

Being a nonprofit operation employing only one full-time staff member, the Miss California Pageant is unique in the field of popular entertainment in that it is entirely free of profit motive. This independence attracts a staff of volunteer workers whose dedication is not diluted by financial concerns. It also means that the pageant can exist unfettered by a need for the approval of popular or monied interests. Ironically, the events and the queens they produce continue to be a product the public purchases. A total of 2.8 million people watched Deanna Rae Fogarty receive her crown on twenty-four percent of California's televisions. The ratings from 8:00 to 9:00 P.M. on June 23 were the highest in the west. Had she been chosen as a finalist in the national pageant at Atlantic City, more than sixty-five percent of the television-viewing audience across the country would have watched her belt out "Mein Herr" and "Wilkommen."

The Miss America Pageant remains a cornbelt phenomenon which focuses on the amorphous middle of America. It demands community involvement and tends to establish itself best in those small communities where the involvement is highest. San Francisco sent no candidate to the 1979 Miss California Pageant, while such places as Morro Bay, Reedley, San Luis Obispo, Fresno County and Lake County were represented. In general, the geographic distribution of the local pageants coincides with the political distribution of the population, with the more conservative areas producing the most contestants. Out of the thirty-three contestants participating in the Miss California Pageant, nine came from the Los Angeles–Orange County area.

Local pageants begin in July of the year previous to a given Miss California Pageant and continue through April of the next year. Some, such as the San Joaquin County Pageant, involve thorough and rigorous screening processes. In 1978, 125 applicants were interviewed, and twenty-nine were selected to compete. Ten finalists selected from preliminary pageants were then given ten weeks of intense training in such required areas as walking, dress, hair styling and developing their talent. Then on a final night of competition, Parlisha Sophia Watts, a nineteen-year-old student at San Joaquin Delta College, was selected. One of three black candidates to make it to the state finals, she sang a rendition of "I've Got Love" that was spunky, brazen and "Black." She eventually came in third in the state, winning the $1,000 scholarship award for second runner-up. To put on her local pageant, the people from the Miss San Joaquin County Pageant Association raised $19,000, of which $15,000 went to producing the event and $4,000 was divided up in scholarship prizes.

Irony was not lacking in the selection of Gil Stratton, a well-known Los Angeles television sports commentator, as a cohost for the final night of the Miss California Pageant. In fact, the pageant bears greater similarity to a sporting event than to any other recognizable genre of public entertainment. The highly specialized behavior demanded in a pageant requires a special training without which no woman stands a chance. There is no such thing as a "natural" in the pageant just as there is no such thing as a person who has a natural ability to pole-vault. Such behavior must be learned and can only be developed through training. Similarly, during pageant week, a Miss California candidate is required to perform activities and present herself in ways which are unlikely to be repeated in her life.

Despite this, one of the ideological themes of the pageants is individualism. At the outset, the general chairman of a pageant receives a memo from the executive secretary, Ruth McCandliss, headed "Re: Let the Contestants Be Themselves," which encourages them to allow the candidates to nurture their individuality:

> We encourage the National Finalists to show their individuality, and this holds true where dress is concerned. We strongly advocate "good taste" in the selection of wardrobe, a hair style which is becoming to the contestant and comfortable for *her* to wear, and a reminder that what is worn under her dress or swimsuit is her own decision . . . If a young woman can enhance her appearance (within the confines of good taste) then the more power to her.
>
> So please do not permit anyone to question any addition(s) to wardrobe (swimsuit or dress) which the modern woman considers an aid in making her a more attractive person.
>
> You must, of course, operate within the framework of instructions from State Pageant Headquarters when selecting wardrobe. Certain requirements are made regarding type of swimsuit, dress for Judges Interview, rehearsal clothes, etc.

Allowing contestants to wear padding as they choose is hardly an expression of individuality. As it is, all the 1978 Miss America candidates came within an inch or two of the standard 36–24–36 or 35–23–35 measurements (the twelve-inch hourglass), and padding merely serves as an aid to conformity, rather than individuality. Nonetheless, the rhetoric of the pageant continues to stress the American ideal of individuality, and a late 1960s style belief that a person's success depends on the development of her own individual potential. Deanna Rae Fogarty expressed this ideal when asked about her role in the women's movement. "We all do it on our successes. I'm not out to fight for them. Women will have to draw their own strength from within. This [indicating her body] is only an exterior."

Despite the rhetoric, serious pageant candidates have very little room for personal expression in dress, hair, makeup, or even self-presentation. To begin with, each must conform to the numerous conditions of a twenty-nine-page rule book, with five full pages on swimsuits alone, which they are given upon arriving at Santa Cruz. This book contains such a stupefying list of stipulations that a pageant week promises less freedom for the participants than basic training or state prison. During the stay in Santa Cruz, each contestant is attended by a close entourage of chaperones from their local pageant area and hostesses from Santa Cruz. The hostesses—"outstanding women of the community who are selected because of their abilities, graciousness, and joy in being with others"—act as constant companions to the contestants, picking them up at their motels, delivering them to the Santa Cruz Civic Auditorium, the site of the pageant, and returning them to their motel. They have full charge of all the contestant's activities, interviews, pictures, recordings and any other appearances and must accompany her at all times unless she is in the company of her chaperone. The chaperone is described as a "companion and friend, buffer, champion and watchdog." Her particular function is to be on constant surveillance for the possibility of "unacceptable and uncomfortable situations." Except onstage, no contestant has contact with the outside world except through the mediation of a chaperone or hostess. In particular they are protected from men—even fathers. As the rule book states:

> So many fathers are handsome and young looking, and could easily be taken for your "gentleman friend." Therefore, we limit then as to contact with you, as we so all other males.

This constant guard also assures adherence to a conduct code which prohibits attendance at unscheduled parties, meetings, or social events, smoking in public, imbibing alcoholic beverages or entering any establishment where alcoholic beverages are served, taking unprescribed drugs or tranquilizers, or being in the presence of judges or men.

The pageant has a history of being attacked by conservatives and liberals and it has become so defensive that it obsessively protects the contestants. If anything, it has erred on the conservative side of the issue, but this has been, in part, stimulated by a desire to distinguish itself from a host of imitations that have spun off from the Miss America Pageant over the years: Miss USA, Miss Universe, Miss Rheingold, Miss Subways, Miss Chinese-America, Miss California Rodeo, and so on. Anyone on the staff of any Miss America Pageant would be quick to explain that these are merely "beauty" pageants whereas the Miss America Pageant (and its state and local counterparts) is a "scholarship" pageant. These women are selected on the basis of the "whole person," not just their bodies.

The swimsuit competition is the area where the Miss America Pageant is forced to be the most defensive. In the 1970s the contestants were finally allowed a choice which extended beyond the one-piece paneled swimsuit, but the regulations which still apply don't amount to much of a liberation. Above all, the regulations steer clear of any hint of sexiness in the suits with such guidelines as "the fit of the suit in the bust and crotch areas must be smooth and trim and not revealing. Pay particular attention to these areas when making the selection." It is this concern which probably resulted in relaxing the requirement of the "panel" suit and not the fact that it had been long outdated. In effect, the front panel served to call attention to the crotch rather than hide it.

A woman parading on a ramp through the Santa Cruz Civic Auditorium in front of two thousand fully clothed spectators wearing an outdated single-piece swimsuit with matching four-inch spike-heeled shoes (in style again) while Jack Fisher and the Miss California Orchestra play cocktail-lounge music presents an absurd image. Although the pageant took place on the Santa Cruz beach until 1954 where swimwear was more appropriate, its history does little to justify its present form. The stated justification announced to the audience during the pageant is that "it enables our judges to determine health qualities, the attitudes our contestants portray while meeting this more difficult part of our program, and the self-discipline she possesses in caring for herself." The contestants are told that the swimsuit competition is the "health portion" of the competition permitting the judges to evaluate their "form, carriage, proportions, skin tone, etc.," while the judges' instructions direct their attention toward such abstract qualities as "beauty, figure, grace, poise and posture."

Despite the confusion about the purpose of the swimsuit competition, there can be little doubt that the pageant would lose its appeal without it. Joseph Merkel, the press director of the 1979 Miss California Pageant, inadvertently revealed this attitude when he said jokingly of the swimsuit competition, "It's the name of the game." It is the element of the Miss America Pageant most often included in the imitation pageants. However, in their effort to distinguish themselves, the Miss America Pageant has not been able to abandon the swimsuit competition, realizing that it is essential to its popularity. As the judging goes, the swimsuit competition carries one-sixth of the weight. Each candidate has a personal interview which carries an equal weight, as does her appearance in the evening gown competition. The talent competition is given an importance equal to the total of the other three parts, thus allowing it half the emphasis, but it is difficult to imagine any woman with a less than shapely body possessing enough talent, poise, or personality to be Miss America.

Five judges sit at an elevated table by the stage-left side of the ramp. Normally composed of three men and two women, the panel is drawn from "pageant family": producers, directors, chaperones and fashion and grooming specialists involved in other state pageants. They are also experienced judges, having developed an expertise in recognizing the specialized behavior demanded. Because the judges are longtime products of the pageant system, they tend to pick winners who perpetuate the values previously encouraged. Their aim is toward conformity with other judges. Being housed in the same hotel, the Dream Inn, it is understandable that the judges spend time together and discuss candidates, influencing one another with comments about their favorites. Veteran judge Al Castagnola supports this behavior. "It's natural to talk about the job, and it's better to openly discuss the merits of each girl. That way the judges' decisions are more considered and more informed."

The most abstract judging comes in the evening gown section of the entertainment. Each contestant steps up to a microphone and is given fifteen seconds to introduce herself to the audience, present her background, ambitions and philosophy of life.

> Good evening, I'm a twenty-one-year-old senior at Cal Poly-Pomona. My major's elementary education because I would like to have a part in molding the young children who'll be our citizens of tomorrow into integrated persons: physically awake, mentally alert, spiritually alive. I wish to further my education by obtaining my master's degree in music at USC. Thank you.

She then steps onto the ramp and parades across, making two stops, one in front of the judges, one across from them, where she then executes slow-motion militarylike turns, stopping periodically with her feet poised at right angles to each other. As in the swimsuit competition, contestants move with a special motion like models; their shoulders drawn back a little farther than normal, their heads a little higher. There are specific technical qualities to these walks which the beauty experts among the judges (usually the two women) recognize and evaluate and points can be gained or lost depending on the amount of scapula showing or skin tone, but usually the judges respond to instructions which tell them to evaluate poise, grace and general appearance.

Since such qualities are difficult to quantify, it is hard to imagine the judges remaining totally objective. Judges develop their own way of looking for the required qualities. "I don't look at the gown," says Al Castagnola, "I look for poise, presence, command of the stage, how a girl radiates. I look at what she's doing when she's not in the spotlight. Is she onstage? Is she smiling?" It is evident that a lot of outside behavior is counted in evening gown competition and the contestants are instructed never to appear during pageant week without makeup, proper dress and a smile.

Another aspect of the contestant's performance that spills over is the personal interview. "The interview keeps coming back all the time in your mind," confirms Castagnola. The contestants appear before the panel of judges for a five-to-seven minute interview in which they are asked questions ranging from "Who is the Prime Minister of Canada?" to "What is your opinion of [California's] Proposition 13?" or "What are your feelings about marriage?" Interviews are scheduled over the two days of preliminary judging and, as they are videotaped, they have the added formality of TV lights and cameras, as well as the presence of the panel of judges set up like a press conference. Such conditions would normally be intimidating to candidates, except for the fact that, like all other parts of the competition, they have had thorough coaching from a trained and experienced team which probably included hours of practice interviews and briefings on current events. The judges are instructed to evaluate "personality, mental alertness, vocabulary, voice, general knowledge, personal appearance, sincerity and manners," but they also look for specifics. For instance, they will ask questions which the contestant cannot answer to see how forthrightly she will acknowledge her ignorance. They will also test the political inclinations of the candidates, and few will risk their chances by offering anything but guarded conservative responses.

The easiest part of the judging is also the weightiest—the talent competition. Often the talent displayed is one which is developed, with considerable coaching, for the occasion, and since it must be demonstrable through performance, singing and dancing are the most frequent choices. Out of thirty-three 1979 Miss California finalists, twenty-five sang or danced or did both for their two-minute, forty-second presentation. In past years, certain talents have been more likely to produce winners. Classical musicians have a higher probability of winning than the practitioners of such unusual talents as roller skating or baton twirling. Very unusual talent displays, such as the sign-language presentation of poetry, stand very little chance of winning. Those who sing tend to do songs popularized by well-known singers such as Garland and Streisand in the style of those singers, and looking at this portion of the pageant, one often sees the shadows of other more famous performers onstage. In effect, the competition inadvertently serves as a homage to the popular heritage of women.

What the judging aspires to in all its aspects is a Miss California who is talented, beautiful and intelligent. There is a functional aspect to this, since the judges remember that they are selecting someone who will serve as unofficial state hostess for the coming year, presiding at numerous civic functions as well as other pageant functions and commercial engagements. Furthermore, the Miss America–Miss California pageants have identified themselves as "scholarship" pageants since 1945, serving the cause of women in their totality rather than that aspect which is represented by the bathing beauties of the original 1921 pageant.

Despite the fact that they attracted vociferous opposition from the women's movement in the late 1960s, the pageant represents the largest scholarship organization for women in the world. Between 1950 and 1980 the Miss California Pageant awarded over $144,650 in scholarships. As of 1980, local and state pageants throughout the United States handed out approximately $2,000,000 annually, and the Miss America Pageant alone offered another $116,000 in scholarship prizes. As a result of the diligence of volunteer fund-raising efforts, these figures are rising. The local pageants of the Miss California Pageant increased their awards from $16,325 in 1970 to $48,000 in 1978. The Miss California Pageant prize monies increased from $8,000 to $13,500 in 1979 alone—these funds coming from the Campbell Soup Company, the Gillette Company, the Kellogg Company, Santa Cruz financial institutions, the Shoong Foundation and others. Contestants are allowed to put their winnings toward any form of instruction they select, and the choice normally ranges from law school to voice lessons or beauticians' school. All are met with equal favor by the pageant organization. In addition to scholarship prizes, pageant winners collect thousands of dollars' worth of gifts such as cars, furs, wardrobes, free hair styling, free travel, free room and board, etc., and they are capable of earning a considerable amount from their modeling or appearance fees as a reigning queen. In all, the awards are sufficient to attract many contestants who would not otherwise be part of a beauty pageant. Feminists can find numerous reasons for objecting to the mode of selection of scholarship recipients and to the compromises involved in creating this public image of women, but they are still obliged to acknowledge the amount of financial support that can be gained.

The Miss California Pageant at the Santa Cruz Civic Auditorium is now structured for TV, a change that affects the contestants and the whole spirit of the "live" event at the same time that it extends the audience from 2,000 to 2.8 million. Despite nostalgia for the old days when the pageant was held on the beach, and evident problems arranging the current format, the "pageant family" remains committed to the event for the "civic involvement it generates," in Al Castagnola's words. It is now an institution so thoroughly established that it exists of and by itself.

TAKE BACK THE NIGHT

Starhawk

Rallies, meetings and demonstrations raise power—but rarely do organizers think about grounding it afterward. Grounding does not have to be elaborate—simply remembering to formally end each working session will help earth the power. Group members might simply take hands in a circle and sit quietly for a moment. Recently, there has been a growing tendency in the feminist movement to incorporate ritual into conferences and demonstrations, for the express purpose of grounding and channeling the power raised. The following is an account of a ritual several women and I created in November 1978, as part of a conference on violence and pornography, with the theme "Take Back the Night!" The climax of the weekend was a march through the North Beach section of San Francisco, the heart of the topless-bottomless and massage parlor scene. The ritual took place in Washington Square Park, at the end of the march.

The women pour in from the street. It takes so much longer than we expected. I had no conception of three thousand women in a mass.

Witches, at the front of the march, aspurge North Beach with salt water. They chant Laurel's couplet:

> Wipe the slate clean,
> Dream a new dream!

At Broadway and Columbus, the artists create a mini-ritual around their float. In the front, it is a giant, candle-lit Madonna; behind, slabs of dead meat and pornographic magazines. A strong symbol of images that squeeze women into narrow, hurtful roles. They bring out the float, chant, tear the pornography into confetti. Holly Near sings.

We wait at the park, too nervous to leave and risk not getting back in time. The witches arrive at the entrance to the park, form a double line, a birth canal. They hold lighted candles and incense and sprinkle the women with salt water as they enter:

> From a woman you were born into this world,
> By women you are born into this circle.

We are onstage (the back of Anne's truck). Our backdrop is the lit facade of the church: an irony. Lennie Schwendinger of Lighten Up has created beautiful lighting for us—it is the first time I have done a ritual so theatrical, where the bright lights cut us off from the crowd, who become "audience." Our pool of light seems the only world—and I'm not sure I like it. Behind us, in the trees, a woman's acrobatic troupe, Fly By Night, perform a slow, aerial dance.

Nina leads the chant:

> We're taking back the night,
> The night is ours!

The women are not dancing, as we had hoped. The audience-performer image is too strong—they are watching us. I feel awkward, unsure of what to do. The chant dies away—still, crowds are flowing into the park . . .

Toni Marcus begins to play her violin. The sound carries over the park, electric, magical . . .

We can put off starting no longer. I take the microphone, and say that we should turn for a moment and look at each other, at how beautiful we are, how real we are . . .

I say, "We have been taught that women's bodies are unclean, that our sexuality degrades us, that we must either be virgins or whores. But we accept neither image! Instead we raise the banner of the naked goddess, whose body is truth, who is within us, in the human spirit.

"We say that our bodies are sacred, because they bring forth life, because they are life, because they give *us* pleasure, because with them we make, build, think, laugh, create and do . . ."

Lee and I lead the responsive chant:

> Our bodies are sacred,
> Our breasts are sacred,
> Our wombs are sacred,
> Our hands are sacred . . .

It builds and builds.

Our voices are sacred,
Our voices carry power!
The power to create!
The power to change the world!
Let go—let them become sound—
Chant without words—let them be heard!

The voices roar into the night. Not a cone—it is too strong, too amorphous—
a tidal wave sweeping out of the park.

It stops. Quietly, I lead a soft, low chant. A humming—the buzz of two
thousand bees, a deep throb.

Over it, Hallie leads the meditation:

"Softly, softly now begin to feel the earth's energy beneath your feet as She
dances with us.

"Close your eyes . . . feel your strength sparkling through your body and
women around you. This is the power generated by our marching, our chanting, our dancing, our destruction of the symbols of violence. Know that each
of us, and all of us together, have the power to change the world. Feel the
affects of your action rippling out into the world . . . reflect on how your life
will be different.

"Open your eyes and look about you . . . see our strength in one another's
face . . . know that we are strong. Know what the women of old knew . . . that
the night must belong to us. Know that we are women who take back the
night. Know that the night is ours!"

Cheers, laughter, screams, kisses. Some of us touch the earth. The women
follow. The ritual is done.

RITUAL AND THE NATIONAL BLACK THEATRE

Barbara Ann Teer

We didn't do our first piece until '71. But before that the standard of art
was created. The standard was basically what I call the five cycles of
evolution. We went through what I call the "nigger" cycle, the "negro" cycle
and militant, nationalistic and revolutionary cycles. We analyzed each of those
cycles from a social point of view, a religious point of view, a political point of
view. We found out about the colors, the foods, the lifestyle of the family, the
relationships of people within each of those cycles. Each performer was
required to go through each cycle. Each person had to keep a notebook of pictures and experiences when they went into each cycle. They would have to
dress their cycle; they would have to live around those people. It was a total
educational process. Then when we got to the revolutionary cycle we found it
was all the same.

In the meantime, we were having symposiums on Sunday where we invited all of the major figures in the black world to come and address themselves to the community about whatever was going on. Rap Brown, Stokely Carmichael, James Foreman, my sister Fredrica Teer and Congressman Charles Rangel all spent a Sunday afternoon with a hundred people or more. We would rap and talk and exchange and try to get in touch with what this overwhelming force was that was called blackness. It wasn't simply a skin color to me, it never was, but it was what made me unique. We decided to perform after these two-and-a-half years. We realized that we had a standard, but we didn't have a form to hold the standard, and that's when I started creating rituals. Ritual is the theatre. Our first production was *The Ritual* and it was done on Channel 13. It was so popular they got a thousand phone calls, and the show was aired three time consecutively back to back. That caused the show to go national. We then got a lot of different job offers, none of which I took because they were all too commercial, and I thought it would water-down this thing.

In those days people used to get possessed, just go right out, you know. The drums would take them out. They would talk in tongues, and they would tell stories, and they would share with me all kinds of things when they came back. They experienced a freedom I had never seen before. I was just loving every minute of it. I couldn't sleep at night I was so turned on. I began creating exercises and processes and techniques to handle the energy and I continued to go to my mentors, who were church people.

Ritual got us a semi-visibility in the black world. We started touring college campuses and black studies programs performing *The Ritual to Regain Our Strength and Reclaim Our Power*. During the performances people would get so turned on they would spontaneously start running up and down the aisles just celebrating themselves—you never saw anything like it. By this time I had changed all the standard theatrical titles. I said we were not actors, we were liberators. Our theatre wasn't a theatre—it was a temple. Our techniques were in a form I called ritualistic revival—we were doing revival form, we weren't doing play form.

THE STORY OF A MOTHER, A RITUAL DRAMA

Martha Boesing, in collaboration with the women of At the Foot of the Mountain

The Story of a Mother is a kaleidoscope of images which explores the relationship between mothers and daughters. Scripted scenes about the myths, the key memories, the repressed feelings and, finally, the bonding of mothers and daughters are interspersed with structured audience-participation events in which all present are invited to see the world as their mothers did, and to speak both the spoken and the unspoken words which hang in the air between all daughters and their mothers. Music for the production was improvised on guitar, reed flutes and percussion instruments (water glasses, clay pots, temple gongs, sticks). Traditional songs were also sung and three songs were set to music by Roberta Carlson. Following is an outline of the play with its five open-ended ritual segments that change shape from audience to audience. Included with the ritual segments is some actual "audience response" material that Ellen Anthony recorded and transcribed.

A. MOURNING

1. The Big Mother (the play begins and ends with a gigantic Mother figure created by one actress sitting on another's shoulders, the two of them covered by a long white dress with apron, the upper actress wearing a nobcap).
2. The actress wearing the cap takes it off, descends from the other's shoulders, and becomes a daughter who mourns her mother's death.
3. The other actresses, as chorus, catalog the means of her death (she died washing the dishes . . . hanging out the laundry . . . mashing the potatoes . . . flushing out the diapers, and so on to the end . . . reaching out for love).
4. Daughter speaks to the mother at graveside of what she would have done "if only you could have looked at me."
5. All sing "Sometimes I Feel Like a Motherless Child."
6. Images of Loving and Fighting: scenes of familiar ritual interactions.
7. Performers chant and sing, calling forth Mother, which leads the audience into the first open ritual.

Ritual I: The Calling Forth of the Mothers

(One of the actresses speaks to the audience improvisationally, using the following outline:)

ACTRESS: Be aware of your breathing, just breathe. Call for your mother, whatever name you would use, until she appears. See her in front of you. Notice age, standing or sitting, what she is wearing, how her hair is, hands, all physical characteristics what she is doing. Approach her or let her approach you. Look at her, speak, touch. Ask her: Can I enter you? Slowly enter in whatever way is right for you. Turn around. Fit your feet, legs, thighs, genitals, pelvis, hips, stomach, spine, chest, breasts, shoulders, arms, wrists, hands, fingers, neck, head, chin, cheeks, mouth, nose, forehead, eyes, skull, into hers (one at a time). Be aware of yourself as her, what you are doing, where you live, how you feel, and so forth. When you are ready, open your eyes, see the world as she saw it.

(If it is a small group, the actress may call on each person in the group, but with a large group the audience is asked to speak voluntarily.)

ACTRESS, AS MOTHER: There were certain things which I always said over and over again. Are there things that you always said that you would like to say again now?

(The audience members, speaking as their mothers, call out: "I always said" and finish it with a phrase appropriate to their own mothers. Examples from production experience: "I told you so"; "Now don't worry about money, money comes when you need it"; "If everyone else jumps off the bridge, are you going to, too?"; "You made your bed, now lie in it"; "Make your bed"; "But I'm not everybody else's mother"; "Wait till your father comes home"; "I hope you have three just like you"; "You'll never know how much I love you"; "This hurts me more than it hurts you"; "You know they're only after one thing." When everyone has spoken, the actress says:)

ACTRESS: Close your eyes. Get in touch with that part of you which is not your mother. Leave her in the same way that you entered her. See yourself as separate from her. You might want to tell her what it felt like to be her. Say good-bye. When you are ready, open your eyes, see the world again as you see the world.

B. HIDING

1. Hide and Seek: rituals of attention-getting.
2. The Mother's List of Things to Do: a mother sits rocking, listing all she has to do while a daughter begs for attention (take chair to upholsterer, put up storm windows, get driver's permit for Curtis, call furnace cleaner, In a minute!).
3. The Calls for Dinner (the familiar words, phrases, responses of family at dinnertime ["Everything's getting cold on your plates!"; "I hate this vegetable crap—Daddy says crap!"]).
4. Baby Feeding: a pantomime with chorus and song in monosyllables.
5. It Says in the Book: conflict between a mother's instincts and what "the book" says ("It says in the book not to pick her up when she's crying.").
6. Closed Doors: the child overhearing mother's secret sounds, muffled anger, stifled sobs, sexual sighs; the mother finding and comforting the child.
7. Goodnight Rituals.

Ritual 2: The Healing (Redeeming of the Daughter)

(Actress 1 brings a bowl of water and washcloth to Actress 2. Actress 1 chants, "The mother says to the daughter . . ." as Actress 2 says something truthful to daughter and washes her. Other actresses do this. Actress 1 invites the audience to speak as mothers or become their mothers and say something to the daughter, beginning with the phrase, "I want you to know." Actress 2 washes another actress in response to each one who speaks from the audience.

Examples from production experience: "I did the best I could"; "I didn't know how to love you"; "I didn't want to hurt you"; "I envy you"; "I need you"; "Dad and I are glad you're a girl"; "I like you the way you are"; "You're the most important woman in my life"; "Most of the time I felt afraid"; "You'll always have a home.")

C. INITIATING

1. The Daddy Jig: to a square dance, the calls repeat familiar phrases about "Daddy" (Actress 1: Right-hand star if you don't mind the bother; Left-hand star— Actress 2: You're just like your father— Actress 1: Move to the center and give me a shout— All: Your father won't like it— Actress 1: Now move on out—).
2. The Rape Dream: daughter recounts a dream of rape that follows the formula other women who have rape dreams will recognize; the mother comforts.
3. The Shampoo—Ritual Scenes of Preparation: ("We'll make you all pretty for Daddy"); Wetting ("The water is not too hot"); Soaping ("No, I won't get soap in your eyes"); Rinse ("Daddy won't recognize you because you're so clean and sparkling); "Boys, boys, boys, that's all you ever think about").
4. Making Up: the little girl watches the mother get ready for going out ("Can I watch?" "When you die can I have it?" "What's that blue stuff for?" "Are all mothers as pretty as you?").
5. Your Father Is a Wonderful Man: the actress asking the little girl questions was also putting on makeup and at the end of "Making Up" she transforms into a mother who descends the stairs in anticipation of the father as her audience. He isn't there, he's late, so she has a monologue in which she tells her daughter all the wonderful things about her husband ("You're a lucky girl to have your father for a father"; "I could fill a whole book with things you don't know about your father").
6. Menses Image: the daughter throws bloody bandages to the mother, who catches them, crosses to the daughter and slaps her face.
7. Menstruation Scene: mother-daughter interaction on day daughter's period starts.

Ritual 3: The Words Never Said (Giving Voice to the Scream)

(The audience is invited to speak as the mothers they are, or to become their mothers again, and say something that was never said, beginning with the phrase: "I never said."

Examples from production experience: "Sometimes I hate you"; "I'm sorry you turned out to be a girl"; "I'm jealous of you"; "I need a mother, too"; "I believed in you"; "It would be easy"; "I was perfect.")

D. SEPARATING

1. The "Do You Like Yourself" Clichés: familiar female self-deprecation.
2. The Hysteria Transfer: the mother begins with self-hatred ("I hate this chair"; "I hate the cleaning"; "I hate my husband"; "I hate my eyes"); she is countered by the daughter ("Your eyes are beautiful"), but then the roles transform and the daughter takes on self-hatred while the mother consoles.
3. The Chicken Monologue: a daughter at the dining room table recounts a fight between her mother and father, and as the father puts the mother down and the mother retreats from the fight, the daughter chokes on a chicken bone.
4. One actress comes to the choking daughter like an animal mother, licks her all over, the daughter relaxes and is healed.
5. The Big Mother (seen in the opening scene) reappears on a darkened stage and lights six candles that have been set out as another actress sings "Mother" ("M" is for the million things she gave me, etc.).

Ritual 4: The Words Never Said (Adorning the Mother)

(The Big Mother takes center stage and opens her arms as if to invite the audience into them. As the actresses and members of the audience say things they never said to their mothers that they always wanted to say, long colorful ribbons are placed on the Mother's arms and about her neck and hat. Audience members can come out of the audience to do the placing, or they can remain seated and the actresses will place the ribbons for them. Each person begins with the phrase: "I never said."

Examples from production experience: "I want to grow up to be just like you"; "Thank you"; "I'm glad I'm your daughter"; "I realized you had a hard life"; "I don't want you to die"; "I respect your choices"; "You were right"; "You're the strongest woman I've ever known"; "I need you"; "I like you the way you are"; "There's a lot of you in me"; "I'm proud of you"; "I appreciate all you've done for me"; "I want to know who you are."

When the audience response is finished, the Big Mother says, "I lit the candles for you. And he always said . . ." An actress responds as "he": "What-cha lighting the candles for? What a dumb thing to do to light the candles." At that the actresses blow out the candles and Big Mother disappears.)

E. BIRTHING

1. Plate Scene: angry mothers in chain of putting down plates, picking them up, arguing with children, driven to the point of frustration and hysteria ("Do you think I'm a slave? Is that what you think?" "Hired help. I don't do this for pay, I do this for you . . ." "Nobody cares about me. Nobody cares what I feel." "Who am I? I am nobody. That's who I am." "Nobody likes me"). For a moment there is a tableau of images of women killing themselves or their children with broken plate shards.

2. Actress in monologue speaking as her own mother: one actress as daughter whispers repeats of the mother's refrains as the mother recites her own sense of life and how she's come to terms with it.

3. Big Mother enters with teardrops on her face. She goes to center stage and slowly takes them off, dropping them to the floor.

4. A child is born from under Big Mother's skirts.

5. Big Mother sings lullabies to the child.

6. Acknowledging the Woman Hating: mothers and children, in conversation, review familiar comments and phrases ("When my hair was black, they used to say I was a tease . . . but once I started getting these gray hairs, I was a useless old hag"; "Whenever I reached out to touch people, they said I was acting needy, or that I was an easy catch. Just like a woman. But if I kept my hands to myself, they said that I was cold, probably frigid"). The mothers say that this was done to keep women apart, to keep mothers and daughters apart. A mother says, "I'll tell you what, I'll give you my arms. They're damn strong. They've carried laundry and groceries and suitcases and dirty diapers and boxes of books and wastebaskets full of cat shit and all my sleeping children upstairs and down. And they're very soft. They've held all of the people I've loved, sometimes all night long." The daughters reply, "Just like a woman, she said."

Ritual 5: Communion

(The actresses carry bread to the audience and give some to each member of the audience, saying softly to each either: "Nurture yourself with this food" or "Let the mother within feed the child within." They might give bread to one person at the end of a row and ask the audience to pass the bread along, offering bread to one another with these phrases. As they do this, one actress remains onstage and sings "The Song of the Mother":)

ACTRESS:
>
> We will walk through the streets of this city which sleeps,
> which sleeps, my daughter,
> you and I.
> You carry the bowl,
> I'll bring the grain,
> on this parade through the city.
>
> We will walk through the streets of this city which sleeps,
> which sleeps, my daughter,
> you and I.
> I'll take the ashes,
> you bring the jonquils, daughter,
> on this parade through the city.
>
> We will walk through the streets of this city which sleeps,
> which sleeps, my daughter,
> you and I.
> You carry my heart,
> I'll carry you, my little daughter,
> on this parade through the city.

F. THE BIG MOTHER'S FINAL SPEECH:

(One actress becomes a child curled up on the floor and then grows into the Big Mother—a reversal of the opening image:)

BIG MOTHER: How could anyone tell this story? It's too long. It's hundreds of thousands of years long. It's been writing itself since the world began—every day of every year and every minute of every day. I mean, history is so much simpler than this story of a mother. *(Pause)* We've survived. That's something to tell. Through the dirty dishes and the children sitting on our laps and the men leaning on our arms and the tyranny of their myths and their movies and their songs, we have survived. And who could say what it is like? In the end the only thing to say is that we go on living—with all of our beings we go on living. And the entire planet depends upon our ability and our willingness to do it.

G: THE INTRODUCTIONS: THE CONCLUSION

(Each of the actresses introduces herself and her mother's name, inviting the audience to stand and do the same: "I am Cecilia, daughter of Margaret"; "I am Phyllis, daughter of Mary Jane"; "I am Martha, daughter of Mary"; "I am Jennifer, daughter of Martha"; "I am Aurora, daughter of Lena"; "I am Jan, daughter of Marilyn"; "I am Robyn, daughter of Liela May.")

"LESSON I BLEED":
ADRIENNE KENNEDY'S BLOOD RITES

Rosemary K. Curb

"Lesson I bleed" is the opening line of Adrienne Kennedy's play *A Lesson in a Dead Language*.[1] The syntactically ambiguous line might well serve as a slogan for all of Kennedy's plays, since the female characters in other plays are obsessed with blood as well.

To become a woman means to bleed. The phases of progression from girlhood to womanhood all involve bleeding: menstruation, sexual initiation or deflowering and childbirth. The three uniquely female rites of passage are naturally terrifying to a girl/woman experiencing them for the first time because all three involve internal pain never before experienced and the sight of blood coming out of her body. Since blood means life and loss of it means death, the uninitiated girl is frightened that something vital has torn loose inside of her and she is dying. Not only does her changing adolescent body seem an alien and uncomfortable garb forced on her against her will, but she has a sense of being transformed into her mother. Her mother and other older women may contribute to her sense of confusion about becoming a woman by calling menstruation "the curse" and indicating that menstrual bleeding is shameful—a dark female secret that must be hidden from men lest they ridicule and reject her simply for being female. Numerous patriarchal religions regard menstruating women and women who have given birth as unclean.[2]

In contemporary American culture, the adolescent girl discovers that the rituals associated with menstruation, e.g., asking the male druggist for sanitary napkins, can be painfully embarrassing. Popular culture reinforces adolescent insecurity by advertising an array of products to hide the "curse" of menstruation. Where misogyny is the rule of patriarchy, a young woman quickly learns to hate her imperfect and uncontrollable female body. Menstrual blood is the sign—almost the anti-sacrament—of the inherited guilt of womanhood.

In *A Lesson in a Dead Language*, Adrienne Kennedy uses the words *blood* or *bleed* thirty-four times in a play so short that it has only thirty lines of dialogue. The effect of the repetition is to load the word with symbolic significance. Blood is not only the sign of the guilt connected with being a woman, but in the play it is also symbolically associated with loss of innocence and even patriarchal assassination. The play is set in a brightly lighted classroom furnished with ordinary school desks, but there theatrical realism ends. The female teacher is costumed as a huge White Dog from the waist up. The dominating presence of highly colored life-size statues of Jesus, Joseph, Mary, two Wise Men and a Shepherd encircling the room suggests that the play is set in a Catholic school. The extraordinary White Dog costume which makes the teacher's speech seem to come without mouth movements and makes her gestures large and stiff is perhaps a child's perception of the medieval nun's habit and the remote, partly female, creature within.

The White Dog and statues overpower the pupils by their actual bulk and by the weight of tradition and symbolism which they carry and with which they threaten the students to confess and conform. The seven girl pupils wear white organdy dresses, white socks and black shoes. The virginal costumes are school uniforms more appropriate for church processions than classroom work. The number seven (often considered the perfect, magic number) suggests that the pupils represent all girls at the threshold of adolescence.

Apparently a Latin lesson on the assassination of Julius Caesar is in progress. The last line of the play, "Calpurnia dreamed a pinnacle was tumbling down," is one pupil's laborious translation from the lesson. Calpurnia's vision foretells not only the immediate assassination but perhaps the complete downfall of patriarchy in the public sphere symbolically acted out in private as the drooping impotent phallic pinnacle.

The White Dog's opening line "Lesson I bleed" is a dictation to which the Pupils respond in unison: "I bleed." Perhaps punctuating the teacher's announcement "Lesson: I Bleed" would eliminate the ambiguity and clarify that what follows is a brief but bizarre excursion into female sex education. Perhaps the line is also a pun in black dialect summarizing the whole theme of the play: "I better not grow up less'n I bleed an' get blamed for grown-up crimes an' on top a' that get accused a' tryin' to do 'way with my elders an' ancestors." Menstrual blood represents a double curse for adolescent girls.

To bleed is to be cursed with a messy inconvenience, but not to bleed indicates a major alienation from parental and societal approval: unwanted pregnancy, the proof of premarital sex. Therefore, the opening line can also be read as a moral command: "Lesson I (one): Bleed."

In the play, bleeding is associated with the death of the White Dog, Julius Caesar and the figures represented by the statues. The White Dog, who is Mother as well as Teacher, instructs the pupils to write one hundred times on the blackboard, apparently as punishment for their misdeeds, "Who killed the white dog and why do I bleed? I killed the white dog and that is why I must bleed." Large circles of blood are visible on the backs of the pupils' white dresses when they stand at the blackboard. The blood is evidence of their guilt.

Collectively blaming the assassination of the White Dog on the pupils, even though only one of them is guilty, is similar to blaming all Jews for the death of Jesus, the whole Roman Senate for the death of Julius Caesar, or a whole class for a dirty picture of the teacher which only one student drew on the blackboard. Collective punishment for presumed collective guilt is a phenomenon familiar to children, slaves and other oppressed groups. Although the slaughtered dog is described by one pupil as "a charming little white dog [that] ran beside me in the sun when I played a game with lemons on the green grass," the dog is not merely a child's pet whose death is the result of an unfortunate accident.

The White Dog in the play represents the whole world of elders and ancestors from Christianity and classical antiquity down to the two most powerful female authority figures in the adolescent girl's life: mother and teacher. The adult women who have long ago suffered through the adolescent rites of passage seem to derive sadistic satisfaction from the sufferings of those to be initiated into womanhood and thus issue warnings laden with their own fears and repressions: "My mother says it is because I am a woman that I bleed," say the pupils in unison. Furthermore, elders threaten to incarcerate the insubordinate. One pupil says, "Teacher, my mother is sending me to the Asylum if I don't stop talking about my white dog that died and my bleeding and Jesus and the game in the green grass. I asked her who made me bleed. The conspirators, she said . . . And she said everything soon bleeds away and dies. Caesar, too."

Another of Kennedy's adolescent characters, Kay (Sister Rat) in *A Rat's Mass*, is sent to the State Hospital in Georgia by her mother when she fails to accept adolescent changes quietly. Growing up is generally portrayed in Kennedy's play as a dreadful irreversible passage from which death is the only escape, and mothers never console daughters or ease their passage through adolescence.

Set in the memory and imagination of Brother Rat, *A Rat's Mass* chronicles the fall from innocent bliss of Sister and Brother Rat (Kay and Blake). Brother Rat imagines them hiding from Nazi conspirators who leave in their wake dying baby rats and dying gray cats hanging from rafters with sunflowers in their mouths—a suggestion of castration.[3] Although bloody rats certainly present a more terrifying image than the white dog, animal imagery in all of Kennedy's plays is associated with frightening uncontrollable sexuality. Here the animals are not only dead but unsexed as well. However, as in nightmares, the dreadful beasts (adolescent sexual desire), refuse to stay dead but instead return bloody and mutilated to mock their murderer. That Kennedy would identify societal taboos against female adolescent sexuality with Nazis is curiously appropriate. Since the Nazi goal was to achieve a pure (in every way) homogeneous Aryan race, the Nazis condoned hunting down and slaughtering all aliens: Jews, homosexuals, the aged and infirm. For an adolescent black girl to awaken sexually is to become acutely conscious of her alienation from society on many levels. She is warned by her mother to fear premarital sex and pregnancy out of wedlock as a fate worse than death, but the white male-dominated culture simultaneously tells her that she is a promiscuous bitch just because she is black. She acknowledges her bloodiness and her sexual yearnings as proof of her hopeless bestiality. Naturally she expects to be hunted down and slaughtered by those in power.

The female authority figure in *A Rat's Mass* is neither mother nor teacher but a fellow classmate, a white girl named Rosemary, who has worms in her hair and who has so dazzled Blake (Brother Rat) with her Medusa charm that he will do whatever she says. The turning point in the adolescence of Brother and Sister Rat is their fatal act of incest. At some time in the past, Rosemary ordered Kay and Blake to have intercourse on the slide in the playground to prove their love for her. Later, the slide becomes an aisle of blood for Sister Rat, who confuses the slide, slippery and red with the blood of her deflowering with the red carpet runner in church and the blood itself with the Communion wine.[4]

Sexual initiation is a rite of passage into the adult world for both Brother and Sister Rat, who now see sex everywhere. However guilty Brother Rat may feel, the chief victim of Rosemary's plot is Sister Rat, who not only bleeds, and consequently sees blood everywhere, but fears she is pregnant. No real baby ever comes, but Sister Rat is obsessed with the vision of dead baby rats. Furthermore, she tells Blake in her letters from the asylum that she hides under the house (like a rat) and gnaws (like a rat) sunflower petals—a symbolic acting-out of her deflowering and gnawing away of her own genitalia. To force her brother to share her agony, she sends him the gnawed petals in letters.

Before the play opens, Rosemary has gratified her voyeuristic curiosity by pandering to Brother Rat's desire for her approval and has played the panderer in their union. Rosemary appears in the play more like a phantom than a participant in present action. Of course, the only present action is Blake's reminiscence. Because Rosemary is aloof from the rat world (as white and Catholic), she remains untouched by the suffering, which she causes.

Before their fatal incest, Brother and Sister Rat were as innocent as the pupils in *A Lesson in a Dead Language* before the death of the White Dog. Sister Rat remembers: ". . . we lived in a Holy Chapel with parents and Jesus, Joseph, Mary, our Wise Men and our Shepherd. People said we were the holiest children." The same Christian Nativity figures which dominated the White Dog's classroom hover over the two children in *A Rat's Mass* and move on- and offstage in procession, speaking in unison much like a Greek chorus, until they abandon the finally lost adolescents to their rat world.

Sexual sins make Kay and Blake more ratlike; both have rat tails. Blake has a rat head and a human body, and Kay has a human head and a rat belly. The partial metamorphoses are symbolically appropriate since Blake willed the sin which Rosemary counseled, and Kay exhibits it in her belly. After the Nativity figures desert them (loss of grace?), Kay and Blake act more ratlike and their voices sound more like gnawing.

In *A Beast's Story*, set in "the gloomy house of a minister in a drab section of a midwestern city," the beasts are members of a black family obsessed with sensuality. Parental fears and conflicts make it impossible for the budding adolescent Beast Girl, costumed in a white organdy dress, ever to grow into healthy womanhood. Beast Woman, her mother, tries to thwart her daughter's passage into womanhood through sexual initiation. "I keep the ax to maintain her innocence," she says. Like the labyris of the Amazons, Beast Woman's ax is a weapon of defense against male invaders. The mother is obsessed with the blood of her own deflowering. Of her daughter's birth she says, "I went into labor at my dead sister's funeral. Twenty hours later she was born." If the daughter is a substitute for the dead sister, she can only prevent her daughter's death by preventing her going through the rites of passage which lead all women to death. Beast Man says to her, "You spoke of death at our wedding."

The conflict within the Beast family is brought to a crisis when a boy called Dead Human invades as Beast Girl's lover and husband. Although the girl desires sexual union with the boy, her parents' taboos and phobias freeze her budding sensuality, and she drops her bridal bouquet and runs to her mother. About her passage through the marriage rite, Beast Girl says, "It was morning when I awakened, a red sunrise morning, the first day of my marriage. At last I knew who I was . . . no shadow of myself, I was revealed . . . to myself." The imagery suggests that Beast Girl thought herself liberated from her parents' fears, but according to the boy she fled from the marriage bed the first night: "You said I had raped you like your father had raped your mother the night you were conceived. You fled from our bed." Furthermore, no fruitful union of boy and girl is possible since Beast Girl and Dead Human say her parents made her kill (abort?) her baby "with quinine and whiskey." In the end, with great force and fury, Beast Girl smothers her husband with a pillow and smashes her father's skull with the ax.

The Owl Answers reaches a similar but opposite conclusion: mother and daughter grow more and more bestial and deranged as their struggles with sensual desire and repulsion intensify until violent suicide is the only escape for both of them. The mother stabs herself with a butcher knife, which the daughter later uses on herself. Although *The Owl Answers* is longer and more complex than any of the three plays previously discussed, it focuses on the personality fragmentation of She who is Clara Passmore who is the Virgin Mary who is the Bastard who is the Owl rather than on adolescent rites of passage. Nevertheless the Bastard's Black Mother who is the Reverend's Wife who is Anne Boleyn is as reluctant to see her daughter through the sexual initiation and childbirth rituals as Beast Woman.

She says, "On my wedding day the Reverend's Wife came to me and said when I see Marys I cry for their deaths, when I see brides Clara, I cry for their deaths." In the play the death of Mary means the death of the Virgin Mary and every woman's deflowering. The Reverend's Wife carries a vial of blood, the sign of her own passage and perhaps a trophy of survival. Early in the play she holds up the vial and says, "These are the fruits of my maidenhead, owl blood Clara who is the Bastard Clara Passmore to whom we gave our name, see the owl blood, that is why I cry when I see Marys, cry for their deaths, Owl Mary Passmore." The name she gives her daughter carries the curse of her confusion: as owl she is doomed to be obsessed with sensuality and eventually fall prey to it, but as Mary is equally doomed to a sexual frigidity forced on her by her mother's fears. Later when the mother is becoming more like an owl, she screeches what has become a parrot-like incantation—the formula of a ritual spell: "The Reverend took my maiden head and I am not a virgin anymore and that is why you must be Mary, always be Mary, Clara."

Cursed with such a heritage, the daughter cannot pass beyond her mother's fears. Her sexuality is frozen in frustration. Furthermore, she has incorporated her mother's fear of rape so thoroughly that she describes it as if it happened to her. She is conditioned to regard all men as rapists and any expression of her own sexuality as the signs of a fatal disease. Even more devastating to her development is her conviction of her own worthlessness caused by her mother's continual rejection and denial of affection.[5]

Lack of maternal affection also warps Sarah in *Funnyhouse of a Negro* into a rigid, fearful woman who has retreated from reality into a fantasy world populated with alter egos. Like Beast Girl and She who is Clara Passmore, Sarah the Negro is obsessed with the rape of her mother by her father at which she was conceived. All three young women regard their existence as the hated product of their mother's fall from innocence. It is understandable that the mothers express no warmth for the product of their violation and that they try to prevent their daughters from growing up. Sarah's mother goes insane. Her single line is a warning to her daughter: "Black man, black man, I never should have let a black man put his hands on me. The wild black beast raped me and now my skull is shining." Like Sister Rat, the mother is locked up in an asylum for failing to adjust quietly to female bondage to male violence.

Sarah experiences her mother's rape obsession in all of her multiple personalities. The prime fear is the return of the father from the jungle to rape her. Beast Girl and She also fear rape by the father. Sarah says she wants to bludgeon her father to death with his ebony African masks. Instead she hangs herself. Taking out anger against the male oppressor/rapist on oneself and blaming self for being a victim is a response familiar to women under patriarchy. Sarah's first appearance with a bloody face and a noose around her neck foretells her fate. Sarah's bloody face is reminiscent of the bloody circles on the pupils' dresses, exhibiting the guilt of passage to womanhood. The main symbol of impotence and death in *Funnyhouse of a Negro* is loss of hair. Sarah's alter egos carry their fallen hair in red bags, which suggest menstrual blood and the blood of deflowering.

Passage into womanhood need not be a death sentence. The naturally flowing blood of menstruation and childbirth need not be regarded as shameful or terrifying. However, in a culture which makes women alien objects to be used and abused by men, women learn to hate their bodies and their sexuality. In societies where women are bought as commodities and discarded as casually as paper cups, women realize that they have no value in themselves except insofar as they conform to their expected role as detachable and disposable vessels of male pleasure and caprice. Adrienne Kennedy's plays vividly dramatize the horrors attendant on female adolescent rites of passage under patriarchy.

2 | THE ACTRESS

"Women have risen to greater heights of achievement as actresses than in any art," Rosamond Gilder wrote in her landmark 1931 study, *Enter the Actress*. Without doubt acting has been and remains a unique art and career for women, for in performance the very fact of being female is what is being featured. Much is involved in performance, from our awareness of the female body to women's status in society. Acting onstage is intimately tied to the ceremonies and the economics of our collective life and to our social role playing. The many different parts actresses play highlight the many different ways of being female.

Yet until recently, very little attention was paid to the complex dynamics of how the actress uses herself to become or sometimes to challenge what each era means its women to be. Even as general discussions of acting became more sophisticated, explorations of psychic need and social ritual, the distinctive interplay of person and role in the experience of the actress received little special attention. Talk about actresses still sometimes echoed Victorian concern about the morality of women onstage or raised the perennial question of female pulchritude and youthfulness as prerequisites for success. We didn't get much beyond Noel Coward's "Don't Put Your Daughter on the Stage, Mrs. Worthington."

The wide-ranging essays first published in our 1981 edition provide valuable research that helped us begin to understand the neglected interaction between a woman's life and the art she creates. The following introductory remarks highlight some of the important insights gained from this early compensatory history which was inspired by the revolution in women's consciousness of the 1960s and 1970s. As we had hoped, in subsequent years these initial explorations have been elaborated in many new approaches—feminist, gender, semiotic, cultural, psychoanalytic, Marxist and more. These later varied modes of analysis are addressed in the final sections of this edition, with two pertinent samples included here to complement original selections in "The Actress."

From shopgirls to society ladies, the theatre has been a way out for women. In the theatre they have risen up the social ladder, earned equal pay, and developed independence. For those who came from theatrical families, entry to the field was usually taken for granted. One thinks of "Little Minnie Maddern"—later the great Mrs. Fiske—who played bits in Shakespearean productions when she was five or six years old, having earlier made her debut singing and dancing with the Maddern Family Concert Company. For women of working-class origins, the stage has always been a means of moving up socially and economically. In turn, "ladies" fallen on hard times, like the famed Anna Cora Mowatt, found the theatre, despite its taint of immorality, to be the only paying outlet for the good looks, genteel manners, musical skills and elocution lessons that had been part of their social education. Lotta Crabtree's career offers a stunning example from the early days of what was possible. As she made her way from rough mining camps in California to national favorite, she amassed a fortune estimated to be over $4 million at the time of her death in 1924.

With the increased participation of women from all walks of life early in this century, they seemed to turn in greater numbers to the theatre. Anecdotes from the period suggest that daughters were doing what their mothers only dared to dream of—they were trying to go on the stage. By the late 1920s, it would seem that New York was almost overrun by women wanting to act.

There has been much to attract women over the years to the theatre beyond the economic advantages. With few options usually open to them—at least until very recently—most women have led lives marked by subordination and submission. Onstage, however, they saw a chance to exercise a kind of control usually absent from their daily experience. Geraldine Page, for example, spoke of that "most wonderful sense of freedom" that comes when as an actress, you feel "that you, and only you, are in control." Acting allows women to capitalize on those characteristics of emotionality and exhibitionism by which they are usually socially defined. Aware of the dichotomies in their lives and accustomed to playing many different roles offstage, they can find onstage an outlet for personality traits developed by the female experience.

Being on the stage, however, also encourages qualities usually associated with men's lives: initiative, self-reliance, ambition and independence. Traveling on tours, hoisting your own luggage, living in hotels alone or with fellow troupers, competing for parts, bargaining for salaries, angling for career advantages—all these activities have given the actress an independence few women have had an opportunity to acquire. Although many have been concerned to be thought conventionally respectable in a profession said to be morally dangerous, especially for women, actresses have nevertheless been part of a unique subculture with its own standards. Long before most other women were able to do so, they could dress as they liked, smoke cigarettes, take lovers, have children outside marriage, and live a generally liberated lifestyle.

Ironically, however, these "free" women are the very ones who have embodied for their particular era the accepted image of women—the passive heroine, the fallen woman, the flapper, the gossip, etc. Although their profession permits them greater personal liberty offstage, their sexual attractiveness, their dominant histrionic power, and their vibrant personalities are marketed onstage to convey the social stereotypes fashioned for conventional patrons mostly, although not exclusively, by male dramatists. Onstage, paradoxically, the actress has usually been a "commodity," as Jean Dalrymple once put it. She has been used, manipulated, exploited for her talents in a theatre that has allowed her little say about what she does. The structure of show business has provided the actress few opportunities to express her sense of self, despite the control her magnetism can exercise over audiences. Mae West put it crudely but well when she said in looking back at the 1930s that actresses—and actors, too, for that matter—"were considered big hunks of meat to be bought, sold and packaged."

"If the playwrights would just talk over matters with the actress," suggested Mary Shaw, they would not continue to produce those "man-made women caricatures" that most actresses are forced to play. She herself made choices of roles in accordance with her feminist beliefs, as the study of her in our collection reveals.

Actresses have sought to gain personal control over their performances in many different ways. Some by their extraordinary intuitive genius have cut through clichés to expose a unique inner life. One thinks especially of Pauline Lord and Laurette Taylor. Others, more conscious of what they might do, have started their own theatres or managed their own companies where they could determine what roles they would play. From the early days Minnie Maddern Fiske, Eva Le Gallienne and Katharine Cornell come to mind. Others associated themselves for longer or shorter periods of time with important companies or studios whose aesthetic or social views they shared or could help to shape: Lynn Fontanne and Helen Hayes at the Theatre Guild; Stella Adler, Frances Farmer, Phoebe Brand and others at the Group Theatre; Ruby Dee with the Harlem Players and various other black theatres; Kim Stanley, Maureen Stapleton, Anne Bancroft and Geraldine Page among many others at the Actors Studio.

In the 1970s, as leading actresses suffered from "lack of work, inferior plays and short runs," they sought a way out by playing in unique women's vehicles, some written by the actresses themselves. Julie Harris's *The Belle of Amherst,* Estelle Parsons's *Miss Margarida's Way,* Irene Worth's *Love Letters,* Gretchen Cryer's *I'm Getting My Act Together and Taking It on the Road* and Ntozake Shange's *for colored girls who have considered suicide/when the rainbow is enuf* are different responses of women performers. Across the country these and many other notable actresses now began to use their skills to project fresh images of the American woman. Building on this rediscovered heritage, every aspect of acting and actors, as women now began to call themselves, was redefined as the feminist revolution impacted on the theatre in the last decades of the millennium.

HKC

ANNE BRUNTON MERRY: FIRST STAR

Gresdna Doty

On December 5, 1796, Mrs. Anne Brunton Merry[1] made her American debut in her most celebrated characterization, Shakespeare's Juliet. That performance was a turning point for Philadelphia's Chestnut Street Theatre as well as for the professional theatre in the United States. Billed as "late the principal actress at Covent-Garden," Mrs. Merry's appearance gave Americans their first opportunity to witness a talent from the first rank of performers in the English-speaking world. No other actor previously appearing in the United States had ever held a position as a first-line performer at either of London's two patent theatres, Drury Lane and Covent Garden. The significance of the occasion was not lost on theatregoing Philadelphians. Two separate reviews in Philadelphia's *Gazette of the United States* supplied details of the performance. "Dramaticus" praised her for those qualities admired in the British Isles: "feminine sweetness," power to mark the passions, "melodious" voice, "natural, easy and appropriate action." Additional comments referred to her most powerful scenes: "In her speech, act IV, when she drinks the sleeping draught, she thrill'd every heart with horrid sympathy; and her dying scene was inimitably fine. In justice we must say, that this elegant and powerful actress is a most powerful acquisition to the American stage." In the same newspaper another critic signed "W" compared her to Mrs. Marshall and Mrs. Whitlock (Sarah Siddons's sister), both of whom had previously performed the role in Philadelphia. Apparently Mrs. Merry exerted force which Mrs. Marshall lacked, but not the "masculine, coarseness" of Mrs. Whitlock. A decided artistic triumph, Anne could not "fail at once to establish her own fame, and to reflect honour on the American drama."[2] Moreover the debut brought $1,200 into the company treasury and her portrait into many homes. On the day following her debut, *Claypoole's American Daily Advertiser* announced the availability of Mrs. Merry's portrait as Juliet: plain, fifty cents and colored, one dollar.

For the twelve years between that first appearance until her death in 1808, Mrs. Merry, as "the sun of the theatrical solar system," established and maintained a new standard of excellence for actors. In addition, she served briefly as manageress of the Chestnut Street Theatre and became a respected social matron while carrying out the duties of a wife and mother. Accomplished by the age of thirty-nine, her achievements seem remarkable, but they are matched in their unusualness by her personal life and career, more dramatic than any role she ever portrayed. Born in London in 1769, Anne spent her early years in the provinces where her actor father shared the boards with talents no less than those of Sarah Siddons at the Theatre Royal, Bath. When she was only sixteen, her father discovered her talent one day when, returning from rehearsal, he heard her reciting one of Calista's speeches. He learned that she knew the entire role, as well as those of Juliet, Belvidera and Euphrasia. Soon after, Anne's recitations convinced manager John Palmer that he should arrange for her debut on the Bristol stage. Only eight months later, Thomas Harris, manager of Covent Garden, brought her to London hoping that a "youthful wonder" would counter the powerful attraction of Mrs. Siddons at the rival Drury Lane. William Dunlap, who later became manager of New York's Park Theatre and first historian of the American theatre, recorded his impressions of Anne's extraordinary debut, which he saw while visiting in London:

> The extraordinary self-possession of this young lady, not yet sixteen, when she appeared at Bristol the preceding year has been recorded by a witness, and it apparently did not desert her on this occasion. Her voice, never exceeded in sweetness and clearness, did not falter, her action was perfect, she was the Horatia of the poet, and London confirmed Mr. Palmer's opinion that she was "another Siddons."[3]

During the first season, Anne played ten new roles in forty-seven performances, an impressive schedule for a sixteen-year-old girl. She drew audiences described as brilliant and overflowing, but, in spite of her mercurial rise, she did not displace Sarah Siddons, reigning queen of the London stage. She did, however, launch a seven-year career at Covent Garden and learned the rigorous demands of touring when she traveled to visiting summer engagements in Norwich, Birmingham, Manchester, Liverpool and as far away as Belfast and Cork. By the time she was a stage veteran of twenty-two, the course of her life changed dramatically when she fell in love with poet, playwright and politician, Robert Merry.

Wealthy, handsome and charming, and son of aristocratic parents, Merry had attended Harrow and Christ's College, Cambridge, but he soon abandoned his academic pursuits for a social life in London and on the Continent, overlaid with prominence as a poet and a rabid interest in the French Revolution.[4] Merry also attempted playwriting, which ultimately brought him in contact with Anne Brunton when his work was produced at Covent Garden. In August 1791 they married over the protest of his family, who objected to Anne's stage career. Merry told his sister, however, "She ought to be proud he had brought a woman of such virtue and talents into the family."[5]

Whatever domestic bliss the newlyweds enjoyed was soon clouded by Merry's literary and political interests which eventually proved disastrous to the young couple. Although Mrs. Merry terminated her Covent Garden engagement, before long financial worries persuaded the couple that Mrs. Merry should resume her acting career. When Thomas Wignell offered Anne an engagement at his Chestnut Street Theatre in Philadelphia, Anne had little choice but to accept.

When Anne sailed for the United States in October to resume her acting career, she was twenty-seven years old, but no longer the fledgling actress. She was an experienced performer with seven years of successes and failures as a leading actress at Covent Garden earned by playing more than fifty roles in more than 352 performances. Also, she was more sensitive to the emotional range of life, a knowledge acquired through the stress of a marriage troubled by financial and political anxiety.

Anne's success was immediate and continuous. She became the principal attraction and leading actress in Philadelphia, but she also dominated the wider theatrical scene wherever the company traveled: on one occasion to New York, in its annual fall and spring visits to Annapolis and Baltimore, and in its summer engagements at theatres in Alexandria, Georgetown and eventually Washington. Her box-office draw was so clearly established that, when her husband died suddenly in 1798, William Dunlap, manager at Park Theatre in New York, negotiated with her to accept a permanent position with his company. Anne bided her time, however, and corresponded with "connections" in London about her future. At the same she maintained her place with the Chestnut Street Theatre. Anne's ultimate decision to renew her engagement with Wignell in the midst of some of the darkest financial months of the company's history confirms her basic respect for and trust in the manager, whom she married three and a half years later.

Anne's theatrical career took another dramatic turn when Dunlap renewed his attempts to bring her to New York in 1801 for "starring" performances at the Park during the summer. She agreed to a contract stipulating a salary of $100 per week plus a clear benefit, a sharp contrast to the $30 per week offered to other performers. Arranged in March, the appearances were scheduled for July. In June, however, Mrs. Merry requested a release from her commitment because of ill health. When Dunlap begged her to reconsider since he had borrowed money in the belief that her appearances would enable him to repay it, she agreed to make the effort. Soon after, Mrs. Merry journeyed to New York, where the actress "for the first time in America was brought forward as [what is now called] a star."[6] Also impressed by the occasion, a fellow actor, William Warren, noted in his daily journal that "Mrs. Merry is acting as a Star in New York."[7] Anne returned to Philadelphia with $750 from benefits in addition to her salary and had established herself as a "prodigious favorite in New York" and a decided advantage to the box office at the Park Theatre.[8]

Understandably, Dunlap arranged another New York engagement with Mrs. Merry in the following spring when her appearances created the cultural event of the season. Dunlap may have intended a third consecutive starring visit, but several events interfered. On January 1, 1803, the actress married Thomas Wignell, manager of the Philadelphia theatre. The marriage seems to have been the inevitable result of their mutual trust and close professional relationship and, possibly, a change in values for the actress. Evidence indicates differences between the personalities of Mrs. Merry's first and second husbands. From descriptions by those who worked under his management, Wignell emerges as an opposite of the dashing, fun-loving and quixotic Merry. At age thirty-three and in her circumstances, the young widow may have admired and needed the steadfastness which Wignell possessed.

From testimonial and description, Wignell appears to have been a fitting partner for the actress, whose private conduct from her earliest professional years was such "as would grace a woman of superior rank."[9] With a similarity of values, character traits and interests, the newly married couple had every reason to anticipate a happy marriage. But the happiness was short-lived, for only seven weeks after the wedding Wignell died following a brief illness.

On the day after the funeral, the newspaper carried a significant and melancholy announcement which marked the beginning of a new phase in the theatrical life of the now Mrs. Wignell. The advertisement stated that the theatre would continue to operate under the direction of Mrs. Wignell and Alexander Reinagle (Thomas Wignell's partner) with the assistance of actors William Warren and William Wood. Anne performed during the Baltimore spring season, but after its close withdrew to await the birth of her daughter, Elizabeth, in the fall.

The spring of 1803 must have been another difficult period for the actress. Once again, she had the sole responsibility for maintaining herself. She also had the increased burden of the management of the theatre in addition to rearing her child. She faced several choices: returning to England, continuing with the Chestnut Street company as co-manager and leading actress, or accepting an offer from Dunlap to join the Park Theatre company in New York. Her decision to remain in Philadelphia and assume the management of the company for a four-year period may have been influenced by an unfulfilled hope of securing the help of her brother, John, also an actor. Charles Durang commented that he "was sorry to see her harrass'd by some of the performers." He also, however, amusingly describes an instance when, as a youth, he beheld her exert her authority in matters of the wardrobe:

> Cain was extremely careless in his dressing, and even at times manifested a want of cleanliness. His "tights" . . . looked like a loose garment thrown on his person hap-hazard. On one special occasion, he was playing Rome to the Juliet of . . . Mrs. Wignell . . . At the fall of the curtain, at the end of the play, . . . amidst the most thundering applause . . . Mrs. Wignell arose, as we thought, obviously excited, and hastened to the green-room . . . With the rude curiosity of a boy, we followed her to the green-room, for we did love and honor our managerial queen above all others. With evident feeling, she directed the master tailor, McCubbins, to be called to her; she also desired the presence of Mr. Cain, before he disrobed himself of his Romeo habiliments. After the two persons thus summoned appeared before her, she descanted in very strong terms upon the dress of Mr. Cain, rebuking both the actor and the costumer, for their violation of everything like propriety and suitableness in "her Romeo's" dress . . . She concluded by ordering the master of the robes to make an entire new dress for Mr. Cain, and to be very particular hereafter, when he had a principal part to play with her, to see him suitably equipped at all points.[10]

In her personal character Anne also influenced the managing of the theatre, for Durang testified that the greenroom "was a drawing room in every sense of the word; where the presence of Mrs. Merry, Mrs. Whitlock, Mrs. Melmoth, Mrs. Wood and other ladies of cultivated intellect and polished manners, were examples to the younger members of the profession, who felt a restraint and respect before them."[11]

Duties as manager and mother, as well as leading actress, left Anne little time for social life; yet Durang remembered her as the "directress" and social matron, a position not always accorded to actresses. Durang also recalled Anne's impressive arrival at the theatre:

> The coachman was a genteel white man, dressed in a kind of half livery—a gray surtout, buckskin breeches and fair-top boots.[12]

One of Anne's chief contributions as manager was in setting and maintaining high standards of performance, but by April 1805 she turned over her share of the management to William Warren in order to devote herself to serving as the leading actress for the company and to rearing her daughter.

Her withdrawal from the management also permitted her to accept another starring engagement in New York during the summer. She made "an impression such as no other actress in this country could ever make." One New York critic wrote: "When we say we do not think we ever saw Mrs. Wignell play better, it may be readily believed it approached the perfection of histrionic art. Her powers are in full maturity and she gave us last night their best exertion. Who that once has seen her wondrous exhibitions, can afterwards receive any satisfaction from the attempts of any other actress in a similar line that the American theatre can boast of?"[13] At the conclusion of the successful engagement she retreated to Annapolis for the remaining summer, to await Warren's return from England with fresh recruits for the company. With two new actresses from London to share the acting roles in the fall of 1805, Anne reduced her schedule. In the following summer, she again went to Annapolis until late in August, when she married William Warren.

Durang has revealed that "there was some surprise expressed" over the Wignell-Warren marriage.[14] To some, Warren obviously did not appear as a likely husband for Anne Wignell. Such sentiments were expressed as late as 1811 by George Frederick Cooke, the visiting British star, who explained to Dunlap: "So . . . this is the widow's third choice . . . Upon my word the good lady seems to descend with every husband: first Merry, then Wignell & then Warren!"[15]

Dunlap, however, remembered Warren "as a pleasant companion and an upright man," and Fennell identified him as "a man of honour and of trust . . . his name is fixed on a firm base of general integrity." Such descriptions suggest that Warren and Mrs. Wignell were suited to each other in temperament and values. Drawn together by long and close association, they had not only embarked on American theatrical careers at the same time but also had remained with the same company for ten years. During that time they had shared successes and failures of the Chestnut Street company, as well as their own personal misfortunes and now each needed a parent for an orphaned child. Anne Wignell, at thirty-seven, undoubtedly was content to share the rest of her life in the United States with the man who had become one of her oldest and closest associates.

Her new domestic status did not alter her professional life; she continued to perform leading melodramatic, pathetic and tragic roles. During the following February, she interrupted her regular performance schedule in order to return New York to help revitalize a languishing season at the Park Theatre. Once again "very crowded" houses and "boundless solicitude for tickets of admission" were the pattern for her engagement.[16] In the autumn she accepted another starring engagement, this time in Boston. She returned home with $1,350 profit, concluding the last of her starring engagements on a triumphal note. The subsequent year was equally successful, but in June, at the age of thirty-nine, she died in Alexandria, Virginia, after giving birth to a stillborn son. A large cement vault marks her grave in Christ Church yard in Alexandria.

Although Anne is not well known in the American theatre and her career in the United States spanned only twelve years, she deserves to be remembered, for she probably exerted more influence than any other professional woman in America up until the time of her death. Arriving at the Chestnut Street Theatre at the age of twenty-seven, she won acclaim as the "most perfect actress America has seen." Serving as director for only two years, she set the high standards of her own art for the company as a whole. She was the first performer whose artistic superiority made her visiting engagements prestigious events which could command unprecedented financial remuneration. She dramatically demonstrated to fellow actors as well as managers the advantage and the potential of importing actors of great reputation. Thus her stardom was born, and in subsequent years the star system became widespread. She was admired as an artist, but she was equally respected for her own personal character. As her obituary testifies, her "spotless and unsullied Fame" did much to convince the early American public that "an unblemished reputation is by no means incompatible with theatrical life."

ENTER THE HARLOT

Claudia D. Johnson

Few professional situations could be as paradoxical as that of the nineteenth-century woman who went on the stage for a livelihood: the vocational possibilities of a stage career were afforded women in few other segments of nineteenth-century life. The salary of an actress was comparatively good; she was able to compete with men on an equal basis of talent and public appeal; and she could, in the theatre, secure positions of management. To reap these ben-

UNIVERSITY OF WINCHESTER
LIBRARY

efits, however, the actress had, by virtue of her association with a profession blemished in the eyes of the public, to relinquish important valuables of Victorian womanhood—a special, even reverent esteem afforded the ideal mother-wife, as well as the sympathetic support of her nineteenth-century sisters. The lonely gulf which existed between the actress and society as a whole, especially its women, was created and perpetuated by a hostile church which dominated American society and commanded the adoration of its women in particular. Although the attitude of the religious public toward actresses was based on ignorance and gross distortions, it was, irrefutably, a strongly held and widely held view, subsequently, a reality to be dealt with. It is only with a recognition of this climate of hostility that one can appreciate the courage of the nineteenth-century actress and the irony of her situation in the theatre—at the same time the worst and the best of worlds.

Because the Protestant churches and its ministers in America were the principal and admitted opponents of the theatre, the position of the actress and her profession must be regarded in the light of the status of the church. Despite the country's earlier abandonment of a state religion and the clear constitutional separation of church and state, Protestant churches in particular grew to be uncommonly forceful in the century.[1]

Virtually every Protestant sect in America, with the sole exception of the Episcopal Church, officially and unequivocally declared the theatre to be the haunt of sinners.[2] The Reverend Robert Hatfield and the Reverend Dewitt Talmadge, for example, both believed that young men and women were better off dead than in the briefest association with actors. Hatfield puts his case in what he obviously regards as a rhetorical question: "Let me ask you, my young friend, justly proud of your sister, would you not rather follow her to her grave tonight than to know that tomorrow she shall stand at the altar and pledge her faith and trust her precious future to an actor?"[3] The Reverend Talmadge, who in the 1870s officiated over the largest church congregation in New York, declared that most people would rather see their children "five feet under the ground of Greenwood," than "in a month's association with actors."[4]

The exact extent to which the general public actually shared the view of the church about theatre would be difficult to determine, but it is clear that many theatrical people *believed* that the public held the same low opinion of them voiced by the clergy. In short, the actress and actor both worked in what they perceived to be a hostile climate. John Hodgkinson, an actor writing at the turn of the century, speaks of "strong and widely-held prejudices against the profession."[5] Writing in 1827, Mrs. Trollope concluded that the general public in America did not approve of theatrical exhibitions.[6] Albert A. Palmer, one of the most successful theatrical owners and managers in the last half of the century, estimates that at least until mid-century seven-tenths of the population looked on stage attendance as "almost a sin." He observes some improvement in the attitude of the public toward the profession by the 1880s and 1890s.[7] Daniel Frohman, the "star maker," another producer of the period, corroborates Palmer's conclusion that as late as the 1860s anti-theatrical bias was far-reaching.[8]

Actresses, of course, were not blind to these opinions of them. Anna Cora Mowatt, born into wealth and social standing, recognized "the prejudices of the world against the profession as a body." The actor, she wrote, "dwells on the outer side of a certain conventional pale of society, which he is allowed to enter only by courtesy, unless it is broken through by the majesty of transcendental talents."[9] Another actress, Clara Morris, reared at the opposite, lowest end of the social spectrum, reached the same conclusion—that members of her profession had labored under a cloud of disapproval throughout most of her career. "Even the people who did not think all actors drunkards and all actresses immoral did think they were a lot of flighty, silly buffoons, not to be taken seriously for a moment." Although the cloud of public suspicion was slowly lifting in the last decades of the century, Morris leaves no about having felt its presence in the 1860s: "The actor had no social standing; he was no longer looked down upon, but he was an unknown quantity. By the 1880s and 1890s, Morris believes that some members of her profession had "won some social recognition."[10]

The conflict between the large religious public and the stage produced a rhetoric so powerful that it was bound to cause the stage and the actors suffering. Several successful managers, William Wood, Sol Smith and Noah Ludlow, who harbored no little bitterness about the church's antipathy toward actors and thought the matter of sufficient importance to record in their memoirs indicate its destructive effect on the profession.[11] Although the frontier, less tradition-bound, less religious and often eager to attract entertainments and actresses, might be expected to be less biased against the theatre, it was far from free of harassment on the part of religious settlers. Noah Ludlow, writing of Ohio in 1828, Sol Smith, writing of Alabama in 1835, and a minor actor named Watkins, writing of Ohio and New Orleans in the 1840s, all attest to the clergy's stance and its significant impact on the professional and personal life of the actor.[12] As late as Lincoln's assassination, the general public was capable of extraordinary invective, and in 1870 the minister of an Episcopal church in New York City refused burial to an actor. Although the press and much of the public objected to the refusal, the case was certainly not an isolated one.

To work in an age when women were denounced for not remaining sequestered, pure and religious undoubtedly made it difficult for the actress to maintain her self-esteem. There is certainly no denying, in a century that saw the phenomenal growth of the theatre, that good actresses received the plaudits of the playgoing public and that, occasionally, some of them, like Charlotte Cushman, even came into contact with genteel society. But actresses were also aware that such occasions were exceptional and that their professional success was quite another thing from social success or public respect. All the plaudits in the world did not alter the general public's view of the actress as a "low order of society . . . very properly debarred from respectable society."[13] Actresses on the American stage rarely, if ever, whined about social snubs, slander in the press and from the pulpit, or their inability to move comfortably in polite society. This certainly does not mean, however, that they were unaffected by the climate of opinion. Mary Ann Duff, along with some of her family, was compelled to break off all relationships with her former theatrical associates and conceal her identity as the foremost tragedienne of her day.[14] One reads of Fanny Kemble discovering with a shock that her American husband and his family would not allow her friends who were actors and actresses to set foot in the house where she lived.[15] Anna Cora Mowatt writes of being brainwashed against the theatre by her minister when she was a child, of feeling personally insulted when a theatre manager offered her an acting job, and later, being accused of betraying her class when she decided to become an actress. Clara Morris writes of her mother's being "stricken with horror" at the idea of her daughter turning to the theatre as the only likely means of helping shoulder the family's financial burden. Later, Clara, herself, came to feel that actresses were, in effect, barred from going to church. The "exclusive spirit" of churches, as she put it, kept many actresses away from the most significant comfort and meaning afforded most women in the century. In an age when the minister was the Idol of the Ideal Woman, he was the adversary of the actress.

Most of the expressed disapproval of the theatre and actresses could be traced to nineteenth-century sexual mores and the commonly held belief that all or most actresses led immoral lives both on- and offstage. With the sole exception of prostitution, to which it was often compared, no single profession was so loudly and frequently condemned. Olive Logan, herself a nineteenth-century actress and writer, declared that misconceptions about the actress had produced an unhappy result: "The name of a poor stock actress is a synonym for what is lax in the sex."[16]

The religious public rested its case against actresses not only on inappropriately applied historical evidence from Restoration England, but also on their assurances that no "lady" would do onstage what actresses did. In the first place, ministers believed that actresses' participation in "a deception" could not fail to infect their personalities. As the Reverend Robert Hatfield made plain, "men and women whose nightly business it is to act a lie . . . who are trained to assume the most contradictory passions and moral states, have no power to prevent this life of falsity and sham from reaching most disastrously upon themselves." Other objections to onstage behavior can be divided into three categories: first, costumes that revealed too much flesh; second, scenes that required flirtation; and third, scenes that required physical contact with male actors. The few ministers who admitted to having been to the theatre believed that what they had seen there was sufficient evidence to call for the wholesale condemnation of all actresses: "lascivious smiles, wanton glances, dubious compliments, indelicate attitudes, kissing, with a variety of vain and sinful practices."[17] Even worse, women were "twirled and handled" onstage, and their clothing was, by ministerial standards, more often indecent than not.[18] Mention is also often made of such proofs of "immoral behavior" as "heaving bosoms, languishing glances, voluptuous attitudes" of actresses in the execution of their roles. Even worse was the immodest physical displays of falling "into the arms of men" onstage.[19]

The reputation of the actresses for immorality may have come as much from what was reputed to go on behind stage as what occurred onstage. The ubiquitous greenroom was, in the minds of many, a den of unspeakable inequities: "The associations of the greenroom are blasting. It is a terrible ordeal through which but few can pass un-singed. The whole land ever and ever anon rings with some new outcry of shame or cruelty."[20] Even though American theatres had from the beginning banned everyone except actors from their greenrooms, the attitudes of outspoken enemies of the theatre were evidently formed from readings in the history of the Restoration stage when greenrooms were often used as "places of assignation." The same clergy who faulted actresses for "acting a lie" seemed unconvinced, at the same time, that what happened onstage was make-believe. Love scenes that began onstage were, it was suggested, continued backstage, an assumption which caused several actresses to insist that love scenes onstage were often played between men and women who hated each other and refused to speak to, much less touch, each other offstage.

The clergy believed that actresses deserved denunciation on the basis of their offstage as well as their onstage and backstage conduct. No woman could remain on the stage and keep the purity of a saint-like femininity:

> The effect of the kind of life led by players is peculiarly pernicious to female character. It strips it of all its loftier attributes, its softer and more delicate charms. Sensibility, modesty and refinement are gradually extinguished by the unfeminine and indelicate business of the stage, and nothing is left but the hackneyed and haggard form of injured humanity, covered and bedecked perhaps, by false and tawdry ornaments. A few female actors may have preserved their virtue, but, alas! how many have lost it forever by their connection with the stage. And if others have not been entirely ruined by this means, how greatly must their characters have suffered in purity and elevation, by the dark forms of evil with which they come into such close and continual contact.[21]

Not only did the clergy succeed in defaming the actress as immoral in an age which held its women to a virtue narrowly defined—on the same grounds, it drove a particularly cruel wedge between the actress and most "respectable" women of her day by discouraging theatre attendance. Frances Trollope observed in her travels throughout America that the clergy had little influence on the theatre-going habits of American men, but that its influence on women was enormous. Clerical disapproval was, she wrote, the principal reason why women avoided the theatre. Furthermore, it is only women, she writes, and not men who "deem it an offense against religion to witness the representation of a play."[22] Certainly there were many reasons quite aside from theological ones which discouraged wholehearted female attendance at the theatre—the third tier set aside for prostitutes, the rowdiness and the violence—but the church's concepts of morality and female psychology also contributed to the widely held conviction that contact with the theatre and actresses was particularly detrimental to female character. Those human faculties, specifically the imagination, the senses and the emotions, which the actress appealed to in her profession, were precisely the faculties that could be used to destroy womanly virtue.

The aim of any upright Christian, and especially the good Christian woman, was to keep emotion and imagination in quiet, unexcited moderation. The duties of home and church, the simple amusements of reading and attending occasional lectures were not dangerous. One could even read dramas without experiencing notable harm. The danger came in seeing plays onstage, for there the viewer would be excited by scenic effects, by direct and "overwhelming appeals to the senses."[23] The Reverend Samuel Winchester: "The tendency of theatrical amusements is to produce injurious excitement. The passions are inflamed, the sympathies are excited, and a multitude of various emotions crowd upon and often overwhelm the soul."[24]

These warnings were meant for all people, of course, but they had greater meaning for women than they did for men because of the century's view of the emotional constitution of the sexes. Men were perceived as not only stronger in body but in reason and resolution as well. As a consequence men had better defenses against the theatre's corruption. The character of woman, as distinct from that of man, is described by a physician of the day as being intuitive, imaginative, emotional and affectionate. A column in the *Christian Spectator* warned ladies against attending the theatre because their imaginations so easily led them into depravity:

A mother might fear the polluting comedy for her son but the more absorbing tragedy for her daughter . . . and it is not to be imagined that the delicate mind of a female, young and imaginative as she may be, can be agitated by scenes like these . . . and yet suffer no depravation.[25]

Woman was thus more liable to taint from the theatre than was man, and her reputation less likely to recover from stains of any nature. Plays that openly mocked religion and piety, portrayed evil, particularly adultery, in attractive or sympathetic ways, used obscene language or were performed by immodestly clad actresses were distasteful to any decent Christian. However, ladies, more than gentlemen, were blemished in viewing these unholy spectacles. Male critics of objectionable plays were invariably more horrified at the prospect of the language from stage reaching the ears of a wife or daughter than their own ears.

The subsequent double standard meant that what was often publicly pronounced to be sauce for the gander as well as the goose in Christian society was in practice sauce only for the gander. A respectable male's visit to a tavern or his enjoyment of a cigar in public, while reprehensible, was largely expected and easily forgiven. The respectable female, on the contrary, was not expected to break the same rules without serious and lifelong ruin of her reputation.

The perils which women might fall into as a result of association with the theatre were believed to be much worse than those which awaited men.

Theatregoing was actually feared as a kind of addiction very like the addiction to heroin; once having gotten a good dose of it, it was almost impossible to give up. Instances were cited of boys being led to the gallows in their search for money to attend the theatre, or men dying sad, premature deaths from dissipation brought on by association with the theatre. As drastic as these cases sounded, the extremes to which theatre addiction led the average man were not believed to be nearly so disastrous as that which awaited women. For the price of a theatre ticket, poor men pilfered and stole, but women were led to sell their bodies as well as their souls. This is the warning of the Reverend Griscom, frequently quoted in tracts and newspaper columns:

> In the case of the feebler sex, the result is still worse; a relish for the amusements of the theatre, without the means of indulgence, becomes too often a motive for listening to the first seducer; and this prepares the unfortunate captive of sensuality for the haunts of infamy and a total destruction of all that is valuable in the mind and character of woman.[26]

As a result, actresses found few of their own sex, with the exception of prostitutes, in the audiences for which they performed, particularly in the first half of the century. In the first place, the portion of the theatre open to respectable women was very small. The third tier was restricted to prostitutes and their companions, and the pit was restricted by custom to men and boys. Women who were not prostitutes were limited largely to the boxes or portions of the lower tiers. The appearance of "ladies" in any part of the house in the first fifty years of the century was sufficiently infrequent to draw attention to the occasion and was always especially noted by observers. Actors in their memoirs eagerly mention the appearances of ladies in the audiences they played to. It seemed to be proof of the moral acceptability and stature of the company. For example, Tyrone Power, a nineteenth-century Irish actor, made special note of the uncustomary spectacle of "American ladies of the best class" in a New Orleans theatre,[27] and Charles Dickens in the 1840s commented on the very few women in the Boston Theatre, all of whom were sitting in the front of the boxes.[28] Certainly a few very fashionable, upper-class women frequented theatres like the Park and some working-class wives brought their whole families and picnic lunch to the Bowery, but for most of the century, respectable women did not support the theatre in any significant numbers even in the cities. Of the New York theatre in the 1840s, Meade Minnigerode writes, "Ladies in general seldom attended the theatre, except to see a Fanny Elssler, or an occasional opera, or some visiting dramatic star."[29] J. S. Buckingham, Frances Trollope and James Boardman report the same situation in what were then frontier theatres. Although productions like *Uncle Tom's Cabin* and *The Drunkard* opened the theatre to a few more respectable women in the last half of the century, continual clerical attacks would never let the actress be assured of any widespread support from the rest of the female population.

There is considerable irony in the fact that, while the actress endured disparagement and ostracism by reason of attacks on her virtue, she appeared in reality to be no more and no less virtuous than other women, even by narrow nineteenth-century standards. Attacks on the virtue of actresses prompted numerous defenses from the men of the American stage. W. W. Clapp, for instance, claimed that there was "no class in the community more remarkable for constancy and devotion in their domestic relations,"[30] and a stage comedian called William Davidge supported actresses in *The Drama Defended* by writing that "there are now in the city of New York, who have retired from the duties of their profession, those whose chastity, truthfulness and domestic accomplishments, as daughters, wives and mothers, are second to none, not even the most opulent in this vast metropolis."[31] When actresses and ballet girls do become immoral, he wrote, it is no more often than women in other fields and, furthermore, not the fault of their association with the theatre.

Nor, wrote Davidge, is there any validity in the argument that actresses are just naturally sinful because they work in close association with men. Do not men and women work together in factories and churches without being corrupted or maligned?

Theatrical women as well as men rose to defend the honor of their sister-actresses, including the lowly ballet girls who were so often the prey of stage-door johnnies or "mashers" as they were then called. Anna Cora Mowatt came to the defense of actresses after she had acquired some firsthand knowledge of the theatre, indicating how very wrong she had been in her self-righteous disdain for actors. In the theatre, she found to her surprise, "refined and accomplished ladies, exemplary wives." She also declared "My views concerning the stage and my estimate of the members of dramatic companies, had undergone a total revolution. Many circumstances had proved to me how unfounded were the prejudices of the world against the profession as a body." She further found that women in the theatre led lives of "unimpeachable purity, industry, devotion to their kin," and she found them "fulfilling the hardest duties of life with a species of stoic heroism."[32]

The mother of Clara Morris had declared when Clara was a child that she would rather she and her daughter continue as lowly domestics for the rest of their lives than that Clara accept a job as a ballet girl in a theatrical company. But Clara's observations as an adult actress belied everything of which her mother had been so fearful. She claimed that in all her years in the theatre she had never seen but one instance of even a breath of scandal in the theatres where she had been employed.

The truth seems to be that American actresses were as willing to uphold Victorian morality as were other women of the day. Theatre critic William Winter, a staunch defender of conventional nineteenth-century morality, passed harsh judgment on several famous actresses like Laura Keene for what he considered to be irregular personal lives, but it was his observation in *Vagrant Memories* that sexual morality was no better and no worse in the theatre than it was in other segments of society. A modern historian's research has led her to the same conclusion about actresses: Elizabeth Dexter writes, "It appears probable that the majority of them were as correct in their conduct and had as much essential goodness as any other group of women."[33]

In an important way, of course, it does not really matter whether public opinion of actresses was justified; the simple fact of the matter is that they were frequently regarded as little better than harlots. Actresses had economic advantages; they had the applause of a special group of playgoers and in a few exceptional instances they were welcomed into the homes respectable people. None of these things, however, altered the persistent day-to-day reality of the ordinary actress—that for most of the century she labored under the unrelenting scowl of the religious mainstream in an intensely religious country. The courage and, one concludes, the usually silent suffering of the actress in the performance of her professional offices can only be valued properly in the light of this disagreeable historical reality.

WOMEN IN MALE ROLES: CHARLOTTE CUSHMAN AND OTHERS

Yvonne Shafer

In the New York season of 1819–20 there was a performance described by George C. Odell in his *Annals of the New York Stage* as a "futile novelty":

> An early, but unfortunately, not the last female Hamlet in New York was shown on March 29; I cannot conjecture what led Mrs. Bartley to this attempt, on her benefit night. Perhaps Mr. Simpson should have played Ophelia.

Earlier in the century actresses had appeared as Young Norval, Romeo and other characters created for men. Students of theatre history are familiar with the number of actresses celebrated for "breeches roles" and known that Bernhardt and Siddons performed Hamlet, but little attention has been given to the large number of American actresses throughout the nineteenth-century performing male roles in regular commercial theatres with full supporting casts. Why did the actresses choose to impersonate men? Were they successful? What does the phenomenon reveal about the nineteenth-century theatre and women's role in it? By focusing on the foremost impersonator of males on the American stage, Charlotte Cushman, in the context of females in male roles, answers to these questions can be found.

There are several reasons actresses occasionally played male roles. The prime reason for Miss Cushman and others who did so repeatedly was natural inclination toward masculine behavior and appearance. For example, Miss Lydia Kelly, a successful Romeo in the 1820s, was never at home in genteel, feminine roles. One critic said, "her Amazonian walk alone is sufficient to scatter and annihilate a whole drawing room full of dandies."

Miss Kelly was very popular, however, playing breeches roles and male roles. "Though not regularly handsome, though in fact somewhat masculine in appearance and manner, she radiated sunshine to the rear places of the largest theatres." Lydia Kelly's most successful female roles were those which were strong and dominating, such as her "hearty and buoyant, if somewhat masculine" Beatrice in *Much Ado About Nothing*.[1] For actresses whose appearance and manner did not conform to the nineteenth-century conception of femininity and beauty, playing the part of a male provided an opportunity to act in a way which seemed natural and which gave vent to the urge to dominate the action.

Another major reason for actresses to play male roles was the increased opportunity to show off their abilities. It is obvious that in a theatre dominated by Shakespeare, the great roles were those written for men. Compared with Macbeth, Lady Macbeth is a small role. Compared with Hamlet, Ophelia is small role. Also for many of the major female roles in Shakespeare, dominating women such as Miss Cushman were simply not suitable. At one point in her career, Miss Cushman considered the novelty of playing Romeo one night and Juliet the next, saying, "If Fanny Kemble is not too old and fat to play Juliet, then I am not."[2] To her friends, however, the idea was simply laughable, and she continued to play Romeo.

The quest for novelty led many actresses to play male roles to draw a crowd. Odell indicates that it was a fairly standard business throughout the nineteenth century for women to play Hamlet, or other male roles, especially on a benefit night. An example is provided by a Mrs. Barnes, who often played male roles as a novelty, and who played Hamlet many times in the 1820s.

Natural inclination, a wish to display ability, and novelty all figure as reasons for actresses attempting male roles. Perhaps some of them, consciously or unconsciously, shared another motivation with Charlotte Cushman: the urge to take the lead and compete with men in a very direct way. Certainly in her attempt at Hamlet, Miss Cushman presented a direct challenge to Edwin Booth. Actresses playing Romeo, Oberon, Hamlet and other leading male roles undoubtedly found pleasure in playing the central part while men played the roles of Tybalt, Lysander and Laertes.

A final reason for the continued performances of men's roles by women is provided by the answer to the second question, "Were they successful?" The answer is clearly, and perhaps surprisingly, yes. The general public and the critics accepted the convention and the actresses drew large audiences and often received excellent reviews. One indication of success is the large number of actresses, many unknown today, who played men's roles: Mrs. Bartlett, Mrs. Hamblin, Mrs. Shaw, Mrs. Sefton, Miss Ellis, Mrs. Hunt, Mrs. Coleman Pope, Mrs. Brougham, Fanny Wallack, Mrs. Alsop, Miss Glyn, Melinda Jones, Madame Ponisi—to list only some of them. Another indication of success is the large number of male roles performed by women, often throughout their careers. Charlotte Cushman played sixteen male roles, many played by other actresses. These included numerous Shakespearean leading parts in nineteenth-century tragedies such as *The Lady of Lyons* and, of course, the popular role of Norval in *Douglas*. There were also the many character roles in an interesting play, *Ladies at Home, or Gentlemen, We Can Do Without You,* with an all-female cast.

Odell usually described such performances in an ironic or negative manner, using phrases such as "freakish exhibition." But Odell was writing from a later viewpoint, and the critics of the time simply accepted the idea, in general, as they accepted the idea of a fifty-year-old Juliet, or as later critics accepted a two-hundred-pound Carmen.

Audiences, too, responded positively to the ladies playing men. In 1820-21, Mrs. Barnes drew the biggest receipts of the season at the Anthony Street Theatre when she played Richard III. A Miss Clifton playing Count Belino in the 1831-32 season, played additional performances "in consequence of the applause bestowed by a brilliant and crowded audience."[3] When Cushman played Romeo in 1860 many persons could not get seats, and some people in the theatre were forced to retire because of the crowds and the heat.[4]

There were of course occasional jeering reviews, even for some of the great Miss Cushman's performances. Some incidents in the theatre annoy the actresses. When Miss Cushman played Romeo in Boston there was a loud raspberry from a man in the audience during a love scene. Cushman led the Juliet from the stage, and returned to say, "Some man must put that person out, or I shall be obliged to do it myself." The crowd responded with cheers and threw the man out.[5]

In summary, one can say that the ladies who played the many male roles throughout the century received some negative criticism, but for the good actresses who acted not merely for the novelty, the reviews were serious and positive, and the audiences large. On the whole, the attempts were successful, as indicated by the fact that a number of actresses repeated the roles so many times and to such large houses. Fanny Wallack, for example, played Romeo and other male roles as a standard part of her repertoire for many years.

Fanny Wallack and other lesser actresses of the nineteenth century never had the stunning and continued success in male roles which Charlotte Cushman enjoyed. The critical and popular response to this actress seems incredible to a contemporary reader, especially one familiar with the portraits of her in Victorian dress, with a portly figure, a large bosom, and a rather grim mouth. She played these roles first when she was in her twenties and continued to play many of them when she was in her fifties. She began by playing Patrick in *The Poor Soldier* in New Orleans when another actor became ill. She moved to Albany in 1837 and played a number of male roles in a stock company. As her biographer Joseph Leach comments:

> By the end of her Albany sojourn, upstate New York knew Charlotte as an able young actress especially adept in "breeches parts," so skilled in male impersonation that no one seriously objected to a woman's daring in Victorian America to change her skirts for the revealing costumes and aggressive demeanor of men.[6]

Her early success led her to play a great many male roles, including the following: Claude Melnotte in the *Lady of Lyons*, Cardinal Wolsey in *Henry VIII*, Alladin, Hamlet, Oberon in *Midsummer Night's Dream*, Romeo, Orlando in *As You Like It* and Richelieu.

Of all these roles, Romeo was her most popular one and received the most critical acclaim both in England and America. In 1845 she performed the role at the Haymarket in London, with her sister Susan as Juliet. There are many rave reviews in the Charlotte Cushman Scrapbook and in the biographies.[7] Charlotte Cushman returned to America for the 1849–50 season, and as Odell says, "A real thrill must have pulsed through the season when, on May 13th, Charlotte Cushman came in as Romeo [the part in which she had been acclaimed in London, assisted by Fanny Wallack as Juliet]." The *New York Times* reviewer noted the immense size of the audience and the enthusiastic response. His review found in the Cushman Scrapbook was typical of the praise Charlotte Cushman received in America and indicates the style of the performance:

> Romeo is, perhaps, the most difficult character to represent in the whole range of drama, and we know no one who can play the part but Miss Cushman . . . In Miss Cushman's picture of Romeo there is nothing sickly, or subtle, or morbid. It is the love of a young, glowing, unreflecting Italian, rich in passion and tenderness, and yet in its hottest glow chastened with a delicacy—a love not of mere sensuality, but of sensuality spiritualized by imagination, and revelling in the frankness of unhesitating trust. It is such a love as manifests itself where the imagination is ardent, the blood hot, and the soul refined.

Considering these reviews and the enormous audiences which came to see the performances, it is not surprising that Miss Cushman played the role of Romeo throughout most of her career with various Juliets, including her sister and Booth's wife, Mary Devlin. Naturally, not all critics liked her in the role—one wag remarked that her Romeo was so "ardently masculine" and Juliet so "tenderly feminine," that the least Miss Cushman could do, once the engagement was over, was to marry her sister.[8] Negative or amused criticism of this sort, however, was unusual, and although she is remembered today for Lady Macbeth and Meg Merrilies, in her lifetime she was as popular as Romeo as she was in these female roles.

Another popular male role in Miss Cushman's repertoire was that of Cardinal Wolsey in *Henry VIII*. She performed the role in full productions and as part of the readings she gave later in her life. A typical review noted her vocal quality—deep, rich tones which lent reality to her interpretation. Writing in 1870, when Miss Cushman was fifty-four, a Pittsburgh reviewer found in the Scrapbook commended her choice of Wolsey as an appropriate role, and said she "gave her greatest exhibition of genius":

> Notwithstanding her age, which is advanced, Miss Cushman yet retains her physical energy apparently unshaken, while her intellec-

tual fire has certainly not paled in the progress of years. She is fitted, at this stage of her life, for the deepest and strongest emotions that a poet or prose writer has set upon paper. Looking at her upon the stage it would be more difficult to conceive that she could yet portray with any marked degree of appropriateness the tenderer passions. Passages from *King Lear* would be more to her taste than Juliet moonshine.

Neither critics nor audiences liked her in all the male roles she played—clearly, novelty was not enough to make a success. When Miss Cushman played Hamlet, she felt she was quite good, but almost no one else did. Some writers called her performance "bizarre," and certainly there must have been a good deal of merriment over the prospect of this sizable woman struggling into the tights she borrowed from the diminutive Booth when she played the role. Ironically, Booth seems to have loaned Charlotte his costume for Hamlet many times despite their rivalry. The Players Club library has several letters from her to Mary Devlin requesting the use of the costume.

In challenging Booth, of course, she was competing with the greatest Hamlet of the time. On one occasion she wrote to Mary Devlin:

My engagement was cut short in New York, because as they told me Mr. Edwin *would* commence there or act otherwheres—I was to have acted *Hamlet there* but they prevented it because Edwin was going to do it.[9]

There is no doubt that Booth felt her urge to play Hamlet arose from a wish to show that she could play it better than he. She felt that his acting was "flimsy" and "pale," that he was a "mere willow" in *Macbeth*. Booth wrote a friend saying, "Cushman is doing so-so at the Boston. She is down on me as an actor; says I don't know anything at all about 'Hamlet,' so she is going to play it here in February."[10] Lawrence Barrett often acted with Miss Cushman and admired her work so much that he wrote several pieces about her after her death. Barrett's comments on her Hamlet, however, reveal a feeling that the challenge to Booth was a futile effort on her part.[11]

Perhaps not too much should be made of the reactions of rival actors, but their comments do reveal the professional courtesy which actors extended in lending costumes, supporting her in the lesser roles, and offering advice on stage business, as well as the competition which figured in Miss Cushman's assumption of male roles. Booth, at least, regarded her effort as a direct challenge to his interpretation.

A more important consideration than the attitude of other actors toward Miss Cushman's assumption of male roles is her own attitude. Her choice of these roles seems to relate very directly to her physical and psychological characteristics, and to her outlook on the role of women in society. Shortly after Cushman's death in 1876, a close friend, Emma Stebbins, wrote a book about her in which the author attempted to disguise the real reasons that she played Romeo and other male parts.

Although Miss Cushman's early training as a "utility actress" at the Park Theatre had obliged her to make herself familiar with many male parts, it was not her choice to represent such, and notably in the case of this impersonation, Romeo. She was led to her choice of this play as the one in which to present her sister to an English audience by her strong desire to be enabled to support her fittingly herself. By acting Romeo, she would add to her sister's attraction, secure her success, and give her that support which it would be difficult otherwise to attain.[12]

Stebben's view is simply not correct. Writing in 1894, W. T. Price, in *A Life of Charlotte Cushman*, stated: "There is not only no apology needed for Charlotte Cushman's Romeo as her female biographers seem to imagine, but it was one of her most remarkable achievements." He then presented his viewpoint that offstage Miss Cushman was performing the dominating role normally played by a man in terms of supporting all her relatives, handling business affairs, traveling and working in different places, and establishing households of which she was the head. He concluded that it was natural for her to choose to play the dominating male role on the stage, since "she was playing the part of a man in these serious relationships of life."[13]

Her dominating personality and physical appearance led her naturally into such a position. She felt that she had a handicap in traditional roles normally played by beautiful women, and her acting in female roles was characterized by a restlessness and constant movement, because she felt that to play with repose one had to be beautiful. In male roles she was spared comments on her lack of conventional beauty, and was spared invidious comparisons between herself and beauties like Mrs. Siddons. Her size, too, made it difficult for her to play the role of a woman who was dominated by a man, and one critic wondered at the probability of Bill Sykes being able to kill her Meg Merrilies. She herself complained to William Winter, "The actors who come on for Macbeth are, usually, such *little* men; I have to look down at them."[14] Actors who performed with her were keenly aware of her size, too. Booth remarked that when as Lady Macbeth she urged him to kill Duncan, he felt an inclination to say, "Why don't *you* kill him, you're big enough."[15] When Forrest was in the audience and she said, "All the perfumes of Arabia will not sweeten this little hand," Forrest laughed aloud and said, "*Little* hand! Why it's as big as a codfish!"[16]

Obviously, then, it was her physical qualities, and her attitude toward them, that drew Miss Cushman to male roles. Playing Romeo and other male roles certainly did not embarrass her, nor was she embarrassed to dress and behave according to her inclinations offstage, despite the comments of friends and relatives. The writer Melville met her and found her a very masculine "strange creature" wearing a "man's collar, cravat and Wellington boots."[17] Elizabeth Barrett Browning was dismayed by what she described as a "female marriage" between Charlotte and the young actress Matilda Hays, who played heroines to Charlotte's heroes (in the *Lady of Lyons* and *Romeo and Juliet*, for example). In a letter to her family regarding a relationship with the sculptress Emma Stebbins, Charlotte said, "I love her very much, she is the finest nature I have ever been in contact with."[18] In 1858, Miss Cushman temporarily retired from the stage, moved to London, and lived with three other women as, in her words, "jolly female bachelors."[19] That this mode of life was known and accepted is indicated by a number of comments by writers at the time.

Charlotte Cushman's relationships were with women who had aspirations to raise the status of women through writing and art—as she felt she was doing. Price wrote, "Eliza Cook fell in love with her, and read her own poetry to her, some of the sonnets being on Charlotte—and they spent much time then, and in after years, in the company of each other."[20] Another writer Charlotte encouraged was Geraldine Jewsbury, who wrote a novel titled *The Half Sisters*. It was a defense of women's right to free love and the need to prove themselves capable of more than marriage and motherhood. The central character was modeled after Charlotte, and the author wrote to her, "We are touching on better days when women will have a genuine normal life of their own to lead, and no longer feel their destiny manqué if they remain single."[21] Miss Cushman supported and assisted Emma Stebbins, and tried to help her win a major commission for a piece of sculpture, saying, "In this way *women* will raise the statue."[22] Through playing leading roles, Miss Cushman was able to stand as a highly visible symbol of successful and independent womanhood, and in playing roles men usually played, and receiving more acclaim than any other Romeo at the time, she showed that women could compete with men. She must have taken a great deal of pleasure in playing Orlando in the all-female production of *As You Like It* performed by 150 members of the Professional Women's League.[23]

Charlotte Cushman's efforts to raise the status of women, her dissatisfaction with her lack of typical feminine beauty, and her natural instinct toward domination all led her to play male roles. With the exception of Hamlet, these were popular and critical successes. Her male rivals may not have liked what she did, but had to take her seriously, especially in view of her general success. She seems to have made a clear appraisal of herself and her circumstances, and to have played roles which brought her fame and earned her a great deal of money. This gave her the means to live as she chose and to assist other women in various ways and to encourage the artistic efforts of women with independent outlooks. The position she achieved brought her admiration, critical acclaim, a very active social life, and wealth.

There is nevertheless some evidence that however successfully she adapted to her circumstances, she could have wished them otherwise. Although she played men's roles, she would have preferred to play really fine roles written for women. She acted the part of Richelieu, but her real desire was expressed when she wrote to a playwright wishing to have a play with

> a woman of strong ambition, who is at the same time very wily and diplomatic, and who has an opportunity of a great outburst when her plans are successful—in short, a female Richelieu.[24]

Later actresses had the opportunity to play such roles as the American theatre changed. New playwrights and changing social views presented an increasing number of dominating women's roles in realistic dramas such as *Margaret Fleming, Mrs. Warren's Profession* and *Ghosts*. With the increasing emphasis on realism in the theatre, the number of women playing men's roles decreased. In the twentieth century attempts at Hamlet by actresses such as Eva Le Gallienne and Judith Anderson have been regarded as notable oddities, and the former is certainly more likely to be remembered for her portrayal of Hedda Gabler and the latter for her Medea. As a phenomenon of the nineteenth century, the actresses playing male roles revealed a challenge to the male domination of the stage, a taste for novelty, and the willingness on the part of the critics and audiences to accept the process as one of the many conventions of the nineteenth-century theatre. For individual actresses, playing male roles offered the possibility of psychological satisfaction, star billing, public acclaim and increased income—all major advantages for strong independent female performers.

ADAH ISAACS MENKEN IN *MAZEPPA*

Lois Adler

Adah Isaacs Menken "is the sensation of the New York stage," said one review. "Her rare beauty and the tantalizing audacity of her performance defy description. She must be seen to be believed; anyone who misses her at the Broadway Theatre will be denying himself the rarest of exhilarating treats."[1] The penny press went all out for Menken, famous as the first lady to play the male lead in *Mazeppa* while strapped to the back of a real horse—and in the "nude" no less! The date was April 30, 1866. The former "Mrs. J. C. Heenan," ex-wife of the boxer "Benecia Boy," had come a long way from her days at the Bowery.

The Oxford Companion to the Theatre attributes the first playing of Mazeppa by a woman to Charlotte Crampton in 1859; a listing in Odell's *Annals of the New York Stage* for such a performance on January 3, 1859, at the Bowery would seem to corroborate this, although other commentators do not mention it. Odell quotes from a handbill (presumably) which said that Crampton was "the first actress to attempt the part with her two beautifully trained horses, Alexander and Black Eagle; executing the most intrepid feats ever performed by a lady." However, she didn't do it in the nude, nor was she tied to the horse's back, which gives Menken the edge.

Menken first played the role on June 3, 1861, in Albany. *The Oxford Companion to the Theatre* errs in claiming San Francisco, 1863, as the place and date of the initial performance. It also gives Menken's real name as Dolores Adios Fuertes—an absolutely super name—but one of several "real" names that Menken made up along with conflicting tales of her birth and background.

In fact (faulty reportage and crumbling, nonpaginated newspapers aside), the material involving Menken is a mass of contradictory statements, historical inaccuracies, and hearsay provided mainly by Menken herself. She used extensive PR and was also the source of the "facts" behind the publicity—all these having achieved legitimacy through continued repetition, unfortunately. When Adah Bertha Theodore—and that was her real name—married Alexander Isaacs Menken, so one story goes, she claimed she told his devoutly religious family that she was the daughter of a Portuguese rabbi. That this tale undercut the story of her conversion from Catholicism to Judaism seemed not to matter. The penchant for the "Spanish Style" and the related stories seem to have surfaced very conveniently in 1861, right after the death of Lola Montes (Marie Dolores Gilbert), whom Menken identified with and emulated. She began using the name Dolores with her intimate friends at that time and later announced this as her real name to the European press.[2] She was Swinburne's "Dolores."

The idea for Adah to do Mazeppa came from the actor James Murdoch, who had played in *Macbeth* with Adah in Nashville, according to biographer Paul Lewis. Supposedly sometime in 1861, Adah was in a sketch at the Broadway called *Ha Ha Horsie*, in which a group of girls cavorted around wearing imitation horses' heads while one girl rode a horse. At one point the horse reared, and our Adah (one of the horsies) grabbed the reins, helped the girl to dismount, then leaped onto the horse's back while the audience applauded wildly. When Murdoch heard of the incident, he suggested that she do Milner's dramatization of Byron's *Mazeppa or the Wild Horse of Tartary* lashed to the back of a real horse. None of the male Mazeppas had ever done that scene on the horse; they had used dummies. Apparently, no one in New York wanted to chance a woman doing that stunt, although Murdoch had seen her ride (she was trained by her stepfather, supposedly) and he knew she could do it. The manager of a company playing at the Green Street Theatre in Albany, Captain J. B. Smith, was interested, and so they went off to Albany. Once there Murdoch supervised the building of a spiral ramp; it was his idea that she should ride out through the audience on this runway so that everyone could see her. In his book, *The Stage*, he never mentions any of these things, though he gives a vivid account of what it was like to play opposite her improvised Lady Macbeth.[3]

At this point, Adah came up with the second innovation—she would wear flesh-colored tights to simulate nudity while strapped to the back of the untamed horse. According to her account, she was "ordered" never to answer questions from the press or anyone else as to whether she wore tights or was really nude. The wardrobe mistress, Emma Hazeltine, was also sworn to secrecy.

Adah practiced at least an hour a day on the runway. But at the dress rehearsal in the afternoon before the opening, something frightened the horse, which bolted and toppled off the runway. Adah, according to Lewis, "having broken the bands of light paper which served as bindings, leapt out of the way of the horse, grabbed the reins and spoke quietly to the horse—then mounted her and insisted on trying it again and again until it was perfect." News of this spread and the house was sold out by evening. While this is an amusing story, that same Captain Smith, in an interview printed by Mr. H. P. Phelps in the *Albany Mirror* on October 25, 1879, reminisced about how he came up with the idea for Menken to do *Mazeppa*. He had seen her in another company in Albany and thought that it would be perfect for her and that it would be a great success. Certainly for an era bound up with spectacular scenes on the melodramatic stage, this was a good guess. His description of Menken's initial nervousness and what happened in rehearsal when the horse bolted, throwing her and injuring her, is in marked contrast to her account. He does say, however, that she was very plucky and tried until she got it right; he quoted her as saying, "No one ever saw me show the white feather."[4]

On the evening of June 3, 1861, Menken opened in *Mazeppa*, appearing in the "nude" in staid Albany. She followed the tradition of using a black horse popular since the late 1850s; the horse's name was Belle Beauty. Certainly a black horse was more fearsome and wild-looking for a naked lady—even if she was playing a man. There is a marvelous litho in the Townsend Walsh Scrapbook at the Lincoln Center Library of Adah dressed as a Tartar warrior, looking like Brunhilde-cum-Odile. She is on a black horse, wearing a black cape, black boots, carrying a black shield and with black, flowing hair.

The *Albany Express* said, "The house was crowded; we can safely say that it was the largest audience that has been seen for years within the walls of the Green Street Theatre. Miss Menken has proved herself to be a heroine in the fearless manner in which she succeeded to the top of the theatre on the back of the horse Belle Beauty. The place has been got up in fine style."[5] The run was brief, but Menken made a hit in Albany. A clipping in the Townsend Walsh Scrapbook states that the straps used in the "binding scene" were still in view over a bar in Buffalo.

For the next two years, Menken toured with *Mazeppa*, visiting Hartford, Philadelphia, Pittsburgh, Wilmington and Louisville (where she played Pip in a version of *Great Expectations*; she was an ardent admirer of Dickens, with whom she later became friendly), but the dates are difficult to verify. Paul Lewis says she was back in Albany for her return engagement in January 1862 and was earning a high salary playing to capacity audiences. We do know that she brought *Mazeppa* to Baltimore in November 1862, where after a few performances she was arrested as a Confederate spy. She was accused of being involved in some plot with a well-known Confederate sympathizer, who it seems gave her several gifts. This was the story of her most recent husband, Robert Henry Newell, writer and literary editor on the *Sunday Mercury*, who was summoned to Baltimore to bail her out (she had divorced J. C. Heenan, the famous boxer, several months earlier).[6] Her own story was that she was talking to some admirers after the performance and was overheard praising Jefferson Davis.[7] In any event, this scandal produced fabulous receipts at the box office; people flocked to see her despite the tense war atmosphere. It is difficult not to draw the obvious conclusion that Menken devised this whole thing as a publicity stunt—perhaps the initial box-office receipts were not good or she perceived some possible threat to her drawing power.

Offers came from California during the Baltimore run, and Adah knew when to move on, when to conquer new territory. In the summer of 1863, she left for California, where she entertained the miners and sporting men for about a year. She felt San Francisco was her town and the feeling appears to have been mutual; the show was a tremendous success and she was personally very popular. Her friends were the Western literati: Mark Twain, Bret Harte, Charles Warren Stoddard and other writers on the well-known magazine *The Californian*. It was Charles Henry Webb's review in *The Californian* that contained the famous quote: "The Menken is unrivalled in her particular line—but it isn't a clothesline."[8]

Menken was clever enough not to submit *Mazeppa* to overexposure in San Francisco; she interspersed it with performances of *The French Spy* and *Black-Eyed Susan*, playing the male leads. In addition, she toured other parts of California like Sacramento, and at one point took off for Virginia City, Nevada. By doing this, she warded off the possibility of using up her San Francisco audience. She was earning $500 a week in California and was reportedly offered $2,500 down payment for an engagement in Virginia City.[9] In March 1864, Adah agreed to the offer in spite of the fact there was no theatre. She found a substitute and flamboyantly (in the style of the Old West) put her production of *Mazeppa* in an old amphitheatre on the outskirts of Virginia City. As she told it, Lewis reports she had men coming up onstage handing her silver pieces while she dispensed kisses; this was her arrangement, after gently chiding them for throwing money at her—which was their customary way of showing appreciation. After her Nevada triumph, Menken returned to San Francisco that spring for the final run of *Mazeppa*. A new influx of people plus those natives who had not yet seen the notorious lady assured her of an audience and secured the financial success of the run. Adah benefited enormously from this Western tour, not only financially but in terms of star status and future bookings. It afforded a goldmine of erotic adventures for the publicity mill, particularly for the tour of Europe she took in 1864.

Menken returned to the United States and appeared in *Mazeppa* at the Broadway Theatre in New York on April 30, 1866. This is considered by some biographers to be the first performance of Menken's *Mazeppa* in New York, although there is considerable disagreement about where this performance fits into the history of the production. Whatever the case, Menken came to NewYork as a star, having acquired fame in Europe; and this was the best way to arrive, considering the theatrical fare she offered.

Paul Lewis's version of opening night—he dates it June 12, 1861—is based on a mixture of information supplied from books written by Menken's friend, Ed James, and her husband, Robett Newell, and her own diary.[10] She was billed as an "extraordinary artiste": an epithet that appears on an early handbill found in Lincoln Center (*Menken Portfolio*) advertising her appearance as a danseuse in a vaudeville sketch in Louisiana. Lewis says, "The suspense and thrills were built up by posters displaying a black stallion, teeth bared, rearing its front legs pawing the air. Lashed to the animal's back was a cleverly concealed figure of a woman who appeared to be nude, with black hair to the waist, bare arms and with a look of wild terror on her face."[11] There was real excitement and gossip about Menken appearing "nude"; and Menken had cut her hair in a mannish bob a few days before opening night, according to Lewis. The first night was sold out. Boxes were ten dollars each. Booth and Whitman, her friends, were reported to be in the audience.

Just before curtain time, Adah pulled what can only be called a "kitsch" stunt. First, the houselights were dimmed, then they rose again slowly, while ushers passed out copies of Adah's poem "Pro Patria" (poetry and writing in general were her lifelong passion and she got a great deal of it published). After a few minutes, the lights went out and the curtain went up.

Here is Lewis's description of the appearance of Cassimir, based on Ed James's account: "He [she] appeared in skin tight breeches, a deep plunging man's shirt and calf high boots . . . sitting on a pasteboard rock. 'Yonder sits the brooding Cassimir,' says another character." Adah's voice was "uncommonly husky" and her stage speech was something all her own: "a mixture of Southern, Spanish and the rounded English of Edwin Booth." James thought she showed great agility and said her acting style appeared to be distinctly her own: she made up for her lack of polish by her emotional intensity . . . She was a hot-blooded young woman, even if she wasn't exactly the character Cassimir." One gathers from all of this that Menken had presence and tremendous sex appeal onstage as well as off.

As for the big scene, Lewis says, "The horse reached the runway at the rear of the theatre, then cantered down toward the front stage again—Adah giving commands continually. When horse and rider reached the stage, the curtain closed swiftly and the spotlight was extinguished. Cheers rang out."

At her curtain call, Menken proved a real showman. She appeared completely covered from head to toe in a scarlet cape. Suddenly she was sobbing and there was Edwin Booth rushing to her side. Supposedly she took fourteen curtain calls.

While the *Herald* was not enthusiastic, the *Tribune* was positively virulent: "the atmosphere reeked with vulgarity."[12] Horace Greeley himself in the *Tribune* was supposed to have attacked her with statements like, "An actress who uses her naked body to entice audiences into a theatre should be barred by legislation from the stage." Apparently this started a running battle between them, with Adah taking out ads to answer him. The publicity was fabulous and kept her constantly before the public. She called Greeley unfair; she admonished him for criticizing something he had not seen. She urged him to see the performance and when this didn't work, she dared him to show up: "See me in my notoriety!"[13] He finally did show up and ultimately, though he was never able to praise the show, became a friend.

George Wood, manager of the Broadway, answered the critics by saying, "To see Miss Adah in the natural beauty of her womanhood, costumed as she is costumed, is alone worth the price of admission."[14] The *Courier* declared, "the female *Mazeppa* is the sensation of New York. It should continue to draw crowds for months to come."[15] Another of the reviews said: "She is Aphrodite and Diana; a marble statue of exquisitely molded perfection."[16] The *Evening Daily News* said: "May a lady be naked? She lives, she breathes . . . we salute the naked lady of New York." The *Post* said: "She is so lovely she numbs the mind and the senses reel—although we must confess that the play is a dreary excuse for a theatrical entertainment; yet we would be willing to see it again just to see her." The *New York Clipper*, rather than giving an actual review, recapped Menken's European reviews and discussed her previous success in California.[17]

It was said that Menken was popular with the suffragettes. One can see why. Adah, ever the admirer of independent women (she thought Hester Prynne heroic—simply hated little Pearl), espoused the cause or might have *said* she did. Certainly Ms. Menken never hid the fact that she found domesticity distasteful, nor did she conceal her dislike of "good" (obedient) women. She considered them bores. Once, after submitting her writing to *Harper's* magazine, she said, "As for Ladies magazines, I want no part of that flabby, sanctimonious collection of trash which good women read so avidly. If I had a favorite recipe, I would send it to them and they would pay me well for it. But I have never been an accomplished cook, thank the Lord. I will be rich enough to pay someone to cook for me—even breakfast."[18] Adah's most famous comment, made in a letter to her friend Robert ("Racy") Reese after his marriage in 1864, revealed definite insight. She said, "I believe good men should be married, but I don't believe in women being married; somehow they all sink into non-entities after this epoch of their existence. This is the fault of female education. They are taught from the cradle to look upon marriage as the one event in their lives. That accomplished, nothing remains."[19]

Immediately after the New York run of nearly a month, Menken left for Europe. There she repeated her past success, adding to her list of admirers and friends the names of Dumas Père, Gautier and George Sand. She died in Paris in 1868, penniless, at the age of thirty-three, and was buried in the Jewish section of Père Lachaise Cemetery. Later the body was transferred to the Montparnasse Cemetery.

From all of the above material, one thing seems abundantly clear—that Menken's projection of her physical attractiveness, not her histrionic ability, was the dominant theatrical attribute. Newspapers referred to her as "statuesque" and as "Aphrodite." Paul Lewis maintains that she was about five foot seven with a perfectly shaped figure; and with full lips that were painted crimson. He quotes Newell as saying that "Adah was a symbol of desire . . . all who saw her, wanted her immediately."[20]

It is obvious to us that Menken had a real talent for what might be called dramatic display. She had a sense of what her audience wanted whether in the theatre or out of it. In an age that lusted after spectacle and variety (a partial reason for the popularity of breeches roles), when advertising was everything, Menken knew how to advertise. She was her own best publicist. She was the prime female example of that special brand of showmanship which is usually associated with men, specifically those who were engaged in "popular enter-tainments" during the second half of the nineteenth century. Her production had less straight dramatic quality than any of the previous productions of *Mazeppa*; much dialogue was cut and greater emphasis was placed on her "postures" both on and off the horse. This touch of "burlesque," combined with her imaginative, melodramatic approach to publicity, created a product that was closer to a circus or a Wild West show. It was this total approach that made Menken's *Mazeppa* a great hit.

LYDIA THOMPSON AND THE "BRITISH BLONDES"

Marlie Moses

References to Lydia Thompson and her so-called British Blondes are most frequently found in discussions of the "leg business" or "naked drama" of the last quarter of the nineteenth century. Thompson has been credited with, or blamed for, the establishment of "nudity," i.e., the display of female legs, clad in tights and topped by short skirts or trunks, as a box-office attraction in the United States.

The revealed female form had been introduced on the America stage by Adah Isaacs Menken and had reappeared with the *danseuses* of *The Black Crook* and *The White Fawn*, but the phenomenon of women in tights, kicking and dancing onstage, appears to settled into U.S. theatre history with the long run of *Ixion, or the Man at the Wheel*, which opened at Wood's Museum in New York on September 28, 1868, with Lydia Thompson in the title role.

After a highly successful run to capacity crowds, the company moved to Niblo's Gardens, establishing a total long-run record of forty-five weeks. A tour of the Eastern United States followed, the success of the troupe prov-ing so profitable that, with only minor exceptions, for the next six years the company toured as far as California and played to enthusiastic American audi-ences, returning occasionally to New York and making intermittent voyages to England to secure new scripts, recruit new actors, and order new scenery and costumes.

Most treatises on the subject of modem burlesque cite Thompson and the female members of her troupe (which included men as well) as the first "queens" of burlesque—or at least as its "progenitresses."[1] Certainly the several extant photographs of the Blondes appear ludicrously prurient in their intent. And it was true that burlesque was regarded as a substandard literary form. History, however, has been unkind to Thompson and her associates, seizing on the evidence of the photographs and, more significantly, on the scathing reportage of the contemporary American press, and ignoring the contradicting evi-dence—especially the evidence of Thompson's stature in the English theatre.

Remembering that the New York stage of the 1860s was working to overcome its reputation as a rowdy, undisciplined and unclean institution, it is not difficult to imagine the outrage engendered by the appearance stage of women in tights. The scantily clad Parisian dancers of *The Black Crook* had subsided from the stage, and now for the second time in a decade the theatre had been invaded by a *foreign* element,

> an army of burlesque women who took ship for America, and presently the New York stage presented one disgraceful spectacle of padded legs jiggling and wriggling in the insensate follies and indecencies of the hour.[2]

So ran the accusation of the well-known actress-turned-author, Olive Logan, whose lengthy diatribes in magazines and in her books, *Before the Footlights and Behind the Scenes* and *Apropos of Women and Theatre*, consistently attacked the Thompson actresses for their "bleached blonde hair" as well as their "padded limbs." What Logan feared above all else was that the "naked drama" was debasing both actresses and the acting profession.

Others who believed the stage was imperiled by the Thompson company included the editors of *The Spirit of the Times*, who claimed that the burlesque company had

> not only enticed to their exhibitions a new public element from the suburbs, but so drained the old theatrical audiences of a percentage of their followers, that in a little while, nearly all the dramatic houses were forced to recruit their companies with lascivious attraction.[3]

Despite continually swelling box-office receipts and consistently favorable audience reception, Lydia Thompson's burlesque company never enjoyed a prestigious reputation in America. Lavish testimonials and benefits tendered her on her various American tours, as well as occasional testimonials in the press by such respected personages as Shakespearean scholar Richard Grant White did not seem to offset the tarnished reputation which she suffered during her initial engagement.

Theatre historians have unwittingly perpetuated this tarnished view of Thompson and her theatrical associates—a view based primarily on her American reception. When one studies Thompson from the British vantage point, an entirely different reputation emerges. It might, therefore, be useful to examine briefly the life and career of the London actress.

Born in London in 1836, the young Lydia Thompson made her debut at age sixteen as a ballet dancer and won London hearts both as a dancer and later as an actor in Christmas pantomimes. Before she was twenty she had established herself as an outstanding Principal Boy in burlesque, pantomime and extravaganza. On the basis of her London success she toured the Continent, including Russia, to high public acclaim. In later years, after her American success, she would tour India and Australia.

She continued to play her Principal Boy parts for years; well into her fifties she was the subject of unabashed praise and amazement over the extreme youthfulness of her face and figure.

The press in England was as generous as it was calumnious in America. Newspaper and magazine articles contained tributes to her gentility, modesty, kindness, sweet disposition, good humor and flawless good taste. Reviews of her performances unfailingly praised her grace of movement, her singing, her captivating style of comedy. The Victorian press, in short, adored her.

There is no hint of disapproval of her scanty costumes or suggestive dialogue, simply because both of these phenomena were part and parcel of the burlesque/pantomime tradition. The Principal Boy was a beloved part of this tradition, and British audiences loved and revered their Principal Boys. On the question of tights, Thompson was quoted in the *New York Herald* in 1895: "Some ladies upon the stage object to put them on. Why? Shakespeare's most lovely heroines wear tights—Rosalind, Viola, Imogen don them, and Joan of Arc as well." And on legs: "Many aver it was I who brought legs into prominence both in England and America, which statement is ridiculous. Legs were very much in evidence long before I was born or crossed the ocean."[4]

Lydia Thompson continued acting in London and the provinces after her final American appearance in 1891, but following her formal retirement in 1899 she played only a few dowager roles. Neither England nor America recognizes her fully as the popular performer she was, unquestionably because of the fact that she so divided her enterprise between the two countries. She led a full and active stage life that spanned fifty-three years.

She was the first Englishwoman to import her own company to America and the first star of either sex to play an entire unbroken season in New York. She popularized burlesque and extravaganza in the United States . . . and also helped to introduce the word *burlesque* into the language as a term for entertainment which utilizes suggestive songs and scantily clad female dancers. Despite her occasional detractors, she won the hearts of her audience, and she received numerous tributes from a legion of fascinated admirers.

HORRIBLE PRETTINESS: A CULTURAL ANALYSIS OF "BRITISH BLONDES"

Robert C. Allen

In August 1869 Richard Grant White reflected on burlesque's remarkable triumph during the season just ended:

It means something, this outbreak of burlesque acting all over the world. No mere accident has made so monstrous a kind of entertainment equally acceptable to three publics so different as those of

Paris, London and New York. And by monstrous I do not mean wicked, disgusting, or hateful, but monstrously incongruous and unnatural. The peculiar trait of burlesque is its defiance both of the natural and conventional. Rather, it forces the conventional and the natural together just at the points where they are most remote, and the result is absurdity, monstrosity.[1]

William Dean Howells, whose essay on burlesque appeared but only months before White's, was similarly struck by the incongruities that lay at the heart of burlesque and its representation of femininity. Strangely enthralled and repulsed by burlesque performers' impersonations of masculinity, Howells declared: "Though they were not like men [they] were in most things as unlike women, and seemed creations of a kind of alien sex, parodying both. It was certainly a shocking thing to look at them with their horrible prettiness, their archness in which was no charm, their grace which put to shame."[2]

To cast these two insightful characterizations of burlesque in somewhat more modem (and theoretically grounded) terms, we might say that burlesque is one of several nineteenth-century entertainment forms that is grounded in the aesthetics of transgression, inversion and the grotesque. The burlesque performer represents a construction of what Peter Stallybrass and Allon White call the "low other": something that is reviled by and excluded from the dominant social order as debased, dirty and unworthy, but that is simultaneously the object of desire and/or fascination . . . The result , . . is "a mobile, conflictual fusion of power, fear and desire in the construction of subjectivity: a psychological dependence upon precisely those Others which are being rigorously opposed and excluded at the social level. It is for this reason that what is *socially* peripheral is so frequently *symbolically* central."[3]

What were the qualities of this monstrous union, and how were they articulated in such a way as to cause the whole to be infinitely more alluring and threatening than any of its individual attributes? Clearly, the power of Thompsonian burlesque to delight and to horrify is inextricably bound to its status as the most thoroughly feminized form of theatrical entertainment in the history of the American stage of that time. Indeed, no form of American commercial theatrical entertainment before or since has given the stage over to women to a greater degree. In 1868 no other form of theatre had ever put before its audience the issue of the representation of women and femininity as boldly or as inescapably as did Thompsonian burlesque. That it did so not as a "serious" dramatic treatment of the place of women in American society but rather in a form that united "the coarsest fun with the most intoxicating forms of beauty" merely heightened its impact.

What the audiences saw on this stage full of male-impersonating, revealingly attired, slang-spouting, minstrel-dancing women was a physical and ideological inversion of the Victorian ideal of femininity. Lydia Thompson, although not nearly so large as the burlesque stars of a decade later, was certainly statuesque, as were the other principals in the troupe. There was nothing of the frail, ethereal, steel-engraving lady about her. Her corseted costume emphasized her bust, hips and legs, calling attention to the markers of sexual difference the sentimental costume kept hidden. Whereas the sentimental feminine ideal had been consistently depicted as dark-haired, much was made of the blondeness of the British Blondes and the means by which this tint might have been achieved.

In September 1868, when Lydia Thompson and her troupe appeared at Wood's, she faced an audience of clerks and shopkeepers, men and women, for whom theatregoing was, for the most part, socially and morally unproblematic. Theatres had been made safe and respectable, the theatrical experience predictable, and the audience quiescent. Ironically, it was the presence of respectable, middle-class women and men in the audience that made burlesque so problematic, and it was only in relation to what the bourgeois theatre had become since the Astor Place riot that burlesque seemed so transgressive. Mainstream American theatre had by 1869 reached an accommodation with the middle and upper strata of American society. The theatre would continue to be a liminoid space, where things were not what they seemed and where pleasure might be taken in the construction of unreal worlds. At times controversy over the nature and propriety of those pleasures and those unreal worlds strained the accommodation. But onstage and in the audience, the theatre's inherent power to transgress and invert existing power relations was much more circumscribed.

When Lydia Thompson moved to Niblo's Garden in the winter of 1868–69 and into the heart of the middle-class theatrical world, she upset this accommodation. At the historical moment when women had finally become socially invisible as part of the theatre audience, Thompson and her troupe made women visible in a way that could not be ignored. Just when the voices of class division within the audience had been silenced, Thompson and her sisters spoke in the undignified slang of the market place and street. Just when sexuality in the audience had been stifled, the third tier evacuated, and the concert saloon closed, the "leg business" put the issue of female sexuality on center stage. All that had been repressed in the righteous, moral, conservative middle class's conquest of the theatre returned in burlesques. Theatre once again became unpredictable; the relationship between performer and audience became unstably and uncomfortably direct. The fear that even playful ontological duplicity onstage might upset the natural order of things resurfaced. Who could control these women with their "idiotic parodies" of masculinity, their "horrible prettiness"?

HENRIETTA VINTON DAVIS: SHAKESPEAREAN ACTRESS

Errol Hill

The stage career of Henrietta Vinton Davis encompasses all of the promise and frustration experienced by black actors of her generation. She was born in Baltimore, her father being a talented musician who died prematurely. At fifteen she graduated from a Washington school and took a teaching job in Maryland, but was back in Washington in 1878 as secretary in the office of the Recorder of Deeds. She became a student of Miss Marguerite Saxton, an esteemed elocutionist, and made her professional debut as a public reciter at Marini's Hall in Washington, D.C., on April 25, 1883. On hand to introduce her was the man under whom she served in the recorder's office, the leading black statesman in the country, the honorable Frederick Douglass. It could not have been a more auspicious start to a long and brilliant career on the concert platform and legitimate stage.

Miss Davis was advertised as "the first lady of her race to publicly essay a debut in Shakespearean and other legitimate characters." Her recital program included speeches of two of Shakespeare's heroines: Juliet (from *Romeo and Juliet*) and Portia (from *The Merchant of Venice*).[1]

Miss Davis opened in Boston on July 17, 1883, appearing at the Young Men's Christian Union Hall on Boylston Street. Supporting her on the program were two Boston artists, the soprano Adelaide G. Smith and Samuel W. Jamieson, a pianist. She acquired professional managers who announced a tour immediately following her Boston engagement that included a number of towns and cities in the Eastern states. The Boston correspondent of the *New York Globe*, writing of her performance, recognized Miss Davis's potential as an actress but was not much impressed with her impersonations. He thought she would make a stronger impression in scene work with other actors than in solo recitations. However, a few weeks later at the Bethel A.M.E. Church in New York Miss Davis scored a notable success, her commanding presence and deep sonorous voice reminding her reviewer of Charlotte Cushman, first lady of the American stage. As Juliet in the potion scene from *Romeo and Juliet* she was "so true to the concept of a truly great artist as well as to nature, that the audience, electrified by the beautiful acting and the finished elocution of Miss Davis, applauded her to the very echo."[2]

At the end of her first season of performances, Miss Davis showed a marked improvement in her readings. She had added speeches of Rosalind in *As You Like It* and Cleopatra in *Antony and Cleopatra* to her repertoire, and expressed her desire to appear in a regular stage production next season supported by a full company of actors. This ambition seemed close to fulfillment when the *New York Globe* announced on March 29, 1884, that Miss Davis had been engaged by Thomas T. Symmons, manager of the Bohemia

UNIVERSITY OF WINCHESTER LIBRARY

Dramatic Club, to appear at Whitney's Opera House, Detroit, on April 14. The club had evidently acquired an enviable local reputation and Mr. Symmons, himself a baritone soloist who subsequently took over Miss Davis's management and became her husband, planned to put his company on the road in a new drama with her as leading lady. There is no evidence that this project ever materialized. Miss Davis continued to build her reputation in frequent appearances around the country. In the May 3, 1884, issue of the *New York Globe*, an article entitled "Our Dramatic Artists" commented on her development as an actress:

> Miss H. Vinton Davis has shown undoubted talent as a delineator of Shakespearian characters. Her concepts are rich and original, while her stage presence is graceful, easy and natural. In humorous delineations she shows to good advantage, but her strongest forte is in characters like Lady Macbeth and Juliet. This artist is yet in her youth and has plenty of room in which to rise to an honorable position.

On a visit to Cincinnati, Miss Davis had teamed up with Powhatan Beaty in scenes from Shakespeare. The collaboration had worked so well that Beaty was invited to participate in an ambitious production at Ford's Opera House in Washington, D.C., on May 7, 1884. The program consisted of three scenes from *Macbeth*, *Richard III*, "which was performed almost entirely," and a scene from *Ignomar*. Miss Davis played Lady Macbeth, Lady Anne and Parthenia; Beaty was Macbeth, King Henry VI and Ingomar. Completing the company which was assembled for the occasion were a number of local amateurs, among them W. R. Davis, who made his stage debut as Gloster after King Richard, W.H.H. Hart as Earl of Richmond and selected students from Howard University. Citizens and soldiers were supplied by the Washington Cadet Corps. Directing the production was Miss Saxton, the elocution teacher who had coached Miss Davis. The Opera House seating more than 1,100 was filled to capacity with a mixed audience of both races, the honorable Frederick Douglass and family occupying a private box.

The long and ecstatic notice in the *New York Globe* of May 17, 1884, commenced by saying that the three principals covered themselves with glory. It went on to discuss the performances of the leading actors:

> As Lady Macbeth, Miss Davis displayed powers of conception. While we failed to discover in her acting the dull, heavy, declamatory style complained of by some critics, to me it was plainly apparent that Miss Davis has great reserve dramatic powers, which have not been drawn upon because of the influence that always somehow represses the spontaneous outflow of genius in beginners . . . The perfect adaptation of Miss Davis to her chosen profession is undisputed. She has earned the plaudits of professional critics, and her success has opened the dramatic door to many. Thus leap by leap the colored

man and woman encroach upon the ground so long held sacred by their white brother and sister.

Referring to notices in the white press about the production, this reviewer felt that the actors should be highly flattered because they were not criticized as colored people nor as beginners. Instead, they should regard such criticism as a compliment since every paper discovered among a few faults great merit in the embryo actors and actresses.

The review in one of these white papers, the *Washington Post* of May 8, 1884, is illuminating for its description of the atmosphere in the Opera House during the production. More than sixty years had elapsed since the African Company in lower New York was harassed by white patrons and forced to give up playing Shakespeare. The reception accorded these colored Shakespeareans in Ford's Opera House showed how little had changed in the mental attitude of those whites who refused to accept black performers in productions of serious plays. The *Post* critic reports:

> There were many white people in the house who seemed disposed to turn to comedy the tragic efforts of the actors. In this they were not wholly successful, for the earnestness and intelligence of several of the leading performers were such as to command the respect of those most disposed to find cause for laughter in everything that was said or done . . .
>
> The scene from Macbeth went creditably, all things considered, Miss Davis and Mr. Beaty showing a knowledge of the requirements of the parts which they essayed which, it is safe to say, surprised those in the audience competent to judge. The most enjoyable thing of the evening was *Richard III*. Here the "guying" disposition of the audience found ample opportunity to vent itself . . . The combat between Richard and Richmond waked the most derisive plaudits from the auditors, and "Time" was repeatedly called by particularly irreverent individuals.

Over the next ten years, Miss Davis continued to perform regularly in an everwidening circuit of cities, touring the South and West in addition to Eastern states. Her press notices grew more and more effusive. Appearing before a mostly white audience in Evanston, Illinois, in 1888, she held them "spellbound by the intensity of dramatic truthfulness she displayed" and was called "the most talented artist on the American stage."[3] In North Carolina, the *Goldsboro Argus* hailed her as "the greatest living genius of her race . . . Her prodigious memory, her graceful control of every thought, word and action, her powerful delineations and her compass and modulation of voice are truly wonderful."[4] There were renewed calls for her to be accepted into a regular company presenting Shakespeare and other dramatic classics. The *New York Freeman* of January 23, 1886, found it singular that none of the brilliant musical and elocutionary exponents of the race had so far obtained a footing on the legitimate stage and cited lack of money as the principal drawback. It urged some public-spirited individual of means to take an interest in Miss Davis's career. All that was necessary to the fullest development of her dramatic powers, wrote the Boston correspondent of the *New York Freeman*, was an opportunity to be heard by the great devotees of the drama through the competitive arena.[5] T. Thomas Fortune, writing in the *New York Age* of September 19, 1891, included Miss Davis among a few colored women actors who could achieve fame and fortune on the regular stage if only she could find a sponsor.

All appeals were in vain. Henrietta Vinton Davis, despite her manifest excellence as an actress, was unable to gain admission into the ranks of legitimate theatre companies, then exclusively under white management, because of her color. This racial boycott not only denied her professional fulfillment but deprived the theatre itself of a superbly talented actress whose art might have enriched the lives of countless playgoers. One would like to think that Shakespeare himself might have benefited from her interpretation of his heroines in properly mounted productions. The irony of the color bar as it applied to this actress is that Miss Davis was herself light-complexioned and not noticeably different from dozens of other actresses on the professional stage with inferior ability but without the stigma of African ancestry. A description of Miss Davis's physical appearance occurs in the Buffalo *Sunday Truth*:

> Miss Davis is a singularly beautiful woman, little more than a brunette, certainly no darker than a Spanish or Italian lady in hue, with illustriously expressive eyes and a mouth moulded upon Adelaide Neilson's . . . We could not help thinking what a magnificent Cleopatra she would make to a competent Antony. She has made the part a study, we have been informed since seeing her in Association Hall, and hope to view her in it some day. Her reading of *Mary, Queen of Scots* was also very fine and elicited much applause.[6]

Miss Davis appeared but once with the Astor Place Company in its rather cursory production of *Damon and Pythias* in 1884. The next year she was billed to play Desdemona to Beaty's Othello in Cincinnati but there is no mention of the production in the available records and one is left in doubt whether it ever occurred. Then in 1898, after fourteen years of concert recitals, she was at last seen in a full-scale production of a play that she helped to write. This was an original five-act drama of the South entitled *Our Old Kentucky Home*, written in conjunction with the colored journalist J. E. Bruce. In it Miss Davis had the role of a Creole slave, Clothilde, whose courageous attack on a fort helped to bring about the end of the Civil War and reunite her with her lover, one of the freed slaves who had enlisted in the Union Army. The show toured the Eastern cities with marked success. Two years later, the *Colored American* carried a terse and ominous announcement: Miss Davis had signed for *The Country Coon*, one of the best shows to be presented next season. The title of this show would place it solidly among the minstrel-cum-vaudeville type of variety acts that black performers produced regularly for touring in second-rate theatres across the country. It was the last place one would look for an artist of the caliber of Miss Davis. She had done everything that could possibly be expected of a dedicated actress to maintain the integrity of her art, which was directed toward the interpretation of dramatic masterpieces; now in utter frustration she was reduced to playing in the popular music hall. She had presented a range of Shakespearean characters: Juliet, Lady Macbeth, Cleopatra, Ophelia, Portia, Desdemona, Lady Anne and Queen Elizabeth, as well as other tragic heroines from the nineteenth-century drama: Calanthe, Mary Stuart, Parthenia, Leah, not in their completeness—that privilege had been denied her—but in dramatic monologues and selected scenes to universal commendation. Now she would play what? It is small consolation that the details of her assignment in the coon show are not known. The experience must have been soul-destroying, for Miss Davis was back on the concert circuit in 1901, extending her itinerary to the great Northwest and West Coast where she stayed for some three years before returning to her adopted home city of Washington. In 1903 she revived *Our Old Kentucky Home* in Denver and again played Clothilde, recited at the Palm Garden in New York in 1908, and one final appearance occurred at the Trinity Congregational Church in Pittsburgh in 1909 when she doubled in the roles of Zingarella, a flower girl, and Dominique, a comic character, in the production of another original play entitled *Dessalines* written by W. Edgar Easton. She had been acting continuously for a quarter of a century and more. The *Colored American* of February 22, 1902, provides a fitting summation to the career of this distinguished artist:

> Miss Davis is a remarkable woman and had she not been handicapped by unfavorable racial origin, she would today by virtue of her acknowledged talents take rank with dramatic artists of the Leslie Carter, Maude Adams, Julia Marlowe and Henrietta Crosman school. This thought strikes us, since Washington is so honeycombed with prejudice against the Negro to the point that in few theatres can we secure a decent seat and colored traveling companies cannot secure dates—why could not an enterprising manager organize here a stock company on the order of Lafayette Square and produce plays of current human interest, adapted to the refined tastes of our best people who now refrain from attending the existing theatres because of the unjust treatment they are compelled to endure? The natural head of such an organization would be Miss Davis. With such a versatile artiste, capable of assuming roles from tragedy to light comedy, and a few other actors as a nucleus, a stock company of undoubted drawing qualities could be built up in a season. An adequate theatre could be constructed or a suitable hall could be remodeled to serve the purpose at a moderate expense. Now why not a theatre for our people as a solution of the embarrassments that now confront us?

MARY SHAW: A FIGHTING CHAMPION

Robert A. Schanke

> The most marvelous thing in the twentieth century is woman's discovery of woman.[1]

> To me [there is always] the sustaining thought—the equality of woman's value as compared with man's . . . We [women] must develop ourselves and must not allow our habits of thought, our inheritance, to retard our best expression. We must search for things within ourselves, not in our environment, and we must not drug ourselves with formulas and compromises.[2]

These words, modern as they appear, embody the goal of a woman who spoke them nearly seventy years ago, actress Mary Shaw. She led protest marches, organized strikes, founded women's clubs, and addressed international audiences. Flouting both critics and public opinion, she used the theatre as a vehicle for her feminist ideas.

Even before she became a Broadway star, Mary Shaw was an ardent champion of women's rights. On December 6, 1892, she enrolled as a charter member of the Professional Women's League, an organization dedicated to bringing "together women engaged in dramatic, musical and literary pursuits with the purpose of rendering them helpful to each other."[3] Housed in their own building at Sixty-eighth and Broadway, the League sponsored numerous benefits, symposiums, bazaars and exhibits—all focused on promoting the advancing role of woman in society. At monthly meetings, members performed plays, read position papers, and generally sought means to improve the status of the professional woman. By 1902 the league boasted five hundred members, including such leading ladies as Ada Rehan, Mrs. Fiske, Helena Modjeska, Blanche Bates and Lillian Russell.

Shaw served the League faithfully. For over twenty years she sat on the board of directors. In 1893 she starred as Rosalind in the League's all-female cast of *As You Like It*. Mme. Janauschek played Jaques. Scheduled for a single matinee performance on November 21, 1893, it proved so popular that in late January 1894 the League revived the production for one week.

But her work for the League was not limited to acting. In the spring of 1894 she organized a conference and symposium in New York entitled "The Woman of the Next Century." Joining her in reading papers were Maude Banks and Mrs. James Herne, wife of the playwright. Shaw granted interviews and presented speeches. She spoke out particularly on behalf of women artists. She recognized that one of the handicaps facing actresses who want equality with men is "that so many of them are unable to eliminate their sex consciousness."[4] Women have been brainwashed into believing they are inferior, but they must change that image. "Women," she demanded, "exert a tremendous and virtually irresistible influence over the stage. Not only the plays, but also the actors must please the women or fail hopelessly. The women who support our stage may make it, or they may mar it."[5]

Shaw resolved to be a woman who "made it," who influenced the stage. For many years she lacked the necessary credentials. She had played minor roles with the Boston Museum Stock Company for two years, had joined Augustin Daly's New York company for one season, and had supported famous stars in national tours for nearly ten years. Not until 1899, after acting for twenty-one years and promoting the women's movement for ten, did she merge her two interests: theatre and the fight for women's rights. The playwright she first turned to, the one whose female characters symbolized the very apotheosis of the emancipated woman, was Henrik Ibsen.

Her choosing Ibsen aligned her name with the controversial, contemporary theatre. His dramas had polarized theatre-goers. Leading the conservative attack, puritanical William Winter of the *New York Tribune* called Ibsen a writer "of a number of insipid, and sometimes tainted compositions, purported to be plays . . . He is an offence to taste and a burden upon patience." But leading Ibsen's defense was Shaw's friend and feminist leader Annie Nathan Meyer. Detecting "his strong sympathetic belief in the future of woman," she saluted Ibsen as "a prophet of the new womanhood."[6]

Mary Shaw agreed. When she chose to star in Ibsen's *Ghosts* she realized the significance:

> Most of our plays and books and laws are masks. They lull us to sleep, give us moral peace. Ibsen had the courage to lift one corner of the mask and look at the dreadful thing, and there was a chorus of shrieks. Then, when he tore the mask away, pandemonium. The grinning mask which Ibsen tears away in *Ghosts* is the duty of wifely sacrifice in woman.[7]

When she chose to star in *Ghosts*, Shaw believed she had embarked on a holy crusade. Armed with her personal convictions and directed by internationally famous Emmanuel Reicher, stage manager of the Deutsches Theatre and a friend of Ibsen's, Mary Shaw performed one of the outstanding roles of her career. Praising her "cosmic range, suggestive power, profundity and extreme telling simplicity," critic Arthur W. Row hailed her performance as "one of the great moments in great acting."[8] She seemed, thought a critic for the *New York Dramatic Mirror*, June 10, 1899, like "a real woman." The *New York Times*, May 30, 1899, pronounced that "this was Ibsenism's greatest night in New York thus far." Mary Shaw had "achieved a new triumph."

Soon after this professional triumph, Shaw received a personal reward. She was elected to represent the American theatre at the International Congress of Women held in London, June 26–July 5, 1899. Among the other American delegates were Susan B. Anthony, Rev. Anna Howard Shaw and Mrs. May Wright Sewall. The goal of the Congress had remained constant since its formation in 1888: to promote unity among working women of the world and to apply the Golden Rule to all of society. When Mary Shaw arrived in London she joined three thousand other women representing the countries of the world.

On June 30, 1899, Mary Shaw addressed the professional section of the Congress on "Drama as a Field for Women." Before the overflowing crowd, she proclaimed "that the drama was the aristocrat among the fine arts, and was a child of religion." To aspiring actresses in the audience who feared persecution, she declared, "Women who felt the dramatic instinct within them might enter the profession with confidence and hope. In spite of persecution, the drama at the present day enjoys a popularity the equal of which is given to few other institutions."[9] Her listeners were so impressed that they hastened to honor her. Henry Irving entertained her in his theatre. Herbert Beerbohm Tree invited her to act with his company. The honors culminated when she received an invitation to lunch with Queen Victoria at Windsor Castle and to travel there from London in a special train bearing an enormous banner: *Her Majesty Queen Victoria's Guests.*

Ironically, once Shaw returned to New York City after the Congress, she encountered persecution and opposition. Friends and colleagues criticized her diversity of interests; a true actress, after all, should be devoted to theatre alone. Managers chastised her for going to London, arguing "that an actress must be an actress and nothing else, to the public." The moment an actress appears as a lecturer she forfeits "that fascination of mystery" which is important to her art.[10] Indeed, even the critics, wearying of her feminist pronouncements, endorsed William Winter's observation: "Miss Shaw has shown signs of taking a more serious view of herself than anybody else ever has taken or ever will take."[11]

But unwilling to compromise her principles, Shaw resumed her feminist crusade. After a long run in *Ben Hur,* she joined actor Frank Gillmore as codirector and leading lady for George Fawcett's new theatre in Baltimore. In addition to the stock company productions typical of the period, they planned an Ibsen series of *Ghosts, A Doll's House, The Wild Duck* and *John Gabriel Borkman.* Following its Baltimore run, each play would tour major Southern cities. The series opened on November 11, 1902, with *Ghosts,* advertised as "one of the dramatic surprises of the season." And that is was, for the production closed after three performances. A *Baltimore American* critic hailed Shaw's "artistic touches," but he regretted that the large audience had been shown such a "morbid and gruesome drama." In answer to mounting protests, Fawcett announced that since it was "not a play for the majority of theatregoers," he would halt the Ibsen series and send *Ghosts* on the road.

In spite of the setback in her plans, Mary Shaw continued her defense of Ibsenism. As time approached for the five-month tour, she anticipated the public's growing awareness that Ibsen "exerted an influence for good."[12] The critic's reactions during the tour rivaled those she had received four years earlier. The *New York Times,* January 27, 1903, recorded that her "sterling performance" of Mrs. Alving seemed as tragic as Hamlet or Phaedra. Another

New Yorker noted that Shaw challenged with the great Elenora Duse. In Chicago, W. L. Hubbard of the *Chicago Tribune*, May 8, 1903, praised the "spirit of naturalness" and the "harmony of ensemble." He singled out Mary Shaw as an "actress of distinctly agreeable simplicity and directness of method." The production proved so popular with Chicagoans that a special return engagement of three performances was held a few weeks later.

Once the Chicago run finally ended, Shaw began a venture unprecedented in American theatre history: a thirty-seven-week tour of Ibsen's *Ghosts*. In a series of one-night stands, the trailblazing company traveled to Wisconsin, Minnesota, North and South Dakota, Colorado, Wyoming, Nevada, Nebraska, Iowa, Kansas, Missouri, Tennessee and Kentucky. They played to farmers, cowboys, cattle punchers and wheat harvesters. In Genoa, Nebraska, they even appeared before a tribe of Indians! By the time Shaw returned to Chicago in March 1904, she had performed *Ghosts* 225 times in fifteen months and had traveled over sixteen thousand miles.[13]

Fortified by the tour's success, Shaw expanded her repertoire by again attempting an Ibsen series, premiering her ambitious project on March 2, 1904, with *Hedda Gabler*. The determined actress held definitive views about the title character:

> Hedda Gabler is a distinct type of twentieth century woman. She is symbolic inasmuch as she typifies some of the gravest complexities to be met with in certain modern women. She is a skeptic. She has no ideals. She has the twentieth century lust for money and power. Being a woman, she knows that these can only be obtained through a man; she wishes to gain wealth and influence through man, but will give nothing in return.

In her performance of Hedda, Shaw intended to illustrate "the penalty women pay for tampering with social laws."[14]

Regardless of her noble aims, the Chicago reception was decidedly hostile. Critic W. L. Hubbard in the *Tribune* of March 3, 1904, had hailed Shaw's performance in *Ghosts*, but he now berated her for portraying the ignoble Hedda. The *Chicago Record Herald*'s James O'Donnell Bennett in March 1904 denounced her incessant movements, flounces across the stage, constant fidgeting and wringing of her hands. He thought she made Hedda "downright rude." Echoing the attacks of many critics, Amy Leslie of the *Chicago Daily News* on March 11, 1904, charged Shaw with presenting a "gospel of despair, of revolution, of dethroning tenets and creeds." The actress had contracted for an evening run at the large Steinway Hall, but once the theatre owner saw the notices, he persuaded the local fire commissioner to condemn his theatre as a fire hazard.[15] Refusing defeat, staunch Mary Shaw continued with matinee performances at a vaudeville house.

A less decisive woman might have yielded, might have returned to playing safe and popular scripts. But for Mary Shaw, opposition "only spurred her on" to more feminist advocacy.[16] She chose, therefore, to star in what became one of America's most sensational premieres, George Bernard Shaw's *Mrs. Warren's Profession*, a play focusing on a woman who avoids starvation and the bleak life of the factory by resorting to prostitution. Through the title character, the playwright had intended to "advocate moral reform."[17]

Nevertheless, even the intelligentsia opposed the play. Indeed, the editors of *The Theatre* magazine in December 1905 ran a two-page argument entitled "The People vs. George Bernard Shaw." Labeling him a literary anarchist, they insisted that the play was "wholly unfit for public representation." Such attacks created a sensational climate before the Broadway opening. While the play was in rehearsal, the secretary of the Society for Suppression of Vice in New York, Anthony Comstock, warned producer Arnold Daly against bringing the show to Broadway, announcing that "whatever outrages public decency and is injurious to public morals is indictable."[18] William McAdoo, New York City Police Commissioner, echoed support: "If New York should adopt his [Shaw's] moral code I would resign my Police Commission in an hour." He personally censored many lines of the script and threatened to close the production if his orders wernt unheeded. Furthermore, all of the playwright's dramas were banned from the open shelves of the more than thirty libraries in the city.

By the time the company arrived in New York, the atmosphere was tense. On opening night, an estimated ten thousand people crowded around the theatre. Scalpers sold tickets for as high as thirty dollars apiece. Once the play began, all seats were sold, hundreds were standing in the aisles, and nearly three thousand were turned away. Extra police were ordered to handle the curious mob. The following day, however, the press spared no venom:

> The lid was lifted by Mr. Arnold Daly and the limit of stage indecent reached last night . . . It defends immorality. It glorifies debauchery.
> But "the lid" was lifted for only one night. The morning after the opening, the production was closed, and Arnold Daly and the cast were summoned to court to answer charges of appearing in an immoral play. Only after an eight month legal battle were they acquitted. The presiding judge noted that "if virtue does not receive its usual reward in this play, vice at least is presented in an odious light" and ruled that the play could be performed.[19]

Following the court decision, the play reopened on Broadway but created less excitement. Rennold Wolf of the *New York Telegraph* remarked that all seemed comparatively tame now that the play bore "the stamp of the court's approval." Even so, all seats were sold out, and scalpers again sold tickets on the sidewalks. As before, Mary Shaw's performance received commendations for being "a treat in itself." Wolf ranked her as "one of the truly distinguished actresses on our stage." But regardless of the acting, most critics still agreed that the play was definitely "unfit for the general theatre."

When the limited Broadway run closed, Mary Shaw embarked on another crusading, coast-to-coast tour, supplementing *Mrs. Warren's Profession* with *Ghosts* and *Candida*, another feminist play. Soon after the tour, she selected to star in another feminist play, this one dealing with a growing issue in American politics: women's suffrage. She held firm beliefs on the subject. In fact, she insisted that the very "principle of democracy [was] at stake." Votes for women, she argued, meant "one step further toward the goal of self-government.[20]

Little wonder that the play entitled *Votes for Women* attracted Shaw's attention. Written by Elizabeth Robins, an American actress living in London, the plot revolves around Vida Levering, a suffragette who accidentally meets her former lover and his fiancée. Many of Vida's lines provided Shaw with ammunition for the women's movement:

> Some girls think it hardship to have to earn their living. The horror is not to be allowed to.
> We have got to learn [to] get over our touching faith that, because a man tells us something, it's true.

When the character addressed a suffragette rally in Trafalgar Square, she presented an impassioned plea for women:

> We must get the conditions of life made fairer. We women must organize. We must learn to work together. We have all worked so long and so exclusively for men, we hardly know how to work for one another. But we must learn.

Vida's thoughts sounded so much like Mary Shaw's that some theatregoers wondered if she were really acting.

Actually, the opening on March 15, 1909, did appear more like a political rally than a theatrical premiere. Suffragettes representing the Interurban Council of Women Suffrage Clubs, the Union Club and the Equality League of Self-Supporting Women crowded the theatre. Members of the American Suffragettes were conspicuous with yellow buttons pinned to their lapels. Banners flew from the balcony. Women from the Harlem Equal Rights League marched during intermission with placards reading "Women vote in 4 Western States. Why not in New York?" Frequent bursts of applause accompanied entrances and exits, the rise and fall of the curtain, and emotion-filled lines of dialogue added to the excitement.

Although the suffragettes endorsed the production, the critics did not. Charles Darnton chastised the cast for its lack of polish. A writer for the *New York Times*, March 16, 1909, complained that the play was too obviously a propagandist tract that avoided realistic confrontation of the issues. Another *Times* reviewer attacked the characterizations: "The people who are opposed to suffrage . . . are insistently represented as unsympathetic, if not ignorant types, while all the virtue is on the other side." Even Shaw's performance was damned with faint praise. Her acting "was so much the better than the play," wrote one critic, of the *Dramatic Mirror*, that he "felt sorry her . . . *Votes for Women* would have throttled the artistry from a Heaven-sent genius." The

New York Times complimented her attempt at saving the script but recognized she was limited by a "wildly improbable scenario." Perhaps most pointed was Charles Darnton. Shaw's decision to perform the play bewildered him, for it seemed nothing more than an inferior *Mrs. Warren's Profession.*

Unheedful of Darnton's advice to choose better scripts, Shaw continued championing feminist dramas, regardless of their quality. Only a few months after *Votes for Women* closed, she starred in Paul Bourget's *Divorce*, a lengthy discussion of the problems women encounter in common-law marriages. Critics denounced the tedious dialogue, stilted translation, and confusing plot. In addition, they unanimously condemned Shaw's performance. For over a decade Mary Shaw had used the theatre as a vehicle for her feminist ideas. With evangelistic fervor, she had starred in *Ghosts, Hedda Gabler, Candida, Mrs. Warren's Profession, Votes for Women, Divorce* and *New York*, thereby linking her name indelibly with propagandist theatre and with the image of the emancipated woman. Her last three Broadway performances were such critical failures that she did not appear in New York for four seasons. Instead, she toured and wrote articles about the theatre. With the exceptions of her own revivals of *Ghosts* and *Mrs. Warren's Profession*, she never again enjoyed star billing on Broadway. Her politics had marred her career.

As her professional popularity waned, Shaw devoted even more time to championing women's rights. Foremost in her interest was the founding of a new woman's organization, the Gamut Club. A number of professional clubs already existed: the Professional Women's League, which she help found in 1892, the Twelfth Night Club, the Charlotte Cushman Club and the Rehearsal Club. But Shaw found all of these lacking in proper focus. "Tea table tattle, bridge and banalities" had become their chief interest, she argued. Undoubtedly, a major impulse for her beginning a new club was her defeat for the presidency of the Professional Women's League by what she called "Tammany tactics."

Instead of a club for "rich women with fat pocketbooks" Shaw wanted "an aristocracy of brains." She declared the time was right:

> I consider the Gamut Club offers a wonderful avenue of education in tolerance and kindness and Christian charity. These are things women need to learn—loyalty to their sex and patience with each other and appreciation of the individual struggle every woman is making in her particular line of endeavor.[21]

Shaw's goal, therefore, was to provide a meeting place for the busy professional woman, a kind of "halfway house for rest and rendezvous."[22]

With Shaw as president and Lillian Russell as vice-president, the Gamut Club officially began on July 13, 1913. Reasons for the name were twofold: it articulated the goal to represent most of the arts and professions and it bestowed honor on a men's club of that name in Los Angeles that had given Shaw honorary membership a decade earlier. The board of directors drew up unique qualifications for membership. All women were warned that they "must amount to something." If they were not professional artists, teachers, or doctors, they had to prove they were "vitally interested in one of those areas. The board further announced: "Positively no parasites permitted. The Idle Rich are severely debarred."[23] Perhaps aided by these elitist restrictions, applications for membership poured in quickly. By October 1914 the roll books listed 250 members.

As president, Shaw organized a variety of club activities—monthly dinners, dances and skits. At least once each year she directed members in a play. Since many of the women were theatre artists, she sought "to encourage dramatic and theatric material in the club whether in decorations, acting itself, or in playwriting, and to present plays not practical in the commercial theatre."[24] One of her most popular productions was of a play she wrote herself: *The Parrot's Cage*. In the biting satire, Shaw gave five women costumed like parrots the opportunity to perch and to talk of feminism. The feminist Free-Souled Parrot struggled to break the chain around her leg and chattered, "I want to be free! I want to be free!" A sneering Idealist Parrot sniffed in reply, "A parrot's highest mission is to amuse."[25] In her *Impressionistic Sketch of the Anti-Suffragists*, Shaw had the "antis" recite their daily pledge:

I pledge myself to remember each day, at every hour, that there are only two great moments in a woman's life. The first, when she gives her first kiss to her lover; the second, when she kisses her own little baby[26]

But the activities of the Gamut Club had a serious side as well. Shaw urged members to support the "dress strike" initiated by the Women's Political Union in 1912. Women backing the strike pledged to buy no new clothes until 1915 when the suffrage amendment was to reach the referendum stage.[27]

Calling attention to the injustice done to women by the wanton slaughter of their sons, Shaw rallied club members for a Peace Parade to protest against World War I. When the Peace Parade actually occurred on August 29, 1914, Shaw and the Gamut Club led over fifteen thousand women from Columbus Circle down Broadway to Union Square. Wearing black and carrying no flags or banners, they represented a silent "prayer for peace."

Protesting was not the club's only involvement with the war effort. Once the country became involved, members labored with war drives, sold Liberty Bonds, made surgical dressings, helped the Red Cross, and hosted open houses for soldiers every Sunday. The Gamut was the first woman's club in New York to open its doors as a canteen. Drawing on the talents of the members, Shaw presented a number of original one-act plays for the servicemen. One of the plays, *Wrong Numbers* by Essex Dane, toured to almost every camp and hospital within a fifty-mile radius of New York City, performing 439 times.

Yet the years following 1914 were not totally devoid of professional theatre work for Mary Shaw. In 1916 she toured *The Melody of Youth*. She starred in New York revivals of *Ghosts* in 1917 and 1918 and of *Mrs. Warren's*

Profession in 1917, 1918 and 1922. Much of her time was spent working with Jessie Bonstelle to found a Woman's National Theatre. Their scheme called for a parent company in New York with subsidiary companies in other cities. Not wanting to antagonize commercial managers, they decided to limit productions to American authors and American actors. Men could perform for the company, but they would not be connected with the management. As Shaw argued, male managers make it "impossible to 'get across' any real and distinctive feminine feeling or opinions."

> Although seventy-five percent of the theatre-going public is composed of women and consequently the managers are lying awake nights trying to secure productions which will make a hit with them, they obstinately refuse to accept woman's judgment. No matter what an author says, the play is remodelled and whipped into shape by those men in charge, who cause the heroines to talk and act not as real women would but as men think that women ought to talk and act.[28]

The idea for this new theatre was certainly unique. It failed, however, since the goal of raising $1 million to begin the project never materialized.

Shaw's final venture in theatre occurred during the 1927–28 season when she starred in Eva Le Gallienne's twenty-three-week national tour of *The Cradle Song*. Shaw's performance of the Prioress was hailed at every stop. The tour, however, provided Mary Shaw with more than critical acclaim; it opened up more platforms for her to speak out on women's rights. As in past tours, she spoke at many women's clubs. Her theme now—women must save the theatre. "The legitimate stage is in a perilous state," she proclaimed. "And only through the efforts and interest of woman can it be saved."

For over thirty years, Mary Shaw had struggled for the women's movement, using her talents as an actress to reach the public. Her persistent crusading prompted the editors of *McClure's* magazine to claim that she, more than any other actress in the country, stood for what was "new and daring and experimental in dramatic art." At a memorial service at New York's Little Church Around the Corner following her death in 1929, Edwin Milton Royle dedicated America's first stained-glass window in honor of an actress and pronounced Mary Shaw "a fighting champion." He recognized her challenging mind and authoritative performing had created "a distinct influence on the stage of her time." She had devoted both her career and her life to the advancement of women's rights. This pioneering actress, he concluded, had left a "trace on the universe."[29]

AILEEN STANLEY, HER LIFE AND TIMES

Grayce Susan Burian

The life and times of Aileen Stanley are synonymous with the life and times of popular entertainment in America in the first half of the twentieth century. She was a single woman headliner in vaudeville, she starred in three Broadway musicals, and she was among the pioneer performers in recording, radio and television.

She was born Maude Elsie Aileen Muggeridge in Chicago in 1893, during the time of the great depression. She was named Maude after Maude S., the winning trotting horse of the day, but she was called Aileen. Her father died seven months before she was born. He had contracted typhoid from another daughter who died of the disease just three weeks earlier. But Aileen had two older brothers, Robert and Stanley, and her mother was young and healthy and was soon able to move out of the tenements in which they lived into a house that she opened up for roomers.

It was while living in the rooming house, being catered to and petted by immigrant boarders, that Aileen learned to be a great mimic. She used to sing for the boarders and sometimes mimic their accents. Stanley, two years older than Aileen, showed some musical talent also.

Their mother, Maria, being an enterprising woman, saw in her children's talents a way to earn some money and so raise their living standard. She set about getting a little act together which played at the various organizations around Chicago—the Shriners, Eastern Star, Knights of Columbus, all of whom paid the glorious sum of five dollars per show. The act proved so successful that Maria decided to try for the vaudeville circuits.

The act was very rough to begin with, but Maria managed to get them booked on the Western circuit. In late 1903, Stanley and Aileen toured from Chicago through the Middle West, reaching the West Coast early in 1904. Then they toured up and down the coast on the Pantages Time for more than a year.

The traveling continued. Sometimes they'd change their act, but it would take at least two years to get each act perfected. They played in Box Houses, sometimes called Honky Tonks, as well as storefront theatres, and sometimes even real theatres. In some of the out-of-way places in the West, Aileen remembered that the audience, which usually consisted of miners, would throw nuggets sometimes containing specks of gold at them, so she always had a pocket in her costume.

They soon got tired of traveling and since Chicago now had about seventy-five nickelodeons or five and ten cent theatres, Maria decided it might be good to settle back in Chicago for a while and have the children work in those. In 1911, Stanley and Aileen played nickelodeons; they performed about twenty shows a day and received $65 a week.

It wasn't long before they had worked practically every nickelodeon in the area. Stan became restless and ran off with a chorus girl with whom he formed a new act. That left Aileen on her own, with the name Aileen Muggeridge—one that would never do on a marquee when she became famous. So instead of Aileen of Stanley and Aileen, she decided she would be Aileen Stanley, a single-woman act in vaudeville. She had a sweet personality, nice soprano voice, and charm; it wasn't difficult for her to move on to some of the nicer dinner places and cafés in Chicago. However, she longed to make the big time in New York. She made a short trip there but could find work only as a song plugger. Another song plugger she met and worked with for a while was George Gershwin.

An agent from the Orpheum Circuit, Harry Weber, signed her up and sent her on a tour through Canada and the Middle West and West again. After 1919 she toured almost without break on the United and Orpheum Times, perfecting her single-woman act. Soon she even played the Palace in New York and received a page-and-a-half review from Sime Silverman, but she would return later to rave reviews from everyone.

Weber had her audition for a show in New York, *Silks and Satins*, written and produced by William Rock. She got the role, which was nothing more than Aileen singing her own songs. No real book. But while she was in *Silks and Satins*, she decided to try the record companies—maybe she could make Victrola records. At that time the companies were just experimenting with electrical recordings and reproduction. The equipment was still rather crude. There were no microphones as yet—singers had to sing into a huge horn. The first company she tried was Pathé. They could use her. The Victor company wanted her exclusively but she decided only to freelance for a while. So when *Silks and Satins* was closing and about to go on the road, Aileen tossed a coin to help her decide whether she should stay in New York to make records or go on the road. New York and the records won.

But while making records in New York she was asked to tour for Keith and Albee. She had a special contract that enabled her to play in New York after being outside for a certain time so that she could make her records, and for many years afterward, all her touring was planned this way. Usually her recording sessions would coincide with her dates at the Palace or other theatres in New York City. In between shows she would get into a taxi with a sandwich and her sheet music, eat and study on the way to the studio, record almost cold or with a rehearsal or two, and get back to the theatre for the next show.

Between 1920 and 1936 she managed to record over 215 sides for Victor, His Master's Voice, English Brunswick, English Decca and many other English and American companies. By 1923 Aileen was recording exclusively for Victor and did so until 1930, and then for His Master's Voice in England until 1936.

She always continued her performing either on the circuits or in England. She did take a couple of hours off January 4th of this year while she was playing Minneapolis, to marry her accompanist, Robert Buttenuth, but this was done in between shows. She didn't miss a performance. This kind of touring would continue for years. From January to June rarely did she have a week off, and during the summer months she'd play fairs and special smaller engagements.

She did take time out from the circuits to star with Phil Baker in three Broadway shows for J. J. Shubert: *Night in Spain*, *Pleasure Bound* and *Artists and Models*. It was during *Pleasure Bound* in 1929 that the *New York Post* reported on May 18: "When Aileen Stanley sings a new song, that song goes echoing from one end of the country to the other and across more than one continent, for over 25,000,000 victrola records of her songs have been sold, a mark that even Caruso himself never touched."

Why was she so popular? Possibly because throughout her career Aileen mixed humorous numbers with those that were sentimental, nostalgic, wistful. They were always on the light side. There were never any dark or tragic overtones, and rarely is any pain or genuine heartache expressed; even in a song like "It's All Over Now," the dominant tone or feeling is one of charm rather than grief. The main effect is one of unaffected, unpretentious innocence if not indeed naïveté. Even in her novelty songs these same qualities are what stand out.

Aileen also got in on the ground floor of broadcasting. She appeared with Rudy Vallee on the "Fleischmann Hour" and on the Paul Whiteman show many times. She did thirteen weeks of the "Oldsmobile Hour" and starred in many of her own radio programs both in the United States and England between the years 1929 and 1937. Her records had become popular in England, where she performed five different years, from 1925 to 1937.

From August 1923 to April 1935, her husband, Bob, kept a diary of every theatre or club date that they played, and also made significant notations on certain engagements. The diary helps to explain what glorious days those must have been during the twenties and early thirties for American performers in London. Aileen played the intimate supper clubs frequented by the upper crust of society, was one of their favorite entertainers and so joined in their amusements.

Of course, Aileen always had to sing for her supper at those parties.

By 1931, vaudeville was supposed to be dying, but not for Aileen. In 1931 she was booked solid, playing the picture houses which boasted movies featuring such stars as William Powell, George Arliss, Mary Pickford, Laurel and Hardy—but still offered vaudeville in between the showings.

In February of 1934 Aileen was back in London sharing the bill with Ethel Barrymore who was doing a one-act play, *The Twelve Pound Look*.

Aileen was utterly devoted to her career. When she married Bob Buttenuth, there was no notice of it in the papers. She kept her marriage a secret to all but her closest friends. Her life was devoted to her work, to rehearsing and performing. She rarely partied. After performances she went back to the hotel for a good night's sleep. In the morning she'd do some form of exercise, swimming if at all possible. The partying that she did in London was unusual for her.

She was happier when working and would allow nothing to interfere with work—not even her marriage. Bob wanted to relax and play after performances but he had to do so alone. Eventually this led to divorce. But they were always friends, right up to his death.

In 1937 Aileen made her last trip to England, for the first time without Bob Buttenuth, now her ex-husband, accompanying her. It was on her return from this trip, however, that Aileen discovered that vaudeville was in trouble because of competition from radio and movies, and the threat of television. Performers were no longer being offered huge salaries. She refused to work for less than her normal fee, which was quite high. The time did seem right for her to do what she had been thinking of doing, namely, to train and manage young singers. She opened a coaching studio that Bob Buttenuth managed, and from 1937 until 1959 coached and managed young singers from her four-room suite in the Brill Building. Then Bob died. She closed the studio and moved to retirement in Hollywood, where she lived in a little four-room house on Hammond Street.

Aileen Stanley is indeed the epitome of the American success story. A woman with no formal education, who started her career playing one-night stands in storefront theatres and honky-tonks could entertain and be entertained by England's nobility. Hers was a special kind of growth, of education. She was endowed with natural resources that she was able to tap and to build on as she moved from stage to stage of her career and her life. Few people, no matter what the profession, can look back on a life of so much fulfillment and so few regrets. The very fact that she never quite achieved the status of a superstar, that in her prime she received featured billing more often than top billing, makes her career seem all the more representative of mainstream popular entertainment—a revealing chronicle of its performers and its audience.

WOMEN MIMES IN AMERICA

Bari Rolfe

Women pantomime players came to America from France and England at the end of the 1700s. They played in dance companies such as those of Ravel and Alexander Placide, whose ballet-pantomimes were popular fare throughout the new United States. Mime as an art form as we know it today, however, existed primarily in the clown turns of the circus and the comic sketches in music halls and vaudeville. Players were at first imported from Europe; then American pantomime began to emerge in the nineteenth century. It was out of this background that performers, men and women, developed their skills in the direction their artistic sensibility carried them.

Angna Enters (b. 1907–d. 1989)

Although she studied and performed dance, Angna Enters came to mime through painting. Her portraits taught her that "human beings don't always talk . . . they act in certain ways for which no words are the equivalent." In order to find out how human beings acted, so as to better paint them, she began doing motion studies with herself as the character; soon she needed to show her portraits-in-motion to audiences. Even later, as a concert-mime, she prepared a new piece not by rehearsing it but by painting on canvas the images in her mind.

Her extraordinary career, beginning at age seventeen, started with thirteen New York performances in three years, of some thirty-nine sketches. The output continued nonstop: yearly concert tours throughout the United States and Europe; painting, sculpting, with exhibitions throughout the country; writing of several volumes of autobiography, plays, articles, film scripts; composing music, designing costumes and sets, directing plays and teaching, until the mid-1960s.

Enters's unique presentations were hard to label; it wasn't traditional acting, said the drama critics, nor traditional dance, said the dance critics. She tried various terms: dance-forms, episodes, dance-mime; and finally chose "The Theatre of Angna Enters." She also learned that certain strictures obtained on the commercial stage at that time: "a woman comic was either a mimic, doing takeoffs on prominent people, or a grotesque, or a clown." It was uphill work for this artist who did not fall into any of these slots.

She delicately and wittily blended acting and movement, never patronizing, always inventive. Her unusual programs soon elicited enthusiastic response from critics in music, art and literature, as well as theatre and dance.

To Enters her stage pieces were social commentary in the tradition of Greek and Roman mimes, using a past period as a mirror to see/show one's own time. Her characters were women (an exception was "Boy Cardinal," a movement study of a child ecclesiastic) from many times, places and circumstances, for her range was phenomenal: Art critic Louis Kalonyme commented (1925) that "while they are all based on feminine phases" they were all different. Using classical, popular and jazz music (the first to do so) she drew her characters from ancient Greece, the Middle Ages and the seventeenth century on; they were courtly ladies, prostitutes, a pianist, painter, flapper, cook; from France, Russia, the United States, Spain and Asia; and dozens more women from every society, from every period.

Enters's programs were unforgettable, say many who saw her, and not only for their novelty. Her talent, plus concepts based solidly on proven acting principles, resulted in presentations of intelligence, sensitivity and imagination; they were "unique," "subtle," "amusing," "witty," "tragic" and "comic," to quote a few of the critics. In her writing she was simple, clear, poetic and profound; the validity of her ideas concerning mime is confirmed by time—ideas as true today as when she formulated them.

Lotte Goslar (b. 1917–d. circa 1998)

Elfin-clown Lotte Goslar, who has loved elves since childhood, resumed in the United States in 1940 a career cut short in Hitler Germany. She had been especially fortunate in having as guides and colleagues some remarkable people who let her develop in her own, special way: Palucca, from Mary Wigman's school, a dancer highly appreciated by the Bauhaus people, and the two great comics of the Liberated Theatre in Prague, Jan Werich and George Voskovec, with whom she worked for a year. Then she came to the United States for extensive touring in revues, in cabarets and concerts, including ten years at Hollywood's Turnabout Theatre with Elsa Lanchester.

This dancer-clown-comic-mime choreographed for operas, ballet companies, children's theatre and film sequences. She organized her company, Pantomime Circus, in 1954 and toured the USA and Europe, including appearances at various mime festivals.

Critics emphasize Goslar's considerable comic gifts. The truly funny situations were often tinged with compassion and tenderness; a few pieces were tragedies. However, the traditional sad/glad clown was an image she rejected; for her, simply to be funny was itself a gesture of courage. Her serious side was sometimes, not often, offered to the public. Bertolt Brecht wrote a tragic clown scenario for her; she had another story about a soldier, and still another tragic piece about a child.

In some of her sketches the protagonist was a woman: grandma, fond nanny, would-be carny queen; others featured the androgynous clown: a flower, an insect, a mushroom. Goslar saw two kinds of clowns: the one with the personal act, like Grock, Rivels, or Dimitri, and the knockabout rough-and-tumble clown, in which category women are not found. As the first kind, her personal clown originated in her own reaction to nature, people, animals and trees.

Critical comments about Goslar are refreshing to read: "endearing, indomitable dumpling," "irresistible," "inspired madness," "tender poetry," she performs with "humor, grace and understated parody"; "with a face like a gallant, easily discouraged potato and a heart big as a frying pan," in that happy phrase of Clive Barnes.

Her themes were varied: a disgruntled flower at the mercy of sun, wind and rain; a shy, nasty child dance prodigy; a smug nanny ruffling the hair of her concert pianist protégé during his performance; a motherly flower pouring nectar for hungry bees; an aging carnival dancer vainly competing with younger girls.

Goslar also drew, designed costumes and wrote children's books. That her work appealed both to adults and children attests to its breadth, honesty and humanity.

Bari Rolfe (b. 1916–d. 2002)

Like most women mimes, I began as a dancer in dance companies and as a soloist in cabarets and theatres, in the mid-1930s in and around Chicago. After an onstage fall that slipped a disk, and after somewhat recovering, I involved myself in little theatre, some of it political, and gained some acting experience. When I resumed dance on a noncommercial basis, my dances tended to be little stories in movement; not knowing what to call them, they remained "dances."

In 1955 I saw Marcel Marceau on his first American tour. Unforgettable moment! I pointed shakily from my seat in the top balcony to the tiny white figure below: "*That's* what I want!" After some years of relentless scraping and saving, I arrived in Paris where Marceau had offered to supervise my training—although not in his company as planned but with his teacher, Étienne Decroux. But in a few months I knew that Decroux's style of mime was not for me, and I was fortunate enough to find, late in 1963, the school of Jacques Lecoq.

Lecoq's work gave me more than I'd hoped. My motivation had been to become a better performing mime, but there I found so many doors opening into a world of meaningful movement, of mask, clown and physical theatre, that I wanted only to teach this great store of movement understanding and challenge. I managed to live very nicely, first by teaching modern dance, then as part of a three-person mime company at the Crazy Horse Saloon, plus mime classes in theatres and universities and as choreographer for a company of drum majorettes.

After three years of Lecoq's two-year course, where to go? Herbert Blau, over a Paris lunch, advised me to return to the States, for "a new wind was blowing through acting training there," and I could teach in university drama programs despite my lack of any academic degree. This turned out to be true; I worked in professional training programs at the University of California at Los Angeles and the University of Washington, the drama department at California State University at Northridge, and gave workshops at many other colleges, theatre companies and dance studios. The time was right, for mime was beginning to be recognized in the United States both as an art form and as a useful skill for actors for its insight into meaningful movement and its ability to enhance the physical aspects of theatre. In the few years from 1972 to 1978, many American theatre departments introduced mime to their courses; the professional organization, International Mimes and Pantomimists, was formed; the *Mime Journal* began publishing, then *Mime, Mask, and Marionette*, and two major festivals took place: LaCrosse 1974 and Milwaukee 1978. I was fortunate enough to be a part of all these events, writing and teaching mime, and was the first American to participate in a European mime festival, with an invited paper, at Prague, 1971.

THE ART OF RUTH DRAPER

Muriel McKenna

On her casket lay a collection of shawls, not flowers. It was at her own request. To the people who came to mourn her passing it was a fitting symbol of the many characters those shawls had evoked under her matchless performance.

Ruth Draper, the inimitable, had passed away in her sleep at the age of seventy-two, in December of 1956. She had just opened in New York that week for what was an almost annual appearance, and had planned to start on another transcontinental tour with her cast of characters.

Ruth Draper! The name is almost synonymous with solo theatre. And theatre it was, uniquely her own, even though the costume was no more than one of those shawls, the scenery a chair or table on the bare stage. No matter. Her artistry transformed them into whatever illusion she wished to create, the stage was peopled with other characters who were visible in the imagination of her audience as if right there on the stage.

What should one call her? Some have called her a diseuse, but that term, meaning literally "a speaker of songs," suggests Yvette Guilbert and others of that type of entertainment. Although she gave new meaning to the word *monologuist*, that term has connotations of the old-style elocutionists with all their affectations. She considered herself a "character actress." She was a consummate actress and always a solo performer. Probably the best term would be "one-woman theatre," for that is what her performances really were.

Miss Draper was born in New York City in 1884. Her grandfather was Charles Dana, the famous publisher. Even as a small child Ruth was a delightful mimic and entertained her family and friends with her little character sketches.

It was in 1916 that she first appeared as a professional actress. She had a small part in a play called *A Lady's Name* at Maxine Elliott's Theatre in New York. It lasted for one season. After that she never again appeared in anything but her own monologues.

Until this time she had merely entertained family and friends and performed at private parties. It was not until 1917 that she turned professional under the management of James B. Pond, who continued as her agent until 1928. After that Helen Arthur of Actor-Managers Inc. took over the management of her career.

In an interview[1] Miss Draper stated that there were three influences in life that prompted her career. First, she had seen and been very much impressed by the work of Beatrice Herford, a popular monologuist of time. Second, she saw the Chinese play *Yellow Jacket*, which showed her what could be done with little setting or properties. Last of all, she had encouragement from her great friend, Jan Paderewski, who was most persuasive in urging her to go on with her work and to develop her talent to the fullest.

Throughout her career Miss Draper wrote everything she did for the stage herself. The sketches were not really written down; she often changed a number from performance to performance until it met her rigorous standards of perfection. Sometimes this went on for as long as fifteen years before it sounded just right to her ears. One critic, in appraising her performance, remarked that it was "as if Fritz Kreisler were to give recitals every evening playing only his own compositions."[2]

Henry James, a very admiring friend, was fascinated by her work and wrote what he felt would be a very good number for her, in 1913. It was the story of a very pushy American woman in London, determined to be presented at the Court of St. James's. But Miss Draper was never able to perform it or any other piece that she had not written herself, much as she hated to disappoint her good friend who had gone to so much trouble.

Later, when she once asked Henry James for advice on what she should do with her life—whether to try to become an actress, or to go on with her writing, or to continue with her monologues, James is said to have replied, "My dear child . . . you . . . have woven . . . your own . . . very beautiful . . . little Persian carpet . . . Stand on it!"

During World War I she entertained the American and British soldiers. Later, in 1920, she went to England. It was here, on January 29, that she made her first appearance as a professional (she had often entertained there at parties and affairs before that, however). It was the first of many appearances in England over the years—she was a great favorite. She gave a command performance at Windsor Castle in 1926 and was presented at court in 1928.

In the fall of 1921 she induced Aurélien-Marie Lungé-Poë, the director of the Théâtre de l'Oeuvre in Paris, to let her perform at that theatre and to receive sixty percent of the receipts. It was very successful and she made many appearances there up to as late as May 1950, when she gave her last performance. She had a similar sponsorship from Max Reinhardt in Germany.

Her manager, in December of 1928, decided on a very risky venture. She rented the Comedy Theatre in New York—with the specification that it was to be on a percentage basis, in order to make the expected losses as small as possible. Tickets were sold at regular theatre prices, the same as for any good, full-length play.

To everyone's amazement, Miss Draper, alone on the stage, with only a shawl or hat for costume, a table or chair for scenery, gave eight performances a week for twenty-six weeks. Receipts were greater than for most plays with a full cast and several changes of scenery. The next year she had an eighteen-week season with equal success, and over the years she came back to New York, as elsewhere, many times, to the delight of her devotees.

She made many transcontinental tours of the United States and performed in almost every corner of the world in the course of her long, very successful career.

She received many honors—honorary degrees from such prestigious institutions as Smith College, Cambridge and Edinburgh universities, the Catholic Guild of Ireland and was made an honorary member of the Order of the Garter of the British Empire, rank of Commander.

One of the main differences between Miss Draper's work and that of those who came before her in the field is that she developed what one might call the "monodrama"—that is, two or three sketches were put together to make a short playlet of two or three acts. (Cornelia Otis Skinner was to carry this still further by making a full dramatic production of it, with full staging and costume.) These two- or three-act plays were as complete as a full-length play, as if all the characters were onstage and the stage fully furnished with all the stage settings of a play, so great was Miss Draper's ability to evoke the invisible characters in the imagination of the audience.

That was the most astonishing part of her performance. Her consummate artistry gave her complete independence of the ordinary trappings of scenery and stage setting, or even of costume in the ordinary sense of the word. A table or chair, a shawl or a hat, was all she needed to create the scene and the character. Her figure seemed to change, her face almost appeared to grow old or young as the character she portrayed. And, above all, the other characters in the drama seemed equally visible, one was fully aware of their presence also.

It was said that sometimes even the usually bored stagehands in the wings forgot their crap games for a while to watch this lone woman make a large audience see and feel a whole group of people on the stage and a full stage setting. Surely this was almost the ultimate in compliments to her artistry!

She had no superiors and few equals in her chosen specialty, which was high comedy—and high-quality theatre. In the course of her career she created some thirty-nine sketches, which included some fifty parts in all, in six or more languages—and there were about two hundred invisible characters besides. As mentioned before, they had not been written down, but Charles Bowden and Richard Barr, her managers in 1948, finally induced her to record some of the best. Some of the titles of her numbers were: *Three Women and Mr. Clifford*; *In a Church in Italy*; *Three Generations in a Court of Domestic Relations*; *Three Breakfasts*; *A Scottish Immigrant at Ellis Island*; *On a Porch in Maine*; *The Italian Lesson*; *At the Court of Philip IV*; *Doctors*; *Dalmatian Peasant Woman*; *Showing the Garden*; *The Children's Party*; *Opening the Bazaar*; *At an English Country House Party*—to name only a few of the better-known ones.

From the titles alone one can see the wide range of her ability. She had a "camera eye" for the minutest, faintest details of action and movement, and a "camera ear" for the slightest, barest nuances of sound, inflection and rhythms in speech. She would sometimes speak in any of six languages; at other times, as in the *Dalmatian Peasant Woman*, she would indicate the accent and rhythm of the language even though not able to speak it. In one sketch she is said to have spoken French with a Polish accent. Some of these numbers merit further description and discussion, with the opinions expressed by critics.

One of the best known of her monodramas is *In a Church in Italy*. As the scene opens we see an aristocratic Englishwoman who has come with a friend, apparently to copy a painting for which the church is noted. She is having difficulty, so they pack their materials and go off. Soon an old Italian woman enters and wanders among the tourists who have come to see the church and the painting. She is begging, so some give her money, others ignore her, and she goes off muttering to herself. Then a swarm of American tourists comes in, one of whom is equipped with a guidebook, determined that she and all the others will not miss anything they should see there. As they leave, a young Italian girl enters for a quick, clandestine tryst with her lover. Soon a small group of German tourists enters, stolidly viewing each thing as described from the guidebook. Finally, after they have gone, an old Italian woman, obviously troubled, comes to pray, drops to her knees, lifting her eyes in trust and peace as the curtain falls.

All of this, of course, is accomplished by Miss Draper alone on the stage. One is aware of the invisible characters as one is of the speaking parts. The change is accomplished with only a shawl or a funny hat. The variety of accents and language is enormous—from proper upper-class English to the soft, liquid Italian of the breathless girl.

Three Women and Mr. Clifford is a short monodrama in three acts. In Act I we are in Mr. Clifford's office, where we meet Miss Nichols, the perfect secretary. She manages Mr. Clifford's phone calls, soothes his worried aunt, takes orders from Mrs. Clifford, neatly arranges things when his wife and his mistress want to go to the same play on the same night, sees that he knows about his appointments, and then goes off to join her fiancée. About fourteen invisible characters enter the office or can be visualized at the other end of telephone calls in this act.

In Act II we meet Mrs. Clifford, waiting for their car after the theatre. She greets a few friends, works her way to the car, and once inside on the way home begins a long monologue of worries and complaints. We are aware of her husband sitting silently beside her, occasionally chuckling at her recital of the latest escapades of their sons. As they pass the museum, the wife grows sentimental, wishing that they could go there together again since he hasn't been there for ages. Mr Clifford leaves her at the door and goes off for a walk.

In Act III we meet the lovely "friend," Mrs. Mallory. She is no "mistress," just a charming, cultivated woman of middle years. She is seated on the edge of a large armchair. Mr. Clifford, of course, is in that armchair. She chats happily about the busy, pleasant day she has had. She has been to the museum to see their favorite pictures. She laughs at the escapades of the boys, and so on. As to their "affair," well, it will just have to wait till the children need him less and can understand things better. She can wait.

The costume for these three acts consisted of the following: a smock for Miss Nichols, an evening wrap and small bag for Mrs. Clifford, and a lovely shawl for Mrs. Mallory. The scenery was equally sparse: two tables, a telephone, a pad and pencil for Act I; a small loveseat for the back seat of the limousine in Act II; and a large armchair in Act III. Yet the effect was that of a fully produced play with many characters and full scenery. One of the critics wrote of this monodrama: "It came very close to being one of the statements on the stage of the tragedy of many lives—of selfish wives, at least, with the man a weakling."[3]

Three Breakfasts is the story of another marriage, somewhat like the Broadway success, *The Four-Poster*. This one, unlike the Clifford story, ends happily as the couple discover the real values of life. In Act I we see the young bride as they are moving into their first house, an old-fashioned farmhouse. By Act II, fifteen years have passed. The couple is now wealthy, living in a palatial home in the city, but the eager, tender, loving wife is now a bored society matron. By Act III, many years have passed. The wife is now an old lady, somewhat feeble, but alert and happy, back again in their beloved farmhouse. Of Miss Draper's performance in this monodrama, one critic wrote: "Watch the way she stirs a phantom cup of coffee with a phantom spoon. It tells you things about the way human beings stir coffee which we never noticed before, and the discovery interests us and fascinates us."

Three Generations in a Court of Domestic Relations is another monodrama in three acts. One is aware of the three women and also of the kindly judge who is trying to do his best to take all three people into consideration as he makes his decision.

First we see the grandmother, bent and worn, wearing a black shawl in peasant fashion. She is reaching eighty years of age and is very angry with her granddaughter, who wants to leave them to go out west and marry a "no-good" who drinks and has no real job. She and her daughter are completely dependent on the granddaughter Rosie for their care.

In the second act, the shawl has dropped to Miss Draper's shoulders. The mother, forty-seven years old, is tired and discouraged from a life of continuous struggle. Rosie wants to put her crippled mother and aged grandmother in an old ladies' home so she can marry and go out west with the "no-good" young man who drinks and has no real job. Rosie is needed at home; she is their only support.

The shawl drops to the floor. We now see Rosie. The change is impossible to describe; it has happened so suddenly. Rosie is almost twenty years old. She has looked many places and has now found a very nice home for her mother and grandmother, in the country. Her fiancé has a job offer out west; she can't take both old women with her. There is nothing to do but locate them in a nice place where they will be cared for. Her fiancé is a good boy; she is not wild. The judge tells her to bring the boy to see him and also a letter from the uncle who is said to be offering him a job out west. The judge will decide on Wednesday at ten o'clock. Rosie goes off happily with mother and grandmother.

In performance Miss Draper's whole body and face seem to shrivel up and age as the grandmother, become a little younger as the mother—and, suddenly transformed, she is twenty. A masterpiece of conjury.

Miss Draper did not actually write down her monologues, as we noted earlier. She was finally induced to make recordings of some of her better-known works in a series of albums called *The Art of Ruth Draper*. Some of these were also printed in a book about her with the same title. But neither the printed page nor the recordings are completely satisfactory as a measure of her talent. The words, cold on the printed page, do not read particularly well. Gestures, facial expression, slight movements—all those intangibles that complete the performance—cannot be seen from the printed page or the recordings. She was a consummate actress; every movement made the picture more complete.[4] One had to hear and see to fully understand the unusual art by which she alone created many characters on the stage.

UTA HAGEN AND EVA LE GALLIENNE

Susan Spector and Steven Urkowitz

In 1937, when she was seventeen, Uta Hagen wrote to Eva Le Gallienne asking for an audition to join Le Gallienne's acting company. Inspired by the state repertory theatres she had seen in Europe with her parents, Hagen wanted to break into the theatre doing "the classics." In America at the time only Le Gallienne was regularly producing major plays from the European repertory on the professional stage.

Le Gallienne, although she had already interviewed hundreds of young actresses for her Civic Repertory Theatre, sensed something special in Hagen's letter—"The handwriting alone was full of character and individuality . . . The phrasing too was striking; it was forthright, honest and simple, and the choice of words was intelligent and original; one felt a personality there." She invited Hagen to read for her at her home in Westport, Connecticut.

The personality that showed through in Uta Hagen's letter had been nurtured in an extraordinarily rich soil. Her father was a prolific writer, a noted art historian and composer who had been responsible for the revival of Handel's operas in Germany in the 1920s; her mother, was an accomplished concert singer. Their home was a gathering place for professional musicians, artists and the brightest lights of the university and political community in Madison, Wisconsin. As a girl she studied dance and music in Europe and America and performed in school and at home.

Late in April 1937 Hagen traveled to Westport. In the audition Le Gallienne recalls she read a speech from Shaw's *St. Joan* "quite badly . . . I was ruthlessly honest with her . . . talked to her about it, gave her a few pointers, and asked her to think it over for an hour . . . The improvement was startling." In the abbreviated prose of her journal, Hagen recorded her own impression of the interview: "She started drilling me on [*St. Joan*], and finally made me say it right to her. She practically hypnotized me, and it got better. She doesn't like my voice when it goes up and gets breathy, and said I needed more diaphragm control (which she emphasized by whacking me there). Then she talked and yelled at me. Made me sight-read Ophelia and Nina from *Seagull*. She said maybe I could work in her company in the fall. I don't even know if I want to. Oh well."

Le Gallienne planned to play Hamlet in the summer production she would direct on Cape Cod. She would rehearse from the end of June until the end of August, when eight performances would be given in the Cape Playhouse, Dennis, Massachusetts. Most of the cast was drawn from the members of her defunct Civic Repertory Company, but she couldn't find a satisfactory Ophelia.

Early in June she wrote to Hagen, offering her a week's trial in role—no guarantee, no pay, no expenses. On June 23, Hagen arrived to begin work.

Le Gallienne's plan was to have a month of small rehearsals, meeting with groups of actors as they were available to come to her home in Westport. Set and costume designs and the preliminary shape of roles were to be hammered out before the full company assembled late in July.

During her trial week, Hagen spent her mornings studying alone. Her journal for June 26: "Went canoeing, practicing lines and songs as I paddled. At about 11:30 I paddled for shore vigorously because of a wind, and suddenly tipped over and fell in the water. My watch didn't stop but my swell new copy of *Hamlet* and my hair got pretty wrecked. Came back dripping." Afternoons were spent rehearsing and watching Le Gallienne working with other performers. In her free time, Hagen wrote letters, practiced piano and recorder, and exercised in dance workouts. On Le Gallienne's suggestion she began reading extensively, beginning with Karl Mantzius's six-volume *History of Theatrical Art*.

Le Gallienne was *in loco parentis* for Hagen, who had just turned eighteen, coaching her in her role, of course, but also looking after her health and her diet, and even reproaching her after a wild night out. The girl was brought into conversations with the company designer and manager, the actors and production people. She was made to feel part of a fine enterprise with high aspirations.

At the end of the first week, after a long rehearsal Le Gallienne said, "By the way, Miss Hagen, I think you can tell your parents it's all right now. But you've got to work hard." Accepted, Hagen went outside and wept for a quarter of an hour.

To Le Gallienne's steady stream of concern and approval, Hagen's parent's added a flood of supporting letters, cards and packages from home. One box, for example, brought cake, marmalade, cream, a hairbrush, bubble bath and candy. A long letter from her father has this glowing parenthesis: "(By the way, read an ad today at the grocer's; it was about olives. They were distinguished as large, ex-large, giant, jumbo, colossal, ex-colossal and super colossal. Now I wonder what your Ophelia will be like—*super*, or ex-super-colossal?)"

The full company began work in Westport on July 27, and then moved to Cape Cod on August 8. Fencing-master Giorgio Santelli arrived to choreograph the last act swordplay and to give fencing classes to all the actors. Hagen who had woven some of the fabric for the production's costumes, began embroidering during her breaks in rehearsals. She eventually did the decorative work on her own costume and on Osric's. And once the move to the Cape was accomplished, Le Gallienne began giving her twenty dollars per week for expense money. For the first time she was being paid to work in the theatre. In her journal she wrote, "Ahem! Am I proud."

In addition to company rehearsals, Hagen spent time on the set alone— walking, practicing, studying. Le Gallienne took time to affirm her faith in Hagen's talent and to give her perspective on what lay ahead: "Before we started [rehearsing] Eva walked with me and was wonderful. She said she believed in me, that I had great talent, was very good in the part and born for the theatre. But that I shouldn't believe the things people told me because I still had a hell of a lot to learn and in ten years I might be a great actress. I wasn't yet, and she and I knew it. We also had high standards and because I was intelligent she hoped I wouldn't believe praise and let it go to my head."

The work grew more strenuous, approaching the August 23 opening. Le Gallienne's attitudes and graciousness under pressure show up repeatedly in Hagen's journal. After the final dress rehearsal she records her own jitters and Le Gallienne's supportive ease: "I was stinking! Make-up bad, couldn't be heard, felt practically nothing & for the first time did everything in a daze. Also dried up once which has never happened before. Everything else was wrong too. Timing of music, trumpets, etc., very poor. God! It was frightful! Eva stayed sweet and pleasant throughout. How she does it, I don't know!!! I think of her and admire her more as an artist and person than anyone in the world next to mom."

On opening night, Hagen received flowers and telegrams from her family and friends in Madison and Berlin. "I went to the theatre at 7:30 and was rather dazed till curtain time . . . I got more and more excited. As a whole the production went well, with a few technical flaws . . . The feeling and sweep as a whole was better than ever before, but now I can spend the week polishing off thousands of tiny things." (She made meticulous notes detailing changes or reminders for her next performances.)

Hagen's Ophelia was applauded and acclaimed, and, although the reviews were mixed for the production as a whole, audiences were enthusiastic throughout the run. Le Gallienne remembers: "The theatre was crowded every night. I was aware that many people came out of curiosity, expecting to see a freak performance, a ridiculous sort of stunt; quite a number, I suspect, came prepared to scoff. But when the curtain fell at the end of the play, the silence for several moments was electric, and then the storm of applause broke loose and the shouts and 'bravos' brought tears to my eyes. I have seldom been so happy, though I found the eight consecutive performances almost unbearably exhausting."

Critics particularly praised Hagen's work on Ophelia's mad scene. Four Boston writers called it "realistic," "appealing," "excellent" and "clever." The local Cape Cod papers said, "The strength and beauty with which she endows it ranks only second, in the production, to Miss Le Gallienne's last scene." And, "She took the stage to herself for several minutes and in a vague, distracted way that fitted the role perfectly, she won the audience's complete attention and respect. Her exit was the occasion for immediate applause, the only time the play was so interrupted." In her journal, Hagen's response to these reviews was circumspect: "My press notices were good, but I certainly didn't take them to heart considering the bosh they wrote about other things!"

Hagen's second performance was a real letdown after the success of her debut. Le Gallienne had warned her of the second-night dangers, but they were nevertheless a painful shock to Hagen. On later evenings Le Gallienne came to Hagen before the performance to talk about her makeup, to chat about her parents' expected arrival, or to go over a problematic detail. This attention calmed her and eased much of the jittery anxiety she felt.

On August 26 Hagen's family finally arrived, and she was reunited with the source of so much of her talent: "Shortly before twelve I was walking across the street when I heard shrieks and honkings, and there was the family. God, I nearly died of joy." That evening, while her brother Holger was shouting "Bravo's," she took her first "final curtain calls" with Le Gallienne and other leading players.

But the next day's matinee was, in Hagen's estimate, "stinking." The theatre overheated in the sun, and the performers were physically and emotionally drained. "Before the mad scene Eva said, 'You've got to speak up, my girl. The soliloquy was bad.' It threw me way down in the dumps. The whole performance was awful."

Hagen knew that her performances had been erratic, but she worked hard and felt a real sense of her own improvement as the week came to an end: "It was the last performance and [it] made me very sad, but I felt it was the best. Of course there were little things that still left me very unsatisfied, but on the whole it was the strongest. Eva had given me some hints in the afternoon and I took them to heart, regaining a lot of the truth and simplicity I was beginning to lose. Before the performance she said, 'Do your best now!' And I tried. Afterwards, when I meant to give the Ophelia ring back, she made me keep it, and I floated."

Hagen's parents and Le Gallienne spent a long afternoon together in Connecticut a few days after the company left Cape Cod. "I've never seen Eva before as she was this afternoon," Hagen wrote. "Never so alive, so brilliant and witty, and so deep in telling of the past and plans for the future . . . And to hear daddy and Eva having deeply intellectual talks, and to have Eva beg mother to sing, etc., means more to me than I can put down in words . . . Eva said to them, 'You can't know how wonderful it is to be near people who understand.'"

The repertory company Le Gallienne hoped to include Hagen in for the next season failed to materialize. Instead, Hagen went to New York in October and within two months began her Broadway career, starring with the Lunts in *The Seagull*. In *Respect for Acting* (1973), Hagen wrote, "I am grateful to Eva Le Gallienne for first believing in my talent, for putting me on the professional stage, for upholding a reverence for the theatre, for helping me to believe that the theatre should contribute to the spiritual life of a nation." More than any technique or style, in their work together on *Hamlet* it was the sense of the high calling of theatrical art that was passed from one generation to the next.

ACTING TEACHERS

High on the list of renowned teachers of acting are three women: two of our finest actresses, Stella Adler and Uta Hagen, and Alvina Krause, who eschewed the professional theatre but whose teaching earned her the accolade of "maker of stars" like Charlton Heston and Patricia Neal. They belong to a tradition of actress-directors like Minnie Maddern Fiske and Eva Le Gallienne who inspired their actors with an idea of theatre that demanded creative discipline, collaboration, ethical standards and respect for the rich humanity of their art. Adler and Hagen in their notable schools and widely read books are known to a large public, but Krause, who developed her approach in thirty-three years on the faculty of Northwestern University, "has not acquired the fame, public recognition or financial reward . . . of the very few others who have also earned distinction for teaching an art that some believe can't be taught," in the words of Billie McCants and David Downs, her former students, from whose memories these comments have been adapted.

ALVINA KRAUSE ON WOMEN IN THEATRE

Billie McCants

Born in 1893 in New Lisbon, Wisconsin, a little town which then saw few of its young men and none of its women go to college, Alvina Krause knew from an early age that she would go. "I think I wanted always to be a teacher . . . I was drawn to theatre because I was always interested in why people are what they are . . . I would sit back and watch grown-ups, and people would say, 'She's shy. She doesn't talk much.' One summer day, I think I was a junior in high school, I didn't have anything else to read, and I picked up a volume of Ibsen, *A Doll's House*. Great Heavens! What happened to me? I can't describe it. I didn't understand *A Doll's House* but there was something there dealing with women and their society and I read all of Ibsen."

There is a pause. "That smile was over the first marriage proposal I had. On Senior Day we were out gathering stuff to decorate the high school. Here was this young man proposing to me, and I laughed. It was so ridiculous. I said, 'Why, I'm going to have a career. I'm going to do things. I'm not going to get married.'"

But, she is asked, doesn't she believe women can have a career and a marriage and babies? The eyes reveal the extent to which Alvina Krause has pondered this difficult question. "Yes, I do. They'd still better know what's important to them. But it would take a pretty big woman. It would take clear insight. But it *is* possible. As women, we will have to come to an understanding of that."

Is it true, as rumor has it, that Krause is particularly demanding of women students? One recalls the much-repeated story of the night that Patricia Neal was a catastrophe in *Twelfth Night*. Afterward in the dressing room, the beginning actress told her teacher, "I shall never act again. Never." Krause replied. "Never again? You dare call what you did tonight *acting*? See you tomorrow at nine." Krause admits, "I don't take women unless I am convinced that they can take it, from me and from what will come after. The theatre has always been primarily men, and it's getting worse." When women today ask if she was handicapped by being a woman, she answers, "Well, it all depends on what you mean by handicapped. I had to work quietly, slowly." When she joined Northwestern there were only two other women on the speech faculty. One was Winifred Ward, distinguished founder of the children's theatre movement; the other was a costumer. "Oh, yes, a woman could teach costuming. There were the three of us. That was it. Women were not wanted." Krause was the first woman to direct a major university production there. Now she comes forth with her remarkable laugh, "But I did get to do what I believe in."

ALVINA KRAUSE—A TEACHER OF LIFE

David Downs

If Alvina Krause were a violinist, I would probably be a teacher of the violin. When she entered and altered my life, I was searching, however unknowingly, for a human being whose comprehension of life's truths went beyond the obvious. Krause had discovered those truths for herself through theatre. "Theatre," she says, "is life given form, given meaning." And to teach theatre, she had to teach human life. I am not the only student who came "to life" with her guidance. She saw me, she searched me, and she set about the task of helping me. It is her way.

When the opportunity came for me to teach at Northwestern, Krause urged me to pursue it. "Take the job. I will always be at your side." And so she was. The daily acting journal that had formed the mainstay of my training with her in Bloomsburg became a daily teaching journal in Evanston. She returned my weekly installments with extensive notes, suggestions, comments, questions. And behind all of her help was the insistence that I develop my own approach to teaching. "Exercises are nothing," she wrote. "My exercises worked for me. Find your own exercises. So long as the principles you illustrate are true, the goals you exemplify are right, you will find your own way." As the years go on, I am not surprised to discover that she was right. Alvina Krause profoundly exemplifies life in and through theatre. I will ever be thankful it was not the violin that so stirred and compelled her life.

ACTING FEMALE

Faye E. Dudden

"Acting female" is what traditionalists and reactionaries prescribe for women, but an "acting female"—a woman who plays roles—reveals the possibility of escaping that imperative. Whenever a women enacts a part she implicitly threatens the prevailing definition of womanhood: she shows she can become someone else and make you believe it. The very project the actress engages in undermines assumptions about the fixity of identity, and through-out Western culture theatre has been associated with both falsehood and the female.[1] In the words of film critic Molly Haskell, "Acting is role-playing, role-playing is lying, and lying is a woman's game."[2]

An acting, "changeling" woman may in fact seem threatening; her per-formance hints that supposedly meek, mild, domestic woman might really be quite the opposite—though, vengeful, or even demonic. No wonder that for centuries men forbade the stage to women and enlisted boys to play their parts. With the sure instincts of a confirmed misogynist, Rousseau con-demned the theatre because it gave power to women. The effect of plays and players was, he said, "to extend the empire of the fair sex, to make women and girls the preceptors of the public."[3] Thus the discrepancy between seeming and being that is intrinsic to theatre whispers to women about transforma-tion, self-creation, even power. This is theatre's revolutionary normality, its secret-out-in-plain-sight.[4]

There is, however, a problem. Ever since women first appeared onstage they have been associated with sexuality and immorality. The actress has been equated with the whore so persistently that no amount of clean living and rec-titude among actual performers has ever served to cancel the equation. Acting is linked to sexuality because it is an *embodied* art in contrast to the relatively disembodied business of writing, or the decorative arts so long associated with women. To act you must be present in the body, available to be seen. The woman who acts is thus inherently liable, whatever her own intent, to become the object of male sexual fantasy and voyeuristic pleasure. Acting is a particu-larly acute case of the general phenomenon of woman being reduced to sexual object. The theatrical enterprise thus contains two divergent possibilities for women: transformation and objectification. Theatre may enable women to rehearse the most radical projects of self-creation or may reduce them to bod-ies and present them as objects.[5] Theatre may do either of these, or both, or neither: it depends on the conditions under which theatre is conceived, pro-duced and received. It depends, that is, on history.

The story of the American theatre's two standing offers to women is deeply intertwined with the history of modern women and of public life. Theatre is a quintessentially public activity, and traditionally the public sphere belonged to men. In early America, women were confined to the privacy of home and family, and the only "public women" were, as slang neatly indicated, prostitutes. Yet beginning in the late eighteenth century a few women began to realize that the public realm was where economic resources were divided and decisions about social policy were made: the penalty for failure to present oneself in public was powerlessness, poverty or dependency. And so modern women's history revolved around women's struggle to enter public life on terms equal to men—to win the vote, to win access to higher education, to challenge employment discrimination. But women's problems did not end when they breached the barriers and entered these realms. The continuing problem of a woman in public, on the street and in the workplace, is the same as the problem of a woman on the stage: she must be there in the body. To be present in the body carries with it the inherent risk of being taken as a sexual object against one's will—in sexist deprecation, in sexual harassment, in physical assault. Theatre thus exemplifies a general problem for women in public, what we might call the "body problem."[6]

Yet the nineteenth-century theatre also presented a historical opportunity. When actresses showed themselves in public, women had a chance to imagine new ways of acting and being. For although gender is deeply implicated in our identities, is also performative—that is, it is actually achieved or constituted through our actions: we are born with sex, but we must learn to "do" gender.[7] Gender only seems natural: it is in fact assumed or enacted—as sociological talk of "roles" and "scripts" suggests. Routinely permitting women to play male "breeches" parts, the nineteenth-century theatre made this insight potentially available—in a simple-minded way—to anyone who attended. In a major performance like Charlotte Cushman's legendary Romeo, where a woman dressed, talked, and acted like a man, it hit the audience in the face.[8]

Today we live in a society in which one of theatre's two possibilities has won out, especially in its technological descendants, film and television. While live theatre harbors a fringe of avant-garde "gender bending" and feminist performance art, the mainstream of film and TV conducts a multibillion-dollar business involving the commercialized display of the female body, and the pornography industry accounts for billions more. The body problem is perhaps greater today than ever, for we live and work relentlessly surrounded by images that cater to male sexual interest, making it impossible for women to be unaware of their objectification. The ubiquity and verisimilitude of modern popular entertainments, together with their kin in the advertising industry, constitute a hall of mirrors that can rob women of any authentic sense of self. As the art critic John Berger writes: "Men look at women. Women watch themselves being looked at. This determines not only most relations between men and women but also the relation of women to themselves."[9]

The social history of American theatre helps to account for this troubling contemporary problem by charting the origins of the modern entertainment industry from the earliest years of the republic to the days just after the Civil War. This chunk of theatre history explains how entertainment first became a business, how it came to be so thoroughly controlled by men, and how it began routinely to display women's bodies for visual pleasure. The way that theatre evolved exacerbated the body problem by making male visual pleasure and the sexualized image a routine element of commerce and hence of public life. Women were not only objectified but also commodified. *Women in the American Theatre* examines why and how that happened, for the change was neither natural nor inevitable yet it was freighted with enormous consequences for modern women's lives. In charting the significant historical developments, I look at all the ways women were involved in the American theatre, not only as performers and audiences, but also as managers and as characters in plays. I pay special attention to the nature of the "business" and the predominance of commercial concerns. The antebellum theatre's turn toward one of its two inherent possibilities, objectification, provides a critical case study in the relationship of gender, popular culture and American capitalism: women's bodies became products in the entertainment marketplace of nineteenth-century America long before there were "mass media."

I have written about a particular time in American history when each of the stage's seemingly contradictory possibilities was realized. In the early and middle decades of the nineteenth century in the United States, the theatre first reached out to a mass audience, and in that same time and place the first organized women's rights movement in world history emerged. Between 1790 and 1870 entrepreneurs came to realize that entertainment could be produced and sold like other mass-consumption items, and they eventually found that one of theatre's two possibilities was significantly more profitable than the other: exposing female bodies brought in large audiences. Yet the other, more liberating, possibility of theatre for women was never squelched and often was flaunted, for women were always present onstage, often appeared in male roles, frequently took on theatre management, and constituted an increasing segment of the audiences, all while the "woman question" was before the nation as never before.

3 | HERE ARE THE WOMEN PLAYWRIGHTS

A wonderful anecdote in Dore Schary's autobiography, *Heyday*, tells a lot about the difficulties of women playwrights in the American theatre. A play written when Dore Schary was a young man was read by producer Walter Wanger who, misled by the unusual name, sent the following cable to Harry Cohn, head of Columbia Pictures in Hollywood. "Dore Schary should be signed up—she writes tough—like a man."

The ironic inversions in the punch line here make an important point. Playwriting has always been viewed as man's work, and the women who have tried to intrude have found the going rough. Major critics and big-time producers have said it straight out: women can't write first-rate plays. Even Lillian Hellman, without doubt the major American woman playwright, was faulted by George Jean Nathan for the "generic female inability" to master an "economy of emotion." The producer John Golden in a speech giving a "national achievement award" to Rachel Crothers in 1939 insisted that "there were few, if any great women dramatists—the reasons obvious: they were congenitally good, sweet, tender, loving, shy . . . so protected that they could never have seen the side of life . . . that one should know, see—perhaps, even live—to be a great dramatist."

There you have the characteristic answers influential men have offered to the perennial question: Where are the women playwrights? The women writers see things differently. They wonder what there is about the theatre as a medium that has kept women from full participation. Theatre as a highly public expression and a risky investment, they realize, has been outside of what has been defined as women's sphere. Playwriting is a skill that can only really be learned as part of a group working together in a highly technical physical plant, and they know that women have not usually had access to the camaraderie of the production process or the complex instrument of professional theatre.

Although some of these difficulties are shared with male writers who also find theatre a forbidding form, women face the put-down of male producers and directors, the ridicule of family and associates for even trying to make it, and their own guilt and frustration at sacrificing personal needs of self and children for the niggardly rewards of theatre. They are sometimes in a double bind. Brought up to deny themselves and their strong emotions and sexual drives, they find it difficult to expose what they really feel. If they do manage to give form to their "suppressed desires," they are chastised or feared for subverting the accepted female image. If not feared, female subject matter is often rejected as the dull, uninteresting minutiae of domestic life unrelated to the big world of male activities.

Paradoxically, despite these potent obstacles, the number of women dramatists in the history of American theatre is surprisingly large. As always in uncovering women's past, we discover findings that belie what we have been taught. The play list in our earlier editions contained more than 600 women playwrights, and this is by no means a complete accounting. Although the names may not be known to the larger public, these playwrights have played an important and occasionally outstanding and original role in the development of American theatre. They have won Pulitzer Prizes, Drama Critics awards and Obies. From their pens have come some of the all-time hits—from *East Lynne* to *Abie's Irish Rose* to *Harvey*.

One can trace women writing for the stage back to the very beginnings of American theatre to an occasional revolutionary bluestocking like Mercy Otis Warren. Some of the actress-playwrights of the mid-nineteenth century were close observers of the native scene, writing "original society plays" that treated American themes somewhat realistically at a time when most plays were romantic or melodramatic spectacles.

At the turn of the twentieth century, in the wake of the struggle for women's emancipation, women playwrights almost seemed to take over the processing of popular commercial productions for an increasingly female audience. Stories in newspapers and magazines featured the new phenomenon: "The Women Who Write Successful Plays." What many of these women wrote, like the men with whom they competed, were those serviceable melodramas, farces, mysteries and comedies that made up the season during the teens and expansive twenties. Working as "pros," they tended to look on playwriting as a "business."

Important as these professionals were in making a place for women in the theatre, they did not challenge—except by their presence—the conventional views of women and the aesthetic limitations of Broadway. Only a few were able to bring something of women's concerns to the mainstream—the ever-active Rachel Crothers, Zona Gale and Zoe Akins, for example. It was, however, largely in the more congenial atmosphere of the little theatres, art theatres and institutional theatres that the more venturesome women dramatists began to expose aspects of women's lives long hidden from view. They enriched the social dramas of an earlier day with penetrating psychological insights which they tried to project in effective dramatic action. One can find in the seminal experiments of Alice Gerstenberg, Susan Glaspell, Sophie Treadwell, Hallie Flanagan, Gertrude Stein and others, some of the subjects and the structures now widely used by today's women playwrights.

The strong, individual voices of Lillian Hellman, Clare Boothe Luce, Mary Chase and Lorraine Hansberry carried women playwrights[2] into the mainstream during the years from the Depression to the 1950s despite the severe cutback in the number of Broadway shows. In the 1960s the experimental Off- and Off-Off-Broadway theatres, like the earlier little theatres, were responsive to women writers and a whole new generation of exiting playwrights came from these creative nurseries—Megan Terry. Rochelle Owen, Rosalyn Drexler, Adrienne Kennedy, Myrna Lamb and others. Some of these women banded together to produce their own plays in theatres that would, as they put it, be stripped of "sexism and violence," the motto of their Theatre Strategy.

In the 1970s, women, finding theatre a powerful instrument for consciousness raising, began writing plays with great abandon and coming together in feminist theatres. They revived the plays of early innovators, with Gertrude Stein at the head of the new "woman's canon." There was a strong sense that the time was ripe—not for the "great woman dramatist," a concept at odds with the antihierarchical women's movement, but for the varied, insightful plays written by women who would be recognized as major contributors to American drama.

The new consciousness that led some dramatists to reject the traditional, commercial theatre completely also made those who looked to Broadway and the regional theatres more vocal and more visible. By 1985, half the new members of the Dramatists Guild were women, comprising thirty-two percent of the total membership. After almost forty years of neglect, women finally gained some recognition from the mainstream when Beth Henley, Marsha Norman and Wendy Wasserstein won Pulitzer prizes in the decade of the 1980s. The Susan Blackburn Prize for an "outstanding English-language play" written by a woman was established in 1978 and remains active. For the first time significant anthologies of plays by women began to appear—some for forgotten writers of the past and others for the new voices of women. In 1983 the Sunday Magazine section of the *New York Times* featured an article by critic Mel Gussow titled "Women Playwrights: New Voices in the Theatre." He identified "the wave of adventurous young women playwrights" as one of "the most encouraging and auspicious aspects of the current American Theatre."[1]

A number of the better-known of these "adventurous" theatre artists spoke out in 1986 in *Interviews with Contemporary Women Playwrights,* by Kathleen Betsko and Rachel Koenig, the first collection of its kind.[2] Previous anthologies about playwrights almost totally ignored women. From these rich interviews and some others, we can suggest some of the issues of common concern to a wide variety of playwrights.

To start with, the very designation "woman playwright" stirred controversy. As early as 1941, Lillian Hellman had turned on an interviewer who called her "a woman playwright," saying, "You wouldn't refer to Eugene O"Neill as one of America's foremost *male* playwrights."[3] Even for some in the women's movement of the 1970s, the term remained "dicey," "pejorative." Eve Merriam commented, "I *don't* want to be a 'woman playwright,' because I don't want to have my things done in woman's theatre exclusively. It smacks of a certain kind of ghettoization, even if one chooses it."[4] Although Adrienne Kennedy said that she is no longer bothered by the label, she is bothered by the reality behind it, which is that "as a black woman or as a woman writer, or as a black writer, I don't stand in line for the income or the rewards."[5] Wendy Wasserstein concluded that "we are all in it together. I listen to my plays, and as I hear them, I distance myself, and I still think: 'A woman wrote this.'"[6]

Certainly most of the women playwrights interviewed by Betsko and Koenig and others believe that the critics respond to them as "women playwrights."[7] The power of the critics, as many see it, not only closes shows but closes off creativity. Some writers needed several years to recover from being savaged by critics whose attacks seemed "unpardonable." Occasionally the few women critics—Edith Oliver, Marilyn Stasio and Erika Munk, for example—might help the survival of a play, although some writers complained that women critics often accept the male approach and provide little support.[8]

Although some writers spoke of open discrimination in the hierarchical professional theatre, others believed the obstacle to be differences in taste and "incompatible production aesthetics."[9] In 1985, the Dramatists Guild Committee for Women organized a panel to discuss "Plays by Women—What's the Difference?" It became apparent that exploring how "womanhood affects woman's work" would require complex analysis of economic, institutional and cultural values.[10] These tasks would be undertaken by feminist scholars in the next decade, but here are a few parameters of women's life in theatre that were frequently reported.

Getting started as a playwright is always a difficult first step, especially for women. Few recalled available role models. Lillian Hellman was for many the only woman playwright of note. Having children or the decision not to was important to many writers, some of whom fought for day care in their companies or housing allowances for babies and babysitters when they work away from home. Earning a living was a major concern given the limited production possibilities for women, who teach, act, or do films to keep going. Once in production, women report that the "inevitable power struggle between playwright and director is always exacerbated by the male-female situation."[11] A few, like Maria Irene Fornes and Emily Mann, resolved this tension by directing their own work and others sought out responsive women directors.

On the question of a "female aesthetic," most seem to believe that women do share some common qualities but found it difficult to pin down what they were. Some suggestions included the following: Women are "tuned in" to their bodies and are also more responsive to other people, valuing human relationships. There is a recurrent interest in duality and fragmentation, in hearing many voices, locating the individual in the community, and fracturing the conventions of traditional realistic forms. Helene Keyssar, in her study *Feminist Theatre* concluded that "the presence or absence of realism is not *the* central issue" rather she identified the "strategy of transformation . . . of self and world" and "the possibility for change" as central to this new women's drama.[12] Just how feminist or how political women's drama is or ought to be is variously interpreted. Ntozake Shange, whose *for colored girls* . . . was the first feminist play to reach Broadway, concluded, "When I make a personal statement, it is to me a political statement."[13]

Something most women playwrights seem to agree on is the importance of female characters in their work. Marsha Norman pointed out that women can create active women characters now that they have become "the central characters in their own lives."[14] They have "secrets to tell" which have sometimes made their work unwelcome in the commercial theatre. The need "to have power over one's work"[15] brought some of the women writers together as early as 1968, when Maria Irene Fornes organized and ran New York Theatre Strategy. Others have been part of Women's Interart Theatre, which Margot Lewitin headed, or Ellen Stewart's Café La MaMa, or the various Julia Miles's Women's Projects. Although women playwrights vigorously debated their differing views, most of them used whatever hard-won power they had to "tell the stories that haven't been told" about their own experience and the world in which they were living.[16]

HKC

MERCY WARREN: SATIRIST OF THE REVOLUTION

Alice McDonnell Robinson

Although Harriet Beecher Stowe's role in rousing antislavery passions before the Civil War through her novel and the play based on it is well known, the part played by another New England woman, Mercy Warren, in an earlier war is almost totally unknown. In the days before and during the Revolutionary War, Mercy Warren stirred up hatred for the Tories of Massachusetts and admiration for the American Revolutionaries through a series of plays.

Mercy Otis Warren was three years younger than her brother, James Otis, who was one of the most brilliant, and one of the most outspoken, of the early patriot leaders. Like her brother, she had always had a love of study. She had been allowed to go with her brother when as a boy he studied with the Reverend Jonathan Russell, their uncle by marriage. The Reverend Russell had been educated at Yale and was entrusted by Colonel Otis, their father, with the job of preparing his oldest son for Harvard. In the Reverend Russell's library were not only the Greek and Latin classics but also the works of Pope, Dryden, Milton and Shakespeare. Mercy Otis received nearly the same education as her brother, but, of course, she was not allowed to go to college. After his graduation from Harvard, James spent two years at home studying for his master's degree. He seems to have shared much of his reading and his thoughts with his intelligent sister. In 1754, at the age of twenty-six, Mercy Otis married a former classmate of her brother, James Warren.

The home of James and Mercy Warren in Plymouth became a meeting place for the patriots. Through her brother and husband, Mercy met John Adams and his wife, Abigail. She knew Samuel Adams, John Hancock and later Washington and Jefferson.

She might have remained a simple housewife rearing five sons and writing poems on nature and friendship in imitation of Pope and Dryden, had not her beloved brother become, as she was later to write, "the first martyr to American freedom."

James Otis and Samuel Adams led the Massachusetts House of Representatives in the struggle against the strict rule over the Colonies imposed under the rule of George III. In 1769, her brother James, in a rage against some custom officials who had printed scurrilities against him, published in the *Boston Gazette* a notice giving the names of certain men who had "treated the characters of all true North Americans in a manner that is not to be endured." The next evening, Otis walked, unarmed, into the British coffee-house frequented by his enemies. He was instantly threatened, the lights were put out, and his enemies attacked and beat him with canes and swords. Otis never recovered mentally from this attack. He returned to the Assembly in 1771, but he was not himself. In December of that year he was carried off in a post chaise bound hand and foot. It was at this time that Mercy Warren, at the age of forty-four, took up her pen to fight the battle her brother had helped to begin.

In 1772 the propaganda battle by the patriots was at a low ebb. With her brother unable to lead the patriots in their opposition to the English rule, Mrs. Mercy Otis Warren now began to use her pen to keep before the people her brother's ideals. She allowed excerpts from her first propaganda play, *The Adulateur*, to be printed anonymously in the radical paper, *The Massachusetts Spy*, on March 26 and April 23, 1772. In 1773 she published anonymously in pamphlet form a revised five-act version of the play. This longer version was probably published to take advantage of the patriots' outrage over the Hutchinson-Oliver letters in which Hutchinson had written that he doubted that the colony three thousand miles away could enjoy all the same liberties as the parent state and that "there must be an Abridgment of what are called English Liberties." This statement seemed to confirm the patriots' worst thoughts about Thomas Hutchinson, then acting governor. Hutchinson was the arch-villain in Mrs. Warren's play.

Mrs. Warren had never seen a play, for Boston had not allowed the players to perform in their city. She read history and philosophy and, when she felt inspired, she put her thoughts into poems. Her favorite themes for her poems were nature, friendship, philosophy and religion. Most of her poems were written in rhymed couplets imitative of the poetic models of the day, Alexander Pope and John Dryden. But now she used her pen to write in dramatic form, using blank verse. She was familiar with the plays of Shakespeare, Molière and Joseph Addison. The model for *The Adulateur* was probably Addison's heroic tragedy, *Cato*, for she included a quotation from *Cato* on the title page of her pamphlet.

Mrs. Warren's purpose, as she later wrote, was to "strip the Vizard from the Crafty"; those politicians against whom she directed her satirical pen were the wealthy Tory oligarchs who represented the British king and opposed the elected Assembly of Massachusetts. Chief of these men was Thomas Hutchinson who, when the play was published, was governor of the colony. At the time of the Boston Massacre, when the play takes place, Hutchinson was the lieutenant governor, president of the Council, Chief Justice and judge of Probate. As early as 1762, James Otis had spoken out against the same man's serving as both legislator and supreme judge. After Hutchinson became governor, his brother, Foster, became justice of the Common Pleas; his wife's brother-in-law, Peter Oliver, became Chief Justice; and his son, Thomas, became judge of Probate. This was the tight little group of oligarchs who were the target of Mercy Warren's satire.

The time depicted in *The Adulateur* is 1770, just before and during the Boston Massacre. *The Adulateur* follows quite closely the actual historical events. Of the aristocratic oligarchy of Massachusetts, Mrs. Warren uses among her characters:

RAPATIO, Governor of Servia	(Thomas Hutchinson)
LIMPUT, Married to Rapatio's Sister	(Andrew Oliver)
HAZELROD, L.C. Justice, Brother to Limput	(Peter Oliver)
MEAGRE, Brother to Rapatio	(Foster Hutchinson)

The Characters were not, of course, identified in the pamphlet, but the close relationship of the characters made their originals easy to determine.

Opposing these four characters are four Boston patriots, each given an appropriately heroic Roman name:

BRUTUS, Chief of the Patriots	(James Otis)
JUNIUS	(Samuel Adams)
CASSIUS PATRIOTS	(John Adams)
PORTEUS	(John Hancock)

Mrs. Warren's primary purpose in writing *The Adulateur* in 1772 was to arouse the patriots and unite them once again to oppose the "tyranny" of Britain as they had done at the time of the Boston Massacre. She drew her characters in strong black and white. She was, however, surprisingly advanced in her thinking about the human dignity and equality of men. She ranks, along with Samuel Adams and Thomas Paine (who had not yet come to this country), as one of the most democratic of the Revolutionary War leaders. In this play she depicts the wealthy and powerful oligarchs as contemptuous of the common people. On the other hand, Brutus and his fellow patriots believe in the dignity of the common man. Mrs. Warren was well aware of the social revolution that was going on at this time.

In *The Adulateur*, the patriot leaders also stand for liberty and freedom. Through them, Mrs. Warren describes some characteristics of a government which would assure greater freedom to the people. First, no one man should have too much power, as had Rapatio, surrounded by fawning relatives and parasites. Second, a good government should assure justice for all, and judges must be free from influence by the executive branch of the government. Third, the government should have no standing army.

Mrs. Warren seems already to have visualized an independent country, for she has Brutus wish for a "gen'rous, free and independent people." She calls her readers to immediate action, and she seems to encourage physical opposition. Her leaders are resolved that before they will be slaves they will "pour out" their "choicest blood" and with their daggers "force a way to freedom."

Through her depiction of the heroic leaders of the patriots, headed by her own brother, Mrs. Warren attempts to define for the first time in original American drama the "true" American. This idealized American is trustworthy, unselfish, freedom-loving. He scorns title, position and money that are attained at the sacrifice of honor. He respects the common people and believes in a government based on the will of the people. He has a vision of greatness for America.

Mrs. Warren's play seems to have helped to discredit the two chief victims of her satirical pen, Thomas Hutchinson and Peter Oliver. The names of Rapatio and Hazelrod, which she gave them, stuck to the two men.

In 1773, Mrs. Warren published in the *Boston Gazette* some excerpts from a new propaganda play called *The Defeat*. This play was evidently never published in pamphlet form. In *The Defeat* Rapatio and Limput appear once again. The patriots with the names of Honestus, Cassius, Rusticus, Hortensius and Lucius are members of the Massachusetts Assembly. In this play, the patriots are once again victorious. In the third act, which is merely summarized in the newspaper, a battle takes place in which "Rapatio, Abettors and Creatures are totally defeated" and "freedom and happiness" are restored to the people. In the final scene of the play, Rapatio laments his lost peace of mind which he basely sold "for flattering titles and more sordid Gold."

In *The Defeat*, liberty is again set up as an ideal and is even triumphant. Several references are made to native rights or native freedom. This is an early mention of that "natural law" which the patriots were beginning to claim to be over and above mere governmental law. Mrs. Warren enumerates four rights which the government should protect. The government should protect the right of assembly, should assure the right of the legislatures to meet and make laws without intimidation, should allow freedom of the press, and should protect the people from a standing army. Most of all, Mrs. Warren, as she had done in *The Adulateur*, warned against a government in which one

UNIVERSITY OF WINCHESTER LIBRARY

man has too much power. She also helped to destroy the effectiveness of Thomas Hutchinson as governor of the colony, and in 1774 he was recalled to England to report to the king in person.

Before Mrs. Warren's third play appeared, certain important events took place. In December 1773, the famous Boston Tea Party occurred. As a punishment for the dumping of the tea, the British ordered that Boston Harbor be closed. The very next day after the closing of the harbor, the news of Parliament's so-called Intolerable or Coercive Acts reached Boston. Among the Coercive Acts was one that stated that the governor should appoint his Council instead of its members being elected by the House.

The news that the king had signed the Coercive Acts arrived in August, along with the list of thirty-six men who had been appointed by the king to serve as councilors. These councilors at once became the object of the patriots' contempt. The mob "persuaded" all but sixteen of them to resign their appointments. The sixteen who refused to resign had to seek protection from the British soldiers who made of Boston almost an armed camp. General Thomas Cage had now replaced Thomas Hutchinson as governor.

Early in 1775, Mrs. Warren attacked with her pen these sixteen councilors who had refused to resign their appointments. This play, which became her most popular one, is called *The Group*. The first two scenes were printed in the *Boston Gazette* on January 23, 1775, and reprinted three days later in *The Massachusetts Spy*. On April 3 the *Boston Gazette* advertised that the play was for sale in pamphlet form. The pamphlet edition published in Boston included four scenes and an epilogue. A short time later, pamphlet editions were published in both New York and Philadelphia. These pamphlets included only the two scenes which had appeared in the newspapers and may have been copied directly from the newspapers. The last two scenes and the epilogue contained in the Boston edition seem to anticipate the fateful day, April 19, when the British troops marched out of Boston to seize military stores at Concord.

In her prologue to the play, Mrs. Warren set forth her purpose in writing it:

> Hear this and tremble, ye who 'scape the laws;
> Yes, while I live, no rich or noble knave,
> Shall walk the world in credit to his grave;
> To virtue only, and her friends, a friend,
> The world beside may murmur, or commend.

All of the characters in *The Group*, with the exception of Hazelrod (Peter Oliver, formerly the "adulateur") and Sylla (General Gage), are councilors appointed by the king. They are given names like Brigadier Hateall, Hum Humbug, Sir Sparrow Spendall, Beau Trumps, Simple Sapling and Crusty Crowbar. Though *The Group* was published without identifying the characters, there are five extant copies of the play with a key written in. Few of these Tories are known by name today.

In *The Group* Mrs. Warren has no virtuous patriots to praise the ideal of freedom. Perhaps her cry for freedom and liberty sounds even louder by being voiced by the Loyalists. Most of Mrs. Warren's councilors realize that through their own weakness they have rejected the great ideal of liberty.

In the epilogue, Mrs. Warren voices, through "a Lady reclined in an alcove," her faith in the final victory of the Americans over the British troops. Many "painful scenes" will follow, the lady says,

> Till British troops shall to Columbia yield
> And Freedom's sons are Masters of the field.

Mrs. Warren, writing the final scenes of this play just a few weeks before Lexington and Concord, tried to give the untrained militia the confidence to face the British troops.

The success of *The Group* seems to have made Mercy Warren feel a little guilty about the picture she had drawn of the Tories. She began to wonder if such cutting satire was suitable for a lady to write. She wrote her friend John Adams to ask him what he thought. John Adams responded in a letter to her husband: "My most friendly regards to a certain Lady, tell her the God Almighty (I use a bold style) has entrusted her with Powers for the good of the World, which, in the Cause of his Providence, he bestows on few of the human race. That instead of being a fault to use them, it would be criminal to neglect them." Abigail Adams added her own comment to the letter. "I observe," she wrote, "my friend laboring under apprehension, lest the severity with which a certain *Group* was drawn was incompatible with that benevolence which ought always to be predominant in a female character . . . Yet when it is so happily blended with benevolence, and is awakened by the love of virtue and abhorrence of vice . . . it is so far from blamable that it is certainly meritorious."

Perhaps these words helped to reassure Mrs. Warren that her satire was necessary to the cause. However, *The Group* seems to have been the last of Mrs. Warren's dramatic satires. Some scholars have credited her with two more satirical plays, *The Blockheads; or, the Affrighted Officers* and *The Motley Assembly* but there seems to be no proof that she wrote either of them and their style is quite different from *The Adulateur, The Defeat* and *The Group*.

In 1805, at the age of seventy-seven, Mrs. Warren published her three-volume *History of the American Revolution,* which she had begun in 1775.

In 1814, hearing that the copy of *The Group* in the Athenaeum in Boston had been attributed to one Samuel Barrett, Mrs. Warren asked her old friend John Adams to vouch for her authorship. Adams, seventy-nine years of age at the time, traveled to Boston and wrote on the last leaf of the pamphlet: "August 17, 1814. The 'Group' to my certain knowledge was written by Mrs. Mercy Warren of Plymouth. So certifies John Adams."

About the same time, Mrs. Warren wrote at the end of her own copy of *The Adulateur*: "Though many years have elapsed since the above sketches were written and time has meliorated the resentment felt against those who strenuously endeavored to enslave the American colonies, they were in the busy period of the Revolution deemed a just portrait of the characters mentioned in the preceding pages; and all who are acquainted with the historic records of those times will compare historic and dramatic narration and accede to the justice and truth of the description." In October of that same year, 1814, Mercy Otis Warren died. Through her plays she had been an active participant in the struggle for a new nation.

LOOKING TO WOMEN: RACHEL CROTHERS AND THE FEMINIST HEROINE

Lois Gottlieb

In 1931, Djuna Barnes interviewed Rachel Crothers for the *Theatre Guild* magazine. She asked how, from such an early point in her career (around 1908), Crothers had been able to overcome masculine resistance and take charge of the production of her own plays. Crothers referred specifically to several women who had helped her and offered the following generalization: "For a woman, it is best to look to women for help; women are more daring, they are glad to take the most extraordinary chances . . . I think I should have been longer about my destiny if I had to battle with men alone."[1] Coming as late as 1931, Crothers's affirmation of women's capabilities and her assertion that women play an important role in the destinies of other women contradict the generally held belief that by the second half of her career, begnning in the 1920s, Crothers's plays depict the failure of the American women's movement and repudiate the feminism so apparent in her earlier plays.

The term "feminism" in relation to Crothers's plays can certainly cover everything from fearless exposes of sex antagonism and injustices to women to a benign focus on women at the center of the dramas. The role of feminism in her plays clearly changes from a coherent and optimistic ideology to a rather shadowy and amorphous afterimage. Crothers's feminist heroines change, too, from energetic and clear-sighted rebels to women who are confused, dissatisfied with the sense of emancipation surrounding them. These are developments in feminism, as Crothers saw it, however, not reversals or failures. And they can be understood best through the plays themselves, within which Crothers developed the theme of woman's evolution—her purposeful and inevitable progress. In these plays she created aparticular kind of feminist heroine crucial to that evolution: the woman who looks to other women, to give help and to get help, in order to advance woman's development.

Between 1899 and 1906, Crothers's apprentice years as a playwright, her feminist heroines reflect society's views of their specialness. Such women stood out from most other women as a studied contrast in dress, behavior and attitude, with greater intellectual capabilities and a usually recognizable professional or working role. Crothers further emphasizes the distinguishing external qualities of these women by contrasting them with the more traditional women characters, who tend to be unpleasant, difficult, weak, or malicious in these early plays.

The superiority of these incipient feminist heroines is partially a negative factor in their lives. They lose, or almost lose, the men they love, not, ostensibly, because the men devalue their superiority, but because they overvalue it. The superior women themselves often overvalue their strength and competence, and they seem to chasten this excessive pride by giving up the men they love to "needier" women, that is, women whose whole live are love.

The superior sufferer is tacit evidence of woman's evolution, but she does not advance that evolution. When she looks to other women to help them, what she sees are traditional women and what she helps them to are women's traditional goals: marriage, respectability, protection. The social injustices which limit the superior women to lonely nobility are only indirectly commented on. Far from seeing herself in the mirror of other women's lives, the superior sufferer is defined by her unlikeness to the common run of femininity.

Rhy McChesney, in Crothers's first theatrical success, *The Three of Us* (1906),[2] is really a "transitional" heroine and reflects Crothers's difficulty in bringing her feminist out of the closet. She attempts to advance woman's evolution by defying the double moral standard, which insists on man as woman's protector, and she explicitly dissociates herself from the "fear" of a compromised reputation that is supposed to curtail the activity of "all good women." Crothers gives Rhy a forceful declaration of independence by which to demolish the age-old role of the masculine protector. As she says to both the villain and the hero: "My honor! Do you think it is in your hands? It's in my own, and I'll take care of it, and everyone who *belongs* to me. I don't need you—either of you." But Crothers also has Rhy pose as a helpless woman so that her brother, whose ego has been damaged by having a strong sister, can enhance his self-image by defending a woman's honor.

Between 1908 and 1914 Crothers wrote a series of social problem plays, American style, in which the feminist heroine is far more comfortable with her strength than earlier heroines, is consciously motivated by her desire to help other women break out of boundaries, and is explicit in her belief in women's evolution and its beneficial impact on society. Crothers's central women of this period are not "youngsters" and several of the most interesting characters are in their mid-thirties, expressing Crothers's conviction that modern dramatists no longer had to "confine heroines to ingenues, stage age seventeen."[3] These are, in fact, experienced women, successful in business and arts. Bettina Marshall of *Myself-Bettina* (1908) and Frank Ware of *A Man's World* (1909) have traveled and lived abroad; Victoria Claffenden in *Young Wisdom* (1914) is a college graduate; Ruth Creel and Ann Herford in *He and She* (1911) have developed themselves as journalist and sculptor, respectively, through discipline and long apprenticeship; and Beatrice Barrington in *Ourselves* (1913) steeps herself in a personal as well as theoretical knowledge of the causes and cures of the great social evil, prostitution.

Crothers endows these women with more freedom of experience and thought than her earlier characters, and the questions they debate and the battles they fight supply far more abundant evidence of woman's emancipation than one could glean from earlier plays. Bettina, for example, in the manuscript of *Myself-Bettina*, refuses to define woman's honor exclusively by her reputation and condemns marriage as the means to restore a "fallen woman's honor. Frank Ware, in *A Man's World*, writes social protest novels exposing the brutality of women's lives on the Lower East Side, where poverty and prostitution are inextricably linked to keep women in bondage and where both phenomena are traceable to the "man's world." Frank also tackles the problem of woman's sense of psychological inferiority to man and her dependence on masculine attention for status and self-respect. *He and She* questions the impediments placed by men before the artist woman and critically examines the charges of inherent inferiority, unnaturalness, selfishness and injustice to husbands and children which were part and parcel of the emotional baggage the artist woman was forced to contend with. In the manuscript of *Ourselves* the premise is that prostitution is a "man's business"—and a big business at that and that society has been sidetracked from resolving the problem by focusing on the women when the more effective approach would be to start "locking up the men."[4]

On almost every point, these central women are acutely and critically conscious of the status of women, but an equally conspicuous feature of their character is their attempt to impart this consciousness to other women, not only to teach them about their bondage, but also to see the freedom of their own lives reflected in the lives of more women. In two of these plays, *Myself-Bettina* and *Young Wisdom*, Crothers perceives the helping within a family context, as an older, more experienced and more emancipated sister attempts to encourage or hasten the advancement of her more domesticated or confined sister. In three of these plays, women turn their attention to a wider sphere of women, enlarging the notion of sisterhood from a familial to a societal relation. In *A Man's World*, for example, Frank sets up a girl's club on the Lower East Side to provide a center of learning and support in an environment hostile to woman's freedom. Frank's ideal of woman's self-sufficiency and strength does not endear her to all women—particularly women of her own class who are alienated by it. Thus, when Frank tackles the problem of women who are psychologically, though not economically dominated and diminished by the operation of the man's world, her helping meets with some resistance. Lione Brune, a temperamental and haughty opera singer, acknowledges that "All men are pigs," but resents what she considers Frank's "show" of independence from men and refuses to adopt it for herself, since she fears the reprisal of a manless existence. In another dimension, Clara Oakes, a timid, unsuccessful miniature painter, is fearful of Frank's disapproval because she is tired of being strong and self-sufficient and is, in fact, humiliated by her spinster status. Clara does gain a measure of self-respect, however, when she accepts Frank's offer of a job as a resident art teacher in the ghetto girls' club. In *He and She*, Ruth Creel, a success young journalist with an entirely emancipated view of woman's nature, spends a good deal of time encouraging the artistic development of her friend, Ann Herford, a thirty-six-year-old wife and mother who has had a late start developing her considerable talent as a sculptor and is still uncertain of her abilities. As Ann cheerfully contends with patronizing solicitousness toward her work and family interruptions, Ruth argues that Ann has genius and ought to resist everything that threatens it, including her father and her husband. Eventually, Ann acknowledges the inhibitions these men have placed on her advancement, and although she has secretly created designs for her sculptor husband to enter in an important public competition, she follows Ruth's advice to enter them under her own name, and she beats her husband for first prize.

Crothers's portraits of rebels and reformers are more complex than this brief survey might suggest, or to put it another way, her plays are less programmatic than the "dramatic tracts" written by other feminists. Two plays of this period offer insights into some of the drawbacks of the reform movement. In *Ourselves*, for example, Beatrice Barrington is a type of privileged, wealthy, sheltered reformer whose desires to help women needier than herself exceed her ability to do so and blind her to the urgent need to understand the situation of women in her own class. She takes home a prostitute from a reformatory in order to work out theories of the benefits of a refining influence on the lives of fallen women, but Beatrice's housekeeper has far more impact on the young woman and has far more luck becoming her intimate than does the wealthy woman. And the young prostitute, rebelling against being treated as an "experiment" rather than a person, ultimately refuses further "refuge" from her patroness and returns to the slums, convinced that self-help, not patronage, is the best process for freeing women like herself.

In the manuscript of her final play of this series, *Young Wisdom*, Crothers depicts a naïve and breathless heroine who delights in reading aloud from her mentors, such as Mona Caird and Ellen Key—both well-known anti-Victorian critics. Victoria argues for the merits of free love and "trial marriage," and is swept away by an excess of enthusiasm for woman's evolution. As she breathlessly declares: "The future of the world depends on women . . . Men don't evolute at all, you know." Through Victoria, Crothers pursues the possibility that radical feminist thought may misguide woman's evolution, and this play, like the others, displays the moderate position Crothers took as a feminist on the subject of woman's evolution. While the four earlier plays reflect the middle-ground position, "that with the development of society is bound up henceforward the more complete and perfect evolution of women,"[5] this last play shows Crothers's rejection of "the attempt of a few extremists to exalt the wonder woman at the expense of the man."[6]

The heroines of this period bear witness to the increasing numbers of women affected by the women's movement. Their activity reflects what journalists called a growing "sex loyalty" or "sex solidarity" among women, which the women's movement had generated and which could be put to work to aid the evolution of all women. Crothers publicly praised the growing sex-loyalty for its success in closing two particularly divisive gaps: the moral chasm between "good women" and the "woman who has strayed from the path of conventional morality," and the personal division between "the home woman" and her "self-supporting sister,"[7] whom she resented. She also acknowledged that her own progress in the theatre had been aided by sex solidarity: she received important professional help when Maxine Elliott, the star to whom Crothers had sold *Myself-Bettina,* allowed Crothers to stage and direct it. As Crothers noted, Elliott had "such an admiration for and faith in the work of woman, that she was delighted to find a woman who could shoulder the entire responsibility."[8] Sex-loyalty, however, also placed Crothers on the defensive, when some feminists denounced *Young Wisdom* and Crothers took to the papers to defend herself and her play against charges of "hypocrisy" and pandering to the box office. Crothers argued that she had already proved herself a "natural woman's champion," the "most ardent of feminists" and saw no discrepancy between her belief "in women and their capacity to earn their daily bread in the same field and on the same footing with men," and her intent to satirize the "theories involved in the advanced women, to laugh *with* them, not at them," at the funny, chaotic results which would ensue if "the radical ideas" of "the most militant feminist" were at once adopted and acted upon."[9]

Between 1914 and 1919, Crothers wrote a group of six plays, which replaced social problems with sentiment and which were modeled on the popular "gladness" plays, of which *Pollyanna* is probably the best-known example. For the only time in her career, Crothers abandoned both the themes of woman's evolution and the feminist heroine, and their absence makes a striking difference. Women characters in conventional mold, financially dependent on men, once seen in secondary roles in her earlier plays, now took center stage.

With the 1920s, however, Crothers reintroduces a feminist perspective, but the comic mode which she adopted and perfected in this decade complicates her treatment of woman's evolution. As comic figures the central women of the twenties lose their previously idealized characterizations as well as their long hair. Where the rebellious reformers were almost entirely a collection of superior women, the twenties heroines are either immature, ordinary to a fault, or, in some cases, less than ordinary. Two of these heroines, Teddy Gloucester in *Nice People* (1921)[10] and the daughter, Mary, in *Mary the Third* (l923),[11] are frenetic flappers, barely out of their teens. Minnie Whitcomb is a pathetically mousy music teacher in *Expressing Willie* (1925),[12] and Nancy Marshall, a figure in several one-acts published in 1926,[13] is a feminist opportunist, selfishly exploiting suffrage gains to further her political career. The single superior woman, the androgynous female aviator in *Venus* (1927),[14] is a figure of fantasy.

Another important feature of the comic characterization of these women is that Crothers portrays them as products of their flawed society rather than as superior to it. They show an excessive concern with self-fulfillment and personal liberty, the watchwords of their day. When the twenties heroine recognizes a social injustice to women, her solution is emphatically individual.

Along with the comic emphasis on "self," the plays reflect the weakening of sex solidarity. Crothers's women of the 1920s will not look to other women for help. For the flappers in *Nice People*, for example, women of the critical older generations mirror a type of femininity distasteful to the younger women. As sex solidarity weakens, woman's role in helping other women break out of boundaries is relegated to a secondary action or is entirely ignored even while change for women remains at the center of the plays. In two plays the evolution of women is expressed by magic, or fantasy. The self-effacing Minnie of *Expressing Willie* finally achieves power and confidence, but only through the satirized, pseudo-Freudian ritual of digging deeply inside herself, freeing herself from "suppressions," and releasing buried greatness. The female aviator in *Venus*, disgusted by sex antagonism on earth, prepares to emigrate to Venus in order to live the androgynous life.

In looking to the women of the 1920s, then, Crothers highlights their flaws and foibles and plays down their positive qualities. The feminist heroine is a comic character who struggles to maintain equilibrium and identity in the intoxicating freedom of postwar society, and Crothers portrays this as an age which wedged itself between generations of women as well as between women of the same generation, isolating them from the mutual help which had proved so effective in advancing women's progress in the preceding era.

The four plays of Crothers's last periods, 1929–37, do not easily lend themselves to a uniform reading on the status of woman's evolution; what they reveal about the fate of the feminist heroine after the 1920s is certainly too complicated to be supported by general reference to the "demise of the New Woman."[15] The novelty of being an "evolved" woman has worn off; only vestiges remain of the external, man's world to be fought. Therefore, the announcements of dissatisfaction, loneliness, depression and boredom issuing from the most visible exemplars of the "daughters" of the new women are cause for attention. Thirty-year-old Kitty Brown, in *Let Us Be Gay* (1929), and thirty-six-year-old Mary Howard, in *When Ladies Meet* (1932), are both glamorous, creative, well-traveled, financially successful and sexually liberated women, but far from being "completed" by their freedom, these women find their lives lacking and are beset by confusion and anxiety. The thirties home-women, however, make the same complaints. The two middle-aged Iowa housewives in *As Husbands Go* (1931) dread a return to the lifelessness and anonymity of their domestic roles after a revitalizing trip to Europe; and Susan Trexler, in *Susan and God* (1937), confesses to her daughter that she has spent most of her domestic life trying to fill it up with things outside marriage and family.

The evolved woman inherited a "freedom" from gross, external injustices but not a guaranteed place in the sun, freed from internal anxieties and fears. As a consequence, Crothers records a sense of disillusionment with the women's movement and a tendency to blame it for deficiencies in woman's emotional life. As seventy-six-year-old Mrs. Boucicault puts it, in *Let Us Be Gay*: "Women are getting everything they think they want now, but are they any happier than they were when they used to stay home and let men fool them?"

The new challenge, then, for the woman of the 1930s, is to find "happiness" rather than justice or advancement. In the face of the Depression, the rise of Fascism and the onset of World War II, it is not surprising that Crothers emphasizes the difficulty of this task. Her heroines tackle it with all the energy Crothers normally endows her advanced women, but a sense of disillusionment pervades the plays.

Far from being entirely negative about woman's evolution, however, Crothers's last plays deal with the continued process of woman's growth and Crothers carefully identifies her latest challenges. The plays appeal to woman to take a more accurate measure of the dimensions of the human male and discard the idealized myth; they demonstrate the necessity for woman to reject a "man-centered" distortion of reality but, at the same time, to assess honestly man's place in her emotional life.

One play from this period, *When Ladies Meet*, supplies a full and consistent critique of man's place in the emotional life of the evolved woman. Crothers concentrates on two women who have a man-centered reality. They have, consequently, not only inflated and idealized man—as protector, savior and source of transcendence—but they have also accepted a "second-hand image" of woman, as she is reflected through man's eyes, and this is an image that divides women from each other as well as from themselves.

The two central women of *When Ladies Meet*—ladies of the title—are built from the stereotypical models of antagonistic women—since they are the mistress and wife of the same weak-willed publisher. Mischance brings them together, ignorant of each other's relationship to the man. Each woman meets her "rival," without preconceptions and certainly without a predisposing hostility. In fact, the women like each other a great deal. Because mutual affection and trust have built between the women in the absence of the man, Crothers can deliver a far different recognition scene when each finally discovers the other's identity. Claire, the wife, sees that Mary, "the other woman," is not a "vile brazen slut" though throughout the long years of marriage with a philandering husband, she has consoled herself with the image of the "other woman" as a cheap seducer. Similarly, Mary sees that Claire, the "wife," is not the dull, unsympathetic creature of her lover's complaints—an image soothing to Mary's conscience—but rather is a lively, humorous, attractive woman. In short, the man-centered reality does not survive.

By eliminating man as the lens through which to view woman, Claire and Mary have both outgrown an imprisoning myth; the consequence is that rather than fight each other for the man, each rejects him, Claire leaving her husband and Mary ending her affair. Both have taken a more accurate measure of the dimensions of the human male, and Mary is an interesting example of a Crothers woman for whom this reality is not too hard to bear.

In fact, this reality is a prelude to Mary's taking a more honest look at man's place in her life, and she does so with humor. She is the "strong" and "intelligent" woman who "at last persuades herself that a man is *the* thing in life she wants" and as a consequence, she accepts the label of "the biggest fool of all!"[16]

It is one measure of the distance traveled by the evolved woman that Mary can acknowledge man's place in her life, without self-loathing or self-pity. She is no longer bound to the stoical silence that marked earlier feminist heroines, suffering loneliness and isolation. But the spectacle of an evolved woman, aggressively announcing that career, money, and acclaim have not brought her personal happiness or assuaged her loneliness, was disconcerting to those who had judged Crothers a feminist. Eleanor Flexner was particularly distressed by Mary's complaint, at the beginning of *When Ladies Meet*: "I haven't found *anything*. Except to know that I haven't *got* anything that really *counts*. Nobody *belongs* to me—nobody whose very existence depends on me. I am completely and absolutely alone." Flexner saw this as a significant sign of the failure of feminism.[17] For Flexner, "the wheel has come full circle." The progress of woman's evolution had not simply been slowed, but reversed.

When Ladies Meet is not, however, a cry from woman to reverse woman's evolution. In fact, the structure of the play argues that Mary's critical examination and honest assessment of her independent status advances, rather than reverses woman's progress. Mary's declaration of loneliness is heard at the beginning of the play; the action that follows comically exposes Mary's attempt to assuage her loneliness through an idealized lover. Crothers does not mock the loneliness as an unworthy or degraded emotion, but she does make comedy out of Mary's attempt to combat loneliness, mocking Mary's distorted, "man-centered" view of things.

Mary is a new type of feminist heroine in the Crothers canon, and she brings new dimensions of humor and insight to the conflict between the evolved woman and love. In terms of Crothers's career, Mary represents the last stage in the development of the theme of woman's evolution, begun three decades before, but she is evidence that through this last phase of her career, Crothers reiterated the importance of supportive bonds between women in the continuous struggle for woman's progress.

APROPOS OF WOMEN AND THE FOLK PLAY

Rachel France

The first use of the term *folk play* the American theatre appears to have been the Carolina Playmakers' *Carolina Folk Plays* on the program for their initial production at Chapel Hill, March 14 and 15, 1919. Credited with this term was Professor Frederick Koch, who hoped that, by beginning with a specific locale, a writer would eventually find his or her way to the universal. If a writer could view "the lives about him with wonder, why may he not interpret that life in significant images for others?" Koch asked. "It has been so in all lasting art."[1] Hamlin Garland was prompted to say of such efforts that "locality makes the American drama."[2]

There were, however, earlier plays about rural life, many of them written by women for whom the important issue was not locale but, rather, defining exactly who in America could be described as its "folks." These plays, ignored by Koch and Garland, would not be included in the standard canons of Folk Art.

Ruth Suckow's essay, "The Folk Idea in American Life," does much to illuminate this earlier group of plays about rural life. She attacks the view that folk art—especially in America—should be tied to regional peculiarities. Her folk were "hard-working people of a fairly religious call, with a strong belief in education, Protestant and to that extent Puritan."[3] Rather than simple people living close to the land, Suckow's picture of "folks" can better be recognized as "the silent majority."

Her essay, written in 1930, reiterates, with the clarity of hindsight, the effort—most fervent after World War I—to define native American culture as something distinct from and independent of European culture. This effort began in earnest toward the end of the nineteenth century, inspired, in no small part, by the nearly fifteen million foreigners who immigrated to the United States between 1896 and 1914. These newcomers gave rise to the fear that America's boast of a classless society might only be realized at the expense of the native born.

This nativist point of view warrants mentioning because it was also espoused by the most prominent members of the women's movement. Suffragists found it especially ironic that so large a group of "foreign" men could expect to be enfranchised before "American" women. But, more important, it provides an exact reflection of the spirit which informed so many of the folk plays written by women prior to 1920.

In these folk plays middle-class white women bear the cultural burdens of American civilization; they are preserving their small enclaves from the corruption of outside influence. Intellectual or social pressures are brought upon them by men. However, these folk plays reflect the isolation of women from wider social structures. Men who engage in the activities of the world are seen essentially as foreigners to the rural sense of community and are cast aside. The imaginative constructs of folk drama render them negligible. Folk drama becomes, therefore, the drama of the woman's world.

Zona Gale's vision in *The Neighbors* (1912) should be taken as a vision of the upper Midwest which may have existed for her as a young woman. It is also one which she would subsequently reject as hopelessly naive in *Miss Lulu Bett*, written less than a decade later.

Central to Gale's idea of "folks" in *The Neighbors* is the notion that human beings are fundamentally good—or, at least, "folks" are. Their finest instincts might lie beneath a rough exterior, but they can be brought out when the latent sense of community of folks to which they belong is realized.

Implicit in Gale's concept, also, is the idea that the community is led together by women. Of the eight characters in the play, six are women. The are all instinctively aware of correct social behavior. By word and by deed they will educate Ezra Williams, a woodcutter, and Peter, who suffers from unrequited love.

Gale shows how the women's influence comes into play when "neighbors" are faced with a problem. One of them, Mis' Carry Ellsworth, plans to adopt her orphaned nephew. He is to arrive that evening, but Mis' Ellsworth lacks the means to care for him properly. Only Ezra fails to respond to the situation with instinctive goodness. "Well, ain't that just like a woman!" he exclaims. "Always gettin' herself come down by a lot o' distant relatives to support."[4]

Women, however, quickly find the appropriate way to assist their friend and neighbor. Mis' Ellsworth, they know, would not accept money, "even if anybody had any to offer." Instead, they hit upon the plan to give her clothing and other supplies that she will need. The values of the community emerge. Charity, to these self-sufficient people, is indeed "nasty." Of prime importance is to be "folks."

It is Peter who displays the deepest flaw, one that keeps him from the community. Although he is one of them, Peter has yet to learn how to behave properly. "Folks is folks, no matter how different or similar," says Grandma. "They can't fool us. Folks is folks." Peter, with his predilection for lofty discussion, seems to be denying that he, too, is "folks." The women are aware that Peter needs to conform, since it is actions and the shared remembrance of the local landscape and family events which bind the community together.

The women, as Ezra notes, "tend to the society end of this town." His business is seen as inconsequential men's work; however, he is considered a member of the community, if only because of "the few little things my wife just sent over."

At the end of Gale's play, the neighbors learn that another home has been found for Mis' Ellsworth's nephew. The women gather to share her loss. "We all know," Mis' Abel begins. "I ain't had but one, but I know." Mis' Trot agrees, "Yes, I've got seven an' sometimes I'm drove most to death with 'em, but I know." And, although Mis' Moran "never had none," she too knows. "Mine's dead— all dead," Grandma adds. "But I know." And so does Inez know. Their remarks form a chant of "womanhood," the common sensibility which is the foundation of the community.

Although there are two men in *The Neighbors*, their presence plays no part in the women's lives. Only Mis' Moran mentions her husband. Feeling slighted by Mis' Abel, she complains, "If that ain't just like Jake's treatment of me." Apparently, the most useful male contribution, which is not female-inspired, is the eight dollars a month that Mis' Ellsworth receives.

In addition to the stress upon "womanhood," *The Neighbors* touches upon the conflict between the sexes. It is this conflict that is explored quite fully in Alice Brown's *Children of the Earth* (1913), where it is an important secondary theme added to the basic folk drama theme of country versus city. This four-act play has had an impact beyond its stage success, or lack of stage success, because of its subject matter—with the ultimate triumph of woman over man, and of nature over materialism.

Children of the Earth goes well beyond Gale's relatively simple assertion in *The Neighbors* that the sense of community is a natural aspect of rural life. Instead, Brown depicts a rural civilization which is still to be fully formed, focusing on that point in time when the community is threatened both by the materialism of the industrial age and by the unrefined sensuality of frontier days. Her heroine, Mary Ellen Barstow, must integrate the natural aspects of rural life, the feeling of union with the earth, with a profound sense of duty, to morality and the work ethic, to realize a new level of civilization—for herself and for the "children of the earth" for whom it is her special province to care.

It is difficult to comprehend *Children of the Earth* in terms of realistic passion. The play reads like a reconstruction of archetypal themes in American literature—in terms of the unique place of "womanhood." Brown tells her story in terms of Mary Ellen's relationship with two men. One of them, Nate Buell, is a city man who is "always looking out for the main chance."[5] He has been denatured, so no compact with him is possible. Peter Hale, on the other hand, represents the natural man. He is married to Jane, a dark woman of mysterious origin. Mary Ellen could, if she wished, win Peter for herself. However, their union would merely be a sexual one, as Peter's marriage to Jane has undoubtedly been. Instead, Mary Ellen symbolically weds both Peter and Jane. Their combined sexual energies will, hereafter, be sublimated by the need to care for the land and all its people. Thus, Mary Ellen finally succeeds in civilizing the wilderness.

Children of the Earth was an evocation of American life which drew upon certain nativist literary traditions. Brown has attempted to alter existing stereotypes by creating a new formulation for the role which women played in the making of America. The play achieved immediate favorable recognition by Winthrop Ames, who was anxious to promote the work of American dramatists. He offered a $10,000 prize in 1913 for the best play submitted anonymously by an American author. Augustus Thomas, Adolph Klauber and Ames himself selected *Children of the Earth* from nearly seventeen thousand manuscripts. In 1915 the play ran for a disappointing thirty-four performances at the Booth Theatre in New York.

A salient fact about Brown, and authors like Neith Boyce and Susan Glaspell who also wrote about rural life, is that these women had left the small communities of their birth in order to participate in the theatrical life of New York City. Brown, for example, worked extensively with the Washington Square Players, who performed most of her one-act plays. The reality which pervades their work is the reality of remembered life seen through the prism of the cosmopolitan milieu which they had chosen. Part of this milieu was the avant-garde of a triumphant feminist movement.

The women they knew had fled the countryside in order to gratify their desires and instincts. Yet their plays reveal the life of farm women with reverence. While Zona Gale presented women as the triumphant moral arbiters of rural communities, city feminists saw farm women as nobly struggling to gain their rightful ascendancy. For city dwellers, the country became sentimentalized. They felt that it had natural values which were lost in the artificiality and materialism of urban life. In a sense they saw their own freedom as artificial. In the country, women coped with primordial realities. *Children of the Earth* had as its primary objective to show how a woman might transcend these realities. Her heroine gains ascendancy because Brown has made spiritual awakening an adequate tool for coping with sexual and material appetites. But Brown is quite obviously describing the ideal, rather than portraying the realities of rural life. Yet, it is precisely the ideal of woman's having natural moral superiority that informs three "realistic" about rural life which were written shortly after *Children of the Earth*.

Brown's own one-act *Sugar House* (1916), which Margaret Mayorga called "one of the best one-act plays that have been written in America,"[6] appears to be a realistic study of a married man who tries to set up housekeeping in an abandoned sugar house with his lover, a young girl. A mob comes to tar-and-feather the girl. The man's wife intercepts the mob, and by the use of moral persuasion manages to save the girl. Brown makes it abundantly clear that the crude men in the mob have no business meddling in the affairs of women. The husband recognizes that his wife has shown him the path of righteousness from which he must not stray.

Neith Boyce's *Winter's Night* and Susan Glaspell's *Trifles*, both written in 1916, also depict the harsh realities of rural life. Boyce and Glaspell share Brown's optimistic view of women's superior nature. But, unlike Brown, they do not depict happy reconciliations between their women characters and the men who would be agents of their oppression. Both Boyce's heroine, Rachel Wescott and Glaspell's, Minnie Wright, have, in effect, found personal freedom in their lives, but it is a freedom made possible only after the deaths of their husbands.

Rachel Wescott was married to her husband Daniel for twenty-eight years. During all this time the couple lived with Daniel's brother Jacob. Daniel has just died and Rachel confronts her brother-in-law with her plans for a new life:

> I've spent enough of my life here, Jacob, I never meant to stay here forever . . . I've had my ambitions, Jacob, and for all that I'm forty-seven I can't feel that my life's over yet.[7]

Jacob has silently loved Rachel and, with his brother's passing, assumes that he and Rachel will marry. However, Rachel intends to abandon Jacob despite his pleas that she either remain with him or take him with her. She is unsympathetic to his need for her and considers his proposal to be crazy. The situation can only end badly. Once rejected, there is nothing left for Jacob but to blow his head off with a shotgun.

This episode in the play serves to reveal fully the dark atmosphere enveloping the life that Rachel is escaping. The play is notable for the amount of sympathy the author directs toward Rachel and the cavalier way in which she disposes of Jacob. The two men in Rachel's life, her husband and her would-be lover, have existed only to be overcome before she can have a fuller life.

Rachel is unable to articulate why her life has been so barren. Yet Boyce makes it plain that Jacob is fundamentally wrongheaded in thinking that Rachel longed for a man's love. Rachel herself has been aware intuitively of a more profound need denied by her drab existence with Daniel and Jacob.

Boyce's thesis is that Rachel has been yearning for aesthetic fulfillment—the fulfillment available to ordinary women if only they will grasp for it.

Similarly, Glaspell's *Trifles* is about the drab existence of rural wives. Her biographer[8] describes the play as "precise realism," but the term "precise realism" is applied to two characters who never appear on the stage—John Wright, who has been murdered, and his wife, who murdered him. These characters are seen solely through the eyes of two women who accompany the men investigating Wright's death. Glaspell undoubtedly wanted the views expressed by Mrs. Hale, the neighbor's wife, and Mrs. Peters, the sheriff's wife, to be accepted as truth.

While the action of the play is an investigation, Glaspell has skillfully introduced what are two investigations. The men are simply looking for clues to a murder. Glaspell, with a touch of irony, has Mr. Hale remark at the beginning of the play that "women are used to worrying over trifles."[9] Unbeknown to Hale, it is such "trifles" which furnish the substance of the women's investigation.

In fact, it is the men who are, in Glaspell's eyes, interested in "trifles," like the identity of Wright's murderer. The women, on the other hand, with a finer grasp of ideal justice, realize that, although the murder of Wright was indeed "an awful thing," and a crime in the eyes of the law, that act was not the worst crime committed in the Wright house. The keynote to this is description of John Wright by one of the women as a man who "didn't drink, kept his word as well as most, I guess, and paid his debts. But he was a hard man. Just to pass the time of day with him [was] like a raw wind that gets to the bone."

The men are destined to hunt in vain for their clues; the women quickly find what the men have missed. This discovery is not an accident; it is the result of their peculiarly feminine sensibilities which enable them to recognize the importance of what they find, a bird with a broken neck. They guess that Wright killed it. "Wright wouldn't like the bird—a thing that sings. He killed that too." They realize that the bird's death might well have been Mrs. Wright's motive for murdering her husband. "If there'd been years and years of nothing, then a bird to sing to you, it would be awful—still, after the bird was. Still."

Glaspell introduces the idea that the truly "awful thing" was not the murder of John Wright but the life that his wife had been forced to endure, isolated in the Wright home. Because they have neglected Mrs. Wright, the women feel implicated in the greater crime. "Oh, I wish I'd come over here once in a while! That was a crime! . . . Who's going to punish that?"

In partial expiation, the women decide to hide the incriminating evidence. The men, as it happens, are on the right track in their investigation. "It's all perfectly clear except for a reason for doing it. But you know juries when it comes to women. If there was some definite thing . . . a thing that would connect up this strange way of doing things." Their concern with the details of the most readily apparent crime is, in Glaspell's eyes, proof of the superficial masculine view of criminal justice. They casually assume that the women feel as they do. "I guess they're not very dangerous things the ladies have picked up . . . Mrs. Peters doesn't need supervising. For that matter, a sheriff's wife is married to the law. Ever think of it that way, Mrs. Peters?" Truthfully Mrs. Peters replies, "Not—just that way."

In *Trifles* Glaspell has clearly pointed to the dichotomy between men and women in rural life. Men are basically insensitive to the nature of women's lives. More important than that, their proclivity for the letter of the law bars them from a humane understanding of justice. The two women, with their sense of higher purpose, band together to protect another woman from what is clearly the injustice of man's law when applied to women. Glaspell in effect condemns John Wright to death for being insensitive to his wife's aesthetic yearnings.

For critics like Arthur Hobson Quinn, folk drama had a different meaning. It comprised "a significant movement in this country which has to interpret the life of those natives of America who have retained the primitive culture of their ancestors, and whose emotions have remained in that inarticulate and unsophisticated state which allow them free expression and make them therefore well suited for the drama."[10]

Quinn's choice of a play to represent folk drama was Lula Vollmer's *Sun-Up*. This play not only presents primitive folk life located here in the mountains of North Carolina, but places the characters within the larger context of American civilization. Vollmer's heroine, Widow Cagle, reveals that most "primitive" women instinctively discover their essential bond with all other women. Both Widow Cagle and her son, Rufe, thrown by circumstances of World War I into contact with a larger civilization, instinctively formulate the then currently popular rationale for fighting the war.

Sun-Up is a notable departure from the other folk plays mentioned here, in that it places its characters within the framework of current events. Although first produced at the Provincetown Playhouse in 1923, the play was most probably written in 1918. Vollmer had come to New York that same year, at the height of America's war activity. The play was her response to the war while it was still going on. Burns Mantle reports that Vollmer's friends from the South brought her many stories of the reactions of Carolina mountain folk to the draft. "It took two weeks to get the play on paper but she spent the next five years in search of a producer."[11]

Lulu Vollmer's primitive North Carolinians eventually see the war as a means of preserving American ideals. In fact, the war is responsible for Widow Cagle's recognition that she has a common bond with all other mothers. "As long as thar air hate—there will be feuds. As long as thar air women thar will be—sons. I ain't no more to you than other mothers' sons air to them."[12] This theme, readily apparent to less primitive minds, is revealed to the Widow Cagle through her dead son's spiritual message. Her truly womanly nature is awakened. "I heared you, Rufe. I never knowed nothin' but about lovin' anything but ye—till ye showed me hit's lovin' them all that counts."

Widow Cagle, as an example of primitive life, begins by opposing any intrusion by the government into her life. When the sheriff comes to investigate the failure of two mountain youths, one of them Rufe, to register for the draft, Widow Cagle voices her negative feelings about the government. Rufe, however, has had some schooling. "That little bit o' larnin' taught me to respect something a little higher than my own way of wantin' to do things." It has equipped him to understand the need for going to war, even at the cost of his own life.

Rufe's unarticulated feeling of patriotism combines with the only other knowledge he possesses, also unarticulated, of the world beyond his home—religion. Armed with his knowledge of God and country, Rufe can face his mother when she tells him, "It seems a little queer to me that ye air goin' off to fight the Yankees with Zeb Turner, the man who killed yo Pap, still alive."

The point Vollmer is making is that, even though her characters are innocent to the point of simplicity, their intuitive reactions and instinctive wisdom in time of national crisis draw them to the stated purposes of the national government—a government whose very existence is mythical to them, "somethin' a little higher than my own way of wantin' to do things." The government is identical with the "somethin' different outen the Bible."

Before her turn to patriotism, the Widow Cagle makes a very shrewd political analysis of her own. "Thar ain't no reason fer war, unless us poor folks fight the rich uns for the way they air bleedin' us to death with prices for meat and bread." But the newly patriotic Widow Cagle discards these Marxist ideas. Patriotism, Vollmer suggests, brings out womanly sentiment.

Lula Vollmer was the American playwright whose work was most produced throughout the little theatre network, with *Sun-Up* her most popular play. *Sun-Up* brought folk drama into the larger context of American life. If the characters are unsophisticated, Vollmer's concept was not. It held that everything profoundly true must be simple enough to be understood by even the most primitive among us.

Theatregoers could identify with Vollmer's characters in the sense they represented American life in its purest form. Undoubtedly they served as an imaginative release from reality. Archetypes of the native American—simple, basically good, independent and free—they carry over to this day in popular literature, in cartoons and on television.

ANNE NICHOLS: $1,000,000.00 PLAYWRIGHT

Doris Abramson and Laurilyn Harris

If a young woman with an Irish surname marries a young man from a Jewish family, someone is bound to refer to her as "Abie's Irish Rose." Explanations are seldom necessary. The expression has become a cliché, firmly embedded in our language.

It found its way into our traditional speech by way of a play that opened on Broadway, May 23, 1922, and closed—over five years later—on October

22, 1927. Eventually, *Abie's Irish Rose* became something of a national institution. It set a record for consecutive performances (2,327) and held that record for fourteen years. After that comedy had been running three years, Lorenz Hart wrote lyrics for Richard Rodgers's song "Manhattan" that included the line: "Our future babies we'll take to *Abie's Irish Rose*. I hope they'll live to see it close—someday." When it reached its two thousandth performance, the *New York Telegraph* noted that a group of Jewish and Irish children in attendance were not even born when the play started its New York run. Milton Wallace, one of the actors in the company, had cards printed listing *Abie's Irish Rose* as his permanent address.

Who wrote this extraordinary popular hit? The multitudes who have heard of the play usually do not remember (or, more likely, never knew) that its author was a woman—a rather remarkable woman named Anne Nichols. It is estimated that from this single play she earned a million dollars in royalties as author and millions more as producer.[1] The movie rights alone brought in two million. In addition, she wrote over twenty other plays, numerous vaudeville sketches, and was an active producing-manager. Indeed, hers is perhaps one of the greatest commercial success stories in the history of the American theatre. "There were weeks when I made $180,000 net profit," she once told Arthur Gelb. "I bought stocks and bonds and most of Flushing."[2]

Strangely enough, Ms. Nichols's theatrical achievements have for the most part been either belittled or pointedly ignored. She is seldom mentioned in current theatre history textbooks. She rates no separate listing in standard reference works such as *The Oxford Companion to the Theatre* or *The Reader's Encyclopaedia of World Drama*. You won't find much attention devoted to her latest edition of the *Encyclopedia Britannica*, and the *Encyclopedia Americana* lists her name once (under the heading "Abie's Irish Rose"), while several paragraphs are devoted to the accomplishments of golfer Jack Nicklaus.[3]

This neglect may be the result of a deeply ingrained attitude shared by a number of male theatre critics and historians, an attitude perhaps best summed up by George Jean Nathan: "Even the best of our women playwrights falls considerably short of the mark of our best masculine . . . women, when it comes to the confection of drama, are most often inferior to their boyfriends."[4] Thus all American women playwrights, from Anna Cora Mowatt to Lillian Hellman, are casually dismissed as somehow "inferior" to their male counterparts, and one casualty of this bias is undoubtedly Anne Nichols. One has to search out old newspaper articles for any detailed information about her life and works. In most instances, she remains simply the name below the title of *Abie's Irish Rose*.

Anne Nichols was born in 1891 in Dale's Mill, Georgia, and reared in Philadelphia. Despite a rigid Baptist upbringing, her childhood ambition was to become an actress, and, at sixteen, she ran away from home with thirty-six dollars in her purse to pursue her ambition. Down to her last five dollars, she eventually landed a job as a dancer in a touring Biblical extravaganza called *The Shepherd King*. Then came several years of stock and vaudeville engagements, and marriage to a young actor, Henry Duffy. She decided to try writing when she realized that she and Henry were too impoverished to buy vaudeville sketches in which to perform. Her first effort, a melodramatic tearjerker, accidentally turned out to be funny, and the audience laughed hysterically. The embarrassed author fled to her dressing room, only to be met by the delighted theatre manager, who offered Anne her first important contract. That contract marked the beginning of Anne Nichols's career as a professional playwright.[5]

She wrote her first full-length play, *Heart's Desire* (1916), in collaboration with Adelaide Matthews. For various touring companies she wrote *The Man from Wicklow* (1917), *The Happy Cavalier* (1918), *A Little Bit Old-Fashioned* (1918) and *Springtime in Mayo* (1919). She also wrote the books for several musicals in 1919, among them *Linger Longer Letty*, which was constantly revived by its star, Charlotte Greenwood, throughout the twenties and thirties. (Eventually, under the title *I Want a Sailor*, it became Bob Hope's first starring vehicle.) For Fiske O'Hara, with whose company she had toured as far back as 1915, she wrote *Down Limerick Way* (1920) and *Marry in Haste* (1921). She again collaborated with Adelaide Matthews to write *Just Married*, which opened in New York in April 26, 1921, broke all stock company records in New York, Chicago and London, and was apparently made into a movie three times.[6] In one of her infrequent interviews, Ms. Nichols wryly observed that although both *Linger Longer Letty* and *Just Married* were running on Broadway when *Abie's Irish Rose* opened there in 1922, people persisted in congratulating her on *Abie's* success by saying, "Weren't you lucky to have your first play turn out to be such a hit!"[7]

But *Abie's Irish Rose*, while certainly not her first play, nor even her first successful play, was to overshadow all her other work. For it was the kind of popular hit that attracted a great deal of attention and engendered considerable critical response. So, to her surprise and dismay, the author found that she could never again be anyone but "that woman who wrote *Abie's Irish Rose*."[8]

She got the initial idea for the play from Fiske O'Hara, who told her about a young Jewish friend who had pretended his Irish Catholic fiancée was Jewish in order to win his Orthodox father's approval of their marriage. After the wedding, however, the father discovered the truth and rushed in horror from his son's house. Anne Nichols recalled later that the story made a strong impression on her: "I couldn't stop thinking about that mixed alliance, and all the prejudices which it brought in its wake." Ten minutes after the O'Haras left, she sat down to work on the play that was to become *Abie's Irish Rose*. She wrote steadily for three days and most of three nights. Her intention, she said, was "to write a play which might serve to overcome religious bigotry."[9] *Abie*, like all her best work, would be a comedy, but underlying the humor would be a serious message—a plea for religious tolerance.

At first glance, *Abie's Irish Rose* seemed unlikely to cause much of a stir in the theatrical world. The plot was amusing but unpretentious, revolving around the difficulties encountered by Rose Mary Murphy and Abraham Levy in their quest for some semblance of a normal wedding and a happy married life. The complications, including two belligerent fathers-in-law (each of whom makes Archie Bunker look like a model of tolerance), two well-meant deceptions (Abie introduces Rose to his father as Rosie Murpheski; Rose tells her father that she is marrying one Michael Magee), and three frenetic wedding ceremonies (one Methodist, one Jewish, one Catholic), are finally resolved when Rose and Abie manage to produce twins, an event which turns their hostile fathers into doting grandfathers, willing to take the first tentative steps toward tolerance and understanding.

Abie could hardly be characterized as an overnight success. The author spent three years just trying to get her play onstage, but it was rejected by every producer from New York to Hollywood. Finally, Oliver Morosco agreed to try it out on the West Coast. Nevertheless, despite its success there, Morosco was reluctant to attempt a New York production.[10] Ms. Nichols then took matters into her own hands. She mortgaged her home and used the money to produce the play herself at the Fulton Theatre.[11] The initial New York reaction to *Abie's Irish Rose* was lukewarm. Reviews were mixed, though not all were hostile (for example, William B. Chase, reviewer for the *New York Times*, liked the play and hoped for a long run).[12] But the stinging adverse remarks of other well-known critics such as Percy Hammond, Robert Benchley and Heywood Broun did affect the early reception of the play, and box-office receipts suffered.[13] However, Ms. Nichols sank every cent she had into the production, the actors took a salary cut, ticket prices were reduced, and *Abie* managed to keep going for two shaky months until it suddenly caught on with the theatre-going public.[14] The play that Benchley disparaged as the worst in town was on its way to becoming, in the words of George Jean Nathan, "the fourth biggest industry in the United States."[15]

Not that the critics gave up—in fact, some relentlessly hounded the play for the entire five years of its run. Most memorable were the barbs of Robert Benchley. Faced with the task of writing an original description of the play every week for *Life* magazine, the formidable Benchley produced mini-critiques such as, "We understand that a performance of this play in Modern dress is now under way."[16]

Other critics were less clever but equally cutting. Some were disturbed and mystified by the success of such an "undistinguished" play, and wrote lengthy essays in which they solemnly tried to analyze the "secret" of *Abie's* popularity. To George Jean Nathan, the source of the play's success lay in its indebtedness to burlesque sketches such as the popular *Krausmeyer's Alley*.[17] To Robert Littell, it seemed significant that *Abie* "is nice to everybody . . . There is no villain. Everybody on the stage is likeable"; yet, puzzled, he concluded "there must be a deeper reason than all these, a more human, a more subtle one."[18] The author herself put it more simply: "It has the love element, the comedy, and it tells facts, but tells them with a smile."

Anne Nichols had created a well-constructed blend of broad humor, sentiment and gentle caricature and audiences loved it. In addition to the Broadway production, there were performances of *Abie's Irish Rose* all over the United States and Canada. One company was in London; another in Sydney, Australia. The play was performed in Europe in French, German, Spanish,

Portuguese, Swedish and Russian. It was seen in China with an all-Chinese cast. It played eight months to packed houses in Berlin (Hitler didn't like it).[19] There were two New York revivals (1937 and 1954), two film versions (1928 and 1946) and a weekly radio show in the early 1940s. Touring companies continued to stage *Abie* for decades. As Ms. Nichols once said, "It has never stopped playing somewhere."[20]

But ironically, *Abie's* success was to prove a very mixed blessing for Anne Nichols. After an interview with her, Arthur Gelb wrote: "It brought its author spectacular fame and fortune—earning her more money than any single play has ever earned for a writer. But it also put a permanent crimp in her literary career, [and] hounded her personal life for four decades . . . "[21] She went on to write, direct and produce other plays after *Abie's Irish Rose*, but she gradually found herself forced to devote more and more time to the comedy she and others called her "million dollar hit."[22] One problem was that she genuinely loved and believed in her play, and felt compelled to keep an eye on it. "No matter what else I was trying to work on, I had a compulsion to check up on the various companies," she said. "And invariably I'd find that the minute my back was turned, the actors would start distorting the play by ad-libbing lines for laughs. I had to travel back and forth across the country constantly to keep them in check. I hardly found time to write anymore."[23]

Then there were numerous legal battles, starting with Oliver Morosco's attempt to get an injunction to stop the play's opening in New York.[24] He failed, but later there was trouble with contracts, with booking agents, with managers trying to cheat her. She became involved in lawsuits to collect the money due her. In 1929 she sued the Universal Pictures Corporation for $3 million, charging that they had used her play as the basis for their film *The Cohens and the Kellys*. She lost the case when that eminently perverse critic George Jean Nathan testified that the theme of young lovers thwarted by their parents went all the way back to *Romeo and Juliet*. The court then ruled that the idea had been used so often it was in the public domain.[25]

In 1962 she told Arthur Gelb, "I've always been haunted by the ghost of *Abie's Irish Rose*." She was trying to live quietly (she had divorced Duffy in 1924 and her son was living in California), but people still kept trying to meet her, to interview her, "wanting to know what makes me tick." In order to work in peace on her autobiography, *Such Is Fame*, she had finally withdrawn to the seclusion of Harwich, Massachusetts. Fearing further interruptions, she asked Gelb not to reveal where she was, stating that she needed about another three months of peace and quiet to complete the book.[26] One wonders if she ever got them. When she died four years later, her once-huge fortune substantially reduced by the Depression and medical bills, the autobiography was apparently still unfinished.

SOPHIE TREADWELL: AGENT FOR CHANGE

Louise Heck-Rabi

As an agent for change in American drama, Sophie Treadwell never ceased to be challenged by ways of arriving at something different and something new. As a dramatist, she did not identify the type of play she could do best and then refine that form until it was adjusted to that equipoise of playwright's intention and audience acceptance a commercially successful play required. She was never to find the best type of play for her to write to achieve commercial success, as did Maxwell Anderson and Rachel Crothers, for example. Nor could she identify what was best in her work and utilize that aspect of her talent to author hit plays.

There is an endearing lack of deliberation and calculation in Treadwell's addressing herself to what was different and new in the writing of drama. She seems to have been temperamentally bound to an honesty that hurt. She kept up a frenzied work pace as she turned her dramatic impulses into a stage script which she would then refine, adjust, revise up to the opening night or the first rejection from an agent or producer. She would continue to make changes as she marketed her plays. Even over a period of years she would work on a script because she believed in her plays. Once done, however, she would not return to a type of dramatic composition she had already attempted. Indeed, the longhand first draft of a play was always something different, something new.

Her role as agent for change stems from these ongoing new attempts. From the laboratory of her temperament and talent, she would switch from one kind of play to another. These creative shifts were a counterpart to the many moves and changes of address in her personal life. The restlessness impelling her dramatic experiments and the rootlessness of her life experiences combined to cast her in the role of transformer of dramatic writing for the stage.

For Saxaphone [sic] is the most innovative of Treadwell's works. She was intrigued by the prospect of hitting upon a novel amalgamation of music, film and dialogue which audiences would like. She sang and had written for films. The combination of her knowledge of music, film and stage plus her proclivity for innovation resulted in the composition of *For Saxaphone*.

After *Machinal* Treadwell probably wanted to move on to a film-writing career where she could try out the new talking picture medium and also bring home good salary checks. In Box 27 of her papers in the Special Collections of the University of Arizona Library at Tucson, there are six scenarios and two filmscripts. These are labeled "Work for United Artists;" one is titled *New York Nights*. She obviously thought that with the growing popularity of radio and talking pictures in the early 1930s, musical plays would become more successful than straight plays. A musical play rather than a musical comedy is what *For Saxaphone* is. Its use of constantly changing musical sound, frequent lighting and staging shifts and unusual visual and verbal presences, suggest that the play may be more suited to the cinema than to the stage. The technical challenge of the play is, in itself, complex and forbidding. *For Saxaphone*, which was copyrighted June 4, 1934, is a musical mutation of *Machinal*. It centers on a protagonist who is given a core character, Lilly and her three satellite selves. The play follows a progression of her life experiences.

Treadwell's preface to an early version of *For Saxaphone* best explains artistic intentions for the play:

> The script is written to be played with an almost unbroken musical accompaniment. It is really words for music. I did this because I think our audiences' nerves, tuned to pictures and radio, now almost demand it of any entertainment. The music is for the most part typical of music today,—where a saxophone is much heard, but there are also parts of a Brahms Symphony, some Viennese waltzes, Hungarian gypsy innovations, etc.
>
> Also much use is made of voices (of people not seen)—bits of conversation here and there—incomplete—suggestive. I thought this gave a certain way to develop the story as well as giving the whole thing the living effect of something overheard. Anyway, our audiences are now trained to it through radio and have come, I think, to like it. The dialogue is written in a short repetitious rhythm, where I tried to create the empty, blatant blah effect of most of our talk today.
>
> The play is done in fourteen scenes, all of which go one into the other through lights, voices and music, as [sic] that the effect is of something seen, moving-by and something overheard—from all of which, a bit here and a bit there, inconsequential and seemingly unrelated, the audience discovers—writes the play.
>
> All the scenes are planned to be done in different light spots— pools of light on a dark stage—no scenery—a door or a window, when necessary, set up as a separate piece—very little furniture— very few props. It must all create a sense of luxury and taste and the clothes, especially Lilly's, must be exquisite. In fact, her role is a sort of kaleidoscope of a beautiful girl in beautiful clothes.
>
> To stand any chance at all the play must have an exceptional young actress to play Lilly, She must be young and she must be able to create a special mood around herself—a special aura (as some children—doomed to die in childhood—seem to do).

The four characters who comprise the central figure dominate the play, but in all versions Lilly remains the protagonist, while Minnie, Billie, Gilly dart in and out of the action. Chronicling Lilly's reaction to the events of her life as they swirl past her, the play deals chronologically with these happenings, as in *Machinal*. Treadwell's experiments focus on dividing these activities into scenes. From the fourteen scenes in the earlier versions, Treadwell pared the phases of Lilly's life to eight to be performed in two acts of four scenes each.

In Version Eight there is Act I: Engagement, Wedding, Honeymoon, Moon and Act II: Married, Knife, Flight, Flight's End.

In each version, Lilly's death is prefigured when a knife appears in the hands of a male exhibition dancer who is an accomplished knife-thrower. In all versions of the play Lilly is knifed by this dancer at the final curtain. In Version Five, dated December 1941, Lilly is not slain; she dances with a young man after her dancer-lover has departed.

As the characters sit at cabaret tables before and after the exhibition dancing, they converse about personalities in the newspapers, particularly current film favorites: Clark Gable, Ronald Colman, George Raft and Rudy Vallee. Events of the day also emerge in the chitchat, lending a topicality to the play which may now cause it to seem dated. Treadwell lists in her cast of unnamed characters those seen and heard, those heard and not seen (voices) and characters seen, but not heard (visual presences).

Given the experimental factors in the play, the intricacies and difficulties to be anticipated in the sound plot and light plot, plus the difficulties of casting a first-rank Lilly, as well as finding a knife-throwing dancer and other carnival performers, *For Saxaphone* was obviously not a commercially viable product. Treadwell knew this, but, nonetheless, she tried to sell it as a stage or motion picture property. She failed, but the comments of those who rejected it afford a critical look at its strengths and weaknesses.

Treadwell first approached Arthur Hopkins with *For Saxaphone*; he relayed the script to William James Fadiman, a reader for Sam Goldwyn, Inc. in New York. Fadiman wrote the following letter to Hopkins on December 12, 1935:

> This play by Sophie Treadwell is most unusual and might even be called eccentric. The novelty and marked freshness of the background, setting, accompaniment and fusion of these elements with the story are factors that remain exciting in themselves but occasionally hamper the fluid narration of the story . . .
>
> Since the fundamental *raison d'être* of this play is the unique rhythmic synchronization of dialogue with sets and characters, it seems difficult to imagine an important actress subordinating herself to these theatrical requirements . . . I am afraid its presentation on the screen, depending as it does upon sheer story-line, would lose much of the bizarre construction that Miss Treadwell presents in the stage version . . .

On April 20, 1937, Treadwell's agent Richard J. Madden in New York wrote this letter to Treadwell in Los Gatos, California, about the fate of *For Saxaphone*:

> . . . I wonder if you ever heard from Bobby Jones [Robert Edmond Jones], who was almost frothy at the mouth here before he left for

abroad over your *For Saxaphone*. He declared to me that he absolutely "must produce" that play in autumn but at the moment he could not tell where in the world he would get the money except that it must be gotten. Of course, I think it would be swell if Bobby could follow up his promise and enthusiasm with performance. He is expected back here in a few weeks and I know, one of the first things he will devote himself to will be the promotion of *Saxaphone*.

We had, through our coast office, some very exciting correspondence concerning a coast production by one of the Federal Theatre groups out there but I discouraged it, in view of Mr. Jones' attitude . . .

Temporarily defeated, Treadwell replied to Madden from Old Trees Ranch, Stockton, California, on August 28, 1937:

Dear Dick, I got your letter today, and I'm really grateful that you are are not tired of me and mine, but my decision about the script has not changed. I know that you have had them read by all the men that count and that's that—they did not catch. I want them back now . . . In the meantime, *Saxaphone* is really not available. Just four days ago—unforeseen—out of the blue—I had a wire from a friend—in the theatre but not a producer—asking for a short option—which I gave—gladly. Mr. Hopkins gave him the play to read two years ago, but nothing came of it—until this wire.—So that is that.

It seems to be a law with me in everything that I never get anything—not even a chance at anything—until I completely give up . . .

The identity of this friend cannot be gleaned from the papers, but late correspondence testifies to the fact that Robert Edmond Jones remained enthusiastic about *For Saxaphone*, and for a period of three years tried to stage it, but it was in vain.

On April 26, 1940, Jones wrote in longhand to Treadwell from Villa Riposa, Santa Barbara, California, a letter which describes their working relationship and mutual concern over the play:

. . . I think the thing for you to do is to forget about mechanical devices and let *me* worry about the inner and outer along the lines you outline. Don't put down any directions for scenery at all. Let the drama secrete its own form as a nautilus secretes its shell. Something entirely new might happen, never seen in the theatre before— . . . I have always maintained that its only fault (silly word!) from a box office point of view is that it seems a depressed play—not tragic, but depressed. There is nothing wrong with this except that I don't think people would try to see it, and yet there is no adequate experimental theatre where such things could be put on. I dreamed of it for Central City once, but the backers there can't see anything that isn't in the festival spirit. However, *Saxaphone* is perhaps beside the point—I am leaving for New York—address 1 East 53d St. Keep in touch with me. All best in haste Bobby.

Treadwell replied to him May 8:

> The new version of *Saxaphone* on its way to you . . . (The depression of which you spoke to me—and so justly—is surely not in it any more—because the depression is not in me any more.)
>
> You will, of course, see that the form of the thing had come to me from the motion picture and the radio. I think all plays will soon be played to music—whether they are written to be or not. Surely music plays a mighty role in the patience and absorption of a motion picture audience.—Consider sitting before some of that tripe in quietness' [sic] submitting to silence . . .
>
> I have tried to use these things—that have proven their mass entertainment value—to make a real SHOW. If you would like it and do it,—it could be an amazingly beautiful show,—perhaps a great show.

Some five years later, Treadwell tried again. She wrote a brief note, quoted in its entirety here, to Richard Rodgers. Dated March 4, 1942, it does not mention a play title, but does deal with a play with music.

> Dear Mr. Rodgers, I am sending you today the first act of a play I am working on. I am thinking of it as being played to continual music. Would you look through it and let me know what you think of it? Something you said—casually—at Terry's [Theresa Helburn] last Sunday gave me the courage to send this along to you. I hope you do not find it any kind of an intrusion upon your time. I hope you may like i [sic] Cordial regards to you and Mrs. Rodgers, Sincerely,

We do not know if this play was a new venture or *For Saxaphone*. There is no letter of reply from Rodgers in the Papers.

In 1947, Treadwell was relentlessly seeking a producer. Henry Souvaine thought well of *Saxaphone* and his letter comments astutely upon the form of the play:

> I was very happy that I was given the opportunity to read your play *For Saxaphone*. Certainly this is beautifully written and an extremely professional job of creating believable theatrical illusion.
>
> Technically, your form of projecting the plot development was, to me, continuously interesting. In fact, I wonder if the producers of *Allegro* didn't have a little thought communion with your writing studio in Newtown. It is a little unfortunate that *Allegro* appeared on

Broadway before your play, although the similarities in technical treatment are nothing more than a coincidence . . .

Did Treadwell anticipate the Broadway musical play in *For Saxaphone*? Probably not. But her good judgment of the necessary properties for a novel form for the stage or screen has been proved by the multimedia and total theatre shows of the 60s, and she accurately predicted the ubiquitous popularity of music in all stage and cinematic works.

GERTRUDE STEIN: FORM AND CONTENT

Betsy Alayne Ryan

Gertrude Stein's disruption of the alternate reality—or fiction—of the traditional theatre is the unifying principle of all her plays, regardless of period. Insofar as she was able to accomplish this disruption, she rooted the experience of the spectator in the theatrical present, avoiding what she termed "syncopation," and established an immediate relationship between the spectator and the physical world of the stage. This relationship involved no identification with a fiction onstage, but a detachment from it and a focus upon the surface of the theatre experience.

If this description seems to bear some resemblance to the intent of Brecht, it is best to take the analogy no further, for Brecht rendered social and political realities for overtly utilitarian ends. Stein's concerns, on the other hand, lay solely in the realm of epistemology. Interested less in political and social questions than in everyday reality, she sought to transmit her knowledge simply and directly to another mind. This is not to say that her position was not political. As Marcuse has said, "The political potential of art lies only in its own aesthetic dimension."

Stein's plays are first and foremost attempts to call attention to the theatre experience. Forty-one of them refer often enough to themselves and to Stein's writing process to be considered metaplays, or plays about plays. Her inclusion of process as an integral part of her plays makes most of them self-referential at some point.

The fictional aspect of the theatre is undermined by this self-reference. Once a play refers to itself as a play, the spectator acknowledges his presence in a theatre, and disengages from the fictional character of the proceedings. Contrary to traditional practice since the Renaissance, which posited the unreal (a flat painted in perspective) as the real (a town square), Stein posits the actual presence of actors and spectator as real.

Stein's plays are not pure attempts at metaplay, however. All of them have subject matter, however sketchy or disrupted.

Stein's plays can be said to reflect nine broad categories of subject matter: identity, mystery, domestic life, conversation, war, movement, nature, sex, love and religion. Most of the plays, save the ones concerned with identity, should be considered less explorations of topics than distillations of her life concerns.

Domestic life of some kind comprises subject matter of forty-three plays from *White Wines* in 1913 to *The Mother of Us All* in 1946. Stein's overriding concern in these plays, most of which reflect her own household, was in capturing the essence of day-to-day living.

References, usually veiled, to love and sexuality are made in fourteen plays from *Old and Old* (1913) to *Yes Is for a Very Young Man* (1944–1946). These generally take the form of descriptions of Stein's own relationship with Alice Toklas, and become quite explicit once it is understood that her euphemism for orgasm was "cow," and that Alice's nickname for her was "baby."

Nature provides the subject matter for forty plays and ranges from oblique references to birds, animals and landscapes to plays based entirely on nature imagery. Nature was obviously a source of delight and comfort to Stein, and forms the basis of what she termed her landscape plays, many of which are set in an actual nature landscape.

Stein's preoccupation with movement within a landscape finds expression in the subject matter of thirty-two plays.

Twenty-two plays, most of them occurring between 1915 and 1919, reflect Stein's preoccupation with conversation to such a degree that they can be considered metaplays. The number and variety of subjects combined with an overriding dialogue perspective makes these plays intensely conversational in tone.

War is the subject matter of ten plays. *Yes Is for a Very Young Man* (1944–1946) is the most complete depiction of life in wartime, the domestic situation, the love affair and the war itself sketched with a thoroughness not approached in her other plays. The play deals specifically with the activities of the French Resistance and Marshal Petain's "toy" army.

Religion is the subject matter for four plays: *Lend a Hand or Four Religions* (1922), which presents four religions (first through fourth) as personages in a nature landscape, and *Four Saints in Three Acts* (1927), *Saints and Singing* (1922) and *A Saint in Seven* (1922), all of which sketch the saintly life. Stein was interested in saints primarily because of their self-contained existence, their ability to simply be. The use of saints emphasized her static art since she could render them most completely, she felt, by not showing them doing anything.

Seven of her plays are mysteries. The mystery play is a prototype for all of Stein's plays, since she avoids presenting connections between events in all her plays in the few instances that events occur. Anyone who faces the plays and attempts an explanation spends much time reflecting upon what she so deliberately makes ambiguous and equivocal for the sake of her static art. The danger lies in positing meanings and connections for plays that depend on non-connections and non-significance for their very existence.

The subject matter explored most intensively in the plays is identity vs. entity, the overriding concern of her life and art. Does the essence of a person or thing depend upon its connections with extraneous things or upon a quality that issues from within? If the latter is the case how does one establish it? How does one really know who one is? *Identity a Play* (1935) is the first play to approach the question with any thoroughness. Written just three years after her first move into narrative (1932), it addresses directly the question of identity, and indirectly, perhaps, the question of her own integrity during this phase of her career. *Identity a Play* explores the ramifications of the deceptively simple Mother Goose rhyme "I am I because my little dog knows me."

Doctor Faustus Lights the Lights considers the subject in a different way. Doctor Faustus has sold his soul for the knowledge of electric light, and doubts the wisdom of that move from the beginning of the play. In fact, he desires complete darkness after all the light he has seen.

The parallels between the situation Faust finds himself in and Stein's own in the "identity" segment of her career—the time in which she exchanged the complete solitude of some twenty years of writing for recognition by an audience—are imperative to note. After writing her widely disseminated *Autobiography of Alice B. Toklas* and *Everybody's Autobigraphy* in the early thirties, she wrote often about the consequences of fame for a writer, wondering openly in plays and theoretical writings whether it was possible to retain any sense of self in the glare of publicity and with the ever-present awareness of audience expectation.

After the notoriety brought by her identity writing of the 1930s, Stein never wrote so clearly again. To write well, as she stated from the beginning of her career, a writer must have as little sense of her audience as possible. In her later plays, Stein sought to combine writing as it is written with writing according to someone else's point of view. She withdrew from her audience to a large extent to accomplish this, and regained, at least in part, a solitude from which she could write.

There is subject matter in every one of Stein's plays, no matter how skeletal or veiled. As she said of painting, "The minute painting gets abstract it gets pornographic. That is a fact." Her plays always emerge from first-hand contact with things or persons. Still, the subject matter seems to be simple indeed, except for the few plays which explore in detail philosophical questions relating to identity and war. In fact, it is so very simple and multifaceted (ninety-nine percent of the plays reflect combinations of subject matter) that it can hardly be said to distract to any great degree from the surface of the theatre experience. Fictional though the plays are, they present only fleeting fictions, brief evocations of topics for the spectator to take in as he moves on.

Stein's innovation lies in her disruption of the alternate reality of the stage through manipulations of form and subject matter, both of which she expresses in essence, moment by moment, and forces to relate spatially within the landscape of the theatre. Through techniques of juxtaposition, repetition, modification, rhyme, simple language and monotonous sentence structure she is able to keep the focus of the spectator on the present moment of perception.

Through her use of hermeticism, non-logical expression, multiple perspective and multiple stories, she achieves movement within her plays and confines the attention of the spectator to his experience in the theatre. Only four of her plays . . . even risk transporting that attention to fictional stage reality, and those plays need to be considered departures from her general technique and aesthetic.

THE COMIC MUSE OF MARY CHASE

Albert Wertheim

When Mary Coyle Chase won the Pulitzer Prize in Drama in 1945 for her comedy *Harvey*, she was only the fourth woman to win that prize since its founding in 1918. Zona Gale had received the prize in 1921 for the dramatization of her novel *Miss Lulu Bett*; Susan Glaspell for *Alison's House*, a play based on the life of Emily Dickinson, in 1931; and Zoe Akins for *The Old Maid* in 1935. What sets Mary Chase immediately apart from these other woman dramatists is that she does not in her three major plays—*Harvey* (1944), *Mrs. McThing* (1952) and *Bernardine* (1952)—deal with the plight of women in society, and she is, moreover, a writer of highly imaginative comedy. A longtime resident of Denver, Colorado and environs, Mary Chase does not write about New York or other East Coast cities, but sets her plays in what might be any medium-sized mid-American city, though Denver is probably her model. By freeing herself from specific social or political issues and by casting off the restraints of geography, she is able deftly and sometimes brilliantly to use her comic art to present man's eternal conflict between his imaginative world and the constricting world of social forms and social realities. Although at first glance a seemingly lighthearted dramatic gewgaw, a play like *Harvey* shares a common theme with such overtly serious works as Eugene O'Neill's *The Iceman Cometh*, Philip Barry's *Hotel Universe*, or Tennessee Williams's *Glass Menagerie*. Mary Chase's comedies, particularly *Harvey*, deserve the serious treatment they have not yet received from critics and even from their more enthusiastic reviewers.

One is tempted to say, and perhaps with some justification, that, written and produced during wartime, *Harvey* must surely have had immediate appeal to audiences weaned by the grim realities of global war and, consequently, eager to find escape in the fantasy world that Mary Chase offered.[1] Elwood P. Dowd, who takes leave of the worldly society represented by his sister Veta, his niece Myrtle Mae and their friends to share a life with a pooka, an invisible six-foot rabbit, is doing no more, one might argue, than the audiences of 1944 and 1945, who took leave of Germany, Japan and Italy to spend a few enjoyable hours with Elwood and his invisible friend Harvey. Though these judgments may well be true, the fact that *Harvey* has survived beyond the World

War II era, that it is still being successfully performed and enjoyed today, seems proof that the play has more than mere escapism to recommend it.

A usual procedure of comedy is to laugh at the illusions of comedy's central characters and, finally, to restore them to the level-headed, normative thinking of society. In Molière, for example, the Orgons, Argans and M. Jourdains must surrender their illusions and self-delusions to the worldly right reason of the Cléantes and Cléontes. In Mary Chase's *Harvey*, the usual procedure is reversed and we find ourselves identifying positively with the benign fantasy world of Elwood P. Dowd and his pooka, and rejecting the everyday world of social forms and social norms. And it is precisely that everyday, normal world that is the object of Mrs. Chase's satire and the butt of her comedy.[2]

The method of Mary Chase's comic art is one that step by step exposes the ridiculous stiltedness, meanness and sterility of what one might call "normal" or "expected" social behavior. To foster her increasingly negative picture of normalcy, she makes her audience laugh at the comic posturing, insensitivity and stupidity of "good society" and of the arbiters of normalcy, the psychiatrist and his staff. At the same time, she builds up, both in the audience and in her stage characters, an increasing affection for the eccentric Elwood and his invisible friend. It is Mary Chase's triumph that before her play is over, Harvey has become as real to Elwood's sister Veta Louise, to Dr. Chumley, the psychiatrist, and to the theatre audience as he is to Elwood himself. The transference of allegiance through comedy from the world of reason to Elwood's eccentric world of imagination and fantasy is Mary Chase's triumph and marks her sense that the imaginative, visionary world is finally more estimable than the often hollow world of manners.

Appropriately, *Harvey* begins as a comedy of manners but one in which the audience is not made to laugh, as is the usual manners comedy rule, at the outsider but at polished society itself. The curtain rises on a comic picture of the *beau monde* as it exists in Middle America. Veta Louise Simmon and her daughter Myrtle Mae are giving a ladies tea complete with a laughably off-key soprano singing "I'm Called Little Buttercup." She is accompanied by an equally untalented pianist. With the sour notes of the songstress in the background, Veta Louise, full of self-importance, is describing her fete to the society editor of the local newspaper. Both the scene and the dialogue deftly satirize the world of society ladies and the clichés of society column rhetoric:

> . . . a tea and reception for the members of the Wednesday Forum. You might say—program tea. My mother, you know—the late Marcella Pinney Dowd, pioneer cultural leader—she came here by ox-team as a child and she founded the Wednesday Forum . . . Miss Myrtle Mae Simmons looked charmingly in a modish Rancho Rose toned crepe, picked up at the girdle with a touch of magenta on emerald . . . The parlors and halls are festooned with smilax.[3]

Into this caricatured depiction of a high society occasion and into a room dominated by the severe portrait of the late Marcella Pinney Dowd, "pioneer cultural leader," saunters the dreamy, light-footed, socially uncaring Elwood P. Dowd. His gait, his manner and his unfashionable attire immediately single him out as an outsider in the world of social teas and Wednesday Forums. To Veta Louise's stilted telephone conversation with the society column editor is immediately juxtaposed Elwood's delightful and delightfully unpretentious telephone conversation with Miss Elsie Greenawalt, a woman unknown to Dowd who is selling magazine offers to his invisible companion presumably sitting alongside him on the couch. He promptly invites the strange telephone saleswoman to his sister's party as well. The mental delight conjured up at the thought of Elsie Greenawalt's making an appearance at Veta's socially preten-tious tea helps pit Elwood's unaffected, affable world against the pretentious-ness and off-key singing of Veta's.

Although Miss Greenawalt never materializes, Elwood himself comically crashes his sister's festivities. His encounter with Mrs. Chauvenet, society matron and society leader "dressed with the casual sumptuousness of a wealthy Western society woman—in silvery gold and plush, and mink scarf even though it is a spring day," is deliciously comic. Having run through the social forms of inquiring after Elwood's health and inviting him to dinner, Mrs. Chauvenet is rendered speechless as Elwood proceeds to introduce her to his six-foot, invisible pooka. While Mrs. Chauvenet darts from the room aghast, Elwood and Harvey proceed to the parlor, where the invisible giant rabbit will duly be introduced to the remainder of Veta's socially prominent, shocked guests. The comic confrontation between polished society's decorum and Elwood's fancies is brilliantly made at the close of the play's first scene, in which Elwood reaches for a bottle of liquor hidden behind a handsomely bound book in the library. The volume that has served as a screen for Elwood's pint bottle of spirits is, of all things, a deluxe, limited edition of Jane Austen. In a wonderful comic stroke, Mary Chase lets Jane Austen, the novelist most clearly associated with the world of polite society, stand in for the whole world of decorous behavior and become the comic foil to Elwood and his alcohol-inspired but nonetheless charming invisible companion.

During the first scene of *Harvey*, Mary Chase wittily satirizes normal social behavior and *society* in the limited sense of that term used in newspaper columns to describe the aristocratic world. Moving from Veta Louise Simmons's drawing room in scene one to a mental hospital, Chumley's Rest, in scene two, the satire begins to encompass a new and enlarged target. In her comic treatment of the sanitarium to which Veta hopes to commit her idio-syncratic, socially unacceptable brother, Mrs. Chase calls into question the ability of psychiatrists to define what is meant by normal behavior within *soci-ety*, in the more general application of that word, and to ask as well whether what the psychiatrists imply is normalcy is truly a desirable state.

A farcical misdiagnosis by the admitting psychiatrist at Chumley's Rest, Dr. Sanderson, results in a scene laden with comic irony as Sanderson assumes that Veta is in need of admission to Chumley's Rest and that Elwood, her charmingly "normal" brother, is quite understandably committing her. That Veta is forcibly carried off, stripped and put through the rigors of hydro-tubs is her comic punishment for seeking to expose Elwood to these things. More important, however, the action satirizes and exposes the psychiatric establishment that would excise all idiosyncratic behavior, reducing humanity to some preconceived idea of uniform, monolithic normalcy. The psychological jargon so freely employed at Chumley's Rest is an analogous, but insidious version of the jargon found in society columns. The psychiatrists, as arbiters of what is proper in society, are the sinister cousins of society columnists.

The ability of Elwood and Harvey to best the psychiatric staff at Chumley's Rest is a clear comic victory, as the humiliated Dr. Chumley screams at his blundering assistant:

> Doctor—the function of a psychiatrist is to tell the difference between those who are reasonable, and those who merely talk and act reasonably. Do you realize what you have done to me? You don't answer. I'll tell you. You have permitted a psychopathic case to walk off these grounds and roam around with an over-grown white rabbit. You have subjected me—a psychiatrist—to the humiliation of having to call—of all things—a lawyer to find out who came out here to be committed—and who came out here to commit!

But of course Dr. Sanderson's error in judgment is not altogether an error, for Elwood Dowd has far more human feeling, social grace and love of life than his sister or than the psychiatric staff, the arbiters of normalcy, themselves. And as the first scene of *Harvey* ends with the triumph of Elwood and Harvey over the world of good society as represented by Jane Austen, so at the conclusion of the second scene Elwood and Harvey triumph once more. In accord with the widened satiric focus of the second scene, the Jane Austen volume of the first scene is replaced with the published record of civilization itself, the encyclopedia.

Once again Mary Chase supplies a coup de théâtre as the first act curtain comes down on Wilson, the mental hospital orderly, looking up *pooka* in the encyclopedia:

> P-o-o-k-a. "Pooka. From old Celtic mythology. A fairy spirit in animal form. Always very large. The pooka appears here and there, now and then, to this one and that one at his own caprice. A wise but mischievous creature. Very fond of rum-pots, crack-pots and how are you, Mr. Wilson?" How are you, Mr. Wilson? Who in the encyclopedia wants to know? Oh—the hell with it!

The invisible presence of Harvey usurps the pages of the encyclopedia, the product of the Age of Reason, asserting himself and his world of imagination, myth, rum-pots and crack-pots.

In large part, *Harvey* abounds in comic irony as Elwood P. Dowd and his long-eared pooka seem increasingly amiable and rational amid the rest of the characters of the play who are lost in the insane chaos produced by Mary

Chase's excellent farce.[4] Elwood's innocent and accepting attitude, further-more, increasingly wins audience affection, so that audience laughter is directed against the supposedly sane world and audience applause toward Elwood and his imaginary rabbit. In short, Harvey becomes more real than the dramatic caricatures onstage, and the audience, therefore, comes not only to approve of Elwood's fantasy but to share it. Harvey's triumph is made manifest when the portrait of the giant rabbit is hung over the mantelpiece, replacing the severe portrait of the "lantern-jawed" Marcella Pinney Dowd, doyenne of Mid-western cultured society.

Beneath the comedy, however, is a serious questioning of the validity of the imagination. What makes Mary Chase so remarkable a playwright is that she uses the medium of comedy to present an issue that has most often else-where been treated tragically or with high seriousness. In Eugene O'Neill's *The Iceman Cometh*, for example, the playwright's central concern is the question of whether facing reality is better than living in the fantasy of one's pipe dreams. The would-be truth-teller in that tragedy, Hickey, attempts to strip the inmates of Harry Hope's bar of their dreams, forcing them to face reality. Hickey's initial success renders his friends moribund. They are once more revi-talized when they reaffirm the validity of their pipe dreams. With medical metaphors, Hickey tells his friends:

Oh, I know from my own experience it's bitter medicine, facing yourself in the mirror with the old false whiskers off. But you forget that, once you're cured.

Hickey's medicine, however, works no cures and, O'Neill's audience realizes, his is a medicine that can well be lethal to the imagination and the human spirit. The stern truth of *The Iceman Cometh* is likewise the stern truth of Ibsen's *The Wild Duck* and of other serious modern plays. In Mary Chase's hands, it is transformed into sparkling comedy. She, too, has a doctor and patient, but O'Neill's Hickey and his clients become the raw material for laughter in *Harvey*:

DR. SANDERSON: If you'll begin by taking a cooperative attitude—
that's half the battle. We all have to face reality, Dowd—sooner or later.

ELWOOD: Doctor, I wrestled with reality for forty years, and I'm happy to state that I finally won out over it.

Like Hickey, too, Dr. Sanderson and his mentor, Dr. Chumley, have a medi-cine, formula 977, which will drive away Elwood's rabbits and let him instead see his responsibilities and duties. And like Hickey's cure, it dehumanizes, as the wise cabdriver's speech makes patently clear:

Listen, lady. I've been drivin' this route fifteen years. I've brought 'em out here to get that stuff and drove 'em back after they had it. It changes em . . . On the way out here they sit back and enjoy the ride.

They talk to me. Sometimes we stop and watch the sunsets and look at the birds flyin'. Sometimes we stop and watch the birds when there ain't no birds and look at the sunsets when it's rainin'. We have a swell time and I always get a big tip. But afterward—oh—oh . . . They crab, crab, crab. They yell at me to watch the lights, watch the brakes, watch the intersections. They scream at me to hurry. They got no faith—in me or my buggy—yet it's the same cab—the same driver—and we're goin' back over the very same road. It's no fun— and no tips— . . . Lady, after this, he'll be a perfectly normal human being and you know what bastards they are!

The cabdriver becomes the spokesman for Mary Chase's comic indictment of "normal" behavior. As Elwood avoids Dr. Chumley's cure and leaves with his fantasy world intact, with his invisible rabbit still very much there, the audience applauds with delight affirming thereby the necessity of dreams and the vitality of the life of the imagination.

In *Harvey*, Mary Chase makes her mark as a distinguished playwright, not a female playwright with a particularly feminine or feminist point of view, but a playwright willing to tackle an important and serious human problem and to do so through the medium of comedy. She continues to do this in her subsequent plays, although none matches the success and comic genius of *Harvey*. In *Mrs. McThing*,[5] produced eight years after *Harvey*, Chase attempts to recapture her earlier achievement. Again the world of good society, championed by Mrs. Howard V. Larue III of Larue Towers, is pitted against the mythic world of Mrs. McThing, the witch of the Blue, Blue Mountains. Mrs. Larue's world is one of social formalities and her desire is to keep her son Howay isolated within a circumscribed society that is at once beset by social snobbery and devoid of imagination. Her comic punishment is to have Howay replaced by a changeling, an attired stick that embodies the ultimate desires of Mrs. Larue's comically and often farcically sterile world. The real Howay has broken free from the mannered, constricted world of Larue Towers to join a mob of ridiculous gangsters at the Shantyland Pool Hall in the sleaziest part of town. When Mrs. McThing also translates Mrs. Larue into a kitchen helper at the pool hall, the sterile snobbery of Mrs. Larue slowly gives way to a spirit of acceptance and a new vitality as she is humanized by her stay among the fantastic mobsters.

Mrs. McThing was a Broadway success largely because Helen Hayes as Mrs. Larue, together with the precocious Brandon de Wilde as her son Howay, carried the play. This comedy, however, falls short of *Harvey* because it fails to go beyond a criticism of a very limited segment of society. Beginning in the confines of Veta's home and satirizing her Wednesday Forum, *Harvey* proceeds in subsequent action to move to the Chumley sanitarium and satirize normalization of behavior in general. *Mrs. McThing* never goes beyond a satiric criticism of the insulated, over-refined, vapid life of Mrs. Larue and her society friends. After a pre-Broadway run of *Harvey* in Boston, where Harvey was portrayed by an actor in rabbit costume, Mary Chase wisely eliminated the visibility of Elwood's pooka. In *Mrs. McThing*, the fantastic world, the world of Poison Eddie and his gangsters at the Shantyland Pool Hall, is all too graphically represented. Likewise, perhaps distrustful of the audience's powers of imagination, Mrs. Chase, in the final moments of the play, has the powerful but hitherto invisible Mrs. McThing make a double appearance, first as a frightening witch and then as a beautiful fairy godmother decked in rhinestones. The theme of *Mrs. McThing* remains the same as that of *Harvey*: the importance of imagination and fantasy to make human beings more than the stick figures of convention. Yet by giving a local habitation and a name, actualizing the fantasy world, *Mrs. McThing*, although a comedy of merit, falls far short of *Harvey*'s triumph.

Mary Chase's third well-known comedy, *Bernardine*, first staged the same year as *Mrs. McThing*, explores new comic ground. It is a nostalgic, wistful remembrance by a young man, Arthur Beaumont, of the humor and mystique of years when he was "Beau," the acknowledged leader reigning over the special preadult world of teenage boys. Entering in the prologue to *Bernardine* and dressed in his Air Force uniform, a mature Beau recounts his dramatic anecdote of earlier days when he reigned supreme as leader of the Kings. His monologue recognizes—and forces the audience to recognize—the universality and inherent comedy of that special time in the lives of the young just before they enter the adult world of responsibility. It is at once a time rich in pubescent fantasy and a universal *rite de passage*, that, when viewed with hindsight as it is in *Bernardine*, makes one aware of the comic nature of teenage posturing. As Beau explains to the audience in his prologue:

> There are quite a few of us retired Kings flying these days. But often in the service clubs and around we get together and talk about our lost kingdoms; high-school days in the old home town—a Hallowe'en world that is—with its own set of rulers, values, dreams and a cockeyed edge to laughter.
> Here no adult can enter fully—ever.[6]

And it is that "cockeyed edge to laughter" that Mary Chase seeks to recover in *Bernardine*.

There is much wistful comedy in *Bernardine* derived from the intersection of a straightforward adult world with the "cockeyed," exclusive world of teenage fantasy. There is as well some broad comedy derived from the scenes in which one of the teenagers, who is less sophisticated than he thinks he is, comes close to seducing an unusually attractive older woman. But *Bernardine* is a comedy that has higher sights than *Time Out for Ginger* or any number of Henry Aldrich comedies, for it suggests that the special world of the Kings with its concomitant special vision of womanhood and sexuality, Bernardine Crud of Sneaky Falls, is a necessary part of growing up, a desirable prerequisite for adulthood. In both *Harvey* and *Mrs. McThing*, Mary Chase suggests an alternate fantasy for the rigidity and limitation of diurnal existence. Her position in *Bernardine* shifts somewhat, for she suggests that the special imaginative world shared by adolescents can inform their adult lives in such a way that the memory of it will serve to humanize the rigors of adult life and prevent their becoming the stick figures of *Mrs. McThing*. Even the adults like Mrs. Weldy, who urges the young men to act responsibly, seem to understand this, for Mrs. Weldy ultimately advises her son and his friends to make the most of their adolescent years in the Shamrock, "You stay here—all of you—as long as you can."

Mary Chase creates successful comedy from the time spent by teenagers in their idiosyncratic, closed fantasy world. At the same time, she emerges curiously close to a serious poet like Wordsworth, who also, in poems like "Lines Composed a Few Miles Above Tintern Abbey," emphasizes the special scenes of youth, which when remembered in tranquillity have the power to humanize the workaday world. One has the sense in *Bernardine* that those humorous, awkward, but halcyon days spent at the Shamrock visualizing Bernardine of Sneaky Falls will, in later life, bring Wordsworthian "tranquil restoration" and will lighten the "burthen" of a troubled and sometimes "unintelligible" adult world for Beau and his teenage comrades.

Where *Bernardine* falls short is in its ability truly to recapture the adolescent world. Mary Chase is a competent comic playwright, but she is, finally, no match for Wordsworth and his ability to recapture for adult readers the mystique of youth. *Harvey* continues to stand out as Mary Chase's major work, even perhaps her masterpiece, and it is *Harvey* plus *Mrs. McThing* and *Bernardine* that secures for Mary Chase an important place among those American writers who have championed the necessity of dreams, the life of the human imagination.

LILLIAN HELLMAN TALKS ABOUT WOMEN: INTERVIEWS

In Pentimento, *published in 1973, Lillian Hellman wrote that she could not develop the plot Dashiell Hammett had suggested to her for the play that became* Toys in the Attic. *"I can write about men, but I can't write a play that centers on a man. I've got to tear it up, make it about the women around him, his sisters, his bride, her mother." An the last decade of Hellman's life, which was also the decade of the women's movement, interviewers drew from her some intriguing observations about her sense of herself as a woman artist and about women's issues. The following collage is a sampling of what she said on these topics.*

Interview with Nora Ephron (1973)[1]

NE: Ever since *The Children's Hour* opened, you've been called a woman playwright and a woman writer. How do you feel about that?

LH: Irritated.

NE: What do you think of the women's movement?

LH: Of course I believe in women's liberation, but it seems to make very little sense in the way it's going. Until women can earn their own living, there's no point in talking about brassieres and lesbianism. While I agree with women's liberation and ecology and all the other good liberal causes, I think at this minute they're diversionary; they keep your eye off the problems implicit in our capitalist society. As a matter of fact, they're implicit in socialist society, too, I guess. It's very hard for women, hard to get along, to support themselves, to live with some self-respect. And in fairness, women have often made it hard for other women. I think some men give more than women give.

Interview with Bill Moyers (1974)[2]

BM: Why do you suppose there aren't more women writing plays for the theatre today?

LH: Well, of course, there always should have been. God knows why there weren't early. I think there are a lot more women writing now, not only for the theatre; there are a lot more women writing now than when I began or certainly fifty years before me when there were very few women writing anything. There are more women poets, there're more women novelists, aren't there?

BM: You once said I think that women's liberation is a matter of economics. Would you elaborate on that?

LH: Yes. I was misunderstood when I said it in a forum. I don't have to tell you how deeply I believe in women's liberation. I think some of its cries are rather empty cries because I think it all comes down to whether or not you can support yourself as well as a man can support himself and whether there's enough money to make certain decisions for yourself rather than dependence. In that particular discussion that was quoted one of the ladies brought up the point of she was not willing to do the cooking and lift the garbage cans. It seems to me it's not a question of who lifts the garbage cans but whether you have enough money to get somebody to lift them for you or enough money to say to your husband look I've worked as hard as you've worked today, please lift the garbage cans for me; or please do the cooking, I've worked perhaps even harder than you've worked today. I doubt if there'll be any true women's liberation until women are capable of even being paid for bringing up children which I think should carry a salary with it.

BM: You said you were dependent and yet you strike me as always being a fugitive from commitment. I know you lived with Dashiell Hammett for thirty years off and on.

LH: Yes.

BM: And I guess one could say that's a commitment, and yet in your writings and in your life there seems to be a hanging back from commitment.

LH: I don't think from commitment; I think you mean from marriage.

BM: I didn't mean it, but I'll accept that amendment . . . from both. Why from marriage? Then I'll move on.

LH: I've been, as a matter of fact, I think a little too committed. I don't know. I don't know. It isn't even that I had a very bad first marriage. I had a very pleasant first marriage to a very pleasant man called Arthur Kober. It wasn't at all a mean marriage, and we still see each other and are very fond of each other. I suppose I decided that it wasn't right for me. I don't mean that so many people urged me into it, but I thought I was better with no formalities. I was better if . . . I would stay longer if I felt free to go any day. I suppose that was it.

BM: Did he [Dashiell Hammett] help you with your writing?

LH: Oh yes, enormously, enormously. I can't ever pay him enough gratitude for what he did beyond the obvious things that writers can help with. He was so enormously patient. And more than patient, he was honest, sometimes rather sharply and brutally honest. Without that I don't think I would have done very much.

BM: Did he tell you this is no damn good?

LH: Oh yes, indeed. In stronger words than that. In very strong words.

BM: Did you take it from him?

LH: Oh yes, I took it. Once in a while I would get terribly pained and miserable about it. Yes certainly I took it because I recognized that it had . . . I think you can always take what people say if you know there's no malice in it or no self-seeking in it. Then whether they're right or wrong, they've shown that amount of love to take the chance on your hating them which has always impressed me in people.

Interview with Stephanie de Pue (1975)[3]

SDP: You were recently named Ladies' Home Journal Woman of the Year, in the Creative Arts, and cited for "embodying woman's potential as an artist since the production of your first play."

So many women seem to have the conflict, "Shall I be like Mommy, and be safe, or be like Daddy and do something?" I recently read an article which notes that women of noticeably great achievement have often been raised by or particularly close to, their fathers.

LH: Well, I suppose so, but then most girls are closer to their fathers.

SDP: It's an awful, sociological phrase to use, but do you feel you've made a valuable contribution to younger women by being a role model, a woman of accomplishment?

LH: Oh, I wouldn't answer that question for anything in the world.

SDP: You wouldn't?

LH: No. Certainly I don't think I've been—how can you look at yourself that way, looking in the mirror to say, "I've been something." I don't do that, I don't look at myself that way. If it's happened, I'm delighted, and if it hasn't happened, it doesn't worry me. I don't see myself in such terms, they're too high for me.

SDP: Well, you have now lived through two women's emancipation movements. Do you think the second will stick better than the first?

LH: My youth couldn't have been called a women's emancipation movement.

SDP: There were a great number of women who became doctors, lawyers, etc., and in the '40s–early '60s they got lost.

LH: Yes, but I don't think it was a movement, in the sense of women's liberation. There were a great many women for the first time, not even for the first time, it began in the '20s, beginning to work, beginning to sleep around, beginning to live with people they weren't married to.

But I don't think there was any real movement, just a pocket of people in certain cities. Most of the people I went to college with, for example, I don't think went to work.

SDP: Well, it's a common aphorism, that one of the greatest temptations for women is to think they can simply be rather than do. Have you found that so yourself?

LH: I think women almost have to be more sort of interested in a personal life than men have to be. I don't mean because men don't want one, any more than women do, because I think they do.

But I think women, no matter how liberated they are, feel more pressed to look for a personal life, whether it's a husband or a lover or a house or children or whatever it is, than men feel pressed to.

Interview with Christine Doudna (1976)[4]

LH: I was lucky. I was successful, early, I was twenty-seven years old. Women *have* been put down, there's no question of that. For centuries and centuries.

CD: In a speech you said of the women's movement: "Some of its cries are empty cries." You talked about someone who was complaining about carrying out the garbage.

LH: I don't think it's of any great moment who carries out the garbage. I think it is important that people be economically equal. So that if somebody feels like walking out, there's a way for her to earn a living rather than suffering through a whole lifetime because she can't. Most people of decent manners, living together, automatically divide the jobs anyway, whatever they are. My own nature would have forbidden anybody depriving *me* of what I thought were my rights. I would have walked out.

CD: Isn't that an extreme way of resolving a problem? Suppose you don't want to walk out over who carries out the garbage?

LH: I would think in a decent relationship you don't have to keep a daily score of who does what. It doesn't matter who washed the dishes. It seems to me a thoroughly middle-class argument and I have no interest in it.

Are you going to legislate this? Is every mother in the world going to bring up a son who says, I won't put my wife down? And is every mother going to bring up a daughter who says, I don't dislike men and won't make them pay? A great many women put men down very badly. Particularly upper-class ladies.

CD: Do you think some women use the women's movement as an excuse for letting out hostilities which are really a lot more complicated?

LH: I guess many do. But I don't know any. Most women want everything. They want "leadership," they want to be darlings, they want to be Marilyn Monroe and they want to be Madame de Maintenon. At the same time they want to be president. There is no oneness about any movement.

CD: Does the fact that young women have an easier time of it today than fifty years ago make you unsympathetic to their concerns?

LH: I'm not sure young women do have it easier. Yes, there are more jobs available, but for whom? I'm not sure Negro women have it any easier than they did when I was growing up. I'm not sure poor women have it any easier.

CD: As a writer and a woman, how do you feel about the alterations in language that many feminists advocate?

LH: I hate "Ms." There really isn't anything like making small battles in order to lose big ones. That's what the whole women's movement has been about to me. The big battle is equal rights, whether one likes to face it or not. Even that may never solve it, but the small battles just won't do. These are diversionary movements.

Nobody can argue any longer about the rights of women. It's like arguing about earthquakes.

CD: Do you think there's such a thing as feminine sensibility in literature?

LH: Sure. I think sometimes it's extraordinarily good and sometimes it's awful. The present crop of feminine porno writers is below contempt. Masculine stuff is very seldom porno in quite as nasty a fashion.

CD: Erica Jong, for example, is somebody who . . .

LH: I'm not going to discuss people by name. Whoever thought sexual liberation had anything to do with liberation?

CD: Anaïs Nin talked about how a lot of her creativity had been taken up by personal relationships. Have you ever experienced that as a conflict?

LH: Oh Christ, what a silly thing to say. That's like saying a lot of your creativity has been taken up by drinking or going swimming. It's your choice. Silly, self-pitying remark. You chose it, you wanted it.

Interview with Marilyn Berger (1979)[5]

MB: One of the things that I think women forget is that there is a price to be paid for the extraordinary freedom that a woman like you has. Do you feel you've paid a price?

LH: Yes. Yes, I've paid a price.

MB: What price?

LH: Well, I think I said it earlier, that there would have been safer, pleasanter ways to go. And as you get older, of course, perhaps you think . . . I don't think much about them really. Things turned out the way they did. Some prices, but I have no regrets for that price. Prices are to be paid for everything. There's no way to live without paying the price. It would be hard for me to regret my life. It's turned out . . . I was very lucky.

MB: I think people who do well and work hard often say they're lucky, but it's a little more than luck.

LH: Oh yes, it's a great deal more than luck. I don't mean to underplay it. I worked very hard. I don't mean to say it's lucky in the sense of throwing dice.

MB: Was not having children a price you paid?

LH: Yes, it was certainly one of them. I myself should have said it. I hesitate always to say it because it sounds, I don't know. I back away from it. Yes, of course it was a price I paid. However, I could have had the children. Hammett wanted them, as indeed you know I was married once, and my husband wanted them. It was my choice.

MB: I didn't know that Hammett wanted them.

LH: Yes, he wanted them too.

MB: That must have been very difficult not to at a time . . .

LH: Well he wanted to because I was pregnant. I'm very fond of children and I would have had a nice time with children. That I certainly regret. But now they'd probably be grown up and unpleasant.

MB: Do you think in retrospect that your life as a dramatist would have been any easier had you been a man, not a woman?

LH: No.

MB: Was it easier because you were a woman?

LH: No.

MB: Neither.

LH: No, I don't think so. It might've had certain minutes where it would have been easier to have been a man and where I wouldn't have had to . . . so the personal things didn't become quite so personal, if you know what I'm awkwardly trying to say. There might have been that if I'd been a man, but I don't think it would've made much difference.

MB: Another question that's been raised is whether your books, coming out at a time of great movement for women's liberation, have been lucky in their timing.

LH: I think they have been.

MB: And have you found yourself being considered as a standard-bearer for causes that you really have nothing to do with at all because you happen to be a woman and . . . ?

LH: Yes. Yes, I have found that and been amazed by it. But then I have to say that in a sense, I understand it because I'm sure that I also had such people when I was young. I don't remember who they were, but I'm sure I also had such people too who I admired because they had done certain things that I was about to do or wanted to do. Sometimes my admiration was misplaced. Sometimes it wasn't. I am all for women's liberation. I am not, as I said before, not for the offshoots of women's liberation. I mean, I believe it must begin with economic liberation. There must be equal pay for equal work.

MB: You describe without any fuss an abortion you had done in your twenties. What do you make of the anti-abortion movement today, the right-to-lifers in this country?

LH: Well, legal abortion, of course, in my mind is a very necessary and very properly advanced movement for people who either cannot, which is, I think usually the case, or even if they do not want, which is almost the same case since the child would not be loved or cherished if it's not wanted or taken proper care of, as one sees by child abuse . . . constant child abuse, certainly from people who had never wanted the child. It's a very necessary, civilized, proper act. The other is very irreligious to me. I have just the opposite theory. The anti-abortion law is a very irreligious law to me. It's forcing on people that which they cannot properly cherish and understand.

Interview with Sylvie Drake (1981)[6]

LH [about the movement]: It hasn't gotten down to the basic issue.

I said once that I don't give a damn who carries out the garbage. It's not the point of proof. The question should be addressed totally in economic terms: equal pay for equal work. Unless it does that, it's never going to attract any but unhappy middle-class women. It is a working-class woman's problem.

It's almost come down to being a dislike of men, rather than an acceptance of the pleasure of men. Men have brutalized women, certainly, but the issues have been strange issues, often meager, minor complaints. And the enmity is strange.

Childbearing and -rearing is a very important function of women and always will be, please God. Yet it's absolutely absent from the discussion—perhaps because it is in the hands of women with very little interest in bearing or rearing children. I think—I hope—that when it's in the hands of simpler women, if ever, it will straighten itself out.

LORRAINE HANSBERRY: ARTIST, ACTIVIST, FEMINIST

Margaret Wilkerson

Lorraine Hansberry wrote *A Raisin in the Sun*, the first play by a black writer to win, in 1959, the New York Drama Critics Circle Award. She was also the first woman and youngest playwright to win that award. Born in 1930, she lived a brief, intense, socially committed life, dying in 1965 at the age of thirty-four. Her short span of years yielded five published plays (one of which was completed by her former husband and literary executor, Robert Nemiroff), and more than sixty magazine and newspaper articles, poems and speeches. Among her unpublished works are several playscripts, filmscripts and adaptations, including a treatment and preliminary notes for a play on Mary Wollstonecraft, the nineteenth-century feminist and a stunning opening scene for a play on the great Haitian liberator, Toussaint L'Ouverture. She wrote the text for *The Movement*, a photographic essay on the Civil Rights Movement. *To Be Young, Gifted and Black*, a dramatic compilation of her writings prepared by Nemiroff, toured the country after her death, playing to thousands on campuses and in communities, and adding a new and vital phrase to the American idiom. An activist artist, she spoke at Civil Rights rallies, writers' conferences, and confronted Attorney General Robert Kennedy in a controversial meeting with black leaders about the role of the FBI in the Deep South.

Hansberry was a fiercely independent thinker who trusted the intellect instinctively. The roots of her philosophical views lie in Chicago, the place of her birth. Her childhood there held curious contradictions. On the one hand, she grew up in an upper middle-class family; her father was a powerful realtor who built his fortune on the sale and rental of kitchenettes to relieve the crowded housing conditions of blacks. He won a Supreme Court case against housing discrimination. Her mother, at one point a ward committeewoman, helped to manage the buildings and tenants, but had plenty of time for the leisure-time activities typical of the bourgeoisie. The parents taught their four children pride in themselves and in the race, and nurtured in them the belief that their possibilities were (or should be in a fair society) limitless. On the other hand, she lived in Chicago, a city of racial/ethnic barriers and boundaries. The burgeoning population of blacks, increased periodically by waves of immigrants from the South, was literally confined by restrictive covenants to a fifty- to sixty-block-long area with a few small neighborhoods nearby into which blacks had moved. Despite her family's financial resources, they could not purchase any home they could afford, nor could they eat in certain restaurants, nor even try on shoes in some of the city's major department stores. Wealth may have freed her mind and spirit, but it could not free her colored body.

Her abhorrence of narrowness and parochialism later led her to an awareness of the hidden alliance between racism and sexism long before it was popular to do so, and to shape a vision cognizant of the many dimensions of colonialism and oppression. Anticipating the Women's Movement of the 1970s, Hansberry was aware of the peculiar oppression under which women lived and the particular devastation visited upon women of color. Recognizing its devious forms, she argued forcefully that anti-homosexual attitudes were linked to the oppression of women and man's predilection to gain mastery over other men.

For Hansberry, nothing was "more universal in the world than man's oppression of man." This issue is what "most great dramas have been about, no matter what the device of telling it is."[1] Blacks, women, homosexuals and any others whose oppression is profitable will be victimized. Within her highly political and humanistic world-view, all art was social—whether intentionally so or not. And it was her role as artist to expose the myths and illusions of her time and culture so that the human race could achieve its true stature. She believed that "man is unique in the universe, the only creature who has the power to transform the universe [to] impose reason for life on life."[2] Like a sculptor molding clay she could create characters, structure a world in which the beauties and absurdities of human action could be exposed or treasured, as the case might be.

In the early 1950s, Hansberry worked as a journalist and associate editor for *Freedom*, a black, progressive newspaper in New York City founded by Paul Robeson. During this time, undercurrents of social protest were quietly growing, despite the Red Scare, McCarthyism and hearings by the House Un-American Activities Committee. Numerous violations of human rights, brutality of the Deep Southern variety and labor protests filled the pages of *Freedom* as Hansberry gained an education in politics, culture and economics unparalleled in any university curriculum. While she treasured this work, she found journalism ultimately too restrictive—for one had to stick with facts, even if they obscured deeper truths.

In *A Raisin in the Sun* (1959) we see her first successful attempt to transform the experience of her early years in Chicago into a drama which captured the deferred dreams of a race of people, while exposing the materialistic dangers of the society which evokes, then frustrates those dreams.

A Raisin in the Sun dramatizes the seductiveness of American materialistic values by depicting the aspirations of a black family, the Youngers, who live in Southside Chicago of the 1950s. The title and theme are taken from a Langston Hughes poem, "Harlem," which asks: "What happens to a dream deferred?" Three generations of Youngers live in a cramped kitchenette apartment. When $10,000 insurance money is paid to Lena Younger (Mama), the elder of the household, she places a down payment on a house (in a white neighborhood) to the dismay and anger of her son, Walter, who dreams of capitalizing the windfall by investing in a liquor store. Moved by Walter's frustration, Mama gives him a portion of the money—which he promptly loses in a dubious business deal. The financial crisis which he precipitates becomes a critical test of Walter's personal values. "There ain't no causes," says Walter, "there ain't nothing but taking in this world and he who takes most is smartest—and it don't make a damn bit of difference how."

It is indeed a moment of truth for a black man who seeks enough material resources to improve his family's economic situation and to provide his son with a future. Those aims seem acceptable enough. However, Walter's dream is dangerously flawed: he also seeks the kind of material wealth which comes at the price of deceit and oppression.

House, secretaries, cars are all emblems of the success he seeks. But the dreams of Mama and Walter differ dramatically. Mama wants the family to advance materially without becoming materialistic, while Walter embraces materialism and power—of the kind which has already limited his opportunities. He seeks merely a transfer of power, not a change in the systems of power.

Hansberry had seen the dangers of such confusion in her own brothers, who upon their father's death inherited his business, but little of his philanthropic vision, social commitment and business acumen. Eventually, through a series of mishaps (some of which were not of their own making), they lost their property in Chicago and moved west. Despite Hansberry's comfortable life, she rejected the fruits of capitalism and the conspicuous consumption of the bourgeoisie, dressing simply even as a high school student and ignoring her mother's urgings to buy expensive clothes so that she would be in style. Here, in a 1961 interview, Hansberry explains the difference between material need and materialism:

> There are thousands, millions of people in the United States who don't have too much of anything. They don't have enough and there's a fine and important distinction between that kind of material base of life which simply provides what people need to live a decent life and the middle-class preoccupation with acquisition, with affluence, with these things that they can demonstrate to their neighbors to show that they are keeping up with the fashions.[3]

Hansberry, however, was not satisfied simply portraying the economic disparity between the poor and the wealthy. She proceeded to attack materialism even in the midst of poverty.

The Sign in Sidney Brustein's Window (1964), the second and the last of her plays to be produced during her lifetime, offers even more striking examples of Hansberry's objectivity toward her material. The play, which shocked some critics because it was not about black people specifically, focused on Sidney Brustein, a Greenwich Village intellectual, who, through his new and struggling newspaper, supports a local politician's campaign for office. The play charts Sidney's personal odyssey toward self-realization and affirmation of his responsibility to engage and act in this world. Some early notes on this play indicate that Hansberry originally intended the title to be *The Sign in Jenny Reed's Window* with a female character as the central figure. However, over a period of time she decided that it would not suit her purposes. While speculation continues as to why she made this change, her choice demonstrated her ability to write authentic, convincing male characters, if she had not already proven that talent in *A Raisin in the Sun*. One suspects that the final structure of the play with its male protagonist served her social statement as well if not better than a Jenny Reed would have. For while Sidney is the central figure, he is educated to his own chauvinism, intolerance and self-indulgence by three sisters who collectively present a tapestry of women victimized by this society.

The primary woman in Sidney's life is Iris, his wife, who tolerates the "Pygmalion-like" relationship which initially attracted and continues to hold her husband. Despite his progressive outlook on society, Sidney's views on women are nearly Neanderthal. He demeans Iris's attempts at intellectual discourse and reinforces a girl-child image, complete with flowing hair and idyllic ignorance. When Iris begins to rebel against this image (she eventually cuts off her beautiful hair) Sidney is shocked.

Mavis, his sister-in-law, is portrayed as a bourgeois matron—the stereotype of the uptight gentile whose racial prejudice and provincialism come through in the simplest of conversations. Sidney and his friends enjoy many laughs at her expense. Yet it is Mavis who teaches him about courage—she who has lived with the secret that her straitlaced husband has supported a young mistress and illegitimate son for years, and who has made peace with that knowledge. Noting Sidney's shock, Mavis comments on his naivete:

> Sometimes I think you kids down here [Greenwich Village] believe your own notions of what the rest of the human race is like. There are no squares, Sidney. Believe me when I tell you, everybody is his own hipster.[4]

Sidney can only salute this woman whose humanity and intellect he had ridiculed.

Finally, Gloria deals the deathblow to his smugness. Gloria, the high-priced prostitute who had the fantasy that she could leave her mink-lined, sordid profession with its dope addiction and violent repercussions, by marrying Alton, a young black man. Sidney's last illusions are shattered when Alton breaks the engagement and Gloria commits suicide, while Sidney lay in a drunken stupor, wrapped in his own disappointments. Gloria is the most tragic victim, symbolizing the ultimate, perhaps, in the oppression of women. Mavis has reconciled her disappointment and made a life, such as it is, with her husband. And by the end of the play, Iris has asserted herself and forced Sidney to view her and himself in a different way. The possibilities for their relationship begin at the end of the play. But for Gloria there is no new beginning—at least not in this life. She had become trapped in a role which her world made attractive, a role which she continued to accept and to which she became addicted. Her end is inevitable self-destruction. Hansberry places in the hands of this "Greek Chorus," the Parodus sisters, the true "education" of Sidney and reveals the varied permutations of women's victimization.

Her handling of the only homosexual character in the play exemplifies her ability to use material without regard to her personal experience or preference but to expose ignorance and pretentiousness wherever she found it. By the time this play was written, Hansberry had already written some plays, short stories and essays exploring the theme of homosexuality and denouncing homophobia. By this time she had also become comfortable with her own lesbianism and was involved with a circle of intimate women friends. Yet David, a playwright in *The Sign in Sidney Brustein's Window* who is a homosexual, embodies many of the characteristics personally detested by Hansberry. He is a whining, self-indulgent character who wears his sexual preference like a chip on his shoulder, daring anyone to knock it off. Even so, Hansberry later grants David his humanity and complexity by exposing his painful sojourn through his life as a homosexual.

Again, here is Hansberry the intellect, controlling her characters (and her own emotions) and insisting on distance between herself and her subject matter while utilizing the knowledge and memory of passionate encounters. Only in this way can she command her universe to yield the truths which she seeks for her audience.

This imposition of will suggests a "dark" side to Hansberry which is as much aware of the brutal, selfish, irrational side of humankind as she is of its transcendent potential. *A Raisin in the Sun*, in fact, whose upbeat ending sometimes obscures the danger into which the family is moving, had a different ending in an earlier version. This earlier ending showed the family seated in the darkened living room of their new home, shades drawn, family armed, awaiting the inevitable attack by their hostile white neighbors. Probably no other line dramatized this idea more effectively than Sidney's speech near the end of *The Sign in Sidney Brustein's Window*. Now having faced the abyss of human corruption and suffering, he acknowledges his pain—but pushes through it to action. The line is written as one sentence with practically no punctuation so that the words tumble out of Sidney in an emotional outpouring. But even as he is swept up in this passionate response, he imposes his own will and intellect on that rush of words—directing them toward action when they could just as easily lead him to withdrawal from the world.

[I am] a fool who believes that death is waste and love is sweet and that the earth turns and men change every day and that rivers run and that people wanna be better than they are and that flowers smell good and that I hurt terribly today, and that hurt is desperation and desperation is—energy and energy can *move* things.[5]

WOMEN ALONE, WOMEN TOGETHER

Honor Moore

Until women go to war, scale Mount Everest, or have major moral concerns—in short, until their experience becomes less domestic and more dramatic—they will not write great plays. Such were the clichés about women playwrights when I went to college. The women's movement has changed that. It provided the sociological environment for many new female playwrights to emerge and brought about changes in consciousness that enabled women dramatists to bring so-called nondramatic feminine experience to vibrant theatrical life. The catalyst was the consciousness-raising group. Whether or not a woman joined such a group, she inevitably during the last ten years began to experience her femaleness in a new way. If she was a writer, her own experience and perceptions, instead of seeming inappropriate for the theatre, became a rich source for her writing, became also something to celebrate. This change of attitude is, I think, itself responsible for the kinds of plays, both in form and content, that American women are now writing.[1]

Since the plays women are writing do not employ, strictly speaking, new forms and since the dramatic technique seems to come so urgently out of the need to bring specific material to dramatic life, I will speak of strategies rather than forms. Approaching women's experience through the strategy of telling the story of an individual woman's struggle for autonomy results in what I call "the autonomous woman play," while choosing the strategy dramatizing a situation which involves a group of women (or women and men) results in "the choral play."

When autonomy became an issue for many women, women's individual struggles became material for drama. The autonomous woman plays have one female protagonist, a fragment of whose journey toward autonomy we share. Some, like Alice Childress's *Wedding Band* (1973) concern a woman's survival of the death of someone she has been close to. Childress's Julia, a black woman in 1918 in South Carolina, discovers herself in the process of her white lover Herman's death. Others place the struggle in the context of an argument between male and female; in Ruth Wolff's *The Abdication* (1969), a seventeenth-century Swedish queen abdicates her throne and in the course of confessing her sins to a cardinal with whom she has fallen in love, gains spiritual independence. Still other plays like Ursule Molinaro's *Breakfast Past Noon* (1968) and Gail Kriegel Mallin's *Holy Places* (1979)[2] take on the struggle of mother and daughter. Molinaro's is a play of manners in which mother's and daughter's values clash in the context of such issues as smoking and whether the mother approves of the daughter's lover; Mallin's is a poetic play in which the daughter resists her mother's love in order to resist the ordinariness of her adored father's death.

In these plays we are given heroines with a variety of lives and situations, but it is the way these women's inner lives are drawn that gives the plays their power. The feminist movement affirmed for women the truth of their inner lives and gave them a sense of the validity of their perceptions. It is this validation that gives the playwrights a context in which to bring female emotional reality into the theatre. The plays almost never adhere to traditional fourth wall convention. In Corinne Jacker's *Bits and Pieces* (1975), for instance, the heroine, a widow, is visited by her dead husband whom the other characters don't see. He is not a ghost as he might be in a more traditional play, rather a "piece" of Iris's previous life which has continued into the present to lure her to the past, back to a less autonomous self.

Francine Stone puts her heroine Anna (*Dead Sure*, 1977)[3] in a crisis situation: the husband whom she has left holds their children hostage and threatens to kill them if Anna doesn't return. Anna is a feeling rather than a thinking or reflective woman. Stone breaks into the "action" with tiny flashbacks and imaginings, Anna imagining what would happen if she did go back—almost a hallucination. For example, lights come up on Anna alone on the stage:

> *(She is standing at the table, but the shaft of light extends no more than an arm's length around her. As she talks, she pulls a comb through her hair, paying no attention to her grooming. She encounters a bad knot and fights it mechanically. All the while she is thinking:)*

ANNA: I'm . . . back. Is that what you want? *(Starts again)* Should I see
  them? Are they all right? *(Starts again)*

And:

ANNA: Don't sat anything. There's nothing to say. *(Starts again)* No,
  I'm not staying. *(Starts again)* If only you'd said something . . .

Because of the extreme stress of Anna's conflict these solitary moments height-
en the drama. Stone's strategy is effective in dramatizing the sense of being in
two places at once, of suppressing an inner reality to deal with an outer one, a
way of experiencing many women share.

In other autonomous woman plays, the protagonist is divided into several
selves, each of whom expresses different versions of the woman in question.
Usually the conflict is between a self acceptable to (male) society and a savage
self who cannot conform.

A young girl in white sings, "I'm Lise, little Lise from Nuremburg" to a
delicate music-box melody. This is Myrna Lamb's heroine's memory of her
perfect child-self, the self that was pleasing to her Marlene Dietrich–like
mother. For the purposes of her opera *Apple Pie* (1975)[4] Lamb divides Lise in
two, one an idealized child-self, the other the present woman-self who is too
sexual, too ambitious, too much.

In Marsha Norman's *Getting Out* (1978),[5] a violent Arlie batters around
her prison cell while Arlene, Arlie rehabilitated and eight years older, lives her
first day out of prison. Arlie's youthful female life force is expressible only
through violence, her actions screaming her refusal to buckle under to society's expectations of demure womanhood. As if a memory or a present specter,
Arlie bounces, invisible, through rehabilitated Arlene's present apartment: the
two actresses do not acknowledge each other directly, but there is a sense of
forces resisting each other. When the guard who has driven Arlene home to
Louisville after eight years of prison moans, trying to embrace her, "Arlie, Arlie
girl, I'm sorry . . . " Arlene bats back, a mirror of her past, as Arlie seethes in
her prison cell across the stage: "I'm not Arlie. Arlie would have killed you."
Again we as women identify with her sense of being two people, one who
would break all the rules, the other who keeps that rule breaker in line.

In other plays like Susan Miller's *Nasty Rumors and Final Remarks* (1979)
and my own *Mourning Pictures* (1974) the protagonist engages in two dramas,
one with herself witnessed by the audience, another inside the play. Miller's
Raleigh, dying in intensive care offstage, appears vibrant and alive to replay
moments with her mourners or to correct their perceptions of their common
past. In *Mourning Pictures*, Margaret continually shares with the audience
what events in her mother's dying mean to her growing sense of herself as an
adult, a woman rather than a daughter.

If the autonomous woman plays say "This is what we have in common"
by showing an individual woman, the choral plays say "There are many different kinds of women, each unique, but with much in common," by show-

ing us the drama of a group of women. The autonomous woman plays give us women in isolation, women taken apart. The choral plays show us women together, women seeking integration by attempting community, much as women did in consciousness-raising groups. Though plays about individual women are still being written, most of the autonomous woman plays were written in the early seventies, while the choral plays are more recent—as if experience of women's groups had been their impulse.

Some of these plays are actual choral pieces rather than plays. Ntozake Shange's *for colored girls who have considered suicide/when the rainbow is enuf* (1975),[6] which the author calls a "choreopoem," and Susan Griffin's *Voices*,[7] also written in poetry, are two examples. Neither piece has a plot; rather they are communal tellings of several women's lives, rituals in which the women move from isolated, oppressed and painful pasts into a strengthening and newly communal future. At the end of *for colored girls* its characters, six women, come together in pain and slowly emerge to embrace each other and sing, "I found God in myself and I loved her fiercely." *Voices* ends with a young woman turning away from suicide:

ERIN: What held me like a magnet was the possibility of death, but
      I am curious . . .

In other plays, we witness groups of women in actual situations. Some, like Wendy Wasserstein's *Uncommon Women and Others* (1977)[8] and Leigh Curran's *The Lunch Girls* (1977)[9] are realistic; others, like Aishah Rahman's *Unfinished Women Cry in No Man's Land While a Bird Dies in a Gilded Cage* (1977),[10] are more poetic and abstract. Rahman's takes place one day in 1955, alternating between a home for unwed mothers where six women—black, Hispanic and white, all pregnant by black men—have twenty-four hours to decide whether to keep their illegitimate unborn children, and an elegant Manhattan apartment where Charlie Parker, the black jazz saxophonist, is dying in his rich white mistress's "gilded cage." Parker is meant by the playwright to "represent all the reasons why the women's men aren't there." The counterpoint between the world of women (six identically pregnant women on a stage is quite a spectacle) and the death throes of a black male artist who has been exploited and destroyed by white society gives the play a perspective that adds to its power.

In Wasserstein's *Uncommon Women*, a comedy about seven classmates at Mount Holyoke, men are present only as the male voice which, over a loud-speaker, periodically intones ideals of womanhood in the form of selections from the college catalog. These exhortations—that the students be "uncommonly" fine, that they dress properly, etc.—provide the play's comic tension. *Uncommon Women* begins at a reunion lunch years after graduation and flashes back to a year in the late sixties when most of Wasserstein's heroines were seniors. It is a play about a female community which, because it is insulated from the real world, can afford to scoff at the male values which emanate from the loudspeaker, even though falling short of those standards causes the young women considerable pain. Wasserstein has compassion for characters and events (women growing up, rejection by boyfriends, female eccentricity) that would usually, in the theatre or on television, be subject to ridicule or satire: we laugh *with* rather than *at* her uncommon women. In one hilarious scene, three women examine a first diaphragm as if it is some unfortunate variety of jellyfish; in another, all seven women dance joyously to a bouncy calypso beat—the choice of dance music makes the scene poignantly ironic: "If you want to be happy for the rest of your life/Never make a pretty woman your wife . . ." In spite of its truthful view of woman's situation, *Uncommon Women* is a comedy in the classic sense. All is resolved: the young women, however "uncommonly," have survived their college years; their communal act of memory has acknowledged and soothed, shared pain has receded and the past is suffused in golden light.

Curran's *The Lunch Girls* is a darker play. Its characters are women of less privilege than Wasserstein's Mount Holyoke students. They have grown up—some are mothers—and there is little money or glamour in what they do. The play secs them through a day of work—they wait the lunch shift at a seedy Manhattan key club dressed in net stockings, spike heels and skimpy chorus girl outfits. The locker room where we see them transform themselves from ordinary women into spike-heeled, net-stockinged, skimpily dressed kewpie dolls is no utopia. The lunch girls have become hard women and their dreams are charged with desperation: they yearn toward mere survival; a man who, if he couldn't care, would at least pay the way; a chance to play Ophelia; a way out of an unwanted pregnancy. The community these women would form is vulnerable to their own need for what the men—customer, pimp, husband, boss—can give them and what they must betray to win it. This vulnerability is pungently demonstrated when one of them notices the glint of an eye in one of the knotholes in the locker-room wall: she retaliates with hair spray and the peeping Tom howls with pain, a temporary victory. Curran offers no easy healing, and when Vicky, who wants to leave the club and get her kids into commercials, speaks of unity, she is tentative: "I just heard what ya said the other day about gettin' along and how nice it'd be if we all, ya know . . . really made an effort . . . I wanna help ya."

Most of these plays derive at least some of their dramatic impact from the fact that they look at pre-women's movement times from a post-women's movement point of view: this is the way it was, it has not been clearly seen before. There is not yet a body of playwrighting work that deals with the new communal future or that concerns women characters with feminist values and aspirations, if you will, the Mount Everests that women have begun in the last ten years to climb.[11] What are the dramas in a woman's life when her life is a life she has freely chosen? Tina Howe's *The Art of Dining* (1979)[12] is the first such play I know. In form an autonomous woman play, it treats an evening in the life of Ellen, in her mid-thirties the "co-owner and chef extraordinaire of The Golden Carousel."

It is a November night and Ellen and Cal, her husband and maitre d' prepare for the evening clientele. "These are the various works in progress," the stage direction says, hinting at Howe's metaphoric intention: that a woman chef be taken for a woman artist whose works range from "Pears in Contreau with Frozen Cream" to "The sauces, Hollandaise and Velouté." *The Art of Dining* is a comic symphony to the creative process as experienced by women. It is the rare woman artist who would not identify with Ellen when, after raging at her husband's unconscious interference with her art (he compulsively eats her key ingredients), she says:

ELLEN: I can't do it all by myself, I just can't . . . it's too hard . . . so much to do . . . I get lost sometimes, afraid I've done something wrong . . . You're not helping me . . . tell me it's fine . . . tell me it's fine.

But Ellen perseveres with her creation. "Just let me cook," she snaps, and impulsively crowns the evening with crepe suzettes, a second dessert for everyone. "I don't believe this!" one diner says. "It's extraordinary!" says another. The play ends with what is literally a communion in Ellen's culinary art, a communal ingesting of the flaming triumph of one woman artist. Says a stage direction:

(The fury of the November wind increases outside and the light from Ellen's bonfire burns brighter and brighter as the diners gather close to its warmth. Ellen stands above them with a fierce radiance. Purified of their collective civilization and private grief, they lift the fiery crepe to their mouths and start to eat as the curtain slowly falls.)

The women playwrights who have most successfully developed original theatrical voices are those whose work has continued to be put on by one theatre or producer: Joseph Papp has produced more than one play by Howe, Shange, Lamb and Miller; the Actors Theatre of Louisville has done the same for Marsha Norman; the Phoenix, after producing *Uncommon Women*, commissioned another play from Wasserstein; and the American Place Theatre has begun the Women's Project to develop women playwrights and directors. Because a play requires production to be a completed work of art, it is this kind of support, as much as the support of the community of theatre women, that will enable what is probably the strongest surge of women playwrights in history to continue to invent forms to suit their content, characters to express their perceptions, aspirations and visions.

4 IF NOT AN ACTRESS, WHAT? . . .

"If not an actress, what . . . ?" is the big question for many women who want to do something in theatre. While accepted, even encouraged, as performers and occasionally as playwrights, women have largely been excluded from most other aspects of show business. The creative and technical side of the production process and the manipulations of money and public relations have been more or less off limits to them. "Not strong enough," "no technical understanding," "lack authority," "too emotional," "no head for economics" are the sorts of responses made until recently to women who have wanted to work at the various trades and arts of production.

A closer look at what women have actually done in those areas usually labeled "for men only" suggests that it is not the tasks to be done that pose the problems for women but the hierarchical power structure of theatre. If the job is lowly, the organization experimental or community-oriented, or the artistic skill new, women are likely to be found doing the work. Once the job becomes an executive or top administrative one or the organization successful or nationally important, or the skill formalized into a profession, women's role seems to diminish and their original pioneer work often ignored or forgotten. This process is not peculiar to theatre but is endemic to women's participation in American life, as Gerda Lerner has pointed out in *The Majority Finds Its Past*. For women's careers in theatre, it has resulted in both lack of opportunity and a neglected history of accomplishments.

In the nineteenth century, when theatrical production was not highly specialized, women, usually starting as actresses, could become involved in every aspect of production. There was Laura Keene, for example, acting, directing others, making costumes, designing and painting scenery, organizing publicity and writing or adapting plays; or Mrs. John Drew, progenitor of theatre's royal family, brilliantly managing the Arch Street Theatre in Philadelphia; or the early founders of Augusta's theatre described in the following pages.

Greater division of labor and commercialization occurred just as the energetic "new woman" made her appearance at the end of the nineteenth century. Although being male remained an important determinant of success in such new careers as those of director, designer and technician, a surprising number of women turn up in these positions. Obviously they were not among the "men who direct the destinies of the stage," as the new directors of Broadway were hailed, but they were directing in Hull-House, in the Toy Theatre of Boston, in the Neighborhood Playhouse, in the Washington Square Players and in The Provincetown Players. Few recall, for example, that some of Eugene O'Neill's earliest plays were directed by women: Nina Moise, whom he greatly admired, and Ida Rauh, whose direction could be innovative or "punk," as he put it. Rachel Crothers directed all her own plays, feeling as "passionate" about production as about the script, and many other women playwrights as well as actresses have directed and produced their own work and that of others.

From the 1920s on there was almost an "old girls' network" of directors, producers and even designers. The short-lived Woman's Theatre, initiated in 1926, took as its objective "to promote woman's work in the theatre and to render aid and give counsel to all who may apply. Whether she has a voice to be heard—a play to be read—a desire to act—or to paint scenery—whenever a woman asks our advice or seeks our aid in securing an audition, we assist her without charge." There are many examples of women turning to women to break the domination of men in various careers. A notable example of women working together was the American Repertory Theatre of the 1940s created by famed actress-director Eva Le Gallienne, Margaret Webster and Cheryl Crawford. Webster's many productions of Shakespeare made her the best-known woman director in America, and Crawford, one of the founders of the Group Theatre, went on to become one of the top Broadway producers responsible for shows ranging from the plays of Tennessee Williams to *Brigadoon*.

This chapter of our book offers a rare view of the impressive achievements of women who worked backstage and out front over a long period of time—from intrepid eighteenth-century pioneers to settlement house idealists, a Vassar College visionary who created a national theatre out of a Depression federal relief program, to young women who became the matriarchs of the regional theatre, and directors, designers, critics and agents who crashed through theatrical, gender, social and political barriers. Section 6 will deal with these specialists in the context of the Feminist Theatres, where alternative values governed every aspect of theatre production, and you will hear from them again in the final section, Voices at the Millennium.

The feminist impulse and the explosion of alternative theatres, experimental, regional, Off- and Off-Off-Broadway, as well as the limitations of intensifying commercialism on Broadway provide the context for the turmoil of the 1970s and 1980s, which marked a turning point for work in the theatre. Despite the inspirational history suggested here, which unfortunately remained largely unknown, young women continued to be discouraged by their teachers and their socialization from preparing themselves to be directors or producers. Although by 1987 there were over one hundred women members of the Society of Stage Directors and Choreographers and many more outside of its membership, they were not widely employed by producing organizations that repeatedly claimed to be unable to find competent women directors. Women producers felt themselves to be "new kids on the block," who despite talent, training and track records had to pull down many barriers—the most difficult being the "Broadway barrier." At a panel discussion titled "Women on Broadway: Do They Make a Difference?" organized in late 1986 by the Outer Critics Circle at Sardi's famous theatre restaurant, some of those working in the mainstream called the situation "grim." Elizabeth McCann, producer of such hit shows as *Amadeus*, cautioned those interested in producing. "Women in this industry are not plugged into the power network that can make a difference. They're not running the unions, and they're not running the real estate. There is not one theatre that can be booked in the ladies' room. We've got to get plugged into that network and stop letting the men make all the deals." She dubbed Broadway the "last closed door."

One who had gotten through the door became dissatisfied with producing on Broadway. Lyn Austin, who had been associated with the wealthy producer Roger Stevens for years, decided to use her long experience to "commit to an artist." She created supportive structures to enable such avant-garde artists as Martha Clarke and Anne Bogart to stage their venturesome visions through her Music-Theatre Group/Lenox Arts Center. Another who produced plays because of her dedication to an idea is Miriam Colon, who had acted on Broadway and on TV and was the first Puerto Rican taken into the famed Actors Studio. She founded the Puerto Rican Traveling Theatre in 1967 to give her community an opportunity to share "our defeats, our dreams, our rage, our humor."

Producer-patron Lucille Lortel and producer-publicist Jean Dalrymple encouraged talent and innovation. Lortel, who in a long career produced or coproduced some five hundred plays, was honored as the "Queen of Off-Broadway." It was at the Theatre de Lys, later renamed the Lucille Lortel, a gift from her husband, that the Brecht-Weill *Threepenny Opera* played for seven years, the American Theatre and Academy matinee series offered unique theatre events, and plays by Mamet, Shepard, Norman, Churchill and many others found a home. Jean Dalrymple, publicist and producer on Broadway, used her great skills and persuasive personality to realize the dream of low price but very high quality productions at the New York City Center. Under her guidance, the theatre seemed, critic Brooks Atkinson wrote, "like a fresh, exciting, varied form of public art."

A number of talented women found that they had to start or be in charge of their own theatres if they were to have opportunities to direct, for directing was even more closed to women—especially on Broadway—than producing. Lynne Meadow recalled that she was the only woman in her directing class at the Yale Drama School. "There were no women in the class ahead of me or class behind me." Without role models, she nevertheless absorbed the tough professional training at Yale and made her way to New York, where in 1972, she undertook to run the Manhattan Theatre Club. She dedicated her theatre to developing new work like Beth Henley's *Crimes of The Heart*, Richard Maltby's *Ain't Misbehavin'* and David Rudkin's *Ashes*, all of which won major awards and went on to Broadway success. Her discovery of new talent, Mel Gussow, wrote, has made her "a figure of consequence in the American theatre."

Carole Rothman, who with Robyn Goodman started the Second Stage Theatre in New York in 1979, said that "we wanted to take charge of our own lives and create jobs for ourselves." She felt that women were not permitted to make the jump from workshop productions to main stage. As a feminist she thought that, as she said, "it would be a good idea not only to direct myself, but to give other women directors the chance to direct. Doing plays by women was also a goal." She has had a particularly fruitful association with Tina Howe, whose *Painting Churches* and *Coastal Disturbances* she produced, in addition to resurrecting many neglected American plays in her theatre.

Ellen Stewart was and still is "La Mama" of all who turn their back on commercial theatre. When women complained about their "inability to get ahead" in show business, she urged them to get their own "pushcart"—that is, "to start their own theatres"—as she was urged to do at the beginning of her career. "Look into yourself to note where you were shortchanged artistically along the way and make a balance of payments . . . If you aspire to the performing arts, aspire to give what is inspirational to audiences." This "doyenne of Off-Broadway" has worked in her intensely personal, idiosyncratic way as the magician of theatre at her La MaMa Experimental Theatre Club since 1961, a feat acknowledged by the MacArthur "Genius" Award in 1987. She offered playwrights her stage and a place to put their head down, if needed, and no money, but support to try, and if you fail, to try again "until something beautiful comes out." She encourages those who "go beyond the norm," who "stretch the boundaries of theatre." For women, she is a role model who urges them as she does her artists to go out and do what they want. Her accomplishments are far too numerous to describe here except to say that almost every modern theatrical innovation has found a place with her. Her uncritical openness, governed only by her intuition, has literally taken in the whole world.

Women designers and technicians confronted an overwhelmingly male-dominated field. The long hours, the physical labor, and the necessity of supervising male stagehands were all used as excuses to keep woman out. But Aline Bernstein, set and costume designer of the Neighborhood Playhouse and The Theatre Guild from the 1920s on, became the first woman admitted to the Scenic Artists Union, and Peggy Clark Kelley, distinguished especially as a lighting designer, became the first women to be president of this union. Indeed, again and again women's talent and skills have challenged the barriers erected by the male domination of the professional production process.

In lighting, the newest artistic dimension of theatre, women have been the innovators—from the experiments of Loie Fuller to the accomplishments of Jean Rosenthal and Tharon Musser. So, too, as costuming a show became a professional task rather than an adjunct of the actor's stock-in-trade, women like Lucy Barton, Willa Kim and Pat Zipprodt came to dominate what would seem a natural field given women's upbringing.

There is no career in theatre untouched by women, although one must repeat that they are most active and successful where new roles are being defined and where salaries are low but human rewards high. They have been great teachers. They have cast our shows and movies and nurtured talent as agents for plays and actors. They have set standards and transmitted values as critics, and guarded rights as theatrical lawyers. More needs to be done to show that women have been in theatre all the time. More needs to be done to break the hold of stereotypes that continue to keep women out of jobs that history tells us they have done with distinction.

HKC

WOMEN OPEN AUGUSTA'S FIRST THEATRE

Mary Julia Curtis

In 1790 two women opened a theatre in Augusta, Georgia, on the marshy banks of the Savannah River. Pioneers of the Georgia backcountry, they staged *George Barnwell, The Beaux Stratagem*, and other cut-down versions of eighteenth-century dramatic fare. Their theatre was a converted schoolroom, their producers were a debating society, and their newspaper critic a clever Englishman writing under the name of "Zoilus." The two women, Mrs. Ann Robinson and Miss Susannah Wall, professional actresses who had begun their American careers in the civilized city of Baltimore, must have asked themselves time and again during the 1790–91 season in Augusta, "How did we ever end up here?"

Their first performance, which we know about from a review in the *Augusta Chronicle,* was held on June 17, 1790. The women had put together a kind of variety show with sketches and songs, designed to amuse their audience of legislators, jurors, litigants and judges who had assembled in Augusta, the state's temporary capital. Among Mrs. Robinson's selections was a parody of a legal dispute between Farmer A and Farmer B. Farmer A had a bull; B had a boat. *Bullum versus Boatum* had appeared in the *Charleston* [S.C.] *Morning Post* on July 14, 1786. The narrative, interspersed with great dollops of "true law Latin," concluded with the farmers being "non-suited" with the judgment. So the bench permitted Farmer A and Farmer B "to begin again—*de nova.*" Whereupon, Mrs. Robinson caught her breath, gave a yank to her corset, and began again. She "kept the house in a continual laughter." Miss

Wall, the beautiful ingenue, enchanted the Augustans with airs like "Sandy o'er the Lea," sure to please homesick Scots in the house. The reviewer of their opening performance trusted that "those ladies and gentlemen who did not attend will not deny themselves the pleasure of being there on next Wednesday night."

Who was Mrs. Robinson? G.O. Seilhamer in his *History of the American Theatre* wistfully speculated that she was the lady-love of George III and that having lost his attentions she eventually sailed to America. Unfortunately that was another Mrs. Robinson. Our Mrs. Robinson first appears in American theatre annals as Mrs. Dennis Ryan. She and her husband were performing in Baltimore with a company managed by Thomas Wall, the father of Susannah. In 1783 Ryan assumed the management of the Baltimore company and in June of that year took it to New York to entertain Tory and British audiences—a risky partisan business. When the British withdrew, Ryan petitioned the magistrates in Philadelphia for permission to perform but was turned down. Within two years the Ryans sailed for Charleston, South Carolina, which had always been a lucrative stop for earlier touring companies. The Ryans' season proceeded smoothly for three months until smallpox broke out and the company fled back to Baltimore.[1] Ryan died in the following January, leaving his widow with an infant and in charge of the company. She was married again to a Mr. Robinson whose identity remains a blank. Mrs. Robinson, as the "late Mrs. Ryan," returned to Charleston in the spring of 1789 with at least two charges: Charlotte Wall, daughter of Thomas, and her son, Dennis Ryan. The trio struggled to perform in the city which by now had turned its back against theatre people. Thanks to unruly conduct at Harmony Hall, South Carolina passed legislation against theatre in 1787.[2] So Mrs. Robinson and Charlotte Wall labeled their performances "olios," "rehearsals," and "concerts," and offered the legal dodge of the "Lecture on Hearts." In 1790 Mrs. Robinson doggedly moved her "family" on to Augusta. Charlotte, however, had dropped out of the group, and her place was taken by Susannah.

Susannah Wall, if one believes the *Augusta Chronicle*, June 26, July 3 and October 9, 1790, must have been a beguiling creature. There were odes composed to her beauty. Fulsome praise for her singing enlivened the pages; and an acrostic with her name was printed up to amuse her. She may have had some acting experience before her arrival in Augusta and like her sister have been led onto the stage at a tender age,[3] Whether experienced or not, the *Chronicle*, June 19, 1790, noted that she sang "with exquisite taste, judgment and precision."

Mrs. Robinson and Miss Wall elicited support from the newly formed Dramatic Society, which consisted of "gentlemen" who fitted up the theatre, supplied musical accompaniments, and assumed the male roles in the plays.

According to the *Chronicle* of July 31, 1790, the society was the third of its kind in Augusta's early days. Before its appearance, there had been the Academic Society and the Library Society.[4] With the arrival of Mesdames Robinson and Wall, the Library Society was temporarily displaced, however, by the Dramatic Society, which met regularly on Saturday nights. The gentlemen's success as theatrical enterpreneurs can be measured by the ferocity with which they were attacked. One Augustan wrote to the *Chronicle* of September 4, 1790, complaining that "gentlemen have taken up the business of players." That the correspondent spared Mrs. Robinson and Miss Wall may attest to his Old World manners with the ladies. But he contemptuously deplored "the constant buzzing of the theatre, which salutes our ears in every quarter of this little town."

Unlike Charleston, which had outlawed theatre, Augusta opened its doors to Mrs. Robinson and Miss Wall. The "establishment," in fact, provided the facility in which they performed. When Mrs. Robinson and Miss Wall opened their theatre season on June 17, 1790, it was in a building that also housed the General Assembly and the Superior and Inferior County Courts. Five days later, at a meeting of the board of trustees of the Richmond Academy which ran Augusta, the members resolved to enlarge the downstairs room by knocking out an interior wall. On June 23, the evening following their propitious board meeting, Mrs. Robinson and Miss Wall made their second appearance in the "theatre." With the backing of the board of trustees of the Richmond Academy, which included other influential Georgians besides the governor, the actresses enjoyed a legal security and political privilege rare in the new Republic.

Aside from the surprising historical fact that two women started Augusta's theatre and did a wide range of theatrical productions, there is another remarkable feature of the 1790–91 season: the quality of the theatrical reviews submitted by "Zoilus" to the *Chronicle*. Here was an arresting critic whose standards had been set in the English playhouse and whose observations revealed a depth and maturity in his reading of plays. He did not even spare Mrs. Robinson: "It were to be wished that Mrs. Robinson would, in future, pay more attention in committing her parts to memory: In *Deborah* she was very deficient in this point."

Stung by this remark, Mrs. Robinson somehow got word to "Zoilus." In his next review in the *Chronicle* of October 2, 1790, and his last, he added a paragraph which should have placated her:

> Mrs. Robinson, at present, stands in a more delicate predicament than is perhaps generally known: It is not left to her choice to take a favorite Character, or one to which she can render most justice. The play is struck out by the Society; her part is consigned to her without being even consulted; and whether it is acceptable to her or not, she feels herself under an obligation of performing it, by her agreement with the Society.

Throughout the winter of 1790–91, while Miss Wall was worshiped as a muse and the "Sweetest Syren of the Augustan Stage," Mrs. Robinson was trying to maneuver the Dramatic Society to work out a more favorable arrangement. Even though the society met regularly at the Theatre on Saturday night,[5] Mrs.

Robinson was either not welcomed or not listened to. On December 4, 1790, she addressed the society by means of an announcement in the *Chronicle:*

> Mrs. Robinson earnestly requests the Gentlemen of the Dramatic Society to convene this evening, in order to determine on some measures relative to their engagements with her.

A performance of *Douglas* and *Thomas and Sally* followed in February 1791, but it was the last recorded production of Mrs. Robinson and Miss Wall working in consort with the gentlemen. Something in their arrangements had soured.

On May 1, Miss Wall married a local Army officer and settled down to domestic obscurity, no longer to adorn the stage.[6] Her decision left Mrs. Robinson professionally stranded in the last outpost of the English-speaking world. To add to her distress, her ten-year-old son, Dennis, who was subject to fits, disappeared.[7] Sometime during that month Thomas Wall, Susannah's father, arrived in town with Lawrence Ryan, who was Mrs. Robinson son and Dennis's brother. Three of them—Thomas Wall, Mrs. Robinson and Lawrence Ryan—gave the concluding performance in the theatre on May 21.

"A Mental Evening's Amusement"

> Mrs. Wall (of Amherst County, Virginia, and formerly an actor in the Richmond Theatre) will exhibit a . . . Lecture on *Heads* . . . [and] a critical dissertation on Noses . . . Mrs. Robinson will also join . . . in a scene from Shakespeare's Catherine and Petruchio . . . An epilogue addressed to everybody, not aimed at anybody, will be spoken by Lawrence Ryan, in the character of Nobody.[8]

Their final performance coincided with George Washington's presidential progress to Augusta. Three days before, in their theatre, he had been served a banquet and honored with toasts. Visitors from every possum corner had been attracted to Augusta to see Washington and, of course, the actors took advantage of the crowds.[9]

By May 21, the closing night of their season, Mrs. Robinson had decided to make Augusta her home and was advertising the opening of a school for ladies. Three years later the Richmond Academy offered her the use of a Lot 79, which usually included the tenement on it, "for seven years, free of rent."[10] During the winters of 1797 and 1798–99, Mrs. Robinson traveled to Charleston to perform with the Placides at the Charleston Theatre. At the time of her benefit in 1799, she made a plaintive appeal to the Charlestonians:

> Whoever recollects her former exertions, and first-rate theatrical abilities, in the gay day of youth and spirits [when Mrs. Ryan] with her continued attention to please, will contribute their mite to render the evening of days easy.[11]

She returned to Augusta that summer and attempted at least one performance in July and another in October in her old "theatre," also know as the "Court-House." After she reopened her school in November 1800, she too faded into the Augusta community like Susannah. The only possible trace of her existence appears in the City Council Minutes of 1806 in which she received $10.00: "Paid to the Poor of the City."[12]

Two troupers of courage and tenacity, Mrs. Ann Robinson and Miss Susannah Wall sought employment where theatre was not only legal but encouraged by the city fathers. Their stage, fitted up in a large room, continued to be used by the Charleston Theatre company until 1823. Their productions aroused "Zoilus" to print four signed critical pieces of a level "Charleston knew intermittently, and Savannah, not at all."[13] And their audiences, mostly immigrants from the British Isles, devoured their theatrical fare like manna from the Old Country. The two of them made a unique and enterprising team, unparalleled in American theatre history.

ART THEATRE IN HULL-HOUSE

J. Dennis Rich

In September of 1889, two young women, Jane Addams and Elle Gates Starr, moved into a deteriorating old mansion in the middle of an immigrant neighborhood on Chicago's Halsted Street. In this tenement setting, they established Hull-House, one of the first settlement houses in America. The young women hoped to be neighbors to the poor, to share in their life experiences, and to work with them to improve their lot. The cofounders of Hull-House, especially Jane Addams, soon were recognized as pioneers of the modern social movement in the United States. According to Addams, the settlement "was an experimental effort in the solution of social and industrial problems which are engendered by the modern conditions in a great city."[1] The visual arts, music and drama were integral in the effort "to provide a center for a higher civic and social life." "The universal for the portrayal of life lying quite outside personal experience" was encouraged through programs in the arts.

It is significant that their effort to "socialize democracy" began theatrically. Among the first recorded activities at the settlement house was a dramatic reading from Hawthorne by Mrs. Sedgwick, the first resident at Hull-House. In the early years, young people were drawn to the settlement by the opportunity both to observe and to participate in dialogues, cantatas, charades, parlor magic and festivals. Though such theatrical experiences offered a release from the day-to-day circumstances of the slum-dweller, the actual production of plays at Hull-House had to be deferred. Both the people living in the neighborhood and the first residents regarded the theatre with some suspicion. The population attended the theatre, but they did not encourage participation in it. Indeed, they feared the stage even if they were fascinated by it.[2]

Jane Addams wisely turned her attention away from the theatre and toward the development of the other arts. "Picture exhibits, lectures, concerts, classes in handicraft and choral clubs were in part established for the purpose of providing an alternative to the commanding and nearly always insidious appeal of melodrama and vaudeville."[3]

But the "insidious appeal of melodrama and vaudeville" was the source of Addams's conviction that an exposure to the theatre was important in the education of young people. She was aware of "the persistency with which the entire population" attended the theatre. And, she interpreted such attendance as fulfilling a need for imaginative expression. It was the way in which this need was fulfilled that gave her cause for concern.

> The young men told us of their ambitions in the phrases of stage heroes, the girls, so far as their dreams could be shyly put into words, possessed no others but those soiled by long use in the melodrama.

The neighborhood theatre, "such as it was, appeared to be the one agency which freed the boys and girls of that destructive isolation of those who drag themselves up to maturity by themselves, and it gave them a glimpse of that order and beauty into which even the poorest drama endeavors to restore the bewildering facts of life."[4] Addams reasoned that if the theatre had so powerful an impact upon the lives of the urban poor, then Hull-House had to offer an alternative to the popular melodrama. She believed that a theatre which depicted life more truthfully would attract the young people of the neighborhood and would encourage understanding in place of escape. Her belief led to the creation of one of the first art theatres in America.

When the visual arts and music became established at Hull-House, the idea of a theatre at the settlement became possible. A cautious initial effort to incorporate the drama was made with the establishment of the Shakespeare Club in the early 1890s. The purpose of the club was to encourage good reading and to attend professional performances of Shakespeare's plays. In addition, professors and graduate students from the University of Chicago often were invited to lecture about the play club members were reading. The literary approach and the importance of the playwright assured respect for this early venture into the drama. Gradually, the readings brought about the realization that "a very widespread desire existed among the children and young people to act, and that satisfaction of this desire under educational auspices and high standards leads away from instead of toward the professional stage."[5]

Seven years after Hull-House opened, the theatre which Jane Addams hoped could be established materialized. A theatre in which young people might better "understand life through its dramatic portrayal" was created at Hull-House in January of 1896 with the performance of William Dean Howells's play, *The Sleeping Car*.[6] The event marked the birth of the first settlement theatre in America. In the February 1896 *Hull-House Bulletin*, Addams reported, "There seems to be a general awakening on the matter of plays . . . We hope this enthusiasm will be utilized to produce plays of good standard. A simple, healthful play, with real characters is most delightful, and beneficial to both the actors and the audience."[7] During the remainder of 1896, five additional dramatic performances were presented on the stage in the Hull-House gymnasium. Both the productions and the process of rehearsal were praised. And in the following year, Addams suggested the establishment of an agency within Hull-House whose sole purpose was theatrical production.

In April 1897, Shakespeare's *As You Like It* was produced at Hull-House, under the direction of a Chicago advertising executive, Walter Pietsch. The play was so well received that Addams appointed Pietsch director of drama at the settlement. In October of the same year, Pietsch formed the Hull-House Dramatic Association. He immediately set goals for the new organization. First, he declared that the object of the Hull-House Dramatic Association was "to raise the standard of all plays at Hull-House"; second, he sought to recruit the most talented young people at Hull-House to act under his direction; finally, he began working toward the construction of a theatre facility.[8] By October 1898, Addams was able to announce that "Plans are being drawn for a new building."[9] The new theatre was completed one year later, in October 1899.

The completion of the new theatre extended the influence of the drama at Hull-House further into the immigrant community around Halsted Street. Among the events which inaugurated the new stage was a production undertaken by "a large colony of Greeks near Hull-House."[10] The *Return of Odysseus*, a dramatic adaptation of Homer's *Odyssey*, was performed in Greek. Addams reported that it was "a unique experiment to have genuine Greeks portray Homer."[11] This particular production was important to developing theatre at Hull-House for a variety of reasons. First, the production encouraged other ethnic groups in the neighborhood to stage dramas in their own languages. Similar projects were soon sponsored by Lithuanians, Poles, Russians and Italians living in the immigrant community. Second, the play was the first Hull-House production to attract attention outside of the immediate neighborhood. Finally, the production represented the Hull-House commitment to establishing a drama which "gives beautiful and significant expression to local loyalties and traditions,"[12] in other words, to a drama which had a rightful place in the community.

The construction of the new theatre established the drama on an equal footing with the other arts at the settlement. Under the supervision of Jane Addams, the theatre began to serve as "a vehicle of self-expression for the teeming young life" in the neighborhood. But Addams was not content simply to see the facility in use. She wanted the drama to go beyond the goals of "recreation and education." She believed that the Hull-House theatre would be able to provide an alternative to the popular melodrama because it was unfettered by commercial considerations. In lieu of the pursuit of profits, Addams argued for the pursuit of truth, for a theatre in which it was possible to "attempt to expose the shams and pretenses of contemporary life and to penetrate into some of its perplexing social and domestic situations." She hoped that the stage would become "a reconstructing and reorganizing agent of accepted moral truths" in which ideas could be tested.[13]

Addams's strong belief that the theatre at Hull-House ought to encourage new standards for the drama attracted the attention of others. As early as 1899, one of the leading writers and thinkers in American realist literature, William Dean Howells, wrote that the Hull-House stage

> seems to me a real Théâtre Libre, and for us an opportunity for a conscientious drama which is quite unequalled in America, so far as I know. You are not only going to bring a harmless joy into the lives of those poor neighbors of yours, but you are going to give a chance for honest and faithful work to those intending playwrights who are now locked out of the temples of the theatrical trust. Who knows but you are indirectly founding an American drama.[14]

Howells's dream of founding an American drama never materialized at Hull-House. But by the turn of the century, the first American settlement theatre was on its way to becoming an important art theatre. Eventually, the vision which guided Jane Addams in the creation of a theatre at Hull-House also provided the impulse which led to the formation of important American experimental theatre companies such as the Provincetown Players and the Theatre Guild.

Jane Addams's revolt against the values of the monopolized commercial theatre entered a new phase at the turn of the century. Walter Pietsch resigned his position as director of drama at Hull-House. In 1900, Addams appointed Laura Dainty Pelham, a theatre professional, to replace Pietsch.[15]

Pelham became a Hull-House resident and assumed various responsibilities at the settlement. Despite her professional background, the retired actress expressed no interest in transforming the amateur group at Hull-House into a professional company. She realized from the beginning of her association with the theatre that its primary function was to provide an outlet for the young people in the neighborhood. At the same time, Pelham did not compromise her professional standards. It would appear that Laura Pelham was prepared for her role as director of drama by Jane Addams. Pelham's commitment was similar to that of Addams; that is, the promotion of artistic integrity over commercial considerations. Under Pelham's guidance the settlement was able to produce plays which, though performed by amateurs, came to be regarded as "professional" by Chicago audiences and newspaper reviewers. In this remarkable woman, Jane Addams foound a leader capable of bringing her idea of a theatre to complete fruition.

Pelham assumed leadership of the Hull-House Dramatic Association under difficult circumstances. Apparently, Walter Pietsch resigned his directorship because he had, in some way, displeased Jane Addams.[16] Whether or not this assessment is correct, Pelham stepped into her directorship during a period in which plays were not being produced at the settlement, and in which the enthusiasm that productions such as *As You Like It* had generated was dwindling. The new director's first goal was to unify a disintegrating company of young actors. If she was going to create serious theatre at Hull-House, she first had to establish herself as a competent artist.

To achieve this end, Pelham utilized the dramatic form which Addams had so often criticized—the melodrama. Pelham's first production, presented in December 1900, was *A Mountain Pink*, by Morgan Bates and Elwyn Barron. Addams, writing in the *Hull-House Bulletin* of Autumn 1900, strained to find justification for the play. She observed that it "mixed the more usual dramatic ingredients of love and a lost heiress" but that it was of interest to residents and the neighborhood because Mrs. Pelham had acted in the play professionally and would "play her original part" at the settlement.[17] Pelham, in her defense, was pragmatic. She argued that she had chosen the melodrama for practical reasons:

> The company was most familiar with that type of play; my own experience was largely along such lines of work; and the neighborhood from which we expected to draw our audience still loved the old-fashioned drama with virtue triumphing over vice suitably downed in the last act.

Pelham's judgment appears to have been correct. *A Mountain Pink* played to an audience of over a thousand people in three nights, and it created the sense of unity which the director perceived as necessary if she was to build a cohesive company of young actors at Hull-House.

In October 1900, even as she was rehearsing the melodrama, Laura Pelham was working to create an atmosphere in which a different kind of drama could flourish. In support of her cause, she invited the famous actor Joseph Jefferson III to speak to the Hull-House Dramatic Association about theatre as a serious art form. "His advice and encouragement," Pelham reported, "were a great inspiration to us, and the work of our first years was largely based on the plan he outlined."[18] The Hull-House Dramatic Association did not immediately abandon the production of light entertainments in favor of more serious work. Rather, Pelham limited membership in her company and worked to raise the standards of performance.

Beginning in the winter of 1904, literary merit became a criterion for production. Safe entertainments were, for the most part, discontinued. "The first mile-stone" in the new approach to production at Hull-House was the very successful American premiere of Ben Jonson's pastoral drama *The Sad Shepherd*.

The decision to give a new direction to theatrical activity at the settlement coincided with a change in the Halsted Street neighborhood, as the Irish and English-speaking French "neighbors were being crowded out by Italians, who did not care for performances in English."[19] The immigrant community continued to be served by the Hull-House clubs and by productions, but Pelham was more easily able to undertake the production of a different kind of drama. Jane Addams's desire for socially significant theatre could now be satisfied.

Jane Addams's vision and Laura Pelham's professionalism, when combined, resulted in the creation of a true art theatre in Chicago. Plays by Shaw, Pinero, Galsworthy and Ibsen came to dominate the Hull-House stage.

Eventually what was now called the Hull-House Players achieved recognition both in America and abroad as "the first and most important settlement theatre in the United States" and as an "example of Little Theatre with sociological aspects."[20] Maurice Browne, often called the founder of the art theatre movement in America, acknowledged a debt to Hull-House. He wrote, "The Hull-House Players gave plays of distinction with skill, sincerity and understanding. Mrs. Pelham, not I, was the true founder of 'the American Little Theatre Movement.'"[21]

WOMEN DIRECTORS—THE EARLY YEARS

Shirlee Hennigan

The first women to direct on the American stage were actresses. They directed or "staged" the plays in which they acted, sometimes working with another person who was not in the cast—frequently this was the producer, theatre manager, or author of the play and might additionally have been the actress's husband. (Directing the plays they acted in was common practice for male actors as well.)

The actresses in the early part of this century who staged the vehicles in which they starred include Minnie Maddern Fiske, who usually worked with her husband, the producer Harrison Grey Fiske; Olga Nethersole, who ran her own repertory company and was produced by her husband, Louis Nethersole; Margaret Anglin, who was famous for her Shakespearean roles; Marie Dressler, who did primarily farce and revues; Mary Shaw, noted for her Ibsen and Strindberg heroines; Josephine Hull, best known in later years as James Stewart's sister in both the stage and film versions of *Harvey*; and Jane Cowl, Henrietta Crosman, Elsie Janis, Grace George and Margaret Wycherly. Some of these actresses not only staged the shows in which they performed but also produced them, joining the ranks of a number of other women who produced shows, including playwrights Dorothy Donnelly and Rachel Crothers.

It should be noted here that in the first quarter of the century there were a great many plays written by women produced for the commercial Broadway theatre. In the 1925–26 season, a random year chosen for examination, there were fifty-four women playwrights produced in the New York professional theatre. Some were co-authors with male playwrights and some, like Rachel Crothers, Catherine Chisholm Cushing and Dorothy Donnelly, had two or three plays of theirs on the boards that year, in which better than one in eight authors of Broadway plays were women.[1]

Female and male stars continued to stage their own vehicles through the 1930s. Some of the new women who did this double duty were Blanche Yurka, Auriol Lee (who became a director of importance, staging most of the plays of John Van Druten until her death, when he assumed the direction his plays), Alla Nazimova and Estelle Winwood. One actress who stands out as a consistent and persistent director is Eva Le Gallienne. At her Civic Repertory Theatre, established in 1926, she directed herself in some twenty plays. She also directed plays in which she did *not* act at her theatre on Fourteenth Street, where her prolific group was critically acclaimed. After the Civic Repertory Theatre closed in 1932, Le Gallienne staged plays on Broadway at the Shubert and Broadhurst Theatres. In her productions she appears to have consistently used women designers such as Aline Bernstein and Irene Sharaff. In the 1940s she joined forces with Cheryl Crawford and Margaret Webster to found the American Repertory Theatre, where she shared directing chores with Webster. By the later forties the phenomenon of performers—of either sex—directing themselves seemed to die out.

Just as acting seems to provide a natural access into directing, so playwriting offers a similar ingress. Since the beginning of the century there have been women playwrights who have also directed. Rachel Crothers is an early and prolific example. Her first Broadway success was *Myself-Bettina* in 1908; it was produced by Maxine Elliott, who also starred. Two years later her next show, *A Man's World*, was produced by the Shubert Brothers and ran for seventy-one performances. Between 1913 and 1940 she directed nineteen of her own plays and several written by others; some of her plays, such as *As Husbands Go* and *When Ladies Meet*, were long-run hits. This record makes Rachel Crothers one of the most prolific American playwright-directors.

From the opening of the century until the 1980s the list of women writers who directed their own work is a long one, including among many others Margaret Mayo, Anita Loos, Sophie Treadwell, Anne Nichols, Rose Franken, Lillian Hellman, June Havoc, Megan Terry, Elaine May, Julie Bovasso, Amy Saltz, Maxine Klein, Maria Irene Fornes, Elizabeth Swados, Julianne Boyd and Lucia Victor.[2]

The emergence of women who were primarily directors committed to staging plays rather than either acting in them or writing them followed the early actress- and playwright-directors. Such a woman was Agnes Morgan. Although her important career spanned close to a half century, she is almost totally unknown today, something this brief review hopes to rectify.[3]

Agnes Morgan seems to have been interested in theatre all her life. At Radcliffe she acted in plays and upon completing her Master of Arts degree became a protégé of the famous Harvard professor George Pierce Baker. He sent four women abroad to study the continental theatre for a year; Agnes Morgan was the only one to stay the full year and complete the assignment. When she returned she became a member of Baker's seminal 47 Workshop.

After leaving Cambridge, Agnes Morgan met Helen Arthur, who was working in New York at the Henry Street Settlement. She encouraged Morgan to join in the theatre activities started there by the philanthropic sisters Alice and Irene Lewisohn. When their theatre became the Neighborhood Playhouse on Grand Street in 1915, Agnes Morgan's career as a director began in earnest. From that date until 1927 she directed a long list of plays by such distiguished authors as George Bernard Shaw and Harley Granville-Barker that gave the theatre a reputation for artistic achievement. Morgan also wrote the book and lyrics and directed five "editions" of *The Grand Street Follies*, which brought commercial success and popular interest to the Neighborhood Playhouse.[4]

When the Lewisohn sisters, who were also directors, closed the Neighborhood Playhouse in 1927 believing it had completed its period of experimentation, Agnes Morgan and Helen Arthur founded their own company. Originally calling it the Grand Street Follies Company and later incorporated as the Actor-Managers, it existed until 1939. Operating on Broadway and using many of the actors and designers they had been working with, the new company functioned as a cooperative and was among those mentioned in a 1927 newspaper article as part of the "feminist movement in drama."[5]

In 1928 Agnes Morgan directed for the Shuberts a production of *Maya* by Simon Gantillon that caused a uproar. This sympathetic portrait of a French prostitute in Marseilles was closed by the police on charges of corrupting the morals of youth. Protests were made to Mayor Jimmy Walker by leaders of New York society and theatre, and although Lee Shubert deemed the show "beautiful, very, very beautiful," he did not fight to reopen it.[6]

In the next decade Agnes Morgan remained very active, doing new editions of *The Grand Street Follies*, directing on Broadway, in summer theatres and for the Popular Price Theatre of the Federal Theatre Project in New York. Her company also worked at the Casino Theatre in Newport, Rhode Island, where she staged, among others, a play Laurette Taylor wrote for herself to star in. Program credits for their Newport enterprise reveal a unusually large number of women in charge of the operations of the theatre.[7]

From 1934 until the end of her career in the 1960s (she probably died around 1970 in obscurity), she was associated with Frank Carrington at the Paper Mill Playhouse in Milburn, New Jersey. In 1982 the general manager who had worked with her there paid tribute to this forgotten, pioneer woman director. "She was a beautiful person and a real theatre person. She came to rehearsal completely prepared. She knew exactly what every person from the lead to the lowliest chorus person should do, and exactly where they should be . . . She had a great feel for the theatre . . . remarkable . . . a fantastic person."[8]

HALLIE FLANAGAN: PRACTICAL VISIONARY

Pauline Hahn

In an address entitled "The Search for New Standards in the Theatre," Francis Fergusson names four key American theatrical figures: Robert Edmond Jones,

Harold Clurman, Thornton Wilder and Hallie Flanagan. Jones, the poet, he calls frustrated by the parameters of a designer's role. Clurman, ardent prose-lytizer, and his Group Theatre never fulfilled their bright promise. Wilder, metaphysician for the common man, was co-opted by Broadway and his work grew facile. But Flanagan he calls a "Statesman": a leader and a thinker who "in a crucial experiment demonstrated the potential theatre life of this country." Her ability to sustain more than one large concept at a time (rather than settling for a least common denominator of things) resulted, Fergusson says, in the winning of a new audience which grew to trust theatre and found itself transformed in the very magic way of which Jones dreamed.[1]

Hallie Flanagan was a visionary, most eloquent and expansive when communicating with her great good friends, T. S. Eliot and Gordon Craig; but whether with lumberjack or senator, she was unyielding in her use of the broad historical perspective, judging herself and all around her by the highest and best in theatrical history. It is only fitting that our reevaluation of her be conducted within these same dimensions.

"Half a century from now," Hallie Flanagan once pondered in a speech, what will "historians speaking of this period . . . have to say." She imagined what we would know of the Federal Theatre Project, of which she was the national director. She described, in this and in other writing, the vast tapping of artistic energies, the public works, the inspired rejuvenation of the artists roused from abject humiliation and despair, pride restored to them, and the patriotic sense of responsibility which comes with national service. She spoke of the revolutionary movement away from precious, glittering, irrelevant theatre, the switch from "the four hundred to four million," as she put it, to the theatre which, "by a stroke of fortune unprecedented in dramatic history, can fulfill its necessity . . . to help reshape America." She said that historians of the future would point not only to the natural wealth rescued from oblivion, but also to the formation of a national (and by that she means to include every single type of American, from farmer to coal miner) trust and faith and passion for the theatre because of its immediacy its relevance, and its accessibility.[2]

That was a great deal for her to have expected from us, the historians of today, but she depended upon it, no doubt all the more so after her beautiful theatre had been abolished. Little could she have guessed that the Federal Theatre Project would be relegated to a one-line mention in history books, and she to a bored, obligatory, four-word phrase, set off by commas.

How did it happen? How could we as a nation have sustained such an attack of amnesia? How could we have developed such indifference? The major critics of the time—theatre critics and thinkers from all over the world—hailed the Federal Theatre Project and Mrs. Flanagan as of monumental significance, not only to America but to the larger history of world theatre. The best playwrights here and abroad—Eliot, Shaw, O'Neill, Auden, Toller—rushed to have their works performed, for scarcely any remuneration, by the most important theatre of its day. Some of our greatest talents had their start with the Federal Theatre Project, and many of them arguably did their best work there. National theatres of Europe sent representatives to study the workings of a true theatre. Theatre became a daily subject of discussion and a true avenue for dialogue. Everyone who was anyone was sure that this was the making of an American national theatre, with Flanagan as its head. She was recognized to be not only the conceptualizer of a unique, indigenous, American national theatre, but was undoubtedly, for American theatre, the major unifying, international force of her day.

For almost fifty years, however, Hallie Flanagan and her Federal Theatre Project have been ignored, forgotten. How does one get written out of history? This is a complex question, the more so because it is one which must be explored not merely as a unique issue but in relation as well to many other women who have made important contributions to the theatre and to other fields who have likewise been forgotten.

Tentative answers concerning Hallie Flanagan's disappearance fall into two areas of discussion: the political and the conceptual. The political may be easily disposed of, although the details are full of charges and countercharges. It consists of hostility toward liberals; fear of leftism and accusations of leftism, particularly during what Stefan Kanfer calls "The Plague Years"; and the complex mechanisms involved in culturally institutionalized sexual bigotry. The conceptual requires a deeper kind of analysis which I would like to suggest.

Let us begin by examining what Hallie Flanagan meant by theatre and what sort of theatre she attempted to create. Here is how she envisioned a national theatre:

> *The theatre has never been greater than its audience.* When audiences have been big, varied, and exciting, plays have been big, varied, and exciting. When the Greek plays were given in those exposed arcs cut from stone, the audience assembled from all Greece. They came to a festival to see plays chosen by the government and paid for by government money, and they expected the plays to be good. They were good, good enough to last three thousand years. In the Middle Ages the crowds jostling through the streets stopped to heckle and applaud the street players, investing the plays with their own vitality So too, in Elizabethan England it was a noisy crowd and a big crowd that jostled into the pit to see a play by Will Shakespeare. The plays had to be tremendous, and they were.[3]

She then traced the process by which the theatre became small and precious and finally (in America) both geographically and financially inaccessible, until there were only two choices—the worker's theatre or mass media:

> It was logical and it was inevitable that the stage, having become the property of a few, became so special that the masses of people had to turn to the cinema and radio for their theatre. Thus the twelve thousand [unemployed] people in our rolls are not there entirely, or perhaps even primarily, because of the general economic situation [the Depression].[4]

In an address she said:

> No doubt every one of us had thought at some time of some form of
> state or national theatre like institutions in European countries. We
> had thought, perhaps, of careful planning by wise committees, of the
> greatest actors, writers, designers, plays, all housed in appropriately
> magnificent surroundings, of an academy of dramatic training for
> gifted youth.
>
> If the loss of that dream still seems great, balance against its dig-
> nity its danger, the danger from which the American stage has always
> suffered—imitativeness. The pattern for our Federal Theatre has to be
> different, a pattern dictated by necessity, demanded for immediate use,
> utilitarian and functional.[5]

Now she described her audience:

> There is no yawning in the Florida Wheel, where our actors play the
> Turpentine Circuit, audiences coming in barefoot with lanterns to see.
> Forty million people: lumberjacks in Oregon, sharecroppers in the
> South. Nothing is too good for this audience. It is their theatre. Only
> a theatre which springs from or penetrates into city, town, village and
> farm can be called an American Theatre.[6]

That is enough to give us a good notion of where she stood on audience. Now,
let us turn to subject matter:

> Tremendous things are happening in the world of politics, in the
> field of light, in the realm of science; and if the theatre cannot cap-
> ture some of the quality of this excitement in the plays it does and
> the way it does them it will die of yawning, with or without govern-
> ment subsidy!
>
> We must see the relationship between the men at work on
> Boulder Dam and the Greek chorus.
>
> Giving apoplexy to people who consider it radical for a govern-
> ment-sponsored theatre to produce plays on subjects vitally concern-
> ing the governed is one function of the theatre.
>
> The relation between art and necessity lies at the root of the
> Federal Theatre.
>
> Theatre: not the frosting on the cake but the yeast which makes
> the bread rise.[7]

This last should not be taken lightly. In one of Flanagan's articles she described
theatre in an ideal society as explaining economics to the farmer who feeds
starving economist and actor alike. Compare this to her comments on her
own theatre, where "our actors are themselves the protagonists . . . a vital force
. . . not a decoration."[8]

The precondition for Francis Fergusson's correctly placing Hallie Flanagan in theatre history was his having already, in *The Idea of Theatre*, placed theatre itself correctly into history:

> Hamlet's charge to the players expresses the perennial need for a direct and significant imitation of human life and action which can be played as music is played. But though we may assent to Hamlet's definition, if we read it attentively, we shrug it off the next moment.
>
> If he could ask the players to hold the mirror up to nature, it was because the Elizabethan theatre was itself a mirror which had been formed at the center of the culture of its time, and at the center of the life and awareness of the community. We know now that such a mirror is rarely formed.[9]

What Hallie Flanagan was proposing—and what she in fact created for four years—was exactly this sort of a theatre, a real theatre, the kind we know nothing of, but the kind which every great theatre in history has been.

As Fergusson puts it, it isn't easy to even focus upon the *idea* of a theatre. We tend to assent without thinking, and if we do think we confuse it with "lyric poetry or pure music, on one side, or with editorializing and gossip, on the other"; and if we do not confuse it, we "shrug it off the next moment."

In our theatre of marketplace, of "alternating crusading and racketeering" (in Fergusson's words), it is easy to forget and for things to change shape. The regional theatres, which were the legitimate offspring of the Federal Theatre Project, have become as bland and homogenized as the Broadway theatre the '30s. The people's theatres of which Flanagan spoke—radio, film and now television—have only speeded up the dulling process. Then of course, the unexpected and inexplicable occurred. The heart of the Federal Theatre Project records disappeared for thirty-five years. The Dies Committee—HUAC—became fat and ferocious, savaging decades with fear and silence. And, strangest of all, the very generation of historians which should have passed on an understanding of her concepts and her theatre instead rarely mentioned her.

An explanation is required of us. Perhaps Flanagan is ignored because we cannot understand her theatre, while her theatre is ignored because we cannot understand—or categorize—her.

Envied for her fabulous (if fictitious) White House connections, she was the very emblem of *la nouvelle femme arrivée*. Undoubtedly the most powerful theatre producer of her day and, in very truth, a pivotal figure in theatre history then and now, Hallie Flanagan is, in fact, the double object of ironic ill fortune. In the political climate of the '30s, the grotesque fate of a moderate like Hallie Flanagan was to be classified simultaneously as "red" and "red-baiter" (Joseph Losey's characterization of her in a letter to the author), so that it was judicious simply to pass over her.[10] In the equally grotesque sexual-political climate of our (endlessly) transitional period, the status of a woman alters radically as she steps out of earshot, on the implicit principle that, although we all certainly know that some women are superior, any woman whom we have not personally seen to be superior is not one of them. Thus "cultural slippage" allows a key figure in American theatre to fall silently into oblivion.

Yet we must remember that as she looked ahead to the future, she placed her trust in us to see her contributions clearly. In 1986, the fiftieth anniversary year of the founding of the Federal Theatre Project, we are beginning to recover her heritage. The archives of the Federal Theatre, rescued from oblivion by Dr. Lorraine Brown and Dr. John Connor, have been restored and made available at George Mason University. Here the Institute on the Federal Theatre Project and New Deal Culture has become the center for oral history, performances, displays, publications and discussion. Perhaps now history will be able to fulfill properly the injunction Hallie Flanagan gave us a half century ago.

TALENT AND THE TIMES

Toby Cole

How does a theatre agent, beset with the daily concerns of contracts and careers, make an impact trying to steer American theatre away from purely commercial ventures? This was the question I tried to answer as an advocate for socially-relevant work during the sixteen years I ran New York's Actors and Authors Agency out of a small office above Sardi's Restaurant. My agency began in 1957 with the aim of rehabilitating the careers of actors hurt by McCarthy era blacklisting, then went on to represent American and British writing that best reflected the antiwar and pro-underdog sentiments of the 1960s. Looking back, it is clear that my efforts to resist Broadway's philistinism were informed not just by several exceptional talents but also by the tenor of the times.

My Jewish immigrant parents balanced a steadfast loyalty to a Socialist vision of society with their struggle to establish a life in America and their sentimental love of opera. I got my first taste of performing while in high school in 1928, and then in the 1930s in "agitprop" plays with an amateur dramatic group, a part of the Jack London Club—one of the many left-wing clubs proliferating at that time to champion artists' and workers' rights. Lacking formal plays, we honed our abilities with "mass chants" adapted from poetry, such as the popular *America, America* by Alfred Kreymborg that demanded, "What have you done with all your gold, America, America? What have you bought and sold of human flesh and misery?" I recall taking our rousing message to an amateur night at a local Newark, New Jersey, burlesque house.

My training in the basics of the Stanislavski method began across the Hudson at New York's New Theater School. I was inspired by productions such as *Waiting for Lefty* and other Clifford Odets plays flawlessly mounted by the method-trained permanent company of the Group Theater. My own first professional engagement was as an "extra" in Hallie Flanagan's Federal Theatre, which thrived from 1935 to 1939. Soon after beginning acting training, I joined the staff of the New Theatre League, the coordinating office of some fifty workers' theatres throughout the country. There I was the booking agent for appearances of progressive and pro-union folk singers like the now-legendary Leadbelly, Woody Guthrie and Pete Seeger. With the onset of World War II, I closed the League's office and organized the donation of its archives to the New York Public Library for the Performing Arts. On Broadway, I was an assistant to the producer of the successful musical *Finian's Rainbow*. In 1947 I edited, for Lear Publishers, a collection of essays by Konstantin Stanislavsky and other Russian directors from a New Theatre League publication (Theatre Workshop); *Acting: A Handbook of the Stanislavski Method* has been in print for over fifty years.

Spurred on by my husband Aron Krich (a poet and publisher of Lear Books), two years later I collaborated with my sister-in-law Helen Krich Chinoy on the seminal textbook *Actors on Acting: The Theories, Techniques and Practices of the World's Great Actors, Told in Their Own Words*. In 1953 we co-edited *Directors on Directing: A Source Book of the Modern Theatre*. In 1960 I concluded the series with *Playwrights on Playwriting: From Ibsen to Ionesco*.

By the mid-1950s, my son John was ready for school. The worst of the McCarthy witch hunts having subsided, I was ready to seek a more active role in the American theatre. Lacking the drive and experience to pursue an acting career, I learned the ropes of actor-representation at the Lucy Kroll Agency, where I scouted and signed the promising young actor James Earl Jones. Setting out on my own, I was interested in representing some of the many talented performers driven to the margins by the House Un-American Activities Committee's (HUAC) intrusions into theatre and film. Zero Mostel (1915–1977), a gifted cabaret artist and "Borscht Belt" performer, had been blacklisted for a decade from radio, TV and film, and was dropped by the William Morris Agency. At a meeting in my home, Mostel—who had turned mostly to painting—agreed to let me represent him. His actor-director friend Burgess Meredith cast him in *Ulysses in Nighttown*, a stage adaptation of the most lurid episode of James Joyce's *Ulysses*. While I had seen Mostel as a stand-up comic at Cafe Society in Greenwich Village, this was my first experience of him in a dramatic role. Joined by many Irish literary figures at the Bagel Workers Union hall on opening night (June 5, 1958), the audience was riveted to Mostel's brilliant evocation in voice and mime of Leopold Bloom. His performance heralded a new sophistication for the emerging off-Broadway movement and a potentially giant presence among American stage actors. My faith was fully justified in 1961 by his magical switching of species in Ionesco's *Rhinoceros*.

But while Mostel often spoke longingly of tackling Falstaff, Moliere, even Brecht's *Galileo*, the mercurial part-time painter opted, after a year's indecision, for a lucrative musical-comedy career. Enlivening *A Funny Thing Happened on the Way to the Forum*, he subsequently fixed himself in the popular imagination as Tevye in *Fiddler on the Roof*, while in private the actor ridiculed such lowbrow fare. The central character in novelist Saul Bellow's tour-de-force comedy *The Last Analysis* was a "humanities"-ridden comedian turned therapy guru. The part seemed written for Mostel, though Bellow had never seen him onstage. The actor's rejection of the role as too "strenuous" and the play's subsequent poor production and failure caused a disillusionment that would keep Bellow from writing further for the stage. Having represented the future Nobel laureate in the venture, this was my greatest disappointment as an agent. Mostel turned to entertainment lawyers, to revivals and tours of the successful musicals. His enormous talent wasted, Mostel died at 62, ironically, after a single performance as Shylock in the first preview of Arnold Wesker's adaptation of *The Merchant of Venice*.

Faced with the fickleness of some actors and the difficulty of placing them in consistently challenging roles, I turned my attention to representing playwrights. Augured by Julian Beck and Judith Malina's pioneering experimental Living Theatre, the new consciousness of the 1960s invigorated Off-Broadway and gave rise to Off-Off-Broadway. Thanks to my championing of outsiders, the young rock rebel Sam Shepard felt comfortable leaving a successful commercial agency and offering his plays to me. Fostering his reputation by arranging popular stagings of his arresting one-act American-absurdist sketches, Shepard gained wider recognition with the production of *Operation Sidewinder* at New York's Lincoln Center Theater and his collaboration on the screenplay for Michelangelo Antonioni's *Zabriskie Point*.

During the crest of the movement against the Vietnam War, I was proud to be associated with Barbara Garson's "cause celebre" antiwar send-up of President Lyndon Johnson, *MacBird*, which enjoyed a long run at New York's Village Gate. Unfortunately, when I eagerly gave the British rights to Joan Littlewood, an icon of British alternative theatre, her complete revision of *MacBird's* verse parody proved disastrous.

On frequent trips to Europe, I was impressed by the profusion of younger playwrights working with frankly class-conscious themes at London's Royal Court Theatre under the helm of the great George Devine. Among these, I recruited Edward Bond *(Saved)* and John Arden *(Serjeant Musgrave's Dance)*. Lamentably, their stark and visionary plays were not well served by America's inexperienced actors, who were daunted by British accents. Often I felt at odds with rising impresarios whose promotional instincts were stronger than their allegiance to the theatre as an art. In Mike Nichols's hands, however, Ann Jellicoe's *The Knack* proved one of the agency's few financial successes. Also, I took great satisfaction in the poetic melodrama of William Alfred's *Hogan's Goat*, a play whose strong attack on the Catholic Church may have thwarted Hollywood agent Swifty Lazar's attempts to sell the play as a film.

In the early 1970s, the last years of the agency, I arranged the introduction of West End playwrights Simon Gray and David Hare (both then unknown to the U.S.). Increasingly I was drawn to European works in translation, among them the avant-garde Austrian Peter Handke's *Offending the Audience* and English versions of Bertolt Brecht by the noted drama critic and scholar Eric Bentley. Thanks to Henry Popkin and Daniel Gerould, keen observers of the Eastern European stage, I circulated the plays of Slawomir Mrozek and Stanislaw Witkiewicz. Due to my own passion for all things Italian, I also made the rounds of Broadway producers with the wonderful Neapolitan comedies of Eduardo De Filippo, Italy's most beloved playwright, and was appointed U.S. representative of the Pirandello Estate. Another Nobel laureate, Chile's Pablo Neruda, became a part of my list when I encouraged Farrar, Straus and Giroux to publish Ben Belitt's translation of Neruda's opera *The Splendor and Death of Joaquin Murieta*.

With the New York scene dominated by high-budget, low-value revivals and its press—including the *New York Times*—as yet indifferent to alternative developments in the theatre, I distributed my own play catalog and licensed college, university and regional performances nationwide. But my frustration with misguided productions reached its peak with Wooster Street Performing Garage's *The Tooth of Crime*—a sad waste of Sam Shepard's finest work, which I had already seen come to fruition at the Royal Court Theatre, twice.

With the Vietnam War still raging and Richard Nixon at his worst, I left the United States, relocating far from Broadway in the permanent stage set of Venice, Italy. During my expatriate years, I conceived and edited two literary readers: *Venice* (1979) and *Florence* (1981), published by Lawrence Hill and distributed by Farrar, Straus and Giroux. I also became a guide to the Jewish Ghetto of Venice, helping to reawaken awareness of its significance and monuments. Returning to the United States, I settled in Berkeley, California. There, from 1985–1995, I programmed numerous radio broadcasts—including a yearlong series on socialism, portraits of Samuel Beckett, and readings of activist plays such as *The Death of Steve Biko*—for the literature and drama department of Pacific Foundation's KPFA-FM, under the invaluable guidance of my mentor Susan Stone.

Like any good agent, the best I could do for those I represented was to make it possible for their talent to shine. I did this by teaming them with the highest standard of artists, while serving as a buffer against rejection and a guard against poor choices and crass temptations. Through the hurly-burly of so many opening nights, I tried to maintain a standard of seriousness and excellence in keeping with my own tastes and beliefs. At the least Bond, Bellow, Arden, Gray, Handke, Garson and Shepard provided me and American audiences with unforgettable glimpses of how theatre can transform lives, awareness, and a society much in need of transformation.

MATRIARCHS OF THE REGIONAL THEATRE

Dorothy B. Magnus

More than half a century ago, three intrepid women director-producers, Margo Jones, Nina Vance and Zelda Fichandler, led a significant revolution in the American theatre. It was a revolt against commercialism, centralization, the joblessness of theatre artists, and the failure to experiment with the classics or new plays. They were disenchanted with the Broadway theatre for perpetuating these ills. They waged a battle for the survival of good live drama in new regional theatres that sprang up from local impulses and the determination of these strong individuals.

"Neither the building, nor the organization, nor the finest plays and actors in the whole world will help you create a fine theatre if you have no consistent approach of your own, a true philosophy of the theatre."[1] So said Margo Jones, first of the distinguished matriarchs of the regional theatre. On June 3, 1947, modern American regional theatre was born with the opening of Margo Jones's Theatre '47 in Dallas. According to historian Joseph Zeigler, throughout her theatre's history until her death in 1955 she "served as high priestess of the movement and a measure for all others." Margo Jones achieved her eminent position not only through her life and her work, which were the same, but also through her book, *Theatre-in-the-Round*, which has been called "the nearest thing to a bible in the regional theatre world—an extraordinary self-testament which makes awesome reading because it is prophetic and above all pure."[2]

She tells her story in part this way: "My interest in theatre started very early . . . At eleven I knew I wanted to do plays, and up went a sheet in the barn where my sister and my brothers joined me in my first producing-directing venture . . . Until I was fourteen, I did not have a chance to see a professional production of a play. New vistas opened to me in Fort Worth when I watched Walter Hampden as Cyrano . . . I went to a girls' college [Texas State College for Women] where the drama courses were crowded with aspiring actresses, and I was the only student interested in directing . . . I did a certain amount of acting in college plays, but always with the clear understanding that I was doing it to acquaint myself with the actor's viewpoint and problems."[3] She speaks of being an avid reader of the classics and later of new scripts.

At the time, no graduate program in drama was available from her alma mater; she took her master's degree in psychology but held to her interests by doing the thesis on "The Abnormal Ways Out of Emotional Conflict as Reflected in the Dramas of Henrik Ibsen," case studies of the behavior of three of Ibsen's female characters: Hedda Gabler (suicide), Ellida (hysteria) in *The Lady from the Sea* and Irene (insanity) in *When We Dead Awaken*. She had the opportunity to direct one of these plays, *Hedda Gabler*, on her first directing job a year later, after a summer of study at the Pasadena Playhouse. The next step in her education was a trip around the world. She went to theatres in Japan, China, India, England, France before she had seen New York.

While she was abroad, the Federal Theatre was started. Upon her return home, she became assistant director of the Houston Federal Theatre. Following the collapse of that project in Houston, she went abroad again, this time to see the Moscow Art Theatre Festival, which she covered in a series of articles for the *Houston Chronicle*. On this trip, she also saw Berlin and Warsaw and revisited London and Paris.

When she returned this time, she knew she wanted to have a theatre of her own. The Houston Recreation Department offered her a job teaching playground directors to do plays with children in the various parks of the city. The department had a small building with a stage which was used for square dances three days a week. Since she believed her place was primarily in the little theatre movement, she asked to use that small building free of charge to produce plays provided she kept up her other duties in recreation. The moment she received permission to use the theatre, she announced in a press release that the Houston Community Players had been formed and *The Importance of Being Earnest* was to be the first production. The play was done, ran two nights, and she managed to get one review in the newspaper. Since the theatre was not available for the second production, Elmer Rice's *Judgment Day*, the cast performed in a courtroom, which now seems mildly prophetic of what was to come.

The Houston Community Players also presented the classics—Shakespeare, Molière and others. While gathering material for his book, *Advance from Broadway*, Norris Houghton visited Margo's theatre and wrote that one of her most provocative statements was: "My most successful box-office productions have been the classics. I always have to sell standing room for Shakespeare, Ibsen, or Chekhov."

In the spring of 1939 she was introduced to theatre-in-the-round at a theatre conference in Washington, D.C. She saw a production in a hotel ballroom that impressed her so much she felt she could do something similar in Houston. "I remember that on the train back to Houston, I shocked a girl sitting next to me by springing up from my seat all of a sudden and exclaiming, 'Why not!'" Her theatre in Houston was too hot for summer productions; theatre-in-the-round seemed to be the answer. "All I had to do," she said, "was to persuade one of the hotels to give me an air-conditioned room on the mezzanine. I succeeded in this, and we produced six plays during the summer. It was my first directing experience with theatre-in-the-round."[4]

During World War II, she moved to university theatre as a faculty member of the drama department of the University of Texas. There she directed three new plays and worked on several theatre-in-the-round productions, including one of new scripts. At the end of 1943 she decided that her way in the theatre pointed to the formation of a permanent resident professional theatre with a repertory system, producing new plays and classics. In the summer of 1944 she received a grant from the Rockefeller Foundation to develop her plan and do research on the few professional theatres of that time. Besides her theatre in Dallas, she envisioned the creation of similar theatres throughout the country; she was for the principle of decentralization.

Before she had time to get well into the research project, she answered a call from New York to codirect Tennessee Williams's *The Glass Menagerie*. It meant adding the training of the Broadway stage to her experience. Besides, she said, "I believed in Williams and I loved the play."

While the search for a suitable building for her theatre in Dallas was in progress, Margo took two leaves of absence to direct plays on Broadway, one of which was Maxwell Anderson's *Joan of Lorraine*. She returned home with the determination that the job in Dallas could be delayed no longer. An attractive, modern building of stucco and glass brick was finally located on the Fair Park Grounds. It was air-conditioned and adaptable to theatre-in-the-round. In the spring of 1947 all papers were signed with the approval of the State Fair Association and the City Park Department. On June 3, Theatre '47 opened with William Inge's *Farther Off from Heaven*, which, when he became famous, he revised and retitled *Dark at the Top of the Stairs*. Margo considered the search for new plays a great adventure. Williams's *Summer and Smoke* was brought to Broadway directly from its debut in Dallas. Likewise, Jerome Lawrence and Robert E. Lee's *Inherit the Wind* moved directly from her theatre to Broadway in 1955. The two authors now offer an award each year to the person or theatre in America demonstrating the most initiative in finding and producing important new scripts.

Theatre '47 completed its season with enough funds to start Theatre '48 with a twenty-week plan; Theatre '49 ran for thirty weeks and Theatre '50 followed the same plan. As to the name, she says: "Suggested by a theatre in Prague, it is changed every year on New Year's Eve in order to remain contemporary at all times. The audience that night is asked to attend the performance a little later than usual and to join the actors, after the play, in greeting the new year and the new name of the theatre."[5] It was Margo Jones's conviction that "a theatre person is good in proportion to the inspiration, amusement, beauty and education he can give to others. I want for other people what I want for myself; to live life to the fullest, to see good plays, to read good books, to see great paintings, to hear fine music." Until her premature death, this distinguished pioneer made her theatre a place for these passionate beliefs.

Following in the footsteps of trailblazer Margo Jones was a handful of disciples who created the theatres that were to form the backbone of the regional theatre revolution. First of the disciples to make history was Nina Vance, who had worked with Margo Jones and the Community Players in Houston. Reared in the tiny community of Yoakum, Texas, she comes from a background boasting a pioneer spirit typical of the rigorous Depression life in the rural Southwest. She received her B.A. degree from Texas Christian and did postgraduate work at the University of South Carolina, Columbia and the American Academy of Dramatic Art. The same year Margo started her theatre in Dallas in 1947, Nina began the Alley Theatre in Houston, in a friend's dance studio, with the support of more than a hundred interested Houstonians. The inaugural production, Harry Brown's *A Sound of Hunting*, opened late in November 1947 and ran for ten nights. In 1948 the Alley, then an admittedly amateur group, presented five more plays. There were respectable audience-pleasers, among them Lillian Hellman's *Another Part of the Forest*, Clifford Odets's *Clash by Night*, Somerset Maugham's *Caroline*. By 1949 their playhouse was condemned and the Alley found new larger quarters in an abandoned fan factory. Soon Vance decided that star performers were needed to save the Alley from financial crises. They became an Equity company when Albert Dekker came to play in *Death of a Salesman*. Actors and directors like Signe Hasso, Chester Morris, Alan Schneider and William Ball worked on the Alley's "postage stamp stage."

The Alley was selected by the Ford Foundation as one of the first regional theatres to receive major financial help in 1960. The theatre received a three-year grant of $156,000 to enable it to attract known actors away from Broadway with the promise of $200-a-week salaries over forty or more weeks each season. Of the total money needed, the foundation's grant provided half (the first $100 per week per actor), and the theatre was required to supply the other half. The Alley was on its way to full permanence with some national recognition, but still it was limited by its much too small fan factory theatre.

In 1962, the theatre received the largest of a series of Ford matching grants to regional theatres for the construction and running of a new theatre. Nina Vance chose New York architect Ulrich Franzen, and together they set out to design and build a mammoth theatre that looms above the Civic Center in downtown Houston on land donated by the Houston Endowment.

The theatre opened its new $3.5 million two-theatre playhouse in October 1968 with Brecht's *Galileo*. Concurrent with the move into the new theatre came other major changes; from a half-dozen actors in the late 1950s to more than three times that number now and from 225 seats in the fan factory to nearly eleven hundred in the new building, which includes a replica of the fan factory stage.

Zeigler has said of these leaders of regional theatres that they "started their theatres in order to create places for themselves to direct plays . . . It is significant that today most of these people direct plays rarely if at all. Early in the life of their theatres they discovered that no one else wanted to do the 'dirty work' of management, without which the theatre would collapse . . . Soon, however, the dirty work began to get not only cleaner but also very interesting and far more dynamic than the interplay of actors."[6] Nina Vance exemplifies this pattern of moving from director to producer.

Margo Jones once wrote: "The production of classics is healthy, but . . . the seeds of progress in the theatre lies in new plays," and Nina Vance shared this belief. The first new play presented by the Alley Theatre, Ronald Alexander's *Season with Ginger*, was produced in 1950. Later retitled *Time Out for Ginger*, the play became a Broadway success starring Melvyn Douglas. Another Alley premiere, in 1955, was James Lee's *Career*, which the Alley dedicated to the memory of Margo Jones. That play later went on to Broadway success and was made into a film starring Dean Martin and Shirley MacLaine.

The Alley had its first playwright-in-residence, Frank Gagliano, in 1960. His play, *The Library Raid*, was produced in Houston. Later the work went to Off-Broadway as *Night of the Dunce*. Another Alley playwright-in-residence was Paul Zindel, then an unknown writer of novels and plays. His play *The Effect of Gamma Rays on Man-in-the-Moon Marigolds* was premiered by the Alley in 1965. The play then disappeared, except for a showing on educational television, until it was mounted at the Cleveland Playhouse in 1969 and went on from there to Off-Broadway success and the Pulitzer Prize.

Nina Vance's prestigious theatre of the Southwest has been called the most regional of the regional theatres. Full credit goes to the financially astute and successful director-producer who started her penny-postcard recruitment of theatre supporters with two now famous words, "Why not?" Miss Vance died in the winter of 1980.

Zelda Fichandler shares billing with the other two matriarchs of the regional theatre revolution. Indeed she is one of its most persuasive advocates. Looking back twenty years she says, "Some of us looked about and saw that something was amiss. What was essentially a collective and cumulative art form was represented in the United States by the hit-or-miss, make-a-pudding, smash-a-pudding system of Broadway production. What required by its nature continuity and groupness, not to mention a certain quietude of spirit and the fifth freedom, the freedom to fail, was taking place in an atmosphere of hysteria, crisis, fragmentation, one-shotness and mammon-mindness within ten blocks of Broadway."[7] Zelda Fichandler's Arena Stage was, in its inception, like the Alley's, modest in scope but high in ideals. Fichandler named Jones as the person who influenced her most. "She showed me the road. And in 1949 she took the time to talk to a frightened young girl to encourage her objectives and stiffen her right arm." In 1950 the Arena Stage began at a time when Washington's only roadshow theatre, the National, had closed its doors rather than integrate. Its first home was in a dilapidated neighborhood in northwest Washington in the old Hippodrome movie theatre with 247 seats.

Boston-born Zelda, who received her B.A. from Cornell, was finishing her M.A. at George Washington University when her mentor there, Edward Mangum, impressed by her ability included her in his planning for a theatre. She was the one who had the time and the energy to work night and day on the idea. She found the old movie house, cleverly skirted antiquated Washington regulations requiring a fire curtain (an impossibility in an arena theatre) and obtained a special allowance for the new theatre (which prohibited the use of the word "theatre" in its name).

The Arena Stage differed from the Alley in that from the start it was professionally staffed and had an Equity company. Early members included George Grizzard, and Alan Schneider was the resident director. The inaugural production was *She Stoops to Conquer*, followed by *The Glass Menagerie*, *The Hasty Heart* and *The Importance of Being Earnest*. The theatre rediscovered and found success with plays which had been commercial failures on Broadway, notably *Summer of the Seventeenth Doll*, *Epitaph for George Dillon* and *The Disenchanted*.

For five years Zelda forged ahead with Arena Stage despite great financial odds and difficulties, not the least of which was audience support. A narrow percent of the population, upper middle income, highly educated, professional, seemed to form the audience core for regional theatre; the common man, it was found, is fairly uncommon among those who attend live professional performances. Recognizing the need to broaden the base of audience support, Zelda said, "If we wish to attract . . . the 'new working class'—engineers, technicians, researchers and teachers—who are not economically depressed or sensorially dead, then we must attract them with the directness of our work, its abrasion, its physical energy, its source within life."[8] By the mid-fifties, the theatre had gross receipts of $121,000 and outgrown its first musty home. Halfway through a successful run of Agatha Christie's *The Mousetrap* in its American premiere, the theatre closed and the search began for a new location. An abandoned brewery to which clung the stale aroma of long-since-emptied beer kegs became the second home in 1956. The opening play in the "Old Vat" was an expanded version of Arthur Miller's *A View from the Bridge*, directed by Alan Schneider.

In 1961 a new 796-seat Arena Stage Theatre was built, becoming the largest new theatre constructed for a permanent professional company, and the first professional theatre in America built specifically in arena style. It grew out of Zelda's decade of experience with the arena form and solidified her commitment to it. What had started from simple economic and structural necessity had evolved into a positive philosophy of theatre for Zelda who extolled the circular form. The new theatre was the first American professional production of Brecht's *The Caucasian Chalk Circle*.

Like the Alley Theatre, the Arena Stage was an early favorite of the Ford Foundation. When the time came to build the new theatre, however, there was an acute need for funds. The only way to obtain gifts was to be nonprofit. Arena Stage was therefore reconstituted into a nonprofit parent organization, the Washington Drama Society. A stream of funding proposals has emanated from Zelda, who is considered the best writer of grant proposals in the regional theatre and an acknowledged genius of theatrical subsidy on the East Coast. Her Arena Stage has become *the* major nonprofit theatre institution in the East outside New York.

In January 1971 Zelda opened the $1.5 million Kreeger Theatre as an addition to her Arena Stage, "christening it with the American premiere of the British comedy, *The Ruling Class*, by Peter Barnes."[9] For the new addition to her building, Zelda programmed an "Old Vat" Room, in honor of former days, a place for the company and the audience to gather, and wonder, together. During the 1950s Zelda Fichandler's interest in new plays was steady. In the early years of her theatre she presented the premiere production of Robert Anderson's *All Summer Long*, which went to Broadway, Robinson Jeffers's *The Cretan Woman* and Josh Greenfeld's *Clandestine on the Morning Line* (financed by a Ford Foundation Grant).

A stunning leap forward in the growing interest in new plays came with the premiere of *The Great White Hope* at Arena Stage in Washington in 1967.

This one premiere was a major turning point of the regional theatre revolution because it proved the national power of new plays. As director Edwin Sherin later pointed out, "It all happened because of the whimsical and radical genius of Zelda Fichandler . . . she has the vision of a seer. She believed in it!"[10] Howard Sackler's *The Great White Hope* was a gargantuan undertaking for Arena Stage. Despite a grant of $25,000 from the National Endowment for the Arts, Arena Stage lost $50,000 on the two-mont premiere; but the theatre gained something that could not be measured in dollars. It gained for itself a place in the forefront of the modern American theatre, as representatives of the nation's media flocked to a regional theatre to report on the latest rage.

In the fall of 1968, the play opened on Broadway (after having been sold to the movies for nearly $1 million) with Arena director, Edwin Sherin and Arena star James Earl Jones, plus a large portion of the Arena company riding with the play onto Broadway. The show received immediate laudatory reviews and went on to win many theatre awards, including the Pulitzer Prize.

Now Zelda began to concentrate more and more on mounting premieres. The season after *The Great White Hope* she premiered Arthur Kopit's *Indians*. In the next three seasons, Arena Stage offered premieres of Arthur Giron's *Edith Stein* (directed by Zelda); Stanley Greenberg's *Pueblo* (subsequently seen by millions with Hal Holbrook starring in the Emmy award-winning television version); Jay Broad's *A Conflict of Interest* and Michael Weller's *Moonchildren*. For her efforts in new plays, Zelda was given the Margo Jones Award in 1972, by then long overdue. The record of the recent seasons is testimony to her continuing dedication with six premieres of which *The Ascent of Fuji*, directed by Zelda during the 1974–75 season, was only the second play by a Soviet writer to be shown in the West in nearly a decade.

Thanks to the three intrepid women pioneer director-producers who led the revolution against Broadway, theatre in America has penetrated the so-called hinterlands. The shackles of Broadway have been broken, and the winds of change have blown over theatre USA in large part because these three woman have said, "Why not?"

PEGGY CLARK KELLEY: REMINISCENCES OF A "DESIGNING" WOMAN

Peggy Clark Kelley

I always wanted to be an actress. Although both my parents were scientists— my father was professor of anatomy at the University of Pennsylvania and other universities and he and my mother did research on blood circulation and published articles together—they were both active in theatre. Wherever they lived they started little theatres so that I grew up with this love of theatre as well as with exposure to the sciences and to the liberal arts. What got in my way as a budding actress was my height. I just kept growing and growing. I'm five eight and three-quarters. At Smith College I always had to play the men's parts in our all-female productions. I begged Samuel Eliot, our professor, "Can't I be something other than a spear-carrying servant. I really want to act." "Well, Peggy," he replied, "I can't see you as a woman, and you couldn't be a noble, so you'll have to be a slave." This was a rather devastating thing to say to somebody who was just seventeen and having her problems growing up. I said to myself: "If this is going to be the way casting directors look at me, my career as a great actress in the American theatre is over before it's begun. In the big world out there, they won't cast me for men's parts; the men can do it better." I decided to concentrate on my other love, which was painting and design. I *had* to be part of the theatre. I took all the art, costume, lighting, scene design and architecture and drafting courses I could. Smith College gave me all the things I wanted, I thought the theatre in our old Students Building was *mine* and I did everything for the shows we put on. At Smith we had no feeling that if we were in design or production we were being women in a man's field. It was our field; it was our theatre. You were as good as anybody else, and that is a marvelous thing to learn somewhere in your life.

At Yale the situation was rather different. I got into Yale without any problems because Donald Oenslager, who was head of the scenic design program, had studied at Harvard with Oliver (Pete) Larkin who was my professor at Smith. When they found that I had had architectural drafting, they put me to work drafting the first major production of the year. They assigned me to various crews, and everybody was pleased. I thought, "Well, this is fine. I'm going to get to do exactly what I want." It seemed a marvelous extension of the major I had created for myself at Smith. The courses I took on my own, drafting at Smith and extra lighting at Yale, provided the skills that I've earned my living by far more than the courses that were prescribed for me.

When I came back for the second year, however, I had to prove myself all over again. Their whole attitude at Yale at that time seemed to be, "Let's not waste time on the women because they're going to get married and are not going on professionally. We'll use the women on crews if they do well, but we won't give them the extra plums in design because it's the men we're interested in." The women at Yale were mainly in acting or in costume design. There were very few who went into scenic or lighting design.

By the time I got to the third year in the design program, there were two boys and I getting our degree in design. It was the hardest year for the three of us. We had to do sketches to compete for the right to design the major productions, of which there were four each year on the main stage. The first show was about Carlotta and Maximilian. I liked my designs best, but they gave the assignment to one of the men. I was very upset. At that point, I got a note from the vocational office at Smith that there was an opening in Florida in an interior decorating shop for twenty-five dollars a week. It was during the Depression, remember. So I wrote home and I said, "I have been a burden to you all long enough. I'm going to take this job and quit; obviously they're not interested in me. I'm a woman and I'm never going to get anywhere in this man's world." My father was teaching anatomy but he got somebody else to take his classes. He and my mother drove up to New Haven for the weekend and took me out to dinner at Savin Rock. We sat and looked at the ocean, and he said: "Now look here, Peggy; you have talent, you've gone this far, you're doing well, we've talked to the faculty, they're intrigued with what you can do, they think you have promise. Finish and get your degree. You don't have to worry about being a burden, because Granddaddy is paying for it." They said, "Look, there must be some girl who desperately needs that job, and you don't need it. Anybody can sell antiques or interior decorating things but not everybody can design scenery and so, if you'll finish the year out we'll give you the next year, if you want to travel—look at the theatre—even go to Russia [which in 1938 was quite a thought] or go to New York, or whatever you want, since we're not paying for this year at all. And it will mean so much to Granddaddy." My grandfather got the first Ph.D. they ever gave at Yale in Zoology. My father got his A.B. at Yale. They felt I should have that Yale degree. After all, none of us knew any way to go in the theatre except the academic way; we didn't have family connections with theatre or anyone to turn to say: "Here's somebody, can she be an apprentice or something?" That's why I was doing it the academic way, and I knew that once I got through Yale I would need a year of internship, working with a designer, to find out what happened professionally before I could try my wings at designing, even though I was convinced from when I finished high school that I could design better than anyone. What can I tell you? If you don't have that kind of feeling about yourself, do something else, because it's a hard row to hoe.

Anyway, I finished the year out; I got to design the next production, which was most interesting, and I got to light it too; nobody'd ever done the sets and lighting before, at Yale. Then I was mad because I couldn't do the costumes, because I didn't like what the costume designer did, but that's another thing. While I was at Yale I took the exam for the Theatrical Designers' Union and passed it. Young people do that quite a lot now but they don't always pass it. So that, when I graduated, I was also a member of United Scenic Artists, which meant that I could work on Broadway. I was qualified. I stamped my thesis, which was *Sadko*, the opera by Rimski-Korsakov, with the union stamp. Oenslager was so funny, he said, "Well, we all take an oath never to harm a brother member—I had to pass you." Koenig, who was a third-year design student at Yale my first year and took the exam the same time I did, had done some designing professionally, so I said, "Look, next year you're going to get a lot of shows to do and I would like to be your assistant." He said, "Fine, if you pass the exam let me know." We exchanged addresses. When I went up to Green Mansions to design for the summer, I let him know. In midsummer, just when they were going to repeat the things they'd already done, I got a wire from him to hurry on down to New York. I went to work as his assistant. The only thing my family had to help with, and did, that year they had promised me, was to pay the union initiation fee. I went right to work in New York as Johnny's assistant. Also, then, I got some little costume designing things to do. I was very busy. I wouldn't let John pay me as much as he should have, according to the union, because I didn't think I was worth it. That was a nice bargain for him, too.

I learned a lot about where everything was, but I didn't learn enough. I had to find out about the whole union situation with stagehands and how that works, on my own, because nobody at Yale knew anything about it. I learned how important your crew is in professional theatre and how helpful and how wise a good carpenter, electrician, property man can be. For years people came from Yale and got shows to design and only did one. They might've been good but their shows never worked, because they came with arrogance and with this feeling that union crews were a necessary evil. It's terribly easy for the professionals to destroy a young person just entering on the scene. Working with Johnny, I learned these things. I was just his assistant, but I did all his drawing and found his props. I laid out lighting and saw that through because nobody did much about lighting at that point. I learned all about the shops from the good to the bad. I had an important experience working with Johnny on *Here Come the Clowns* with Eddie Dowling. Johnny had an interesting set, but he wouldn't leave me places to get lights in as I had asked him to. I couldn't do anything about it; I was just his assistant. I came in one day and the house electrician warned me that something was going on. They all liked me because I never tried to put on airs. I came with humility and good manners because I figured they'd been paid to do this job for a long time; they must know something, which was not the attitude of the recent Yale graduate at that time. Well, here was Abe Feder relighting the show. You see I hadn't any contract; I was just Johnny Koenig's assistant. I don't know what Abe expected me to do, but I looked it over and I stayed and I watched, but I never liked him very much for it. Also, he was cutting holes in the scenery where I'd asked Johnny, "Couldn't we make space for things?" Being brought in specially, Abe could do that a lot. But then I figured, "Gee whiz, there's more to this than anybody's told me, I'd better find out a little more about the whole situation; who does what to whom and so forth." I worked with Stewart Chaney on some shows, but I waited before doing any lighting on my own until I really found out how it's structured and about production electricians, etc. Nobody told me these things before.

Then, of course, there was always the resentment against a woman. These older men, for the most part, did not want to work with young people, and they certainly didn't want to work with a woman. There were some that were so arrogant, so arbitrary, and so impossible that even though you'd worry through and you'd work it out, you didn't work with them again if they couldn't adjust to you. They also would try each crew—they are like children—to see how far they can go. If they're focusing lights for you and they're up on the ladder and you know where you want the light aimed and you know you want it shaped a certain way, well, they'd swing it, they'd do all sorts of things to see how much you'd put up with. But I had more patience; I had to learn it because I knew that if I were up on that ladder I could do it so fast, but I'm not allowed there, I don't belong to the stagehands' local. They don't have very many women. Once, during the war, in Texas, the wife of a business agent, when he went to war, got taken into the stagehands' local, but I've never heard of any other women. They've had to take some blacks in here and there, so possibly there's hope for us other second-class citizens.

But the stagehands made a lady out of me, I've never appeared in slacks in the theatre. It's much more practical to wear pants when you're lighting a show, but they resent that. Now people don't so much, it's changed; but they did in 1938 when I was starting out. Women who would work in the theatre and would come in practical work clothes—slacks or trousers of one sort or another—all of the men would say, "Aha, a lesbian; she's trying to look like a man, trying to do a man's work." So I always wore, as neat as I could, a suit, but a skirt. It would be much easier to go around with pants but that whole image wouldn't work. I never wanted to have anybody think I was trying to pretend to be anything I'm not; I'm me. Well, I was doing everything. I was painting on the paint frame, you know, assisting designers, designing sets when they came my way, but they weren't hits so they didn't count, and designing costumes. Lighting just finally fell on me and happened.

There are a lot of things that make lighting a very good field for a woman because you have to be patient with these technical people who have to do the manual labor for you. It's no good going up and punching them in the nose; you've got to get it accomplished with a certain amount of cajolery and flattery, but also knowing what you want, and that it can be done. That was another thing in our famous talk, when my family convinced me to stay on at Yale, was that my parents said that I was saying that there was no hope for me, "I'm a woman and obviously they are putting barricades up here." "Well," my father said, "you're a woman, and of course it's harder because there's resentment against that. First of all, however, you've got to know your job better than any man and do it better. Don't have a chip on your shoulder that it's because you're a woman that you're discriminated against. But once, if you've made it and done something right, then it should be easier, because you *are* different."

They were right. They have always encouraged me in whatever I wanted to do and stood by, and that's wonderful. I think not everybody has that kind of family.

But being a lighting designer was hard. Each time a woman comes into the lighting field it's easier for them and eases up for everybody else. Jean Rosenthal had been lighting shows for WPA; she wasn't in the union yet, but she was about four years ahead of me at Yale. She'd also been lighting Martha Graham ballets and she worked with the Mercury Theatre. She had a harder time because she was the first woman to do lighting exclusively. After me, Tharon Musser was the next one to do lighting.

There are many women in the theatre now working in all fields. It was difficult that first year or two when I was doing everything, and we were working out of the Depression getting fewer shows each year. The union had a stewards' list where you signed up to work, and then when you got to the top of the list, they'd have a call for men to work in the paint studios. So, say there were three or four jobs that day, they'd call the three or four top people on the list and you'd draw which studio you went to. The first studio I drew I had to trade, change with another member, because they had no facilities for women. They had no extra toilet or anything there, so that limited the number of shops I could work in. I had to go where there was a separate toilet; that's the state law. Now they have to put them in for everybody, but then you couldn't send a woman where there wasn't at least a place for her to change her clothes and go to the bathroom. But once I got to the studio, no problem at all. They knew I could draw things up so I'd draw out the drops to scale, measuring them up from the designers' sketches. And then, on the paint frame, Joey Deluca was little and I was tall so we'd work along there; he'd paint in the middle and I'd go up high, and then I'd go down, sit below and paint that. But it was all very, very good experience.

Once people find that you know your job and that you're not really making a big issue and can control yourself not to cry at the wrong time or any of those ridiculous things, then they don't worry about your being a woman, at least I don't think they do. I don't worry about it, it was difficult at first; it's difficult for any young and different person to break into a new field. You can look at Ibsen's *Master Builder* and see the resentment of the old for the young; it goes on just as much as the sex problem. There are not as many women hired to design sets as there are women who *could* design beautiful sets. I think there's a prejudice in the minds of the producers or backers. Unless you're very young, you don't necessarily go around showing people your portfolio, but there have been women who designed scenery off and on all through the years. You've had combinations of people like Jean and Bill Eckart who did it as a husband-wife thing, and Helen Pond and Herbert Senn, I don't think they are married, but they've collaborated together. And of course, Aline Bernstein, she was still designing, not only costumes, but sets when I first came into theatre. Irene Sharaff did that lovely production in the thirties of *Alice in Wonderland* for Eva Le Gallienne's Repertory; mostly she's noted as a marvelous costume designer. Of course, *there* people accept women. In terms of hiring designers; if they had the choice they'd rather, all things being equal—equal experience, equal background—most producers would take a man ahead of a woman just because they think they are probably less trouble. I think that you have to learn, when you get into a situation, when you really want to fight with somebody because they're doing it wrong, not to do it because men can say all kinds of things to each other or they can hit each other or something and get something settled, but if a woman starts to yell or scream at somebody she sounds like a shrew, and right away you're handicapped there. I never knew, in certain situations when people would yell at me, just whether I was going to burst into tears or yell back at them and tell them in four-letter words what I really thought of them. Mostly I'd just simply sit and analyze, and then it turned out all right. It freezes you up when somebody yells, if the stage manager gets upset or something. But I wasn't brought up to be a fighter in terms of the words and the yelling, screaming kind of thing; I'm not good at that, I hate it. I hate to have to yell, but I will not give up my idea. I'm a fighter in terms of the bulldog—of holding on— and I do have confidence in myself.

THE LADY IS A CRITIC

Caroline J. Dodge Latta

The lady is . . . a critic? An American female theatrical critic to be exact! Preposterous? At the most a rare species? Yet over seventy women[1] in the United States currently practice this profession full- or part-time although their identities usually are known only to those who live in their circulation area. A few may gain prominence outside of their own particular sphere of influence but national recognition is elusive. There is no woman today who holds a position of national theatrical influence, who has the stature of a Walter Kerr or the household familiarity of a Clive Barnes.

One apparent reason for their anonymity is that female theatrical critics exist almost universally outside the mainstream. If they work in New York (and approximately forty-one percent do, the heaviest concentration of female critics anywhere in the country), either they are to be found as assistants to the regular drama editors or as "second stringers" on the city's major newspapers and magazines. They may also be found as primary reviewers on the many secondary specialized newspapers New York and its environs support. The majority of female critics are, however, far removed from the theatrical center. They are scattered nationwide—in Nashville, Houston, Chicago, Los Angeles.

Yet women do comprise twenty-three percent of the practicing theatrical critics in America today. To understand the range of criticism in our time and to explore the possible uniqueness of female criticism, we need to know who these female critics are, how they entered the field, where and how they work, and what special perspective, if any, they bring to their criticism.

It is interesting to note that women's responses to theatre were among the earliest to appear in print in Colonial America. Despite the social opprobrium frequently attached to women attending theatre, women managed to get some of their views about performances circulated. One of the earliest was one "Arabella Sly" who wrote the *Virginia Gazette* in 1756 asking about the "propriety of laughing at a scene without shielding her face with her fan"[2] at a performance of *The Beaux Strategem*. "Arabella" was generally "highly delighted" with the performance she attended, but another woman writing a few years later earned the distinction of registering in print the first unfavorable artistic critique written in America. In the May 6, 1760, *Maryland Gazette* "Clarinda" chastised "the bad manners of an actor who showed obvious resentment toward the audience when he was hissed, and who stopped the action of the play to instruct them not to applaud." She was also horrified "by the practice of the low comics who, being unsure of their lines, improvised vulgarity. These improvisations were even more offensive because they occurred in *Hamlet*."

Even the artistic battle lines between the sexes were firmly drawn in these early days before dramatic criticism or theatrical reviewing as a profession existed in the Colonies. (Criticism emerged as a separate form of writing in the 1790s.) An exchange of letters in the New York press in 1761 between "Philodemus" and "Armanda" placed "Armanda" in the undignified position of defending her disputed right to view a theatrical piece and express her opinion of it. She found it necessary to mount a personal attack on her opponent, "characterizing him as an old man whose early life was debauched and who now sees evil in everything."

Despite these lively beginnings, women theatrical critics fell curiously silent during most of the nineteenth century. Not until the 1890s do two names dislodge themselves from the anonymous group of women who attended the theatre and who surely discussed in detail its personalities, scandals, shortcomings and artistic merits. Mildred Aldrich contributed pieces on theatre to *Arena* (1892, 1893), the *Boston Journal* (1894) and the *Boston Herald* (1895).[3] Amy Leslie, former light-opera singer and comedienne, wrote a review of a "touring company's [1890] production of *Castles in the Air*, sold it to the *Chicago Daily News* and was hired as drama critic,"[4] a title she was to hold for the next four decades. In 1936 Ishbel Ross in *Ladies of the Press* briefly mentions four other women drama critics—Ada Patterson (*Theatre* magazine), Wilella Waldorf (*New York Post*), Carol Frink (*Chicago Herald-Examiner*) and Leone Cass Baer (Mrs. H. W. Hicks) (*Oregonian*, Portland, Oregon). Ms. Ross laments that "there have been few good women drama critics . . . with the sustained reputation of a Percy Hammond or a Burns Mantle."[5]

Interestingly enough, Ms. Ross's list does not include either Edith Isaacs, Helen Deutsch, or Eleanor Flexner, yet these women expanded the opportunities open to drama critics in general, and to women in particular, further than any of their contemporaries. Mrs. Isaacs, who began her career as a theatre critic, became editor of *Theatre Arts* magazine in 1926 and made it the most influential theatre periodical of its day. Her editorial faculties were acute, her business acumen highly developed, and her critical eye keen, assuring the public of the finest coverage of the performing arts. Nine years later Helen Deutsch, a press agent, not a critic, singlehandedly coerced the New York drama critics into forming a "Circle." Its "mission" was to award a critical prize "for the best new play by an American playwright produced in New York during the theatre season."[6] Unfortunately, however, no women drama critics were charter members of the new society. In 1938 Eleanor Flexner, former contributor to *New Theatre* magazine, an outspoken proponent of social criticism and one of the few effective radical drama critics, published *American Playwrights 1918–38*. Her book was a scathing, often penetrating indictment of the failure of America's foremost dramatists to respond creatively to the economic conditions of the Depression.

It seems appropriate that Rosamond Gilder, critic for Isaacs's *Theatre Arts* magazine (1937–48), first woman member of Deutsch's New York Drama

Critics Circle, and advocate of Ms. Flexner's sentiments that the critic's "gift places him under a social obligation, to be a teacher and a guide,"[7] should head the list of the ten best and most representative women in the profession today. This list was developed during consultations with Joseph Shipley, Secretary of the Drama Critics Circle, and with various critics. The women critics *emeriti* with Gilder are Ethel Colby (*Journal of Commerce*, 1940–70), Claudia Cassidy (*Chicago Tribune*, 1942–65), Clara Hieronymus (*Nashville Tennessean*, 1956–present), Ann Holmes (*Houston Chronicle*, 1948–present), Glenna Syse (*Chicago Sun-Times*, 1958–present) and Edith Oliver (*The New Yorker* magazine, 1968–present) comprise a groups of "old timers" who have served twenty years or more. Marilyn Stasio (*Cue* magazine, 1968–78, *New York Post*, 1978–present), Linda Winer (*Chicago Tribune*, 1979–present) and Sylvie Drake (*Los Angeles Times*, 1969–present) have been at their jobs for a decade or more. Through interviews and analyses of their writings I have sought to suggest how these important women critics see themselves and their work.

America's female theatrical critics feel that their job places upon their shoulders what Sylvie Drake calls an "extraordinary responsibility."[8] They point to roughly five traditional areas of that responsibility. The first is, as Glenna Syse points out, to one's publisher and/or editor. The way to fulfill that responsibility is to be both readable and read. The prescribed method of achieving daily readership varies from individual to individual. Claudia Cassidy admonishes "never be dull."[9] Glenna Syse offers the precise formula "to tell what I saw and liked and why." Marilyn Stasio tries to "communicate a feeling of the reviewer's experience," to so capture the essentials with words that in reading her review, one sees the performance flash before one's eyes.

Editors often see the critic as a consumer guide for the audience, the second area of responsibility. Linda Winer deplores this conception of the critic, yet includes an answer to the consumer query somewhere in her review. Ideally she would like to believe everybody would and should go to anything and everything, but practically she realizes that people do not. Part of her hostility to wearing the consumer guide hat is that her relationship with the audience is more complicated than that. She is a member of that audience and her critique is written from that perspective. She wishes her review to bridge the gulf between audience and critic, to be a continuing conversation that she and the reader might have shared, had they stopped for coffee after the show. She is, she believes, as well informed a member of the audience as she can be.

Ms. Winer does not, however, write to instruct actors or directors, the third area of responsibility. Feeling she is not one of them, she does not presume to tell them their job. If the review helps them, all to the good, but her primary concern is directed to continuing her dialogue with her compatriot-in-arms, the audience. Ann Holmes weights this third area of responsibility— what is owed to director and cast—more heavily. Exhaustive self-study convinced her that she lacked sufficient knowledge to serve as a critic who could make informed judgments of use to performers. She actively pursued funding agencies and received three major grants to enable her to "fill in the gaps." She traveled throughout Europe and America observing theatre and the cultural scene. In 1969 she ventured into territory usually off limits to critics to watch prominent American theatre directors rehearse and mount their productions. Gaining a behind-the-scene's viewpoint made her, she feels, a more astute commentator and opened her eyes to the enormous benefits that could be achieved if cooperation between critic and director was standard.

Feminine critics widen responsibility from concern with a specific production to a fourth area: responsibility to the artistic community as a whole. Such a responsibility carries with it the inherent danger that artistic groups will confuse responsibility and loyalty. They will demand respect and praise where none is due, simply because of their existence. Nothing angers Glenna Syse more than being placed in the untenable position of being criticized by the artistic community for doing her job. Clara Hieronymus echoes her complaint. Theatre criticism in Nashville, up to the time she began writing in 1956, had been primarily social backslapping, a product of a pleasantly patronizing tradition which passed out nearly unanimous accolades to most artistic endeavors. Ms. Hieronymus fulfilled her obligation to the theatre groups in her community by refusing to measure all dramatic activities by anything less than professional standards.

Objectively recording outstanding performances is, to Rosamond Gilder, the fifth and highest level of a critic's traditional set of responsibilities—responsibility to posterity. As she eloquently states:

> The clearest insight that can be attained into the mysteries of this art [of acting] which dies with its creator—dies indeed with the moment of creation—is through the eyes of the observer who has recorded his impressions for our benefit.[10]

In her monthly dramatic reviews and in her book *John Gielgud's Hamlet*, a play-by-play description of the action that occurred onstage, including every facet of vocal and physical interpretation, Ms. Gilder reported clearly, allowing herself to serve as a medium by means of which great actors' performances could be faithfully and accurately transcribed.[11] The recorded echoes of these great performances reverberate throughout future productions. Such memories, Edith Oliver adds, actually enrich performances she is currently watching.[12] They are beacons which light up the past and illumine the future.

In addition to these five responsibilities, female critics cite the following: (1) a responsibility to new performers. Edith Oliver feels it her primary duty to welcome and encourage beginners, for theatre is reborn only with an unending flow of talent. (2) Ms. Oliver extends this responsibility to include encouragement of the fledgling playwright. She served as a dramaturg at the O'Neill Theatre Center new plays program. Lehman Engel in *The Critics* compliments Marilyn Stasio's ability in this crucial area. Ms. Stasio, he feels, presents the new playwright's best qualities and points out what, in her opinion, are his weaker areas, managing throughout the whole discussion not to sound discouraging. Felt responsibility is not confined to novice performers and playwrights. Each of these critics follows the careers of their protégés, hoping to be able to report substantial progress but capable of being brutally honest with both herself and her favorites. Edith Oliver's nine-year vigil over the charismatic but unfocused talent of James Earl Jones finally bore fruit in his rendition of Boesman in Athol Fugard's *Boesman and Lena*. Tennessee Williams's *The Glass Menagerie* was championed by Cassidy in Chicago en route to New York as "honest, tender . . . brilliant."[13] What is not so well known is her 1961 critique acknowledging Williams's failure in *Night of the Iguana*, calling it "a bankrupt play."[14]

There is also (3) an unstated responsibility to the theatre at large. Edith Oliver worries in her October 25, 1969, *New Yorker* piece that "a theatre in which the artists—writers and actors—are subservient to the director seems not revivifying but decadent." Ann Holmes laments in "The Musical Show" the lack of public and private support for this unique American contribution to the theatrical world.[15] One has only to read between the lines to realize that both statements are evidence of these women's concerns about the health of the theatre in general.

Harold Clurman has written, "Critics are parts of communities, each with its own particular history and need."[16] Female critics apparently take this statement to heart, for they express movingly and convincingly the fulfillment they experience when they feel they have met this responsibility. Clara Hieronymus speaks of the necessity of knowing her community, of a twenty-five-year commitment to one place, of her unique niche, of valuing what happens here and of being valued in return, of the reward of watching her comments result in raised expectations and ultimately better theatre. Lehman Engel notes Claudia Cassidy's "courage . . . in behalf of her charge: Chicago."[17]

Rosamond Gilder carries responsibility to one's community a step further. (5) She reminds the theatre of its (and by extension her) responsibility to society. Such a responsibility often requires a critic to serve as a scourge compelling all concerned—be they artists or not—to "try to understand more clearly the satanic workings of the world around . . . [them] and attempt, at least, to use . . . [their] gifts to elucidate its meaning and thereby contribute to a better future."[18]

During World War II Rosamond Gilder focused her criticism on an analysis of the effects—adverse and advantageous—of the war upon the theatre and conversely the effect of the theatre on the war and its wearied participants. She reminded her readers that "this war will not stay out of the theatre as others have." Yet as "comedy followed comedy," she did not accept the apparently inescapable conclusion that the theatre influenced the war only by providing "momentary escape from fear and care." She contended that the theatre was capable of affecting the war in much more positive ways, as a powerful propaganda weapon.

In the end, however, she tempered her enthusiasm for propaganda. Rather, the critic should encourage the theatre to be filled with action designed to affirm the dignity and nobility of man. (6) This statement translates into a sixth level of responsibility: a responsibility to take, whenever possible, the optimistic viewpoint, not in the spirit of naïveté with head buried in the sand but honestly to find, delineate and affirm the good. Sylvie Drake's definition of the art of criticism as an act of construction, of discrimination, not of enmity, and Marilyn Stasio's fine essay on the theatre's "vital resources,"[19] are examples of positive, courageous, deeply thought and deeply felt expressions of affirmation.

In his book *Creativity in the Theatre* Dr. Philip Weissman speaks of the critic as lacking nurturing qualities. He points out that many renowned critics have been biologically childless and suggests that this barrenness may "extend from his personal to his artistic self."[20] Yet the articulated concerns of these women critics—the necessity to watch over the charge, to follow its progress, encourage its growth, remind it of its duty to others, and provide it with the best of all possible worlds—seem to be variations of nurturing behavior. Have learned feminine behavior patterns unconsciously influenced the viewpoint and writings of female critics? Ann Holmes, long-standing drama critic of the *Houston Chronicle*, would contend that women bring no special perspective to their work and that the job of reviewer demands sensitivity, not gender. We are certainly not yet ready to answer any of these questions about female or male critics; indeed we are just beginning to try to formulate ways of looking at critics and criticism.

The women's movement of the last decade has brought about a new consciousness and understanding of the problems feminine acculturation has created for female critics. For instance, part and parcel of the need to affirm is the need to affirm the self. As Linda Winer states, "I was raised to make people like me, to not make trouble, to please people, to make them more comfortable." Such admonitions are, of course, directly counter to the job of a critic. "It is irrelevant," she continues, "if they like you, yet it was a hard lesson for me to learn that my job was not a popularity contest and that professionally I must do all the things I was taught not to do in polite society." The affirmation of the self is made more difficult because men, not women, are the accepted authority figures; there is an ingrained trust in men's opinions that has given them the credibility edge. These realizations have made female critics, like all minorities, harder on themselves than on others. Women critics have often in fact so steeled themselves to a man's world that hearing another woman's voice in the theatre is a revelation. Linda Winer cites the Chicago production (not the television version) of Wendy Wasserstein's *Uncommon Women and Others*: "Listening to a woman's concerns as a woman really touched me."

Interestingly enough, most female critics, with the vocal exception of Linda Winer and Glenna Syse, do not acknowledge experiencing any difficulties in being a woman in the critical profession. Sylvie Drake feels women have always been more readily accepted in the arts. Ann Holmes points to her grants as evidence of the lack of discrimination she has experienced. Clara Hieronymus attributes any resentment toward her as due to a "southernism" (resistance to professional standards), not to her femininity. Rosamond Gilder states that she arrived on the scene after the vote had been won and as such never experienced male prejudice. And Claudia Cassidy suggests that being a woman had given her certain advantages.

Still one wonders whether women critics pay a higher price than men. Linda Winer suggests that pressures on a female critic's personal life are enormous. "We have the crazy schedule of a doctor always on call but not the excuse we are saving lives." In a traditional marriage, the male critic's nightly absences are covered by the understanding wife and mother; but in a dual-career marriage, the strains of two competing careers (especially when the woman's demands so much time) can lead to collapse.

Although the price may be great, it is evidently not great enough to deter these women. They find their profession fascinating. "I am," says Sylvie Drake, "finding myself lately more and more interested in expressing what the critical process is to me." Claudia Cassidy points to the challenge of searching for the right chemical combination that would make a production perfect.[21] At the best of times Ann Holmes considers herself a creative artist when she succeeds in abstracting the performance into another form that will make almost as great an imprint as the production itself. Marilyn Stasio speaks of the fun of it all,[22] and Linda Winer of the continual excitement of knowing there is always so much more to learn, the factor that after all is what makes any job worthwhile. As she describes it: "We are performers with the typewriter, not parasites of the arts, but rather part of the process, part of the circle of performance." And what is more, she adds, "We are beginning to be admitted to the critical fraternity." The year 1979, for instance, saw two breakthroughs into this fraternity. Glenna Syse became the first woman critic (and the first critic outside the New York area except for Eliot Norton in Boston) to be on the nominating committee for the Tony Awards (five people who see everything on Broadway) during its thirty-three-year history. And Linda Winer was the first woman to be asked to participate for an entire week as a master critic at the National Critics Institute, Eugene O'Neill Theatre Center, Waterford, Connecticut.

Although women have traditionally found equality and advancement easier in the arts, this has primarily been as actresses who would seem to professionalize the emotionalism usually identified as female. Women critics, along with women playwrights and directors, have had to combat the stereotypes in order to practice the "masculine" intellectual skill of judging. Those women who have had the courage to open up the critical "fraternity" need to be studied and celebrated. This paper offers a start on that task.

CASTING BY JULIET TAYLOR

An Interview with Helen Krich Chinoy

As the credits flash by at the end of films like Julia, The Turning Point, Close Encounters of the Third Kind, Interiors, An Unmarried Woman, *you may not notice the name of Juliet Taylor, but "Casting by Juliet Taylor" has become the hallmark of some of the best films ever made. Paul Mazursky praises her "offbeat ideas." Woody Allen says, "She towers over other casting directors. She is not just a packager or someone who moves bodies through; she is someone who is sensitive to the performers."*

The job of casting director is one of those little-known tasks that is essential to making movies today. As an independent casting director, Juliet Taylor brings together actors, directors, screenwriters and producers, often providing a link between those who work onstage and those in films. This histrionic matchmaking requires very special personal qualities and skills, ones Juliet Taylor has in abundance. In the following interview, she talks about her background, her work and her own sense of herself as a woman in a special job.

I suppose that somewhere in me at the start there must have been the desire to be a performer because I get such vicarious pleasure out of working with actors in casting. At Smith College, however, I was interested in all aspects of theatre which I was given a chance to study. That's how Smith contributed to what I am doing now since there's no specific training or preparation for casting directors. I gained a sense of theatre and performance; my critical faculties were developed as well as my ability to read a script and interpret it appropriately, which is very important.

After graduating from Smith, I took a six-week secretarial course and came to New York. I got my first job, as a receptionist for David Merrick, through someone who had gone to Smith. It makes a big difference, getting that first job. After all those years in school, I thought it was fine being in the world, earning ninety dollars a week, working six days a week. I felt I was fortunate to get a paying job in the theatre where it wasn't easy to find work. After six months a former Merrick casting director whom I had gotten to know asked me if I wanted to become a kind of secretary-apprentice in the office of Marion Dougherty to which she was moving. Marion Dougherty who had been the biggest casting director for live television for a long time, was now so busy doing film casting that she was setting up her own company. She was interested in someone who wanted to learn about casting but would do the secretarial work as well. I took that job, and never left—I stayed longer than anyone else. I ended up inheriting Marion Dougherty's business just by hanging in for five years.

Marion Dougherty was a wonderful person to work for. Interestingly enough, at first I found her more exacting than a man would have been. In a way, I was quite intimidated at first. But as time went on, that changed.

She's one of those people who once she knows and trusts you is very generous. She would share with me what she was thinking and how she felt about different parts and different actors and directors. She would include me in the process and let me sit in on things. It was a small office. She was also very generous with credit. She would tell a director that a certain actor had been my idea. That's very rare. Most people don't do that. When she left New York, she essentially left me her business through an agreement we made. It was very nice.

I've thought a lot about whether being a casting director is a career that is particularly congenial for women. Marion used to say women did it because men couldn't make enough money in it. Women would accept the pathetic salaries that men would not. That is partially true, but not entirely because men are doing other jobs in theatre that aren't that lucrative. I think that some of the personality ingredients that are needed by casting directors tend to be associated with feminine qualities. To enjoy casting and to be good at it, you have to be interested in people. You spend an awful lot of time getting to know other people. They never get to know you really. It involves a lot of curiosity and patience. I think women tend to have more of these qualities than men.

I couldn't put my finger on just what attracted me to the work except that it was a way of becoming very emotionally involved in a project. You're not always talking about concrete things; you're talking about people and feelings about them. In casting you are working on this instinct about someone, a feeling about whether they are going to project a certain quality. You develop a close relationship with directors and actors. You give them a sense of bringing something to life. Casting requires other capabilities as well. We do a lot of negotiating. There are a couple of casting directors who won't do negotiating. The ones I can think of are women. Maybe they don't feel comfortable. But I enjoy that aspect. I don't really understand what it is to be a casting director unless you have to cast within a specific budget. Anyone can cast anything if you have enough money. You have to have a sense of what the finances are. I find that interesting and challenging.

Marion taught me that you can create an environment that makes everyone comfortable. Her office was in a cozy brownstone. It wasn't at all officey. This would make the director feel relaxed. Most important was what went on in the reception area. I think that everyone who is a casting director has usually started out as a secretary. It's the way you learn to be kind and friendly to the actors who are usually very nervous. You learn not to overbook the day so that people don't have to wait a long time.

What Marion did which was really innovative in casting was that she eliminated the "grocery list" style of casting using huge numbers of people. Everything became very personal. Only people who were specifically right came in. By not having that cattle-call feeling, you eliminate a lot of the tension. You explain the scene to the actor so well that he or she feels comfortable with it. You give them the most information they can possibly have before they go in so that they don't feel like pawns in a game. They don't feel so vulnerable and at a loss. They feel like it's a one-to-one-situation. That's really important. I think it's the whole key.

Casting women—I don't know if I have cast enough women's pictures to speak about the problem, although I did cast *Julia*, *An Unmarried Woman* and *The Turning Point*. I do enjoy casting good women's roles, but I don't get much opportunity to do that. You really don't, even now. Even when the women's roles are leads, so many of the supporting roles are not. It seems as if all the background characters are always men. You don't get that many opportunities to cast an interesting group of women. I'd enjoy doing that. What goes into the choice, I guess, is my own instinct about what certain kinds of women are. To a certain degree I feel that there are only certain kinds of images of women that are acceptable to American audiences. As their leading ladies or their men's love interest, they seem to prefer women who are kind of vulnerable. That is the difference between the women who star in films in Europe and those who star in films here. There is much less variety and much less strength in the women in films here. There is an image problem. I've several times come up against directors who say that some woman is too strong. That's the reality we work with. I don't know if that's something to criticize. I think our vision is somewhat limited.

A woman to be cast has to be very lovely looking and between the ages of twenty and thirty-five. A few who have proven themselves go on working but most just stop working by the time they get to be forty. Whereas the men over forty, if they are talented at all, are starring in every television series in America. That is when they become most valuable and get paid fortunes. For women there's no counterpart to that experience.

A picture I thought really captured the female experience was Claudia Weill's *Girlfriends*. It was a very low-budget film. I helped her sort of off the record. That's a film that never could have been made by a man. I've also worked for another woman director, Joan Silver. Each director—male or female—has a very different style. I think, however, that the women do have different ideas of sexuality. I think that they are a little bit courageous in both the casting of men and of women, in terms of who they think is attractive. They are far less predictable in their choices.

Although most of my work is for films, I am a theatre person. I really enjoy theatre. I'm interested in new playwrights. I spend most of my time looking for actors in the theatre. All the new people are in the theatre. Once people get into films, they have already made it. Most successful film actors are stage-trained. You have to be because after you get by on whatever your personal charisma is that makes you magical and interesting on film, you have to have something to draw on. You have to have resources. Unless you're really an actor, you run out and the work becomes very thin. The only place you can learn is on the stage. The only film actor I can think of who didn't have any real stage background is Jack Nicholson. Not all actors who are talented on the stage have a big impact on film, but most do at some point in their careers. Very few good actors aren't personable on screen. But there are a few who aren't.

To young women who find casting an intriguing job, I'd say that it's a wide-open field. In New York now, there's more work than there are casting directors to do the job. The difficulty is getting training. There are very few casting directors to work for. Most of them can't afford to have more than one or two people working for them. Some people start as agents and switch to casting. Some start out at advertising agencies, casting commercials or soap operas. I'm glad I didn't have to do that. I think it warps your point of view.

For myself, I find working with so many different people and different points of view very interesting, really lots of fun. I like working independently. I have a two-and-a-half-year-old son and a twelve-year-old stepchild. I try to balance my personal life and my business life. I close my door after six P.M. My husband, Jim Walsh, who's a theatrical producer, and I share the household responsibilities and we have an old-fashioned Scottish nanny to help out. I'm glad my job doesn't require me to travel these days. In the future there might be other possibilities—production, etc., but right now my life is full and busy. I'm enjoying what I'm doing.

5 | IMAGES

Theatre is an imagining of human life and relationships. A theatre event displays apparent experience in such a way that those who witness the event may have their beliefs about human behavior confirmed or challenged, or both, possibly even inspired. When we prepared the first two editions of this book, theatre studies had only begun to explore the nature of image making in performance, the relationship of theatre images to social reality, or the difference between the stage image and the suggested visuals embedded in literary text. Then as now, though, there was wide consensus that gender display in theatre, as in other arts and media, has a very powerful effect on the hearts and minds of a society. Sociologist Erving Goffman's *Gender Advertisements* demonstrated with pictures taken from magazine ads how images that those who dominate society have determined to be socially useful can stifle members of both sexes. In her introduction to that book, Vivian Gornick notes that Goffman "shares with contemporary feminists the felt conviction that beneath the surface of ordinary social behavior innumerable small murders of the mind and spirit take place daily."

In the 1970s and early 1980s, many people insistently expressed indignation over what were perceived as restrictive and inaccurate images in popular culture of women, minorities and other people who experience themselves as oppressed and second class in society. As the issue came to light and research efforts were launched, theatre critics looked first at identifying negative portraits, usually static concepts, in dramatic literature (woman as whore, woman as shrew, woman as passive). There is a preponderance of theatre that displays women as either whore or madonna, foils to male heroes or Beatrice to Dante, sex objects and confections (as in a pseudo-burlesque show even titled *Sugar Babies*), frivolous and not to be taken seriously. Even those women with strong characters must conform to patriarchal rule—Shakespeare's heroines, the Duchess of Malfi, Hedda, or even poor Nora, who walks out with no place to go and must surely in actual life be destined for the paternalism of welfare.

Some changes have occurred in the society at large that may shift the norms governing mainstream theatre practices. The emergence of women as serious athletes in professional basketball and World Cup soccer as well as tennis and other sports has gone a long way toward transforming how people perceive "woman." However, a 1998 study of television, movies, music videos and teen magazines by the Kaiser Family Foundation and Children Now indicates disturbing trends continue. For example, while sixty-three percent of all the television ads targeting women were for appearance-related products, only nine percent of the ads aimed at men concerned themselves with a man's looks.

In the second edition we called for research into gender that might analyze what gender values are being reinforced or created by the stage picture alone. In addition, we argued that research should take into account male roles and various gender relationships to perceive the full implications of gender images for society as a whole. When males are themselves weak or absent (consider *Awake and Sing*), what might such a presentation say to audiences? Many questions arise as we recognize the relationship of gender display to sex-role socialization on the part of both men and women.

In our new Chapter 7 we offer a sampler of some of the most important image theory to emerge since our last edition—theory that addresses the psychosemiotics of theatre production and spectatorship as well as aspects of socioeconomic imperatives that affect gender imagery. The theories of the 1980s, though, do not fully mine the arena of gender representation onstage. Theory of another sort might be found in collections of plays by women, especially women of color that have been published in the past ten to fifteen years; see, for example, *Shattering the Myth: Plays by Hispanic Women* (1992), edited by Linda Feyder, or *Contemporary Plays by Women of Color: An Anthology* (1996), edited by Kathy A. Perkins and Roberta Uno. The topic remains ripe for exploration.

This section, surveying some of the image studies done before the mid-1980s, is a kind of historical record. It suggests approaches that see the female character in dramatic action rather than in a still image; it delineates aspects of the black female in drama, shares Susan Glaspell's clever feminist twist on the male detective image and explores the use of (and problems with) creative drama to wrestle with sex-role stereotypes. The new Chapter 7 exemplifies the predominant image studies in the years since the second edition, and the last chapter is a forum for many women in theatre today who boldly and inventively chart new paths for our imagery.

LWJ

UNIVERSITY OF WINCHESTER
LIBRARY

THE SECOND FACE OF THE IDOL: WOMEN IN MELODRAMA

Rosemarie K. Bank

To a measure, scholarship in each generation sees within the phenomenon it studies the image of itself. Thus, to the nineteenth- and early twentieth-century reader or critic, American melodrama presented female characters who epitomized the ideal woman of that period—chaste, virtuous, nurturer of home and family, charitable servant and defender of the weak and downtrodden, loving wife, sister, sweetheart and mother, loyal friend and the cornerstone of a stable, productive and decent society. This image of women supported cherished preferences for certain kinds of female behavior, behavior which was rewarded by idolizing women as kinder-hearted and morally superior to men, albeit thereby more naive and dependent, less rational and self-motivated and unfit for the world of making and doing. This view of the women in nineteenth- and early twentieth-century stage melodrama can still be found in contemporary scholarship.

There are female characters in melodrama who confirm this interpretation, but scholars today, given the general social-intellectual climate, need not automatically dismiss the idea that the image of women in American melodrama has more than this one aspect to it, just as theatrical scholarship in the past two decades has revised the general notion that melodrama and popular theatre did not merit scholarly attention.[1] Though as yet little contemporary cultural history of nineteenth- and early twentieth-century drama has emerged, a gradual shift in the depiction of women in American melodrama in the decades after the Civil War has been identified, a shift toward action. Much of the earlier, more passive, portrait of female characters has been delineated by David Grimsted in *Melodrama Unveiled*[2] (although that work is not primarily concerned with the image of women in the American plays from 1800 to 1850 which it examines). From his analysis, however, a shift appears to exist in the later melodramas of the century and those of the early twentieth century. Twenty-one of these comprise the sample for this discussion.[3] Although the selection is partial and does not isolate all variables, it is suggestive and illuminates the thesis at issue, namely that the image of woman in American melodrama from the Civil War to World War I has two aspects or faces.

The traditional view of the melodramatic heroine, and the one shared by those who do not know the form well, is of a kind, charitable, virtuous woman in trouble, usually of the villain's devising. Accordingly, the heroine is most frequently pictured wringing her hands in helpless frustration and anxiety, throwing herself desperately and impotently at the feet of a cold and indifferent villain, or tied to railroad tracks or a sawmill—the ultimate victim—to be rescued in the nick of time by a man. These pictures—virtually a poster concept of melodrama—are remembered because they are striking (precisely the reason why managers used them in their publicity in the first place), but the vision they present of women in American melodrama is, at best, a partial one.

The female characters in late nineteenth- and early twentieth-century American melodrama often play an active role. They determine their fates in three major ways: they work at jobs outside the home, they play an active role in solving the problems that beset them and they define the moral climate within which the action takes place. For example, in the sample, almost half of the heroines work outside the home. Their employment ranges from working as maids and domestics,[4] telegraphers, entertainers and teachers[5] to those who own their own businesses.[6] In addition to heroines, many other female characters are employed, largely in menial capacities such as cooks, washerwomen, maids and the like. The criterion is simple: those who need to work do so.

No concept of long-term careers for women exists in the melodramas of this period, to my knowledge, nor any sense of work for wages as pleasurable and desirable in and of itself. On the one hand, this view is socially realistic, since many of the labors performed by the female characters in melodrama who must work are neither pleasant nor fulfilling, while on the other hand, the goal for women in these plays is to be good wives and mothers, not to have careers. Accordingly, any employment which prepares women for or which does not conflict with these roles is an acceptable preliminary or stopgap activity. In short, when the female characters in these plays have no other means of support or cannot live on what their men provide, they are expected to support themselves and to do their jobs well—and they do. A number of women in American melodrama can say with their British sister May in *The Ticket-of-Leave Man* (1863), "I pay my way."[7]

In addition to employment, the majority of heroines in late nineteenth- and early-twentieth-century melodrama play an active role in solving the problems that beset them, for this is an area which vitally concerns even those female characters who need not work. In the twenty-one sample plays, for example, the central plots of one quarter (six plays) are resolved partly or fully through the actions of the heroine or another female character. This proportion is significant because the action of almost half of the samples (nine plays) is resolved by secondary characters or without the help of any agent (for example, by the death of the villain from accident or natural causes). The hero resolves the central action partly or fully in the remaining six plays. When plots are resolved through the action of secondary agents in melodrama, those agents are frequently women, and when a central plot is resolved by *one* major agent acting alone, that agent is as likely to be the heroine as the hero. It is not uncharacteristic of these plays that it is the heroine Laura in Augustin Daly's *Under the Gaslight* (1867) who breaks out of a toolshed to untie a man from the railroad tracks seconds before the train rushes by (in response to which he remarks, incidentally, "And these are the women who ain't to have a vote!").[8]

The specific things the female characters in melodramas do to solve the problems that beset them give the lie to the traditional view of a submissive, un-enterprising or defenseless creature. Deeds range from the exposure of corruption, to bringing the police, to tying up the villain or untying the hero, and so on, for examples of female courage and inventiveness abound in these plays, even though the characters are in most respects conventional women of their times. Indeed, the picture of a heroine slapping the villain smartly across the cheek or telling him off in public is a salutary antidote to the posters of heroines as victims.

The female characters in late nineteenth- and early twentieth-century American melodrama define the moral climate within which the action of the play takes place. Ethically, the heroine has the same moral status in these plays as the hero. She is considered not only capable of making moral choices, she is expected to act upon those choices and to defend her right. Socially, women are viewed as predominantly domestic beings, yet within the context of their own times melodramas give great importance and status to female characters as full partners not only in the domestic arena, but also in the vital business of securing virtue and exposing vice in society as a whole.

Poetic justice, that is, the rewarding of virtue and the punishment of vice, or the statement that this ought to be the case, is the cardinal ethical tenet of melodrama. Punishment for villainy may include death or imprisonment, but in many cases the villain is simply exposed and sent away. The reward for virtue for both men and women in melodrama is not great fortune; it is the establishment of happy family life. This is the goal for which all virtuous characters strive and it is the most frequent reward for their labors at the end of a melodrama. That reward is a heavy weight upon women, however, for the didactic devices of melodrama stress over and over again that if the family fails society falls, and women are the family. It is no accident that so few of the heroines of melodrama have mothers, for life was perilous indeed, as the hero of Bartley Campbell's *My Partner* (1879) says, for the "poor gal 'as had no mother to guide her."[9]

If the image of women in late nineteenth- and early twentieth-century American melodrama is highly proscribed and conventional in domestic matters, there is, as I have suggested, yet a "second face" to the idol. The moral force of women as people in these plays is considerable, for the female characters more than any other define what is right and wrong in life. They are actively concerned with human values in the broad sense: they help the poor, aged, sick and helpless, often at great personal expense and risk; they are tolerant of frailty (even of their "fallen" sisters) and assist those who wish to reform; they are kind, loving and hardworking when they or others are in need. What is more, the female characters in the melodrama of this period tell men what they ought to think and do morally and the male characters— unless totally depraved—follow their advice. Such advice is easily overlooked in these plays because it tends to be expressed in the form of maxims, such as "Stick to your resolution to do right, and this funny old world that trampled you underfoot yesterday will receive you with open arms today."[10]

One may argue that such moral exertions—and they abound in all nineteenth-century melodrama—do not alter the course of the world, but these plays are, for the most pare concerned with a fairly intimate sphere, a world in which not even the male characters are involved with the "big issues." Within this sphere, personal moral questions *are the* questions, and it is significantly the female characters who give them utterance and definition. This image of women as moral forces in the world is, it would seem, a more positive picture than that shown by countless contemporary cinematic and televised melodramas in which female characters urge their male counterparts to do the wrong thing because it is safer, or in other ways give testimony to, seemingly, an innate inability to tell right from wrong much less to act when a moral imperative presents itself.

Thus far, I have suggested that the women in late nineteenth- and early twentieth-century American melodrama determine their fates by working for wages, by playing an active role in solving the problems that beset them, and by defining the moral climate within which the action of the play takes place. My objective in doing so has been to challenge the view of these characters as uniformly passive, helpless, naive, irrational and uninventive. Ethically and socially this case needs to be made so that we may gain a more accurate view of the depiction of women in literature and so discharge our obligations as social historians in our own times. Accordingly, there are many unasked questions to claim the attention of cultural historians in the coming years, such as, for example, the relationship of working heroines to employment patterns in American society, whether there really is a shift away from passivity in heroines' behaviors in melodrama after the Civil War and, if so, is there a similar shift in the novel and popular fiction, and the tensions produced by the seemingly contradictory assertion that women are to be moral arbiters and yet may not participate in law or politics. The benefits of reading a play as a social document, as has been argued elsewhere,[11] are particularly evident for understanding the image of women which these plays project, and in relationship of that image to the sociocultural historical context out of which it grew.

There are also aesthetic questions which must claim the major attention of theatre scholars because to conceive of the female characters of nineteenth- and early twentieth-century melodrama, particularly of the heroine, as active affects our understanding of the structure of melodrama. The commonly accepted view of the action of melodrama envisions the hero and the villain in a tug-of-war for possession of the heroine or the heroine as a buffer between the hero and the villain. The tug-of-war concept is not supported by the facts. In this sample alone, for example, the villain has no designs upon the heroine's person or fortune in over half the plays. Further, there are a number of plays in which there is no readily identifiable villain, either because the villain and the hero are the same character or because the villain is something nonhuman, such as external circumstances or hard liquor. Though the triad appears in most melodramas of the period, then, it is not a structural necessity, since there are a number of melodramas both without villains, per se, and without a tug-of-war over the heroine.[12]

The concept of heroine as buffer[13] reflects an overemphasis upon the hero, which the action of many melodramas of the late nineteenth and early twentieth centuries does not appear to justify, for it is at least as frequent the case, if not more frequently, that action is centered on the heroine—what she does, what happens because of her, how she responds to actions initiated by others, and so forth. It is not, of course, wrong to see the hero as the central figure in the action when that is the case, but we ought not automatically assume that he is central. The male emphasis inherent in the concepts of tug-of-war and heroine as buffer slants the action of melodrama in the direction of sexual rivalry, whereas the central conflict actually appears to be ideological.

I have said here and elsewhere that poetic justice is the cardinal ethical tenet of melodrama, indeed that poetic justice is a structural necessity in melodrama (that is, that melodrama does not exist as a form without it). Since poetic justice is a statement about the world as it ought to be, the action of melodrama may actually reward virtue and punish vice, or simply establish the premise that this is the way things ought to be in the world. Given that the central conflict of melodrama is ideological, meaning, in this case, concerned with ethical matters, and given that this conflict is structural as well as ethical, then it follows that the character who is most involved with poetic justice is the character most central to the action of melodrama. I have stated that when an agent resolves the central conflict, that agent is as likely to be the heroine as the hero, and that the heroine is more likely than the hero to define the moral climate of the play. Given the close relationship between the ethical and the aesthetic in nineteenth-century melodrama, then, the *active* heroine would be the character most likely to determine the structure of the play and to exemplify and express its cardinal ethical tenet. This is an orientation toward melodrama which defies the conventional picture of heroines and female characters as consistently submissive prizes in a male-oriented sex conflict, but it is an orientation which the data appear to justify.

Melodrama is a very cohesive form. Its dramatic and theatrical aspects are closely bound to ethical and social considerations. Nowhere is this clearer than in respect to the image of women in nineteenth- and early twentieth-century American melodrama, where structural interests lead to ethical considerations, the ethical to the social, and so forth. That we have seen only one face of the idol thus far is likely due to the general neglect of melodrama by scholars through most of this century, and to some critics it still seems a bizarre idea that anyone would devote the same analytical seriousness to the characters and action of a melodrama as to those of a comedy or a tragedy. Fortunately, this attitude has begun to change in the past fifteen years, and a more equitable and complete portrait of melodrama is emerging.

Less explicable is the constant neglect of melodrama as a data source by cultural historians who have freely turned to other popular American literary sources from the nineteenth century. Perhaps that attitude will also change as contemporary theatrical scholarship in the area increases and becomes available to other disciplines. Certainly, active intellectual cross-fertilization seems particularly appropriate in the areas of popular culture and the historical depiction of women. A significant piece of that picture, it seems to me, is the "second face" of the idol, a face which will define itself through studies more extensive than this summary essay, and which the present volume does so much to encourage.

WOMEN IN PULITZER PRIZE PLAYS, 1918–1949

Judith Louise Stephens

The rapid and continuous change which characterizes the twentieth century is reflected in the life of the American woman. Female characters in the literature of the century in turn reflect these many changes. Many books, articles and scholarly studies have focused on the portrayal of women in American fiction. By comparison, few studies deal with women characters in American drama. Although there has been some critical examination of the women in the plays of a few of our leading playwrights, Eugene O'Neill, Tennessee Williams, Lillian Hellman, Rachel Crothers and S. N. Behrman, a broader and more thorough analysis of women characters in a selected body of twentieth-century American drama is needed.

I selected the Pulitzer Prize plays for study because they offer a wide range of female characters in a variety of situations, and because they occupy a fascinating position in American dramatic history. The Pulitzer Prize plays have been praised and maligned but seldom ignored.[1] Although controversy has surrounded the prizes, they have become a firmly entrenched tradition.

This study covers the years of 1918 to 1949, from the Pulitzer Prize for drama awarded to Jesse Lynch Williams in 1918 for *Why Marry?* to the award given to Arthur Miller for *Death of a Salesman* in 1949.

It seems appropriate that the first Pulitzer Prize for drama was awarded in 1918. This year begins the postwar era which is frequently chosen by historians (as well as social and literary critics) to denote America's entry into the modern period.[2] According to John Gassner, "it is one of the commonplaces of contemporary American criticism that we have been in possession of the best drama in the world since 1918."[3] Thus, the awarding of the first Pulitzer Prize signals a new tradition in an American theatre determined to break with the old. There are several reasons for terminating this study after the decade of the forties: a span of those decades with twenty-seven prize plays is sufficient in scope for one investigation; John Hohenberg notes that after Columbia University President Nicholas Butler's retirement in 1946 "no succeeding president of Columbia University sought to exercise the power that Nicholas Murray Butler has applied to the granting of the Pulitzer Prizes"[4] and the prize plays of the forties do include the fresh new talent of playwrights such as Tennessee Williams, Thornton Wilder and Arthur Miller, whose works reflect some of the societal changes brought about by World War II. In some of the chosen plays the female character is the protagonist of the play; in others she is a central figure or she is one whose action and presence figure most predominantly. This study does not aim to compare the position of American women as seen in the plays with the existing social conditions of each decade: it is not a sociological but a literary analysis. Each character was analyzed according to selected dramatic criteria and critical reviews of the plays were examined with particular emphasis given to commentary concerning the female characters.

The two specific aims of my study were: (1) to determine whether some of the criticisms pertaining to the women characters found in American fiction were valid when applied to female dramatic characters; and (2) to analyze the central female characters in the Pulitzer Prize plays from 1918 to 1949 according to traditional dramatic criteria, noting what traits or characteristics were shared by those characters and what, if any, changes occurred over each decade.

I identified four major characteristics of female fictional characters which form a partial compendium of traits regularly assigned to women characters based on conclusions reached by authors of books, articles and dissertations who have explored modern literary female characters in some depth. These characteristics are as follows:

1. *A preoccupation with love.* Most of the writers found that female fictional characters are predominantly or exclusively concerned with love. Joanna Russ, in an article entitled "What Can a Heroine Do?" found that women protagonists have been restricted to the confines of the "love story," which can have a number of variations such as falling in love, courtship, marriage, or the failure of courtship and marriage. Sample plots are:

   > How She Got Married. How She Did Not Get Married (always tragic). How She Fell in Love and Committed Adultery. How She Saved Her Marriage But Just Barely. How She Loved a Vile Seducer and Eloped. How She Loved a Vile Seducer, Eloped and Died in Childbirth. As far as literature is concerned, heroines are still restricted to one vice, one virtue and one occupation.[5]

   After analyzing the women characters in five major Western authors, Simone de Beauvoir concluded that the woman is "required in every case to forget self and to love."[6] It seems that a woman character can be the protagonist of a love story but little else.

2. *Irrationality and emotionality.* June B. West studied the women characters appearing in the literature written between the two world wars and found that they were portrayed "as being slaves to their emotional natures"[7] Similarly, Katherine Rogers found, in all but the early novels of Sinclair Lewis, "the assumption that it is absurd for women to compete with men professionally, since they lack the necessary mental equipment—judgment, common sense, rationality."[8]

3. *Selfishness or selflessness.* The Eve-Mary Syndrome, or the prostitute-Madonna complex, is a phrase used to describe a certain dichotomy found in female literary characters. It refers to the tendency of writers to portray women as being one of two extremes:

either extremely selfish (Eve) or extremely selfless (Mary), either a demon or an angel. Leslie Fiedler notes that the women in American novels are traditionally "bifurcated into Fair Virgin and Dark Lady, the glorious phantom at the mouth of the cave, and the hideous Moor who lurks within."[9] Judith Montgomery documents the favorable presentation of the dependent, selfless heroine in the works of Nathaniel Hawthorne, Henry James and Edith Wharton. Montgomery places the demise of such heroines between 1900 and 1920, which marks the emergence of the bitter, destructive heroines of more modern times.[10]

4. *Passivity*. Mary Anne Ferguson documents the persistence of the submissive wife as a literary type. She cites examples ranging from Griselde in Chaucer's *Canterbury Tales* to the women characters of such modern writers as D. H. Lawrence, Dorothy Parker and Sherwood Anderson.[11] Carolyn Heilbrun asserts that especially after the thirties, women characters tended to become only an event in the life of a man. She quotes a contemporary novelist as saying, "What do you do with women characters, except have the men characters make love to them? Then either they marry them or they don't."[12] It appears that women characters are commonly presented in the form of "being" rather than "doing."

I integrated these four characteristics with four traditional dramatic criteria for character analysis. These criteria are a character's basic motivation, the deliberation the character engages in, the decision that a character makes (or fails to make) and the action that the character performs.[13] A character's *motivation* is her basic goal or desire. It is what she wants above all else. It is the driving force, the underlying reason for decisions and actions. A character's *deliberation* is a mental process which involves a weighing of alternatives—a considering of different courses of action and their possible consequences. A character's *decision*, then, is the choice she makes. A character's *action* is the actual deed she performs as a result of her decision. Through performing this act she may or may not reach her initial goal. These aspects of character analysis were applied to each character by asking the following questions:

MOTIVATION: What is it that the character most strongly desires? Does her goal or desire remain consistent throughout the play?

DELIBERATION: Is the character shown in the process of deliberation? If not, are periods of deliberation on her part referred to in the text? Is her deliberation exclusively of an ethical nature (based on moral values) or an expedient nature (based on practical considerations and individual desires)?

DECISION: What is the nature of the character's decision? Are her decisions predominantly ethical or expedient? Is the character portrayed as extremely selfish or selfless through her decisions?

ACTION: Does the character carry her decision into action? What is the nature of that action? Is the action physical or verbal?

These four criteria of motivation, deliberation, decision and action are related to each of the four major characteristics of fictional characters. In examining the *motivation* of each character, I can discover if she is predominantly concerned with romantic love. Irrationality-Emotionality can be related to *deliberation*. If a character is shown in the process of deliberation, she is not portrayed as a totally irrational being; even if her deliberation is referred to in the dialogue, there is still some indication of a thoughtful mental process. The Eve-Mary Syndrome, or a character's tendency toward either extreme selfishness or selflessness, can be related to the dramatic characters through an examination of their *deliberation and resulting decisions*. If a character engages in expedient deliberation, she is considering a way or a means of obtaining her goal. If she engages in ethical deliberation, she is considering her actions in the light of moral or ethical standards, and this is not considered selfish. I examine women characters to see if they engage exclusively in ethical or expedient deliberation and if their resulting decisions indicate a consistent selfish disregard for others or an attitude of self-abnegation. Finally, passivity can be related to *action*. If a character's decision results in her taking an action of some sort, she cannot be thought of as a "passive" agent; if her action results from her own decision, which in turn was reached through her deliberation, the character will most likely be seen as one with power and force. This approach provides a basis from which the traits of female dramatic characters can be compared with those found in fictional characters.

This analysis is applied to twenty-eight female dramatic characters in the Pulitzer plays. From the first decade (1918–29), the characters are: Helen in Jesse Lynch Williams's *Why Marry?*, Ruth Atkins in Eugene O'Neill's *Beyond the Horizon*, Lulu in *Miss Lulu Bett*, Anna in Eugene O'Neill's *Anna Christie*, Jane Crosby in Owen Davis's *Icebound*, Jude Lowry in Hatcher Hughes's *Hell-Bent fer Heaven*, Amy in Sidney Howard's *They Knew What They Wanted*, Harriet Craig in George Kelly's *Craig's Wife*, Goldie McAllister in Paul Green's *In Abraham's Bosom*, Nina Leeds in O'Neill's *Strange Interlude* and Rose Maurrant in Elmer Rice's *Street Scene*.

From the second decade (1930–39): Elsa Stanhope in Susan Glaspell's *Alison's House*, Mary Turner Wintergreen in Kaufman and Ryskind's *Of Thee I Sing*, Bus Nielson in Maxwell Anderson's *Both Your Houses*, Laura Hudson in Sidney Kingsley's *Men in White*, Charlotte Lovell in Zoe Akins's *The Old Maid*, Irene in Robert E. Sherwood's *Idiot's Delight*, Alice Sycamore in Hart and Kaufman's *You Can't Take It with You*, Emily Webb in Thornton Wilder's *Our Town*, Mary Todd Lincoln in Robert E. Sherwood's *Abe Lincoln in Illinois*.

From the third decade (1940–49): Kitty Duval in William Saroyan's *The Time of Your Life*, Miranda Valkonen in Robert E. Sherwood's *There Shall Be No Night*, Mrs. Antrobus and Sabina in Thornton Wilder's *The Skin of Our Teeth*, Veta Louise in Mary Coyle Chase's *Harvey*, Mary Matthews in Howard Lindsay and Russel Crouse's *State of the Union*, Blanche Dubois in Tennessee Williams's *A Streetcar Named Desire* and Linda Loman in Arthur Miller's *Death of a Salesman*.

First, I compared the female dramatic characters with the four general traits of female literary characters and concluded that a *preoccupation with love* is the most common characteristic among the characters. Of the twenty-eight analyzed, all except Bus, a secondary character in *Both Your Houses,* were involved, to some extent, in a love story. Of the remaining twenty-seven, fourteen were primarily motivated by love. That is, they were making decisions and acting primarily on the basis of love. Out of these fourteen, eight were primarily motivated by romantic love. These eight are: Helen in *Why Marry?*, Ruth in *Beyond the Horizon*, Jane in *Icebound*, Jude in *Hell-Bent for Heaven*, Goldie in *In Abraham's Bosom*, Laura in *Men in White*, Mary Wintergreen in *Of Thee I Sing* and Alice in *You Can't Take It with You*. The remaining six of these fourteen characters were primarily motivated by love of their husband and/or family. These six are Charlotte in *The Old Maid*, Mrs. Antrobus in *The Skin of Our Teeth*, Miranda in *There Shall Be No Night*, Veta Louise in *Harvey*, Mary Matthews in *State of the Union* and Linda in *Death of a Salesman*.

Although not fundamentally motivated by love, four of the remaining thirteen characters find their ultimate goal or are "saved" through love and marriage. These four are Anna in *Anna Christie*, Lulu in *Miss Lulu Bett*, Amy in *They Knew What They Wanted* and Kitty in *The Time of Your Life*. Also, two characters actively seek their goal in life through love or marriage. These two women are Harriet Craig in *Craig's Wife* and Nina Leeds in *Strange Interlude*. Neither woman is successful in her search but neither ever considers the possibility of pursuing any other course.

The seven remaining characters are not primarily involved in a lover story, however, each of these seven women is in some way involved with love during the course of the play. These seven are Rose in *Street Scene*, Elsa *Alison's House*, Irene in *Idiot's Delight*, Emily in *Our Town*, Mary Todd Lincoln in *Abe Lincoln in Illinois*, Sabina in *The Skin of Our Teeth* and Blanche in *A Streetcar Named Desire*. For these seven women love is shown as a part of their life but does not play as predominant a role as it does with the women mentioned earlier.

All but one of the female characters in this study, irrespective of status or role, were involved, to some extent, in a love story. For most of these characters, the story focused on their success or failure in love or marriage. Thus, the contention that female literary characters are preoccupied with love is also true for most of the female dramatic characters in the Pulitzer Prize plays, 1918 to 1949.

Although most of the women in this study could not be called totally *irrational and emotional beings*, certain conclusions can be drawn from the analysis. Fourteen of the twenty-eight characters are significantly developed on the level of deliberation, or are clearly shown engaging in deliberation. But by itself, deliberation is *not* an accurate measurement of a character's irrationality or emotionality. Even though some characters are shown in scenes of thoughtful deliberation, three of them—Blanche, Sabina and Mary Todd Lincoln—are portrayed primarily as highly emotional characters. All three engage in deliberation and Sabina is a very emotional character; Mary Todd Lincoln and Blanche are both studies of mental decay.

Sixteen of the twenty-eight characters engage in highly emotional scenes. That is, they are shown crying hysterically, sobbing incoherently or in some respect losing control of their emotions. Thus, the conclusion that women tend to be portrayed as emotional rather than rational beings holds true for the majority of the female dramatic characters in the Pulitzer Prize plays from 1918 to 1949.

Of the twenty-eight characters, only nine were found to suffer from the Eve-Mary Syndrome. Harriet in Kelly's *Craig's Wife*, Laura in Kingsley's *Men in White*, Sabina in Wilder's *The Skin of Our Teeth* and Blanche in Williams's *A Streetcar Named Desire* were essentially selfish characters while Goldie in Green's *In Abraham's Bosom*, Charlotte in Akins's *The Old Maid*, Kitty in Saroyan's *The Time of Your Life*, Mrs. Antrobus in Wilder's *The Skin of Our Teeth* and Linda in Miller's *Death of a Salesman* can be seen as selfless. However, we should note that Charlotte, Mrs. Antrobus and Linda exhibit a brand of selflessness on which they seem to thrive; they lose self-identity but at the same time seem to take on an awesome and pervading power which becomes both a nurturing and destructive force. Nineteen were more complex than the terms "selfish" or "selfless" would indicate. Therefore, the contention that female characters are usually portrayed as either extremely selfish or selfless beings does not hold true for the majority of characters analyzed in this study.

Most of the characters in this study are physically passive. Out of the twenty-eight only two women—Rose of *Street Scene* and Veta of *Harvey*—complete a physical action which is a result of their own decision and which is not supportive of a male protagonist's more crucial action. The rest of the characters either perform their major action only verbally, or begin an action which is left uncompleted or unfulfilled, or perform an action which is in an auxiliary position to the male's. Thus, the female dramatic characters can be seen as passive when qualified in this respect.

In considering the four literary traits, then, the female dramatic characters conform to one on an unqualified basis: most tend to be preoccupied with love. The characters conform to two of the traits on a qualified basis: most tend to be emotional but not necessarily irrational and most are, in certain respects, passive. Although there are some examples of the Eve-Mary Syndrome, the female dramatic characters do not tend to conform to this one trait. So, in these ways the female dramatic characters generally conform to three of the four traits which impose limitations on female literary characters.

In comparing the women characters in one decade to the others, it appears that the women in the plays of the first decade (1918–29) possess a stability, independence and strength not generally found in the later decades. Out of eleven plays studied for the first decade, all but three have a female protagonist. In contrast to this, the Pulitzer Prize–winning plays of the 1930s include one drama in which no female characters play a significant part. Out of the nine plays analyzed for that decade, only three characters can possibly be considered protagonists. During the 1940s a female protagonist is even more rare: among the seven Pulitzer plays, only one character, Blanche in *A Streetcar Named Desire*, can be considered the protagonist.

The most popular occupation of the women characters is that of wife or mother or both. In the decade of the forties a female character was more likely to be portrayed as a wife or mother than in the other decades. One character in each decade was portrayed in the role of a prostitute or mistress: they are Anna in O'Neill's *Anna Christie* (the twenties), Irene in Sherwood's *Idiot's Delight* (the thirties) and Kitty Duval in Saroyan's *The Time of Your Life* (the forties).

Of the twenty-eight characters, ten are portrayed as having an occupation outside that of wife or mother. Only two of these ten work in a profession: Helen, a laboratory assistant in *Why Marry?* (1918) and Blanche, who had been a high-school English teacher, in *A Streetcar Named Desire* (1948). Three of the ten women are domestic workers or maids: Jane in Davis's *Icebound*, Lulu in Gale's *Miss Lulu Bett* (the twenties) and Sabina in Wilder's *The Skin of Our Teeth* (the forties). Alice in Hart and Kaufman's *You Can't Take It with You*, Bus in Anderson's *Both Your Houses* and Mary in Kaufman and Ryskind's *Of Thee I Sing*, all of the thirties, are secretaries. Rose in Rice's *Street Scene* works in a real-estate office and Charlotte in Akins's *The Old Maid*, of the thirties, a day nursery for indigent children. Amy in Howard's *They Knew What They Wanted*, of the twenties, had worked as a waitress. In tabulating the number of women working at an occupation other than that of wife, mother, or prostitute, we find that five out of eleven characters did so in the twenties and four out of nine characters did so in the thirties. In contrast, only two out of the eight characters analyzed from the forties would fit into this category: Sabina, the maid, and Blanche, who was a failure as a teacher.

Another change over the decades is that the characters of the thirties and the forties show less deliberation than those of the twenties. This decrease in deliberation might be related to the fact that fewer were protagonists of the plays. In any event, there was a marked decrease in the scenes of and references to deliberation for the female characters of the thirties and forties.

Probably the most obvious characteristic shared by all the female characters is that except for Helen of the first decade and Blanche of the final decade, none of them was a professional person.

In overview, then, it seems that love for boyfriend, spouse or family member is the most common motivation for the dramatic characters plays surveyed. The tendency to portray women as being primarily motivated by romantic love was most prevalent in the first decade. The tendency to portray the women as being primarily motivated by love of husband or family increased over the three decades. None of the characters analyzed from the forties is primarily motivated by romantic love but five out of eight of them are primarily motivated by a love for their husband or family.

The tendency to portray a female character working at an occupation other than that of wife, mother, or prostitute remained steady over the twenties and thirties but decreased during the forties. The tendency to portray a female character *successfully* working at a profession remained practically non-existent for all three decades. The one exception is Helen, a laboratory assistant in the prize-winning play of 1918.

The majority of women are portrayed as emotional rather than rational beings. The female characters are most fully developed on the level of deliberation in the plays of the first decade. Scenes portraying women in the process of deliberation decreased in frequency during the thirties and forties.

The majority of women do not conform to the Eve-Mary Syndrome: that is, most are not primarily selfish or selfless individuals. However, there are nine characters who do conform to the syndrome. Since five of those nine were from the decade of the forties, it seems that the tendency to characterize women as being either selfish or selfless increased during this decade.

The majority of women are, in certain respects, passive on the level of physical action. Chances of the female character's having the status of protagonist tended to decrease after the first decade (1918–29). This suggests that the central female characters in the Pulitzer Prize plays, 1918–49, have generally received limited development, which accords with assumptions that women are primarily interested in love, are emotional and are passive. I do not suggest that the playwrights have presented an inaccurate or false picture of women but only the repetition of a partial or limited picture. I do not suggest here that the use of love, as a character's main motivation, necessarily implies a repudiation of the playwright's creativity. But from this study I conclude that playwrights need to discover ways to express what women think and feel *other than* those thoughts and feelings centered on love, home and family. They have long been accepted as part of a woman's life but they are not necessarily her whole life. I also conclude that the criteria of motivation, deliberation, decision and action provide a workable basis for dramatic character analysis from both the traditional and feminist viewpoint.

THE WOMEN'S WORLD OF GLASPELL'S *TRIFLES*

Karen F. Stein

Susan Glaspell's murder mystery, *Trifles*,[1] explores sympathetically the lives of middle-aged, married, rural women characters who would usually be minor figures in a play. In this way, *Trifles* (published in 1920) is a uniquely female and, indeed, feminist document.

Two New England farm women gather some personal belongings for Minnie Wright, jailed on suspicion of her husband John's murder. Observing the details of daily life in the bleak Wright household, Mrs. Peters and Mrs. Hale deduce the events which led Mrs. Wright to hang her tyrannical husband. The lack of a telephone, the shabby furniture, the much-mended clothing and a canary with a broken neck bear mute but telling witness to the harsh meanness and cruelty of John Wright. Considering Minnie her husband's victim (like her symbolic analogue, the strangled songbird), the women conspire to hide the evidence they discover.

Trifles is an anomaly in the murder mystery genre, which is predominantly a masculine tour de force. We are used to seeing the detective as an active hero, proving his skill and ruthlessness in a brilliant intellectual game. In the classic sleuth story, the detective is hired by a desperate victim, frequently a woman, to solve a problem through his expertise. The hero may incur risks in his investigation, but his willingness to do so is further proof of his courage and power. In solving the mystery, the detective demonstrates his shrewdness and acuity. His successful investigation is the piecing together of a difficult puzzle; his reward for success is a handsome fee, the admiration of all who have observed him, and frequently, the love of the woman who hired him. But he remains intriguingly aloof, uncommitted.

The scenario of *Trifles*, however, is quite different. Here, the detectives are the very women that the powerful police, sheriffs and detectives see as trivial, even ludicrous. Two middle-aged married women, lacking all glamour, unravel the mystery from positions of weakness, not strength. Furthermore, as we will see, they utilize their intrinsic "femaleness," their triviality in the eyes of men, their concern with the minutiae of women's lives, to solve the mystery. What is most unusual, however, is that they do not remain objective observers; they become personally involved, and, through their successful investigations they gain human sympathy and valuable insights into their own lives. This growth, rather than the sleuthing process, is the play's focal point.

The women themselves are "trifles" to the busy, efficient men who leave them behind to tidy up while they (the men) investigate the murder of John Wright, searching upstairs in the bedroom for clues to the motive. The county attorney, intent on finding physical evidence, fails to pursue two references to Wright's meanness. But, as the women attend to the trifling details of packing clothes and cleaning up the kitchen, they observe carefully and come to understand the mystery of the missing motive. The clues are a strangled canary and the irregular stitching, indicative of tension, in a piece of patchwork Mrs. Wright was sewing. Thus, while the men search for—and fail to find—external signs such as forced entry into the house, their wives interpret the emotional significance of small details, learning of the narrowness of Minnie's life, her frustration and her anger.

Interpreted similarly in its social and psychological contexts, the patchwork process becomes an objective correlative for the lives of these New England matrons. The patchwork quilt, composed of remnant fabrics scraps and salvaged bits of old garments, is a uniquely American solution to the dilemma of keeping warm in an economy of scarcity before the introduction of central heating. Patchwork is a task demanding patient and painstaking attention to repetitive, minute details: a quilt may contain as many as thirty thousand pieces, each one-half inch by three-quarters of an inch in size.[2] To women, in their homemaking role, went the task of hoarding the fabric scraps and stitching them into quilts. Girls were set to sewing samplers and quilt squares as soon as they were old enough to hold needles; they were expected to busy themselves with needlework whenever they had no urgent chores. Through this apprenticeship, girls were trained in the docility and discipline which society values in its women. At the same time, the apprenticeship in quilting and other household tasks in a society with sharp gender-role differentiation bound women of a household together. Networks of female friendship and mutual assistance were central in the lives of eighteenth- and nineteenth-century women.[3]

Quilts were made primarily for their utility, but they also offered an outlet for creativity that often had no other available channel of expression. For the many women who had no knowledge of reading and writing, and who could not have spent their time in such nonproductive activities, patchwork became a means of artistic self-expression. In the quilt patterns and the names for them that their makers devised, women told the stories of their lives. Such names as "Baby's Blocks," "Log Cabin," "Corn and Beans," "Covered Wagon Trail," "Underground Railroad" and "Union Star" give us an insight into the daily routines and political sentiment of their creators.

The patchwork squares are pieced together in solitude, often in between and after the completion of the round of chores which was women's lot. The quilting itself, however, the joining of the patterned patchwork upper layer to the lining and the backing, was done in a communal setting, the quilting bee. Groups of women, friends and skilled seamstresses, would gather around the quilting frame to cooperate in the tedious task of quilting. The quilting bee was one of the main social events for women whose daily lives kept them isolated from each other. For many years, we have thought of the quilting bee as an occasion for idle gossip. But, we are gradually learning to understand and appreciate the importance of these parties as vehicles for sharing knowledge and camaraderie, for developing and strengthening social support groups, and for accomplishing a difficult job effectively.

Quilt-making brought neighbors and friends together in a holiday spirit to cooperate in the production of useful and beautiful artifacts. In *Trifles*, as Mrs. Wright's neighbors view the separate fragments of the incomplete quilt, the mood is not festive but funereal. They have come not to join in the warm and social act of creation, but to clean up the debris of destruction. Through the sympathetic eyes of her neighbors, we are made to see the frustration of all Mrs. Wright's hopes for beauty, order and happiness.

Observing the bits of evidence, a strangled bird which John Wright must have killed, the tight stitching which was the woman's reined-in response to this act of wanton cruelty, the women become poignantly aware of the emotional poverty of their neighbor's life. We feel with them her thwarted needs for song and companionship. Mrs. Hale reflects, "Wright wouldn't like the bird—a thing that sang. She used to sing. He killed that, too." Through the women's identification with her, we understand Minnie's desperate loneliness which drove her to do away with her brutal husband.

> MRS. HALE: If there'd been years and years of nothing, then a bird to sing to you, it would be awful—still, after the bird was. Still.
>
> MRS. PETERS: I know what stillness is. When we homesteaded in Dakota, and my first baby died—after he was two years old, and me with no other then—

Out of their sympathy for Mrs. Wright as a woman they perceive to be more sinned against than sinning, the neighbors conceal their discovery of the motive from the male investigators. After ripping out the uneven stitches and removing the strangled canary, they respond with terse irony to the county attorney's patronizing question about Mrs. Wright's quilting, "We call it—knot it, Mr. Henderson."

In their decision to conceal the evidence, the women in *Trifles* affirm their ties of loyalty and affection to other women. Mrs. Hale laments her guilt in letting this communality lapse: "Oh, I *wish* I'd come here once in a while! That was a crime! That was a crime! Who's going to punish that?" The need for cooperation is manifested throughout the play, in the references to shared tasks such as quilt-making, and in their remarks about their own needs for companionship. In fact, the discovery and interpretation of the clues and the suppression of the findings is a shared process, diametrically opposite to the solo virtuosity usually displayed by male detectives. Further emphasis on the mutual understanding and aid women offer each other was inherent in Glaspell's title for the short story from which she derived this play, "A Jury of Her Peers." The women here realize, through their involvement in the murder investigation, that only by joining together can they, isolated and insignificant in their society, obtain for themselves and extend to others the support and sympathy that will help them endure the loneliness and unceasing labor required of them. For these women, solving the murder is not a disinterested act, but a cooperative endeavor which leads them to a knowledge essential for their survival as females in a hostile or indifferent world.

BLACK WOMEN IN PLAYS BY BLACK PLAYWRIGHTS

Jeanne-Marie A. Miller

In 1933, in an essay entitled "Negro Character as Seen by White Authors," the brilliant scholar-critic Sterling A. Brown wrote that blacks had met with as great injustice in the literature of America as they had in the life of their country. In American literature, then, including the drama, blacks have been depicted most often as negative stereotypes: the contented slave, the wretched freeman, the comic Negro, the brute Negro, the tragic mulatto, the local color Negro, and exotic primitive.[1] Black female characters have been scarce in only one of these categories—the brute Negro. They have been most plentiful as the faithful servant. In American drama, where, seemingly, many more roles have been written for men than women, black or white, it is the black female character who has faced double discrimination—that of sex and race.

As early as the nineteenth century black women were written about by playwrights of their own race. Melinda, in William Wells Brown's *The Escape*, for example, is a mulatto who is not tragic,[2] and Rachel, in Angelina Grimke's early twentieth-century play of the same name, is a young, educated middle-class black woman who protests against the indignities suffered by her race.[3] Although there were many plays written by blacks after the dawn of the twentieth century, the Civil Rights movement of the 1950s and the black consciousness movement of the 1960s produced many new black playwrights who brought to the stage their intimate inside visions of black life and the roles that black women play in it.

Alice Childress, a veteran actress, director and playwright, in several published plays, has placed a black woman at the center. Childress noted early that black women had been absent as an important subject in popular American drama except as an "empty and de-characterized faithful servant."[4]

Childress's *Florence*, a short one-act play, is set in a railroad station waiting room in a very small town in the South.[5] The time of the play is the recent past. Emphasized is the misunderstanding by whites of blacks, brought on by prejudice and laws that keep the two races apart. The rail separating the two races in the station is symbolic.

In the station a black woman of little means, with a cardboard suitcase and her lunch in a shoebox, has a chance meeting with a white woman also bound for New York. In the conversation that takes place between them, the prejudices of the whites and their myths about blacks are exposed, such as that of the tragic mulatto. Revealed also is the determination to keep blacks in the places set aside for them by whites. Marge, the black woman's daughter living at home, has accepted her place; Florence, the daughter seeking an acting career in New York, has not. Because of the revelations of the white woman, Florence's mother, en route originally to bring her daughter home and end her fumbling New York career, changes her mind and instead mails the travel money to Florence so that she can remain where she is. Thus, a docile-appearing black woman, who stays in her place in the South, acts to help her child transcend the barriers placed there by those trying to circumscribe her existence.

Childress's two-act comedy *Trouble in Mind*, while concentrating on discrimination in the American theatre, also brings into focus the troublesome conditions in the United States of the 1950s.[6] The framework of *Trouble in Mind* is the rehearsal of the play "Chaos in Bellesville," a melodrama with an anti-lynching theme, in reality a white writer's distorted view of blacks. The principal character, Wiletta Mayer, a middle-aged black actress, a veteran of "colored" musicals, appears at first to have found a way to survive in the prejudiced world of the theatre. Coerced by the white director, however, she explodes and reveals her long pent-up frustrations. Specifically, Wiletta disagrees with the action of the character she is playing—a black mother who sends her son out to be lynched by a mob seething with hatred because the black man had tried to vote. Wiletta, alone among the play's interracial cast, demands script changes that will portray black life realistically. Though she loses her job in the attempt, she in no way seems to regret the stand she has taken after a lifetime of acceptance.

In *Wine in the Wilderness*, Tommy Marie, a young black woman from the ghetto, teaches real pride to her newly acquired middle-class acquaintances.[7] This play is set during the black revolutionary period of the 1960s. It is one of those Harlem summers popularly described as long and hot. A riot is taking place outside the apartment of Bill, a black artist currently engaged in painting a triptych entitled "Wine in the Wilderness"—three images of black womanhood. Two canvases have been completed: one innocent black girlhood and the other perfect black womanhood, an African queen, this artist's statement on what a black woman should be. The third canvas is empty because Bill has not found a suitable model for the lost black woman, the leavings of society. Unknown to Tommy, she has been picked out by two of Bill's friends to serve as the model for that hopeless creature. At first sight Tommy is unpolished and untutored but is essentially a warm, likable human being. Once a live-in domestic and now a factory worker, at the present time she has been burned out and then locked out of her apartment as a result of the riot.

Later, dressed in an African throw cloth and with her cheap wig removed, Tommy undergoes a transformation as she overhears Bill, to whom she is attracted, describe his painting of the African queen. Believing that he is referring to her, she assumes the qualities he praises: "Regal . . . grand . . . magnificent, fantastic." For the first time she feels loved and admired. While Bill is trying to get into the mood to paint her, she recites the history of the Black Elks and the A.M.E. Zion Church, all part of her background. With her new look and the new knowledge he has gained about her, Bill cannot now paint Tommy as he had intended, for she no longer fits the image he sought.

The next day Oldtimer, a hanger-on, unthinkingly tells Tommy about the three-part painting and the unflattering role she was to play in it. She, in anger, teaches Bill and his middle-class friends about themselves—hatred they have for "flesh and blood blacks"—the masses, as if they, the others, have no problems. To the white racist, they are all "niggers" she tells them. But she has learned—she is "Wine in the Wilderness," "a woman that's a real one and a good one," not one on canvas that cannot talk back. The real thing is inside, she states.

Bill changes the thrust of his painting. Oldtimer—"the guy who was here before there were scholarships and grants and stuff like that, the guy they kept outta the schools, the man the factories wouldn't hire, the union wouldn't let him join"—becomes one part of the painting; Bill's two friends—"Young

Man and Woman workin' together to do our thing"—become another. Tommy, the model for the center canvas, is "Wine in the Wilderness," who has come "through the biggest riot of all . . . 'Slavery,'" and is still moving on against obstacles placed there by both whites and her own people. Bill's painting takes on flesh. Tommy has been the catalyst for change.

Unlike Childress's other plays, *Wedding Band* is set in an earlier period— South Carolina in 1918.[8] The central character, Julia Augustine, the black woman around whom the story revolves, is an attractive woman in her thirties. A talented seamstress, she has only an eighth-grade education. The play opens on the tenth anniversary of her ill-fated love affair with Herman, a white baker who has a small shop. This illegal love affair is the theme of the play. In direct violation of South Carolina's laws against miscegenation, the pair has been meeting and loving clandestinely for years. On this day, in celebration of their anniversary, Herman gives Julia a wedding band on a thin chain to be worn around her neck. This day, too, is the first that Julia has spent in this impoverished neighborhood. She has moved often because her forbidden love affair has caused her to be ostracized by both blacks and whites.

A series of encounters clearly delineates the kind of woman Julia really is. Though she is lonely between Herman's visits and sometimes allows wine to fill in the void, she is a woman of strength. She endures the criticism of her affair. She is unselfish, warm and forgiving. With compassion she reads a letter to a new neighbor who cannot read. Unknown to her lover's mother, Julia sews and shops for her. When confronted by this woman who hates her and whose rigid racism drives her to exclaim that she would rather be dead than disgraced, Julia rises to her full strength and spews out the hatred that momentarily engulfs her. And even in her sorrow she is able to give a black soldier a fitting send-off to the war and the promise that the world will be better for all blacks after the war's termination. In the end, Julia forgives her weak, timid lover who is dying from influenza. He could never leave South Carolina for a region more suitable for their love and marriage, he explains, because he has to repay his mother the money she gave him for the bakery. In reality, history stands between Julia and Herman. South Carolina belongs to both of them, but together they could never openly share the state. The promised escape to the North and marriage never materialize. Julia stands at the end of a long line of Childress's strong black women characters. In this backyard community setting of *Wedding Band* are other images of black womanhood— the self-appointed representative of her race, the mother protecting her son from the dangers awaiting him in the white South, and the woman abused by a previous husband, waiting loyally for the return of her thoughtful and kind merchant marine lover.

The promising talent of the late Lorraine Hansberry was perhaps best displayed in the well-known *A Raisin in the Sun*, which portrays an interesting variety of female characters, none more so than Lena Younger, who has grandeur, strength, patience, courage and heroic faith.[9] She is strong in the belief of her God who has sustained her throughout life. She mightily loves her family to whom she teaches self-respect, pride and human dignity, protects them, sometimes meddles in their affairs, and does not always understand their needs and desires. Above all else, she wants a home for her family, a physical structure large enough to house them all comfortably. Acquiring this home would mean the realization of a long-deferred dream. She wants, too, to help Beneatha, her daughter, fulfill her dream of being a medical doctor. But the attitudes of the younger generation Lena does not fathom—Beneatha's toward religion and Walter's toward money, which to him symbolizes success. The wise, sensitive woman that she is, Lena Younger realizes before it is too late that her son, in desperation, is reaching out to manhood at the age of thirty-five, and she helps him by making him the head of the household over which she has presided since the death of her husband. Theirs is a household of working-class people struggling to survive with dignity.

Beneatha, young, spoiled, spirited and sensitive, has social pride. Her ideas about women's liberation and her interest in her African heritage were in full force in the decade that followed the production of *A Raisin in the Sun*.

Ruth, Lena's daughter-in-law, a gentle woman, weary with life, loves her husband, who at first falsely blames her for his lack of materialistic success. She wants him to have that chance to be a man. In this household Ruth acts as a peacemaker between the generations.

A Raisin in the Sun is a drama of affirmation. Man's possibilities are manifold and in this work this family, with the help of the women, changes its world, if only a little.

Like Childress, Hansberry turned to the past for materials for one of her plays. In *The Drinking Gourd*, a drama about slavery, written for television, one of the principal characters is Rissa, a cook who is also one of the more privileged slaves on Hiram Sweet's plantation.[10] On the surface, she is like the cherished, fictionalized image of the black mammy who philosophically accepts her status, showers love and devotion on her white master and his family, forgives her white family of all wrongdoing, and hums or sings away all personal pain and sorrow. But unlike that unrealistic mammy, Rissa is concerned about her own family. To make life easier for her son Hannibal, she obtains a place for him in the Big House, only to have him refuse the favor. Slavery to him in any form is repulsive. After Hannibal is brutally blinded at the order of the plantation owner's son—for daring to learn to read—Rissa seeks vengeance for the crime. Though the fate is unknown of one son, Isaiah, who ran away from slavery, she assists blind Hannibal, his sweetheart Sarah, and Isaiah's son, Joshuah, in escaping from slavery to freedom. Moreover, for protection, she gives them a gun that she has stolen from Hiram Sweet's cabinet. Thus Rissa reverses the myth of the faithful, contented slave—faithful to her master and contented in her servitude. Unlike Carson McCullers's Berenice in *The Member of the Wedding*, who continues to care for her white charge while a mob seeks to murder one of her own family, Rissa rivets her attention on her son, while her white master, calling to her for help, dies outside her cabin.

Unlike the majority of black American playwrights, who use realism in dramatizing their ideas, Adrienne Kennedy, an avant-gardist, experiments with expressionism and surrealism. A poet of the theatre, she uses impressions and images rather than treat plot and character in a traditional manner. Despite the mode of treatment Kennedy draws her material from the black experience. Her female character Sarah, in *Funnyhouse of a Negro*, is a young, tortured black woman who has nightmarish agonies about being black.[11] The action takes place on the last day of her life—before she commits suicide. The fantasy characters, all well-known historical figures—Queen Victoria, the Duchess of Hapsburg, Patrice Lumumba and Jesus—represent the various selves of Sarah. In a monologue she reveals pertinent information about herself. The daughter of a light-skinned mother and a dark-skinned father, she spends some of her time writing poetry. She also spends time with a Jewish poet interested in blacks. Because of guilt feelings about her treatment of her father, whose black skin she abhors, she imagines that she has killed him with an ebony mask and believes, at other times, that he committed suicide when Lumumba was murdered. After her own suicide, it is revealed by her Jewish lover that, in reality, Sarah's father is married to a white whore. The material possessions he has are those which Sarah herself craved—European antiques, photographs of Roman ruins, walls of books, Oriental carpets and a white glass table on which he eats his meals. The pressures of being black in America are the subject of this work. These pressures, in turn, have produced madness in this sensitive black woman as an identity problem as well as a problem with love, God and parents.

In a second play by Kennedy, *The Owl Answers*, the racial identity problem is repeated.[12] The scenes, a New York subway, the Tower of London, a Harlem hotel room and St. Peter's, are fantasies in the mind of the principal character, a black woman named She Who Is. Her mother, a cook, was impregnated by a white man of English ancestry, who declared the child a bastard. But the child, now a woman, dreams about her white father's world. The English ancestors whom she claims—Shakespeare, William the Conqueror, Chaucer and Anne Boleyn—in rejecting her, jeer her. She cannot find her place in either the black or white world.

Thus black women in plays of many black playwrights receive varied treatment, and their images, for the most part, are positive. The women often have great moral strength. In contrast to many of the white-authored dramas in which black women have appeared, usually as servants dedicated to the families for whom they work, in the plays of black writers, these women's concerns are for what interests them, mainly their own families. In many of these plays it is their lives that are onstage. In black-authored dramas depicting ghetto lifestyles, black women hold on to life, however harsh it may be, and sometimes work for a better future. In the dramas written by women, except in the plays of Kennedy, black women often look to the future with optimism. Even Childress's Julia Augustine's plans for a move to the North with her lover terminate only with his death. In the plays written by black males, black women's happiness or "completeness" in life depends upon strong black men. Thus black playwrights bring to their works their vision, however different, of what black women are or what they should be. Missing, however, is a wealth of dramas with positive images of black middle-class women, black middle-class women who work to improve the quality of life for themselves, their families, their race—the Mary McLeod Bethunes, the Mary Church Terrells and the unsung black women who help to improve the world, if only a little.

WHO PUT THE "TRAGIC" IN THE TRAGIC MULATTO?

Winona L. Fletcher

My old man's a white old man
And my old mother's black.
If I ever cursed my white old man
I take my curses back.

If I ever cursed my black old mother
And wished she were in hell,
I'm sorry for that evil wish
And now I wish her well.

My old man died in a fine big house,
My ma died in a shack.
I wonder where I'm gonna die,
Being neither white nor black.

—*Langston Hughes*
"Cross"[1]

Nowhere is the spirit and tragedy of the mulatto captured with more poignancy than in this impassioned creation by Langston Hughes. The main character of his poem, however, should by no means be misconstrued as "a figure of a poet's imagination." With or without public sanction or recognition, there exists in America a product of racial admixture known as the mulatto—in the flesh. This is no recent phenomenon since there is considerable evidence that "miscegenation doubtless took place from the first."[2] After the emancipation of slaves, the rate of increase among mulattoes accelerated more rapidly than among the darker members of the race, and the 1910 census revealed more than two million persons who admitted belonging to this group.

It is generally known, however, that no census can reveal an accurate tint of mulattoes, since the process of tracking down racial admixture is about as nebulous as the genetic phenomenon that permits one drop of black blood to make a person "colored." It is difficult, if not impossible, to determine where black leaves off and white begins or vice versa; yet we have become so obsessed with our attempts to make this distinction that long ago the question of color was catapulted into a national problem. This fact is the basic tragedy that underlies and permeates all the other "tragic" elements of the tragic mulatto. The myriad associations of "white" with right, might and superiority and "black" with backwardness and inferiority set the stage for the entrance of the tragic mulatto. Playwrights, both white and black, have grappled with the theme of miscegenation for over a century and a half. This theme is directly responsible for establishing myths, stereotypes and traditions both on- and offstage—all of which have at one time or another been used, abused, refused and manipulated by anybody who chose to do so.

Somewhere along the way there sprang upon the stage a convention that declared that the treatment of the mulatto must be sentimental, given to evocation of pity (and sometimes real fear); that the character must possess virtue and nobility; that the figure must be resigned to alienation from society and acceptance of a fate that results in shame for the possession of one drop of black blood. Melodrama, the favorite of nineteenth-century playgoers, dictated the creation of this virtuous, noble, sentimental agent. The perfect real-life model for this dramatic character was the female mulatto slave. Already a victim of the white master, whose whims dictated her existence, her presence as his concubine aroused jealousy in the white woman, envy and hate in her darker sister and despair in her own soul when she was prohibited by society from passing for white. She offered limitless dramatic possibilities. It was, therefore, generally agreed that the thus created "tragic mulatto" should be female although there are notable exceptions to this last mandate.

Harriet Beecher Stowe is credited with establishing the tragic mulatto stereotype in her creation of Eliza (*Uncle Tom's Cabin*, 1852). The image of the fair-skinned mother clutching her young child as she frantically jumped the ice floes to freedom is one of the few pieces of "black history" recognizable to most Americans. But Stowe is not wholly responsible for putting the "tragic" in the tragic mulatto—as researching and soul-searching reveal. While Stowe's infamous black Uncle Tom overshadowed all other prototypes in the dramatization of her novel by George Aiken, the mulatto archetype remained popular throughout the Civil War and Reconstruction periods. Dion Boucicault discovered the figure and granted her a seat of dramatic prominence in his popular nineteenth-century drama, *The Octoroon* (1859). *The Octoroon* is a melodramatic treatment of a much beloved female whose discovery of her black blood foils her plans to marry the white man she loves, and in one version of the play, leads her to sacrificially take her own life.

Other nineteenth-century white playwrights were captivated by the tragic mulatto (octoroon, quadroon) also: John T. Trowbridge, *Neighbor Jackwood* (1857); Charles Barton Hill, *Magnolia* (1862); Bartley Campbell, *The White Slave* (1882); Margaret Smith, *Captain Herne, USA* (1893). Nearly all romanticized the physically beautiful, near-white girl and her struggle equality and understanding. In *Neighbor Jackwood*, for instance, the beautiful Camille, a runaway slave so white that her New England neighbors are unaware of her black past, remembers:

CAMILLE: To be a thing, a chattel, a slave—then to feel for the first time that I can call myself a woman, and in such an hour to find . . . Oh this is the beginning of life.

As late as the first decade of the twentieth century, Edward Shelton was keeping the tradition alive with *The Nigger* (or *The Governor*, 1909). The hero of this drama possesses a drop of black blood that is so infinitesimal that he fooled even himself and would have spent his entire life "passing" had not his black genealogy been revealed for political reasons. This unfortunate revelation instantly reverses his life and sets him on the new tragic course of the mulatto.

Despite society's attempts to check miscegenation by statute, playwrights continued to deal with the theme—more frequently with the process (miscegenation) than with the product (the mulatto). Plots more believable than the action of *The Nigger* were attempted in the twenties by such major playwrights as Eugene O'Neill (*All God's Chillun Got Wings*, 1924), and on through the next decades to the sixties, when Howard Sackler permitted black Jack Johnson to flaunt his sexual habits with his white woman onstage and onscreen in *The Great White Hope* (1968).

Black playwrights have not been silent on this theme either. Editors James Hatch and Ted Shine seem to think that "miscegenation is the one theme on which both black and white playwrights have always agreed: 'mixing is bad.'"[3] The point of view differs, but the product usually remains tragic, and the participants in the process are forced to accept the poetic justice meted out in the form of punishment or reward for the "sin."

William Wells Brown, black contemporary of Mrs. Stowe, led his mulatto heroine through melodramatic, if not tragic, ordeals of resisting her white master before permitting her to escape to Canada with her black husband. Melinda is permitted to preserve her virtue, at least, since as a tragic mulatto not preserve her racial purity:

MELINDA: Sir, I am your slave; you can do as you please with the avails of my labor, but you shall never tempt me to swerve from the paths of virtue.

—*The Escape or A Leap for Freedom* (1858) Scene 5

Brown also permits his white antagonist to chuckle over his guest's mistaking of a servant child as the master's and replies, "If you did call him my son, you didn't miss it much. Ha, ha, ha!" (Scene 3)

Events in society and in the theatre conspired to keep the black playwright's pen inactive during the sixty-odd years following Brown, and the real-life female mulatto joined the song and dance routines and found fame as a "high yeller" chorus girl helping to paint the picture of the "exotic Negro." Then, in the twenties, some black writers rejected the exotic image and chose to use the stage for race propaganda. The mulatto shed another tragic tear.

In 1926, black playwright Myrtle Smith Livingston used a black man and a white woman as chief figures in *For Unborn Children*. Her treatment of character and point of view were different from O'Neill's 1924 approach, but there would be no difference in the resultant product. In Livingston's drama the black hero rejects all family pleas:

> GRANDMA CARLSON: Before we can gain that perfect freedom to which we have every right, we've got to prove that we're better than they! And we can't do it when our men place white women above their own!
>
> MARION (SISTER): Stay with your own race if it's color you want—we have women who are as white as any white person could be—My God! What is to become of us when our own men throw us down?
>
> —*For Unborn Children*[4]

Leroy defies all customs and laws in is determination to marry his white beloved one, but oddly enough, makes the supreme sacrifice to give her up when he is told that he is himself a tragic mulatto. As he walks out into the threatening screams of the lynch mob, he consoles his grandmother with the words:

> LEROY: Don't grieve so; just think of it as a sacrifice for Unborn Children.

Livingston felt it was tragic for a black man to marry outside his race, especially while he was still trying to prove his equality. The paradoxical nature of all of this compounds the tragedy which pervades the mulatto (black, in general) attraction-rejection syndrome.

Writing three-quarters of a century after the appearance of *The Octoroon*, Langston Hughes, as did his predecessor Boucicault, left no doubt about the thesis of his play when he named his compelling drama *Mulatto*. Drawing upon society's early affirmation that an admixture of white blood tended to improve the black breed,[5] Hughes created several mulatto characters to dramatize this belief. While the female mulatto appears briefly in Hughes's drama, the playwright chooses as his protagonist the tragic male figure Bert. Perhaps Hughes felt that this explosive assertion of manhood better suited the era of sociopolitical writing that characterized the thirties and, thus, he relegated the female to a place of subordination. It is both ironic and tragic that this early assertion of manhood was not a statement of *black* manhood in the sense of the dramatic assertion of black manhood of the 1960s.

Nevertheless, Hughes raises his drama above the level of a mere problem play when he presents a strong-willed, rebellious, proud mulatto son of a white plantation owner and his Negro mistress. Convinced that his near-whiteness makes him superior to other blacks, he defies his white father, loses control and kills him during a fight; he is then forced by the lynch mob to take his own life.[6] The playwright's underscoring irony that Bert is too much like his white father to live brings real pathos to Bert's final recognition of the totality of his tragic situation. One is moved to ask—is there no other way? Or to pick up the lament "we have learned forever how well they die—cannot we learn now how to let them live?"

But there is yet another ironic twist. The female mulatto, Sallie (Bert's sister), is permitted to live, to suppress her outrage and revolt and to outwit her white father by preparing herself, at his expense, to "educate her way out of his control." But Hughes knew that her story had less dramatic value—at least to the audiences of the thirties. Failure to legitimize miscegenation, to permit the products of the act to live normal lives without circumvention only added fuel to their futile efforts to survive in a supercilious society—both on- and offstage.

The docile, saintly, noble, forgiving mulatto of Boucicault's day is certainly not present in the twentieth-century treatment of the character—but then neither are the same motivations for manipulation of the traditional stereotype. The black revolutionist of the '60s is a good example of this change. Convinced that integration was never intended to be a two-way street and that many whites feared that it meant "mongrelization of the benefactors' race," the revolutionists began screaming "Black Is Beautiful" and rejecting everything white. In the midst of this movement of black identity, the product of miscegenation became tragic for reasons totally different from Boucicault's octoroon who admonished herself for "the shameful single drop of black blood which poisoned all the flood."

This new tragic mulatto is developed with horrifying intensity in the plays of Adrienne Kennedy. Ms. Kennedy turns from realism to a surrealistic world that can display the tortures and nightmares of her female character— a tragic mulatto searching for an identity that is trapped in conventions and torn by the paradoxes of living in a no man's (nor woman's) land. Symbols of these paradoxes are hurled out in rapid-fire order: smooth lily-white skin, black kinky hair, laughing white figures, pale yellow skin, ebony masks, etc. Sarah in *Funnyhouse of a Negro* and Clara in *The Owl Answers* are trapped in blackness, desperately struggling to resolve their love/hate for black/white, caught in the never-ending attraction/rejection syndrome.

> SARAH: . . . he haunted my conception, diseased my birth . . .
> —*Funnyhouse of a Negro*

All of Ms. Kennedy's plays should be required reading for anyone seeking insight into what it means to be a tragic mulatto.[7]

As was the Little Red Hen in the well-known fable of that name, we are finally forced to face the issue: Who put the "tragic" in the tragic mulatto? Society, if forced to reply, would probably be as noncommittal and evasive as the Red Hen's followers. Their answers might go something like this:

> "Not I," said the Blackface Minstrel as he covered his face with burnt cork—denying white audiences a chance to see real black folks in all their living colors onstage.

"Not I," said the Abolitionist as she created one more "idealized abstraction" and penned one more sentimental phrase for the mulatto—evoking pity from white America who sighed, "There, but for the Grace of God . . ."

"Not I," said the Lawmaker as he wrote another law against racial intermarriage.

"Not I," said the Theatre Audience, clinging to its safe and satisfying old stereotypes.

"Not I," said the Klansman as he spewed out racial superiority and cut another length of rope.

"Not I," said the Maker of Beauty Standards as she made millions selling skin whiteners and hair straighteners.

"Not I," said the Black Revolutionist as he rejected the "polluted mainstream" and started his own brand of "racial purity."

And the beat goes on! . . . Conventions have a way of hanging on, especially when they are deeply rooted in traditional thought patterns. As long as the mulatto is viewed as a social problem rather than a human being, as long as blacks are caught up in the benevolence/malevolence, identification-with-the-aggressor-phenomenon, as long as "white" is elevated above "black,"[8] there will be tragedy in miscegenation, and the resulting mulatto only an extension of this tragedy.

The tragic mulatto is a living product of society's conscious/unconscious attitudes and values and is willfully or unknowingly created by all of us. No matter how many laws we make—or break—until we escape first from our own conventional traps, we cannot effectively free her from the myth and conventions which engulf her; therefore, playwrights (and anyone else who chooses) will continue to manipulate her at will.

CREATIVE DRAMA: SEX-ROLE STEREOTYPING?

Lin Wright

Creative drama is improvisation with children. It is a group process. The leader helps the children perceive their world and then express themselves through the dramatic medium. The content of the drama can be based on curriculum materials or it may be developed around the personal interests and concerns of the children. Once the topic is chosen, the children under the guidance of the leader create the plot, characters and settings. As they perform the improvisation, they create the action and dialogue. Participant evaluation of the improvisation is also an important aspect of the process. If creative drama is sensitively handled and the content carefully chosen, it should be fun for the children and an excellent means for their intellectual, aesthetic, emotional and social growth. Empirical research should verify these claims.

Relatively little research, however, has been conducted to verify the effect of creative drama with children, and the results in the few existing studies are generally less positive than anticipated. In all of the studies that include sex of student as a variable, boys have received scores different from those of girls on social, creative and communication instruments after sessions in creative drama.[1] This sexism in the creative drama process was unexpected since the practitioners in the field claim to work with the individual child within the group for the maximum growth of each child. There is a need to discover the cause of these results and to develop means to assure nonsexist sessions for the children.

Dr. E. C. Irwin (1963) taught fifteen sessions of creative drama to 149 third-grade children to test growth in personal development from the drama process. The experimental boys made significant gains in social adjustment on the California Test of Personality. The girls made significant gains on personal, social and total adjustment.[2] Elissa Goforth (1974) discovered that fifty kindergarten boys and girls scored significantly higher on the Wallach and Kogan Creativity Series after sixteen creative drama sessions. She also found that boys in the classes with the least structure scored significantly higher (.001 level of confidence) than the children in the other drama classes.[3]

Dr. Lin Wright (1972) found thirty sixth-grade boys showing more growth in perception (a greater awareness of and a better interpretation of another's acts within a situation) than an equal number of girls after fifteen drama sessions. Feffer's Role Taking Task was the measure used.[4]

Mary E. Lunz (1974) found, after ten creative drama sessions, seventh-grade boys and girls showed significant improvement in communication effectiveness. When the data was analyzed for the effect of sex of the communicator, a trend appeared implying that "males responded more positively to creative dramatics activities than the females."[5]

Dr. Irwin concluded that "a program of creative dramatics may possibly have a greater applicability to girls than to boys" in the third grade.[6] Lunz made a much stronger statement:

> The social and cultural implications are incredible . . . The trend opens questions of preferential treatment for males by leaders, or the tendency of males to dominate the group activity. Experimentation with lesson structure in regard to how this factor is manipulated during activity is necessary to gain insight into the question.[7]

In the creative drama session, the leader most often uses literature, history, current issues, other curricular materials, or the ideas of the students to motivate the improvisations. The literature used is often folk or fairy tales and characters from these stories are hopelessly stereotyped. Many children's books are also sexist. Leaders attempt to overcome this bias by having the girls play some of the stronger men's roles. This is not a real solution for the children know that the girls could not perform the tasks in "real life." Leaders can search for the few stories with strong roles for both boys and girls. New "nonsexist" stories are being published but care must be exercised with these materials because they often lack exciting characters and dramatic tension and will not play well. Text writers of history and social studies often suggest class activities involving role playing. History texts usually record the events of the brave men and supportive women from our past. The social studies problems are based on current social norms—which are usually sexist. Improvisations based on the children's ideas often reinforce sex-roles. The ideas the children bring to the drama session are based on the current TV fare and whatever else they experience, see and read. Most of this material is replete with stereotypes. The leader is a product of our sexist society and may have as much difficulty as the children envisioning non-stereotyped roles.

Solutions to stereotyped material are not easy. No one may really know what constitutes a nonsexist role, a role that respects the differences between the sexes but one that does not limit the activities either sex can perform. The leader can search for playable "nonsexist" material. *Pippi Longstocking, Charlotte's Web, The Courage of Sarah Noble, The Pushcart War, A Wrinkle in Time* are a few stories with strong roles for males and females.[8] There are historical female figures of dramatic stature, such as Harriet Tubman, Sojourner Truth, Clara Barton, Susan B. Anthony, Helen Keller, who moved beyond the stereotypes of their era. If the leader can ask appropriate leading questions and conduct a discussion with tact and insight, it is possible to help children create their own stories in which the characters are not limited by sex.

Since both the participants and the leader of the creative drama session are products of our sexist society, often the process of planning, playing and evaluating the improvisations reinforces sexist behavior. Anne Thurman, at a convention session examining sex-role stereotyping in children's drama, raised four questions related to this issue:

1. Do we give equal opportunity to boys and girls when we discuss, play and evaluate our scenes, or do we let the boys dominate and the girls acquiesce?
2. Do we call attention to sex distinction and role by allowing too many all-boy or all-girl scenes? Do we allow, acquiesce, or foster a large amount of small-group planning in single-sex groups?
3. Do we discipline the boys more harshly than girls? Do we praise boys more than girls? Do we expect the boys to be more aggressive and noisy than girls?
4. Are we conscious of sexist remarks or slurs as we have become of racist remarks? "Just like a girl, women drivers, dumb blonde, jock, my father says women are the weaker sex."

Trying to keep these questions in mind, David Saar[9] and I set out to team-teach boys to move beyond the typical roles they usually play and to see what techniques and materials might be of value in this process. We were concerned with the material we used, the roles we played in the entire drama context, the attitudes and expectancies we had for the children, the general group ambiance. The process of planning and evaluating with the children was every bit as important as the actual playing of the drama in dealing with sex-role stereotyping.

Sixteen children were selected by their teachers from four fifth-sixth grade combination classes. The teachers selected the students who they felt would benefit most from the creative drama project. The students were told that the leaders were making a video film of the process of creative drama, a film that would be used to help train teachers and college students and show them "how much upper elementary students are capable of doing." The group met in the media center three times a week for four weeks. Each session lasted one hour.

The goal of the sessions, as stated to the students, was to develop an "improv troupe." Such a troupe is composed of individuals who are willing to share their ideas and also are willing to support the ideas of other group members. Each is willing to act out any ideas presented and to work to play off of any other member within an improvisation. The individual is always initiator and supporter in all three stages of improvisation, the planning, playing and evaluating. This was an "adult" challenge and the students responded well to the approach.

All class activities—warm-ups, theatre games, pantomimes, story dramatizations and original improvisations—were selected to help the students develop the dual roles of initiator and supporter. Means were devised to help as many students as possible develop their own ideas and present them to the group. The corollary of this was to help all students listen to their classmates, respect their ideas and be willing to support ideas from everyone.

The sessions started with small group pantomimes. We then created improvisations based on the idea of "what if" there were a series of unrecorded adventures of some of the sailors who became separated from Odysseus. This left us without the male leader and we hoped to "readapt" the story so the format could allow some nonsexist roles. Finally the children created a modern Odyssey: they chose to create a space journey.

Prior to the sessions we met with the children to explore their drama backgrounds and attitudes toward one another and apparent willingness to lead or follow. An outline of content and procedure for the twelve sessions was developed.

During the first two sessions the children were allowed to work in groups of their own choosing. The boys played with boys and the girls with girls. For the next session the children worked with those from their "pod." This placed them in groups of four, two boys and two girls each. While playing out the "unwritten" incidents from the Odyssey, the entire group worked together. Both boys and girls played sailors and monsters.

As we approached the creation of the children's space odyssey we evolved a scheme that put the children in boy/girl pairs. Each child had to develop an idea for the play, then combine her/his idea with that of the opposite-sex partner. These ideas were written and then presented to the entire group. Small groups volunteered to prepare these scenes under the direction of the initial pair of creators. These scenes were presented to the entire group and best segments were selected to incorporate into the final improvisation. One day was spent working on the final version which was filmed during the final class session.

The classroom teachers using informal observation felt that the drama experience had been very positive for the students and that there was carry-over into the classroom. They noticed an improvement in the students' listening abilities. The students were more willing to listen attentively to others and then develop their ideas in relation to what had been said. Some of the students conversed more easily with adults and one boy with a learning disability had found his experience with drama a heady and unusual success. They reported discovering new abilities to perform and socialize in their students. In relation to leadership roles, they perceived greater changes in the boys, feeling that they had grown most in their ability to both lead and follow. They perceived a difference in leadership roles assumed by the girls.

The creative drama leaders noted that during the initial sessions two "natural" male leaders dominated the group. One girl acted as a leader with a small group of girls. By the end of the twelve sessions this had changed. Of the eight boys, there were the original two strong leaders and one newly emerged strong leader; two boys had assumed minimal leadership roles; three were followers. Of the eight girls, three strong leaders emerged; four assumed minimal leadership roles; one was a follower. Leadership qualities for the girls emerged most definitely in the final, original improvisation. All but one girl developed usable ideas and helped the group work to dramatize their ideas.

The girls had little difficulty supporting others' ideas throughout the sessions. The original female leader usually sought support for her ideas but if it was not forthcoming would willingly help develop the ideas of others. Of the boys, the three followers supported anyone's ideas; three boys tended to automatically support the ideas of their male peers but would support female peers only if the support of the whole group seemed strong. The newly emerged male leader was very group-oriented and very instrumental in bringing out everyone's ideas. The two original male leaders had difficulty supporting the ideas of other children. One tried, but retreated to "aloofness" when it became difficult. The other male leader would support other's ideas only if he could develop a means of gaining attention for himself in the process.

Three of the most successful male/female pairs were composed of a girl with leadership ability and a passive boy. In the fourth productive pair both the boy and girl were leaders but neither was acknowledged as a leader outside the drama group. The other pairs suffered in varying degrees from the boys' allegiance to each other rather than to the group.

The roles that the students were willing to play indicated some shifts in attitude. Initially the children tended to choose "male football player, female cheerleader" type roles. At one point one of the males commented that girls would have to stay in the boat because "girls don't fight." In the final story, the girls fought, played major roles and were supported in these roles by most of the boys.

In conclusion, it is possible to effect positive change in the roles that boys and girls will assume in the drama process and playing, but this new flexibility will not carry over into the classroom unless the teachers create an atmosphere that will encourage these new roles. It is difficult to take basically sexist material (i.e., the Odyssey) and "turn it around" by an enlightened presentation. Original material, developed by the group under the leaders' guidance, can more easily be nonsexist. Presently, it appears that creative drama is as sexist as our society and is a means for continuing sex-role stereotyping. From the work started in the Mesa schools it seems possible to begin to reverse that condition.

FEMALE PROTAGONISTS IN THE PLAYS OF SUZAN ZEDER

Susan Pearson-Davis

Before the 1960s, most scripts in the field of theatre for young audiences were adaptations of traditional folk and fairy tales or popular children's fiction. Most fit neatly into the category of the well-made play; were realistic in style; had very familiar titles, few contemporary topics and no controversial issues. Characters were usually less than three-dimensional since social and educational attitudes put narrow limits on what was considered suitable for children, and depth of characterization was thought to be confusing to them. But when television began bringing regular coverage of war and social unrest into most living rooms, society's view of children and what was suitable for them began to change. As it did, innovative scripts for young audiences began to appear.

Prominent among this new wave of innovative writers is Suzan Zeder, the author of eight plays for young audiences. Zeder, a Fulbright Scholar who teaches playwriting at Southern Methodist University, has won numerous awards for her scripts, including the Children's Theatre Association of America's Charlotte Chorpenning Cup for Best Playwright of the Year in 1978 and the same organization's Distinguished Play Award for *The Play Called Noah's Flood* in 1985 and for *Doors* in 1986. Although her scripts are innovative in many ways, perhaps her greatest contribution to contemporary theatre is her creation of child protagonists, particularly young female characters, who are recognizably contemporary and fully three-dimensional. Unlike the doll-like, passive, or sweet and sentimentalized girls in the traditional repertoire of plays for young audiences, Zeder's young female protagonists elude sex-role stereotypes, struggle with difficult and contradictory thoughts and feelings which often lead to rebellious behavior, and grapple actively with the problems that confront them. In addition, these young protagonists are written in such a way that both children and adults can identify with them on their own level.

Probably the best of these young female protagonists is ten-year-old Ellie Murphy in *Step on a Crack* (1976). Ellie has been raised by her single father, Max, for six years since the death of her mother. Max's remarriage to an attractive woman named Lucille fills Ellie with jealousy, brings out all her insecurities, and makes her behavior far from that of the "perfectly good little girl" she used to be. Ellie copes with her angry feelings and attempts to prop up her dwindling self-esteem by retreating to her own room where, with the help of two imaginary friends, Lana and Frisbie, who enter her room through her toy box, she creates and enacts fantasies of being rich, famous and far superior to Lucille. A third imaginary character, Voice, who represents Ellie's own dark side, lives in Ellie's mirror. It is Voice that starts all the fantasies by reminding Ellie that she is not as pretty, talented, or smart as Lucille.

Zeder's externalizing of Ellie's fantasies is highly theatrical and holds the attention of even very young children by turning Ellie's thoughts into visible action. But the psychological complexity inherent in the fantasies, such as the use of Voice to represent Ellie's over-active self-criticism, also makes Ellie easy to identify with on an adult level, in spite young age.

Zeder's adaptation of L. Frank Baum's *Ozma of Oz* (1981) gives another good example of the complexity of her young female characters. Baum's original Dorothy is brave, strong and positive, but thoroughly one-dimensional. Even when she is adrift on a raft in the middle of a stormy ocean, the read sees Baum's Dorothy struggle with fear or any other attitudinal obstacle. By contrast, Zeder has updated her play to the present and made Dorothy a teenager with weaknesses and negative attitudes that get in her way. She is accompanying her aging Uncle Henry because she has to, not because she wants to. She is bored to tears by his ramblings about Australian history and terrified when the storm strikes. Once they have been washed ashore in Oz and her uncle taken captive, Dorothy has to do things she never dreamt she could do in order to rescue him. In the process, she learns that she has the ability to think her way through a problem and that she has courage she can act on in spite of feeling afraid. With the help of Ozma—who also differs from the original in having the power to make people see "behind the mind and into the heart"— Dorothy discovers that there is more to Uncle Henry than the helpless old man she thought he was.

Not all Zeder's major, three-dimensional characters are children. Two of her most fascinating and well-developed characters, one of whom is over forty, appear in her 1985 script, *Mother Hicks*. The play is set in a small town in Southern Illinois during the Great Depression. Girl is a thirteen-year-old foundling who has been passed from family to family all her life, alienating most of them with her headstrong willfulness and refusal to follow rules. At the beginning of the play she has just been left behind by yet another foster father and forced to move in with the town mortician and his wife, whom she does not like.

Mother Hicks is a mysterious woman in her forties who lives alone outside this small town. She was a midwife in the town until a time ten years earlier when the townspeople, in fear and ignorance, blamed her for the death of several babies and ostracized her as an accused witch. In the atmosphere of fear and loss brought on by the Depression, tales of her witchcraft spread; the townspeople, including Girl, look on her with dread. But the two are destined to meet when Girl is severely injured and brought by a young deaf man named Tuc to be nursed back to health by Mother Hicks.

Both of these characters have to deal with the most difficult kinds of losses. Girl, who had begun to hope that Mother Hicks was really her long-lost mother, discovers that although Mother Hicks can help her in some ways to heal the wounds of her repeated abandonment, she must "find her own name" and create her own identity before she can feel comfortable being defined as part of a particular family. Mother Hicks's own infant daughter died in the same epidemic that killed the babies she is accused of having witched. Her mysterious midnight visits to the graveyard every week, which have been used by the townspeople as evidence that she is a witch, are eventually revealed to be visits to the unmarked grave of her dead child.

Zeder's plays run the gamut from comedy to serious drama, from fantasy to realism and from ancient to modern historical periods. Her young male protagonists, especially Jeff in *Doors* and *Other Doors*, are written with as much depth as the female characters. Zeder is primarily concerned with ordinary people coping with problems of everyday life, but these problems are ultimately universal in their scope: communication breaking down when one person withholds information from another "for the other's own good"; people searching for a sense of identity and meaning in life; and people struggling to have a voice in the decisions that are made about their lives.

Zeder maintains that she writes about rather than for children, and does so not for any particular social or educational purpose, but because she finds children fascinating and dynamic dramatically. She feels that it is extremely important for adults to "respect the child as having both magnitude and significant emotions" and refrain from condescending to children or trivializing their emotional difficulties, even in the well-meaning attempt to protect them. She carries this belief into her writing and validates the child's mind, world and perceptions, emphasizing the universal presence of the child within the adult.

FEMINIST
THEATRES
AND THEORIES

6 | FEMINIST THEATRE

Although there is evidence of some feminist theatre activity during the beginnings of the women's suffrage movement and in Greenwich Village early in the twentieth century, it is only since the late 1960s that we have witnessed and documented a continuing feminist theatre. Approximately 150 feminist groups have produced theatre events in the U.S. since the '60s, and in the mid-'80s more than thirty were still active, with new groups forming as older ones closed. For example, Lilith Women's Theatre Collective, founded in San Francisco in 1974, served feminist energies in the Bay Area through performances, readings and workshops until its closing in 1986, which many see as the end of the phenomenon of feminist theatre groups.

Some feminists have chosen to create theatre with troupes which define themselves more broadly as "political theatre" and often include men as performers and cocreators. In our second edition we profiled Joan Holden of the San Francisco Mime Troupe, Maxine Klein of the Little Flags Collective and the "street adventures" of Berkeley-based Ladies Against Women in a chapter on "New Practices, Problems, and Perspectives." Having dropped that chapter for this new edition, we add the "Feminism and Political Theatre" essay to our sampler of feminist theatre activities. It directly precedes essays by and about Martha Boesing, Roberta Sklar and Megan Terry, all of whom have been pioneers in theatre both political and feminist.

We end our third edition of this chapter with selections from Charlotte Canning's wide-ranging and thorough 1996 tapestry of interviews and research, *Feminist Theatres in the USA*. Canning thoughtfully observes "feminism's constant state of change and the vigorous debate over that change,"

framing her history of feminist theatres and feminism with a wise maintenance of "the tensions between history and feminism, celebration and critique, and change and stability."

Why this need for feminist theatre? Certainly women have acted, managed companies, chosen scripts and written for the professional Western theatre at least since the days of the *commedia dell'arte* troupes, but any feminist
consciousness in their work was rarely acknowledged or encouraged.
Although there are feminist notions in plays by women before the twentieth
century, writers were not able to assume responsive women or sympathetic
men as their primary audience. Even today, feminist drama created for the
commercial theatre has to please men in power aesthetically and politically to
achieve recognition and status. Feminist dramatists who work outside feminist groups often still have to struggle with social suppression of their speech
and sexuality. *The Search for Signs of Intelligent Life in the Universe*, written and
directed by Jane Wagner, first performed by Lily Tomlin, produced by the two
of them in Broadway's Plymouth Theatre in 1986, seems an anomaly—an
award-winning feminist piece in the heart of the traditional commercial theatre district. The achievement is explained, perhaps, as much by its noncon-
frontational style as by the talents of its creators.

More often, feminist theatres provide an alternative to the establishment.
From the beginning, feminist theatre has been compensatory by necessity.
There is much to compensate for: oppression in almost every arena of society
(including both radical politics and the avant-garde theatre movement); the
invisibility of women's history and culture; an absence of active roles for
women; little access to, and/or equality in, the professional theatre; the continued omission of women's life and language in men's theatre; a lack of visibility and validity for lesbian experience; and the repression of ancient feminist ceremonial traditions.

While seeking to compensate for these frustrations, lacks, and repressions, feminist theatres have fostered consciousness raising and used theatre to
build sisterhood among women and bonds with feminist men. Though there
is no universally accepted definition of "feminism," there is general agreement
on the necessity of valuing and asserting female experience for personal and political change. A feminist theatre provides an environment in which a female artist
can define herself in her own terms. Many women need to create in an atmosphere where the language of female experience prevails. Even if a woman
intends to work in the male-dominated world, her own authenticity and possibilities for survival might be nurtured by experience in a feminist situation.

In the 1980s, several feminist theatre festivals spread "the psychic news"
(Megan Terry's term). The Feminist Amerikan Theatre coproduced the 1980 and
1981 Boston Womyn's Theatre Festivals. In 1985 the Boston Women in Theatre
Festival assumed the task. The National Festival of Women in Theatre gathered
feminists in California annually in Santa Cruz, 1981–85. Women's One World
Festival, produced in 1980 and 1981 in New York City, was the genesis for the
East Village's WOW Cafe. These festivals also drew feminist theatres from other
countries. Although feminist theatre festivals ceased to thrive as companies

dwindled and the women's movement shifted foci, a touring festival of women's music called "Lilith" was popular at the turn of the twenty-first century.

Many feminist theatres and writers in the '80s began asking questions and attempting projects that grew out of the groundbreaking work in women's studies—exploring engendered use of space, gesture and imagery for example. Some addressed political issues of concern to both men and women with approaches informed by female experience, such as Minneapolis-based At the Foot of the Mountain's *Ashes Ashes We All Fall Down*, which put nuclear issues into the context of a woman's life while emphasizing a positive approach to the future.

There have been controversies and splits within the feminist theatres, some of which are suggested in this chapter. Many of the conflicts are just as common in nonfeminist companies, particularly the alternative theatres that began forming in the '60s: Is the art of the theatre more important than or separate from political goals or social ends? Should the group be organized communally, or with specialization of labor, or along more traditional hierarchical lines? How much effort should be expended in fund-raising and marketing? Should the group be open to anyone willing to work or should it be selective? Other disagreements arose over questions particular to feminist groups: Should men be allowed to perform or attend? How should one deal with sexuality within the company, the audience, the material selected for production?

Some feminist theatres are composed solely of women who perform exclusively for other women; there are others in which women-only companies perform for audiences of both sexes (sometimes holding women-only events); and in some companies men and women perform for mixed audiences. There is considerable variation in the type of performance space used, in the process by which decisions are made, and in the style and tone of the work done. But despite those differences, feminist theatres invite everyone to remove sex-role limitations and stereotypes from habits of thought—conscious and unconscious. It is the possibility of this new understanding that suffuses and motivates the work of feminist theatres.

LWJ

FEMINIST THEATRE: A RHETORICAL PHENOMENON

Patti P. Gillespie

Since the formation of the first feminist theatre groups in 1969, increasing numbers of people, mostly female, have joined together for the purpose of doing theatre—by, for, or about women.[1] Although the companies vary markedly in size, organization, repertory, working methods and artistic excellence, all advocate or promote equality of opportunity *for* women, and all call themselves feminist theatres. Their nationwide and apparently spontaneous formation from coast to coast—without encouragement, leadership, or direction from a national organization—makes them an example of a grassroots movement seldom witnessed in the American theatre.

Although constituting a populist activity of considerable strength and vitality, feminist theatres have been largely ignored by established reviewers, critics and scholars. Local media occasionally review individual productions and generate stories on indigenous groups, but newspapers and magazines with national circulations have, for the most part, neglected the phenomenon. For example, of the more than fifteen feminist theatres active in New York City between 1969 and 1977, the productions of only the Women's Interart Theatre were regularly reviewed by the *New York Times* and *The Village Voice*. Five articles exhausted the attempts of established periodicals to deal with the theatres nationwide before 1977. Even underground newspapers and radical feminist publications treat the theatres and their works only occasionally rather than regularly; none attempt an analysis of the national phenomenon. Such inattention has predictably resulted in a public largely uninformed, or misinformed, about the nature of those theatres calling themselves feminist.

Reasons for the inattention are several. The most important can be briefly suggested. Feminist theatres, considered collectively, lack the unity and cohesion necessary for identification as a movement; their very diversity in size, repertory, format, and budget makes analysis and subsequent generalization difficult. Furthermore, the newness of the phenomenon, the inconstancy of the groups and the decidedly experimental thrust of several have impeded inquiry by obscuring sources of information. Moreover, the artistic quality of the productions is often quite mediocre when judged by traditional criteria; established reviewers and media may consider coverage a waste of their time and space. Finally, the term *feminist theatre* appears now to engender controversy: some rather traditional producing organizations are beginning to embrace the term while other theatres, obviously devoted to the goals of feminism, are beginning to reject it outright.

But neither the inattention of the media nor the difficulty of the research excuses a casual dismissal of these theatres. The works of such feminist playwrights as Adrienne Kennedy, Myrna Lamb and Megan Terry are now known, anthologized, and produced in nonfeminist theatres. Obies have been earned by plays and performers first seen in feminist productions.[2] But beyond such individual contributions, the national phenomenon itself has an importance not yet recognized and acknowledged by scholars. The formation and rapid development of feminist theatres nationwide is a rare example of an unpremeditated and vigorous people's theatre, a theatre apparently formed in response to strongly felt and shared needs. Whether by encouraging an adversary relationship with contemporary society or by promoting new images and possibilities for women, feminist theatres are credited with radically changing the perceptions of some viewers and the very lives of others. The most tantalizing questions, then, relate not to individual practitioners and theatres but to the national phenomenon. Why did these theatres form in such numbers and with such suddenness? Why did the theatres assume such diverse, and often quite nontraditional, characteristics?

Feminist theatres and feminism. Discovering answers to these and related questions requires recognition that all feminist theatres are rhetorical enterprises; their primary aim is action, not art. Each company is using theatre to promote the identities of women, to increase awareness of the issues of feminism, or to advocate corrective change.

The groups, if agreeing on little else, appear to share two convictions: that women in this society have been subjected to unfair discrimination based on their gender, and that theatre can provide at least a partial solution to certain problems arising from such discrimination. Did the groups not agree on the former, their public statements would be far different from those expressed. Did they not agree on the latter, they would have chosen strategies other than theatre for the exploration and promotion of their beliefs.

Certainly the suffragettes had their Bloomer plays,[3] and the 1920s and '30s were replete with agitprop dramas. But in neither instance were the *theatrical* (as opposed to the *dramatic*) practices so removed from those of the mainstream. Feminist theatres, on the other hand, sprang suddenly, spontaneously and in relatively large numbers from no tradition and no political organization in particular. Such activity, at first, seems inexplicable. Analysis, however, suggests that the emergence is due to a peculiar confluence of historic circumstance and rhetorical need.

Formation of the theatres. Although theatre's potential as an instrument for education and change has been well known for centuries, the range of its possibilities was rediscovered and widely popularized during the 1960s. Experimental theatres arose to contradict long-held views of what drama and theatre could be. Attention centered on new kinds of plays, new sorts of organizations, new spaces for producing, new methods of training actors and new audiences for performances. Asserting the political ends of art, the New Left developed street theatres and guerrilla events; probing the boundaries of life and art, the avant-garde focused on theatre as discovery, as process. The delayed appearance of the women's movement made possible its appropriation of certain theatrical practices popularized by the New Left and the antiwar demonstrators: performing in unusual places, presenting pithy and provocative skits, confronting audiences, proselytizing. During the 1960s, too, groups such as the Open Theater, the Performance Group and La MaMa focused on self-exploration, group improvisation, collective organization, nonverbal communication and physicalization; these techniques, too, became available to the feminists.[4]

Significantly, many women active in feminist theatres had prior experience in the avant-garde or the New Left. For example, women figured prominently in the Open Theater. Of the fifteen women identified by Joseph Chaikin as particularly significant members of his group, ten are now, or have been at some time, involved in feminist theatre.[5] More telling, however, is that many women active in feminist theatre lacked prior training or experience in theatre but had been active in the New Left and antiwar coalitions which used theatrical tactics for the promotion of their causes.[6] In sum, by 1970, not only were new techniques of theatre available, but also by then many women had experienced the techniques firsthand.

But history alone is insufficient to explain women's ready adoption of theatre. The peculiar nature of the rhetorical problems facing advocates of women's equality also contributed to the grassroots movement. Recent studies have demonstrated several ways by which the rhetoric of women's liberation differs from other kinds of persuasive efforts.[7] First, the gender roles assigned to women at birth are not congruent with those deemed necessary for a successful rhetor. In fact, according to Campbell, "Insofar as the role of rhetor entails qualities of self-reliance, self-confidence, and independence, *its very assumption is a violation of the female role.*" Second, elimination of sex-role stereotyping requires both individual and social change. Thus, "All of the issues of women's liberation are simultaneously personal and political"; therefore, its rhetoric must be at once personal, dealing with the particular experience of individual women, and political, treating the organizations and structures affecting all citizens.[8] Third, as McMahan has shown, the rhetorical situation generated by liberationists is a paradox: even while proclaiming their equality, women are asking society to grant it to them. The responses to a rhetorical paradox are severely limited and may restrict communication through ordinary channels. It will be argued that theatre provides a mechanism by which women advocating radical change can overcome this particular combination of rhetorical problems. The question, why did feminist theatres arise in such numbers, is answered by considering them as tactical responses to problems faced by women advocates of equality.

Women chose theatre, in part, for the reasons that others proposing radical change have found it helpful. In conflicts where competing groups have vastly unequal power, the weak group often finds traditional forms of argument and public discourse inadequate. Low-power groups, therefore, often resort to techniques of violent confrontation and/or symbolic protest.[9] Women, a low-power group, tend to reject violent confrontation as a means of persuasion because they believe it to be based on male-dominated values, values which they question and strive to change. When violent confrontation is eliminated as an option, symbolic protest assumes a central position in planning.

Theatre is itself a kind of symbol. Like other art, theatre is a hypothetical construct to be appreciated and judged by its adherence to internal principles rather than by its fidelity to external "reality." Since theatre is performed for groups of people, its social component is stronger than that of most other verbal arts. Moreover, since living actors speak and act in front of a live audience, the sense of immediacy and urgency is greater than that of music, painting, lyric poetry or the novel. In fact, the power of theatre to teach and convert has been recognized by figures as disparate as Plato and the Panthers, Bishop Ethelwold and Adolf Hitler.

But theatre remains a symbol, and thus deals in a world of hypothesis, not "reality." It therefore permits revelation of events, characters, and ideas without actually threatening either participants or viewers. A logical construct, theatre encourages reflection and empathy but does not require an immediate defense of, or attack upon, the world of the play. In a word, theatre is not debated. It does not demand (although it does permit) an agile exchange of ideas in the "real" world.

As a symbol, theatre says more than its literal meaning and means more than a single thing. Public address and debate are more nearly confined to the presentation of systematic arguments. Theatre has no such obligation: it can present a version of "reality" in all its complexity and contradiction. Thus theatre is particularly suited for promoting radical causes, causes which call for a restructuring of relationships and transactions, causes which lack specific, well-defined goals—in short, causes such as the liberation of women.[10]

Moreover, theatre is, by its nature, especially well able to cope with an unusual demand of feminist rhetoric. Campbell argues effectively that an intimate interaction proceeds between the experience of a single woman and the public issues of all women. In fact she concludes that this inevitable relationship between the individual and social, the personal and the public, is a cornerstone of liberation rhetoric.[11]

Theorists as remote as Aristotle and as recent as Langer have observed that theatre is at once particular and universal, historic and philosophic. History deals with the real actions of real people; philosophy treats ideas and ideals; but drama constructs hypothetical, individual characters acting in invented situations. That is, within the play *Oedipus Rex*, Oedipus is a particular man-in-action; but *Oedipus Rex* is an artistic hypothesis, and so Oedipus, a logical universal. Because theatre, at its essence, displays both the particular and the universal, the individual and the totality, it is a strategy well selected to capture the intimate connections between the experience of a single woman and the political issues of all women. Whereas public speaking and debate can only assert such connections, drama can embody them, presenting them in all their intricacies and incongruities.

Finally, theatre permits a woman to function as a persuader without violating either her own past conditioning toward passivity or society's expectations regarding her appropriate behavior. The role of actress, unlike that of rhetor, does not violate gender-based expectations of conduct. Women have performed in the theatre at least since the sixth century B.C. and regularly in most countries since the late seventeenth century. True, actresses have been viewed by some as living on the fringes of respectability; but no one now is shocked by the presence of a woman onstage and few view the role as inappropriate.

Moreover, in the hypothetical world of the play, a female character can, with society's acquiescence, expose a social problem, defeat a male adversary and experience economic and political success. Thus, an actress can, with a minimum of threat to either herself or members of her audience, embody traits, participate in situations and articulate conclusions which in real life would be deemed unsuitable or threatening. While nineteenth-century audiences, for example, condemned the character Nora in Ibsen's *A Doll's House*, few attacked the actress for assuming the role. As a fictional character, then, a woman is free to decide, to take action and even to attack contemporary practices with little reason to fear the renunciation or retribution of the audience upon her personally. Able to present a "view of reality" with no need personally to explain it logically or defend it rationally, even a timid woman may become bold enough to function actively as a persuader.

The formation of feminist theatres nationwide, then, can be appropriately viewed as response both to the historic possibilities of the 1970s and to the peculiar problems related with liberation rhetoric.

Characteristics of the theatres. The confusing tangle of expressed goals, diverse structures and varied methods of working likewise unsnarls when feminist theatres are viewed as particular responses to perceived problems. The traits of the theatres vary consistently with the answers to three questions: (1) What problem does the theatre target for solution? (2) What role is the theatre to play in its resolution? (3) What is the degree of social upheaval required for its correction?

Although the specific features of individual feminist theatres are, to some degree, unique, two major kinds of groups can be identified: those which are intent upon promoting women artists in particular, and those committed to assisting women in general. While the groups may overlap, theatres representing the two extremes can be cited and their practices compared.

Although less numerous, theatres which concentrate on the problems of women artists are often among the oldest and best known.[12] Such groups as Women's Interart, in New York City, observe that women artists have inadequate opportunities to show their work. There are too few women playwrights, for example. Of the several hundred plays produced in New York between 1969 and 1975, only seven percent were written by women.[13] Women writers complain publicly that they are made to feel guilty about writing, that they are encouraged to consider their own efforts as mere "self-indulgent folly."[14] There are too few, and too inconsequential, roles for actresses. An analysis of Broadway and Off-Broadway plays produced between 1953 and 1972 reveals that only one-third of the available roles in the some 350 plays were for women.[15] There are too few positions open to women directors, women producers, women designers and women technicians as well.[16] Feminist theatre, for groups such as Women's Interart, becomes a showcase for the works of talented women and a place of employment for female artists. Except for their preference for women artists and for plays which present women in non-stereotyped ways, these sorts of feminist theatres are largely undistinguishable from other professional, commercial or community theatres. They tend to organize themselves into traditional producing units, with directors, designers, writers, and the like. Since their goal is to display art and artists in a favorable light, excellence becomes a major goal of each production. Generally these feminist theatres receive the most favorable notice from the established media and are most likely to be financially solvent, with permanent homes and organizations.[17]

But feminist theatre applies as well to the more numerous and amorphous performing units around the country whose aims coincide roughly with those of women's liberationists. These groups are often transitory and, to an outsider, may appear unorganized, haphazard, formless. These groups are apt to reject the traditional theatrical organization—a director atop a hierarchy of artistic specialists—in favor of loose aggregates of equal persons working collectively. Some aggregates include even the audience as part of the collective experience. A representative of such groups, It's All Right to Be Woman Theatre, considers that feature a central one: "Whereas theatre has been, to date, a combining of specialists, the essence of our theatre is to convey the collective experience . . . a theatre without separation of roles . . . a theatre without a stage to separate audience and players.[18] By and large the groups practice what they preach, and some go to considerable lengths to assure democracy within their theatre. Womansong Theatre, for example, omits the names of individual performers and switches parts among the performers at different productions.[19] Both the Cutting Edge and Women of the Burning City develop their scripts collectively.[20]

These groups often select plays and tactics designed to command attention, to shock, to alienate. Common confrontative techniques include attacks both on the norms of femininity and on basic gender-role expectations. *The Saga of How I Lost My Hairy Legs* assures a reaction by its treatment of a subject previously considered tasteless and unfeminine.[21] Myrna Lamb's play *But What Have You Done for Me Lately?*, depicting a desperate pregnant man in search of an abortion, forces a recognition of the issue of personal freedom by transposing gender roles.[22] Short guerrilla events performed in elevators of office buildings and department stores shock by their verbal assaults on familiar persons and institutions.[23] The New Feminist Repertory was praised by one feminist for giving "validity to ideas that have been expurgated from the range of attitudes permissible to 'healthy' people in the past few decades" and for understanding that "it is society that needs 'adjusting,' not the individual."[24] With such strategies, feminist theatres are merely using techniques already established as successful by the street and guerrilla theatres of the past decade.

In certain other respects, however, the feminist theatres are quite unlike their agitprop predecessors. The performance materials in feminist theatres, for example, are unusually personal. Such material serves to highlight the groups' informal, even vulnerable, style of production. It's All Right to Be Woman summarizes its practice:

> We make theatre out of our lives, our dreams, our feelings, our fantasies. We make theatre by letting out the different parts of us that we have pushed inside all our lives . . . We make our music out of the tunes we hum to ourselves and the beats we tap out on a table top. Making theatre out of these private parts of ourselves is one way we are trying every day to take our own experiences seriously, to accept our feelings as valid and real . . . To believe that what happens to us or what we feel or dream is important enough to share with each other and other women, that it is, in fact, the most important thing we have to share.[25]

Whether building scripts from interviews with the performers' mothers[26] or from dreams related by members of the audience,[27] the groups seem determined to make the theatrical event intimate, and from this intimacy to build a sense of common experience and, therefore, political commitment. A critic at a performance reports: "The personal voices of real women become the expression of feelings known in all of us . . . Watching we were drawn into a sense of closeness with performers' lives, not just with their work."[28]

Women's movement and feminist theatres. Interestingly, the two kinds of feminist theatres parallel an observable division within the women's movement at large. Organizations such as the League of Women Voters and WEAL promote specific economic and social reforms. They are characterized by their moderate stance, their traditional methods and their commitment to work through established channels of change. Similarly, moderate feminist theatres such as Interart, Los Angeles Feminist Theatre and Washington Area Feminist Theatre aim to lessen the economic deprivation of women artists. The problems they address are the definable and practical problems of employment and salary. Their solutions are straightforward: to give women work, to show their art to the general public, to present that art in the most polished and acceptable way possible. Since the problem is to provide opportunities for theatre artists, the existence of the theatre is itself a partial solution. Moderate theatres, therefore, adopt traits which promote the continuance of the theatre. Since a high quality of artistry is important for the accomplishment of their primary goals, such groups contribute to the world of theatre as well as to the world of women—accounting for most of the significant new plays and playwrights, and serving most successfully as a conduit for introducing new female talents into the mainstream of the American theatre. Inasmuch as the social changes they advocate are not very profound, the existence and practice of these groups represent no threat, are readily acceptable to the media and to other theatres and can exist in comfortable parallel with the theatrical mainstream.

On the women's movement at large, groups such as SCUM, WITCH and Weatherwomen strive to change the whole fabric of society by attacking its attitudes and institutions. The approach is radical, the rhetoric combative, the aims revolutionary. Similarly, radical feminist theatres such as It's All Right adopt traits designed to cast doubt on accepted conventions of both content and form.[29] The radical theatres tend to reject traditional (scripted) plays, normal patterns of organization, accepted critical standards, polite language. The specific characteristics chosen as replacements depend, of course, on whether the theatre strives to promote lesbianism, explore the black experience, raise consciousness[30] or name the enemy.[31] But in every instance, radical theatres select strategies which cultivate solidarity among adherents while encouraging antagonism, or at least apathy, toward previously accepted social norms. They do not practice persuasion of the many by the few; instead they organize themselves into leaderless groups which strive to break down traditional distinctions between the leader and the led, the actor and the audience. They do not strive to adjust their presentation to the expectations of an audience; rather they jolt the audience into new perceptions, new ways of looking at the world.[32] They do not promote a single program of change nor answer the question, "What do women want?" They present instead the different experiences of many women without attempting to resolve the consequent contradictions. In fact, theatres such as It's All Right incorporate all of the features which Campbell argues are unique to the rhetoric of women's liberation.[33] Consciousness raising, the "paradigm that highlights the distinctive stylistic features of women's liberation" rhetoric, can also serve as a model for understanding the radical feminist theatres. Both use affective as well as logical proof, rely on leaderless persuasion, resort to "violating the reality structure" and effect a transaction between the personal and the political. To such a posture established media and theatres predictably respond in kind: they attack, or ignore, the radical groups.

Summary. The phenomenon of feminist theatre grew out of a unique blend of historic circumstance and rhetorical problems. Politically powerless, many women chose to air grievances, explore possibilities, advocate change through the medium of theatre. They did so for some of the reasons that low-power groups of the past have exploited its persuasive capabilities. But the additional rhetorical problems confronting women (the conflict between the role *rhetor* and the role *woman*; the paradox inherent in the demand/request of equality; the peculiar interaction between the private and the public issues of liberation rhetoric) made theatre an unusually attractive option.

CARAVAN THEATRE

Bobbi Ausubel

Unlike most feminist theatres, Caravan was not founded as a result of the women's movement by a group of assertive women ready to do theatre. The fact that we were already in existence as part of the '60s experimental theatre movement, with a consciously political direction and with both men and women, colored the work we did. Caravan (1965–78) probably was the first feminist theatre to produce.

We were called Caravan because Stan Edelson and I, as cofounders and codirectors, organized it as a touring summer project of the American Friends Service Committee. We got a school bus, and we'd go perform for food and twenty-five dollars. The first summer we hit on what was to become the Caravan style, alternating between known published scripts and company-created original works, all of which raised questions about personal relationships to social and political happenings of the times. That first summer, in an elaborate environmental setting, we produced Max Frisch's comment on the stockpiling of bombs amidst an indifferent public. That was followed by a company-created script, *We Shall Overcome???*, our multiracial ensemble piece that described the difficulties blacks and whites had coming together.

In the beginning the nature of our work was small. I didn't know it could be big. I come from a non-achieving working-class family, and it was just wonderful to perform in little coffeehouses. One day we got a review in the *Boston Globe* that said, *"The Maids* [Genet] is near genius." It seemed to me people were just rushing in. We had no chairs. I turned around and suddenly we had a business manager who spent my pennies on a roll of printed tickets. I was furious! What right had we to spend good money on tickets when you could give people pieces of cut-up colored paper instead? I had to learn to get paid for the work I do. Sometimes I wish I could go back to the old way when the stakes were lower.

The play that transformed me, and the theatre, and influenced Boston the most, was *How to Make a Woman.* At a Caravan planning meeting in my living room in January 1967—before the women's movement was dreamed of—I said, "I want to do a play about what it's like to be a woman in this culture, and how it is different from being a man." The men were supportive and the women cool, not wanting to be classified as "women," but as "people." We went into rehearsal. My role was to design improvisations and direct. Stan wrote the script from the improvs and from his wonderful imagination.

When we opened it at Club 47 in Cambridge, June 1967, the audiences came, clapped and left. This is in strong contrast to what happened one year later. The world outside the theatre was beginning to quake while we were re-rehearsing and changing the script before reopening it for our first full season at what became our permanent home, the Harvard Epworth Church in Harvard Square. Joe Volpe, an actor in the company, told me a friend had come back from the SDS (Students for a Democratic Society) meeting in Chicago and she had participated in a female liberation group that had formed there. We were stunned. Gradually what I had been saying in the play became clear to me, as it did to the rest of the group. We learned and understood, and relearned with the audiences, and rewrote for the next three years of the run.

How to Make a Woman was an "Aha!" experience for many. People began to stay for discussions, compelled to reexamine their lives. Both women's and men's groups were formed right there in the theatre. Then the women from these groups would come back and lead discussions for audiences at subsequent performances. The play made Caravan into a center of feminist energy in Boston. People would come back and squeeze into a space that held two hundred people and sit on uncomfortable wooden benches, even during the anti-war riots when street lamps were broken outside our windows and tear gas went off. What a way to do theatre! Alive! We were feeding and being fed.

How to Make a Woman tells the story of two women who find themselves in a dress shop (symbolizing the world) run by men. The men seduce the women into certain garments (gender roles) they have designed. The humorous hanky-panky of the designers' offerings begins to work on Mary, but is cut off when Aili prevents her companion from taking the "boob" baby girl's dress and instead forces her to make a dreamlike descent into the beginnings of time, from her birth through her girlhood, sexuality, marriage, and even old age. Then Aili too is forced to make a descent. Her fantasy recreates the terrifying role of Big Mama and the pseudo-liberated marriage. The women flee the shop at the end. The dreamlike sequences were expressed in physical movement-based acting, which was popular in the experimental theatres of the time and which often served as the basis for Caravan's acting style.

Looking back over the years I notice that I have always chosen to create plays about what has been most hateful or painful to me. The theatre process is one of exorcism, of transforming pain. I often start from confusion I have no distance from. For example, *Focus on Me* is about the part of us that hates women. It is an all-women's play; it had to be. For me it was about learning to accept my mother (and all seemingly "weak" women), to accept being a mother, loving my child self, my children. In the play a woman filmmaker is trying to make a film with another woman. She keeps putting her partner down. Like the society, she does not value nurturing and motherhood. So *Focus on Me* was about the process of loving another woman. It ran for eight months.

Caravan's successes were many (I couldn't have said this years ago when the theatre closed and I felt like a failure.) We created new scripts centering on women, on male/female roles, for at least ten years. We recreated known dramatic literature (Brecht, Beckett, Euripides) in feminist terms. *Tell Me a Riddle* (an adaptation from Tillie Olsen's novella) and *Family* each won praise in Boston as one of the ten best plays of their respective years. Often, we got both mainstream and counterculture press coverage, which brought in a wide variety of audiences. We regularly got NEA and Massachusetts Council of the Arts grants. We influenced, among other theatre people, Megan Terry and Martha Boesing, who came to see *How to Make a Woman* at early stages in its run; Earth Onion, a women's theatre group, formed because we traveled to Washington, D.C., in one of our tours. Caravan took feminist ideas to Poland, where we toured for a month as part of the International Polish Experimental Theatre Festival. We nourished many actors and directors; we changed from a hierarchy to a collective.

Caravan transformed men and women together, understanding through painful and exhilarating group process that we were all socialized and forced into polar experiences. We, together, gave an artistic voice to the best of feminist politics: the uniting of the personal and the political.

OMAHA MAGIC THEATRE

Linda Walsh Jenkins

Jo Ann Schmidman founded Omaha Magic Theatre in her native city in 1968, determined to create innovative theatre by and for the people of the Midwest. In the early 1970s she was a performing member/collaborator with the Open Theater, while keeping the theatre going in Nebraska. In 1970 she played the title role in *Approaching Simone*, which won Obie awards for director Maxine Klein and writer Megan Terry. Schmidman's association with Terry has continued since, with Terry first writing for Omaha Magic Theatre, then joining full-time in 1974 as a playwright, literary advisor and sometime designer. Schmidman writes and performs in addition to providing artistic direction and fiscal management.

Besides many skilled performers, a large group of Midwest painters and sculptors work with them, and they have four composers in residence. They have converted three storefronts to total theatre environments, produced more than seventy new plays and musicals and televised many of these shows. The company produces a newsletter, *Magic Dust*, and tours the country, including schools, prisons and Indian reservations. Omaha Magic Theatre has never had a deficit, and in 1981 was named "One of America's Best Regional Theatres" by *Better Homes and Gardens*.

The theatre serves as a catalyst for the community while working closely with it. Megan Terry describes this relationship: "The audience tells us what they want to deal with. We do one piece a year which we think of as lending our skills to give voice to community concerns. The other seven plays we produce are for our own and our audience's artistic growth." *American King's English for Queens* (1978) voiced concern for sexism in language by examining it in family dynamics. Audience discussions after performances acknowledged domestic verbal violence, and led to *Goona Goona* (1979), an examination of physical violence in the home. Terry designed *Goona Goona*, creating a soft-sculpture "house as a gigantic quilt." Terry describes her costume design "as a combination of puppets and football uniforms with padding so the actors wouldn't get hurt. They hit each other with baseball bats while depicting family violence."

Kegger, a portrayal of alcohol use and misuse among young people, was performed as a "model program" at the 1983 "Secretarial Conference for Youth on Drinking and Driving" in Washington, D.C., and televised by Omaha's NBC affiliate during prime time. To prepare the production, the company met with neurosurgeons, neuropsychologists, biologists and drug counselors as they researched alcoholism. *Kegger* then toured through the Midwest and played to over forty-five thousand people. "Everyone is working now to find ways to have chemical-free fun. They've formed positive peer pressure groups within the schools to let kids know it's okay not to drink," Terry asserts. Schmidman adds, "The play is really about the ability of young people to make decisions: When do we become mature enough to know right from wrong—is there a magical age? Respect for the young and myth promoted by media are also dramatically set straight."

Omaha Magic's productions cover many performance styles and topics. For example, *100,001 Horror Stories of the Plains*, produced for the U.S. Bicentennial, collected stories from across the plains via a contest, then performed them in a family dinner-style setting for which people could either pay money or bring food to share. *Running Gag*, an exploration of the American fascination with running and jogging, was commissioned by and performed at the 1980 Winter Olympics in Lake Placid, New York, before touring the country. *Sleazing Toward Athens*, a transformation play dealing with earning versus learning among today's college students, had sold-out runs in Omaha and toured the Midwest.

Not all of the theatre's work is overtly political or social critique. *Objective Love* is a musical performance event about love and the games lovers play; *Family Talk* is a play with music showing positive ways to create effective communication within the family; and *Astro*Bride* is a "McCluhanesque" sci-fi performance musical for one woman, three robots and a synthesizer. Terry emphasizes that for herself, Schmidman, and the Omaha Magic Theatre, "Art is about taking action. I believe in taking creative action. Theatre reminds you that you can transcend this discrete unit, the body, by combining imaginatively with your community in reacting with, for, and to the presentation on the stage that is meaningful to the community."

THE WASHINGTON AREA FEMINIST THEATRE

Mary Catherine Wilkins and Cathleen Schurr

The Washington Area Feminist Theatre was formed in 1972 to provide theatrical opportunities in an atmosphere that would not limit women, to train women in theatre skills, to produce plays designed to broaden the perception of women's capabilities on- and offstage and to promote an understanding of women's experience in society from a woman's point of view. WAFT produced three full seasons of plays—all written by women, a number of them world or Washington premieres, others revivals of shows that are part of the heritage of women in theatre. In 1976 WAFT's major production activity ceased because of both the termination of its relationship with a local college and an internal organizational breakdown.

As a feminist theatre, WAFT always aimed at a high level of artistic accomplishment while exploring the complexity and diversity of women's lives. All production work was performed by women; WAFT's primary commitment to women did not exclude men from audiences or casts, but they rarely functioned on production crews.

Successful production of two short plays for the Washington, D.C., chapter of the National Organization for Women as a part of the anniversary of women's suffrage during the week of August 26, 1972, encouraged some of the women who worked on the shows to discuss the formation of a feminist-oriented theatre. The only other women's theatre group in the Washington area at that time was Earth Onion. This women's collective, closed to new members, toured with an improvisationally-based piece. The organizers of WAFT planned a different kind of theatre—one which would produce scripted plays and involve as many women as possible.

The six women who met initially included some who were attracted by the theatrical potential and some by the political potential. This mixture remained fairly consistent throughout WAFT's history. The initial group consisted of middle-class, college-educated, heterosexual, white women. The social class and education level of the group never changed substantially. However, by 1974 there were a number of lesbians working with the theatre. This change was disturbing to some of the heterosexual women, whose feelings were discussed at meetings of the WAFT board. There were continuing disagreements between those who wanted WAFT to be more politically radical—mostly lesbian—and those who wanted WAFT to remain moderate—mostly heterosexual.

By 1976, there were some black women working with WAFT and attending productions. Most of the founding board members were in their twenties, but one was in her forties, and two in their mid-fifties. Most of the women who took part in productions, especially as crew members, tended to be in their twenties or early thirties. The interchange between age groups proved to be valuable to the board and to the productions. New members were recruited at public meetings and workshops.

The outcome of one early workshop is illustrative of some of WAFT's basic principles in action. The workshop on "Technical Theatre" evolved into an "introduction to scene design" because of the interests and talents of two of the participants—an artist and an interior designer—who continued to work together, designing and constructing sets for the next three major WAFT productions. It was central to WAFT's definition of itself as an experimental theatre that women were supported in their ventures into new areas.

One of WAFT's problems was locating scripts by women playwrights. Finding the names of women writers and the titles of their plays involved extensive searching—of catalogs, anthologies, theatre histories, and library stacks. Then, finding the plays themselves was an additional problem. Contacts made by WAFT's script director, playwright Elizabeth Wilson Hughes, eventually brought in numerous original works.

These are some of the criteria that were applied to scripts: Is it written by a woman? What is its artistic merit? Are there more roles for women than men? Has it been produced frequently by other theatre groups? How does it fit with the other possibilities for the season? WAFT never produced a play written by a man, or one with more and/or better parts for men than women, or one of the commonly produced plays by women playwrights. Judgments about artistic merit and political content were most difficult because both are subjective. Frequently there were as many opinions as there were women in the room, but eventually, through compromise, a consensus was reached.

Although WAFT did not differ radically from traditional theatres in its production structure and process, it did differ in spirit. Feelings of self-confidence, self-reliance, mutual trust, and community were generated among the women who worked on productions because they were in an atmosphere in which women were in authority and where competence and achievement were the norms. This was sometimes difficult for some of the male actors; others, however, seemed to learn and grow from the experience. Conflicts also arose because some of the women resented the presence in a feminist theatre of even the few men who acted in productions. Although this issue was discussed frequently, WAFT continued to include men in the cast and in the audience.

During "Sound-Off" sessions after performances, the audience, including critics from metropolitan dailies and community newspapers, had a chance to exchange comments and questions with WAFT team members. Among the many disparate views, two comments were repeatedly voiced—that the play was too radical and militantly feminist, and that the play was not militant and radical enough. Men in the audience as well as in the cast were openly "astonished" that women were able to design and construct sets, hang light plots and manage an intricate theatre schedule while carrying on other jobs. Some critics consistently focused on WAFT'S name and politics rather than on the artistic merit of the productions. Nevertheless, WAFT maintained generally good media relations, received the same coverage as other D.C. experimental theatres, and had its fair share of good and bad reviews. The theatre enjoyed the support of local feminist groups and publications, and by the time it stopped producing, it had achieved a reasonable degree of recognition throughout the Washington area.

In addition to its regular theatre schedule, WAFT also sponsored special events with the goal of encouraging women artists. These included a play contest, a Clearinghouse Bulletin for unpublished plays and a program for women students from Antioch College. A grant from D.C.'s Commission on the Arts and Humanities, as well as organizational specialists brought in by the board of directors, helped the organization expand and work through problems.

WAFT began with no initial capital, but was able to raise money from box-office receipts, donations, small grants, workshop fees, contractual arrangements and special fund-raising activities. The financial arrangement with Mount Vernon College, a women's college, was a great boon from 1974 to 1976: WAFT received free office, workshop and rehearsal space, and was paid between ten and fifteen percent of box-office revenues for productions and special events.

That arrangement was not renewed in 1976 when new administrators were not receptive to a feminist theatre on campus. At the same time, WAFT's board experienced an internal breakdown. These two factors forced a cessation of WAFT's major production activity. During the 1976–77 season WAFT produced a series of short productions, discussions and workshops designed to explore the impact of combining theatre with feminist politics.

A focal point of dissension during the period when the board of directors was trying to reorganize was WAFT's production of Lillian Mortimer's Victorian melodrama *No Mother to Guide Her*. During its run it was attacked by members of the board as "sexist" and "racist," and was said to lack redeeming artistic or political content. In an atmosphere of great confusion and many recriminations, the board decided that it could no longer function effectively as a group.

Since 1976, there have been a number of different small transition groups working to revitalize the organization, but the phoenix has not yet risen from its ashes. Whatever lies in WAFT's future, it can be proud of its concrete accomplishments. It has passed on a legacy which is alive in the groups that it inspired and in the women who worked with WAFT over the years.

WOMEN'S INTERART THEATRE

Helen Krich Chinoy

The Women's Interart Theatre functions as part of an extraordinary complex known as Women's Interart Center in New York City. The Center began around 1969 "with a group of women from several art forms meeting in lofts and in a Lower East Side firehouse," as Margot Lewitin, its long-time artistic director, recalls. "Each of us was supposed to present or perform some piece of work: a painting, a poem, a piece of music." Lewitin was asked in 1970 to help write a grant for a permanent home. When the group received some funding from New York State Council on the Arts, it moved into a then-abandoned city-owned building.

The participants used their $5,000 grant to renovate four floors of an industrial building on West 52nd Street, creating a theatre along with an art gallery and work facilities for artists. The Center dedicated itself to supporting independent women artists from different disciplines and to integrating the visual arts, music, dance and theatre. Its participants believe that all the arts are interrelated and that to create them or present them in isolation is to limit their appreciation and growth. In addition to encouraging artists to work together, the Center supports efforts on the part of its participants, who include men as well as women, to learn new skills and experiment with new media and offers innovative training programs for both professional and beginning artists.

The Interart Theatre evolved within the context of the Center, coming into being more than two years after the Center itself had been formed. Lewitin recalls its informal beginnings:

> I'd been working at La MaMa, stage-managing for a number of productions. After La Mama, I worked for Mobilization for Youth, but one day my job disappeared. I began spending a lot of time at the Center. Indeed I had nothing else going that particularly interested me. It was a good place to be . . . Not until the 1972–73 season did we do our first theatre piece. I directed a play by Jane Chambers called Random Violence . . . Whether I would ever have moved from stage-managing without Women's Interart I don't know. But being here somehow gave me the courage to begin directing plays.

The women's work nurtured and presented in the Interart Theatre is notable. As one of the oldest theatres in New York emphasizing the work of women playwrights and directors, Interart has staged over fifty productions, more than half premieres, almost all written or directed by women, whose creative growth remains the theatre's primary concern. Novices like Wendy Kesselman, who went on to win the Susan Blackburn award for *My Sister in This House*, wrote her first play, *Becca*, on a commission from Interart. The actress Estelle Parsons made her major directorial debut there in 1979, directing a large-scale *Antony and Cleopatra*. Other playwrights and directors who have worked at the Interart include Joyce Aaron, JoAnne Akalaitis, Kay Carney, Beverley Eamonds, Corinne Jacker, Salome Jens, Adrienne Kennedy, Françoise Kourilsky, Myrna Lamb, Lee Nagrin, Meredith Monk, Elinor Renfield, Amy Saltz, Nancy Rhodes and Susan Yankowitz.

Interart Theatre's dedication to women has brought them important awards: in 1984, both a special Obie grant and a Drama Desk Award. In 1985, the Women's Committee of the Dramatists Guild gave its annual award to Margot Lewitin for her contribution to the development of women playwrights and women in theatre.

In addition to the recognition and the awards, this dedication to fostering women theatre artists has also brought the Interart Theatre a lot of headaches. "We walk a tightrope," Margot Lewitin told Arthur Sainer in a *Village Voice* interview in 1984:

> Some believe that the organization, with its many women artists, is inherently too feminist. Others think the Center isn't feminist enough. Some women's organizations feel that Women's Interart, by virtue of its existence as a women's cooperative, ought to be fashioning a very particular feminist ideology. It's true that we don't necessarily explore feminist issues . . . In fact, the feminist community as a whole isn't that interested in art . . . The truth is we don't have an anti or pro ideology. If we have a bias, it's simply in favor of supporting women artists rather than men.

The Interart's relationship to the projects of the Women's Experimental Theatre, which Roberta Sklar and Sondra Segal codirect, exemplifies their approach. Lewitin explains, "They develop, we house." But Sklar says that "they don't just leave us alone, they leave us alone with love and support." Yet Lewitin insists that Interart is "more than a collection of doting parental figures and discipline-free offspring." Over the years "we had to find a balance between being supportive and being stupid. At some point you have to make a judgment, you have to take responsibility for what you're putting up."

As a result of its open, supportive, responsible approach, Interart has offered productions that vary greatly in content and style. Its biggest "hit," ironically, was a play by a man, Franz Xaver Kroetz's *Through the Leaves*. But it was staged by a woman, JoAnne Akalaitis, and featured Ruth Maleczech and Frederick Neumann; all the artists involved won Obie Awards in 1984.

UNIVERSITY OF WINCHESTER LIBRARY

Another notable project was transforming *Tongues* by Sam Shepard and Joe Chaikin for television.

Because women's work tends to be less well received by audiences and critics, there has been some concern that Interart may be playing down its women's aspect. Lewitin has said that "there are foundation people who genuinely feel that any organization that has the word 'women' in its title can't be serious about art." Without being dogmatically feminist, Interart fights this accusation by their continued dedication to providing a place for women artists.

Their major energies are now devoted to preventing the demolition of their building as part of the attempted gentrification of the Clinton Hill area, where the Interart Center's presence had brought other arts organizations like Ensemble Studio Theatre to the building and to the neighborhood. Having won the first stage of a battle with the city government to remain in their building in April 1986, Women's Interart is trying to implement an alternative community development plan, purchase the building and continue to operate their multi-discipline center with its primary dedication to women in the arts.

NEW YORK FEMINIST THEATRE TROUPE

Claudette Charbonneau and Lucy Winer

We two founded a radical, all-women's theatre company, the New York Feminist Theatre Troupe, which began in December 1973 and gave what turned out to be its last performance in the spring of 1976. We and the other six original members of the troupe had, on a moment's notice, submerged ourselves in a whirlwind of planning sessions, rehearsals, and performances. In the first months a script was written, troupe members found and performances staged at women's centers, churches and colleges in New York and New England. This period culminated in a summer tour of western Canada, only six months after our first meeting. Though we went on to do a great deal more—we made a film, *Jeriann*, and staged a second theatrical production, *In Transit*—we were never again to match the energy, enthusiasm and sheer productivity of those first six months.

It is hard to reconcile our knowledge that the troupe no longer exists with the feeling that it could still all be possible. And nothing—no amount of analysis, nor hours spent rehashing the probable causes of the troupe's dissolution—can mitigate the overriding sense of loss. If not for ourselves, then for those who come after us, there may be value in uncovering the problems.

Alternative groups, inevitably, confront a great many problems in our society. Much of what we faced would be shared by any troupe attempting to do political theatre. Yet certain problems were more acute because we were a group of women. Imbued with a sense of feminism, we wanted our troupe to be an arena into which any woman could step, even if only for a short while. Thus for one New York City production we encouraged a Frenchwoman briefly visiting the United States to join our cast. Knowing no English, she sat on a high stool in white face, playing an organ grinder, welcoming the audience to our show.

This flexibility was invigorating, even though the "polish" of the show might suffer. In fact, it was this kind of spontaneity and openness that the troupe sought. But it was much harder to attain in our permanent membership. We had hoped to create a troupe that would not only portray onstage but embody in its membership the various phases and modes of women's lives. Originally, our group had some range, particularly in terms of age. Some members were lesbians; others were heterosexual. But we never achieved the fully representative group we had envisioned.

Despite the fact that we were all involved in the women's movement, we had not fully and concretely grasped the actual constraints under which most women live. Child care, housework, husbands, unrewarding jobs—all would conspire to make it exceedingly difficult for most women to join an itinerant theatre. But we never did give up: a woman on welfare, mother of twins, joined us to work on the film and the second production. By then we had learned how difficult and consuming it is to sustain a theatre troupe, and how rare it would be for any but a very young woman to be free enough to jump in. The severe limits placed on most women's lives came sharply into focus when the troupe suddenly decided to embark on our tour of Canada. Who could dream of such a journey? Only women who were unmarried, women who had no set careers, women who weren't working to support others—only they could pack up and leave for two months.

Aside from the physical constraints, what of the emotional risks? All the original members had shown a daredevil courage simply in joining. The prospect of an extended tour in a different country seemed a wonderful opportunity and we all knew it; and yet hours upon hours had to be spent in "emotional meetings," not discussing the very real practical issues like money and transportation, but unraveling vague and unidentifiable fears. In fact, whenever the troupe asked us to venture into new territory, to consider a new possibility, most of us experienced a ridiculously disproportionate amount of anxiety—a measure of just how strong and tenacious societal lessons of conformity and non-assertiveness can be. Joining the troupe meant overcoming more hurdles, both physical and psychical, than we had at first anticipated.

Lack of funding presented us with other, obvious kinds of difficulties. If nothing else, money provides a buffer. It can make the daily life of a troupe less harrowing, solving some of the constant, nagging problems—how to pay for adequate rehearsal space, how to transport props or the players themselves to out-of-town engagements, etc. Not to seek funding had been an early and a conscious decision. The troupe had arranged the first performance with no outside help or guidance and that sense of independence gave us tremendous energy. For a group of women to eschew the ordinary, established paths of support in itself made a political point. Clearly, our financial goals had to be modest. The fees we earned were small and the money made from one show had to be put toward the next. But we proved that an audience of women did exist and could be relied on to sustain radical feminist theatre. Our sense of independence was, of course, at the cost of other, important ideals. With money we might have been able to hire some of those women who could not join otherwise and thereby have given the troupe the broader representation we wanted. Nevertheless, if we were starting out again today, we might yet abide by our original decision.

The material the troupe performed centered on issues—the harmful and sometimes lethal side effects of available birth-control devices, the lack of equal work and educational opportunities, the sterilization of Third World women, the fear of lesbians, the medical treatment of women, etc. We used statistics and cited names. Our tone was not self-righteous; frequently, in fact, it was humorous. But there was no way the audience could avoid confronting in specific terms what it means for women to live in a male-dominated world.

Our first show, Lucy Winer's *But, Something Was Wrong with the Princess*, opened as a circus, a device offering many possibilities for exaggeration, slapstick and improvisation. The scene culminated in a sideshow of freaks: Abortion Annie; Birth Control Bonnie; 'Lectric Lizzie, the survivor of many electric shock treatments; and Wonder Woman, the perfect housewife. The play also included original music, poetry and scenes such as "The Socialization of Mary," 'A Psychiatric Consultation," and "Dear John," a song describing a married woman's emotions as she decides to leave her husband. In contrast to the color and flair of the opening, the play closed in darkness: from all sides of the performance space we whispered and shouted the proverbial statements that have shaped women's sense of themselves—excerpts of anti-women passages from the Bible, fragments from the marriage ceremony, lines from television commercials, refrains from folksongs and finally a mounting barrage of catcalls and sexual comments from men on the street.

None of the problems we faced had easy or obvious solutions. Those who were more committed found themselves pushing those who were not—a situation that drained and hurt everyone. The problem in our case was exacerbated, ironically, by elements which were assets: the substantial range in age and the dynamic qualities of several members. Because the most forceful were also the oldest, the sense of disparity was magnified. The troupe had trouble handling the different levels of energy and commitment in a way compatible with feminist ideology. "Emotional meetings" were helpful at times, but their effect was not lasting. There are limits to what consciousness-raising can do in the short run and the troupe lived very much in a short run crowded with the demands of rehearsal and performance schedules. Our failure to achieve a more equal and spontaneous involvement from all the members was a major cause of the troupe's decline. Those who felt "hammered away at" pulled back emotionally. Those who envisioned something more than a brief experiment began to lose heart at the prospect of constantly urging others on.

The disparities in involvement might not have been so debilitating if other divisions had not emerged. As a feminist theatre troupe we had a dual commitment—to politics and to theatre. How to maintain a proper balance became more and more problematic. The divisions arose subtly, as a question of emphasis and not of clear-cut choice. (Not even those who came to see acting as a lifelong pursuit wanted to be part of traditional theatre.) As the troupe got over the initial exhilaration simply at having put on a show, some began to have different expectations. Everyone wanted to put on a good production; but slowly the definition and conception of "a good production" began to change. The shift in expectations led to a shift in values. Spontaneity, flexibility, open membership had to be rejected if the "polish" of the performance were to come first.

The division between a grassroots political orientation and increasingly professional artistic hopes posed our most serious problem. Can the two be reconciled? A sensible balance might have been struck—if the troupe had had a more holistic sense of theatre and a clearer recognition of what the members really wanted and if, while we were trying to develop our range and depth as performers, we had also put more energy into being just as creative politically.

To dwell on difficulties, however, may obscure the most important point of all—that a group of women without experience or help created a feminist theatre troupe that lasted three-and-a-half years. We played every place and any place: in cafeterias, bars, prisons, day-care centers, classrooms, gymnasiums, ballrooms and even a laundromat. The very real sadness we feel because the troupe no longer exists must not be allowed to cloud that reality. In this country and Canada, we reached thousands of women. Certainly we had wanted to build a more lasting structure. But it is perhaps a mistaken value to stress permanence, particularly if it detracts from the recognition that in existing at all we achieved something very hard and very wonderful.

THE LAVENDER CELLAR THEATRE

Dinah L. Leavitt

The Lavender Cellar Theatre was founded in Minneapolis in 1973 by eight lesbian women; its final performance was given less than two years later. During that time the theatre collective performed six original productions for about two thousand people. The members had few theatre skills, little experience, no money, no scripts, no theatre building and no clear idea of what a lesbian theatre was.

The founders originally intended their theatre to be a vehicle for telling the story of lesbian oppression and lifestyles. Complications arose immediately. Some of the women, fearing reprisals, refused to perform publicly outside the gay community; others, involved with gay rights, were unable to commit sufficient time to produce a play; and no one knew of a lesbian play to produce.

Floundering, the core members decided to join the Alive and Trucking Company, a local socialist agitprop theatre. However, this plan was abandoned because the Alive and Trucking could not devote enough time to lesbian issues.

In September 1973 the group, led by Marie Kent, gathered at the Lesbian Resource Center to reorganize. This time the women decided to use the theatre to explore and present the lesbian experience for lesbians. Member Nythar Sheehy says:

> It started because lesbians needed something tangible to validate their experience; they needed something to get people to work together and as an alternative social function to bars. It also developed creativity and raised our own and our audience's consciousnesses.

One crucial element in the development of a cohesive lesbian community in Minneapolis was the Lesbian Resource Center, which in turn played an important role in the establishment of the Lavender Cellar. It provided rehearsal and performance space, acted as a financial backer for productions and gave emotional support to group members; its own collective structure became a model for the theatre's organization.

Members adopted the collective structure because they wanted to overcome the usual management politics, competition and hierarchy of established theatres. Besides collective responsibility for all work and decisions, the group used the concept to share both the group's and individual members' problems. Collective administration usually worked well because the group was small and stable in membership; its business-management needs were minimal; and its major production style—the revue—was well suited to group direction. However, members stated that the cooperative process was often overly time-consuming and that arriving at a consensus was often chaotic.

The company rehearsed an average of twice weekly with five rehearsals a week before each opening. Any member could submit a script for consideration or offer ideas for a collaborative piece. Following auditions, shows were cast and staff assigned by collective approval. Direction was cooperative:

> People explored parts as they interpreted them and the director was more of a coordinator. When a total interpretation was necessary, a discussion was held with the entire cast.

The company employed a variety of acting and directing styles and techniques "as a means of getting in touch with the feelings the characters were expressing which had also been our own feelings." This developmental process, begun with *Prisons*, was expanded and refined through subsequent productions.

The first play, *Prisons*, a one-act by member Pat Suncircle, depicted the roles in which people are willingly and unwillingly cast and the consequences of defining one's role. Presented first at the Lesbian Resource Center in spring

1973, before the group's reorganization, the portable production was kept in repertoire and toured to conferences and meetings.

In December 1973 the group performed an occasional piece, *Scene at the Center*, a musical parody reflecting interaction and activity at the Lesbian Resource Center. This piece, intentionally limited in its appeal, was performed only at the Center.

In February 1974 the company performed, again at the Center, a modern dance revue, *Isidora Is Arisen,* coordinated by Nythar Sheehy, and in May it presented *Women's Struggle Throughout History*, a reader's theatre production based on the writings of such women as Sojourner Truth, Gertrude Stein and Susan B. Anthony. In fall 1974 the group put together a musical revue of eight short acts titled *Cabaret '74*. Like *Scene at the Center*, it was a celebration of the lesbian experience, designed to entertain and provide a social basis of unity for the lesbian community.

Cory, by Suncircle, presented in May 1975, was about a sixteen-year-old girl's struggle with family, friends, society and self in dealing with her lesbianism. The realistic two-act drama employs a cast of ten, including two male roles, Cory's father and her friend, Douglass. The Lavender Cellar cast women in the male roles, costuming them as men. The audiences accepted the role/actress sex reversal as a convention of the theatre. The presence of non-lesbians would have created a group dynamic that the theatre believed would have been counterproductive.

Cory was enthusiastically received by audiences at the Center, and they remained after performances to discuss the play, the production and lesbians' and women's issues. *Cory* fulfilled the group's objective of accurately presenting the lesbian experience. It also was successful as a meaningful exploration and experience for cast members. After *Cory* closed, the Lavender Cellar Theatre became inactive and remains so to date. Marie Kent explains, "After working on *Cory* for five months, we were exhausted, and no one came forward to relieve us."

The influence of the group was small by some measures, but if one considers the special, unique and difficult goal it attempted to accomplish without role models, society's approval or financial support, its limited appeal is both understandable and valuable. Lavender Cellar Theatre reaffirmed lesbian values and goals, contributed significantly to the Lesbian Resource Center's activity, engendered a sense of community through its performances and discussions, became a rallying point for women, fostered sisterhood and gay solidarity and entertained, but the most important thing it did was simply to exist. For two years it performed lesbian drama, and that alone is a unique accomplishment.

AT THE FOOT OF THE MOUNTAIN

Linda Walsh Jenkins

When Martha and Paul Boesing, Jan Magrane and three others formed a theatre ensemble in 1974, they consulted the *I Ching*. The hexagram for "the springs at the foot of the mountain" gave them both a name and an image of sustenance. Although the composition and the direction of the theatre have shifted over the years, its evolution has been guided by that central idea of a theatre as necessary as water.

Organized in Atlanta, the group moved to Minneapolis to begin their politically committed work with a production of Martha Boesing's first two plays, *Pimp* and *The Gelding*. By the fall of 1975, all but Martha and Jan had left. Phyllis Jane Rose (then Wagner) saw their production of Boesing's *River Journal* that fall, returned to her job chairing a university directing program to direct the play there, but then quit her job and moved to Minneapolis to forge a collective with Martha and Jan. For Phyllis, Martha Boesing's play "crystallized the lesson of experience: that women and men relate hierarchically."

During the second half of the 1970s, At the Foot of the Mountain explored, and helped create for the rest of the country, the concept of a feminist theatre. Phyllis Jane Rose explains:

> Through the performance of Martha's plays (and "songs"), through the performance of scripts by other women, and through community events and rituals, we work *collectively* asking such questions as: How can we connect theatre with life? What is the correlation between the choices we make as performers and the choices we make as persons? How can theatre work as a spiritual and healing force in our community? How can theatre best serve radical political change? How can we stop giving in to a system in which power over others is the common standard for success? How does a women's theatre differ from the theatre of our heritage (theatre written and produced by men)?

The initial trio remained as the core of the theatre while many others passed through; by 1980 they needed to rest and gain perspective from the exhausting challenge of collective administration. Phyllis Jane Rose continued as managing director, and Martha Boesing returned as artistic director after taking a leave of absence. Jan Magrane resigned but a year later became producing director. The entire theatre reorganized using a board-of-directors structure similar to that of other not-for-profit groups so they could better compete for grants and other patronage. A full-time administrative staff allowed the artists not only to focus on such new plays as *Junkie!*, *Ashes Ashes We All Fall Down* and *Haunted by the Holy Ghost*, but also to expand the programming to include such new projects as the Summer Workshop Program (culminating in the production of Martha Boesing's *Antigone Two*), the *Junkie!* film, the Broadcloth program (staged readings of new plays by women) and Jan's Coming of Age project (plays with adolescents and senior women). Nevertheless, Martha and Jan finally needed to move in other directions. Jan left in 1985.

In 1984, a decade after the founding of the theatre, Martha Boesing received a $20,000 Bush Foundation fellowship that allowed her an eighteen-month break from the company. She continued to work in association with ATFM, however, playing Fefu in Maria Irene Fornes's *Fefu and Her Friends* (directed by Fornes in 1986), and developing a new multiracial production of her *The Story of a Mother*; but she began reshaping her life as an artist. A National Endowment for the Arts grant in 1987 allowed her to develop further as a playwright.

Phyllis Jane Rose has taken the theatre in a new direction, creating a multiracial, multigenerational and multicultural theatre company. The 1985–87 seasons included plays by Fornes, Adrienne Kennedy, and Marilyn Seven, a series of staged readings of historical scripts by African American women playwrights, staged readings of new plays, performances by feminist comedian Janice Perry (aka "GAL"), a Mother's Day pageant created by performance artist Suzanne Lacey and codirected with Phyllis featuring over six hundred older women, a residency by Spiderwoman, and a touring repertoire of reprises of *Raped* and *The Story of a Mother* (scripted by Martha Boesing with the company's collaboration). In this way, the theatre continues to be a source of sustenance for the feminist political community—"the springs at the foot of the mountain."

SPIDERWOMAN

Linda Walsh Jenkins

Muriel and Gloria Miguel and Lisa Mayo, the core members of Spiderwoman, are three Cuna-Rappahannock Indian sisters, born on the floor of their grandmother's house in an Italian neighborhood in Brooklyn. Central to their creations are their multicultural and female experiences, their political ideas and the concept of "weaving" they take from their Native American heritage. The sisters describe the source of their name and the inspiration for their work as follows:

> Spiderwoman or Spider Grandmother Woman is one of the familiar household gods of the Hopi. Her divine powers, her unlimited wisdom and all-encompassing knowledge have made her a culture heroine of Hopi tradition. She has prophetic access to the future and is

familiar with all the languages of the world. Being a common spider she is ever present and ever ready to intervene, assist, counsel, guide and save.

We take our name from Spiderwoman, goddess of creation, the first to create designs and teach her people to weave. She always wove a flaw into her designs to allow her spirit to find a way out and be free.

We call on her inspiration in the development of our working technique "storyweaving," creating designs and weaving stories with words and movement. We work onstage as an ensemble, basing our productions on life experiences. We translate our personal stories, dreams and images into movement, and refine them into the essential threads of human experience. In seeking out, exploring, and weaving our own patterns, we reflect the human tapestry, the web of our common humanity. Finding, loving and transcending our own flaws, as in the flaw in the goddess's tapestry, provide the means for our spirits to find their way out, to be free.

Challenging the "one size fits all" view of feminism, [we] . . . use our diverse experiences . . . to defy such generalizations as "blondes have more fun" and "all women's theatre is the same." Our stories can be told or thought of at any time—on the street, over meals, in the tub. Then we rehearse, improvise and brainstorm to investigate various aspects of our stories, dreams and images. We usually begin with a theme, someone tells a story, another repeats it, and we work together to transform it into movement or reduce it to its essence.

Muriel Miguel, as director, makes the final decision as to what works and what doesn't with an eye to the creation of an entire production, but everyone in the group has a voice and doesn't hesitate to use it to express herself. This technique insures that a Spiderwoman production will be lively, entertaining and exciting. It also makes for a moving experience within each individual in the audience, as the personal chords sung, whispered, screamed or muttered by the performers strike up resonant reactions with the audience, who become a part of our web, as we become a part of theirs.

The idea for Spiderwoman began with a workshop of Indian and non-Indian women organized by Muriel Miguel at Washington Square Methodist Church in New York in early 1975, to explore this concept of storyweaving. They taught the audience Indian handgames, then one actress became Spiderwoman as she was fingerweaving and began to create a story. Others started weaving in their stories, dreams, and dances, as The New Wilderness Band (men and women) played gongs, bowls, rocks, a saw, flutes and handmade instruments.

This experiment grew into Spiderwoman, as Muriel involved her sisters and others. They produced *Women in Violence* in June 1975, at New York's American Indian Community House. "I wanted to work with anger, with feelings about being boxed in, feelings about the Indian situation, the Indian

Movement today, my own violence as a woman and as an Indian," Muriel has explained.

Their productions have been consistently original, unconventional, transformational events that weave together music, poetry, performance art, fantastic characters, dreams and environmental art. For *Women in Violence* they used a prologue of Indian songs against a backdrop of quilts received in Sun Dance giveaways and large fabric "webs" sculpted by Donna Hennis. Diane Cartwright described their clown personae:

> Pamela Verge's militant-nun clown sprouted a grammar school nativity-play halo. A scrub brush for cleaning up the world protruded from a bandolier of bullets. Lisa Mayo . . . was garbed in clinging black—essential equipment outlined with white paint, long blonde locks topped by an oversize glitter bow. As the circus's strong woman, Gloria Miguel kept a flashlight hidden between the shiny metal-like strips of her skirt so that she might search for herself beneath the reflected image.

Other productions have included their semi-autobiographical *Sun, Moon and Feather* (three Native American sisters in Brooklyn plot to cross the bridge to Manhattan); *Grandma* (a Kiowa mother plans a giveaway, written by Hanay Geiogamah); *The Pause that Refreshes* (a risqué song-and-dance act about menopause); *Neurotic Erotic Exotics* (seven women of color explore experiences of oppression developed in collaboration with At the Foot of the Mountain); *The Lysistrata Numbah!* (performed on European tour), *I'll Be Right Back* (an exploration of global survival, using folk tales, music, dance, animal sounds and performance art chants); and *Three Up, Three Down* (a portrayal of tragic relationships, combining a contemporary love triangle among three women with a song about a withered plant and intermittent scenes from *Wuthering Heights* and *Jane Eyre*).

THE WOMEN'S EXPERIMENTAL THEATRE

Sondra Segal and Roberta Sklar

We founded the Women's Experimental Theatre in 1976, together with Clare Coss, out of an insurmountable desire to discover our own voice and express it in a theatre where women spoke to women about what was important to them. It was started in a rush of seeking survival as we, alongside of thousands of other women, set out to tell our story.

For more than a decade we dedicated our time, energies, creative and economic resources to WET, where we reached out to an ever-widening audience of women who needed our work. The urgency and the desire flowed between theatre-maker and audience member in a charged, palpable and powerful relationship. The subject of our work, though not topical, was always political. We addressed the subversive impulse in women's minds, an impulse to change, to seek expansion of being and a place in the world. We sought to delineate the interaction between the psychological and social worlds. Along with other feminist theatres, theoreticians artists, and activists, we thought—and at WET, we made thought into theatre. Never before had we used ourselves so fully; never had we even imagined such use.

The three of us collaborated, working together and separately through several stages to create our first series of plays, *The Daughters Cycle Trilogy.* We started with research culled from hundreds of women who participated in workshops and interviews. After an inventory of what we had gathered, we wrote separately, exchanging ideas and material to develop a rough draft. More workshops and rehearsals were followed by more writing, as we also took on more specific roles.

In the research period, we were all actors, putting forth our ideas through improvised images. Sondra and Roberta each directed and acted, inventing exercises to create and generate material. Clare Coss, too, actively entered the actor research as well as writing dialogue and poetry that often extended beyond the parameters of the plays. All three of us wrote material and collaborated in decision-making.

Once the play was in rough-draft form, we would move into a more recognizable phase: the rehearsal of a new play. Roberta concentrated on directing; Sondra focused on performance, looking at the work from within; Clare revised the script. Up to this point we had been doing what we called "inspired writing," but now we would see specific problems in the text. Clare, who was brilliant at rewriting, would go home and fix it.

In performance you'd see Sondra onstage together with Mary Lum and Mary Lyon, the two other actors, who worked with us throughout the trilogy (other actors performed in only one or two of the plays); you would see Roberta and Clare in the audience taking notes. We three assessed the work from our unique perspectives. Our roles as performer, writer and director became more delineated but we continued to collaborate very closely, even as we learned to name what we did individually, to claim our work.

Over more than a decade we created two series of plays through this process: *The Daughters Cycle* and *Woman's Body and Other Natural Resources.* Throughout the work our use of humor was a frequent and deliberate choice to ameliorate the pain of seeing the experience of women in patriarchy. Our intention was to disturb, to challenge ourselves and other women and to create good times—not to forget, but to remember through humor. We also sought to develop a feminist actor, one who gives testimony to the ability of women to change. Performer and audience member became partners in a process that moved toward change on both sides of the performing line.

The early years of work were devoted to mining our history of daughterhood. All women are daughters—what could this simple universal truth mean? We were not alone in our passionate research. The mother-daughter relationship, and within it the commonality of daughterhood, gripped feminist thinkers in every field during this second wave of twentieth-century feminism.

The result of our labor was *The Daughters Cycle Trilogy: Daughters, Sister/Sister*, and *Electra Speaks*. *Daughters* is a ritual that moves through themes of birth, the ambivalent and interchangeable nature of mother/daughter roles, the commonality of all women as daughters, and a reclaiming of all our matri-lineage: "I'm Sondra,/daughter of Lille,/Daughter of a woman from Austria." *Sister/Sister* is a search into the relations between sisters and how their child-hood realities impact on their adult sisterhood. The third play, *Electra Speaks*, is an explosive work cutting across history and theatrical forms. Its transformational characters, Clytemnestra (the archetypal mother) and Electra and Iphigenia (archetypal daughters and sisters), confront domestic violence and its links to violence on a larger scale. Our Electra, however, does not collude in the murder of her mother. In a Chaplinesque gesture she attempts to sever her ties with the House of Atreus by flinging herself through the Greek archway of Home: "Electra steps out the door/she had never done this before." Separation leads to survival for Electra, the daughter born under a feminist sun.

In 1980 we turned our theatrical attention to another arena. Clare Coss left WET to continue her practice as a psychotherapist and to pursue her writing, while Sondra and Roberta began new theatrical research on the theme of woman's body and "obsession" as a state of mind. *Woman's Body and Other Natural Resources* is a humorous, compassionate, sometimes musical, series of plays about woman's profound relationship to food. Woman's body is food; she provides food; she binges and starves; she struggles to feed herself. *Food* focuses on the daily, unrelenting Family Dinner. After each performance, we were surrounded by audience members urgently reporting to us on their relationship to food. *Foodtalk* combines scripted "Testimony" by an actor with opportunities for the audience to join the actors onstage in naming the daily, unique, but universal concern with food. *Feast or Famine*, the culminating play, portrays woman's relationship to scarcity and plenty on a global scale. It was written and performed by Sondra and directed by Roberta; visual artists and musicians collaborated also, so that this work overlapped the field of performance art.

When *Feast or Famine* was performed in 1985 for an extended run at Women's Interart Center, our home base, we found ourselves reassessing the demand for, need of and response to feminist theatre in the increasingly conservative 1980s that seek to put women back "where they belong," a period that the *New York Times* was calling the "age of post-feminism." Although thinking seriously about women's lives is as important as it was a decade ago, it no longer seems to be a conscious, pressing part of a mass movement. The Women's Experimental Theatre is not currently active. The decline of economic and audience support tells us this is not the time. We have decided, however, not to formally close up shop. We want to remain open to the rumblings of a distant thunder—that of an old, or new, feminist need.

REBECCAH: REHEARSAL NOTES

Karen Malpede

Rebeccah is a tale whose theme is the birth of the feminist imagination. It is a history of this century from 1905 to 1932, told through the life of one woman, Rebeccah, who becomes a bag lady. As Rebeccah sees how a new community can be built out of the garbage of this civilization, the tale changes tone from grief to joy.

The people who perform this play are workers. They carry all they need into the space with them. And all that they need has been found amidst the garbage on the streets of New York City. They tell a simple story directly. *Rebeccah* is meant to be performed in a circle, the audience surrounding the performers. The story is composed of narrative, song, chant and moments mutual turning—when characters exchange thoughts and feelings so deep their ways of being alter.

Rebeccah's tale begins in Kishniff, Russia, 1905. In a pogrom Rebeccah sacrifices her infant son, to save the rest of her family. The tale continues on the Lower East Side of New York City, March 25, 1911. Rebeccah's daughter, Sarah, is caught in the Triangle Shirtwaist Factory fire. Rebeccah becomes a bag lady; she dresses herself in the charred clothing of the victims of the fire. November 1931, Depression winter, Rebeccah founds a shantytown for homeless women and dies.

The *Rebeccah* company in April 1976 consisted of Tina Shepard (director), Karen Malpede (playwright), Linda Gutierrez (associate), and performers Sybille Hayn, Ellen Maddow, Gloria Mojica, Lois Weaver, and Pam Verge. After these rehearsal notes were made, Marcie Begleiter (designer) and performers Jan Cohen and Ann McGinnis joined the company.

April 4. We meet at the Chelsea Theatre. (Burl Hash, then a producer at Chelsea, had lent us rehearsal space.)

Rebeccah's beginning: the suffering. Tina is correct to say that the temptation of the company is to rush through to the Depression where the play flowers, but that we won't be able to fill that part out until we go deeply into the beginning and middle sections where Rebeccah feels the sorrows that lead to her transformation.

The actors take apart the first narration, reading it a dozen different ways. Sybille beats out a steady rhythm, reading over it. Tina and Ellen try to sing it different ways. They try to *daven* (the Jewish prayer rhythm). They try storytelling where each person adds a sentence when they feel the need, that is, when they are motivated by their own remembrance of the "event."

April 7. After the warm-up we hide onstage. First in the dark and then in the light and then we stand in a circle for a long time and speak about the experience. From the hiding two contrary emotions emerge that will resonate throughout the play—a sense of responsibility for everyone else and a wish to dissociate one's self from the others' fates. And another that some people speak of: waiting to see at what moment what you do will make a difference, hoping always for the chance to act. Then the reverse of this (which I feel!) of having hidden and then not wanting to look—of hoping not to be seen because I have stopped seeing.

April 8. The play as a series of concentric circles converging at a center point, the most subjective, the turnings—which, however, would not be possible without the sense of historical and social reality. A cycle in this way, too, beginning with the songs: the most direct connection between actors and audience and material; then the narratives, the survivors speak; the chants are the victims undergoing the psychic changes necessary to end their victimization. The true subjective center is when the victim renames herself or himself survivor.

April 12. Today the warm-up is a Balkan sound, or several. Tina says she feels like she's coming home to sounds she used to make but stopped because they were not music. The Balkan sounds are a folk tradition carried on by women—men's voices, I'm told, cannot do the thing. It is a sound made far forward in the face and not supported by the breath. A strong, somewhat harsh, nasal sound which combines in quite wonderful harmonies. This kind of singing is part of many cultures—Gloria says it sounds Indian, and it also sounds somewhat Appalachian.

Now I can see the large cycle in the play: the pogrom is the recognition, the Triangle fire is the renunciation, and the Depression is the rebirth. Or, like the ancient seasonal rites from which the theatre once derived, and in which women played a major part, first the battle, then the lamentation, then the regeneration, the rebirth. Within this large cycle there are many smaller ones. So the play is a series of circles in this way, too.

April 27. Ellen has composed a beginning pogrom song. I am delighted with it. In Balkan mode it is vibrant and angry and in it I suddenly feel the seeds of all the play becomes—as though in this first song of defeat and despair there is also all the energy for the later struggles and for Rebeccah's triumph.

As Gloria sings a Balkan song her voice trembles and slips from flat to sharp on the note and I see before me the courage of the person seeking to create—that blind faith that the shape will be attained if persistent effort is made. And when she's done, Tina utters my thought, "There was a nice edge about it, as though you were almost falling off, but didn't." Yes, the danger was very present and rang through all of us.

April 28. Art is about the coexistence of opposites: good and evil, pain and joy, temporal and eternal time. The opposites coexist in a balance. Our work is to shift the balance from evil toward good, from misery toward joy, from prose toward poetry. To weigh good in the balance before the mind, the eye and all the aspirations of the heart.

So I see more and more the different balance in the parts of *Rebeccah*. Today, the factory chant becomes a work song. It reminds us of the unused creativity inside these young women workers; each of them takes a turn supplying a line to this song and from the catalog of their ills, they have crafted together an ironic and bitter, but consciously created song—they have put themselves into the world this way, beyond the harsh limits of their deadening work, they speak.

I think, too, that the Depression chant is—and is in actual fact since its first verse was literally chanted into my ear by a homeless man as I crossed the Lower East Side one day—another expression of this creativity which lives inside of the oppressed, and another manifestation of the force of conscious shape.

I remember what Rebeccah says to the women while she dies:

REBECCAH:
    Now you've found the edge of brave emotion,
    stay there,
    surging up with each new wave of feeling,
    working away at the shape of the world—
    though the refashioning takes forever—
    no more considering stopping
    than a wave in the middle of the ocean
    considers not reaching shore.

SPLIT BRITCHES

Linda Walsh Jenkins

Lois Weaver, Peggy Shaw and Deborah Margolin are the ongoing members of the Split Britches company, which began in 1980 with a production by that name, now considered a masterpiece of feminist theatre. They have created remarkable, witty and provocative women-centered work since then from their home in the East Village and the WOW (Women's One World) Cafe. Their collective vision has been described as being "at the overlapping point of Sapphic poetry, *Mad* magazine and the Talmud."

Lois Weaver's entry into feminist work was with Spiderwoman; she began with the original storyweaving project and remained with the group for over seven years, directing, acting and touring Europe and the U.S. Peggy Shaw met Lois and Spiderwoman in Europe (their second tour) while traveling with the gay cabaret Hot Peaches. The only woman in that group, Peggy built sets and costumes and performed. Spiderwoman invited her to help them with a cabaret they were creating, *An Evening of Disgusting Songs and Pukey Images*. Peggy recalls:

I wasn't used to doing all that emotional kind of stuff. We spent our time [in Hot Peaches] writing new material, sewing on sequins, working with a piano player, changing all the he's to she's and she's to he's in all the songs. In Hot Peaches if you were mad at someone you could yell about it onstage and that was part of the show, but you weren't supposed to do that in Spiderwoman. Me and Spiderwoman kinda went like this [crashing noise] for the two years I was in it. But we all learned a lot and we're all still doing theatre.

Meanwhile, Lois Weaver had begun to conceive of the Split Britches project. Based on stories about her family—especially about three of her aunts—in the Blue Ridge Mountains, what finally emerged was a three-actress tour de force organized by the device of tableaux resembling family photos, with Lois narrating. The stories and gestural performances demonstrated the company's trademark—the split subject. The sisters struggle with their dependencies and their need for independence as they give the audience a funny, thoughtful, touching, sensuous theatre experience.

The original work on this project was done within Spiderwoman in 1980; they brought in Deborah Margolin to script the piece in 1981, and she eventually took over one of the roles when an actress left. With Lois directing, the three actresses told stories in character, told personal stories, sang and worked transformationally, with "gesture leading from one world to another world."

Work on *Split Britches* inevitably caused a break from Spiderwoman in 1981 because it was hard to have two directors in one company (Lois Weaver and Muriel Miguel), and because the two groups were growing in different directions. Later Lois joined the show as an actress. In 1982 her family saw the piece and were so excited they corrected and embellished certain details. After each show, her father could be found in the lobby with the family album, telling stories to the audience.

Each of the three women in Split Britches brings complementary skills to the company. Peggy Shaw contributes a visual eye and design artistry. Moreover, "She's our political thermometer, our radical," Lois explains. "Peggy can cut through a lot of bullshit and say, 'Get real.'" Deborah Margolin brings a wild sense of humor and strong writing skills. Lois Weaver is the director and acting teacher, combining her college Stanislavski training with sound and movement impulse work growing out of her participation in experimental theatre in the early 1970s. To Lois these approaches are the same system: "I felt they were different words, but they were talking about the same things. So I tried to make some connections in order to use sound and movement as a solid base for teaching acting in a traditional setting." In rehearsals and in the workshops the group offers, Lois teaches what she calls "multiple-choice acting":

You stand in the center of a wheel in the moment of performance, and at that center you have many things you can choose from. That moment of choice creates a live moment-to-moment performance. When you pre-choose, that is, when you take on a character which is very structured, you lose that moment-to-moment breathing.

Since 1982 the company has created several shows, taught workshops and worked with the Cafe WOW to establish a genuine community theatre. *The Tennessee Waltz* involved eleven WOW women who developed original scenes, monologues and music using Tennessee Williams's characters (they were unable to get rights for actual text).

Other productions include *St. Joan of Avenue C* (based on Brecht's *St. Joan of the Stockyards*, developed with dramaturg Alisa Solomon), *Patience and Sarah, Cinderella* and *Upwardly Mobile Home.* The latter features three women living in a van near the Brooklyn Bridge while a friend tries to win them a new mobile home in a camping-out contest. The three women are rehearsing a revenge play, "The Shanghai Gesture," which they hope will be their big break. *Upwardly Mobile Home* explores what it takes to survive in America; in one memorable image the three of them are in one skirt, singing "I Like to Be in America" in Yiddish. Playing femme and butch respectively, Lois Weaver and Peggy Shaw have also created roles that parody conventional gender representation, which they play on the street and in performance-art and cabaret venues as well as in their theatre productions. Theorist Sue-Ellen Case describes the strategy and the effect:

> On a given day, the butch may be wearing a man's blue suit from the 1950s, complete with shirt and tie. She may also imitate the walk and gestures of the kind of man who would have worn that suit. She disrupts the image with earrings, pant legs that are too short and a flamboyant, Elvis-style haircut. The femme might be wearing turquoise high heels, a turquoise cocktail dress (also from the 1950s) and a turquoise feather boa. Her colors complement the colors of her partner's suit. She, too, may imitate the walk and gestures of the woman who might have worn such a dress. She disrupts the image by relating to her lesbian escort and by wearing the dress in wrinkled, dirty condition, with no nylons and dirty shoes.

They transport these same costumes onto the stage, replete with gestures and characterization, as part of one of their performances. Their local audiences are familiar with their roles both on the street and on the stage, connecting the public persona with character, or drawing connections between stage and street, public self and theatrical character. Onstage, these costumes and gestures last only a short while, as part of a series of images the actors assume and then shed. Or, in some of their plays, these costumes remain on the actor, overlaid with other costumes, until the audience perceives layers and layers of differing gender-wear, differing period pieces, differing ages and differing class and ethnic accoutrements.

During their production of *Beauty and the Beast*, some of the roles played by the femme include a Salvation Army officer, the character of Beauty, Katharine Hepburn and Lady Macbeth. Some of the butch roles are an old woman sometimes allied with the Salvation Army, the Beast, Perry Como and James Dean. The Jewish actress takes on the characters of a rabbi, a Jewish stand-up comedian, a ballerina representing Beauty and Beauty's father. At one point, the butch is wearing the dress of the old lady, the cape of the Beast and Perry Como's sweater, while the Jewish actress is wearing the clothes of the rabbi, a tutu and, at one point, a dress hanging around her neck on a hanger.

What is the difference between an actor, a celebrity, a social role or a self-conscious system of gestures? Which character is the owner of the play, the protagonist, the "lead," the subject of the drama? If there is something like a subject position in this kind of performance, it is that of a collective subject.

Here's how the members of Split Britches describe their work:

LW: We just tried to tell our stories the best way we could and we wanted to be funny and loud and raucous and crazy. And we wanted to reclaim a lot of roles that had been denied us—to be fat if we wanted to be fat, and to be a country western singer even if we couldn't sing, and to be Juliet if we were sixty. We consciously talked about those things. And we talked about our own experiences most all the time. We rarely ever talked about technique or theory or certainly politics. Our lives are political. In fact, sometimes we were intimidated by the feminist community. After the show we'd be putting on makeup and the women in back were going, "Oh, no!" We were closet women. We were the women they'd been talking about all this time. We were questioned about our "dialectical thesis" and we didn't know what they were talking about, because we were just trying to create theatre from our experience as women.

PS: This woman in Lexington was going to report in the *Times* and *Newsweek* about the work we do, and we said, "No way, honey, if that's your intention, forget it." Because that's the end of us as we know ourselves. It would be all over.

LW: We choose to love the characters we play: In *Beauty and the Beast*, a Salvation Army uptight sergeant who thinks everybody should be Christian, and an Hassidic rabbi who hates women and thinks she's a man and doesn't want to be with us in the first place. We have an eighty-six-year-old lesbian vaudevillian who thinks everything is a show and she's James Dean and she's senile.

DM: Everybody has a scene where they break loose. Lois is a Las Vegas–type singer in San Jose giving a reading from *Macbeth*, building up to "unsex me here." Peggy does Perry Como, lip-synching to "It's Impossible"—she misses the chair and the sound shuts off. The rabbi does a stand-up comic routine. You see the desperate wishes they have for themselves.

LW: The criticism we get from men is, "Nothing happened, there's no climax, there's no plot."

PS: This guy came and he hated the show. He said, "Even Shakespeare didn't have the nerve to have three women alone onstage without men for over an hour."

DM: A lot of our strength comes from not looking around to see, "What do people think?"

LW: We are really lucky. We are able to do our own work. The thing that we're most worried about is being true to ourselves. We're not worried about getting cast, about someone deciding to produce our play. It's personal. It's like what I always thought it meant to be an artist.

FEFU AND HER FRIENDS

Beverley Byers Pevitts

Maria Irene Fornes explores basic feminist issues in her play *Fefu and Her Friends*. Although set in 1935, the play explores lives of contemporary women. The sensibility, the subject matter, the "universal" female characters and the very structure of the play are clearly feminist. The women's lives viewed in *Fefu* are seen, especially in the second part of the play, as being repetitive and capable of being viewed in any random sequence; yet even as women we do not respond negatively to this suggestion. In the very repetition of the four scenes that are played simultaneously we view intimately women's need for women. Although the title character says women need men because we cannot feel safe with each other, the other characters prove her wrong as they interact.

In *Fefu and Her Friends* Fornes defines what can happen when women recognize their own worth, and each other: "And if they shall recognize each other, the world will be blown apart." The play is fluid, structured like music, a "fugue," says the playwright. The play takes place in an affluent New England home. Eight female characters are introduced: they discuss woman's loathsomeness, settle relationships among themselves, rehearse speeches and recount visions. Fornes's characters speak as selves, not in the stereotypical roles of mother, daughter, bitch, witch or virgin. She breathes into her characters humor and intelligence. The loving of one's self and the despising of one's self are both examined, as well as woman's inclination *not* to trust other women.

As they are moved from room to room of Fefu's house during Part Two, the audience is brought into the play. The cyclical four scenes reveal the characters tenderly interacting, bound up in each other's lives. By moving to the characters' spaces, the audience comes to know the reason(s) all eight of these women are getting together. One discovers intimately with the performers "how woman feels about being a woman."

Fefu is cinematic, in both structure and acting style. Part One and Part Three, both set in Fefu's living room, contain all of the characters. The four scenes that nest between the two framework parts each contain only two or three characters. These "substance scenes" present not plot but character development and relationships. The play incorporates stop action, jump cuts, and replay as the audience moves from room to room to see the four scenes in Part Two. As each scene is repeated four times, the rooms have simultaneous life. The scenes and the parts of the play are interrelated by accretion. The through line of action, the passage of time, is merely the sequence of events. The women arrive, they greet each other in Part One. They separate, they read, they share, they rest, they discuss, they play croquet in the second part. Part One is morning, Part Two is afternoon, Part Three is early evening, and contains the climactic event scene.

There are five different environments. Moving from room to room, kinesthetically experiencing the play, becomes more important than following a story. The movement is special because the audience is enclosed with the performers within the four walls. It is, as Fornes expressed it, rather like being a witness. The audience is experientially involved in the play, not following a linear story.

Scenes are intricately interwoven. Cindy and Christina are in the study through which Sue passes on her way with the soup to the bedroom where Julia lies in bed hallucinating. Paula and Cecilia revive and resolve an old relationship in the kitchen while Fefu and Emma play croquet on the lawn. The linkage of the four scenes is both linear and vertical. A rhythm of involvement and disengagement works through all six scenes of the play. Fefu, like Sue, weaves through two other of the four playing areas during the simultaneous scenes, linking the scenes together. Fefu moves through the study/living room to the kitchen for lemonade and back out to the lawn. The fourth (last) time she takes other characters with her while Paula moves to the study/living room to play the piano, and the audience comes together for the third part of the play.

Fornes says that with plot we are concerned with the mechanics of how we manage in the world; a play without plot deals with the mechanics of the mind, some kind of spiritual survival, a process of thought. The temporal awareness of the characters is related to the segmentation of the play's structure.

The central scene of the play is Julia's hallucinating scene in bed in Part Two. It is a moving scene in which the character speaks clearly thoughts many women know:

> The human being is of the masculine gender. The human being is a boy as a child and grown up he is a man. Everything on earth is for the human being, which is man . . . Woman is not a human being. She is: 1—A mystery. 2—Another species. 3—As yet undefined. 4—Unpredictable; therefore wicked and gentle and evil and good which is evil. —If a man commits an evil act, he must be pitied. The evil comes from outside him, through him and into the act. Woman generates the evil herself.—God gave man no other mate but woman . . . —Man is not spiritually sexual, he therefore can enjoy sexuality. His sexuality is physical which means his spirit is pure. Women's spirit is sexual . . . Their sexual feelings remain with them till they die. And they take those feelings with them to the afterlife where they corrupt the heavens, and they are sent to hell where through suffering they may shed those feelings and return to earth as man.

Julia's thesis in *Fefu* is "the mind like the body is made to suffer to such a degree as to become crippled."

In the opening scene of *Fefu,* the title character points out that "women are loathsome." She gives the proof by reasoning the rational male way, by comparing woman to a rock that on the exterior "is smooth and hard and dry and clean" and is on the internal, interior, underneath side "slimy, filled with fungus and crawling with worms." This represents, she says, "another life that is parallel to the one we manifest." She continues, "If you don't recognize it . . . it eats you." This exterior appearance of woman can be readily compared to the image woman has been made into—the commercial view of the world (provided by men) into which women re-create images already created for them. The two sides of the rock represent how women feel about the image. If women do not realize it and recognize it, the underneath side does rot with the fungus and worms found there. If we do recognize this image, as Fefu later tells us, if we recognize ourselves as women, "the world will be blown apart." When this does happen, the reflection that was made by others will be destroyed and we will be able to rebuild ourselves in our own image, created by woman. The character Julia, trapped and oppressed, who at one point of her life was "afraid of nothing," and about whom the others wondered how one so young could know so much, is the one who is symbolically killed in the end of the play so that the new image of herself can emerge.

For many women becoming a feminist has caused a personal transformation. *Fefu,* like other contemporary plays by women, expresses this transformation, the transformation of the personal into mythos.

A RAINBOW OF VOICES

Phyllis Mael

In 1975 three plays by women were produced which displays striking similarities in form and theme: *Voices* by Susan Griffin, *Out of Our Fathers' House* by Eve Merriam in collaboration with Paula Wagner and Jack Hofsiss, and *for colored girls who have considered suicide/when the rainbow is enuf* by Ntozake Shange. All three utilize the format of the consciousness-raising group to present a feminist variation of the archetypal journey in search of the self.

This journey has been depicted in myth, and in contemporary psychology it has become a paradigm for self-realization. Carl G. Jung has termed the goal of the journey "individuation," which he defined as the process of "becoming one's self."[1] Jolande Jacobi describes individuation as "a way to self-knowledge . . . to find meaning in life."[2] Through individuation the individual comes to know herself for what she really is and finds the god within.

In myth this journey was usually that of a single male hero guided or aided by females (or female symbols). If a female was the hero, she was usually aided by males (or male symbols) or often by negative female images such as jealous sisters or jealous goddesses. ("Amor and Psyche" in *The Golden Ass* of Apuleius is an example of the female journey in mythology.)

In these three contemporary plays, however, men are present only insofar as the women speak of them (the casts consisting solely of women), and the men are viewed generally as having blocked the self-realization of the women. In contrast, the women in these plays function as positive images (either as role models, comforters or spurs to complete the journey to the self). There are no single heroes, nor is there a differentiation between traveler and guide, each woman being both.

This nonhierarchical, mutually supportive structure is typical of consciousness-raising groups. The basic purpose of such a group is to help each woman to break through her conditioning by enabling her to understand how society has prepared her to play certain roles. The group also breaks down her feeling of isolation by helping her to "recognize that what she had thought of as her unique experiences are . . . shared and understood by other women . . . Her sense of frustration, . . . futility and helplessness [thus diminishes and she can] begin to work positively toward altering and improving her own life."[3]

These goals are accomplished by "getting women to speak—only when they name their experiences can they begin to grow."[4] In these plays, the voicing of experience is achieved through what I call a rainbow of voices: as a rainbow presents a unity (light) and a diversity (the varied colors into which the light is separated), so do the voices in these plays. We hear individual women's voices moving from hope to disillusionment to despair to awareness. At times the individual voices merge to speak of the collective journey of women, and previously separate voices transform the isolated experience of a single voice into the mutually supportive and collective experience of Woman. The distinct voices thus interact with and respond to each other, either directly or obliquely, to create "a common language [which has the power] to create connections."[5]

This rainbow effect is most apparent in Griffin's play:

> Five women of different generations and circumstances seem to be conducting five monologues . . . Each at first perceives herself as uniquely trapped . . . Never do they actually engage each other in dialogue. Yet they are, in a deep sense, *conversant* with each other; at times their actual words echo each other, and at other times they speak words in unison . . . no longer spiritually isolated.[6]

The first to speak is Maya, thirty-five, divorced, with two children, working on her dissertation on "The Death of the American Family." She opens the initial fugue of voices with a question: "What am I going to do?" During the play, she moves from hope through anger, despair, and awareness that her situation is not unique, to an informed acceptance of her situation. For Maya, who had fantasized the American Dream by marrying a young man who represented "Middle American Decency" and had played out all the fantasies of women—"sex queen, nymph, matron, lady in waiting"—the voicing of her situation enables her to arrive at a qualified serenity, from which she states: "There is a kind of/stunning beauty/to the irrefutable truth/of . . . the/actualities of life,/uncovered from/veils of/myth and prejudice." The fantasies perpetuated by society can cause pain. Unmasking them is the first step to confronting the truth of the self and helps to mitigate that pain.

Kate, in her late sixties or early seventies, echoes Maya's "What am I going to do?" with "What is one?" Although living very different lives and belonging to different generations, both Maya and Kate arrive at similar truths about themselves as women. Both move from solitude to a sense of a shared experience with other women (Maya through a link with her grandmother mother, and daughter; Kate through an unforeseen connection with her mother). This bond with other women seems to provide them with the courage to persevere, for despite approaching old age, Kate considers "death . . . irrelevant./One goes on/with courage/and when/one loses courage . . . one goes on/anyway."

Whereas Maya represented "The Death of the American Family," Grace represents "The Death in Life of the American Family" For although still married, she can barely remember who she was before she became a wife and mother. The marriage has survived, but Grace's sense of self is in jeopardy. Through voicing her memories (of a strong, daring, active young woman), she acquires the strength to let the remembered self out of the metaphorical closet to which it has been relegated. And as she opens the door to that remembered self, she hears voices: "Strange women/speak to me./Women I have/never/met. Women who/I would never/know even/if they lived/next door to me. And I hear my own voice singing back."

Although in the staging the women do not hear or see each other, their shared experience is demonstrated theatrically in three ways. First, the individual voices interlock so that what one voice says is picked up or echoed by another voice. A second way of sharing and hearing voices is the repetition of a statement by each voice. At one point, each says separately, "I was frightened" and then all say together, "I was alone." But they are no longer alone, for the voicing erases their common loneliness. A third method of sharing is through voicing the collective experience of the American woman (expressing the outrage of women in slavery, dying as early settlers, suffering as pioneers in the West, or humiliated as adolescent sex objects in a sexist society). By voicing their common experiences and their shared history, each woman can listen to her inner voice and find her previously hidden self.

Like Griffin, Merriam presents the voices of specific individuals "whose life stories alternate and intertwine . . . We hear women's voices testifying to struggles for maturity, independence, and relationships much like our own, reassuring us that the journey 'out of our fathers' houses' is worth taking."[7]

Unlike Griffin, however, Merriam takes her voices directly from diaries, journals and letters of the historical characters portrayed. The six women, from the nineteenth and twentieth centuries in the United States, range from a little-known schoolgirl to Elizabeth Cady Stanton, founder of the National Women's Suffrage Association.

In the introduction to her book *Growing Up Female in America*, from which the play was adapted, Merriam explains that she selected these particular women in order to "restore our sense of the past . . . to give our lives today a continuity that has been lacking."[8] She wishes her audience to listen to "the striking contemporaneity" of the voices. She thus creates a "hypothetical conversation" or "consciousness-raising group among women who probably never met one another."[9]

Merriam describes the setting of the play as "the secret place where one would run off to think and be alone" and, at the end of the play, the need to "make the voyage of life alone" is voiced by all the women. But the play presents a "timeless interaction in which these women act out for both themselves and each other the stories of their lives." Thus, as in Griffin's play, the individual voices blend to create a collective experience without in any way obliterating the unique qualities of each individual experience. "Both together and alone they make the journey into a world of self-sufficiency and the 'solitude of self.'"

The play opens with a song depicting the house of the fathers as a "brick house . . . a high stone wall . . . a gate with a lock" from which the women must escape. Each rebels in her own way, for each has a different prison from which to escape. Whether radical (as that of Mother Jones and Dr. Anna Shaw) or hesitant (as that of Elizabeth Stern), the journey out of the house of the fathers to the self has been completed by the end of the play, and the voices join to speak of the loneliness of the journey. Merriam is not being ironic when she joins the voices to speak of solitude. For although the voices say "Nature never repeats herself," and they speak of "the solitude of individual life . . . and the need to cherish that individuality," the journey is shared in that it is a journey all must take in order to be fully human. The knowledge of the shared experience (just as the hearing of other voices) eases the journey for the individual.

In contrast with *Voices* and *Out of Fathers' House*, in *for colored girls* we no longer hear individual voices but individual poems which produce a cumulative effect: "The words of a young black girl's growing up, her triumphs & errors, our struggle to become all that is forbidden by our environment, all that is forfeited by our gender, all that we have forgotten."[10] Although Shange speaks in her Introduction of a "black girl" and although originally the play had Latins, Asians, blacks, but no whites,[11] Shange later acknowledged that the play "is a flash of humanity about women of all kinds at different times in their lives."[12]

Through the poems, seven women, wearing different colors of the rainbow, sing the songs, voice the lyrics and bring into being the self that has been denied. The poems cover rite of passage, the search for identity and various aspects of love relationships. As the poems move from youth to adolescence through adulthood, the journey moves individually and collectively from searching to finding.

The denial of the self occurred because "ever since i realized there waz someone calt/a colored girl . . . /i been trying not to be that." By attempting to avoid a stereotype that the woman has been raised to consider repugnant, she fails to become herself. Only when the women refuse to debase themselves and are able to share the pride of being women, colored and in love, can they continue their journey to individuation. Each can then recognize the self behind the stereotype and voice the price and conviction that affirm that self: "This is mine/that aint yr stuff . . . this is a woman's trip & i need my stuff . . . you cant have me less i give me away . . . wat i got to do/i gotta have my stuff to do it to."

That "stuff" is the essence of the self. And in asserting her right to her "stuff," the woman arrives at the end of her journey with a positive affirmation of self. "I was missing somethin/somethin so important/laying me open to myself . . . i found god in myself/ . . . & i loved her fiercely."

In an essay on *for colored girls,* Toni Bambara has pointed out that "sister sharing" (or sisterhood) enables one "to master pain and betrayal."[13] It also enables one to arrive at the god within, which is the inner voice that is not controlled by society but emerges from within the individual. That sharing may occur through singing and dancing the individual and collective experience of the American woman as in *Voices.* It may occur through voicing the anxiety of oneself and of others as in *Out of Our Fathers' House.*

In all three plays, both separately and together, as the colors of a rainbow, the women help each other to articulate their own thoughts and feelings in order to move "out of their fathers' house" "to the ends of their own rainbow" to find the treasure worth the struggle—the self. Through the techniques and structures of consciousness raising, the plays transform the archetypal journey in search of the self into an experience that speaks by, of, and for women in the final quarter of the twentieth century.

FEMINISM AND POLITICAL THEATRE

Linda Walsh Jenkins

While it can be argued that all feminist theatre is political, some women in American theatre combine feminist consciousness with theatre that is specially and consistently concerned with political change. For Maxine Klein, producing director of the Massachusetts-based Little Flags Theatre, political theatre "deals with large collective economic, social and political issues that working people face—such as automation, nuclear proliferation and joblessness." Political theatre has a legacy of at least fifty years in the U.S., with the strongest surge occurring in the workers' theatre movement of the 1930s. Among the companies exemplifying feminist political theatre strategies in the 1980s are the San Francisco Mime Troupe, the Little Flags Theatre and the Berkeley-based Ladies Against Women.

The San Francisco Mime Troupe, begun by R. G. Davis in 1959, evolved into the country's major political theatre first through participation in

Vietnam street protests and then most decisively with two plays: *A Minstrel Show, or Civil Rights in a Cracker Barrel*, by Davis and Saul Landau, and their "commedia dell'arte" adaptation of Goldoni's *L'Amante Militaire*, writer/adapter Joan Holden's first work with the group in 1967. The play won an Obie during its New York residency. When the theatre reconstituted as a collective and Davis departed in 1970, Holden became the company's primary scriptwriter. Although she has sometimes performed and now usually travels with the group, her forte has been political scripting from collective concerns. In an interview with Bernard Weiner, she described the troupe's work:

> In those times ['60s], we were seeking moments of confrontation, seeking outrage. We thought we were guerrillas—Che was our model—and that spontaneous outbreaks would occur wherever we performed. We truly expected to see a revolution in America within two or three years. We had no long view of the struggle. It never entered my head in 1967 that I'd still be here in [the 1980s].
>
> We used to end our plays with explosions. One time we shouted out phony credit card company phone numbers to use. This was symbolic of our image of revolutionary action. Now, our shows tend to end on people struggling to keep in the struggle—people faced with the dilemma of giving up or making an immense effort and continuing the fight. Our message—whether the show is about nuclear disarmament or poverty or U.S. militarism or whatever—always is that people can change, that individuals do make history.

Over the years the Mime Troupe (once pronounced "meem" but now usually pronounced conventionally) has built a reputation for broad physical humor and musical satire designed for outdoor settings, always intended to provoke an audience to take action to make changes in their own lives. In the summer they always perform free theatre in parks, supplementing this through the year with indoor and outdoor shows across the U.S. and Europe. Their 1967–68 Obie citation salutes them "for uniting theatre and revolution and grooving in the park." In 1987 they won the Tony for "outstanding regional theatre."

The troupe has become multiracial and multiethnic, with strong guidance from women. Actress/director Sharon Lockwood has performed with them since 1969; Wilma Bonet plays Latina (*Last Tango in Huahuatenango, Steeltown*) and non-Latina roles (robot in *Factwino Meets the Moral Majority*); Audrey Smith plays a variety of black roles. All three often play men. María Acosta Colón was administrative manager from 1979–86.

NEA granted them $90,000 for the 1986 season, allowing them to provide health benefits and increase salaries of the approximately ten-member company to $230 a week. Families and other jobs are juggled with the demands of the collective, which owns its own building in the Mission District. Holden, for example, who has three daughters, teaches playwriting on and off at the University of California at Davis and the People's School of Dramatic Arts, and received a Rockefeller playwriting grant in 1986.

The very titles of the theatre's productions signal the political issues they've taken on. Some titles connote their stories' content, such as *The Independent Female, or A Man Has His Pride* (Holden's first feminist work and the first work of the new collective in 1970), *Soledad* (1971), *Frozen Wages* (1972), *Americans, or Last Tango in Huahuatenango* (1981), *Factwino Meets the Moral Majority* (1981), and *Factwino vs. Armageddonman* (1982). *Seize the Time* (1970) was a documentary presentation of Black Panther Bobby Seale's Chicago 8 trial; *The Dragon Lady's Revenge* (1971, revived in 1987) attacked CIA involvement in Vietnam drug traffic using a combination of comic-strip style and spy-movies parody; and *Steeltown* (1984) approached steel mill closings and the history of the American labor movement with a more serious format designed solely for indoor playing in a conventionally darkened audience house.

Joan Holden explained her and the Mime Troupe's feelings about politics and theatre in the 1980s in an interview with William Kleb:

> The politics of the '60s and ours in the '70s were very programmatic. We knew what the issues were, we were Marxists, the message was clear, the foreign models were clear. We're still Marxists, but the models aren't clear anymore. The American Revolution is going to be homemade, and nobody knows what it's going to be like. Theory isn't going to convince people that it needs to happen, they have to be convinced out of their own experience. So we're dealing with people's experience at a more particular level, trying to join the personal with the political.
>
> I don't feel either in myself or in other people in the company any fundamental change in attitude. Yes, we have to get subsidy. No, we can't live at the welfare level for the rest of our lives . . . I don't feel that I'm coming from a different place than I ever was coming from since I started doing this. I still know who the enemy is, who is poisoning us and starving Africa, who is getting ready to blow up the world if we don't stop them! I know who I want to kill in my plays and who I want to exalt. Who I think deserves to die and who produces the wealth and should have the power. Those things that come from inside you aren't changing.

Little Flags, a company of men and women committed to "people's theatre," originated in Boston in 1974 but moved to Belchertown in 1986. Founder and producing director Maxine Klein had written and directed experimental and political theatre for years as a faculty member at the University of Minnesota and then Boston University. Her direction of Megan Terry's *Approaching Simone* won an Obie in 1970. She resigned from BU to produce with Little Flags plays dealing with and for "segments of society usually not treated by establishment drama." Her husband, James Oesterich, is the company's composer, and she is director, writer, acting teacher and frequently performer.

Members of the group (which takes its name from a poem by Ho Chi Minh) do not have to espouse one political ideology, but, Klein says, they are bonded by a "belief in the 'struggle,' the right to be heard, and workers' control." Productions have included *Tania* (their first show, based on one of Che Guevara's comrades), *Fanshen*, *The Furies of Mother Jones* (about the famous mine-workers organizer), *Winds of the People* (celebrating the labor and liberation movements), *Marx on Her Mind* (about a fast food waitress who is a union organizer and writes jazz), *The New Rise of the Master Race*, *Emma* (a portrait of Emma Goldman), *Split Shift, Windfall, Ah, Woman!, To the People, Mysterious Death of C. T. List* and *Boston Remembers* (a composite of histories of Boston's working class). Although the stories and character conflicts are political, the work itself is musical and humorous, with an emphasis on giving an audience a very good time. Songs and scripts are published by and available through South End Press and the company.

An itinerant group based in Klein's and Oesterich's home, Little Flags owns its own bus, which it uses to go into neighborhoods, workplaces, prisons, union halls and factories where the audience often participates in a play. They have toured the U.S. and in 1983 performed at an International Peace Festival in Baku, Azerbaidzhan and in Moscow. When creating a performance in a factory, Klein helps the workers create their own material. She explains, "It takes a while. You sit around and tell stories about all of your lives. This is one way I do it. I tell stories about my life, they tell stories about theirs, and then we start improvising on common themes and create plays out of their lives."

Klein's notion of people's theatre is expressed by the title of her book, *Theatre for the 98%*. In an interview she amplified this concept:

> Theatre until now in this country has been extraordinarily elitist, not only in terms of its subject matter but in terms of whom it includes. We're living in a large society; we can't do art for the one or the two or we exclude most of the people, which is what art in this country has done. So I'm part of the movement that is concerned about finding art in all of us and bringing art to all of us.
>
> We've been taught to despise ourselves. That's what celebrity theatre does. You look at all those celebrities onstage and think, "Oh, dear, I could never be like that. There's something wrong with me; either I smell or my hair isn't combed right." That's what I call a theatre of protest—against the individual human form and need and spirit. Quite the contrary, people's theatre is a theatre that gets people involved, that celebrates human values. I mean the values of the majority. Now, it may at the same time take issue with something that's oppressing them. That's perfectly legitimate. But it is not only about what oppresses them; it is also about what exults them.

Ladies Against Women is a subgroup of the larger satirical collective, the Plutonium Players, which formed in San Francisco in 1977 as the Theatre

Collective of People Against Nuclear Power. The women, and sometimes men, of L.A.W. perform stage shows and theatrical events (which they call street adventures) dressed as antifeminists (1950s dresses, pillbox hats, white gloves). For Women's Week at Northwestern University in 1986, they held a "Bake Sale for the Pentagon" and handed out flyers that read:

> We are Ladies Against Women, an organization dedicated to the notion that women of quality don't need equality! We know that what all college-aged women really want is that wonderful man to fill your life with his career and an array of avocado green kitchen appliances! Quit wasting your father's hard-earned $15,000 a year and get yourself a man—that's what we say. In the past we have held campaigns to establish a national dress code and to make virginity a high school graduation requirement. We have struggled for the rights of the unconceived ("Sperm are people, too!") and have been proud sponsors of the "Myth Northwestern" pageant.
>
> Our current project shows that even real ladies can be concerned with doing God's will while never having to leave our kitchens! At our Bake Sale, we are offering our sugar cookies, made only with the finest white sugar and white flour at $3 billion dollars apiece, or $15 billion for a half-dozen. The all-American Twinkie is $9 billion, and Ho-Ho's will be only $6 billion. And just look at what your money will buy! One Twinkie will buy *nine* nuclear submarines, and a single sugar cookie will purchase torture instruments for fifteen thousand Nicaraguan freedom fighters. (May God bless them! We're not talking about some place like Vietnam this time—these boys are fighting communism that we can drive to!!)
>
> As real patriotic Americans, we know that you will want to help us in this endeavor. Remember, nuclear families support nuclear arms.
>
> Our efforts are encouraged by: The Bedtime for Bonzo Anti-Evolutionary League, Mutants for A Nuclear Society, American Society for the Advancement of Rich, White, Straight Men, Students for an Apathetic Society, No Pinkos in Academia, Inc.

Ladies Against Women encourages chapters to form for street-action projects such as local demonstrations and picket lines; anyone interested should write them to register the chapter and obtain some of their scenarios and suggestions. But only the original Berkeley-based group has the copyright to appear at political rallies and fund-raisers around the country.

PROCESS AND PROBLEMS

Martha Boesing

During its first decade of life (1974–84), At the Foot of the Mountain developed a process of working which sprang out of the feminist banner of the times: "the personal is political." But the roots of the work were to be found in the radical theatre of the sixties.

I worked at the Firehouse Theatre in Minneapolis during that time. Like the Living Theatre, Open Theater and The Performance Group, we were involved in everything the sixties offered us, from politics to drugs, from burning draft cards to running around nude on the stage. The political was personal, the belief in change as an end in itself our private war cry. We were aggressive and brave and willing to experiment with our own hearts and psyches to create our art. Resistance amounted to cowardice and we faced each other with an unspoken challenge to make each act more outrageous than the last. It was exciting. It was frightening. Some of us went crazy. The central aesthetic which emerged was that of transformational theatre. One actor often played many roles; characters transformed mid-scene into alter egos, animals, even trees. We questioned the notion of a single or static personality as we began to notice that each of us is really made up of many different images, feelings, attitudes and styles that are constantly changing depending on whom we are with and what is expected of us. And we tried to create theatre that reflected this multitude of personalities within. We moved away from linear plays to ones built like mosaics or patterns on a quilt.

This transformational theatre became the aesthetic format of many women's theatres in the seventies. Plays were often layered, imagistic, nonsequential. Companies of five or six actors were called upon to play twenty to thirty roles in an evening. We gathered across the nation in consciousness-raising groups to tell our stories and talk about the many facets, the many roles we had been asked to play—wife, daughter, mother, lover, colleague, nymph, crone. We were "getting our feelings out"—some of us for the first time. And we were finding friends, sisters, who shared these feelings—anger, grief and a common sense of having been silenced.

So, in our theatres, instead of asking each other to "leave your garbage at the rehearsal hall door," we invited ourselves to bring it all in—our personal problems, our headaches, our memories, our feelings toward each other. We were creating plays out of our own lives, our own issues, and there was no way that we could create characters and situations which had a true life unless we were willing to share the emotional fabric of our own lives with each other.

At the Foot of the Mountain started a practice which continues to this day. Before every rehearsal and every business meeting, we would sit in a circle and say what we were feeling. A simple practice; but not so simple. We discovered that we often didn't even know what we were feeling, although there aren't many different basic emotions. I had a friend who called it the "six-pack": glad, sad, mad, scared, loving, and we added ashamed, because as women we have learned to feel ashamed of almost every move we make. Sometimes we'd get into the thick of a complicated network of emotions about the work or about each other and "feeling circles" would go on for three hours. It seemed important to all of us to stay with each other through the difficulties in order to get to the truth of the work. Sometimes we'd identify the feeling, then reach out to establish the whole condition around it, the memories, thoughts, muscular tensions which arose from that feeling—and from that would emerge the day's character and scene work. Often we would work non-verbally, creating images of sound or movement out of the feelings shared in the circle. The social and political issues we were creating our plays about (rape, prostitution, madness, addiction, war) were always rooted in our own feelings and our own stories. "The personal is political." We took the banner literally and we explored it as deeply as we were able.

The process showed itself in the work in different ways. In an early production of my play *River Journal*, for example, we experimented with improvising the emotional line of the subtext of the play from night to night. We learned the lines and blocked the play, but allowed the actors complete freedom to improvise the feelings of the characters, responding to their own real feelings in the moment. A scene which was filled with rage one night might be played sweetly and deliciously, or etched in fear, on the next. It was invigorating, filled with surprise. Some of the actors loved the challenge, others felt the ground too loose beneath their feet.

When we worked on *Raped: A Woman's Look at Bertolt Brecht's The Exception and the Rule*, a production exploring the economic base of permissible violence to women, we began by sharing our own stories. "Well," we each began, "I'm one of the lucky ones—I've never been raped." But by the time we opened the show each of us had shared one or more rape stories. Some of us were victims of emotional rape; some were incest victims; some had lovers who refused to take "No, not tonight" as an answer; some had experienced mind rapes. For example, in college a creative writing teacher whom I adored said to me: "You're bright. You ought to do something you can do well. But you'll never be a writer. It's a genetic problem. Women's minds are filled with trivia. They can never be great artists." I didn't write again for ten years. That's a rape story.

Through the years we worked on plays about prostitution (*The Life*), addiction (*Junkie!*), nuclear war (*Ashes, Ashes We All Fall Down*), invasion (*Las Gringas*), always beginning with the premise that the personal is political, always using our own denials, our own fears, our own stories as the starting point for the larger social issues we were exploring. It sometimes meant horrendous encounters—with each other and with our own personal demons. For instance, I went through a profound depression while preparing the piece about nuclear war—several months of hiding under my bedcovers, desperate to avoid confronting the despair and helplessness I felt in the face of global death. It was never an easy choice, this plummeting.

And we didn't make it much easier for our audiences. We called these pieces "ritual drama" because in each work there were places where the audience was invited to enter in and take an active part in the event. There were litanies, written stories read aloud, testimonies. This work, again rooted in the aggressive audience encounters of the sixties, began for us with *Raped*, a popular piece which had a long run. One night when performing for an audience of friends in the women's community who had seen the play before, we invited anyone in the audience to stand up at any time and freeze the action by saying "Stop"—which we did—and share a rape story of her own. And they did. Many did. The play took on a different energy. The room was electrified by suspense. Both the wonder and the fear that the person sitting beside you might suddenly give witness, perhaps for the first time in her life, to her own oppression, brought a tension and a presence to the production which gave one the sense not that we were watching a play about change, but that real change was happening right here and now in this very room.

In *The Story of a Mother*, a play about the mother-daughter relationship in our society, we developed a practice in which we went into a trance state and entered into the bodies and minds of our own mothers in order to see and relate to the world as our mothers did. We then would improvise and rehearse whole sections of the play as our mothers. Then—as if we hadn't tortured ourselves enough—we worked with a therapist, a friend of the theatre, with all of us attending six or eight therapy sessions in which we were inside the bodies/minds of our mothers. It was frightening, revealing and profound work. Most of us went into the play having conflicts with our mothers. We came out in a place of understanding of what their lives had been like, a place of forgiveness and love.

The secret of audience participation is to find a way to invite them in without coercion. It is never easy. I think it's important to admit from the start, by the way in which entry is offered, that the actors know more than the audience does, and that we are inviting them to take part because we have found the experience to be very rich and want to share this part of the journey. In *The Story of a Mother*, we led them through the meditation in which they would enter into the inner lives of their own mothers and then share in certain litanies such as "I always said . . ."and later "I never said . . ." Within five minutes the audience had doubled—everyone was there with their mothers. At the end of the play we would say our names and our mothers' names ("I am Martha, daughter of Mary") and the audience would voluntarily join in until the room was ringing with women's names as the matriarchal lineage tumbled out into the space. I think that was our most successful personal work with an audience—direct, radical and healing. It was beautiful to experience the power of the theatre to change people's lives.

One problem that emerges when working so closely and so intensely together is that a family system develops. We were committed to the work, but commitment to become a family had not been part of the contract. We met with resistance and fear. Some of us felt invaded, longed for more privacy, needed separation from the group. Others felt betrayed. We didn't always have the tools to deal with these problems as they arose. Today, I would urge a group working collaboratively to establish clearer boundaries between openness and privacy, to clarify expectations from the start and to limit the shared personal life to that which is usable in the work, taking the rest, if need be, to a therapist. I would also encourage all company members to maintain a strong alternative life, a place to go for friendship and activities outside the theatre. Without it, we grow inwards as a group, elitist, incestuous and often surprisingly lonely.

Our work was in the theatre and our goal was to become the finest theatre artists possible. To approach the material through the personal is not to negate the hours of labor involved in honing our skills—acting, moving, writing, singing, training new company members and pushing the old beyond their limits. It is important to mention this dedication to the craft because I think those of us involved in political theatre, or with any revolutionary art form, tend to become a little lazy. We say, "Well, the important thing is that we're women and we're getting our stories out. If the acting is a little sloppy, it doesn't matter." But it does matter. People's hearts and minds are opened because they are engaged and inspired by the images, the language, the artistry of the event they are watching. At the Foot of the Mountain tried to be diligent, though I often saw the mistakes and failures of the work. Then we were on to the next play before I had the opportunity to rewrite. When I left the theatre in 1984, I looked back over all my scripts, over twenty-five of them, and I said, "My God, I have created an entire body of work which consists of first drafts!"

So we need time. And a great deal of patience. The older I get, the tougher I get on myself. As women we must get tougher, we must put ourselves in situations where we are challenged by artists who have more highly developed skills than our own. At the beginning we needed the support and the love from each other that would give us a standing ovation simply in honor of our survival against overwhelming odds. But women's theatre is almost twenty years old now. We must sharpen our critical faculties and be willing to plunge in deeper. I still believe that women working together collaboratively have something to bring to the art—some real questions about both the form and the content which seem to limit much of our mainstream theatre. There is a kind of work that emerges from this intense, collective longing to communicate which is never attained in the plays by a single writer, mounted as a single production in a season. It has to do with community, with Jung's ideas about a collective unconscious perhaps, and it is a healing voice which is sorely needed on our planet right now. There are stories residing in the deepest parts of our souls which continue to be wrapped in silence. Our tale is not yet finished.

REFLECTIONS

Roberta Sklar

When I was an undergraduate student at Hunter College in 1959, free speech, civil rights and "Peace Now" were not yet household words. Off-Off-Broadway had not yet begun. Feminism was unheard of. The sixties had not yet occurred. This was the world I entered as a young adult. My goal was to be an exceptional woman, for only in that way did I think I would get to do something!

In more than two decades of creating, writing and directing theatre I've had the privilege of living and working during three extraordinary phases of the American theatre. In the founding years of the Off-Off-Broadway movement I directed new plays at the young Caffe Cino and Cafe La MaMa. (As a novice I naively sought a career as a theatre director in a field virtually closed to women.) In the sixties as co-artistic director at the Open Theater, where we collectively created *The Serpent*, *Terminal* and the *Mutation Show*, I shared the vision of an alternative theatre for an alternative society. I've always experienced theatre, and myself within it, in a collaborative way—as a collective effort, a relationship, deeply interactive with its members, its audience and its time. For me theatre is most itself when it is integral to social change.

After working with the Open Theater for several years in the development of a collective approach in American theatre, it slowly dawned on me that while I was speaking collectively, I neither understood my own voice nor had something specific to say. The women's movement, through individuals and groups such as the It's All Right to Be Woman Theatre, suggested to me not only that I had a voice, but that I had a history of experience and a future that warranted articulating. There was reason to speak. It was in the context of feminist theatre, and especially within the Women's Experimental Theatre, speaking solo and in unison with other women, that I found my voice.

Sondra Segal and I began working together in 1973 at the Womanrite Theatre, and in 1976, together with Clare Coss, founded the Women's Experimental Theatre. To work in a woman-identified way, a self-identified way, was the task. It took a lot of pain and it took rigor. We had been acculturated to a male world. We spoke in tongues. The language we had was not fully our own. We tackled the trivialization of our lives, resurrecting domains made small by sexism—the domestic sphere, the kitchen, childbirth, women's relationships, the female psyche, our bodies, our sustenance, our place in the world.

Women's theatre is a theatre of conversion. It's populated by women like myself who've converted through some sort of emotional or psychological "Aha"—a sense of revelation. We've been converted to ourselves. The "deity," if you will, that I attend is the woman within me. What I seek is a woman-identified theatre, one that serves me.

Like several other feminist theatre teams, Sondra Segal and I have worked together since the early seventies in a flow of artistic roles, attempting to create a women's theatre that would be a viable alternative to the aesthetic and economic structures of a male-dominated commercial and avant-garde theatre. Some say we should have first sought the money and power that would have given our institutions an enduring foundation. There may be wisdom here, but I think that the very process of consolidating power and wealth would have preempted the women's culture we sought to create.

Now in an age of conservatism equal to the 1950s, supported by the new economics and the movement of history, we are living again in an era unfriendly to the advancement and equality of women, an era at best dubbed "post-feminism." Once again women are disappearing from the horizon. "Exceptional women" with "exceptional careers" are reappearing, and concurrently, feminist theatres are no longer surviving. Many of the women's theatres of the seventies and eighties have folded. So have the alternative health centers, day-care centers, consciousness-raising groups, women's presses, and women's production companies. Theatre does not exist in a vacuum. We are not unique, nor must we blame ourselves. I believe we are in a still period in the theatre, and as theatre so often does, it reflects the condition of the larger society. At this moment the path to creating feminist theatre may not be clear, but we must ask "Why?" and determine some of the tasks before us. What is the mission? What do we want to say? What do we want to change?

Although this wave of women's theatre has had a healthy life span, we are left with an incomplete legacy: a small number of groups creating and performing new works; a cache of largely unpublished plays; forays into feminist acting techniques, research methods and new forms that might better express our unspoken experience. We are sorely missing an articulated theory of feminist dramatic criticism to carry into the future. As a theatre movement we suffered dearly because such a criticism did not develop while we were more actively producing plays. We lack a substantial codification of our methods, of how we gathered material and information. The process in many of the women's theatres cut across race, class and position and brought housewife and worker, lesbian and straight, secretary and executive into the same workshop, the same consciousness-raising group, the same audience, each seeking self-knowledge and female universality. How these women came together and the process of research that informed us and created women's theatre are extraordinary parts of an untold history.

I hope that women, in every field, will not allow our work to fade from history; that we will record, not simply what we did, but what we intended. Feminism and women's culture have had a utopian aspect to them, and that's good. Our theatre is transformational; it changes something. When we create theatre, we must consciously ask: What is it we seek to change?

To focus attention rigorously on the questions that arise out of womanhood—that's the hardest thing. The temptation to join the male tradition is even greater than it used to be because more women have been allowed in. But the themes and the forms to be explored by women from a woman-identified perspective have barely been let in. Women require new forms to bring forth that which has so long been silenced. If we create only in existing forms, we can say only what has been said before. The theatrical articulation of more than half of the world's population cannot possibly be carried out in a decade by a handful of under-funded women.

For many years I worked exclusively at creating theatre with women, dedicated to women. I hope that in this work I did not only redress the past or ferret out silenced truths. I hope that I dreamed aloud a vision of a woman-loving future that would transform our theatre and our lives.

MAKING A LIFE IN ART: MEGAN TERRY

Interviews with Dinah L. Leavitt, Kathleen Betsko and Rachel Koenig

Megan Terry's more than fifty plays have broadened the American idea of theatre. She is a founding member of the Open Theater and, since 1974, has been playwright-in-residence at the Omaha Magic Theatre. In 1983 she received the Dramatists Guild's Committee for Women Annual Award in recognition of her "work as a writer of conscience and controversy and [her] many lasting contributions to the theatre."

B/K: Megan, what message would you most like to send round the world?

MT: It's worth it to make a life in art. I want to tell everybody it's *possible* and it's worth it. I've lived long enough now to see what happens to people who don't follow their hearts.

DL: Do you identify yourself as a feminist?

MT: I am a feminist, but I'm many things. I'm a humorist and a humanist. I've been in the theatre since I was fourteen; I'm really a theatre person.

DL: What do you think a feminist theatre is?

MT: Everyone is an individual and each theatre company projects a different image. People want to try to determine that there's some kind of party line in feminism and there isn't. The most marvelous thing about the feminist movement is that there are no leaders. The leaders that the media has tried to make they've soon killed off, but it hasn't stopped the feminist movement at all. I think the reason for this is the lack of leaders. Each woman is her own leader. That's why it has such tremendous energy.

I was raised by women. I've always been interested in writing about women. I'm crazy about acting. I was brought up with very fine actors and many of them were women. There were no roles for them to play.

I saw their pain and their struggle when they couldn't get jobs, not because they had no talent, but because there were no parts for them.

The women's movement enabled me to leave New York and give up that whole careerism business—the man's world of career stuff. I was always acting as the woman behind a man anyway. I was giving my energies to male careers. The movement also made me see really clearly that there's a necessity to write about very strong women so women can know that there have been strong women in the past. I'd been wanting to write about Simone Weil for fifteen years, but the women's movement gave me the courage to do it. Plus I'd built my technique to a point where I felt I could attack such a vast project.

If feminism is going to really move ahead, it's got to explore the possibilities of what a woman could be. We don't know what a woman could be like because we've had so many outlines and definitions forced on us. That's the most exciting thing to me. That's the true frontier. Women have got to take over the education of other women, because for too long we've been fitted into something that men want and the definitions that men have made. My own father refused to send me to college because I refused to join a sorority and reflect his values.

With the playwriting techniques we discovered or rediscovered in the sixties you can explore interior states. You can dramatize the interior state of being. Once inside one's head, body or soul, it's vast. Dramatizing that or showing all the possibilities, the ways to go, can really be done in the theatre and acted out in front of people. That's what's important for them to see. It can start a chain reaction. More and more people will come and say, "Ah, I can build on that."

DL: I'm not sure what we are considering to be feminist drama.

MT: Anything that gives women confidence, shows themselves to themselves, helps them to begin to analyze whether it's a positive or negative image, is nourishing.

DL: How do you feel about the idea that if feminist drama is going to say anything new it has to say it in new forms?

MT: It doesn't matter what the form is as long as you're telling the truth. The form is the least important thing. Telling the truth is the main thing. People get hung up on form because they've been to school too much.

I'm always fighting against critics because so many are biased whether they are feminist critics or male critics. They always want you to conform to whatever party line they're putting out. They want to use artists. It's the duty of the artist to criticize everybody including herself and her attitudes. The feminist movement really needs some criticism from artists so that we don't get so hidebound and serious. I refuse to be used.

DL: Is there male and female art or is art just art?

MT: It's art if *I* say it is. Art has always been whatever the establishment says it is. When I finally figured that out, I started proclaiming who I felt were artists, and I began praising and propagandizing all the work I liked. That is what women should do and stop worrying about rules.

B/K: You teach playwriting. Are you spreading the word about women dramatists?

MT: Constantly. Recently, I taught Emily Mann's *Still Life* at a university in Minnesota. My students were *outraged* that they'd never heard of this play, nor the work of Maria Irene Fornes, nor Roz Drexler, Rochelle Owens, Adrienne Kennedy, Sybille Pearson, Caryl Churchill, Pam Gems, Ntozake Shange, Julie Bovasso, Jo Ann Schmidman, Tina Howe. They knew none of these people, and they were getting their master's degrees! They were really angry by the time I finished with them.

B/K: Do you believe that there's a female aesthetic in playwriting?

MT: A female aesthetic could only happen if the next generation of women were raised all together on a desert island.

B/K: So you don't think the innovations of women are in any way organic?

MT: I really don't. How would you measure it?

B/K: We don't know. That's why we're asking women playwrights this question. What we do know, after reading tons of women's plays and hundreds of their reviews, is that there are certain elements common to all: many of their plays are woman-centered, with a much higher percentage of female roles than plays by men.

MT: This will probably continue until the balance is redressed. But after there's a balance, and we have the female characters living up there on the stage that we haven't had for a long time, that may all change again.

B/K: There are some people who feel that there is a renewed but more covert war going on between men and women now . . . a deeper malaise setting in, separating us.

MT: I think that men are negative because women are positive and on the rise! It's driving men crazy! Martha Boesing was telling me that in the thousand plays she receives each year, most have hopeful endings! Women are feeling positive and forward-looking. Plays men are writing often end with everybody dead, dying or neurotic to the point of no return.

B/K: What can we do to heal this polarization?

MT: Live your life as if the revolution had been a success!

B/K: What advice do you have for young women in high school and college who are thinking about becoming a playwright?

MT: Do it. See all kinds of performance, from polka dances to basketball games. Do you know what I miss in the world? Singing. There's a lot of noise, but there isn't enough singing lately.

DL: What do you see as your future work?

MT: I'll be in theatre. I'll be as surprised as you. I plan to keep Omaha as a base because the cost of living is reasonable here, and there's the chance to really understand how a whole community of this size [500,000] operates. I'm fascinated. It's not so big that you can't understand how it works. Also I got out of touch with America by going on so many world tours. I'm a great lover of our country in spite of what the critics or the CIA or FBI may think, so it's thrilling for me to be in the Midwest. Too many people go to New York and get caught up in the hierarchy of moving ahead, the male syndrome of success, and they forget their roots and write themselves out of what they came there with and then they start repeating themselves. They write the same play with different names. Once they get success they get isolated from people.

People in the East are always saying, "What are you doing in Omaha?" I answer, "I'm living a real life."

STAGING WOMEN'S EXPERIENCE: FEMINIST THEATRES IN THE USA

Charlotte Canning

Distrusting traditional theatre practices that sought to divide performance from audience, house from stage, feminist theatre creators and performers looked for ways to emphasize the similarities and blur the distinctions between audience and performer . . . For feminist theatres, the melding of audience and performer came from a feminist belief in bonding women into a community to resist the divisive patriarchy. The emphasis was thus on ideas held in common by a larger group that included both audience and performer.

It's All Right to Be Woman Theatre (IARTBW, 1969) set aside one part of every performance to enact "Dream Plays." Audience members were encouraged to come forward and share their dreams. As the individual related her dream (men's dreams were never dramatized) the performers would mime it onstage. The group would first portray one of their own dreams to encourage the audience to participate. This exchange was based on the belief that "what happens to us or what we feel or dream is important enough to share with each other and with other women, that is, in fact, the most important thing we have to share."[1]

This goal of communality was pursued in other ways, such as seating the audience in a circle and performing for an all-female audience. Members of Women's Experimental Theatre (WET, 1977, New York) believed, "An all-woman audience has the space for unfettered response, and it can take off in celebration of itself. And it does." Twila Thompson, a member of Women's Collage Theatre (1976, New York), said her group also preferred all-women audiences, believing that otherwise women would be more concerned with what the men thought than what they themselves felt.[2]

The feminist theatre event began with the research in the community, continued with performance, was further developed in postshow discussion, and was extended by workshops with the audience. The practice of researching for performance by using women as the primary source, both company members and women outside the theatre, was based on the feminist belief that women were the best resources for information on women. Cultural myths, books, and accepted wisdom about women were viewed with suspicion and thus the only potentially accurate research materials available were the women themselves. Gradually, however, by the mid-to-late 1980s published material began to replace firsthand research with women.

By the mid-1970s the works of many influential feminist authors, such as Kate Millet, Shulamith Firestone, Mary Daley, Nancy Chodorow or Helen Dinerstein, were or tended to be analytical and theoretical, providing frameworks for practitioners and spectators rather than personal narratives and first-hand testimonies. When the Rhode Island Feminist Theatre (RIFT, 19730) developed their play *Internal Injury* in 1978 there was little material available on the subject of battered wives. While they read what was published they also used "real stories" of battered women or, as another review put it, "personal contact with Rhode Island battered wives." Privileging interactions with women who had lived experience with the topic under consideration often brought theatres into contact with facets of the feminist community previously unknown to them.

Spiderwoman has a workshop on their storyweaving technique they usually offer while on tour, in which they share physical exercises to put women in control of their bodies and techniques for turning life stories into theatre. Women are asked to tell stories from their lives and the members of Spiderwoman theatre gradually move participants from telling their individual stories to working together to enact stories emerging from the group.

The Audience as Creator/The Audience as Critic

Many women experienced feminist theatre as a transforming moment, as a near-religious feeling. Certainly this was encouraged by the use of ritual and the stress on community. The often celebratory nature of the shows themselves could move women; as one woman in the audience of the Women's Collage Theatre show *Sirens* put it:

> By the end of the play I had and have a very strong sense that I know you, I know your faces, I have been playing with you and screaming, singing, ripping, dancing, killing and hugging with you all my life.[3]

Postshow discussions provided a venue for the expression of reactions, feelings and dialogue. Most groups believed, as the Rhode Island Feminist Theatre did with *Persephone's Return*, that the "play . . . is not the entire production."[4] There was always a postshow discussion to provide an open dialogue between the audience and the performers. RIFT's talks were not meant to be informational, since background materials were provided in the program, but rather to encourage "an exchange of mutual growth and consciousness-raising."[5]

Feminist theatre could be very powerful, could often evoke strong reactions, and had the potential to change lives. But the same investment that led audience members to praise also led them to critique as well. The reactions could be just as strong when women felt that the theatre had misrepresented feminism, abused their power or not fulfilled their mission correctly. Feminist theatre had endeavored to create a brand of theatre that defied the more common audience/performer dynamic and in doing so found that their audiences, once included as part of the spectacle, took their involvement seriously.

To be feminist was no more than to identify one's self as such and that meant that there were always serious disagreements as to what was and was not feminism. There were different kinds of feminism and arguments among feminists about the different approaches. Feminism belonged to everyone and most feminists believed that every woman was accountable to every other woman. Despite the fact that a feminist theatre group or playwright had put significant labor into a performance piece there often was the assumption that authorship did not necessarily confer absolute authority over the material.

Members of Spiderwoman found the prescriptive attitudes of many feminists constricting and racist. Implicit in the critique was the assumption that all-white groups that created theatre did so based on the celebration and positive images of women who they envisioned as being like themselves. These were then the models for feminist theatre and subsequent groups often followed in their footsteps. The tendency to universalize ignored the problem that many of the early groups relied on the unquestioned assumptions born of their white privilege. Miguel described this as having "to be perfect for all those women who say that one size fits all." But she countered: "That's what our pieces mean, one size *does not fit all.*"[6]

The notion of accountability, of shared responsibility for the images and representations onstage, and audience investment could lead to serious disagreements as to the proper subjects, approaches and group composition for a feminist theatre. Audiences, whether as a whole or as individuals, often felt compelled to work with the theatre to create performances acceptable to feminist politics at the moment.

In 1987, at the Women and Theatre Program (WTP) Conference in Chicago, the new multicultural ensemble of At the Foot of the Mountain presented "The Story of a Mother II," utilizing rituals from the play's first production in 1978. Some of the women present in 1987 found these rituals implicitly coercive. The arguments that ensued focused on the questions of universality and the concept of implicit racism.

What this rancorous post-show discussion played out were the conflicts among differing feminist ideologies, animosity between theorists and those opposed to theory, and the problem of racism and its history in the feminist movement. Feminism had changed since the show was first produced in 1978 and the foundations of universality and commonality were eroded by questions of the differences implicit and explicit in race, class and sexuality. What had not changed, however, was the investment in feminism on the part of the audience and the performers. Women expected to see their experiences onstage and when they did not they expressed their disagreements with the group. This could be productive and yield a new text impossible to imagine without the audience intervention, or it could be negative, emerging either from racism or homophobia or from conflicting notions of feminism. However, these are proof that feminist theatre is a powerful catalyst for feminists, that the reactions it elicits are profound, and that meaning and representation are controversial categories within feminism.

CHANGES AND LEGACIES

Linda Walsh Jenkins

Wherever one places an end date and however one formulates a "period" for the feminist theatre groups, It Is not inaccurate to say that by the end of the 1980s few groups remained. The absence of a large number of theatre groups that can be labeled or label themselves "feminist" is not indicative of the end of the intersection of feminism and theatre. Instead, it is about change. There is a general agreement that the changes in the political situation in the United States during the 1980s severely limited the arts funding available to the feminist theatre groups. However, growing conservatism alone cannot account for the demise in theatre groups any more than it fully accounts for the shifts in feminism as a whole. There were other, larger factors besides the economic situation that signaled an end to the existence of feminist theatre groups as a movement.

One of the strongest reasons was burnout and fatigue as evidenced in feminist organizations across the board; what Flora Davis calls "the graying of the women's movement."[1] The collective structures favored by the groups meant that every woman was supposed to share equally the burden of running the company. In many cases this came to mean that a few of the women would unofficially do all the work or that the company was so small that the work, even when fairly distributed, was considerable. Another factor that contributed to the "graying" was that things had changed enough that younger women were not facing the same kinds of discrimination women before them had, and they were not as inclined to do theatre based on feminism in similar ways to their predecessors.

The feminist theatre movement enjoyed fifteen years, more or less, of activity. During that time women turned to theatre to express their politics, communal bonds and artistic visions, and viewed material factors such as funding, business managers, or production and design resources as of secondary importance. They used spaces never architecturally intended to serve as theatres, performed in their street clothes and advertised by word-of-mouth. This was all accomplished in the context of the feminist community because it provided the audiences, material and emphases. The greatest strengths and the most debilitating weaknesses of feminist theatre came from its community base. The community gave the theatre a clearer meaning and purpose than most theatres enjoy.

The community could also limit what a theatre might achieve. In many cases theatres were not encouraged to go beyond what were commonly accepted as proper subjects for feminism to investigate, nor were they encouraged to present other than positive role models.

Also, ensemble work requires a very delicate balancing act between the group and the individual member. Trust is always a major issue and often women of color and lesbians experienced moments of oppression and discrimination that made them profoundly wary of the other members of the group. Terry Baum's desire to make the lead character in *Sacrifices* a lesbian brought the homophobia in Lilith to the surface, and AFOM's change to a multicultural ensemble foregrounded problems around racism. These problems confronted women with differences that could not be contained within the structures they had constructed and eventually forced them to dismantle their organizations.

The changes and confrontations described here were not isolated in feminist theatres. These shifts were symptomatic of the changes feminism as a whole was undergoing. Identity politics emerged as one critique by women of color of racist feminist practices. Based on the differences of race and ethnicity, these feminists posited that their experiences were radically dissimilar from the white middle-class model and could not be explicated within it. White women did not usually experience the same interactions of racism and sexism that women of color did and therefore rarely created structures that were responsive to the complex concerns of multiple oppressions. Anti-racism has always been a tenet of feminism, but in their eagerness to combat the sexism with which they had had firsthand experience, many white women glossed over the insularity of their experience and were often inclined to present it as a universalized sisterhood. As the community began to lose much of its coherence and to cast about for new organizing principles, the theatres that were inextricably linked to them began to founder. Sondra Segal spoke of the doubt and confusion that she experienced as WET ended its operations. "I don't know what I have to say that women want to hear."[2]

Currently three of the feminist groups discussed here are still operating with a measure of success. Spiderwoman still tours and creates shows, although they are turning their attention more and more to Native American issues with a feminist perspective; Split Britches also continues to produce works, recently celebrating their tenth anniversary; and Horizons: Theatre From A Woman's Perspective, founded in the Washington, D.C., area as Pro Femina in 1976, is still very active. This cannot help but raise the question, is this the entire legacy of feminist theatre? Are the three groups still in existence the only trace of a movement that spanned the United States for more than a decade? On the contrary, the legacies of the feminist theatre groups are far more rich and diverse than the survival rate of the groups might indicate.

The fact that people assume that feminism and theatre can intersect profitably was originated by the theatre groups. While it was often negatively characterized by many of the same stereotypes as feminism itself—shrill, didactic and man-hating—it brought feminist ideas and images to places that might never have had them. Theatres toured to small towns, community centers, churches, synagogues, colleges, universities, women's centers, schools and conferences across the USA. Many of the practitioners are still active in theatre and brought their politics and discoveries with them to their later careers and activities.

Probably the most enduring legacy of feminist theatre for the women who were part of the movement is a commitment to women-centered or women-oriented theatre. Another legacy has been the producing organizations that have emerged to support women's work. In New York the Women's Interart has existed since 1969 and was initially founded to support "independent women artists and present their work to the public."[3] By 1971 the organization had its own space and was producing theatre, sponsoring shows in their gallery, and offering women rehearsal and studio spaces.

Brava, in San Francisco, was founded in 1986 to "help emerging and professional women artists gain greater visibility and increase audiences for their work, and to help them increase their professionalism."[4] The organization provides services to women in the arts community, including acting, writing, directing, grant writing, and production workshops and underwriting for productions. However, their mission is not as generalized as Interart's because they focus on "socially conscious work" that is "feminist and antiracist."[5] To this end they have devised specific strategies to support those commitments. Any panel sponsored by Brava, whether to review work for possible production or in a conference setting, must be at least fifty percent composed of women of color, and the majority of the women who serve on the board are women of color.

Many of the feminist theatre groups of the 1970s came from a sense of urgency supporting a utopian vision of a new feminist world. The average existence for a theatre was three and half years, scarcely enough time to develop complex and intricate theatre experiments and theories, especially when caught in the quotidian requirements of a theatre company.[6] Often, after the theatres closed down, the women who founded and ran them used the knowledge and experience gained from their work to push further the boundaries of the possible intersections between feminism and theatre.

Like most overtly political theatre, feminist theatre was a product of its historical moment. Its location within feminist community dictated certain interests, forms and approaches. As that community dispersed, the performance derived from it began to seem outmoded. Women either shifted their focuses to reorient their theatres toward new ideas and new conceptions of feminism or they closed the theatres and moved on to new ventures. Whatever the solution of individual women and theatre companies, they took with them the experiences, knowledge and contacts they had gained during their work in feminist theatre groups.

7 FEMINIST THEATRICAL THEORIES

Theatre feminists began serious investigations in the 1970s into how the American stage constructs and perhaps challenges social notions about "Man" and "Woman." That cultural systems themselves are constructed, and therefore open to "de-"construction, never has been at issue; most religions long have suggested that the phenomenological world is a shifting fabric of socio/culturally-determined "illusions," or, as Calderon de La Barca wrote, "La vida es sueño." Like other primates, humans create social rules, what psychiatrist Anthony Storr helpfully refers to as "nomos," "our way" or "we are," which changes over time in response to environmental and other natural circumstances, charismatic figures, new technologies, economic conditions, and so forth.[1] Since procreation is fundamental to animal behavior, primates evolve engendered "codes" for sexual liaisons and familial units. Xicrin women of central Brazil literally paint a "second skin" of black paint on their children to symbolize this imposition of culture on biology.

Those who want to change the "nomos" in American society now, whether for the "feminist agenda" or other purposes, question *who* determines these rules, *how* and *why*. Who has the power to decide how persons should dress and behave, and how do they obtain this power? Who enforces these decisions and why? Are the enforcers different from those who determine the rules? How do theatre and other symbolic expressions participate in these dynamics? Can theoretical "answers" for one culture be applied to others? In the United States' porous and vibrant multicultural society, imprinted by traces of European colonial cultures while woven tightly with non-European threads, can substantial and useful explanations be derived?

This section offers a sampler of major definitions and theoretical deductions from leading feminist theatre scholars who have shaped discussions about gender construction in the field since the mid-l980s. Selections from Patti Gillespie's historical and critical survey bookend key passages from writings grounded in linguistic and film semiotics, Marxist/materialist analysis, and Freudian/Lacanian psychology. Often these analyses are in combination as materialist psycho-semiotic theories, so they resist tidy separation into linear organization. As primary crafters of new feminist theatre theory, Sue-Ellen Case, Jill Dolan and Elin Diamond illustrate semiotic and materialist thinking, while Janelle Reinelt and Esther Beth Sullivan elucidate fundamental premises derived from Freud and Lacan. Other important contributors to new theoretical directions are cited in these authors' essays.

Theories as enacted in performance are exemplified by Diamond's essay on Robbie McCauley, director Rhonda Blair's narrative of her own intellectual evolution and Jeanie Forte's insightful observations about performance artists. Postmodern materialist psycho-semiotic theorizing crested in the late 1980s and became academically de rigeur; then by the 1990s it was being questioned by a new generation of scholars chafing at the theories' limitations, some of which Gillespie analyzes. More porous and less rigid theories are evolving as a finite system's ability to describe itself is by definition limited.

The final two essays in the chapter point to the future as independent veins of exploration. Ethnographer Dorinne Kondo employs some postmodern theory while transforming it with Asian American cultural inquiries. Sandra Richards stands outside the postmodern vocabulary to use African hermeneutics in her original approach to African American studies. These concluding selections suggest a transition into the book's concluding section, where women theatre practitioners consider their past, present and future challenges.

In the 1970s, some scholars asked, "Is There a Feminist Aesthetics?" Most agreed that there are too many situational ways of being "feminist" to settle on one ideological mindset and that "aesthetics" is a broad field that may resist such qualifications; "feminisms" might contribute to aesthetics, however. In those early years of the feminist movement, there seemed to be an imperative to find structures or accents in every field that could be women's unique or "authentic" contribution. In a keynote address for a 1984 conference at Stanford, later published in *Women & Performance*, I wondered aloud that since most writers draw on what their bodies have known for kinesthetic imagery, there might be a "Language of Gender Experience" for men and women. Females, acculturated to be "Women," might have learned a psycho-sociolinguistic vocabulary that differs in some ways from "Men," speaking generally and historically but not universally. Perhaps, I offered, that difference could account for some of the structural and imagistic choices some women playwrights have made in the past, as well as for some of the audience-reception differences between men and women. This concept may apply also to the somatic influences of racial, regional, religious, and other acculturations that affect the ways in which people move, talk, listen and respond. My intention was to describe, not to prescribe.

As further attempts to find anything that could be said to be "woman-made" resisted universalization, deconstruction proceeded on the abstract notion of gender itself. Since the mid-l980s, most questions about social rules affecting women have looked to European explanations for the cultural architecture of gender. Sigmund Freud's and Karl Marx's postulates for what drives human choices were extrapolated into provocative ideas that, unlike theories in physical sciences, cannot be proven. The formidable psychological and economic speculations of Freud and Marx, which emerged from their specific modern urban European contexts, have stimulated passionate arguments throughout the twentieth century. Theatre feminists followed a few paths branching off from these "postmodern" theories.

In the introductory essay, Patti P. Gillespie briefly defines the "sex-gender" system and describes historical factors behind the emergence of postmodern theory within theatre academe. This edited version of her survey, published in Karen Laughlin and Catherine Schuler's 1995 anthology, *Theatre and Feminist Aesthetics*, introduces some of the vocabulary and concepts used in the remainder of this chapter. Gillespie observes that African American questionings of Eurocentric aesthetic standards served as a rhetorical foundation for early feminist questionings. Inspired as well by academic European and American literary and film studies, some theatre theorists combined the Marxist, aka "materialist," imperative to examine economic factors implicit in the production of theatre with the signature political theatre "gestus" of Bertolt Brecht, analytic tools such as semiotics and psychological theories derived from Freud by way of Jacques Lacan and French feminist "correctives" to Lacan. Also influential to this theory are Michel Foucault's *History of Sexuality* and writings by Jacques Derrida and Roland Barthes, among others.

In her broad-ranging benchmark study, *Feminism and Theatre* (1988), Sue-Ellen Case explains materialist feminism and psycho-semiotic analysis as it was understood in the mid-1980s. Case's introduction to semiotics may help the initiate encounter what could be the most gender-neutral set of tools in postmodern lingo. Semioticians make useful distinctions between different kinds of "signs," such as metaphor and metonymy, to enable a more precise discussion of how "meaning" or "signification" is generated or interpreted. For anyone who is interested in "deconstructing" any "systems of representation," semiotics provides a seemingly objective set of wrenches, though its mechanistic nature itself may trigger subjective responses on the part of the user.

Case then illustrates how distinctions between a written text and a performance text can be made semiotically, so that one might reflect upon and even attempt to "decode" the ways in which gender and culture are "encoded" in theatre. Now using semiotic tools subjectively, she asks Marxist questions of the encoded written and performance texts, and she ruminates on the deduction that it is the audience as "Male" who "gazes" at "Woman," herself a fictional construct. With Case's guidance, one observes how making distinctions among the signs, investigating the production of signs and discerning the gender rules dominating the "gaze" can contribute to feminist efforts to revolutionize systems of representation.

Jill Dolan further probes the implications of the Male Gaze and the Male subject position. Published in 1988, Dolan's *The Feminist Spectator as Critic* asks what happens when the one gazing is female and lesbian. She argues that "it is the exchange of women between men—buttressed by psychoanalytic processes that reify gender positioning—that works to deliver gender encul-turated meanings through representation." Dolan defines the materialist feminist theoretical ground for her examination of spectatorship. She then organizes and defines the ideas of "other" feminists as "liberal" and "cultural," titles which imply they lack analytic probity. That step of defining other positions invites controversy, as it recapitulates the very practice materialist feminism decries by gazing at and naming the Other from a privileged position. Nevertheless, Dolan's provocative and astute writings, directing and academic leadership have been instrumental in shaping the implementation of materialist feminism.

To revolutionize systems of representation in keeping with materialist feminist ends, Elin Diamond champions the Brechtian "gestus," a concept for creating sign systems that can be utilized in any production style, perhaps even realism. The "gestus" interrupts the traditional mimetic gaze, foregrounds ideology and exposes "character" as a construct of historical conditions. This might jolt spectators into personal epiphanies and motivate individuals to change their own sociopolitical circumstances. Accompanying Diamond's essay on the "gestus," from her *Unmaking Mimesis* (1997), is a description of New York–based performance artist Robbie McCauley's use of the gestus in her startling "Indian Blood," which predates Diamond's theorizing. "Appearing" as "African American" to audiences accustomed to the black-white racial binary, McCauley reveals in her production that she is also Native American, and her black soldier "forefathers" participated in warfare against Indians as part of their understandable effort to support their families and improve their social status in segregated white society. McCauley's performance exemplifies Diamond's call for stage gestures that transform "auratic body into dialectical image."

The other major cluster of ideological propositions that materialist feminist theatre theory merged with Marxism and semiotics is built from Freud via Lacanian psychoanalysis. Janelle G. Reinelt's introduction to basic Freudian and Lacanian precepts has been excerpted from *Critical Theory and Performance* (1992), an intellectually substantial postmodern primer edited by Reinelt and Joseph R. Roach. From Freud's speculations about the nature of "the unconscious," Lacan limned linguistic and symbolic structures within the unconscious. His concept of the "mirror stage," in which a person sees "the Other" as "ideal self," has generated original investigations into the mirror stage's role in topics such as audience empathy, an actor's identification with character and the alienation effect.

Aided by Reinelt's reminder of how Lacan is grounded in Freud, Esther Beth Sullivan's "Women, Woman, and the Subject of Feminism: Feminist Directions" plunges the reader into feminist extrapolations from Lacan. Written as the introduction to Ellen Donkin and Susan Clements' impressive anthology about feminist directing, *Upstaging Big Daddy* (1993), Sullivan's essay firmly posits performance as a form of theorizing. For Sullivan. psychosemiotic theory might explain how "Woman" has been constructed in Eurocentric symbolic language as "other-than-man," and "how the world is defined in a way that privileges some subjects over others." Amending Lacanian-derived analysis by suggesting that "Woman" is denied entrance to phallocratic discourse, feminists can describe margins of ideology and culture, as well as intersections which confound ideology.

"Identity politics" has emerged from this recognition of intersection, ambiguity and marginalization. For example, writing "In Defense of the Discourse," Dolan notes that "through theory, I can articulate the roots of my own identity in the conflicting discourses of lesbianism and Judaism and know that there is no comfortable place for me within any single discourse. Theory enables me to describe the differences within me and around me without forcing me to rank my allegiances or my oppressions."[2] Yvonne Yarbro-Bejarano points out that Chicanas similarly must negotiate a maze of culture-specific identities: "An Aztec woman, Malintzin Tenepal, was Cortes's mistress; she is 'La Malinche,' the Mexican/Chicano Eve who betrayed her people and represents La Vendida (the woman who sells out to the white race). La Virgen is constructed from the Catholic Madonna, the Mother who is pure and asexual."[3]

For Sullivan, African American playwright Adrienne Kennedy and the Split Britches company display and inspire innovative approaches to the female "subject" in theatrical story as well as in the ongoing real life drama of gender liberation. Kennedy has used performance to "focus on how race and gender are produced rather than natural." In plays such as *A Movie Star Has to Star in Black and White* (1988), her "acts of the mind" have developed independently of psycho-semiotic epistemology and yet cannily articulate the constructed nature of "identity" in a manner congruent with that school of thought. Creating separately from academic theory in 1983 and yet in sync with materialist feminist premises, Split Britches performs a provocative "collective subject" in its *Beauty and the Beast*.

Striking demonstrations of applied theory can be found in director Rhonda Blair's "'Not . . . but'/'Not-Not-Me': Musings on Cross-Gender Performance," also published in Donkin and Clements. Narrating her own evolving awareness of the intricacies of cross-gender casting as she employs psycho-semiotic tools and the Brechtian gestus, Blair shares her discovery that the "oscillation of identity an actor moves through in performing the other gender is in fact a process of finding that ostensible Other in the self." Cross-gender projects such as Blair's were widespread in the 1980s and 1990s. In the second edition of this book, Susan Ogden Malouf describes Role Over Productions, a theatre laboratory she and Pamela Carter Joern ran in Minneapolis in the late 1980s "to examine contemporary gender/cultural roles through open casting." Deanna Jent, Meg Swanson, Sande Zeig and Monique Wittig, among others, have employed cross-gender exercises in the classroom to expand actors' range of expression. Building on her dissertation research into nonverbal gender display in acting classes, Jent argues that students who physically enact gender constructions achieve both greater self-perception and a new awareness of stereotyping in gender, race and ethnicity in the extracurricular reality.[4]

Instead of revealing gender codes by "crossing" into the Other, some performers challenge "the gaze" solely by delving into the female body. Jeanie Forte investigates how performance artists Karen Finley and Marianne Goldberg use their iconically female bodies to disrupt viewers' predictable erotic responses. In her essay published in Reinelt and Roach, Forte suggests that Finley defies "consumption as object by aggressively destroying both the object of fantasy and the potential alternative." Goldberg's dance-text performances focus "on her subjective pleasure in her own body" without invoking "masculinist" notions of "sex or sexual desire."

By the 1990s, this "preoccupation with the body" has supplanted critical theory's "preoccupation with language," James Atlas observes. Writing about academia's "embrace" of pornography, Atlas cites literary theorist Laura Kipnis's belief that radical politics in the university "has largely become sexual politics . . . Loss of faith in traditional ideologies as a potential agent of social change" has led "the left" to look at "the ways that subjectivity gets produced in conformance with social norms" in order to produce political change by "discovering the true nature of one's sexuality" as a fundamental step toward "inner change."[5] The calls for inner change and micro-political action on the part of the erudite "left" are unintentionally congruent with Confucian, Stoic and other ancient philosophies, which advise that one must change within to change others. And, although this academic discovery of "the body" purports to be radical, in theatre haven't bodies always told the tales—with priapic comedians, masked tragic figures and dancers of the seven veils?

In the conclusion to her essay in Laughlin and Schuler that begins this section, Gillespie thoughtfully critiques materialist feminism and suggests further feminist investigations in other modes. From her scholarly base in rhetoric, Gillespie summarizes concerns many have about materialist feminism, primarily that it places male subjects at its center by valorizing nineteenth-century patriarchs; it rests on shaky logical premises adapted from or built on speculative conjectures which have no conventional proof; its dense jargon excludes populist participation in its arguments; and its Eurocentric encoding may preclude diversified "play" with its precepts.

Marxist-inspired feminism successfully generated intellectual "capital" for itself in academic discourse, as postmodern epistemology achieved during the 1980s and early 1990s a site of kingly prominence on the scholarly hill. This propelled many women deservedly into department chairs and deanships. Atlas points out, though, the irony in the academic tradition of "criticizing the premises of cultural authority from within the confines of the very institution that most embodies it: the university."[6] Sue-Ellen Case echoes concerns about postmodern theory in a 1995 interview, noting that the Lacanian discourse that "has pretty much taken over the new study of performance" ironically "reconstructs" a "Master Discourse" that is like an orthodox "Bible."[7] She writes in *Performing Feminisms: Feminist Critical Theory and*

UNIVERSITY OF WINCHESTER LIBRARY

Theatre (1990) that the Lacanian critique produces a kind of closed circle in which "woman as Other" is the "Object," regardless of efforts to make her a "subject." Case advises people to read "theory that is political" with the understanding that it is situated in a specific historical moment; rather than adhering to a fixed notion, Case sees herself engaged in "ceaseless revolution."[8]

Where else might feminists look for provocations, tools and information regarding gender rules, transformation of those rules and theatre's role in both codification and revision? Organic chemistry's findings deserve attention, since hormonal tides and basic electro-chemical attractions and repulsions among people undergird procreative impulses, probably are significant any time bodies perform before other bodies, and seem to have been forgotten in the rush to deconstruct culture. Also, since the urge for social order probably is inherent genetically in primates, primatology and ethology may assist theatrical theorists. In addition, *Feminist Economics*, the official journal of the International Association of Feminist Economists, may provide new models to refresh ground overtilled by outdated Marxism.

Bridging primatology and the social sciences, ethnography provides multidisciplinary methodologies well suited to theatre. Anthropology continues to wrestle with biases arising from the differences between a field observer and the "object" of investigation. In her provocative 1989 essay, "Can There Be a Feminist Ethnography?" Lila Abu-Lughod summarizes lively and often conflicting feminist thoughts regarding "objectivity," reminding us that "all knowledge is partial and from an embodied perspective."[9] Having grown up "between two worlds" with a white American mother and a Palestinian father, "halfie" Abu-Lughod calls for "discussion in feminist circles" on "how to develop a politics of affinity built on the recognition of difference." She suggests that some of the most exciting ethnography is being done by indigenous anthropologists and halfies, who know that their selves are multiple and can unsettle boundaries of "self" and "other," revealing "the multiplicity of the self, and the multiple, overlapping, and interacting qualities of other," showing that "we are always part of what we study and we always stand in definite relations to it."

Abu-Lughod's reminder that we live in "one interconnected world" evokes cosmological beliefs such as the Hindu precept that the individual is not just the body, not just the mind, but something else that always has been and always will be. Some Christian theologians see the "self" as defined by Western psychology to be a shallow concept bred by looking outward at material reality rather than inward. Buddhism suggests that "it is our belief in this self, our identification with it that causes us to suffer," postulating that the self and related "illusions" of the phenomenological world are nothing but "habitual behaviors and reactions."[10] Or, as Carlos Castaneda's Native American "Don Juan" observes, the world that human beings perceive is "an illusion created by the description that was told to them from the moment they were born." "Reason," the old shaman suggests, makes people "forget that the description is only a description, and before they realize it, human beings have entrapped the totality of themselves in a vicious circle."[11] It may be that psycho-semiotic materialist deconstruction projects and ancient world religions meet at this juncture of self and illusion, not unlike atomic and quantum theories, gazing at each other in a psychosomatic maze of mirrors.

The final two essays in this section suggest possibilities for theatrical theory through intriguing directions being taken by feminists who draw on Asian and African cognitive and aesthetic processes. In *About Face*, ethnographer and dramaturg Dorinne Kondo explores "the ways Japanese fashion and Asian American theatre illuminate the politics of pleasure, the performance of race, and the possibilities for intervention in a regime of commodity capitalism." She playfully "problematizes the black-white binary and essentialist notions of racial hierarchy" and challenges materialist feminist presumptions regarding politics and the presentation of self on the theatrical stages of fashion and theatre. Kondo takes as a given the complexities and ambiguities inherent in theatre studies, and by employing field work at geographically diverse locations, she reminds us that such studies usually cannot presume a static "single culture."

While Kondo negotiates postmodern epistemology in giving wing to original thoughts, African American scholar Sandra L. Richards takes the reader directly into African thought and aesthetics—"in short, cultures"—as she suggests in her essay published in Reinelt and Roach how "the principles of Sixteen Cowrie and Ifá divination" may have been reformulated creatively by African American playwright Ntozake Shange. Based in the non-gendered language of Yoruba, in contrast to the heavily gendered French of Lacan, traditional Ifá hermeneutics have "remained relatively free of gender bias," Richards observes. Shange's dramaturgy "signals a concept of feminism which significantly departs from those definitions advanced by white European and American theorists." Diasporic dissemination of African cosmological and intellectual thought has permeated and influenced American society immeasurably. Perhaps Richards and Shange can invigorate feminist theatrical theories with this decidedly non-European "interpretive hegemony that can extend from the symbolic to the socio-political order."

What remains for feminist theatrical theories? Shifts in the twenty-first-century American "nomos," a multicultural "we are," might be enabled not only by continuing the process of dismantling what "we" have been into distinct differences but also by molding "what we might be" with inclusive original visions.

LWJ

A FEMINIST THEORY OF THEATRE: INTRODUCTION

Patti P. Gillespie

Throughout this study, I will be showing how the sex-gender system operates within the art and scholarship of theatre. First identified by the anthropologist Gayle Rubin, the sex-gender system has been briefly—and well—defined by Gerda Lerner as "that institutionalized system which allots resources, property, and privileges to persons according to culturally defined gender roles. Thus, it is sex which determines that women should be child bearers, it is the sex-gender system which assures that they should be child rearers."[1]

In using the words *male* and *men, female* and *woman* in this essay, I refer to people positioned within this system, not merely to biological sex. I shall use the word *feminist* to mean someone, male or female, who wishes to transform the sex-gender system. By *feminist scholarship* I mean scholarship that is "distinguished by the systematic inclusion of women, by an absence of language and/or perspective that degrades women or minorities, by rigorous testing of assumptions that hark back to stereotypes and social mythology, and by a concern to rectify the omissions, the degradation and the errors of the past."[2]

Despite considerable variety, theatrical theory displays two unvarying traits: men have proposed the answers, and the answers have been accepted as gender-neutral. The advent of feminist theorists therefore brought with it three new questions: What produced such a male canon? Why was its gender-neutrality assumed? And how might its validity be challenged?

In the nineteenth century, a changing sense of history (historicism) and a growing fascination with the then astonishing proposals of Darwin, Mendel, Freud, and Marx caused some theorists to reconceive theatre: It was *neither* an object *nor* an instrument; it was instead a product of its age and heritage. Theatre was conceptualized as *expression.* Theorists were soon probing authors' lives, social conditions and presumed evolution in order to explain theatre. The idea of theatre as an expression of something antecedent to it soon expanded to include various extraliterary explanations of the art as well. Among those extraliterary explanations favored were ritual (e.g., Gilbert Murray), psychoanalysis (e.g., Freud) and economic conditions (e.g., Marx). Feminist theorists would, about a hundred years later, adopt two of these, Marxism and psychoanalysis, for their own discussions of theatre. Although the early twentieth century popularized several of these new theories, as well as those of the neo-Aristotelians and new critics,[3] none questioned (or even saw) the male domination within theory. Marxist theory did offer two insights useful to later feminists, however; first, that the historic moment accounted not only for the art and artist but also for the critic, and second, that spectators were supremely important to the art of theatre.

Marxists argued that the historical moment shapes and limits the artists and the critics in much the same way as it shapes any other product: neither drama nor criticism could be a pure, disinterested act, for the men making both art and criticism grew out of particular, definable situations whose interests and institutions inevitably shaped their products. Observing, and insistently pointing out, that both playwrights and critics were overwhelmingly upper- or middle-class and educated, Marxists asked repeatedly, "Who profits?" from the work of art or from the opinions expressed in a piece of criticism. *(Cui bono* did not extend to women.)[4]

Their second proposal—that spectators were central to the event of theatre—also emerged from Marxists' commitment to political action, for only spectators could turn the virtual actions of the stage into real actions in the world. Thus spectators, not only as individuals but also as members of a social group (the audience, the society), figured importantly in Marxist theories.

Most influential among the Marxists for theatrical theory (at least outside of Eastern Europe) was Bertolt Brecht. Brecht objected to Aristotelian theatre (especially as practiced by the realists) on the grounds that it dulled a spectator's capacity for political action, supposedly by lulling him into an unquestioning acceptance of the stories he saw onstage. Thus, central to Brecht's Epic Theatre was a call for *Verfremdungseffekt*, making the familiar seem unfamiliar, in pursuit of which all of the resources of the theatre—actors, scenery, costumes and lighting—should be engaged in the task of empowering spectators to see political implications and to seek change. This shifting emphasis from *the play text* to *the play in performance* in front of spectators, launched the first influential theories of *theatre*, as distinct from those devoted more or less exclusively to drama.[5]

The Marxists' emphasis on a spectator as an agent of political change, and on the inevitable contamination of both artists and critics by their own socially constructed presuppositions, appealed to groups that sought to understand and explain both their exclusion from the great historical tradition of theatre and their relegation to the margins of today's theatre.

Prefiguring feminists, African American theorists alleged in the 1950s and 1960s that traditional art and criticism were simply one more mechanism of the powerful to deny respectability and acceptance to the powerless. With increasing stridency, they questioned the relevance of Western (white) art for African American (black) people. Out of this questioning grew, for some, a repudiation of traditionally accepted artistic standards for judging the works of black artists. In less than a decade, feminists would substitute the word *woman* for the word *black*.

Theatre—let alone a theory of theatre—remained outside major discussions within feminism. For example, all issues of *Signs, Feminist Studies* and *Women's Studies*, from their origins through 1989, included only five articles on theatre (excluding literary studies) and none at all on theories of theatre.

Indeed, even within publications devoted to theatre, there were few articles on feminist theatrical theory before the mid-1980s. Essays on feminist theories of theatre appeared mostly in *Women and Performance*, founded in 1983 as a journal of feminist theory. (The major forum for the discussion of feminist theatrical theories has probably been, since the mid-1980s, the Women's Program of the old American Theatre Association (now the Association for Theatre in Higher Education). Feminists in academic theatre, unlike their peers in literary and film studies, are as likely to be artists as scholars. Among the relatively few feminists who chose to be scholars were those with interests in history and criticism as well as theory. Consequently, the pool from which to draw feminists dedicated to theatrical theory has been extremely small.

Theory was controversial among feminists in theatre, just as it was among feminists generally. Although some saw theory as the best way to answer critics and to insinuate feminism into both the academy and the agenda of the political left, others saw it either as a diversion from more important political work or as an elitist activity incompatible with the goals of feminism—or both.

By the 1980s, feminist critics had developed a wealth of materials upon which theorists could work. Studies treating cross-gender playing probably received the most attention. Feminists studied the implications of those theatrical conventions that had male actors playing female characters (in, for example, Greek and Elizabethan plays), and female actors specializing in "breeches roles," major female stars who routinely played leading roles written for male actors. By the end of the 1980s, deliberate, self-conscious gender manipulations (where the spoken words contradicted the visual depiction onstage, for example) prompted both new perceptions of gender and new explanations of its implications.

Many studies were clear attempts to formulate theories about specific phenomena within theatre. For example, the growing attention to gender manipulation brought forth proposals that lesbian theatres might be the most promising source of a new, genuinely feminist, theatre and drama.[6] Feminist scholars in theatre early observed that contemporary female playwrights often abandoned causally organized plots and psychologically driven characters in favor of plays described with words like *circular, modular, contiguous* or with images like *patchwork, quilted, web-like, montage.*[7] They disagreed, however, on the reasons for this shift. Some sought answers in biological sex, arguing (for example) that causal, linear plots—with their rising action, climax and falling action—reproduced male orgasm; modular or contiguous plots reproduced female sexuality—with their smaller, contained, repeating patterns.[8] Others sought answers in gender by linking writing style to theatrical practice and economics, arguing (for example) that female playwrights appropriated forms already explored by contemporary male playwrights of theatre's avant-garde, in which female artists tended to cluster because of a more welcoming production situation.[9]

As differences among female playwrights grew clearer, distinctions among women and between sex and gender also grew clearer. Such clarification, in turn, refocused attention on differences among feminists—their assumptions and working methods. By the mid-1980s, biological explanations (most often associated with radical feminism and standpoint theories) were greeted with increased skepticism, and explanations based on historical and economic circumstances gained favor.

A turning point came in 1988, when two major books treating feminism in theatre appeared: Sue-Ellen Case's *Feminism and Theatre* and Jill Dolan's *The Feminist Spectator as Critic*. Both stressed theory, and both approached their subject from a postmodern perspective, using methods and language derived from feminist work in film and literature. Case explained, "I have borrowed from works on film and on the novel to begin an application of these theories to theatre practice;"[10] and Dolan echoed, "As many feminist film theorists have shown, it is the exchange of women between men—buttressed by psychoanalytic processes that reify gender positioning—that works to deliver gender enculturated meanings through representation . . . [These theories] have distinct and important applications for materialist feminist performance criticism."[11] These works were followed in 1989 by a third, Lynda Hart's *Making a Spectacle*, a collection of essays many of which were theoretical and many of which, according to Hart, used the methods and vocabulary of film and literary study.

After 1988, feminist theorists of theatre turned insistently to consider how ideology (especially that connected with gender) was embedded in texts and performances, how spectators were positioned to accept such ideologies unquestioningly, how feminists might best come to understand texts and performances in order to subvert them, and how performances might contribute to the disruption of such ideologies.

Thus, from among the variety of voices and approaches heard in the early days of feminist scholarship in theatre there emerged, on the eve of the 1990s, a strong preference for materialist explanations and postmodern methodologies. Among traditional theorists of theatre, only Brecht continued to be viewed favorably, probably because he combined a Marxist's commitment to political change, an interest in empowering spectators and (in his *Verfremdungseffekt*) a theatrical means for "deconstructing" messages.

So long as theatre theorists studied only plays and playwriting, they needed only patterns of analysis already established in literary studies, where semiotics, deconstruction and reception theory were the current fashions. As they moved to study production rather than (or in addition to) text, however, they needed explanations of how visual, auditory and temporal as well as verbal elements could serve ideological purposes. They therefore turned to film theory and found there a ready-made explanation drawn from an inventive blend of semiotics, Lacanian and Althusserian Marxism. At about the same time, feminist theorists in theatre, again following trends in film theory, moved away from piecemeal theorizing and toward a general theory of feminist practice in theatre.

SEMIOTICS AND THE GAZE:
TOWARD A NEW POETICS

Sue-Ellen Case

Feminism began in the streets, with demonstrations against the oppression of women. The commitment to change was taken up by women in all professions, including academics and critics. Academics transformed the social issues of the movement into themes and methods for research and criticism. For theatre, the basic theoretical project for feminism could be termed a "new poetics," borrowing the notion from Aristotle's *Poetics*. New feminist theory would abandon the traditional patriarchal values embedded in prior notions of form, practice and audience response in order to construct new critical models and methodologies for the drama that would accommodate the presence of women in the art, support their liberation from the cultural fictions of the female gender and deconstruct the valorization of the male gender. In pursuit of these objectives, feminist dramatic theory would borrow freely: new discoveries about gender and culture from the disciplines of anthropology, sociology and political science; feminist strategies for reading texts from the new work in English studies; psycho-semiotic analyses of performance and representation from recent film theory; new theories of the "subject" from psycho-semiotics, postmodern criticism and post-structuralism; and certain strategies from the project called "deconstruction." This "new poetics" would deconstruct the traditional systems of representation and perception of women and posit women in the position of the subject.

Keir Elam, in his book *The Semiotics of Theatre and Drama*, defines semiotics as "a science dedicated to the study of the production of meaning in society . . . its objects are thus at once the different sign systems and codes at work in society and the actual messages and texts produced thereby."[1] Semiotics, when applied to theatre, explores how theatre communicates, or how theatre produces meaning. The basic operatives in the production of meaning are the signifier (or sign) and the signified. The signifier is the ensemble of elements in a theatrical production that compose its meaning—the text, the actor, the stage space, the lights, the blocking and so on. The signified is the meaning or message which is derived from this signifier by the "collective consciousness" of the audience. So, for example, semiotics seeks to describe the way in which the set becomes a sign: how it signifies place, time, social milieu and mood. Semiotics also identifies and explores those elements of the actor's performance that signify character and objective to the audience.

Since the signified is produced by the recipient of the signifier, semiotics identifies several texts within a performance situation. The written text is only one of these and is not necessarily the definitive one. There is the text printed in a book and read as literature, the text the director reads preparing for rehearsal, the rehearsal text the actor uses, and the production text the audience receives as it watches the play. Semiotics proposes that each of these texts is different and discrete, retaining an equal status with the other ones and representing appropriate material for a critical response. The constitution of a performance text, separate but equal to the written one, implies new dimensions in the coproduction of the text. The importance of the author's intent gives way to the conditions of production and the composition of the audience in determining the meaning of the theatrical event. This implies that there is no aesthetic closure around the text, separating it from the conditions of its production. The performance text is constituted by the location of the theatre, the price of the ticket, the attitude of the ushers and the response of the audience as well as by the written dialogue and stage directions.

This semiotic constitution of the performance text is useful to a feminist poetics. Because the composition of the audience is an element in the coproduction of the play's meaning, the gender of the audience members is crucial in determining what the feminist play might mean. The practice of performing before all-women audiences excludes men from the coproduction of the play's meaning. Within a patriarchal culture, this exclusion may provide the only way certain elements of women's experience can be signified within the "collective consciousness" of the audience. The insistence upon an all-woman audience, then, becomes an essential part of the composition of the theatrical event, rather than a social statement of separatism or reverse sexism. Likewise, ticket prices, child care, the time of the performance and the location of the theatre also coproduce the performance text, positing the accessibility of the production to working-class women, single mothers or women of color as part of the meaning of the play. The gender, class and color of the audience replace the aesthetic traditions of form or the isolated conditions of the author's intent within the interpretative strategies of dramatic theory, firmly allying poetics with feminist politics.

Perhaps even more important is the notion of the cultural encoding of the sign (or signifier), the semiotic discovery that provides a radical alteration of poetic strategies of performance. This notion positions a feminist analysis at the very foundation of communication—in the sign itself. Cultural encoding is the imprint of ideology upon the sign—the set of values, beliefs and ways of seeing that control the connotations of the sign in the culture at large. The norms of the culture assign meaning to the sign, prescribing its resonances with their biases. For a feminist, this means that the dominant notions of gender, class and race compose the meaning of the text of a play, the stage pictures of its production and the audience reception of its meaning. By describing the cultural encoding in a sign, semiotics reveals the covert cultural beliefs embedded in communication. Thus, the elements of theatrical communication such as language or set pieces no longer appear to be objective, utilitarian or in any sense value-free. The author's or director's or actor's intent ceases to be perceived as a singular enterprise; insofar as it communicates. It works in alliance with the ideology or beliefs of the culture at large.

The notion of encoding shifts the political implications of a theatrical performance from the interpretative sphere of the critic to the signification process of the performance, thereby assigning political alliance to the aesthetic realm. For example, there are cultural encodings in casting decisions. Juliet, in *Romeo and Juliet*, usually conforms to certain standards of beauty found in the present-day culture. These standards control her costuming and makeup in foregrounding her beauty for the audience. Since Shakespeare wrote the play with a boy actor in mind, the common casting of Juliet does not proceed from the text; rather, it's determined by the cultural encoding inscribed in the image of the female love object. For feminists. these discoveries help to illuminate how the image of a woman onstage participates directly in the dominant ideology of gender. Social conventions about the female gender will be encoded in all signs for women. Inscribed in body language, signs of gender can determine the blocking of a scene by assigning bolder movements to the men and more restricted movements to the women, or by creating poses and positions that exploit the role of woman as sexual object. Stage movement replicates the proxemics of the social order, capitalizing upon the spatial relationships in the culture at large between women and the sites of power.[2]

Overall, feminist semiotics concentrates on the notion of "woman as sign." From this perspective, a live woman standing onstage is not a biological or natural reality, but a fictional construct, a distillate from diverse but congruent discourses dominant in Western cultures.[3] In other words, the conventions of the stage produce a meaning for the sign "woman," which is based upon their cultural associations with the female gender. Feminist semiotic theory has attempted to describe and deconstruct this sign for "woman," in order to distinguish biology from culture and experience from ideology. Whereas formerly feminist criticism presumed to know what a woman is, but rejected certain images of women, this new perspective brings into question the entire notion of how one knows what the sign "woman" means. At this point, the entire gender category "woman" is under feminist semiotic deconstruction.

Given the assumption that stage and audience coproduce the performance text, the meaning of the sign "woman" is also created by the audience. The way the viewer perceives the woman onstage constitutes another theoretical enterprise. In her book *Women and Film*, E. Ann Kaplan characterizes this enterprise as "the male gaze."[4] Kaplan asserts that the sign "woman" is constructed by and for the male gaze. In the realm of theatrical production, the gaze is owned by the male: the majority of playwrights, directors and producers are men.

The concept of the male gaze asserts that representations of women are perceived as they are seen by men. Here, the term "men" represents the male subject in capitalist patriarchy. A simple example of how everyone sees a play as a male would see it might be the way a play induces the audience to view the female roles through the eyes of the male characters. When the ingenue makes her entrance, the audience sees her as the male protagonist sees her. The blocking of her entrance, her costume and the lighting are designed to reveal that she is the object of his desire. In this way, the audience also perceives her as an object of desire, by identifying with his male gaze. This example illustrates one major cultural assumption—that the male is the subject of the dramatic action.

Women become fixed in the position of object of the gaze, rather than as the subject directing it; women appear in order to be looked upon rather than to do the looking. In that sense, "woman" is constituted as "Other." For women, one of the results of this representation of woman as "Other" in the male gaze is that she also becomes an "Other" to herself. Within the patriarchal system of signs, women do not have the cultural mechanisms of meaning to construct themselves as the subject rather than as the object of performance. A wedge is created between the sign "woman" and real women that insinuates alienation into the very participation of women in the system of theatrical representation or within the system of communication in the dominant culture.

Both the study of woman as sign and the study of woman as object are deconstructive strategies that aid in exposing the patriarchal encodings in the dominant system of representation. Yet the potential for women to emerge as subjects rather than objects opens up a field of new possibilities for women in theatre and its system of representation. Constructing woman as subject is the future, liberating work of a feminist new poetics.

Psycho-semiotic strategies may provide a new kind of revolution, for in the late twentieth century the mode of production which is central to the oppression of many peoples lies within the ghettos of signs and codes. In the age of television, computer languages and communication satellites, the production of signs creates the sense of what a person is, rather than reflects it (in the traditional mimetic order). The mode of cultural production is reversed: signs create reality rather than reflect it. This condition means that artists and cultural theorists may be the activists and the revolutionaries.

THE DISCOURSE OF FEMINISMS: THE SPECTATOR AND REPRESENTATION

Jill Dolan

In the illusionist tradition that dominates American theatre practice, performers and spectators are separated by a curtain of light that helps maintain the fictitious fourth wall. Performers facing the audience are blinded by the workings of the apparatus that frames them. The blinding lights set them apart from the sea of silhouetted heads without faces toward whom their words flow. The spectators' individuality is subsumed under an assumption of commonality; their differences from each other are disguised by anonymity. The spectators become the audience whom the performers address—albeit obliquely, given realist theatre conventions—as a singular mass.

The performance apparatus that directs the performer's address, however, works to constitute that amorphous, anonymous mass as a particular subject position. The lighting, setting, costumes, blocking, text—all the material aspects of theatre—are manipulated so that the performance's meanings are intelligible to a particular spectator constructed in a particular way by the terms of its address.[1] Historically, in North American culture, this spectator has been assumed to be white, middle-class, heterosexual and male. That theatre creates an ideal spectator carved in the likeness of the dominant culture whose ideology he represents is the motivating assumption behind the discourse of feminist performance criticism.

The feminist critic can be seen as a "resistant reader," who analyzes a performance's meaning by reading against the grain of stereotypes and resisting the manipulation of both the performance text and the cultural text that it helps to shape.[2] By exposing the ways in which dominant ideology is naturalized by the performance's address to the ideal spectator, feminist performance criticism works as political intervention in an effort toward cultural change.

This study concentrates on spectatorship. It represents an effort to bring up the lights in the theatre auditorium, as it were, to illuminate the differences between spectators positioned in front of the representational frame. Since it directs its address to a gender-specific spectator, most performance employs culturally determined gender codes that reinforce cultural conditioning. Performance usually addresses the male spectator as an active subject, and encourages him to identify with the male hero in the narrative.[3] The same representations tend to objectify women performers and female spectators as passive, invisible, unspoken subjects.

The feminist spectator viewing such a representation is necessarily in the outsider's critical position. She cannot find a comfortable way into the representation since she finds herself, as a woman (and even more so, as a member of the working class, a lesbian, or a woman of color), excluded from its address. She sees in the performance frame representatives of her gender class with whom she might identify—if women are represented at all—acting passively before the specter of male authority.

She sees women as mothers, relegated to supporting roles that enable the more important action of the male protagonist. She sees attractive women performers made-up and dressed to seduce or be seduced by the male lead. While the men are generally active and involved, the women seem marginal and curiously irrelevant, except as a tacit support system or as decoration that enhances and directs the pleasure of the male spectator's gaze.

Finding her position compromised if she allows herself to identify with these women, the feminist spectator contemplates the option of participating in the play's narrative from the hero's point of view. She empathizes with his romantic exploits, or his activities in a more public sphere, but has a nagging suspicion that she has become complicit in the objectification or erasure of her own gender class.

Ruminating over these unsavory positions, the feminist spectator might find that her gender—and/or her race, class or sexual preference—as well as her ideology and politics make the representation alien and even offensive. It seems that as a spectator she is far from ideal. Determined to draw larger conclusions from this experience, she leaves the theatre while the audience applauds at the curtain call and goes off to develop a theory of feminist performance criticism.

Feminism as the Site of Differences

Feminism begins with a keen awareness of exclusion from male cultural, social, sexual, political and intellectual discourse. It is a critique of prevailing social conditions that formulate women's position as outside of dominant male discourse. Feminism loses some of its polemical force if it is not linked to a coherent ideological structure. Therefore, it is crucial to identify common characteristics that describe the differences among the feminisms.

American feminism can be separated generally into liberal, cultural or radical, and materialist segments, each of which presents a different critical approach to the issue of exclusion from male discourse and the representations in which it is embodied. There are many gradations within and among these categories—some of which are socialist feminism, lesbian feminism, spiritualist feminism—but I find these three most inclusive and most useful for clarifying the different feminist ways of seeing.[4]

Liberal feminism takes its cues from liberal humanism. Rather than proposing radical structural change, it suggests that working within existing social and political organizations will eventually secure women social, political and economic parity with men.[5] In theatre practice and criticism, liberal feminist efforts are responsible for the wider visibility of women playwrights, directors, producers and designers, and the creation of richer roles for women performers.

As liberal feminism gains a foothold for women in the male-dominated institutions of American theatre, however, an insidious backsliding sometimes occurs with regard to feminist politics. Some women in theatre suggest that women's advocacy groups and workshop spaces are temporary measures that will no longer be necessary when women truly achieve parity with men. Many working women playwrights vehemently resist the feminist appellation, because to survive economically their plays must be produced widely in commercial venues. The analogy between feminism and politics is seen as threatening to the universality of their work.[6] Their desire to become part of the system that has historically excluded them forces some liberal feminists in theatre to acquiesce to their erasure as women. Little changes, even as stronger women characters are written into their plays, because the universal to which they write is still based on the male model.

Cultural feminism, the second segment of American feminism I am delineating here, proposes that there are, and should be maintained, clear differences between men and women which might form the basis of separate cultural spheres. Cultural feminism is sometimes called radical feminism. At the start of the second wave of American feminism in the late 1960s and early 1970s, radical feminism was based in a theoretical struggle to abolish gender as a defining category between men and women. Cultural feminism, on the contrary, bases its analysis in a reification of sexual difference based on absolute gender categories. Cultural feminism is founded on a reification of sexual difference that valorizes female biology, in which gender is an inmutable, determining and desirable category.

An inquiry into sex and gender categories is the primary focus of feminism in general, but within each of the feminisms, the investigation manifests different ideology and different forms. Liberal feminism, as we have seen, would subsume the female gender into the (male) generic, or universal, category. Cultural feminism proposes instead a fundamental change in the nature of universality by suggesting that female gender values take the place of the generic male. It seeks to reverse the gender hierarchy by theorizing female values as superior to male values. The oppressions wrought by gender polarization constructed through dominant theories of sexual difference remain peculiarly unattacked in cultural feminist thought.

Cultural feminist performance critics and practitioners are suspicious of both male forms and contents, since they equate them with male meanings that are alien and oppressive to women. These critics look instead to women's culture for female significations. In cultural feminist theatre, the imaginary formation of "Woman" becomes the text's point of entry and the female spectator is constituted as the new ideal, generic spectator. But while her sexual difference from men is reified, her differences from other women are largely ignored. The flattening out of lived differences between women compromises the position of this transcendent female spectator.

I have found the materialist approach outlined below most reasonable and suitable to my own ideological beliefs. But in the discussions of liberal and particularly cultural feminism above and in the chapters that follow, my intent is not to "trash" the work or to imply that it is ranked lower on a political or theoretical hierarchy that elevates materialist feminism to its apex.

Materialist feminism, however, frames the debate over gender in more gender-neutral terms than either liberal feminism, which would absorb women into the male universal, or cultural feminism, which would overturn the balance of power in favor of female supremacy. Materialist feminism deconstructs the mythic subject Woman to look at women as a class oppressed by material conditions and social relations.

Where cultural feminism sees knowledge as transcendent, ahistorical, and therefore universal, materialist feminism inquires into the flux and material conditions of history. It views women as historical subjects whose relation to prevailing social structures is also influenced by race, class, and sexual identification. Rather than considering gender polarization as the victimization of only women, materialist feminism considers it a social construct oppressive to both women and men.

In materialist discourse, gender is not innate. Rather, it is dictated through enculturation, as gender divisions are placed at the service of the dominant culture's ideology. Far from reifying sexual difference, materialist feminism works to understand how women have been oppressed by gender categories. It attempts to denaturalize the dominant ideology that demands and maintains such oppressive social arrangements.

Material feminist performance criticism is not strictly Marxian, as it focuses its analysis on material conditions of gender positioning, rather than privileging economic determinism. Some borrowing of Marxian terms, however, is apparent in materialist definitions of ideology that structure the critique of representation. Cultural production is viewed as a framework for the imposition of ideology, a framework which can be dissected and exposed as complicit in the formation of systems of social relations.

Materialist feminist criticism emphasizes the ideological nature of all cultural products. Dominant ideology has been naturalized as nonideology, since the perceptions of the more powerful have come to serve as standards for the less powerful, who do not have the same access to the media and artistic outlets that create public opinion. Ideology is implicit in perception, and therefore in any critical or creative act—analysis, description or interpretation. The intersection of materialist feminist criticism and postmodernism emphasizes that forms cannot be productively changed without an attendant change in ideology. Deconstructing the performance apparatus in postmodernist terms is not politically progressive unless the gender assumptions that underlie representation are also denaturalized and changed.[7]

Feminist theory suggests that representation offers or denies subjectivity by manipulating the terms of its discourse, images and myths through ideology. As a system of representation, ideology is related to social structures not as a simple mimetic reflection, but as a force that participates in creating and maintaining social arrangements.

Neither is representation simple mimesis, to reverse the equation. The theatre, that is to say, is not really a mirror of reality. A mirror implies passivity and noninvolvement, an object used but never changed by the variety of people who hold it up and look into it. The theatre has in fact been much more active as an ideological force. Materialist feminism focuses on the construction of ideology in social formations influenced by gender, race, class and categories of sexual preference. It views the power base in these relationships dialectically, as capable of change.

If power is a term that can be wielded fruitfully by women, as it sometimes is in materialist analysis, the passive, objectified nature of women as performers and spectators might be fundamentally changed. Chapter 4 looks at just such a possibility for change by proposing an alternative to narrative structured by male desire. This study recuperates the lesbian position from its desexualized stance in cultural feminism to suggest that if lesbian sexual desire motivates narrative, the lesbian spectator may be able to find a subject position vis-à-vis lesbian representation. The lesbian model of alternative spectatorship might hold clues to developing a more tenable position for feminist spectators of any ideological persuasion.

This study deconstructs the privileged position of the ideal white, middle-class, heterosexual male spectator from a feminist perspective. By displacing his hegemonic position and stealing his seat, as it were, for a feminist spectator who can cast an eye critical of dominant ideology, representation can be analyzed more precisely for the meanings it produces and how those meanings can be changed. The intent, by extension, is to affect a larger cultural change in the ideological and material condition of women and men.

Afterword

Envisioning a space-off of representation leads inevitably to a kind of utopianism. Where do you actually stand when you step outside of representation, and who stands with you? My text ends with the lesbian subject because I believe that personally, artistically and spectatorially, hers is closest to the view from elsewhere, and offers the most radical position from which to subvert representation.

Many lesbians "perform" themselves in everyday life as well as in the performance space. If all the world is in fact a stage—that is, if people are continually caught up in representation and ideology, and if we read the ideology of gender only through its representation—lesbians who assert their identity and their right to exist through their self-representations clearly have quite a lot at stake. The danger of representing lesbian sexuality in an era of political intolerance and sexual prudence requires an enormous personal investment from those willing to continue their public, gender-bending masquerades.

A lesbian on the street representing a subversion of gender ideology through a butch or femme role is in some ways the perfect illustration of the Brechtian "not . . . but," foregrounding for her unwitting spectators the in-betweens of nonpolarized gender identity. How this radical meaning can maintain itself in a more formal representational situation might be the continuing question for feminist performance criticism. How can radicalism be maintained in a representational economy that works to neutralize radical meanings?

This question implies a continual consideration of form, content and context in feminist work. For example, how can the formal experiments with old contents evidenced in the WOW Cafe work truly contribute to cultural change? How radical is the work if it continues to take place in an alternative context in which its spectators are mostly lesbians with a predisposition to the meanings the performances construct? Selling a lesbian text to mainstream spectators seems incongruous, but in the best of all possible worlds those spectators will come away from the performance thinking differently about their sexuality and gender assumptions.

Or maybe not. Perhaps the context will prevail, and the desire to consume the glittery Broadway product that hangs like an aura over that excited group of spectators waiting on the ubiquitous TKTS line in Times Square will obscure the meaning of what they see. Perhaps the precedent set, ironically, by the long Off-Broadway run of drag-performer Charles Busch's production *Vampire Lesbians of Sodom* will allow the spectators to contextualize a truly lesbian performance piece as just another incidence of harmless transvestism. Or maybe because the production does not fulfill spectators' expectations of traditional, realist drama, they will be angered and alienated for the wrong reasons, and will fail to achieve a more Brechtian state of understanding.

Time, as they, say, will tell. The larger question might be, How does social change really happen through cultural production? There is an attendant issue here. If the objective—idealistic though it might sound—is social change, what is the position of the feminist critic in relation to feminist cultural production? Economics and context once again loom into the picture. Precarious feminist theatre and performance groups need favorable documentation of their work to persuade funding organizations and audiences to continue their support. The feminist critic who writes frankly of a feminist production's problems risks a certain ostracism from the creative community. In the spirit of progress, however, it seems necessary to point out the limitations of even the most well-intentioned feminist work to institute a dialogue that resonates beyond the confines of an insular feminist community.

The process of reception and the entire hermeneutical endeavor will—and should—be different for different spectators. The meanings derived from any one performance will vary endlessly. For a feminist theatre to dictate a proper meaning is as ideologically and politically suspect as any of the mystifications implicitly condoned by the dominant culture's theatre.

But here, again, I bump against a contradiction in my own discourse. Several times, I have pointed out the dangers of pluralism, yet I seem to be arriving at it (although not advocating it) as I write the coda to my text. I do not believe that all feminist critical methodologies or performance practices are equally insightful or efficacious. I have explained my hesitations about liberal and cultural feminist approaches. I maintain that the materialist feminist approach to criticism and spectatorship has the most to offer in the effort toward radical cultural change.

Materialist feminism at least acknowledges the varied responses of spectators mixed across ideologies of gender, sexuality, race and class. By admitting to this heterogeneity, strategies for how to thwart the white, heterosexual, middle-class male's hegemony as the subject of representation can be formulated. Under materialism, these formulations will not include subsuming spectator differences under some comfortable, homogenous classification. On the contrary, the materialist creative and critical project will be located within those differences, which will inevitably demand new forms and provoke new meanings when they are inscribed in representation.

TOWARD A GESTIC FEMINIST CRITICISM

Elin Diamond

Gender, *Verfremdungseffekt*

The cornerstone of Brecht's theory is the *Verfremdungseffekt* ("alienation-effect"), the technique of defamiliarizing a word, an idea, a gesture so as to enable the spectator to see or hear it afresh.

A feminist practice that seeks to expose or mock the strictures of gender, to *reveal* gender-as-appearance. as the effect, not the precondition, of regulatory practices, usually uses some version of the Brechtian A-effect. That is, by alienating (not simply rejecting) iconicity, by foregrounding the expectation of resemblance, the ideology of gender is exposed and thrown back to the spectator. In Caryl Churchill's *Cloud 9*, cross-dressing that is not quite perfect, in which the male body can be detected in feminine clothes, provides broad A-effects for a gender critique of familial and textual norms in Victorian and present-day society.

The character is never the focal point on the Brechtian stage, but rather the always-dissimulated historical conditions that keep her from choosing and changing. The actor *shows* this, and shows his showing, displacing attention from virtuosic impersonation to demonstration—demonstration not *of* authority, but as praxis. A-effects are not easy to produce. But the payoffs, especially where gender is concerned, can be stunning. When gender is alienated or foregrounded, the spectator is able to see what s/he can't see: a sign system *as* a sign system. The appearance, words, gestures, ideas, attitudes that constitute the gender lexicon become illusionistic trappings that are *nevertheless* inseparable from, embedded in the body's habitus. Understanding gender as ideology—as a system of beliefs and behavior mapped across the bodies of women and men which reinforces social status quo—is to appreciate the continued timeliness of *Verfremdungseffekt*, the purpose of which always is to denaturalize and de-familiarize what ideology—and performativity—makes seem normal, acceptable, inescapable.

Dialectic in Brecht is a "zigzag" of contradictions. Each action must contain the trace of the action it represses, thus the meaning of each action contains difference. The audience is invited to look beyond representation—beyond what is authoritatively put in view to the possibilities of as yet unarticulated motives, actions or judgments.

The Brechtian "not . . . but" is the theatrical and theoretical analogue to "differences within." As such it ruins classical mimesis: the truth-modeling that produces self-identical subjects in coherent plots gives way utterly to the pleasure and significance of contradictions—and of contradictions that, at any given moment, are emerging but unseeable.

Historicization

Brecht understood social relations, particularly class relations, as part of a moving dialectic. The crux of "historicization" is change: through A-effects spectators observe the potential movement in class relations, discover the limitations and strengths of their own perceptions and begin to change their lives. Historicization is, then, *a way of seeing*, and the enemy of recuperation and appropriation. Realism disgusted Brecht nor only because it dissimulates its conventions but because it is hegemonic: by copying the surface details of the world it offers the illusion of lived experience, even as it marks off only one version of that experience. This is perhaps why the most innovative women playwrights refuse the seamless narrative of conflicting egos in classic realism. Consider, to name only one example, Suzan-Lori Parks's *The America Play* (1994), which stakes the real in memory, fantasy and verbal repetition not because historical experience is fragmented (which is true enough) but because, as Parks puts it, there isn't "enough history" for her or her African American characters.[1] Parks concretizes historical gaps by turning the stage into a "black hole" in which a mother and son commemorate their "Foundling Father," a composite of President Lincoln, absent father and minstrelsy impersonation.

Gestus

The explosive (and elusive) synthesis of alienation, historicization and the "not . . . but" is the Brechtian *gestus*, a gesture, a word, an action, a tableau by which, separately or in a series, the social attitudes encoded in the playtext become visible to the spectator. A famous *gestus* is Helene Weigel's snapping shut her leather money bag after each selling transaction in *Mother Courage* (1939), thereby underscoring the contradiction in profiteering and survival for Brecht, the social reality of war. In *Mother* (1994), Patricia Spears Jones's multimedia reimagining of Gorky's novel (and Brecht's use of it) in collaboration with Mabou Mines, spectators sit in fully functional kitchen areas surrounded by television sets, enabling them to watch live action or watch TV, or both. In her closing soliloquy, an educated embittered Mother (Ruth Maleczech) grabs a video camera and films herself face pressed up and distorted against the lens while speaking of her yearning for "transcendence"—a revolutionary leap beyond the suffering she witnesses.[2] In this agonized moment spectators' eyes dart uneasily between video screen and performer, creating with the latter a *gestus* that powerfully displays the contradictory relation between political agency and media manipulation, between humanist traditions of protest and postmodern environments.

Looking at the character, the spectator is constantly intercepted by the subject/actor, and the latter, heeding no fourth wall, is theoretically free to look back. The difference, then, between this triangle and the familiar oedipal one is that no one side signifies authority, knowledge or the law. Brechtian theatre depends on a structure of representation, on exposing and making visible, but what appears even in the *gestus* can only be provisional, indeterminate, nonauthoritative.[3]

This feminist rereading of the *gestus* makes room, at least theoretically, for a viewing position for the female spectator. Because the semiosis of the *gestus* involves the gendered bodies of spectator, subject/actor and character, all working together but *never harmoniously*, there can be no fetishization and no end to signification. A gestic feminist criticism would "alienate" or foreground those moments in a playtext when social attitudes about gender and sexuality conceal or disrupt patriarchal ideology. It would refuse to naturalize or valorize female dramatists, but would focus on historical material constraints in the production of images. It would attempt to engage dialectically with, rather than master, the playtext. And in generating meanings it would recover (specifically gestic) moments in which the historical actor, the character, the spectator *and* the author enter and disrupt the scopic regime of realist representation.

Robbie McCauley, *Indian Blood*

In Robbie McCauley's *Indian Blood*, the dream highway of upward mobility encounters the geography of racism and dispossession. Her narrative fragments cast back to a father's and grandfather's military service in various U.S. wars and a daughter's effort to rethink the psychic and political costs. The auratic images of a "father who was always in somebody's army, navy, air force, national guard" and who "longed to be a policeman" are given a dialectical "shock" in the daughter's stories. The father's and grandfather's devotion to and participation in the U.S. military gave them a public means of expressing citizenship, of supporting their families, of achieving a social status otherwise denied them, even as, by their very participation, they helped reproduce the institutional apartheid of the military they served. Charging up San Juan Hill with Teddy Roosevelt's Rough Riders, McCauley Senior served in the All Black Regiment in the Spanish-American war—a war that produced definitive U.S. hegemony in Central and South America, and intensified the killing and the expropriation of the culture and land of indigenous populations. "And always there were the Indian Wars": her grandfather helped ambush Native Americans returning from Canada. While McCauley sees these military triumphs as service to the racist white supremacy that has destroyed African American life during and since slavery, these accomplishments, duly recorded in her grandfather's discharge papers, save his son's family (barely) from racist attacks in 1950s America. Most excruciating, with the military honors accorded her patriarchs for helping to annihilate the Indians, comes McCauley's recognition that she and her forebears on her paternal grandmother's side have "Indian blood." Annihilation of the Indians is self-annihilation. The shedding of "Indian blood" signifies not only the brutality of capitalist expansionism in U.S. history and in McCauley's family history but also the inevitable self-destruction that racism produces, and always disavows.

The multiple temporalities of memory, history and embodiment are laid bare in McCauley's opening moments of *Indian Blood*, an "opening" that, in the traditions of experimental theatre since the 1960s, she makes spatially indeterminate. As the audience take their seats, the McCauley persona is in our walkway cutting apples, munching a sandwich, watching us, nodding, being watched. The musicians, a pianist/singer, a clarinetist/saxophonist and a guitarist, who will improvise on a score ranging from free jazz to soul to banjo picking, begin to play and McCauley removes the apples. She stretches and, almost as an afterthought, as though the mode of address between herself and her spectators had not yet been settled, announces:

> Sometimes I think that if I could get my body free, I could be free. 'Course that's not the way it is. A regular old socialist can tell you that one can't be free till all are free.

This wishful mimesis between the one and the all, the promise of American democracy, and its inevitable disappointment in American life, generates mimetic correspondences throughout *Indian Blood*, between fragments of McCauley's life and patterns of social and political oppression.

For McCauley, the historical systemic roots of racism breed the ubiquitous wars her military patriarchs fought (wars—and honorable service that did nothing to alter racism either in or out of the service). For the Marxist McCauley all wars are imperialist, especially the Indian wars, whose expropriations of land and life mark her life experiences ("It took me years to figure out reasons for Daddy's anger") and extend beyond her conscious experience.

The mold of the late twentieth-century cosmos is set by war-times and her decades are locked into correspondence with them. McCauley tells stories and tells history as interwoven exercises. But what stories and how to tell them?

> I told you about San Juan Hill like Grandfather was some kind of hero. I said he went up that hill and talked it over with his Indian brothers, that he apologized for taking their land to give to the Americans . . . that Grandfather and 'em were just doing their job in order to survive. Well history not remembered gets told anyway.

McCauley demonstrates that it is only experience as it arises *involuntarily*, through mimetic associations, through unguarded correspondences, that can deliver the meaning of unremembered shocks. It's the historical richness of experience, of history *as* experience, that McCauley longs for.

> I remember seeing chain gang trucks down in Georgia. Black men in prison clothes huddled down. White men standing with a gun. I remember the [military] convoy trucks too. Black men in fatigues up inside. I used to get the chain gang trucks and the convoy trucks mixed up. I used to run 'longside looking for my Daddy. Everyone said he was off in somebody's war when I was born.

Invoking a complex loved father is, for McCauley, a destructive act; to seize hold of his memory is to find herself again in a moment of danger. A disciplined performer, McCauley pushes her voice into dissonant scat-singing, clutches her head, wrings her hands, explodes in rage, whirls, collapses. In the rush of images above, "Daddy" is not the performer's madeleine but rather seeking him (again and again) is. And in this angry memorial, she, like all desirers, seeks him ("run[ning] 'longside") where she can never find him: in his "male mythology" of hard-drinking, chain-smoking homo-social heroism, his world of uniforms, guns, honorable discharge papers, and American pride, "He loved America!" she shouts.

To redeem that love (as his legacy) is to *recognize* its dialectical pain: the strength and self-betrayal that underpin loyalty to America's government and institutions.

McCauley wants to wrest non-bourgeois traditions of black survival—visionary politics, ingenuity, wit, artmaking, spirituality, community awareness—away from the old/new modes of mythic thinking. She refuses to endorse a progress fantasy that tolerates so much suffering. McCauley's techniques of transformation—images and music—display the history of experimental theatre in the twentieth century. Full-sized projections are expanded images from historical documents, private and public of the Middle Passage, of meetings between early American colonists and Indian tribes; of her father in uniform, of the black regiment under Teddy Roosevelt, of the young McCauley and Daddy leaning against the family Buick. The images of public and private documents, evanescently projected, document McCauley's effort to expand experience through historical memory—through memories that we cannot consciously remember. The projections, then, are also projections in the psychic sense, flickering pieces of internal trauma that await their redemption: "I turn around," says McCauley, "and there they are" (a daguerreotype of the black regiment suddenly appears).

McCauley's performance makes clear that her redemption of these unsung heroes has nothing to do with what is officially remembered; she will not and cannot narrativize the fragments of memory that these images convey. Instead she offers us glimpses and tries to catch us off guard. Moving between two microphones that establish the key playing spaces, McCauley's words, both spoken and scat-sung, pointedly mime the dissonance of one of the musicians' jazz phrasing—

When we moved *up*-south-to D-C it was the stran-*gest* a-part-*theid* town

—a syncopation that, as Brecht wanted, alienates the line's disturbing content. Such A-effects in turn open the spectator to the social vista of black culture's (particularly jazz's) commodification as well as its continuity as a source of communal inspiration. To give it the appropriate dialectical turn, a Marxist homily needs to be sung *and* swung.

Ra-ci-sm is based on class, is *caste* biased, *is* class, *is* class, is cla-ss biased

But in this instance she can't keep up her part in a jazz improvisation. She speeds up, blurs the words till one of the musicians summons her back. Far from sugarcoating the message, the music intensifies its strangeness.

Having established from the outset an experimental Brechtian style for her piece, she dons army gear and comments on the problematic of survival. Miming her grandfather, she stands at attention with her gun-prop raised:

The blood was everywhere
Grandfather took a deep breath.
He'd got one more Indian
Now he was alone with his thoughts and a smoking gun
[Speaking loudly in the voice of her grandfather]
"To be on guard like this is a great opportunity for a colored man."
[Returns to her own voice.]

Grandfather was a Father Courage with the paradoxes of parents who lead their tribe through the wars.

[She sits and slowly removes the Army coat from her shoulder and resumes her narrative tone]:

It was my grandmother P's grandmother who had Indian blood. Actually they said she was half Indian. That's what they said when one of the parents was a full-blooded Indian and one was real black . . . she was a full-blooded half-blood [McCauley rolls her eyes] . . . and they said that everyone down that line on that side was 1/2 Indian. They used to tell me *I* had Indian blood [she opens her arms to audience], that I had orange undertones to my skin, that I looked good in green . . . [audience laughs nervously].

Gently mocking family and folk rhetoric on bloodlines, McCauley helps us produce her dialectical image. Having gazed with detached interest at old photographic reproductions of Indian tribes, our eyes are suddenly riveted on the body that brings those images "to life," a body no longer instantiating the racial "substance" we had taken for granted. What really do we see? orange undertones? "mixed" blood? Is this a "black" woman?[4]

The transformation of auratic body into dialectical image shocks our consciousness. McCauley, by displaying her body as auratic object, subtly causes us to racialize her, to identify (and *fail* to identify her) by race. Which means we all take a tiger's leap into the past. We suddenly glimpse the performer's body not as unique, separate, esoteric, but constellated with an unknown black woman on an auction block, a site where blood amid skin once spoke with perfect clarity to those invested in maintaining racial markings.[5] In the closing moments of the performance, McCauley opens for the first time that battered suitcase that has come to signify her "full-blooded half-blood" great-grandmother. As the music grows loud and cacophonous she reads from a sheaf of yellowed government documents the official commendation to her grandfather for helping to exterminate the Indians. The soldier's achievement is dialectically intertwined with the extinction of his ancestral family. In a reprise of the moment described above, McCauley shouts: "They say I have Indian blood, well I think I have it on my hands!" Shaking her head the performer reaches out for the catharsis. But for the spectator the transformation of auratic body into dialectical image has offered another pleasure, that of experiencing "historical existence": the relief of awakening.

FEMINISM AND PSYCHOANALYSIS

Janelle Reinelt

Perhaps because performance directly involves corporeal individuals breathing, thinking, speaking, moving in front of other similar organisms, the intimate questions of human behavior have always been central to performance.

Sigmund Freud, the foundational theorist of psychoanalysis,[1] viewed human life as a materially grounded struggle to ensure survival. The pleasure principle, in dialectical relationship with the reality principle, determines individuals to forgo personal gratification in order to obtain other goals, ultimately connected with survival. Freud divides the subject into unconscious and preconscious in *The Interpretation of Dreams* (1900) and into id, ego and superego in his later work (e.g., *New Introductory Lectures* [1933]). For the earlier Freud the unconscious was the seat of primary processes seeking gratification in the most direct way possible, while the secondary processes of the preconscious mediated and delayed gratification, responding to cultural determinants by insisting on circuitous ways of achieving pleasure. Since the two reacted to one another, the unconscious as well as the preconscious (and of course the conscious) were materially grounded in culture. In his later work Freud tended to stress the overlap between conscious and preconscious and to describe the id as pure drive for pleasure, uncontrolled by cultural prohibition. The ego is the seat of adjustment to the reality principle, and the superego is a kind of bank of repressions and taboos which also functions as an image of the ideal other, usually based on the father.

We have certain basic needs that are mediated by our dependence on a "family" who meets these needs in infancy; enter the oedipal crisis. Since children are learning language at about the same time that they discover sexual difference, sexuality and language become intertwined. The child must learn how to negotiate the desire for the mother (source of direct pleasure. e.g., the breast) over and against the authority of the father. Simultaneously, he or she must learn the symbolic order, the determinate network of social roles that are legitimated by society and authorized by the father. Repression of desire is thus the price for successful socialization.

While this semiotization of the psyche was only implicit in Freud, Jacques Lacan significantly modified the intimate geography under discussion through his insistence that the unconscious is structured like a language.[2]

For Lacan, transcending Freud, the oedipal crisis is not just a crisis of the body; it is refigured as a social crisis of language acquisition. The fear of castration is not just the fear of losing or lacking the male appendage; it is the fear of not having the power to participate in the male-determined logic of signification.

The "mirror stage" might be seen as one of the Lacanian enhancements of Freud which is especially useful for performance theory. Here the individual child first "sees" his image (always "his" with Lacan) outside of himself and identifies this "picture" of a unified self as itself. It is, however, utterly Other, an ideal self, a culturally constituted self (since by now perception too has been conditioned). The child will henceforward desire to recapture and to be congruent with this image of self, will also mourn for the lost self, which is forever absent. This notion of the mirror stage has been especially useful for performance studies because of the analogy between it and the mimetic mirror of the stage, which reflects representations of the self and its world.

Besides demystifying the nature of such representation, however, Lacan provides an explanation of why spectators are in thrall to these representations, why their desiring apparatus is set in motion each time a stage mirror simulates this experience. Many of the basic theoretical questions of dramatic theory touch on this psychological process: the role and purpose of aesthetic experience, the Aristotelian notion of catharsis (what happens to spectators when they view), the Platonic/Aristotelian debates about the danger/good of mimesis, the question of presence in acting theory (or, more historically, the association between the character of the actor and the character of the play), the modern discourse on the role of empathy, and the benefits of alienation in receiving representation. All these topics can be seen as intimately linked to the paradigm of the mirror stage.

WOMEN, WOMAN AND THE SUBJECT OF FEMINISM: FEMINIST DIRECTIONS

Esther Beth Sullivan

The notion of *feminist* theory did not spring to life with poststructuralist discourse. Rather, feminists have been theorizing subjectivity by means of their work, struggle and/or "practice" for years, and post-structural theory—with its attention to how we know what we know—has augmented the already ongoing feminist project of understanding the effects of sociopolitical and epistemological structures. The notion that feminism would find its direction by affirming identity is still a vital and fundamental point of coalition among feminists. Moreover, because theatre is essentially tied to identity and identification, or tied to seeing who we are in flesh and blood, feminist theatres and dramatists have found themselves dealing concretely with issues of identity politics. But, if ideology is pervasive and its very nature is to mask the force of its power, can one trust "herstory" to be any less influenced by ideological assumptions than "history"? Can one assume that women-centered contexts are safe from the forces that institute privilege, hierarchy and oppression?

While feminist dramatists continue to focus on the legitimation of women's experiences and the underrepresentation of such experience, some feminists have augmented that focus by undertaking analyses of how gender is ideologically constructed. This inquiry into gender as construction resulted in a distinction between real, historical beings who are women and the fictional Woman who has been drawn in and by dominant ideology supposedly to represent them. According to theorists such as Teresa de Lauretis, while this Woman has been taken as a representation of women, she more accurately represents "other-than-man," "site of sexuality and masculine desire" and "object of men's social exchange."[1] Incorporating this new direction, the project of deconstructing Woman has been undertaken by feminist scholars and dramatists in order to evidence its oppressive ideology—an ideology that causes women to think of themselves as "objects" rather than "subjects," as passive rather than active, and as an effect of meaning rather than a producer of meaning.

Extrapolating from Jacques Lacan, psycho-semiotic theory is taken to be an examination of subjectivity that is grounded in the primal, psychological impact of the subject's entry into language, or the oedipal experience. According to Lacan, in order to achieve discursive mastery a subject relinquishes its experiential access to the world, or the "real," when that access becomes mediated by language, or the "symbolic." Inasmuch as entry into the symbolic is predicated upon an exchange of "fullness of being" for "fullness of meaning," this exchange is metaphorically symbolized by Lacan as relinquishing the sign of masculine fullness, the penis, for symbolic fullness, the phallus.[2] Feminists look to Lacan's explanation of subject processes in order to understand how the world is defined in a way that privileges some subjects over others. Such investigations then proceed into the realm of discourse, and they examine the effects of discursive practices in the formation of gender identifications and privileges. In doing so, such critiques question Lacan's process of definition. While Lacan stresses the metaphoric character of the penis/phallus image, even as an abstraction the phallus invokes explicit notions of possession: one either has the phallus or one doesn't. In this case privilege is established by the process of oppositional definition: there is only the one difference of having or not having, of being the subject *or* the object, of penetrating/producing *or* being penetrated/objectified. Kaja Silverman points out that "the male subject 'pays' for his symbolic privileges with a currency not available to the female subject" and furthermore that "male subjectivity is defined in terms which rigorously exclude women both at the anatomical and cultural levels."[3] Silverman goes on to argue that this characterization bespeaks a "cultural projection by means of which man can always be assured of having the phallus" as well as "justifying the exclusion of the female subject from symbolic authority and privilege."[4] Consequently, in her difference Woman comes to represent everything other than and opposite to Man. Woman is constructed as something to be acted upon as contrasted to the masculine actant, as a space or territory to be penetrated as contrasted to the masculine penetrator, and as a sight to be gazed upon as contrasted to the Man who does the gazing.[5] Inasmuch as real women come to identify with this representation of Woman, de Lauretis argues that women are "coerced" into submissive, deprivileged experiences, and while "women's consent may not be gotten easily [it] is finally gotten, and has been for a long time, as much by rape and economic coercion as by the more subtle and lasting effects of ideology, representation, and identification."[6]

In large part the momentum to understand how ideology functions has come from Europe by way of Marxist and post-structuralist theory. But the project of figuring out how consciousness is conditioned by the messages that are ideologically implanted in our minds has certainly not been ignored by American scholars and dramatists. In relation to this project Adrienne Kennedy's work comes to the foreground with plays such as *Funnyhouse of a Negro, The Owl Answers* and *A Movie Star Has to Star in Black and White* (1988). Kennedy focuses on the way in which characters constructed by the texts and contexts of their lives [and] presents the complexity of identity that has been claimed as well as ideologically affixed to African Americans, and particularly African American women.

Unlike early surrealists, who relied upon sexual bipolarity as the paradigmatic problem for Man's inability to reconcile the conscious and subconscious worlds, Kennedy foregrounds sexual bipolarity as a cultural construction fostered by desire-producing industries such as "Hollywood" and "great literature"—industries that have made it clear that to be a movie star you have to be white and to be great you have to be a man or be desired by a man. In her "acts of the mind" she focuses on how race and gender are produced rather than natural,[7] therefore exposing ideology and its power to overtly and covertly discriminate against all "others." The psychosocial consequence of this discrimination surfaces in Clara in *Movie Star*: "Each day I wonder with what or with whom can I coexist in a true union?"

Critiques of ideology have expanded our awareness; however, in a strange way they have also had a paralyzing effect. If ideology is assumed to be everywhere and always pervasive and its powers absolute, the best that any of us can hope for is consciousness. For feminists who continue to ground their theory/practice in the affirmative stance that action can be taken to change circumstances, the belief in an unalterable and omnipotent ideology is untenable. Without ignoring the force of ideological conditioning some feminists are now beginning to assert the existence of margins in which women, in particular, are both inside ideology, being objectified according to the construction of Woman, and outside ideology, noting that they are not the Woman of dominant discourse. It is in these marginal spaces that some feminists are placing the possibility for affirmative theory/practice and for disruption of the more centrally dominating forces of ideology.

At the same time, though, feminists were forced by their own increasing understanding of ideology to question the single-mindedness of analyses that focused solely on sexual difference. That is, while women focus solely on the effects of patriarchal oppression and the effects of gender ideology, they de-emphasize the many different forces that impact and oppress women—forces that produce class structure, racism, homophobia and the like.

Theresa de Laurentis posits that there is a space created at the point at which we recognize that we are not what ideology would have us be. Such awareness exists in margins that provide a vantage from which to understand our differences—that is, our difference from ideological constructs and imperatives as well as the differences that constitute community and individual identities. Micro-political practice is that activity that aims at understanding the margins, empowering those who inhabit such margins to represent themselves, and encouraging critiques that account for the ways in which ideology works first and foremost at home.

While marginalized experience has served as the thematic thrust of several feminist theatre groups and many feminist plays, a micro-political practice implies more than plots that deal with racism, sexism and homophobia. It involves the investigation of discursive practices—ways of seeing, defining and understanding experience—and their relationship to marginalized experience and micro-political agency. Keeping this in mind, I turn to *Beauty and the Beast*, a production that was created by the Split Britches company beginning in 1983.

Beauty and the Beast conflates dramatic genres and asserts its difference not simply as a classic fairy tale nor as a vaudeville show. The play opens with a Salvation Army troupe attempting to dramatize "Beauty and the Beast" in order to raise money. Tina Margolis describes the ensuing action: "To fill out the bill—and escape the grave seriousness of their morality tale—the troupe performs specialty numbers as entr'acte material. The characters and roles include a pious-yet-repressed Salvation Army sergeant/elocutionist/Beauty (Lois Weaver); a Hassidic rabbi/father/stand-up comic, who is performing to pay for new Torah scrolls for his shul (Deborah Margolin); and an 86-year-old hoofer, the Beast, who thinks she's James Dean (Peggy Shaw)."[8] Through the course of the play, the tale of "Beauty and the Beast" is broken up with a reading from *Macbeth*, an impersonation of Tony Bennett songs such as "Kitty from Kansas City" and "It's Impossible," and a section of classical ballet featuring the Beast and the Jewish rabbi, who sports a tutu.

Sue-Ellen Case argues that in this interrupted narrative a different subject position is realized. Theorized as a "collective subject," this subject is not characterized by the traditional attributes of wholeness and coherence, nor is this subject constituted/contained within or even across the texts of the drama.[9] Rather, a subject position is established that collects significance from the text, context and personae of the performers in the specificity of their intentional margin. The collecting of subjectivity is most obvious in *Beauty and the Beast*, as performers collect characters one on top of the other. Loaded with highly contextual signs that mark the specificity of this marginal space, *Beauty and the Beast* does not offer the possibility of an unspecified, universal subject nor even the possibility of a universalized female subject. It is the subject of feminism that one finds in this kind of theatre—a subject marked in both theory and practice by its micro-political intent.

PERFORMING GENDER DISRUPTIONS

"NOT . . . BUT"/"NOT-NOT-ME": MUSINGS ON CROSS-GENDER PERFORMANCE

Rhonda Blair

We use cross-gender performance to challenge traditional representations, to illuminate gender-as-construction and to provide actors (especially women) with access to a broader range of roles than they would otherwise have. Cross-gender casting expands a director's range in conceptualizing a production and can subvert conventional representation and realism. Crossing genders is also simply a way to increase the pleasure and fun of theatrical work.[1] This work is more complicated than just having a man play a woman or a woman play a man. A binary view of gender, which divides us or the characters we play into "Woman" and "Man" along comfortable, normal lines, may feel convenient because it is familiar, but it does not account for the subtle permutations that gender takes on in life or art. The oscillations of identity an actor moves through in performing the other gender is in fact a process of finding that ostensible Other in the self.

Viewing gender as an active construction linked to other sociocultural factors denaturalizes it and makes it possible to see it as a flow of signs, rather than an essential attribute of a character that must be mirrored or duplicated by the performer.

In the past twelve years I have directed productions that crossed gender more or less consciously in various ways and with various motives. The first was *Waiting for Godot* in 1978, which I naively called a feminist production because I changed the characters into women and because the company was composed entirely of women.

Technically, our Godot was more a cross-gender translation than a cross-gender performance of the text, although both strategies call into question gender relations and hierarchies.

When I directed Pavel Kohout's *Poor Murderer* I had not intended to play around with gender at all. At auditions, however, there was more strength among the women than the men, and I had difficulty finding a man to play the Doctor, a key role. My vision was limited by the blinders of realism and compulsory heterosexuality. Though valid as far as they went, my choices for *Poor Murderer* and for *Godot* were rudimentary and rather generic: I inserted women into male texts and simply got more women onstage.

But I was slowly becoming more aware of how a theatre production functioned as a semiotic system and how one change in that system (e.g., casting a woman rather than a man in a role) would affect the meanings of relationships in the play as a whole. The fact is *any* configuration is possible if one can find the right code for the production.

I played with this more consciously in *The Zoo Story* in the early 1980s. I cast two women and two men. Under the influence of Megan Terry's *Comings and Goings* and Spolin's theatre games, the actors alternated in and out of roles and spoke simultaneously at certain moments to punctuate certain points and to provide compositional variety to the piece. The performance style was dynamic and kinetically oriented, rather than realistic, due to both the gender switching and the multiple/split characterizations: actors stepped in and out of roles with great frequency and even moved directly from one role to another.

The way we played with permutations of gender and aggression recast the erotic and sadomasochistic elements of the script. As the configuration of actors changed from male/male to male/female to female/female, the audience was confronted with their own responses to aggression, anomie and desire; they were "reading" the surface male/male text against the gender permutations going on beneath it. The actors did not disappear into the characters; they showed us the story—performing, rather than "being," the character. The foregrounding of difference between actor and character was further enhanced because the actors remained onstage throughout the performance. The actors were passionately invested in playing intentions strongly. In short, we were playing with the semiotics of a Brechtian/feminist *gestus*.

In 1985 I staged Caryl Churchill's *Cloud 9*, which deliberately uses cross-gender casting to illuminate gender-as-social construction; it plays with contradictions between actor and character gender and between the characters' mandated social roles and their desires. The cast was impressive, but their very competence gave rise to an interesting issue in relation to cross-gender performance and the critical *gestus*. A reporter who saw a dress rehearsal and who knew in advance about Churchill's cross-gender role requirements asked, "Why did you have Betty in Act I played by a woman?" "I didn't," I replied. "That was a man."

Does cross-gender casting count if the gender of the performer is erased? I do not think it did in this case, for the discrepancy between the gender of the actor and the gender of the character is where much of the meaning of the play lies. At least one moment early in the performance needed to present this actor as a biological male.

The actor who played Betty/Jerry in *Cloud 9* was gifted and well-trained, yet in early rehearsals his approach to Betty was not working. He initially played Betty as being extremely aware and angry about her lot; that is, he played his *response* to Betty rather than playing Betty; more directly, he had difficulty imagining things from inside of *her* body, seeing things through *her* eyes, with *her* history. Much of the humor authenticity of the character resides in the contradictions between her conscious and unconscious impulses. In this phase of rehearsal the actor was projecting his own consciousness onto Betty. He had to shift his performative identification from his own awareness of the workings of social/gender hierarchies to that of someone caught within them unawares and struggling to make the best of a bad lot. In seeing her as not-me-but-my-mother he could not see Betty as a not-not-me, i.e., someone contained within himself. We took our solution directly from Stanislavski. We focused on specific given circumstances in the text, defined a simple, active super-objective—"I want to be liked, I want to be accepted"—and found substitutions from his own experience.

While the purpose of a cross-gender performance for an audience might be to illuminate the cultural and political implications of a *not-me*, the actor must still embrace a *not-not-me*, taking a mental and physical leap into the Other. The director's task is always somehow to help the actor find that Other, the *not-me*, in her- or himself. It is still all about the director creating an articulate, theatrically compelling production and the actor successfully making the transition into playing a *not-not-me* with conviction and panache. But feminist cross-gender performance is set apart from many other theatrical modes because it is simultaneously committed to a conscious critical perspective *and* to the contingent and highly personal nature of performance.

FOCUS ON THE BODY: PAIN, PRAXIS AND PLEASURE IN FEMINIST PERFORMANCE

Jeanie Forte

The artist as erotic agent can operate to dismantle the appearance of sexual offerings, as in Karen Finley's transgressive performances. In *The Constant State of Desire* (1987) the very title promises a protracted stimulation of our innermost urges, a furtive titillation of that mysterious state, when instead we are bombarded with horrific descriptions of noxious sexual acts, incest, suicides, degradation, torture and male castration for revenge.[1] While Finley sometimes disrobes in her work, her body is not the passive nude of classical representation, as she covers herself with food, candy, ashes, or feathers, curiously evoking both self-abuse and sensual self-pleasuring. The myriad, usually perverse forms of sexuality are described in first person but from different personae, including male teenagers, small girls, old men, etc.—the effect of which is to put "Karen Finley" under erasure, deconstructing the problematics of representation and throwing into question the spectators' relationship to desire.[2] Here her erotic agency is expressed through refusal, a defiance of consumption as object by aggressively destroying both the object of fantasy and the potential alternative.

Marianne Goldberg's dance-text performances (what she calls her Body-Word Series), in marked contrast, provide another mode of erotic agency, her sensual exploration of her body's impulses and pleasures. Whether speaking a text herself or working with voice-over, Goldberg uses her body to intervene with unrehearsed movement, breaking the illusion of cohesive narrative through the assertion of bodily pleasure in gesture. In one performance of *Hudson Rover* (1989) she rolls on the floor, slowly wrapping and then unwrapping her (clothed) body in blue fabric, seemingly oblivious to anything other than the feel of hard and soft surfaces. A video camera is passed among the audience members as each is invited to tape a portion of the performance—a move that foregrounds the act of spectatorship, also serving to exaggerate Goldberg's representational status as performing body. By constantly interrupting the text with various forms of "body," she further counteracts the gazing process, creating an erotic atmosphere of body awareness, breaking the audience's identification with the abstraction of language. Rather than invoking sex or sexual desire, Goldberg's work focuses on her subjective pleasure in her own body and its possibilities for movement, a focus that nevertheless generates a kind of tension some spectators apparently find disturbing. I feel it is her ability to demonstrate pleasure, her refusal of objectification in her articulation of body as artist-agent which disturbs, which confronts the masculinist ideology embedded in conventions of representation.

CRITIQUE OF POSTMODERN THEORY, CONCLUSION: 1990s AND BEYOND

Patti P. Gillespie

In the 1990s, several major shifts within feminist theories of theatre seemed to be underway.

One: A Shift from Women in Theatre to Theatre in Feminism

Recent studies stress the relationship of theatre to feminism, exploring ways in which theatre ignores, rejects or promotes the political goals of feminism. This shift, dimly visible by the late 1980s in books by Case and Dolan, was made clear and explicit with the publication of Gayle Austin's *Feminist Theories for Dramatic Criticism* (1990), whose very title captured the changed relationship among feminists, theory and criticism in theatre. One important sign of this shift is that contemporary theories of feminism, rather than traditional theories of theatre, now dominate feminists' discussion of theatre.

Feminism itself is apparently only one part of a tendency emerging in the larger intellectual community, where theory seems to be taking the place of philosophy and where "intertextual references" are taking the place of traditions of inquiry.[1]

To jettison the tradition of theatrical theory in favor of contemporary networks of reference may be unwise, however. Feminist historian Gerda Lerner suggests a danger: "It is the relationship of women to history which explains the nature of female subordination, the causes for women's cooperation in the process of their subordination, the condition for their opposition to it, [and] the rise of feminist consciousness."[2] Nonetheless, if the admittedly small sample offered by recent books is representative, we can expect feminist theories in theatre to ignore or repudiate the long tradition of theatrical theory (excepting Brecht) in favor of contemporary theories derived from other fields and adapted for theatre.[3]

Two: A Shift from Feminism to Feminisms

Feminist studies in theatre are paralleling trends within contemporary feminism and within film and literary studies. According to life-cycle theories of development, a rhetorical or social movement (of which contemporary feminism is certainly one) forms when a period of unfocused dissatisfaction gives way before an energetic cohering, a stage marked by a sense of *urgency* (the problem needs attention now) and *community* (together we face an external enemy).

As a movement expands, however, its sense of community and urgency erodes in the face of organizational requirements and increasing membership. Issues thought simple are found to be complex. The group's attention turns in on itself. Then, unless new factors intervene and reenergize it, the movement will most likely either collapse or accommodate itself to the system.[4]

Feminism's current emphasis on celebrating difference can be understood as a response to the emergence of strong conflicting claims within feminism's enlarged community.[5]

Despite diversity in discussions and performances, however, diversity in theorizing actually seemed to decline. By 1990, feminist theorists of theatre seemed to be deeply committed to post-structural epistemology and materialist conviction. While feminists in general and in theatre are celebrating difference, those publishing in the area of feminist theatrical theories, although talking about difference, are displaying a single point of view, one drawn from a special kind of postmodernism and a special kind of socialism. The emerging theoretical hegemony in theatre thus appears at odds with both current feminism and traditional theatrical theory.

Three: A Shift from Drama to Theatre

Feminists see the shift from an aesthetics of text (which affects spectators) to an aesthetics of reception (where spectators are central to the event) as an opportunity to study and celebrate difference: whereas defining text as central to the theatrical experience means conceptualizing a single element in control, defining spectators as central means stressing the different responses of individual spectators. By adopting an aesthetics of reception, therefore, feminists in theatre lend support to feminism itself, which is now dedicated to honoring difference.[6] Second, explaining diverse responses in terms of diverse experiences (experiences that are themselves rooted in time and place) underscores the historic nature of life (and art) and so the possibility of change. Thus, feminists' interest in spectators embraces not only their role as makers of aesthetic experience (as in theatre studies generally) but also their role as makers of political change.

Four: A Shift from Originals to Derivations

Feminists ignoring or rejecting two thousand years of (male) dramatic theory as a source for a new feminist poetics is understandable. Their heavy reliance on about fifty years of (equally male) literary and film theory however, is less understandable. Postmodernism has been attacked from several sides, both for its detachment from the real world and for its reliance on a dense technical jargon.[7]

Postmodernism is not alone in being condemned: contemporary film theory (from which feminist film theory derives) has been under sustained, perhaps even lethal, attack. Noel Carroll, for example, concluded that contemporary film theory depends on basic assumptions, crucial ones of which are highly implausible; it rests on little evidence and much of that is hopelessly flimsy; it depends for many of its central tenets on arguments by analogy, arguments dangerously weakened inasmuch as neither one of the terms of the analogy is well understood; it unfolds in language so systematically ambiguous that the theory turns out to be nothing more than an "extended exercise in equivocation."[8]

Finally, feminists in theatre are adapting adaptations. That is, they are adapting feminist theories in politics, literature and film that are themselves adaptations of (male) theories, altered to make them take women's experience into account. For example, feminists have adapted traditional Marxist analyses of class so that the analyses can explain women's oppression (by defining women as a class, for example).

Raising such issues is in no way meant to demean the efforts or accomplishments of feminists now working in theatrical theory. The problems facing any feminist theorist of theatre are severe indeed. When a feminist amends an existing theory to make it take account of women's experiences, as did feminist film theories with Lacan's work, she still, inevitably, places male names, male ideas and male voices at the center. To adapt a theory is not to erase its (male) authors. Feminist theorists indeed have a dilemma: If men remain at the center, then women remain at the margins and feminist scholars do not disrupt patriarchal patterns. If, on the other hand, feminists reject or ignore tradition, they lose the wisdom of the past.

Feminist theatrical theories can revitalize theatre studies. By daring to see and name the gender-locked theories of the past and by challenging women's marginal roles in drama and theatre, feminists' theories of theatre can restore to cultural consciousness the history and the present position of women in theatre, onstage and off. By returning to theories developed earlier (for other purposes) and teasing from them insights about women, feminists can bring new life to old theories—those that they deconstruct as well as those that they amend. In this way, they will revive both women and theory for theatre.

Finally, by seeing both women and theatre in new ways, such theories can even risk new visions of what theatre might become.

INVENTIVE ANGLES OF VISION

ABOUT FACE: PERFORMING RACE IN FASHION AND THEATRE

Dorinne Kondo

In these essays, vignettes and interviews, I explore the ways Japanese fashion and Asian American theatre illuminate the politics of pleasure, the performance of race and the possibilities for intervention in a regime of commodity capitalism. Fashion and theatre provide illuminating points of entry into this complex nexus of issues. Both are key arenas for the performance of identities, from the "individual" to the "national." Spectacle and staging are necessarily elements of each, whether on the theatrical stage, on a runway or in the more mundane settings of everyday life, as we perform ourselves with the costumes, props and theatrical conventions at our disposal. Accordingly, both fashion and theatre highlight the performativity of gender, race and nation. And through enacting/subverting familiar tropes of these and other identities, Japanese fashion and Asian American theatre in turn become interventions—contestatory and/or problematic—in circulating Orientalist discourses.

Orientalist discourses are racial discourses, for Orientalist tropes figure "race" for Middle Eastern, Asian and Asian American subjects in the U.S. context. When "race" is enunciated at the contemporary historical moment, the black-white binary is immediately invoked, and race becomes the marked term designating "black" or "people of color," while "white" remains the unmarked site of privilege. *About Face* implicitly problematizes the black-white binary and essentialist notions of racial hierarchy, which create separate, bounded racial groups and place them on a single continuum along the black-white axis.

In the 1960s, "Asian American" emerged as a political coalition that united under a single banner people from many different nations (including former historical rivals, antagonists and colonizer/colonized), who were marked by different immigration histories and positioned differently with regard to class, gender and sexuality, in order to combat the specific racisms that face "Asian Americans" in the United States.[1] In part, the term is a more politically vigorous replacement for "Oriental" and the latter's racist mystifications and exoticisms.

I am concerned primarily with what I call counter-Orientalisms: specifically, the ways in which Asian American theatre and Japanese fashion might mobilize this subversive potential. They create sites for the production and performance of contestory wish-images in the form of racial, gender, national and transnational identities. I seek to reclaim pleasure as a site of potential contestation that might engage, and at times be coextensive with, the critical impulse. How we dress, how we move, the music that accompanies our daily activities and that we recreate and refashion, our engagement with—and not simply the passive consumption of—media or commodities, do matter and can be included in a repertoire of oppositional strategies.

Pleasure, aesthetics and popular culture can all motivate a culture politics that makes a difference. They can be part of what gets you through the day, what my mother calls "giving you a lift." Can you wear lipstick and still think? Can you care about design, color, texture, cut, draping, drafting techniques, display—that is, about clothes—and still be political? Of course, concern with the aesthetic production of the subject re-inscribes certain class and gender stereotypes. The mistake is in thinking that the other position—ostensibly not caring about clothing or appearance, which in itself is a form of preoccupation with appearance—is politically innocent. Such a position is over-determined in terms of its re-inscription of masculinities, and as some women of color (both gay and straight) would argue, of race. After all, who can afford to be unconcerned about his/her appearance? Who is *allowed* to ignore it with impunity? Gender, sexuality and race may condition the degree to which we are conscious of the ways we perform ourselves in everyday life, of the ways fashion and theatre perform *us*.

Clothing can have a political edge as signifiers of subcultural style and as components of ethnic/racial pride: indeed, I would argue that in the early 1980s Japanese clothing design enabled a valorization and eroticizing of Asian bodies as stylish in a contemporary way, rather than merely exotic or an inadequate imitation of Western bodies. At times, the surfaces of the body are the most readily available sites for inscribing resistance, and some of us on the margin want to say that style is one battleground among many others.

Yet of course the fashion world is politically problematic. The battleground of style is suffused, indeed constituted, by commodification. The garment industry is deeply enmeshed in an intense semiotics of distinction and a global assembly line on which many Third World women and men toil. The fashion and cosmetics industries promote aesthetic ideals that often oppressively re-inscribe normative codes of gender, race, class and sexuality. Fashion's planned obsolescence is inseparable from complicity with capitalist production and the mobilization of desire. Such complications demand a critical, multilayered consideration of fashion's contradictory implication in a politics of pleasure, avoiding the temptations of dismissive condemnation, on the one hand, and power-evasive celebration on the other.

Like fashion, theatre is a contradictory site of pleasure and contestation. "Theatre" is itself a diverse phenomenon, encompassing many kinds of venues, artists and levels of accessibility: it matters centrally who is writing, who is performing in what venue for what audience. Theatre and fashion disrupt the notion of fieldwork as a continuous sojourn in a single locale. Instead, both require intensive, short-term investigations, sometimes in widely scattered parts of the globe. For me, this meant spending time between 1989 and 1993 in Tokyo, New York, Paris, San Francisco and Los Angeles, among other sites. Geographic dispersal shifts the focus from a single culture, anthropology's Master Trope, to what has been called the transnational, especially to transnational circuits of capital, and to cultures in the plural.

I would suggest that those of us on the margins are trying to "write our faces" with the tools at our disposal: theatre, design, cultural production, political organizing, academic writing. Our faces, in turn, can speak back to Orientalist hegemonies.

UNDER THE "TRICKSTER'S" SIGN: TOWARD A READING OF NTOZAKE SHANGE

Sandra L. Richards

When Africans were forcibly transported to the "New World," they did not travel alone. Systems of thought, technology, aesthetics—in short, cultures—traversed that Middle Passage, transforming and being transformed by the environment and other cultures with which the slaves came into contact. The present work participates in what might be characterized as a second-generation critical move that, in capitalizing upon earlier studies, seeks to connect *specific* African cultural practices with their literary reformulations in the Americas.[1] It argues that, through a creative deployment of the principles of Sixteen Cowrie and Ifá divination, Ntozake Shange and Femi Osofisan construct dramaturgies that empower audiences, challenging them to impose an interpretive hegemony that can extend from the symbolic to the sociopolitical order. Additionally, it suggests that the figure of Osun, who is said to have taught mankind Sixteen Cowrie divination, serves as an appropriate representation of the ways in which African women, on the continent and in the diaspora, conceptualize feminism.

The present essay attends to redeployments of specific African traditions, leaving unaddressed at this point the ways in which Shange and Osofisan manipulate their Western identities.

Born in New Jersey in 1948, Shange was brought up in a middle-class environment in which Pan-African values were inculcated and artistic expression encouraged. Shange grew up aware of a larger frame of reference wherein skin was not a badge of stigmatization.

Shange's familiarity with Yoruba culture may be dated to the early 1970s, when radical political activists in Boston and New York introduced her to Yoruba religions through the study of dance.[2] Both Pearl Primus and Mercedes Baptista commanded significant respect among African American dancers at that time: not only had Primus incorporated blues and spiritual motifs into her modern dance choreography of the 1940s, but she was also the first African American to research and concertize West African dance in the United States.[3] Journeying periodically from Brazil to New York's Clark

Center, Baptista taught Afro-Brazilian dance, itself a Yoruba-Dahomean–based synthesis of African, Portuguese and American Indian cultures. Leaving New York in 1973 to join the Bata Koto dance group headed by Trinidadian Gloria Toolsey and African American Luisah Teish of San Francisco,[4] Shange also studied with Raymond Sawyer, who had trained in techniques pioneered by Primus and Dunham. The famous choreographer-anthropologist Katherine Dunham had established a basic vocabulary for black dance instruction based upon her field research in Haiti; it emphasized the transmission of knowledge of the social function of dance as well as mastery of technical form. Through the technique Shange would have been exposed to some of the basic concepts of Haitian *vodun*, which synthesized the belief systems of the peoples of Yorubaland, Dahomey and the Congo with Roman Catholicism. In addition, she associated with other dancers and musicians who practiced *santeria*, the distinct form that these religions took among African slaves in Cuba.

Undoubtedly, the literary examples of Amiri Baraka, Ishmael Reed and Zora Neale Hurston should not be overlooked as factors conditioning Shange's appropriations of Yoruba cultures. Valuing black folk practices as a point of origin for their artistry,[5] all three employ conjuring as both formal device and subject matter. Indeed, with it, Hurston established the conditions of literary authority for African American women writers.[6] A general belief in the transformative power of language would find specific corroboration in Yoruba culture's sophisticated acknowledgment of language as a multivalent, ambiguous force. Seemingly, Shange's opposition to racism and imperialism, rejection of Western cultural hegemony and commitment to recuperating marginalized folk traditions of "New World" Africans and of women in general were born out of this early background.

The Theoretical Frame

Common to Yoruba worship, Brazilian *candombié*, Haitian *vodun* and Cuban *santeria* is a metaphysics centering on the concept of a life-force that pervades all elements of the universe. Known in Yoruba as *àse*, this power-to-make-things-happen is a morally neutral energy that manifests itself in discrete entities often in opposition to other distinct entities. Women are thought to possess an additional "bird power" (*eye*), a prophetic ability that, like *àse*, allows them to accomplish whatever they wish.[7] Though force fields often compete with each other, coexistence and equilibrium are also possible. Human communities are assumed to strive to replicate the natural order so that, while harmony represents a desired objective, considerable latitude is allowed for difference and tension. Concepts related to human agency or identity and difference are instantiated in seminal narratives whose signification is replicated throughout the social order. Thus, for example, an individual is said to kneel and choose his destiny in the spirit world: in assuming physical form, he forgets that knowledge and uses divination, sacrifice and ritualized dance as devices to discover the life he was meant to lead. But, in the divination process especially, the individual supplicant remains supremely active, for it is she or he who formulates the problem, selects the most applicable among a variety of explanatory scenarios presented and chooses to make sacrifice.

Central to the divination process are three gods. Orunmila is said to know the secret of existence of both humans and divinities, for he is present whenever a human is created and his or her destiny sealed. His geomantic system of divination, which remains in use today, is known as Ifá. Encoded within two hundred and fifty-six "volumes," or *odu*, each with its own distinct divination signature and related to a specific Yoruba deity, Ifá's discourse is intensely poetic.

Òsun, as she is known in Yorubaland, Cuba and Brazil, or Erzulie, as she is called in Haiti, is regarded as the source of power for most of the Yoruba male-dominated cults because she is reputed to have rendered the original male gods impotent and plunged the world into near-chaos when they refused her admission to their deliberations.[8] Through her actions, Orunmila is said to have learned the necessity of making sacrifice, which reestablishes the unity of natural and supernatural elements. Other divination verses assert that Òsun learned the art while living with Orunmila, and, when he discovered that his wife was divining for clients in his absence, he banished her from his home. Known as Sixteen Cowrie divination, Òsun's system of prophecy, unlike Ifá divination, is open to female as well as to male diviners. It is also the preferred system in the Americas. In that Òsun's Haitian equivalent, Erzulie, is associated with desire beyond satiation, this godhead is said to represent the human capacity to conceptualize and to dream, creating both art and the very idea of divinity.[9]

While Òsun encompasses a necessary animating force, and Orunmila, or Ifá, speaks the truth, the god who presides over its decoding in either system is Esu. Functioning as a "special relations officer," or liaison, between heaven and earth, who exacts retribution on both wayward humans and gods, Esu is also represented as a trickster who seemingly delights in engendering chaos.[10] Said to be both small and large in stature, male and female in gender, Esu is the embodiment of paradox. He functions in part as "a generating symbol who promotes change by offering opportunities for exploring what possibilities lie beyond the *status quo*."[11] As his central position on the divination tray attests, Esu

> challenges, shatters, and redraws the structures of life. In so doing, both [Esu and his Fon counterpart, Legba] reveal the sacredness of ambiguity itself and enlarge the total pattern of meaning that is society, shaping it more closely to the design of the cosmos itself.[12]

Knowledge of that design, however, whether articulated as a religious or scientific narrative, is a social construction reflective of man's apprehensions at a given point in time.

Within the Yoruba performing arts one locus for the manifestation or *àse* is the spectacle. Encompassing the ideas of mental images, mystical visions, and even generations, or lineages, the spectacle is said to constitute a periodic (re)introduction of a "mysterious, permanent dimension of reality which, until revealed, is shut off from human view."[13] In unmasking a transcendent reality, the spectacle strives to increase the collective life-force, or potentiality of all those present, by reasserting the link between the living community, departed ancestors, the yet-to-be-born, and the entire cosmos.

Supernatural contact is valued even in secular entertainment because experience is posited more in holistic than categorically distinct terms. Research on Yoruba secular performance traditions or on African storytelling indicates that principles of categorization are more fluid in these discourses than in Western thought. That is, genres are determined not so much by the presence (or absence) of formal properties as by the effect of that property. Not only may a dramatic event contain sequences that are intended as representational and others that are presentational, but it may also include segments that are liminal, that is, neither material nor supernatural. The application of an analytical label to a given sequence varies, dependent upon its contextual placement in relation to other units and, even more important, upon individual audience members' beliefs.[14] Thus, the dynamic interaction of material-performer-audience is foregrounded within this cultural framework.

The aesthetic means employed to enhance the collective life-force are varied. Dance, mask, totem, the spoken word, chant and song may commingle; tragedy, comedy and pathos may mix within a single, dramaturgic event because they stimulate different, affective responses that together constitute an experiential totality. A polyphony of narratives, shifting perspectives and complementary oppositions with the potential of resolution into equilibrium may feature prominently in the spectacle. Clearly demarcated openings and closings, seriality, repetition, discontinuity, interlocking of energies or values, and, density of meaning may also signify the active presence of àse, or life-force.[15]

Shange's *Spell #7*

In structure and potential effect *Spell #7* replicates the divination process, wherein a supplicant is offered a number of poetic narratives from the volume prescribed by the divining instruments and then asked to choose the scenario that best speaks to his or her need. Shange's text functions like an *odu*, or book, on the construction of black identities within an exorcised space, freed of the dominant culture's stereotypes. Thus, the performers present a series of narratives whose tones vary and whose relationships to each other initially appear tenuous. There is Fay, for example, a Brooklyn housewife, who, contrary to the societal categorizations allotted black women, is not a prostitute but is looking for a fun night out on the town. Alec wants a day of national apology for the dehumanization blacks have suffered at white hands, while Lily dreams of brushing an abundant head of hair from which pomegranates, ambrosia and Ishmael Reed essays flow.

Two narratives placed at the end of each act threaten to rupture the whimsical or contained quality of most of the other scenarios.[16] They instigate instances at an interlock of conflicting energies whose resolution is problematic, heavily dependent upon audience members imposition of an interpretive choice. I am referring to Sue-Jean, who kills her boy-child named "myself" and thinks herself perpetually on the verge of giving birth, and to Maxine, who buys gold from South Africa in atonement for black people's willful perversions. Both women arrest processes of self-discovery, opting instead to remain in a liminal state on the verge of creative action. Their narratives exemplify what critic Barbara Christian terms "contrariness,"[17] or they are structured so that audiences are likely to be engaged by elements of the familiar and yet disturbed or repelled by the transgression of behavioral norms. Sue-Jean's and Maxine's histories challenge audiences to consider valuable energies that lie outside communal boundaries, energies that, if fully acknowledged, would disrupt these norms and force their redefinition. Thus, within these moments of contrariness Esu is potentially at work.

Furthermore, Maxine's monologue is followed by another interlock of oppositional energy, for the master of ceremonies reemerges to reassure spectators that they will love his "black" magic. He initiates among cast members the refrain "bein colored & love it." Stage directions indicate that the chant is supposed to be handled like a celebratory moment in a black church. But this is an extremely hard moment for performers to achieve, occurring, as it does, immediately after Maxine's anguished confession that she has been stripped of her childhood belief that black people were immune to certain immoral practices because "surviving the impossible is sposed to accentuate the positive aspects of a people."[18] She has introduced the suspicion that salvation will never come, that the victims of oppression will become as inhumane as their oppressors, but the cast, like members of a church choir, must deploy language as a percussive instrument and perhaps dance as a vehicle for the manifestation of the invisible in order to massage into being a moment whose force, or emotional signification, will counteract the effect of Maxine's narrative. Whether they accomplish that task depends upon how the audience reads or interacts with what they are doing. Shange comments obliquely upon this foregrounding of audience response when she answers complaints that the production was "too intense":

> both *spell #7 & boogie woogie landscapes* have elements of magic or leaps of faith in typical afro-american fashion; not only will the lord find a way / but there is a way outta here, this is the litany from the spirituals to Jimi Hendrix; "there must be some kinda way outta here."[19]

Thus, the near-final moment of *Spell # 7* is left open, dependent on the triangulation of material-performer-audience at any given performance.

It is further complicated by the reappearance of the minstrel mask, reminding spectators that whatever vision they have chosen within the symbolic realm of theatre must compete against the dominant culture's definition of blackness awaiting their exit from the performance space. Faced with that distorted grin, individuals may succumb to despair or project a will (*àse*) to somehow make life different. As the divination supplicant is required to make sacrifice, that is, to carry out magical-material acts designed to affirm his new perceptions, so too is a *Spell #7* audience challenged to envision and enact some realignment of social relations. But, whereas in the religious context the instability of interpretation may be masked by specific prescriptions and institutional pressures toward priestly self-preservation, in this theatrical appropriation of Yoruba divination, the spectators' freedom remains painfully apparent.

Shange not only utilizes divination as dramatic structure but also incorporates some of its gods into her plays as characters. The "passion flower of southwest los angeles," who lures and then rejects men in *for colored girls who have considered suicide/when the rainbow is enuf*, is perhaps the most stunning example of Shange's revision of *vodun*'s sacred lore surrounding Erzulie.

More important perhaps than concrete instances of imaginative redeployments is the fact that such usage signals a concept of feminism which significantly departs from those definitions advanced by white European and American theorists. Because Yoruba is a nongendered language, traditional Ifá hermeneutics has remained relatively free of gender; thus bias to a certain extent. Shange is guided or constrained by its perspectives.

8 | VOICES AT THE MILLENNIUM

To close this third edition of *Women in American Theatre*, we have brought together the voices and views of some of the many women making theatre at the beginning of the new millennium. It is not a Who's Who, or a compendium, or a scientific survey, but a kind of channel-surfing to catch some of what women working at different creative tasks, in many different venues, with many different perspectives are speaking out about in interviews, conferences, exchanges, scripts, articles and biographies. All of them have been touched in various ways by the feminist transformation of women's consciousness, and they are out there, questioning, validating and celebrating women's lives in and out of theatre.

The number of women involved in charting different and often new directions in theatre and the variety of their organizations, theatres, styles, dramatic forms, triumphs and disappointments are extraordinary. I think of the selections that follow as brief conversations with small groups from this vast cohort, whose numbers it is not even possible to suggest. They have been gathered to talk about some of the challenges involved in such topics as Staging Diversity, Intimate Solos, Addressing the Canon, Artistic Process and Professional Power (Acting, Playwriting, Directing and Managing, and Designing), and Documenting America. These divisions are issues of widely shared interest and concern; they are not meant to pigeonhole artists who have been busily breaking down gender, genre, race and career boundaries in this postmodernist era. The work of most of these women could be discussed under several rubrics. My introductory notes to each section will briefly highlight, as needed, some issues raised by the material, as well as occasional biographical or bibliographical data. The compensatory history, the praxis of the feminist theatres and the thinking of feminist theorists explored in the previous sections of our book provide some large contexts and offer varied, wide-ranging perspectives that help us to listen in an informed way and with sharpened attention to what these women in theatre have to say.

Despite many positive changes, one thing hasn't changed. Most women still function largely outside of Broadway, although a small number occasionally crash through New York's "glass prosceniums." Show business has been much slower than other industries to open up managerial and professional positions to women, despite the fact that, as of the end of the twentieth century, women comprised 62% of the Broadway audience.[1] What has been changing is the relationship between Broadway—so often designated as *the* American theatre—and what used to be derisively dubbed "the sticks." With the Great White Way now increasingly given over to big musicals, corporate megahits and the bottom line, the hinterland has become our major source of theatrical creative energy. Despite struggle and temptation, some of the theatres Off- and Off-Off-Broadway, and in communities across the country, still commit themselves to nurturing new plays, deconstructing old ones, testing innovative theories of acting and design and challenging audiences as active participants.[2] It is here that most of the women in the following pages have been able to contribute their unique values and vision to the redefinition of theatre needed for the new millennium.

HKC

STAGING DIVERSITY

Empowered by the American civil rights and black power movements of the mid-twentieth century, women of color felt deeply the need for a theatre of their own. They saw themselves as outsiders, whose very different views of their needs as women and their relationships to their men were not represented in the white, largely middle-class feminist theatres. In *This Bridge Called My Back*, Cherríe Moraga's powerful 1983 anthology of protest works by women of color, Moraga noted the irony that "reacting to what they felt was the racism of white feminism . . . became a positive affirmation of the commitment of women of color to our own feminism."[1] The struggle of many dramatists and performers of color and other diverse groups as they turned inward toward their own lives and communities is what this section briefly samples. These women had to discover or recover their own voices and devise new dramatic forms and new theatrical organizations, not only to encourage and accommodate the new audience for whom and with whom they wanted to speak, but also to recognize differences within their own community.

Sydné Mahone's tribute to Ntozake Shange's "*colored girls* phenomenon" pulls open the curtain on this dramatic transformation.[2] In 1976, Shange's innovative "choreopoem" projected the beauty, anguish and joy of real black women. It also "created a bridge from the black agenda to the women's agenda," an act which Mahone believes precipitated a crucial "collective mind change for many black women—a leap in consciousness, a discovery of voice."

For the Chicana Cherríe Moraga, too, Shange had been a catalyst whose poetry spoke "a language I knew—in the deepest parts of me, existed, and I had ignored." She believed that her "best shot" as a poet and dramatist was to write in her own Chicana voice, which "had never found its way to the page or the stage." The 1980s gave Moraga, a theorist as well as a playwright, the opportunity to find affirmation not only as a Chicana but also as a lesbian. "My lesbianism is the avenue through which I have learned the most about silence and oppression."[3]

Lesbians comprise an important segment of the growing diversity among women in theatre. As articulate theorists and academic leaders as well as outstanding creative artists, they are well represented in these pages. They have raised many of the basic questions about sexuality, gender, class and race; about identity and representation. As lesbian scripts began to move from lesbian community venues like WOW to the stages of colleges and even to Broadway, they have faced the contradictions of assimilation and appropriation.[4] Lesbian actors and playwrights also broke new ground in the 1990s, when the 1995 Tony Award for Best Actress in a Play and the 1998 Pulitzer Prize for Drama were won by "out" lesbians Cherry Jones and Paula Vogel.[5]

Cindy Lutenbacher's "So Much More Than Just Myself" highlights the growing dedication in women's work to community needs and participation, along with the importance of a creative home, topics that recur throughout this book. Pearl Cleage exemplifies an activist whose stagings are her "emotional response to oppression" and a means "to incite" audiences to action in what she calls "the worldwide struggle against racism, sexism, classism and homophobia." For many years she wrote for black audiences as playwright-in-residence with the Just Us Theater Company in Atlanta. Sydné Mahone was director of new play development at Crossroads Theatre in New Jersey, one of the few long-lived black theatres in the country. Cherríe Moraga, after formative work with Irene Fornes at her Latino Playwrights Lab at Intar Theatre in New York City, was for a long time playwright-in-residence at Brava! For Women in the Arts in San Francisco.

Playwrights of diversity often confront the disparity between the needs and responses of their specific community audience and those of general theatregoers and critics. In her book *Performing Asian America*, Josephine Lee explores the relation of dramatic form to feminist and ethnic content.[6] She explores the reasons realism has remained a popular choice among Asian theatre artists, although it is frequently rejected by feminist theorists as a form that objectifies women and minorities and replicates rather than challenges the oppression in life outside of the theatre. The Asian community is in itself diverse, comprising among others, Chinese, Japanese, Korean and Filipino Americans and Amerasians. War, labor exploitation and prejudice have made these people "perpetual foreigners," and Asian women are stereotyped as geishas or dragon ladies. It was Asian American actors who rejected the demeaning roles in which they were cast and founded theatres for the Asian community that stimulated the writing of plays. Only then were Asian women able to bring to the stage "a presence, a participation, a point of view from a segment of America that has been traditionally viewed as silent."[7]

Suzanne Bennett's introduction to her comprehensive *Women Playwrights of Diversity* highlights many of the issues related to diversity in our increasingly multicultural society, including some dangers, like labeling individuals or ghettoizing artists. In the brief section excerpted here, she also reminds us of what her sourcebook so amply demonstrates—namely, that women of diversity have helped to bring the cultures of America alive for us in all their vitality and complexity. Our theatres and our classrooms have been enriched by new resources, especially the pioneering anthologies of Margaret Wilkerson, Kathy Perkins and Roberta Uno, among others.[8]

HKC

THE "*colored girls* PHENOMENON"

Sydné Mahone

> I write as a sista witness / a woman of african descent living in north america / who came of age and came to artistic and political consciousness in the mid to late 1970s . . . / a bright comet crossed the cultural landscape . . .
>
> —ntozake shange, author of *for colored girls who have considered suicide/when the rainbow is enuf*

In literature and in performance, Ntozake Shange freed herself from Western convention and delivered on the promise of a liberated and liberating black female voice. Within the context of the African American female dramatic canon, this choreopoem was the theatrical event of the decade. It was developed in the early 1970s through workshops in the West Coast women's collectives, won an Obie Award in 1974, and opened at the Booth Theatre on May 17, 1976, where it ran for 747 performances.

Cultural history is shaped by the experience and documentation of events that galvanize (or perhaps illuminate) the masses of people. During the 1960s, the ideals of freedom, equality, peace and justice were translated through the civil rights movement into the particularly empowering ideas of black pride, black beauty and black power. The marches, sit-ins and songs of the civil rights movements offered a model for subsequent liberation movements.

Similarly, the dramatic art of Ntozake Shange created a bridge from the black agenda to the women's agenda. It symbolized a collective mind change for many black women—a leap in consciousness, a discovery of voice. It became clear that women's dramatic texts could be different from men's texts, and it also became evident that there was a tremendous diversity within the chorus of black women dramatists. The final beat of the choreopoem rang triumphant and transcendent in all its gorgeous piety, its sounding of a private battle cry—a new anthem; a victory prayer song, and a shout; a testimony:

I found god In myself / and I loved her Fiercely

Ensconced in the lyric was the pure holiness of women loving women—a dangerous concept for a patriarchal society dependent upon the control of women. Within the thought was the deed: we heal when we let ourselves love each other. We tell the truth. It heals us. It frees us. For me, *colored girls* did that.

Ntozake Shange's voice shook up the theatre world, not only because she disrupted the syntax with candid and complex poetry, but perhaps most profoundly because she changed the face of heroism. Unlike Alice Childress, Lorraine Hansberry and Adrienne Kennedy, her dramatic foremothers, Shange made herself—a black woman—the subject of the drama. The intellectual, erotic and spiritual dimensions of black women were rescued from stereotype, represented for the first time in the matrix of character and identity. Incorporating poetry and dance, the piece was also distinguished by its beauty. The spectacle of seven beautiful black women on a stage, furnished only with a large flower suspended upstage, unleashed a new aspect of performance from the cage of Western theatre. Character, plot action, time and place were thrown off for a more fluid, poetic, ritualistic experience of theatre.

FINDING PLACE AND VOICE AS A CHICANA LESBIAN

Cherríe Moraga

I was privileged to come of age as a writer in a time when people of color, lesbians, feminists were writing in the context of a social change movement. Art and cultural affirmation were critical aspects of that movement and allowed me to find place and voice as a Chicana lesbian. I learned early on that trying to write like white people (if you weren't white) would simply make you a cheap imitation thereof, that my best shot as a writer was to speak with a Chicana voice that had never found its way to the page or the stage.

Giving Up the Ghost was my first play and reflects my transition from poetry to theatre, a Chicana lesbian love story. I worked with Maria Irene Fornes for one year in her Latino Playwrights Lab at Intar Theatre in New

York City. In 1990 Fornes directed the play I had developed in the lab, *Shadow of a Man*, in a San Francisco Eureka Theatre/Brava! For Women in the Arts production. *Shadow* was my "family" play, in which I tried to expose the secrets and silences affecting both men and women in the traditional Chicano household. Moving from the intimate relationship of lovers to the familial face from which lovers are created to the community that houses them both (*Heroes and Saints*), I feel that my plays have always occurred in the dialogue with the Chicano/Latino community. They provide an intra-cultural critique and celebration. They are not written with the Anglo audience in mind because to do so would mean writing in translation. As any writer of any culture should, I try to write as specifically as possible of the complexities in our lives. In that the universality of the Chicano experience is found and the work becomes "cross-cultural" in the deepest sense.

Since 1990 and the coproduction of *Shadow*, I have continued my relationship with Brava! For Women in the Arts. Being the playwright-in-residence at Brava has been the greatest blessing for me and my work. Without a stage, the writing remains on the page and playwrights eventually return to their poems and unfinished novels and may despair of ever seeing their drama take flesh. I know this could have easily been my scenario. Brava changed that for me. As a multicultural women's theatre organization especially interested in premiering works by lesbians and women of color, Brava became a home, bringing together my concerns as an artist and cultural activist. Through Brava, my plays have been shown to audiences as diverse as the city of San Francisco itself. In addition, the teaching aspect of my residency has provided me with the opportunity to help produce a new generation of American theatre artist and writers, including gay and lesbian youth, Chicanas, Latinas and Native American women.

The plays which I have written are drawn from people I have known, people I have imagined and people I have interviewed for the express purpose of writing a play. They are, for the most part, people I have never read a line by in a book or have never seen not wearing a maid's uniform in a film, TV show or play. They are my people. My subject. My heart.

FAST-TALKING, QUICK-THINKING BLACK WOMEN

Pearl Cleage

As a third-generation black nationalist and a radical feminist, the primary energy that fuels my work is a determination to be part of the ongoing worldwide struggle against racism, sexism, classism and homophobia. I approach my work first as a way of expressing my emotional response to oppression, since no revolution has ever been fueled purely by intellect, no matter what the boys tell you; second, as a way to offer analysis, establish context and clarify point of view; and third, to incite my audiences or my readers to action. My work is deeply rooted in, and consciously reflective of, African American history and culture, since I believe it is by accurately expressing our very specific and highly individual realities that we discover our common humanity.

My response to the oppression I face is to name it, describe it, analyze it, protest it and propose solutions to it as loud as I possibly can every time I get the chance. I purposely people my plays with fast-talking, quick-thinking black women since the theatre is, for me, one of the few places where we have a chance to get an uninterrupted word in edgewise. It is my firm belief that exposing my audiences to these African American Nationalist Feminist Warrior women, innocently ensconced within the framework of the well-made play, will quicken the swelling of our ranks by creating an exciting alternative view of what black women—what free women—can and should be.

As a black artist, my cultural heritage is a rich legacy of protest and resistance. As a woman artist, my cultural heroes cross racial and national boundaries, joined together at the womb by a sisterhood based on the worldwide presence of sexism in our lives and the unbroken legacy of our struggle against it. I embrace these twin traditions as a lifeline to the past, a leap into the future and the best possible hedge against the terror of writer's block. For me, the challenge is never what to write about but how to find time to say it all.

THE ASIAN AMERICAN SPECTATOR AND THE POLITICS OF REALISM

Josephine Lee

Recent reassessments of realism have been most critical of the ways in which realism calls not only for a particular level of detail in the theatre set, props and acting style, but also for a particular relationship between the spectator and the stage event.

If instances of modern dramatic realism, plays that pass for a reflection of preexisting reality, are increasingly regarded with suspicion or dismissed entirely as a species of political theatre, then Asian Americans who write realistic plays are subject to the same kinds of criticism. The question becomes why Asian American dramatists choose theatrical realism, as so many have done, rather than the more overtly presentational techniques that have the potential to interrupt the illusion of reality and directly interrogate spectatorial privilege.[1]

The question demands that we consider not only the paradigm of the white spectator and the objectified Oriental onstage—a model of oppressive viewing practices that is frequently evoked these days—but also how Asian American spectators might be positioned in diverse ways. If the model of the realistic spectator—placed in uninterrupted mastery over a passive feminized object onstage, and taking pleasure in his complete knowledge of that object—is no longer fully relevant, what other pleasures might Asian Americans find in a recognized "reality" onstage? I suggest that the desire for the authentic might be satisfied with a lesser degree of mastery, and spectators might identify with the reality in even grossly insufficient characterizations of Asian Americans.

The intense desire for stage presentation to validate, through public performances a vision of authentic reality seems to spring from the desire for the solidarity of ethnic and racial identity. Realism holds the promise of public validation of a "real" self insofar as it appeals to a vision of performers and audience united in their recognition of common meaning. The power of realism, then, is that it allows audience members to see themselves as symbolically whole within the presentation of the drama.

The constant pressure toward the real and the authentic accounts for the frequency with which Asian American readers call for a "true voice" or "our own stories." We should not underestimate the power of this desire, for it may be driven not so much by a naive need to see literal reality as by the desire to authenticate through public performance a vision of ethnic community hitherto erased from public view. The theatregoer who concludes, "that is authentic experience," may not be judging the play or player on the basis of its resemblance to any offstage reality; rather, she might be satisfied by the theatrical allusion to what otherwise remains unseen. Modes of authenticity and realness rely on a complex identification, on viewers' needs to find themselves as whole in the constructed vision performed before them. That need comes out of the fragmented, traumatized situation of marginality.

In this constant return to the idea of the real, I acknowledge its power, however diversely articulated, not only among those identified as Asian American, but also among those marginalized in other ways. In this sense, contemporary realistic plays and films by Asian Americans share some affinities with the peasant plays of the early Abbey Theatre, in Dublin, or the folk plays of the Harlem Renaissance, where the spectacle similarly fed a hunger for authentic or true experience and plays strategically positioned their viewers to create anew the image of community and identity. In this sense, we can better understand these particular versions of realism as the products of wishful thinking, a complex mimetic impulse that at once articulates the powerful impulse to find solidarity in shared experience and at the same time exposes the tensions and contradictions in these perspectives.

"SO MUCH MORE THAN JUST MYSELF": WOMEN THEATRE ARTISTS IN THE SOUTH

Cindy Lutenbacher

Most contemporary southern women theatre artists I have interviewed are affiliated with ensemble companies that also have at heart the commitment to community. All wear several theatrical hats at once (writer, performer, director, etc.). Their primary work grows from the indigenous culture of each individually defined constituency; their art not only makes the audience a vital participant in the performance, it also heightens the audience's awareness of itself as a community. For example the last "act" of Pearl Cleage's and Zeke Burnett's performance is an onstage dance with the audience lasting until some unordained hour of the morning, and Road Company's *Echoes and Postcards* concludes with a community's honoring of its dead.

Jo Carson, a writer and performer living in Johnson City, Tennessee, writes in almost every genre—plays, stories, essays, and a blend of anecdote, talk, commentary, memory and local voices that she has named "People Pieces." She has performed her People Pieces over two hundred times all across the United States, as well as in Nicaragua and on National Public Radio's *All Things Considered*. Carson performs many of her works as a solo artist, as well as in collaboration with theatre groups, especially Road Company, also of Johnson City. Road Company's 1986 work, *Echoes and Postcards*, revolving around the images and ideas of Tennessee life, is a collaborative collage of scenes, memories, songs and anecdotes. For example, Carson performs a piece about youthful attempts to sing like Patsy Cline while atop her grandmother's corn bin and in the family car. "Jo, honey, *please*," says her mother. Late in the show, when Carson finally does sing, with unabashed fervor, Hank Williams's "Your Cheatin' Heart," the entire audience cheers, as they share in the experience of childhood-wish fulfillment. Carson's work is deeply rooted in the language, images, thoughts and feelings of the mountain region. She believes in knowing the place from and in which you write because otherwise, as she says, "I suspect about the best you'll be able to do is gossip."

Pearl Cleage has lived in Atlanta for eighteen years and has spent four of them as playwright-in-residence with Just Us Theatre Company. Cleage writes in several genres, but always with the idea of performance: "I don't think so much about the form. I just talk to people." Her plays include *Puppetplay*, *Good News*, *Essentials* and *Hospice*, which won five AUDELCO awards in 1983. Cleage primarily writes for a black audience; her voice and concerns are those of a black woman. In her piece about buying her first 45 record—The Temptations—Cleage writes of the desires, fears and treasures of a black girlhood: "I was looking for the music that made you know something good was coming to you in the next couple of years."

Linda Parris-Bailey is artistic director of Carpetbag Theatre in Knoxville, Tennessee, one of the oldest continuously operating black companies in the country. Carpetbag tours the region, playing in the usual theatre spaces as well as in many nontraditional places such as churches and prisons—"wherever the people are." The company develops original works that speak from the heart and history of the community, in order to "give something back to the community—its own positive image reflected." Carpetbag's repertory includes *Red Summer*, based on the Knoxville race riot of 1919; *Cric? Crac!*, a collage of African, Haitian and American southern black folktales; and *Dark Cowgirls and Prairie Queens*, originally created in part as a response to requests by teachers and principals in Knoxville for a performance for Black History Month. Written by Parris-Bailey in collaboration with the rest of the ensemble, *Cowgirls* is based upon the stories of black women who were part of the move west.

Angelyn DeBord is one of the mainstays of Roadside Theatre, a touring, teaching, tale-telling company out of Whitesburg, Kentucky. Roadside, now entering its sixteenth year, performs stories and tales from Appalachia, as well as original, ensemble-created plays based upon characters and stories from the mountains. Roadside's repertory includes *Pretty Polly*, a play based upon the real life of Polly Branham, a 'mountain woman tale-teller' who took her stories into the mountain schools and communities in the 1930s. *Pretty Polly*, explains Debord, "begins with an introduction of how we are each the *history* that school history books know nothing about. The piece is a series of stories creating the saga of a woman's experiences; dark and light sides of life are shown from her youth until her ancient years when she reaches a state of acceptance and of grace. The show ends with a hymn which the audience joins in singing: "Bright mornin' stars are risin'/Where are our dear mothers?/They have gone to heaven a-shoutin'/Day is a-breakin' in our souls." Debord acts Polly; she was also one of the collaborators in the creation of the script. In addition to her position as performer-director-writer, shared with the three men and two women of the company, DeBord is an artist-in-residence in the public schools in eastern Kentucky's hollers and way-backs. She teaches storytelling and performance, always drawing students to their own heritage of stories and mountain living.

And there's so much more: Lee Heuermann recreating political cabaret in Atlanta, Jan Villarrubia's plays and "characters" from New Orleans, Rebecca Ranson's works in Atlanta, Cynthia Levee writing in "the Cajun-Jewish tradition," Marsha Jackson and Jomandi, Sallie Bingham in Louisville, Maya Levy in Louisiana, Rebecca Wackler with Southern Theatre Conspiracy, and Linda Gregoric of Contemporary Arts in New Orleans. Then there's *Cabbagetown: 3 Women . . . An Oral Play with Music*, which depicts life in a mill village now part of Atlanta; and *Louisville 200*, the celebration based on 250 oral history interviews created by TriCenter Theatre Company for Louisville, Georgia's two hundredth celebration; and . . .

One has the sense that wherever a noncommercial theatre has arisen in the South, its goals and commitments have been based in the needs, issues and inheritance of a community. Women are invariably either leading or participating in these theatres.

THE CHALLENGES OF DIVERSITY: QUESTIONS AND COMPLICATIONS

Suzanne Bennett

In introductory essays to each of the sections of *Women Playwrights of Diversity*, Jill Dolan, Tiffany Ana Lopez, Sydné Mahone and Chiori Miyagawa highlight accomplishments and trace concerns occurring within the lesbian, Latina, black women and Asian American women playwrights. From their essays and a reading of the plays some similarities emerge: the women protagonists more often find ways to control their destinies; more women write outside the realistic style prevalent onstage in the 1970s and early 1980s; and, interestingly, a significant number of diverse playwrights are constructing character by multiple factors and often excluding race or sexual preference as a defining feature. The central figures in plays by women of diversity are asserting themselves in often bizarre and compelling ways.

Is a play written by a lesbian playwright without any lesbian content (or a play with lesbian content by a heterosexual) a lesbian play? As Jill Dolan admits, "definitions of 'lesbian playwright,' 'lesbian play,' or even 'lesbian' are complicated to attempt." Anna Deavere Smith's best known works, the solo performances *Fires in the Mirror* and *Twilight: Los Angeles 1992*, have black and white racial divisiveness at their core, but present an array of characters from a wide ethnic spectrum. Thus for a playwright to be classified as Latina, Asian American, African American or lesbian, must her drama have characters who are racially delineated with sexual preferences made explicit? Must multicultural theatre speak only of racial and sexual politics? Must it serve a demand for the exotic?

The largess of the major foundations toward a multicultural agenda has certainly helped to increase the number of diverse voices in the theatre. Have they also created a situation in which theatres competing for ever diminishing amounts of money will commit to plays by nontraditional writers only if they demonstrate an ethnic or cultural identity? Artists are more forward-thinking (and amusing) than administrators. The many multicultural collaborations of playwrights and directors point the way toward truly diverse artistic marriages.

Issues surrounding diversity are further confused by ethnic configurations that are more complicated than any categories are capable of representing. Several of the playwrights included remind us how varied a multicultural-multiethnic menu can be: Caradid Svich, for example, lays claim to Cuban, Croatian, Argentine and Spanish. In order to promote and educate people about multicultural, multiethnic playwrights, however, "naming" is useful. It is a way of being counted. The danger is when categories become excuses to limit inclusion in specialized circumstances, such as festivals of ethnic plays. The plea of women playwrights to be recognized simply as playwrights is compounded by nontraditional writers who want to be recognized not as lesbian, Asian American, Latina or black women playwrights but simply as writers who choose to write for the stage.

A further complication is that ethnic and lesbian theatres, while important in developing, cultivating and building an audience for diverse playwrights, remain essentially ghettoized—artists writing for their own audiences in what Jill Dolan calls "site specific" venues. All too frequently the writers who work and hone their crafts in these alternative spaces never make the journey uptown to Off-Broadway, much less Broadway, theatres.

Recently, however, we have seen important exceptions in New York and many of the playwrights are well represented on the major regional stages. Theatre that has been clearly polarized is beginning to pollinate.

The alphabetic ordering which compromises the primary structure of our book is a way of saying that what brings these playwrights together is that they are women who work without a recognized theatrical tradition who because of the dominance of white males historically and contemporarily, still are underrepresented on the stage. An informal survey of the Theatre Communications Group (TCG) theatres in 1995 revealed these figures: out of more than one thousand plays presented, twenty-six percent or a little more than three hundred were written by women; of these plays, sixty (approximately eighteen percent) were by lesbians or women of color. These sixty plays, however, represented only thirty-eight playwrights or approximately five percent of the total number of playwrights. (These figures include children's and young adult theatre.)

We all like to see ourselves reflected onstage. And we deserve to see our cultures and issues occupy a meaningful place in our contemporary mirrors—television, film and the theatre. While television and film have begun to accommodate, often begrudgingly, the new demographic realities, the theatre is slower to make changes. Still, the influence of strong feminist theoretical writing by women in theatre and their presence in our classrooms have provided a foundation from which we will continue to see change. There will be more anthologies and collections of diverse women's plays; a new audience is being educated in ways almost unimaginable twenty years ago when the plays we were reading in American drama classes and seeing on our stages did not speak directly to the lives of those sitting in the desks. The playwrights included in this volume challenge existing norms and accepted definitions of our drama of diversity.

INTIMATE SOLOS

Although the development of solo performance was sparked by aesthetic experimentation in the art world, women performers and feminist theorists have also played an important role. Denied access to or control of the major stages, women have a long tradition of using alternatives to conventional forms and venues—from Ruth Draper's many "monodramas" to Whoopi Goldberg's solo performance on Broadway in 1984 (which was revived in 2004) and Lily Tomlin's 1985 show *The Search for Signs of Intelligent Life in the Universe* (which started the new millennium with a tour and a second Broadway opening).[1] They are all performance artists whose use of characterization and narrative retains some affinity with traditional theatre.[2]

Deborah Lubar belongs in this tradition. She uses her skills as a healer to tell women's stories that bridge cultural divides. Some are based on research and participation with women in crises, in Israel and Palestine and, more recently, in Bosnia, and some are solo pieces of robust ethnic humor and deep feeling.[3] In *Eve's Version*, Lubar's imagination gives us a hilarious, touching feminist deconstruction of what happened in the Garden of Eden. When God, the original patriarch, silences the lively, earthy, sensuous Eve, she painfully realizes what being a woman means.

The women's movement was, of course, all about the rejection of definition by male authority and institutions. With a new consciousness of themselves, and especially of their bodies, some women artists forcefully broke through the confining conventions into what is called "performance art." Influenced by the explicitly sexual creations of women in the visual arts, they made woman's intimate self—her body, her sexuality, her repressed emotions, her ethnicity or race, her daily existence and the "trifles" in it—public art, totally under their own control.

Working with Lois Weaver and Peggy Shaw as the Split Britches company, Deb Margolin developed those qualities that mark her other original plays and performance pieces—her talent for words, her wild sense of humor and her Jewish sensibility.[4] Taking her audience into her confidence, Margolin shares with them the glimpses of the Messiah she experiences in the unexpected, intimate, weird, painful or wonderful little sagas of daily life. The ever-present possibility of spiritual blossoming fills her performances with a rare spirit of wonder and hope.

In contrast, Karen Finley has been dubbed the "performance artist as provocateur," although she thinks of herself as a dreamer "who tries to fix things."[5] She uses the many voices that come to her in trancelike moments, and her body, often nude and covered with eggs, glitter, feathers, or chocolate, to project sexual or political issues the audience doesn't want to hear about. Her "transgressive" performances have made her famous—and "infamous." She was one of the "NEA Four" who fought Senator Jesse Helms's effort to muzzle artists supported by the National Endowment for the Arts grants. After a long, painful litigation, the Supreme Court eventually ruled against the artists. Ironically, as the case made Finley widely known, she faced another kind of risk. Her performances started to be "associated with striptease or live sex, and not at all the feminist or subversion strategy that theory might endorse." Although she persevered, Finely was depressed by what happened, feeling that "it was taking away a part of my soul."[6]

Rebecca Schneider closes "Intimate Solos" with a brief section from her challenging study of *The Explicit Body* about the porn star Annie Sprinkle.

Sprinkle claimed that she took up the life because "there just weren't many girls who would do what I would do back then," but she reacted against "the less savory aspects" of "male-manufactured, genitally-focused raunch."[7] She nevertheless wanted to continue her sex work in order to heal our "sex-negative culture." In performance art classes at New York's School of Visual Arts, she decided "to make art from what had previously been strictly business." Using these new experiences and her porn background, she created *Post Porn Modernist*, which has been described as "a trippy, funny-scary dissection of her career in sex, the first act of which climaxed, so to speak, when she inserted a speculum into her vagina and invited audience members to come have a look." It is this extraordinary moment when she made her most private part public art that Rebecca Schneider theorizes for us.

HKC

EVE'S VERSION

Deborah Lubar

People have often asked me if God was really the way they wrote about him in the biography. "It all depends," I say, "on where you hear God's voices." That shuts them up for a while.

"What was it like to be the first woman?" I don't know, I didn't know I was a woman—until the day we were sent packing. Then I found out. I thought I was the earth.

So I knew I was made of dust and breath. But a woman? A woman? Who had ever heard of this word? I sat up, and I looked around myself—my eyes were still new and clouded—but I could make out all manner of beauty—all manner of shapes and textures and colors and forms—and I knew right away, don't ask me how, that I had come to wake on the Great Earth. And then with myself (*hands*). I began to feel myself (*body*). There were hills and valleys (*down torso*), soft places (*thighs*) and hard places (*knees*), meadows (*cheeks*), wet pools (*eyes*), long grasses (*hair*), and one large boulder (*nose*). The winds were blowing in and out (*from mouth*)—and inside me I could feel the rivers, flowing, flowing, flowing—and I thought, "Oh! I *too* am the earth!"

There was something lying beside me that looked a lot like I felt, only not exactly. Not so many hills and valleys. More like the Nevada Salt Flats, with a southern peninsula down there that I did not have. But clearly it too was of the earth. Of course, it turned out to be Adam, but I didn't know that yet.

And then all of a sudden, a Great Voice From Outside Me was bellowing down from what turned out to be the sky, "**Eve!**"

I looked around myself. I did not know what I was, an Eve.

"**Eve!**" said the Great Voice. "**I am talking to YOU!**"

"Oh," I thought. "I am being talked to!" I had never been talked to before.

"Who are you?" I said.

"I am that I am."

(Pause) Years later, I came to appreciate the gold in that answer, but at the time, it gave me hives.

"Oh that's great. That's really helpful. How about another clue?"

"Don't you talk back to ME," said the Great Voice. "Oh!" I thought. "I am talking! It's my first talking! The earth speaks!" I thought.

"Eve!" The Great Voice was on again. **"I have created you to be unto the Man a helpmate!"** I looked over at the Nevada salt flats. I thought, "I'll bet you anything that's the man."

"His *what?*"

"HIS HELPMATE!"

"What kind of a word is that? Who in the world ever uses this word? 'Helpmate?? Helpmatey' . . . ?"

"DON'T YOU TALK BACK TO ME!" said the Great Voice.

Oh ya. The trouble between us began right there. I don't want to think about it, or talk about it, look, I'll get to it later, all right? Let's change the subject for now.

I'm standing at the base of the Tree, and I am holding it with both of my arms, and I am yearning with all my soul to hear God's voice in my own bones, so I am reaching up and reaching higher, and I take the reddest apple from its branch—and I bite. *(Pause)*

And at that moment—all the world changed.

This apple of blood red, it tasted both of sweet *and* of sour. Both of beauty *and* of pain. All in the same bite! You have to understand—that everything in Eden was *sweet,* and we thought everything outside must be bitter or sour. But here they were together in the flesh of this one fruit, and the taste of it, the taste of it broke my heart into a thousand pieces, some of them went scattering on the ground like seeds. And I am filled up to bursting. The fire inside me is rising so fast, I think that I might split in two from the tension of this sweet and bitter bliss . . .

And I don't know how to contain it, this sweet and the bitter together—and I don't know how to *do* this. I call, "ADAM! AD AAAAMM!"

He comes hopping along one foot to the other—he thinks that I have found another fruit we have not yet tried. And he sees it. And then he freezes where he is.

"What have you done, Eve? What is that in your hand? Now you will die, Eve! And what will I do without you?"

Ya . . . That was the day we began to love.

And I wanted him to know the truth, so I held the apple out to him. "It doesn't taste like death, Adam. It tastes like life!"

But he stepped away from me in fear—and I saw him struggling, struggling, between what to do with me, and the echo of God's voice!

And then . . . I felt his rough, warm hand on mine. And he took from me the apple, and smiling a strange smile, as if to say "good-bye," he ate.

It was the kindest act I have ever known. My Adam.

And then I saw. That as he tasted of the bitter-sweet fruit, something broke inside him, too. Only with Adam, I don't think it was his heart.

And I wanted to run to him, to cleave him, to hold him with all of my body, to tell him, "Adam, I love you!"

But he was staring at my body in fear, disgust and shame. And he turned his eyes to the ground.

"Adam, what is it? What is the matter with me, Adam? What are you doing?"

He goes running off and comes tearing back with the biggest leaves he can find. And still he wouldn't look at me.

"Put these on your body, Eve."

"What for, Adam? What is wrong with me?"

"Put these on your body NOW!"

And he pointed—to the heart and to the fire.

"Why, Adam? *Why?*"

"COVER IT!" And I did. And then he covered himself too . . .

And then Adam is grabbing my hand and throwing me onto the ground beneath the fig tree. "God is in the garden!" he whispers. I say, "God is always in the garden. God *is* the garden." *(Pause)* and I knew that it was true.

But Adam is slamming his hand on my mouth, and he is looking up to the sky, and he hears the Great Voice from Outside of Us.

And then he does a terrible thing. *(Pause)* We have all sometimes done terrible things. Forgive each other.

He takes his cold and shaking hand from mine, and he points his finger, as he used to do when he taught me the names of the animals, only now his finger is hard and sharp as a knife, and he turns it toward me.

"The woman made me do it."

Ya. That was the day I found out I was a woman.

I SEE MESSIAH

Deb Margolin

I see Messiah where he refuses to see me: in the tranquillity of a young girl whom I saw roll over onto a tiny kitten, killing it with her weight in her sleep, and still sleeping soundly, and waking refreshed; in my father's sense of his heroism, crushing the head of the mouse my mother hated so much, crushing it with a rock in the dark and mustiness of the basement. I see Messiah in a Snickers bar, biting in, negotiating the excruciating texture, the peanuts crushed against my palate, the caramel defining with pain the points of dental decay. I see Messiah where he won't see me.

I felt someone push me up against the wall of 600 Third Avenue about twenty-two years ago. That dates back. I was working for a market research firm to make money during college. My job was to cut names out of the phone book on an elaborately random basis and paste them on a form for future torment by so called "interviewers."

On my way back from lunch break to this stimulating environment, a man pinned me to the glass wall outside the building. My belly to the wall. I twisted my neck around, and there, behind me, against me, was the frantic face of a young Hasidic man, and his breath, and the smell of his eyes, the criminality of them. I was unable to speak, I was so stunned, so he said: have sex with me. You've got to have sex with me. Now. You've got to have sex with me right now. I can't . . . I will never have sex. No one will marry me. I can't have sex without marriage. You have to have sex with me. I have no prospects. I'll die. You must. Sex. Now. Immediately—and other exhortatory-type phrases like that. He talked so much that I could see he wasn't a rapist, because rapists are terse, aren't they, I mean, why waste time chatting? So my fear lowered, and I just looked at him with many feelings: contempt, pity, revulsion, curiosity, and hey, how ya doin'. And I said the appropriate: no, absolutely not, or whatever, and I went up in the elevator, picked up my razor blade, and slashed strangers for a sanitary napkin study from the Dayton white pages. I was slicing and slicing and thinking about this man. This man with the pais and tsitsis and glasses and shoes and top hat and gruff, music-less voice, pushing me against this building, and the nerve of him, etcetera. But none of those feelings had any durability. What stays with me half a life later is what was truly gross about this man. And it wasn't his desire for sex with a stranger. Desire is the force of the world, the life force really. It wasn't his presumption that any non Hasidic woman was a whore and could be reasonably talked into sex with some weirdo in broad daylight on the sidewalk in front of an office building. It was his loss of faith! It was his loss of faith in Moshiach, damn it! What kind of Jew is this, I ask you? He had lost faith! That was his sin!

Then you have people who see Messiah where even I, ever vigilant, have not opened my eyes to the possibility. It is one such man I married. Very visionary. What an interesting man. He is very compelling. He's handsome, which is fun; but that's truly a small element. I've known him for twenty-one years, and yet there are times when he's like that Hasidic man against the wall, only in a revelatory, consensual way. His lips are bowed; his upper lip is God's harp. Our son has those lips, and it's divine, not genetic. I can't stop talking, and my husband never says a word, it's so bizarre, so annoying; he has no idea where his body is in space, steps on things, breaks things, is more verbal about alternate side of the street parking than almost anything else, and yet: I am against that glass wall, panting as if for the first time, seeing his face, hearing his voice, contemplating his essence. It's because he sees Moshiach where I am blind. He's got Messiah by the beard in my sleep, in my blind spots. He asked me to marry him on the second floor of the Riverside Funeral home on 76th Street and Amsterdam Avenue. We had just buried his mother. I rode in the black car. The wheezing grief of his father, the choked grief of her two sons, it was all sound: Kaddish, the dirt, the motor whispering inside the limousine. I was wearing a long-sleeved dark dress, with stockings; I was a stranger to myself in that dress, in such lovely weather, in such an emotional situation with a silent man. When we returned after the burial, he said: can I talk to your father? And I said, My father? And he said: I want to marry you. Right away. And I think of the Hasidic man in mirror negative, and I say: Don't you think we should wait until you're thinking more clearly? or something like that. And he says: No, on the contrary. I've never seen anything more clearly, on this day, it makes such sense to me: I must marry you. As soon as possible. Now. And, true to the Hasidic man's vision, his last hope, I threw my arms around this grief-stricken friend and we made out like you can't believe, in the bathroom of the Riverside Funeral Home, with sounds of crying, giggling and negotiations for coffins going on in waves just outside, just beyond us. Now is Moshiach there, or not? Fifteen months later, December 20th, our son was born. Like I told you, he had that upper lip, like his father, and everyone said he was a Christmas baby, which I accept because I must, and before we knew it, it was New Year's Eve, our new, gorgeous, tyrannical baby asleep in the next room, and finally midnight came. I wanted to dance with my husband. He's really handsome. But I didn't know how without waking the baby, and there really wasn't any way, since there were no doors in our house, but Messiah appeared to my baby's father, he turned on the TV. He found a station with hot jazz; we both love jazz; he found first one, then another set of headphones. He plugged both sets of headphones into the TV, put on one, gave me the other. Feeling those phones come round the top of my head like a white horse around the edge of a mountain: the sound of a saxophone, bass, drum, something low and luscious, maybe Lester Young or something: looking up, and there's my husband, and I can tell by his eyes that he hears the same low, lovely thing. So he grabs me and we begin to dance. We hear the same song from two separate sources. A stranger walking in that door would have seen two exhausted lovers swaying together in complete silence. Moshiach, or not?

KAREN FINLEY: A CONSTANT STATE OF BECOMING

An Interview with Richard Schechner

KF: People are scared of my information. They really don't know what I'm going to do, they don't like me dealing with sexual issues or political issue.

If I was doing porn they'd be very happy. When they book me they think they're going to get some kinky chick from New York going out there shoving my tits in their face. When they find out I'm more than that—well, in London I was canceled out this summer, I was banned by the Westminster Council and Scotland Yard.

I've gotten letters from institutions—whose names I won't mention—telling me that I just could not perform there, that their city is just not ready for me. In Philadelphia I really want to perform at

Painted Bride, but I was told they said, "Oh, Karen Finley, there's no way that she's going to perform here."

I think I stir people to be responsible for what's going on in their own personal lives, in their one-to-one relationships, interweaving this into the whole society's corruption. That's very disturbing. I destroy the games people live on, a very yuppie world where security is having a $40,000 a year job, or $120,000. People really don't want that questioned. What happened to the motivations of twenty years ago of having a much more socialist-humanist society? We're supposed to have more time on our hands because of technology. But I don't see it going toward culture or helping people.

I'm talking about abuse. I talk about how old people are disregarded—that if they've only got ten bucks to their name they're lucky to have ten. Also we're really scared of our own sexuality which is no longer a sexuality of love but a sexuality of violence.

The Constant State of Desire

Act II

(Easter baskets and stuffed animals sit on table. Take off clothes. Put colored unboiled eggs from basket and animals in one large clear-plastic bag. Smash contents until contents are yellow. Put mixture on body using soaked animals as applicators. Sprinkle glitter and confetti on body and wrap self in paper garlands as boas.)

SCENE 1
Hate Yellow

I hate yellow. I hate yellow so much. And I see you walking down my neighborhood with your new teeth and solid pastel colored shirts. Yuk.

Don't you know that I'm only happy when I'm depressed? Don't you know I'm only happy when I'm wearing black? That I'm only happy at night. Yes, I'm a creature at night.

Nothing Happened

So I put my head in the oven and nothing happened.
So I fucked you all night long and nothing happened.
So I went on a diet and nothing happened.
So I became macrobiotic and nothing happened.
So I went to the Palladium, the Tunnel, and nothing happened.
So I went down to SoHo and checked out the art scene and nothing happened.
So I quit drugs and nothing happened.
So I worked for ERA, voted for Jesse Jackson and nothing happened.
So I put out roach motels and nothing happened.

So I petitioned, rioted, terrorized, and organized and something is going to happen. Something is going to happen 'cause I'm not going to let you gang rape me anymore walking down my streets that I built with my soul, my creativity, my spit. And you just look at all of my art, Mr. Yuppie, as just another investment, another deal. My sweat, my music, my fashion is just another money-making scheme for you. You are the reason, Mr. Entrepreneur, why David's Cookie McDonald's is the symbol of my culture.

You are the reason why fast food is the only growth industry of this country.

ANNIE SPRINKLE: DIALECTICAL IMAGE

Rebecca Schneider

Contemporary feminist performance artists present their own bodies beside or relative to the history of reading the body marked female, the body rendered consumptive in representation. In this sense, the contemporary explicit body performer consciously and explicitly stands beside herself in that she grapples overtly with the history of her body's explication, wrestling with the ghosts of that explication. Given this, feminist artists can be understood to present their bodies as dialectical images.

"Dialectical image" is a phrase coined by Walter Benjamin to refer to an object or constellation of objects which tell the secret—which reveal or expose the traces of their false promises, their secret(ed) service to the dreamscapes of capitalism. Dialectical images are objects which show the show, which make it apparent that they are not entirely that which they have been given to represent—the way cracks in face paint or runs in mascara might show the material in tension with the constructed ideal. Like secrets bared, dialectical images evidence commodity dreamscapes as bearing secrets, as propped by masquerade. For Benjamin, prostitutes present prime dialectical images. As "commodity and seller in one," prostitutes show the show of their commodification and cannot completely pass as that which they purport to be. Dialectical images such as prostitutes (Benjamin also cites used or outmoded commodities) can talk or gesture back to the entire social enterprise which secret(e)s them. For Benjamin, reading dialectical images for the secrets they tell and the memories they hold provides a counter-history to modernity's myriad promises. Objects accumulating in the cracks of dreams, in the promises of "progress," can be read back against pervasive myths of nature, value and social order.

Dialectical images provoke a viewer/reader to think again—to take a second look.

I had been running the [Annie] Sprinkle performance of *Post Porn Modernist* I had seen at The Kitchen in Manhattan in 1990 across my memory in a kind of eternal return. I kept replaying the image of Sprinkle's spectators standing in the line that bridged the magic gulf between the stage and the house, waiting to accept Sprinkle's invitation to shine flashlights through the speculum she had inserted into her vagina. Sprinkle called this scene a "Public Cervix Announcement." As she labored in the awkward project of inserting the speculum—bent over herself, easing it in—she joked and smiled at her audience, explaining that any spectator who wished could come to the edge of the stage to See the Big Show. She had already held up a hand-drawn diagram, explicating the female parts in anatomical proportion, describing their junction and placement like an excessively compliant Sex Education nurse of Junior High School fantasies. Now she sat spread-eagled at the edge of the stage, speculum inserted, with an attendant or two (sometimes male, sometimes female) ready to pass out flashlights to brave audience members.

Spectators had to choose either to join the line of spectators leading up to the stage to peer through the speculum one by one, or to remain in their seats watching other spectators spectating Sprinkle's cervix. Spectators who chose to stand in line would find themselves rubbing shoulders with all kinds of expectations. Sprinkle's shows in art venues generally draw a mixed crowd: porn fans as well as art-world connoisseurs, sprinkled with a batch of New Age sex positivists. Distinctions have the opportunity to blur. Interestingly, porn aficionados often came to The Kitchen armed with large zoom-lens cameras, ready to step right up and snap their private shots, an action welcomed by Sprinkle as "OK" and even "fun." Avant-garde seekers came expecting the shock or the rush of this encounter—the "slumming" so familiar to the cutting edge. New Agers waited for the holy masturbation scene, in which Annie croons and masturbates in the name of self-transformation and accepting love. But whether one chose to remain seated, or joined in the line of expectations, everyone had the opportunity to observe their own choices.

For many in attendance, those choices became fraught with unexpected complexities. Theatre director and academic Richard Schechner told me that on the night in 1990 when he attended Sprinkle's show at The Kitchen, he chose to stay in his seat. Schechner himself had mounted such sexually open avant-garde pieces as *Dionysus in 69* with the Performance Group, and had even cast Sprinkle in his *Prometheus Project* in 1985 (having "discovered" her Nurse Sprinkle show on 42nd Street when he took a graduate class in performance studies on a field trip to Times Square), but because of the complex repercussions involved in choosing to look, he found himself remaining in his seat. "I chose not to look. That was an interesting choice for me. I was curious. But I was also with [female companions] and feared that my looking would be construed as 'being sexually excited'—and why not?—but I did not want to suffer the outcome of that 'accusation.'" Still, the choice not to look was as interesting and fraught as the choice to look. From their seats, spectators viewed the cervix from another angle: the wide-angled view of the cervix as show. Indeed the cervix itself was hardly any more of a show than the showing was a show, and this concatenation of display left no spot in the theatre uninvolved—complicity was broadly based.

The first time I attended *Post Porn Modernist*, I was the only one of my companions (two women) who decided to join the line. Standing in line, however, I felt a mounting sense of confusion about my choice. How was I to focus my particular gaze? Who was I when I looked? And how would my looking be any different from the man with the large camera several spots in front of me who blurted out in a state of excitement: "It looks just like the head of my penis!"? These questions were not answered as I was ushered before Sprinkle and handed a flashlight. Neither were these questions answered when I saw Sprinkle smiling down at me from the stage like some kind of priest with a wafer in hand, beckoning me to "take, look." Neither were they answered when I saw the round pink cervix peeking back at me. Nor when I returned to my seat. Nor, really, to this day. Rather, the questions remain, in all their visceral tactility, the most fascinating aspect of the performance.

ADDRESSING THE CANON

Although the Shakespeare industry is still very much alive in summer festivals, and even in the movies, our postmodernist rejection of universal meanings and our heightened concern with the ideological implications of gender, race and class have made staging the classics increasingly problematic. The voices in this section explore different approaches to making Shakespeare part of an evolving, new, inclusive canon of old and new works of art.

Tina Packer left the spot she was making for herself as an actor at the Royal Shakespeare Company determined to be a director, so that she could ask the questions of Shakespeare's plays that she considered important from a woman's perspective. With a Ford Foundation grant in 1973, she began to train young American actors in her evolving version of classical acting. Actress and voice teacher Kristin Linklater joined Packer and others in what would eventually become the much-admired Shakespeare & Company, located in the Massachusetts Berkshire Mountains.

In their training and rehearsal, Packer and Linklater developed an original exercise that captured the essential thrust of their work. They called it "dropping in the word," a process in which an actor's lines from Shakespeare's text were "dribbled" or dropped word by word into the consciousness to acquire deeply personal resonance.[1] Packer and Linklater used Shakespeare's "language as a generative tool" to develop "a real balance of the spiritual, the intellectual, the sensual and the gut."[2] It is this same combination of qualities that distinguishes Packer's popular yet challenging major productions. She has brought her woman's point of view to the Shakespeare canon, probably directing more of his plays than any other woman director has done.

When Packer asked her to join in the founding of Shakespeare & Company, the Scottish-born Kristin Linklater was teaching at New York University and was much in demand as a consultant to theatres and schools.[3] She taught a method, originated by her London mentor Iris Warren, that linked the voice with the actor's body and emotions. In 1976, in response to many requests, she published *Freeing the Natural Voice*, which became *the* book on voice for actors. In 1990, she joined with Harvard psychologist Carol Gilligan, whose *In a Different Voice* challenged old prejudices about women's moral development,[4] and together they formed The Company of Women, a theatre troupe that was a logical extension of Linklater's longtime interests. Linklater believed that their work with women and girls was "political as well as therapeutic," and that "when women find their own voices and believe their own sense of the world, they'll be free to say and do things about the world they live in." Workshops revealing how women's voices transformed the words of Shakespeare's male characters led to the preparation of a full-scale, all-woman production of *Henry V*, which was performed at Shakespeare & Company and at Smith College. The acting in their *Henry V* and in a subsequent staging of *Lear*, especially Linklater's performances, won high praise. Some critics and spectators, however, questioned whether their interpretation of *Henry V* could realize their hope of turning Shakespeare's "quintessential war play" into the "quintessential antiwar play."

Alisa Solomon and Sarah Curran Barrett both address the problems and possibilities of staging the classics according to new social, intellectual and theatrical paradigms. In one of her excellent essays, Solomon observes that we have to acknowledge that the "issues addressed by new historicist, feminist, and cultural materialist critics are more easily rendered in writing than in production."[5] A thoughtful scholar-critic like Solomon is able to alert us to the complex thinking that guided the experimental Mabou Mines production of *King Lear*, in which all male characters became women and all female characters became men. Having served as the dramaturg for the production, she analyzes themes and structures in the text of *Lear* that make it "deeply in tune with the times," providing grist for the postmodernist work of Lee Breuer and the loose but important collaborative that have worked together at Mabou Mines since 1970. In addition to featuring a woman as Lear, the production was set in 1950s Georgia, adding racism and class hierarchy to the list of issues being challenged. I was fascinated to find that Ruth Maleczech, the remarkable actress who played Lear and suggested the project, was animated mainly by a desire she shares with many women in theatre "to say those words. To have the *right* to say those words."[6]

Gay Gibson Cima's "Strategies for Subverting the Canon" is a very useful analysis—abbreviated as an outline in our text—for finding ways to rescue the plays of the traditional canon for our theatres today.[7] By enlarging the context—theatrical, semiotic, social, financial, historical, organizational, etc.—in which plays are rehearsed, produced, and received by the audience, we "articulate and dismantle the processes and apparatus that attempt to control theatrical representations of women and, in turn, real women." Her comments draw on a wide range of theoretical sources and theatre practice. In addition, she suggests that the productive, if complex, relationship between theory and theatre allows the director to "simultaneously stage theoretical concerns and theorize through practices."

HKC

A WOMAN'S PERSPECTIVE ON SHAKESPEARE

Tina Packer

What we are talking about today is a woman's perspective on Shakespeare, and, of course, what I really mean is *my* perspective.

I became a director, in part, because as an actor I felt I was going slightly crazy and I made everybody else go crazy with me. What would happen to me when I was working on plays was that my perspective was rarely the perspective of the person that I was working with. And I was working with very good people—the Peter Halls and John Bartons. The only way to resolve it was to start directing myself and asking the questions that I felt were important.

The Tempest, for example—my questions are Miranda's questions. She asks her father, "Did you raise up the storm? And if you did, stop it now. The people are suffering. Stop it." She keeps asking questions, but once she's got some hold on the situation, he puts her to sleep. She's not allowed to ask any more questions. She's an adolescent girl now and her father no longer feels that she has to be free. He has to find a young man for her to marry, which is one of the reasons he creates the shipwreck. But she goes back into captivity. What I see then is Miranda going back to civilization, where she's going to be civilized and where she can't any longer be the free spirit.

Miranda's voice, which Shakespeare puts in early, becomes a very major voice for me, and the fact that her father tells her to stop asking questions, taking her voice away, becomes a major influence on my interpretation. There are many story lines going through each play, but this is what has me come alive. Each generation brings out different themes.

If we go to *Hamlet* for a moment, we can ask questions about his treatment of Ophelia. She betrays him by doing what her father says, only to be accused by Hamlet of not being honest, of being a prostitute and a whore. He's dreadful to her and he's really dreadful to his mother. If you start looking at the plays from the woman's point of view, a very different story is told. The only way this will come out in a production is if the director is interested in what's happening to the women. If you really get Gertrude's point of view, if you really get Ophelia's point of view, then the level of the play really deepens.

In *The Merchant of Venice*, what I see about Portia comes out in the first scene. She and Nerissa are talking about her potential suitors. Here's this woman who's clever enough to win a law case that has flummoxed everybody else in the city. She's clever enough to pull this off and be assured in her argument. Yet she's not clever enough to choose her own husband? What is this? She's terribly rich; her father probably thought she needed some form of protection.

In our current production, when the actress Tod Randolph playing Portia comes on, the first thing she does is scream. You see that this woman is in captivity. Every day someone else comes up to her house, decides whether or not he's going to apply for her hand, and maybe hangs around for two or three weeks while he's making up his mind.

This is her life, bound by these fortune hunters. She can't get out of it because this is the way her father tied it up. Her first line is, "By my troth, Nerissa, my little body is tired aweary of this great world." In her first long speech, the third time she speaks, she says, "So this is the will of a living daughter curbed by the will of a dead father." In Elizabethan England *will* means last will and testament, but it also means sexual desire. Her father's will power goes beyond the grave and so organizes her life. I've never seen Portia played as somebody caged in, dying to get out. And for me it rings really true.

It seems to me that although Portia is a wonderful woman, she ultimately fails in my book because she doesn't make the connection between her having to disguise herself to go into the court to fight the case and the fact that as a woman she couldn't do it. She doesn't make that connection or the fact that Shylock as a Jew is an alien and doesn't have the rights of a Venetian citizen. Hopefully the production makes that connection on some level, but she doesn't. Yet her voice comes out when she's disguised as a man. She can say what she thinks, she leads the court; she organizes it. But once she goes back to being a woman again, she allows the voice that spoke out so forcefully to be somewhat muted. She says to her lover Bassanio, "But now I was the lord of this fair mansion, master of my servant, Queen o'er myself; and even now, but now, this house, these servants and this same myself are yours, my lord." If Portia is getting married, what's Nerissa going to do? There's no social security. If she's going to survive, she too needs a husband. So she grabs the biggest jerk of them all . . . I call him a buffoon-thug.

What fascinates me most about what happens when you shift the emphasis of the plays from the themes we have been traditionally taught into what it is that's happening to the women, a whole series of other questions starts coming forward and a different level of investigation takes place. I've done nearly all the plays now. I don't think there's been another woman director who's directed as many of Shakespeare's plays as I have, or been in them. What's happening for me is that I start seeing these themes coming through again and again. I think that Shakespeare's voice starts coming through the women who are the outsiders and often the creative force.

IN THE COMPANY OF WOMEN: CAROL GILLIGAN AND KRISTIN LINKLATER COLLABORATE TO FREE WOMEN'S VOICES

Sarah Curran Barrett

Intrigued by what she calls the "physics" of voice, Gilligan became interested in the physical voice work that Linklater and her colleagues were doing. Gilligan observed one of Linklater's voice classes during a Shakespeare & Company workshop held at Wellesley College in 1987. As Linklater, who co-founded Shakespeare & Company nearly two decades ago, loosened up someone's tongue and jaw through movement and breathing exercises, suddenly a whole story came out about something that had happened in this person's childhood that had blocked her voice. Gilligan realized that everything she had thought about psychological voice was now tied to physical voice. "I thought it explained what I was observing in women's development when girls seem to shift their voices."

In 1990, Linklater along with Daniela Varon and Frances West, both associate directors of The Company of Women, put together a daylong event, "Women Love Shakespeare," inviting 150 Boston actors to perform all the male speeches they had longed to do.

Out of that interest in how these women, who were playing men's roles in Shakespeare, had shifted the resonance so that the same scenes and the same language were somehow different led to the idea of forming The Company of Women. But Linklater, Varon, West and Gilligan realized there was no point in doing an all-female Shakespeare company unless it was connected to the whole question of strengthening the voices of women and girls. The company decided not only to bring women's voices into the world, but also to connect with local groups of women and girls wherever they performed.

While the company's vision has been tempered by limited financial support and logistical difficulties—the eighteen members of the Boston-based company are scattered throughout the United States and Europe—its spirit is indefatigable. According to Susan Clark, the company's executive director, the company members have a "tremendous amount of belief" in the work that they do.

Clark hooked up with Linklater and Gilligan in the summer of 1991 when she helped launch the company's two-week pilot workshop at the University of Southern Maine in Portland, where she had taught.

The success of the Maine workshop had the company jumping for joy. They led additional workshops in Los Angeles; Blacksburg, Virginia; New York City; and Boston. Their dream of raising a million dollars to put on a full production of *Henry V* still seemed possible.

But the company fell through the cracks when it came to securing large sums of grant money. The Ms. Foundation loved the work the company was doing with women and girls, but doesn't support cultural events. Arts and humanities organizations found the project fascinating, but felt it sounded more like a psychology experiment. Feminist groups questioned why the company was focusing on Shakespeare, a dead white male, instead of women playwrights. The company's answer? "If you're going to bring women's voices into the world, one of the places you need to start that process of transformation is to go right into the center, into the cathedral of culture—that's Shakespeare," says Gilligan.

Despite its financial woes, The Company of Women raised enough money to produce a nine-night run of *Henry V* in September. *Henry V* played to sold-out houses at both Shakespeare & Company in Lenox, Massachusetts, and Theatre 14 at Smith College. "It took four years to get enough funds together and enough solidity in the group to get a sense of what the implications of Carol's work intertwined with Kristin's work were going to mean," notes Clark. "Basically developing a way of approaching a text had been evolving for four years."

The company had a limited budget for equity salaries, $135 per week per actor, so ten women ended up playing thirty-one roles. Through costume, movement and, most importantly, vocal clarity, the actors could distinguish the characters sufficiently so the overlap did not prove confusing for the audience. Linklater stressed the amount of profound work and vocal training that enables these actors to speak Shakespeare's verse as well as they do. "The analogy is always with the musician. If you're a talented piano player, you don't just go out and play Beethoven, you do five-finger exercises and you do scales and arpeggios," says Linklater. "You have to apply that level of discipline with Shakespeare's language in order to get to the same point of clarity."

In the opening notes of the play's program, Linklater and Gilligan write, "The women actors in our company are not pretending to be men; rather, they are playing characters who are men. They are pursuing male objectives and male action." But as clear as the language was, several critics didn't find that the all-women cast lived up to its promise, with one critic calling it "male caricature."

However, Linklater garnered rave reviews for her ability to embrace brilliantly the four roles she played. She transformed each of her characters with slight shifts in vocal rhythm and key. "Whatever it is that I do, that people seem to think has a transformed element to it, has to do with my feeling about the text," says Linklater. It's the way the words create the character, which is a fairly subtle entry into character work . . . It's not on a muscular level or an observing level, it comes from an internal, imaginative place, this meeting of the male and female."

By choosing *Henry V*, Shakespeare's "quintessential war play," the company, through the voices of women, hoped to make it the "quintessential antiwar play." What one local critic found most unique about the company's production was that in "their reevaluation of this glorification of patriotism and conquest, rather than 'feminizing' it, they throw themselves into its very maleness, creating a theatrical spectacle that is just as muscular and dynamic, and even more violent than most man-made productions."

UNIVERSITY OF WINCHESTER LIBRARY

The company considers *Henry V* a work in progress, so they have listened carefully to their critics. "A number of people don't see why we call this an antiwar interpretation. It's not until the end, the last scene, that the message comes through," says Linklater. "We want our audience to understand the pity of war and the vulnerability of humanity in the face of conflict when Shakespeare's words are revealed through the voices and psyches of women."

Nowhere did the audience feel the pity of war more strongly than in the final act. What is traditionally played as a wooing scene between Henry and Katherine, "his capital demand," becomes political rape in the company's version. Maureen Shea, *Henry V*'s director, points out that she did not alter any of Shakespeare's text. "What struck us most about Henry's wooing of Katherine," says Shea, "is that Katherine never says 'yes.'"

MABOU MINES' RUTH MALECZECH PLAYS LEAR

Alisa Solomon

> RM: I was the person in the company who wanted to do it, but it wasn't so much that I wanted to do the *play*—I wanted to do the language. I wanted to say those words. To have the *right* to say those words. Playing this part takes everything you've got and even a bit of what you don't. The notion that a mere human being can ever do this play is a bit of a stretch. We got the worst reviews of any play Mabou Mines ever did. And I got the worst of all. That's something I am very proud of.

From the opening moments of the Mabou Mines' production of *Lear* (for which I served as dramaturg), the play takes on the dubious familiarity of a dream reread months after it was recorded. The relentlessly American setting—Georgia in 1957—immediately dislodges the play from hoary classicism and makes it feel uncomfortably close. At the same time, the reversal of the characters' genders—all the men have been changed to women, and all the women to men (except for the Fool who is played, like a French *folle*, as a man in drag)—makes it startlingly strange and provocative, even paradoxical. After all, to posit a female at the center of *Lear* is to offer a resistant, ever parodistic, reading of Shakespeare's grandest tragedy. Yet the text remains virtually unaltered; only pronouns, references to royalty, and sexually marked epithets and images have been changed—with care to sustain the meter as much as possible . . .

The setting in the American South of the 1950s tugs at two directions. In addition to evoking that old, mythic world, it allows [Lee] Breuer to address some aspects of race relations in the U.S. A longtime detractor from the notion that "nontraditional casting" means that an audience ascribes no significance to the race, ethnicity or gender of an actor, Breuer insists that in some contexts, anyway, such invisibility is undesirable, if not impossible. Here, Gloucester is a black neighbor of Lear's. Edna (Edgar) is played by an African American actor; Elva's (Edmond's) illegitimacy is marked by her whiteness and blond hair. When Edna throws off her goody-goody crinoline to disguise herself, she turns Tom O'Bedlam into Mad Marie, a dreadlocked Rastafarian. Thus her personal rejection by a duped mother parallels her marginality from the colonialist state. Racism and class hierarchy become legible in this production, adjuncts to the patriarchal order the gender switch reveals . . .

Though the characters come to us as recognizable types, they are heavily psychologized (even as Breuer repeatedly admonishes the actors "to find the delicate balance between characterization and lyricism. Don't blow the meter just to make a character point. On the other hand, don't give me a poetry reading"). In the opening scene, he tells Maleczech, "Lear is activating her will before she dies. She's not going to have the right to live in her houses or drive her cars. Not even her own car—which is a '57 Chevy." . . .

As Lear offers shares of her estate to her sons, she snakes deliriously across the stage, waltzing to [Pauline] Oliveros's accordion accompaniment and trailed by a comet of her sycophantic family and followers. Only Cordelion stays put. Activity stops dead when Lear holds out a slice of cake to her youngest son. But Cordelion refuses to represent his love falsely; his true feelings cannot be accommodated by the phony vessel of an exaggerated language, "that glib and oily art." Indeed the play repeatedly makes the deconstructive point that language does not express thought or emotion or represent actions faithfully.

Turning Lear, Gloucester, Edgar, Edmond and so on into women goes beyond the tradition of casting women as Hamlet, where the tragic hero remains a male. Actually changing the sex of the *characters* brings to the foreground assumptions about gender that usually go untested, even unnoticed.

The first question the Mabou Mines production raises, as Breuer puts it, is "what happens when women are the ones with power?" This necessarily encompasses issues of bourgeois feminism. As women have risen toward (but rarely to) the top of corporations and nation states, they have taken on roles defined and traditionally held by men. In doing so, have they adopted the values of these institutions, and if so, inevitably? Or as one disapproving colleague once asked, What's the point of this production, to show that women can be as bad as men? But beyond issues of women in the boardroom, the cross-gender (and, with it, interracial) casting of the Breuer/Maleczech *Lear* contemplates the construction of gender (and other categories)—and does so very much within the play's own terms.

In the heath scene, *Lear* offers the most pointed expression of one of its most compelling thematic questions: What is it to be human? When Lear, deciding to "unbutton here," strips off the last vestiges of social roles, what remains? This production throws one more element into that stormy question: does gender matter? . . .

Though the production has not set out to explain the difference between a father's relationship with his daughters and a mother's with her sons, the gender reversal twists the emotional context of the parent-child theme into new places of pathos and depth if only because seeing a mother at the center of a family offers a more accurate description of social relations as they exist: The family struggles seem in some sense ordinary—Cordelion (who is played by Maleczech's real-life son, Lute Ramblin') recoils from his mother's first-act demands with the silent querulousness of an embarrassed adolescent. And Lear's severing from her son rips through the taboo of motherhood as it is constructed in this culture, with wrenching agony—Lear makes her final entrance huffing under the weight of Cordelion's body, draped lifelessly across her arms. "Howl, howl, howl!" she cries out, her voice collapsing into a gravelly, grief-struck groan.

STRATEGIES FOR SUBVERTING THE CANON

Gay Gibson Cima

As feminist directors, many of us consider the theatre a laboratory in which we prove the validity of experiences previously excluded from or subordinated on the stage. We direct new or recently rediscovered feminist scripts and create our own collectively built plays. Some believe that this is the only way to accomplish feminist goals, that directing the canon—no matter how subversive the director's tactics—simply reinscribes patriarchal values. Others, like myself, think it necessary to adopt *both* strategies: directing the new and redirecting the old. These two projects can proceed simultaneously, enabling us to reach the widest possible audience and allowing us to contribute to the process of creating real material change.

To subvert the canon, then, we must examine the way we finance, house, cast, rehearse and publicize our revisionist stagings, and we must think carefully about the reception of the work. What is the social function and effect of our directorial work? Which specific strategies—design interventions, cross-casting, textual changes, for example—might enable the particular audience of an individual production to see themselves anew? There is no universal formula or combination of strategies that will work best in every situation.

Subverting the Canon: Show What Is There and/or Show What Is Not

1. Usurp the means of production, or, failing that, stage one or more of the major forces that financed your particular show, selected the script, and set the parameters of its staging.
2. Discover and stage the "social script" of the original production.

3. This leads to the idea of restoring historical consciousness to our work by staging the historical conditions, relationships and influences that shaped it.

4. Find stage images that raise questions about why the characters are represented as they are.

5. Look for the underlying myth and represent it as serving the patriarchy rather than acting as a psychological reality.

6. Another way of thinking about this process is to stage the original "interpretive community" that made meaning of the premiere production or of any subsequent production.

7. Focus on demonstrating and critiquing the acting style of the period as it controls female bodies.

8. Employ and critique, or parody, the historical blocking patterns that marginalized women in the premiere productions of classic scripts.

9. Represent in your production the women who enabled the male writers to create works that have been canonized.

10. Write beyond the ending of romance plots.

11. Cross-gender, cross-racial, and cross-generational casting tactics can also aid in the process of subverting the canon.

12. Produce a double bill that will undermine the patriarchal dictates.

13. Unusual sets, choreographic interludes and vocal arias can also subvert a script in performance.

14. Produce your show in a non-theatrical space or highlight the conventions implicit in the theatre that you use.

15. Ask your dramaturg to seek out unusual means of access into the period of the play.

16. Be aware of your rehearsal techniques: Do they promote a questioning attitude, empowering your actors, or do they turn your actors into powerless female characters?

17. If you build your directorial work upon actors' improvisations, plan carefully, because improvisations can inadvertently reproduce the dominant ideological structures that you are trying to critique.

18. Reinvent the audience-actor-director relationship, striving for a sense of "improvised directing."

19. As an antidote to the emphasis on the individual in most of the humanist drama within the canon, stage the wider social context of the conflict, the community out of which the characters emerge.

20. Be aware of the "hidden" semiotics of your production.

21. Make your production into what Stanley Fish has called a "self consuming artifact," a performance text that moves dialectically to contradict its own truths, and thereby challenge the audience to make meaning out of it.

22. Adopt strategies from feminist performance art.

ARTISTIC PROCESS AND PROFESSIONAL POWER

ACTING

By the opening of the new millennium, women performers had abandoned the designation of "actress," which implied someone confined within the traditional cultural assumptions about female behavior, in order to take their proper place under the generic rubric of "actor." The transition to "actor" was not just a change of label, however; it involved questioning and transforming every aspect of the artistic process to enable women to use themselves and their lives to create a theatre free of gender-based oppression.

As early as the 1970s, Roberta Sklar began to explore "the distinct acting problems women have," something that had not been done before.[1] "How do you act as a performer and a person when you have been taught not to *act*, not to do, not to take action." Exploring an exercise used in the Open Theater, where she was a director, she realized that "for women, the internal reality is filled with the social suppression of womanhood . . . rage . . . suppressed self-knowledge." Instead of the conventional approaches of "breaking down defenses," women needed support to build up "strengths, literal and psychic." "Women have to hear their own voice, bodies, impulses, to take them and use them," observed Sklar's collaborator Sondra Segal. "What I am doing is I'm telling what I know." Their words recall those of Viola Spolin, creator of theatre games and author of *Improvisation for the Theater*, a seminal but often forgotten influence whose anti-authoritarian techniques helped to open up acting practice to women's newly articulated aspirations.

Lois Weaver of the Split Britches company, who opens the discussion here, credits her liberation to do whatever she wanted onstage to her early days with those three remarkable Cuna-Rappahannock Native American sisters who are known collectively as the Spiderwoman Theatre.[2] Weaver's teaching encourages a creative freedom that validates women's individual desires, vision and daily experiences, as well as their fantasies, and gives them "a voice in the acting." In the Split Britches performances that she, Peggy Shaw and Deb Margolin have created, the actor's "subtext becomes the text." Their dedication to exploration, empowerment, humor, challenge, relationships and inclusiveness in handling themes, genres and genders injected new dimensions into the acting process.

Glenda Dickerson and Breena Clarke, who had worked together as professor and student at Howard University, became collaborating professionals for their play *Re/membering Aunt Jemima: A Menstrual Show*.[3] In their creative project, they intended to "take apart the stereotype of Aunt Jemima, tear it apart, examine it, and put her back together as the archetype she originally was." They developed the layered "Triune Voice" acting process of "I Am/Who Was/Who Am" to make each actor fully present in the history of women of African American identity, touching "something deeply hidden and ineffable in the student." They used music, historic texts and improvisation to help them discover the voices of their foremothers.

In her extensive experience as a director of more than seventy plays, Anne Bogart has always been on the lookout for more creative approaches, combining influences from Germany and Japan and from the discipline of dance. Her current postmodern "Viewpoints training,"[4] derived from the work of dancer-choreographer Mary Overlie, with whom Bogart worked at NYU's Experimental Theater Wing in the 1980s, provides "a vocabulary for working collaboratively with actors in the creation of the mise-en-scène." It allows the actors to become "the individual and collective choreographers of the physical action." Viewpoints exercises are part of Bogart's preparatory "source work," empowering each company member to contribute in a personal, subjective way to the basic "question" of their new piece and participate in what she calls the "collective dreaming" of the work. With actors trained in these ways and texts that interest her, Bogart creates the striking stagings that have made her a pivotal figure in contemporary theatre.

Several much-admired leading actors conclude the discussion of acting, speaking directly to us of their careers and their craft. They differ in age, background, training and style, but all have won coveted awards, and all share a broad vision of theatre. Ruby Dee broke many barriers for black actors, combining creative accomplishment and social activism in the many defining stage productions and films in which she appeared and the stories and poetry she wrote. Joanne Woodward and Estelle Parsons, best known for their film roles, have a deep interest in the acting process; both teach, deriving their approach from the Actors Studio and the heritage of the Group Theatre, which also combined activism and acting. Both have made serious major commitments as directors to important playwrights and unconventional productions that can "change people's minds." Cherry Jones was a founding member of Robert Brustein's American Repertory Theatre, where she grew as an artist through more than twenty-five productions, working with innovative masters like Andre Serban. Kathleen Chalfant redefined what being a character actress meant in her multiple roles in *Angels in America* and in her triumph as the dying college professor in Margaret Edson's surprise Pulitzer Prize–winning hit, *Wit*.

These artists also share with us the common frustrations of women performers. Some found it difficult to combine motherhood and career; others challenged homophobia by publicly revealing lesbian relationships.[5] Hollywood tried to turn them into commodities when young, and monsters when mature. Even in the theatre, an actor's options diminish when she moves out of the "heroine stage." Yet these women have remained active, sustained by their talent and their commitment to their experience as women and to a compelling idea of theatre.

HKC

LOIS WEAVER ON FEMINIST ACTING

An Interview with Elizabeth C. Stroppel

ES: How do you go about teaching acting and then performing in order to foreground feminism?

LW: A real basis for my work started with Spiderwoman. I learned there that I could do whatever I wanted to do onstage, and very often, that was our starting point. That is my starting point when I teach acting and when I create work with women. Those things run tandemly. I work on encouraging the independent artist rather than teaching an actor. That's probably a feminist root, that we have a voice in the acting. We're not simply puppets for someone else's vision. So the beginning point is desire: What do I want to do? Who do I want to be onstage? If I wanted to play Juliet, and I was a fifty-year-old Native American woman, I could play Juliet. If I wanted to be a country western singer and I couldn't necessarily sing, I could play that. And that was the starting point that we used when we worked in Spiderwoman; it is an underpinning of the work that I do now, to start from that point of desire. That fantasy often takes us outside of the realm of roles the way they are designed for us by the outside world.

Another fundamental is that the minute, mundane details of our life and our imagination are important, viable, and potentially usable in the theatre, either as material or as what you bring to a character. And those details function mostly around relationship, not necessarily around action. "What is the relationship to my environment, my teacup, the other people onstage?" There's a lot of power in what I see, and not necessarily in what I do.

The final fundamental, or theory if you want to say that, is that I work from an associative place rather than a cognizant place, not exclusively, but to try to bring up images and impulses that come out of an associative side of the self rather than what you know. What that does often is to create a sense of logic that's not logical. I don't think that we sit around from a Stanislavskian point of view knowing what we want from one second to another. Life is much more chaotic than that. Our desires, wants, images, and feelings change immediately, from moment to moment, and by working with images—impulses which are more abstract than literal—you can depend on that rather than a literal logic of saying, "Okay, on this line I want to do this."

I've created what I call a "multiple-choice acting" where you can stand in the middle of a pie and in that moment, you have lots of choices. One of them could be an intention, an "I want to," or an action, but it could also be a physical impulse or an image that doesn't necessarily relate to that moment. You can use that and work from that to create moment-to-moment acting by being responsive to moment-to-moment stimulus, some coming from the associative side of your brain, not the cognitive side. I do a lot of impulse work, and I guess this is another place where feminism comes into play. You use the body as a resource, so that you can work through impulse to find a character. Impulse for me is a sound and movement. This is very much inspired by work from the Open Theater, work that Joe Chaikin did. From a sound and a movement, you can create an abstract impulse that can lead you to create a character out of your imagination—a job, a place where they live—but you can also use that work as a subtext for a character already written. I also use a lot of image work. You walk into a room and say, "I see something and that reminds me of . . ." and in that is an emotional memory, if you want to relate it back to Stanislavski. To work and to write from images: those are the fundamentals from [which] I start.

ES: In creating a character already within a text, do you give any guidelines for that?

LW: I start from the body, and look for the place where my body, my imagination, my memory intersects with that character, rather than trying to put my body and my mind *into* that character. It's an aesthetic as well, a kind of acting which I prefer, more closely related to performance where you can see the actor in the character. I never really lose myself to a representation of that character. It's a particular style of acting. You have a character like Nora. and you say, "Where does she exist in my body?" Maybe in the shoulders, so then I try to work abstractly with impulses in those shoulders, first to ultimately create gesture, but secondly, to find the body of a character.

ES: Through its use then, what would you say feminist acting is?

LW: For me, feminist acting is when a woman brings herself to the character and never completely loses herself to the character. She doesn't create a representation of someone else's ideas; she brings her own ideas into that space. Also, feminist acting is not necessarily naturalistic, so, in other words, it wouldn't create a naturalistic or realistic character. It would go outside that realm, break the "fourth wall" for lack of a better term, so that you would see the actor in the character. Again this is an aesthetic where you could see the character coming out and sitting down with you.

ES: Does feminist acting distinguish itself from traditional acting in your mind?

LW: That's hard to say because there are lots of traditional actors who are feminists, and they bring a real power and strength to a real traditional approach. I'm thinking in particular of some English actors, Fiona Shaw and Juliet Stevenson. It's very clear that they bring a feminist consciousness to their work which is incredibly traditional.

THE TRIUNE VOICE

Breena Clarke and Glenda Dickerson

Our task in this essay will be to describe the Triune Voice. The Triune Voice is our term to describe the dramatic voice which we, as African American dramatists, employ in creating original vehicles for the stage from found sources. Uncovering the Triune Voice in the classroom or during a rehearsal process provides a new challenge for instructors/directors and students alike. When exploring the Triune Voice, a whole new approach to resource material takes place. The instructor/director is striving to touch something deeply hidden and ineffable in the student/actor. Therefore, previously unrelated materials may be employed; materials ranging from a snatch of poetry, to a riff of music, to a recounting of a real woman's words. These bits and pieces of stimuli can be used as improvisational devices which the women apply to their own lives.

The Triune Voice is not naturalistic, though it is rooted in reality; it should not be considered choreopoetic, though it employs the poetic voice; rather the Triune Voice is expressed through culturally specific archetypes and calls upon a racial idiom in verse form as revealed in the words of spirituals, folk rhymes, blues, and other spontaneous utterances.[1] We will explore the Triune Voice specifically as we have used it to reclaim the lost voice of the stereotypical figure Aunt Jemima in an original dramatic event entitled *Re/membering Aunt Jemima: A Menstrual Show.* The Triune Voice can be charted this way:

I Am/Who Was/Who Am

Nineteenth-century African American women's emancipatory narratives are the best sources to begin an examination of the elements of the Triune Voice.[2] Beginning with the emancipatory narratives, literary works by African Americans have first and foremost sought to establish an identity for the author as a human being by Western standards.

> Black people, the evidence suggests, had to represent themselves as "speaking subjects" before they could even begin to destroy their status as objects, as commodities, within Western culture. In addition to all of the myriad reasons for which human beings write books, this particular reason seems to have been paramount for the black slave.[3]

Thus, the bondswoman who put pen to paper or who caused others to set down in her own words the facts of her life in slavery, created herself as a reasoning human being capable of reflection.[4] This act killed the slave and created the free woman. Therefore, the first component of the dramatic Triune Voice is this emancipatory voice, the voice which asserts the existence of a reasoning human being:

I AM (I stand before you in person or on the printed page)

Central to the bondswoman's concerns in relating an account of her life is the assertion that she was born in such a place, in such a year, of such people. These simple statements create the bondswoman as the subject of her own narrative. If she says no more, she has given lie to the idea that she is incapable of speaking for herself because of her African ancestry. She has irrevocably changed her status from that of an object, owned and identified by another, to the subject of her own discourse. This first, large step is the foundation of a voice, a perspective, a point of view which had not existed before. This author/narrator creates an a clear, bell-like, subjective voice of identity. What must be understood is that the author/narrator, the enslaved African woman, had never existed as a subjective voice of authority until she created herself.

When the writer/performer discovers this foremother, her heart leaps up. This voicing of **I AM** is the rebellious, revolutionary, courageous act which reveals the drylongso[5] woman she always hoped for, sprung not from the imagination of the solitary playwright, but from flesh and blood. When the foremother goes further to describe the person she was when these events took place, she employs the second component of the Triune Voice, the voice which remembers and is compelled to record:

> **WHO WAS** (This is the person I was when these events took place. This is the voice which remembers our foremothers' recollections and lives by example.)

From her courageous first assertion, the bondswoman proceeds to the well-spring of memory to draw for us the contours of slavery. A second voice emerges from within the text, a voice which enlarges upon the initial assertions to reflect and comment on the particular circumstances of her bondage.

This dual voice, which remembers and is compelled to record, is the **I AM/WHO WAS**. Here the bondswoman provides the crucial first-person, eyewitness account of the institution of slavery. A fundamental understanding of the institution of slavery depends on the authority of an eyewitness account. No scholar trained in the patriarchal tradition which created the "peculiar institution" can be completely trusted to relate its history. One does not interview the fox for a history of hens. Even African American women scholars, who must by necessity distance themselves from the true horrors of the experience, cannot speak for the bondswoman. Also, accounts by male bondspersons must be examined for their exclusions of women's experiences in bondage. Though Frederick Douglass relates the horror of the system of sexual exploitation and forced breeding, he cannot say, "*I am*" the woman "*who was*" the woman who experienced this. Understanding this concept of dual-voiced discourse is crucial to recognizing the secret/dramatic voice. It is upon this foundation that we develop the Triune Voice.

The third component of the Triune Voice is the dramatic voice. This third component enlarges upon and adds "one full measure" to the dual voiced discourse of our foremothers. This is the performer's voice:

WHO AM (I am the woman who was and who am able to express it.) This is the playwright's/performer's voice.

Thus, the Triune Voice: **I AM/WHO WAS/WHO AM.**

This Triune Voice is the synthesis of the dual voice of our foremother with the performer's voice. The playwright/performer who employs the Triune Voice functions as Rescuer. She rescues her mother's words from the trap of submerged memory and the tyranny of the printed page. She stands before us and speaks of her mother's memories. Embracing the words of her foremother and agreeing to speak them, the performer literally speaks with the foremother's tongue—she puts her mother's tongue in her mouth. The action of acknowledging the mother's tongue and words, agreeing to embrace them and synthesizing them with the voices of contemporary African American women is the rebellious/revolutionary/emancipatory act of the performer.

ANNE BOGART—VIEWPOINTS

An Interview with Elizabeth C. Stroppel

ES: When you direct a piece, how do you approach it? How do you then present it to the actors, for example, through exercises?

AB: Well, in terms of how I approach a play—I've done about seventy plays, and each one has been different. I can put it into a rough formula but the details are different for each one. I do a tremendous amount of research first, on the question that the play or the project is asking, and a lot of dreaming. Then I try to allow all the collaborators into that collective dreaming, which involves a great deal of discussion but also something that I call sourcework. This has nothing to do with staging but with getting in contact with what the dreams related to the question that the play asks are. And those will be different depending on all seventy different productions. Then I do a great deal of analytical work, both psychological and sociological analysis of the material around a table. Once that's done, I forget all of that and just turn into a staging factory. I start working physically in terms of choreography, and spend a lot of time just on choreographing details. Hopefully, all of the research and the sourcework that we've done feeds into the vehicle, which is the staging or the choreography, so the question is living on the stage.

ES: Can you explain a bit about "the dreaming" of the play?

AB: It's associating. Each great play has a question that it's asking. Say you're doing *Spring's Awakening*, and the question is about how young people's sexual vitality and life is eaten out of them by older, bitter people. You then ask the question, "How does that happen in your life?" or, "What kinds of associations do you have on that?" That's the dreaming. I have to do a lot of dreaming, and it might take me to certain visual things—magazines, pictures, etc. Then I do the same thing with the actors. I try to create work in which they dream that question; they think about it; they have free association; they remember things from their lives that relate to that question. So the actors can now embody the question, which has been asleep on the shelf like a spore, and bring it to life with their own associations and present-time awareness of the question.

ES: So when you actually start working on the staging, the physical part of it, what kind of exercises do you do to empower the actors?

AB: I do a training called "The Seven Viewpoint Training" which was originally six but then went to nine, so now it's just called "The Viewpoint Training." It's a system of movement, a philosophy of movement on the stage. The viewpoints are: spatial relationship, gesture, kinesthetic response, shape, repetition. architecture, duration and topography. They're all different things that the actors' bodies are making decisions on in the moment. They're trained in that philosophy of movement, so when we actually get to the staging factory, they're basically making up all the movement based on this philosophy.

ES: That is very specific. It's from this training, then, that they come up with the gestures, images, etc. through their own bodies?

AB: Exactly. I'll refine it, or make it more visually clear for the audience, but they essentially make all the movements.

ES: One of my other interviewees [Meredith Alexander] said that you referred to yourself as a "sieve" through which the actors can work. Is that what you mean?

AB: Yes, the actors' or anybody's ideas. I don't particularly think that my ideas are very good. I think they're a way to start but I'll basically use whoever has the best idea at the moment. I'm not very territorial about ideas which I think is somewhat feminist.

ES: Is there a way that you try to bring women's experiences or women actors more to the forefront through, for example, gestures, and so on?

AB: Well, I mix the genders a lot. I did *A Streetcar Named Desire*. One Stanley Kowalski was played as Marlon Brando played him, but another of the Stanleys was a woman. There were twelve Blanches and two of them were men. In the sense that there are more men's roles in most plays, I try to do something, like in my production of *Danton's Death*. Robespierre was played by a woman and Danton by a man, which made it a very gender-related argument between the two.

ES: Yes, playing around with gender is often mentioned as a useful technique because it does bring the construction of gender to the foreground. Can you give any examples of acting that you've seen which struck you as feminist or subversive in some manner?

AB: The most extraordinary performance that I've seen was Jeff Weiss doing Gertrude Stein, but that's because it was so extreme in his portrayal of her and her writing.

ES: A number of respondents have stated that they find it difficult to get women actors to take center stage, and that maybe that might be a part of what feminist acting is.

AB: I totally disagree. I find that women actors are not afraid to take center stage. They're artists. They're working and dealing with the material at hand.

ES: So you don't sense any feeling of the cultural inscription of women being the passive ones?

AB: Yes, in body language and in life, women take up space differently. They try to show that they're not taking up space so as not to look like dykes. It's really intimidating for a woman to stand with her legs apart. The codified behavior of men is not as demanding as women's, so I think that transfers onto stage. It is a stereotype of our society that women do bring to the stage, but everything on the stage is a stereotype. You sit down, pick up a teacup, turn to your right, etc. I guess if I were to say what would be feminist acting, it might be that the stereotype is awake instead of asleep. So instead of blandly repeating behavioral gestures without any awareness of them . . . in other words, if it's done with a vengeance or awake, maybe that's feminist. It questions behavior onstage, the status quo.

ES: Yes, so the audience can question it. Do you make your actors aware of stereotyped gestures?

AB: Yes—I think a great actor, a woman playing, for instance, Madge in *Picnic*, won't just blindly do the stereotypical Madge gestures and behavior. She'll actually fight them, inside, which makes those gestures very awake. So an actress that can bring that to the role makes us ask the question of why Madge is Madge. Why is she doing that?

ES: How important do you think the written text is in being able to act in a feminist manner?

AB: Oh, I'm most interested in doing canons, or subsets of canons. To me the theatre is about memories. Although I am interested in new plays, a huge part of my work is about bringing back things that reside in our cultural history. So, for me, it's almost more interesting to take the canon and awaken it because it is ours; we're weighted down by it. To do *Picnic* is really a great thrill because you ask all the questions from the point of view of now. A huge percentage of my work is devoted to history because memory is what we're in danger of losing.

ES: What would you do with Linda Loman in *Death of a Salesman*?

AB: Faaaabulous! Her state is incredible. I actually did some work with my students at Columbia on that play because I think it's amazing. You can have so much feeling for her. Her life is in shreds. What an amazing role.

ES: So you can actually be a feminist actor in that role?

AB: Absolutely. As a matter of fact, it's part of your job as an actress to deal with those roles. That's our inheritance. That's where we come from. We have to ask where we're going but we can't be Stalinists as feminists and pretend that the past didn't exist. The plays are part of what we're weighted down with. Linda Loman is our family, and we have to deal with our family.

ES: And how do we do that with a 1994 awareness?
AB: You attack it as artists, with resistance, anger and revenge.

FROM RUBY DEE'S MEMORY BOOK

Ruby Dee

Ruby Dee tells of her long career of creative accomplishment and social activism in the joint autobiography with her husband, playwright and actor Ossie Davis. The vivid memories create an unusual informal history of American theatre, films, radio and TV from the perspective of this extraordinary African American couple. Ruby Dee participated in many of the defining events from early movies and the American Negro Theatre in the 1940s and '50s to leading roles in original productions of A Raisin in the Sun, Purlie Victorious, Boesman and Lena *and* Wedding Band; *she was the first black actress of her day to appear in leading Shakespearean roles, has won Obies and Drama Desk awards, and has been inducted into the Broadway Hall of Fame. The stories and poems she has performed over the years when called upon to make a speech have been published and became part of her 1998 one-woman show* One Good Nerve: A Visit with Ruby Dee. *A few telling moments from her witty but moving memoir and a bit from her poem "Calling All Women" suggest the spirit of her more than fifty-year career in movies, television and onstage.*

In Hollywood Filming *No Way Out* in 1950

The day before the beginning of principal photography, some test footage had been shot for the purpose of examining our faces. The makeup people were not quite satisfied with me. They spoke aloud to each other while viewing the results.

"I really don't think she needs any makeup at all. Some powder? But these brows. Yes, let's take the brows down." I felt like a thing, not a person—a heathen from Harlem. Everybody out here is so beautiful. So trim, slim, and perfect looking. How can they bear to touch us black Neanderthals from New York?

Nevertheless, the makeup they put on my face each morning did please me; but hair was a different matter. On the third day, I could sense that the hairdresser assigned to me was not well practiced in handling hair like mine. Despite efforts to relax, I grew increasingly tense. I found myself inquiring about a colored hairdresser. Was there one on staff? Finally, I suggested that perhaps it would be appropriate to bring in somebody who would be more familiar with my kind of hair. "Of course," they said, with a smile that seemed to spring from relief—"It could be arranged."

Elizabeth Searcy, a colored hairdresser, came that afternoon, which certainly made me relax, but not completely. I was still uncomfortable because

I felt those in wardrobe straining to be normal, working with people that, were it not for their jobs, they would not touch.

Every day at work on *No Way Out*, I was conscious of the film's political and social themes. I was also vividly aware of the discrepancy between the fictional world of the film and the reality of racist discrimination on the lot, and in the film industry.

Films like *No Way Out* have widened the crack in the door through which other cultures have entered the previously lily-white film industry, and I was pleased to have had even a small part in this one. It was the best I could do, I'd say, for a colored girl at the time.

Playing Lena in Athol Fugard's *Boesman and Lena* Opposite James Earl Jones in 1970

That glorious trip to the Moscow film festival in 1969 yielded another blessing: I got to know [the agent] Lucy Kroll. About a year later, she called to say that James Earl Jones would be playing Boesman in *Boesman and Lena*, a work by the acclaimed South African playwright Athol Fugard. She asked if I would like to read the script and consider the role of Lena. I confess I didn't understand the part at first. Ossie read it, and talked about its very real social, political and gender significance. He helped open my eyes to the beauty of the text and to the genius of the author.

The work in *Boesman and Lena* became one of the most satisfying investigations of a character I'd ever done, thanks in part to John Berry, the director, and to Ossie. The word "investigation" may be only halfway accurate. The acting process is more reciprocal, I think. You dig as far as you can into the character, while at the same time, the character digs as far as it can into you. The rehearsals and the discussions about apartheid, coupled with my own familiarity with the frustrations of racism, the brutality of sexism and the desperate need for comfort and joy that we all share—all this began to wear away and to crush out my reserve, anxiety and uncertainty until, finally, I relaxed in gradual surrender.

The door to myself flew open one day, and Lena walked in and climbed all over and through me, holding me fast from the beginning to the end of the performance. After the final curtain, she would let go, and I would feel happy and relieved. Lena was an extraordinary, multidimensional person, carrying me into places in myself where I had never been, stretching me enormously as an actor.

Playing Julia in *Wedding Band* by Alice Childress in 1966 and 1972 and on TV in 1974

Alice Childress was one of the first members of the American Negro Theatre. She was the original Blanche in *Anna Lucasta*, and a good actor. It is as a playwright, however, and as an author of short monologues, that I remember her best. *Wedding Band* is her most produced play, and I was Julia Augustine in the first four presentations.

Wedding Band was a challenging play. The story caused eight local TV stations, mostly in the Southwest, to ban the show for content. It was an interracial love story, tender, sad, and, also in that aspect, vicious. But the most profound lesson Julia taught me, as an actor, had nothing to do with race.

When it was being televised for ABC in 1974, I discovered for the first time that it is possible to work twenty-five hours straight without any sleep. Joseph Papp, founder of the New York Shakespeare Festival, directed the teleplay with Alice Childress, as they had also codirected the stage version at the Public Theatre, and he was way behind schedule. We had to finish by morning and that was that. We dared not sit or lie down or stop talking or stop moving around for too long; and we ate only enough to put something besides hot coffee in our stomachs. Tempers were tightrope taut, the work was intense, but we did it because we had to.

Looking back, I think the relentless nature of the work added an excitement to the finished product. I really didn't know I had it in me, or why all of us didn't drop dead. I count *Wedding Band* among some of my most rewarding work.

Playing in Adrienne Kennedy's *The Ohio State Murders* in 1992 and Pearl Cleage's *Flyin' West* at the Kennedy Center

Among some things I would like a retake on is my relationship to Adrienne Kennedy and her work. When I first read her play *Funnyhouse of a Negro*, I didn't understand it, and chose not to do it. When I was invited in 1992 to do the role of Suzanne Alexander in *The Ohio State Murders*, which Gerald Freeman directed at the Great Lakes Theatre Festival in Cleveland, I realized that indeed one of the reasons I was born was to perform in plays written by Adrienne Kennedy. I feel that we have a spiritual and artistic kinship that escaped me at the time. Her characters have, in a sense, been warped by racism. They seem off center, askew. They are people I now recognize immediately not only from intuition, but also from experience.

I'm glad Pearl Cleage was on my dance card to meet as an author and to know as a friend. Rick Khan invited me to perform at Crossroads Theatre in *Flyin' West*, her play about spousal abuse, and about some of the black women who went west to claim land and settle on it. Since it dealt with such an important slice of American history, I wanted it to have an extended run. The play was well received by audiences at Crossroads and at the Kennedy Center Eisenhower Theatre.

Thoughts About the Past and the Future

These are some of the thoughts that crowd my mind, that instruct what I write, that inform whatever humor escapes from me, and that I hope my grandchildren will investigate while they are young.

As a senior now, as mother now of the tribe, I feel that we can't just run off and leave it to the children. We who helped to create this mess still have an obligation. We must ring the bells, call attention to the dangers that stride in full daylight because too few are rehearsing the ways of Struggle and drawing up the demands of Victory. It is time now for envisioning that vastly different future, where food, clothing and shelter can be taken for granted as we get on with that next revolution—the revolution that speaks to the largely unexplored divinity within us, that would relegate all other revolutions to precursors of the main event.

From "Calling All Women":

> Calling all sisters. Calling all
> Righteous sisters.
> Calling all women. To steal away
> To our secret place. Have a meeting
> Face to face. Look at the facts
> And determine our pace. Calling all
> Women.

JOANNE WOODWARD: CHANGING PEOPLE'S MINDS

Helen Krich Chinoy

Joanne Woodward, actor, director, teacher, has brought images of women usually ignored or forgotten to television, the screen, and the stage. From such films as *Rachel, Rachel* and *The Effect of Gamma Rays on Man-in-the-Moon Marigolds* to stage interpretations of *Candida* and *The Glass Menagerie* and television performances in *See How She Runs*, *Do You Remember Love* and *Mr. and Mrs. Bridge*, she has endowed "complex, sometimes downtrodden women" with her own sensitivity, intelligence and power. Collette Dowling, author of *The Cinderella Complex*, paid tribute to Woodward's ability to "reflect the shifting, evocative aspects of Woman as she has emerged in the culture in recent years."[1]

Perhaps Joanne Woodward has been able to use her beauty and talent in this way because she herself has gone through the many changes that have marked women's lives. Brought up to be a southern belle, married for over thirty years to America's reluctant male sex symbol, Paul Newman, she seemed to have been torn in the early years between an upbringing that told her she should have "babies and be supported" and her desire for a career. She speaks of herself as something of a rebel when she came to New York to study acting at the Neighborhood Playhouse and struggled for acting jobs. But despite her stunning, Oscar-winning performance in *The Three Faces of Eve* early in her career, Hollywood had her playing the usual succession of "glamorous, or sexy and voluptuous types."[2] She faced the dangers of being turned into a "commodity" by the industry.

Woodward says of herself, however, "I never really had the personality to be a superstar . . . I was having babies, staying home, studying philosophy at Sarah Lawrence, feeding the pets." She rejects the notion that she was taking a back seat to her husband's career. It was he who "literally shoved me out of the house to work. He directed *Rachel, Rachel* to revive my career when I was a total has-been."[3]

She confessed some time ago that "I've come very late to a great many issues—probably in my thirties. And as far as the whole women's issue was concerned, probably not even until my forties . . . We are confused now, especially women my age. We were raised with certain attitudes and mores that just don't function anymore."[4] Without abandoning the traditional roles of wife and mother of a large family, however, she "has come into her own" in her personal life and her career. As she and her husband turned their backs on the Hollywood scene, her career took a different direction. "I've tapered off, but not by choice, I assure you," she quipped. "There are not many roles that come along that are right for me—unless you're willing to play a mechanical monster or be relegated to playing somebody's mother or as in my case now, somebody's grandmother."[5] Instead, Woodward gradually began the exploration of neglected women for which she has gained acclaim, and in the 1980s she started directing plays for the stage, where she can do what she loves best, work with actors and communicate her strong feelings on social and humanitarian issues.

Her 1986 project directing Shirley Knight in a short one-woman play about nuclear disarmament, *The Depot*, written for Woodward by Eve Ensler, engaged audiences in discussion at the Interart Theatre and toured for two years, even being performed at a nuclear test site in Nevada. Her dedication to reviving the plays of Clifford Odets comes out of the same idea of an engaged, activist theatre. She first learned of Odets from her teacher, Sanford Meisner, who was an original member of the Group Theatre, for which Odets wrote his early plays. Her fascination with this 1930s theatre of social activism and intense actor training led her to produce an award-winning documentary, *Broadway's Dreamers: The Legacy of the Group Theatre* in 1989. In the next decade she directed *Golden Boy, Rocket to the Moon, Waiting for Lefty* and Odets's post-*Group* play about Hollywood originally written for John Garfield, *The Big Knife*. The headline, "Championing Odets, Unfashionable as That Is" does not dim her enthusiasm.[6] "He is one of our finest playwrights. He's just fallen out of fashion." Critics who "applaud" her "audacity" encourage her to continue her honest explorations, and her actors relish Odets's "unerring instinct for how actors work." The "tenacity in the face of hardship" that she recalls from her own Depression experience is also "what makes *Waiting for Lefty* contemporary." Joanne Woodward believes that "we still haven't figured out how to pay people living wages for a day's work . . . To me, this play is not just about the Depression. It's about changing people's minds. Which is what theatre is for."

THE INTEGRITY OF ESTELLE PARSONS

Helen Krich Chinoy

Estelle Parsons has played many roles onstage and off in her long career. Although the general public probably knows her best for her 1967 Oscar-winning performance in the film *Bonnie and Clyde* or her comic turns as the mother of *Roseanne* on television, her talents and interests have ranged widely. She studied law but worked instead for a number of years as writer, feature producer and commentator on NBC's *Today* show. She left television work after her twin daughters were born, although initially she tried to keep going just as men do. "It was not possible to be married, have kids and stay in television." She turned instead to her longtime interest in singing and acting. "I went on the stage so I could work nights."[1]

After her big screen success in *Bonnie and Clyde*, she did several films, which, she has said, "put my kids through private school and college," but there were not many scripts offered to her that she thought worth doing. "I was asked to do horror movie parts with Bette Davis, Piper Laurie, Shelley Winters and others, but I've refused. The characters are not real—I have to have a really grounded character, one that is psychologically sound and logical. Otherwise, I wouldn't know how to play it. I did a small part in the movie with Whoopi Goldberg, but it was funny and I like very much to be funny. When you get older, most of the movie offers are just a joke. Writers' attitude toward older women is ridiculous. The parts are small or if big, not really tasteful or not meaningful to me."[2]

The stage has been more congenial to her talents as a singer, actor and director. She sang leading roles early in her career, and musical theatre remains important; in the summer of 1999 she was in the musical *The First Picture Show* at Los Angeles's Mark Taper Forum. *Miss Margarida's Way*, her "tour de force" one-woman show, won an Obie award in 1978. Because she has found that "most roles for women are stupid, stereotypical, male-written," she was attracted to the "sharply delineated, full-bodied characters" in *Orgasmo Adulto Escapes from the Zoo* by Dario Fo and Franca Rame. She devoted over a year to translating the play herself in consultation with the authors, working on the marathon role intensely by herself in a loft with a dedication that felt like a "religious experience," and then producing and directing the show.[3] "One reason these plays are particularly important to me is because they're saying things, that as a woman, I don't say publicly, that I don't dare express in real life."[4]

It is not too surprising to discover that Parsons turned to directing after *Miss Margarida's Way*, which was "a transitional leap" from being an actor who "can't make decisions."[5] She directed Susan Griffin's *Voices*. Developing trust and courage with her actors, she used "organic American acting—method acting . . . to work out of the inner life into the external form." With the encouragement of Margot Lewitin of Women's Interart Theatre, she directed a multiracial, multilingual production of *Antony and Cleopatra* in 1979. "The effort was to use the best of what every culture could offer, not to do what is so often done, turn all the other cultures into little America. Joe Papp was very impressed. It got a good review. We used mostly Hispanics who gave their own cultural take on things—even using some Spanish language.

"Then I had a company for Joe Papp to do Shakespeare in the schools and also for grown-ups. It was performed in a theatre and the performances were all free; half supported by the city, the Board of Education, and half by some private money. On the weekend we would have a fully integrated audience when families came along with the children. From babes-in-arms right through to great-grandparents on the weekend—we were always just about full. It was an extraordinary couple of years. I took six months to train the company, which would come out in sweat suits, like an athletic team that the kids could root for. We were down at The Public Theater about half a year. Then we went to the Belasco Theatre—Shakespeare on Broadway. That upset me because the theatre was much too large for the kind of Shakespeare I like to do and the kind of acting I am interested in. Still, it worked beautifully—we did *Macbeth*, *As You Like It* and *Romeo and Juliet*. I know it was meaningful to those kids in all kinds of ways—it was a wonderful experience for everybody.

"But it couldn't go on. I had serious family commitments. There were other problems as well with financing, the unfamiliarity of the school system with theatre culture, the discomfort of this audience in a Broadway theatre, etc. I should have done more to continue by myself, I had the whole Board of Education behind me and a lot of private money. But for personal reasons I never could.

"I think often if I were a man I would have been asked to do a lot more. I've achieved a lot of things, but being a woman, the offers have not come in. It's not because of my talent; I think it's simply because I'm not a old boy and can't operate like an old boy. I suppose I'm resigned to the fact that I am a woman and am discriminated against, not listened to, by men that I work with every day. In order to be heard, I have to use certain wiles; whatever a woman has to do. I think it's good that a lot more women are doing more theatre, but I haven't seen an awfully big change in the attitude toward women and what they do."

When Parsons was the 1983 keynote speaker for the Women's Program of the American Theatre Association she suggested that "the problem for all women in theatre is maintaining your integrity, succeeding in the theatre according to your own vision."[6] Interested in acting and in actors and in creativity, part of her vision today involves reinvigorating the famed Actors Studio, of which she is now acting director.

I LOVE HEROINES: CHERRY JONES

Janice Paran

"I love heroines," Jones says, in explaining why, despite a tendency to throw the script across the room in frustration when she first read *Pride's Crossing*, she relished the opportunity to take on Tina Howe's flinty protagonist. A good heroine—one who struggles with her own soul at the same time she tilts against a societal windmill or two—is hard to find, but *Pride's Crossing* apparently met the criteria. Jones grants that, at least in much of the classical canon, heroines do battle on a more personal scale than their male counterparts, and their quarry tends to be of the romantic variety. "In Shakespeare," she notes, "the conflict for the heroine can't be the country you're about to lose, it's always this obsession with one of these really lackluster guys."

Still, Jones never met a heroine she didn't like (well, she holds a bit of a grudge against Major Barbara for being so "power-crazed"), and she's worked her way through their ranks like they were merit badges. "I've gotten to play so many great heroines," Jones says, "and that's one thing that's kept me in the theatre."

Growing up in Paris, Tennessee, Jones was stagestruck at an early age, a passion supported by her family and fostered by a childhood spent "in the woods, playing everything from Tarzan to cowboys-and-Indians to *Romeo and Juliet*." It didn't hurt, she adds, that she was "given a big, tall, strong frame," and that she is gay. "That androgynous thing probably helped," she ventures. "As a kid in the woods, as a baby lesbian, I could be anyone, man or woman, very successfully, and when I graduated to those breeches roles in Shakespeare and Calderon and Brecht, I felt like I'd been training for them all my life."

A local celebrity named Ruby Crider ('Miss Ruby") was responsible for coaching young Cherry (along, it seems, with about half the town's juvenile population) in "creative dramatics," but Jones takes pains to credit her high school speech teacher ("just put a big star next to Linda Wilson," she implores) with her first real preparatory work.

Jones went on to train at Carnegie-Mellon, where supernatural moments took a back seat to a regimen of movement classes, a revolving door of acting teachers and the painstaking process of having her southern accent "beat out" of her. After graduation, she moved to New York, settled into the itinerant life of the regional theatre actor and never really looked back.

As a founding member of the American Repertory Theatre in Cambridge, Massachusetts, Jones appeared in more than twenty-five productions there, including *Sganarelle*, *Three Sisters*, *The Miser*, *Major Barbara* and *Twelfth Night*. "Before then," she insists, "I didn't know what I was doing, I didn't have any technique to speak of. I had a lot of promise, I think, but I wasn't an actor. And then right around the age of thirty-three, I finally felt I could tentatively hang out my shingle and say, 'Alright, I'm ready to set up shop.'"

Twelfth Night comes up frequently in the conversation; it was during that production, says Jones, that she learned the lesson of simplicity from director Andrei Serban. "People who know his work might think the last thing he'd be able to teach an actor is simplicity," she acknowledges, "but he was the one who stayed on my back *nonstop.*" She demonstrates with a Romanian-inflected harangue: "Cherry, what's wrong with you? You so good in rehearsal, but you come before an audience and all you want to do is please them. Please them, like a whore!" Serban's exhortations to "stop acting!" finally hit home, says Jones, persuading her to "strip away the showy, act-y part" of her performance and concentrate instead on feeling "completely alive."

Working with Serban was "like a drug," Jones says, but she chooses a different simile for her experience with Gerald Gutierrez, another director she ranks among her favorites. "Like a laser" is how she characterizes his work on *The Heiress.* "He's very bold, very, very funny, and ruthless in his criticism."

Asked to name actors who have had an influence on her, Jones has a ready answer. "Maureen Stapleton was the first." She does express her admiration for performers who share an "Everyman" quality, who convince you that "on a good day, that would be your response to a situation. People who bring you generously along with them to the story. And cleanly, without a lot of fanfare. The performances I remember most are the simplest ones."

Achieving that simplicity in her own work is a hit-or-miss affair, she concedes, but others are effusive in their appreciation of her ability to do so. "You feel all the time with her that there's an extraordinary light shining on the work," the Old Globe's Jack O'Brien says. "It's her intelligence. Her health. By that I mean her clarity as a woman, the same clarity that she manifests in the characters she plays. There is nothing between Cherry and the characterization—no hiding, no shadow, no fear, no editing."

Healthy is a word often used in describing Jones, onstage and off. She radiates health and wholesomeness and unassailable common sense. She's happy," says O'Brien. "She loves what she does, and her life, her ethic, is an open book. What a brilliant, simple, reassuring way to move through your life."

Jones herself isn't so sanguine about how she moves through her life, except when it comes to her relationship with Mary O'Connor, a New York architect who has been her companion for eleven years. "We're very much a unit," she says simply. But on the subject of career management, Jones is content to watch and wait. "I thought after *The Heiress* I would be more in control, instead of just going with the flow, but I think I'm better going with the flow." She still worries that her technique is inadequate, confessing that every new role brings its attendant anxieties.

However it's arrived at, Jones's guilelessness is at the core of her stage persona. Her craft is assured but not grandstanded; its display is never an end in itself, but an invitation to the soul that animates it. That sense of transparency was there in *The Baltimore Waltz*, Paula Vogel's antic tribute to a brother dead of AIDS; it was there in *The Heiress*, in Catherine Sloper's meek and memorably coiffed resilience; it was there in *Night of the Iguana*, in Hanna Jelkes's compassionate pragmatism, and it is there in *Pride's Crossing*, Tina Howe's homage to old age. There is something disarmingly pure about Jones's meticulous stage presence, which manages, even at its most unruly, to suggest an inner decorum. "She does what Duse must have done," says Gutierrez, quickly apologizing for the lofty comparison. "But in the right role, with the right support—the right costume, the right light, everything—there is finally something mystical, something spiritual about her."

The Heiress was certainly the right role at the right time for Cherry Jones, garnering her Tony, Drama Desk, Outer Critics Circle and Drama League awards, and the kinds of reviews most actors only dream about—but her success in the role was no fluke. As Gutierrez puts it, "She waited forty years to make that entrance."

Jones insists that her comparative neglect of film and television is not unusual among her peers, but in the same breath jokes that three-fourths of the actors she's ever known have moved to Los Angeles. She has a small role in the upcoming film *The Tears of Julian Po,* and is angling for more of the same. "My fantasy," she says, "is to get the "housekeeper/Agnes Moorehead/Thelma Ritter film parts of the twenty-first century, so Mary and I actually have something to retire on."

"I'm starting to move into that age range where I don't know what's going to be there for me in the theatre. I'm moving out of my heroine stage. Now I'm going to have to do the Greeks and the Scandinavian guys," she laughingly laments. On the other hand, her status as a baby boomer may work to her advantage. "We're going to keep wanting stories about ourselves," she says. "We are the 'me generation,' after all. I'm counting on that selfishness to help me have a career into my dotage." The rest of us should live so long.

THEATRE ROLE MODELS

Cherry Jones and Paula Vogel

In 1995 Cherry Jones became the first lesbian actor to thank her partner from the stage as she accepted a Tony Award for Best Actress for her role in the play The Heiress. *In a joint interview with Paula Vogel, who became the first out lesbian to win the Pulitzer Prize for Drama, the actress and the playwright openly discussed their careers and their lesbianism. They had worked together on Vogel's hit* The Baltimore Waltz *and her failure,* And Baby Makes Seven.

Q: Were both of you out from the beginning?

PV: I assume you mean from the beginning of our careers? I was out before I had a career.

CJ: I was out from my first Equity show, when I was 21. I was telling everyone because I was trying to get a date.

PV: It sure is a lot easier to be out. Especially if you're living somewhere where you're allowed to be.

CJ: Exactly. If you're not living in a small town, or, for me, the South. I keep saying every year that living up North is very liberating. And every year I want to move one degree farther north. Someday I may end up in the Arctic.

Q: How did it feel to win the Pulitzer, Paula, and the Tony award, Cherry—knowing you had broken new ground?

PV: There's a headline I keep laughing about that was in *The New York Blade*: LESBIAN WINS PULITZER. In big red letters. That's so funny.

CJ: Had no known lesbian ever won a Pulitzer before?

PV: No out lesbian has ever won a Pulitzer before. But there have been Elizabeth Bishop and Willa Cather and who knows. What do you think in terms of the Tony?

CJ: Eva Le Gallienne, Katherine Cornell . . . There's such a great list of actress lesbians, more than I've ever dreamed of.

Anyway, I know that [in winning our awards] we were breaking ground. And isn't it wonderful that it didn't have one iota of an impact on my life except in my hometown. It was a minor backlash of letters to the editor: "Happy for Cherry's success, not her lifestyle."

That's what's so humbling. It doesn't mean that much to us that we were out as we receive these lovely awards. But it means the world to all of those people in all of those places we can't be out.

Q: You're both in long-term relationships. Could you talk about how your lives at home have shaped your success?

CJ: I have a blissful, amazing home life that I cherish and cannot imagine ever living without. Mary is the source of everything I do, because in drama you have to put yourself in very dark places. And the most horrible thing in the world I can imagine is losing Mary, and I have used her onstage more times than I care to count to take myself to a desolate place, the thought of no Mary. It'll be thirteen years now, you realize.

PV: Annie and I are celebrating our tenth this year. The Stella Adler quote that I always use—she said that it takes three things to make it in this business: the tenacity of a bulldog, the hide of a rhinoceros and a good home to come home to. I don't think I would have made it as a writer—I don't think the success would have happened—without Anne.

Q: Paula, you've noted that it's difficult for lesbian artists to attain national profiles because they have trouble getting their work seen in national venues.

PV: The problem with visibility for lesbian artists (compounded on the problem of visibility for women artists) is that our work is seen as being less universal. And how do you break through that?

There is a different perception for gay artists than for lesbian artists. I think we're struggling with two problems: misogyny and homophobia. Everyone keeps saying, "Gee, when are there going to be lesbian playwrights on Broadway?" And I'm like, "I have no idea." A lot of people tell me, "Oh my God, you're the tenth woman to win the Pulitzer." To me, it's shocking that there have only been ten women in this century to win it.

KATHLEEN CHALFANT: CREATIVE LIFE AND DEATH

Robin Pogrebin

When, after five years, Kathleen Chalfant left the last of various productions of Angels in America, *she said, "I feel like my MacArthur grant is up." She had played multiple roles with such skill that she was nominated for a Tony Award, but now she had "no immediate plans . . . to go back to being an actor looking for a job." She played various roles Off-Broadway and in the regional theatres across the country. When she was sent the script of Margaret Edson's* Wit *she thought she was to read the supporting role of Professor Ashford, not the lead, Donne scholar Vivian Bearing, who is dying of cancer. "Triumphing in the role of her career," wrote Vincent Canby in the* New York Times, *"Chalfant becomes a star." Robin Pogrebin explores facets of Chalfant's creative process.*

Somewhere between the production of *Wit* at the Long Wharf Theatre in New Haven last November and the production of *Wit* that reopened at the MCC Theatre in Manhattan, Kathleen Chalfant says, her performance got better because her older brother—a mentor and close friend—died of cancer.

In *Wit* Ms. Chalfant, fifty-three, plays a woman who herself is dying of ovarian cancer. And after living through the death of her brother, Alan Palmer, on Good Friday, she said, she approached the play with a new level of empathy and insight. "I'm finding that playing the play is now a kind of memorial to Alan," said Ms. Chalfant, who was wearing a blond wig over the head she keeps shaved for the role. "It's somewhere to put both my grief at his loss and what I learned about dying from him." Not only did Ms. Chalfant's experience with her brother help her in reapproaching the play—it was he, in fact, who read the script and told her to do it in the first place—but she said that having done the play helped her help him.

Ms. Chalfant slept in a chair in her brother's hospital room during her brother's final days and was there when he died. "He was my glamorous relative," she said. "He encouraged me to be an actor. He took it seriously." Among the things her brother's experience taught her, Ms. Chalfant said, was what happens at the end. In the play, she collapses into bed the way her brother did, remembering how his body simply stopped working. And she plays her final scene—in which her former English professor reads *The Runaway Bunny* to her—with an understanding of how the mind of an ill person makes its own reality.

"In the last few days of his life . . . he began to tell stories to people who came that were hallucinations, but he narrated them in a perfectly clear way. I realized that at the end of your life, it doesn't matter whether something is objectively real to the outside world or not. There isn't any experiential difference between what we call reality and hallucination."

The play has also allowed Ms. Chalfant to draw on her experience studying the classics in graduate school at Stanford University. In *Wit* her character specializes in the Holy Sonnets of the late seventeenth-century poet John Donne. She read a great deal about Donne, including a 1989 article mentioned in the script.

To better understand the medical details in the play when they were performing at the Long Wharf, Ms. Chalfant and her fellow cast members took field trips to Yale–New Haven hospital and talked with nurses, who evaluated the play's medical procedures for authenticity. Ms. Chalfant also had her brother reread the play to make sure it rang true to his experience, and he saw it performed twice before he died. The play's director, Derek Anson Jones, said he had noticed a change in Ms. Chalfant's performance from one production to another. "There was a level of true fear and dislocation that she brings, which I think adds greater resonance to the work," he said.

She had not expected to be so warmly embraced, particularly in the role of a dying woman who lectures about Donne. "When we first did the play, I wasn't sure whether or in what way it was redemptive," she said. "Here, the response to the play has been overwhelmingly powerful, and overwhelmingly positive. I'm very happy for everyone."

PLAYWRITING

If we go back to the recurring question, "Where are the women playwrights?" the news at the end of the last millennium was heartening. In a 1987 study, only 7% of the plays produced on Broadway, Off-Broadway and in the regional theatres that come under the umbrella of Theatre Communications Group were by women. In 1997, the count was about 20%, with increased representation of women of color. Some of the women playwrights who speak to us in the following pages have made cracks in the "glass proscenium" of Broadway, notably Wendy Wasserstein and Emily Mann, but most women's plays are still found Off-Broadway and in various venues across the country. The Women's Project of New York, headed by Julia Miles, which has been gathering these statistics, explored the sources of women playwrights' creativity, as well as what helps them or hinders them in realizing their vision on the stage, at their 1997 New York conference, "Women in Theatre: Mapping the Sources of Power."[1] A panel of articulate playwrights was asked: "Where do plays come from?" Their brief responses were deeply felt and ranged across the gamut of aesthetic, gender and institutional issues—from "daydreaming" in order to create a "real life" onstage, to documenting why people survive the Holocaust and other perils, to a search for community, encountering one's own wilderness, writing directly for performance or writing from character (especially women characters), and much more. Tina Howe's keynote address dealt with the widely shared frustration that women's wild and wonderful creativity does not reach the stage without the distasteful "subterfuge" of wearing "white gloves."[2] "The fellas get to work with their bare hands, but we have to don white gloves," she charged. She turned her personal saga of how gender defines women's work and its reception into a hilarious performance. Her liberating conclusion turned the "white-gloves-or-bare-hands dilemma" into a plea for many different kinds of gloves that will protect the playwright and the integrity of her work, and protest the theatre that demeans them.[3]

As the old millennium closed, several women playwrights working outside the big commercial theatres won major awards for "bare hands" plays that challenged popularly accepted gender and theatrical conventions. Paula Vogel's *How I Learned to Drive*, winner of the 1998 Pulitzer Prize for Drama, is a postmodernist exploration of a young girl's coming of age in sex-crazed Middle America, where lust and love paradoxically combine to give her control over her adult life. It made its way from Off-Broadway to become the top choice in colleges and regional theatres across the country. In 1999, the Pulitzer Prize went to Margaret Edson's *Wit*, a far-Off-Broadway production of imaginative simplicity, vivid language, wit and emotion. They join the earlier women Pulitzer Prize winners who continue to enrich our theatre: Wendy Wasserstein (1989), Marsha Norman (1983), and Beth Henley (1981). Naomi Wallace, whose political, historical, class-conscious drama *One Flea Spare* won a number of awards in 1997, was chosen for a MacArthur "genius" grant in 1999.

Theresa Rebeck concludes the section by urging playwrights to rethink their attitude toward film and television. She argues that playwrights working in films or television are not "selling out" art for commerce. For women especially, these media can provide an opportunity to work and extend one's talent at a time when the creative artist, especially the playwright, is no longer "king," and theatre is no longer a popular people's art. Indeed, many see theatre today as part of a continuum with mediated performance in film and television.

At the opening of the 2000 fall theatre season, the *New York Times* brought together Arthur Miller, Edward Albee, John Guare, Horton Foote and Maria Irene Fornes to talk about each playwright's experience of having a season of his or her plays staged by the Signature Theatre Company.[4] All expressed warm appreciation for Signature's "emphasis on the creative act." The male playwrights, whose names once gave Broadway its luster, all confessed that they no longer "dream of being on Broadway." For them, the commercial theatre has become a world of "hype," "pressure" and "money," a world in which "what's up onstage becomes this ancillary thing." Fornes, the only woman, countered with a striking assessment of creative work outside of the commercial empire. "I am, in some ways, lucky that I'm not as successful or well known as the gentlemen who are with me here. What I mean by that is simply my work is not done on Broadway, and not even Off-Broadway . . . it's almost like a different type of work." This "different kind of work," done outside of Broadway, has been the lot of many woman playwrights. Fornes's positive perspective deserves attention from all playwrights, as show business continues to resemble big business.

HKC

WHERE DO PLAYS COME FROM?

In November 1997, as part of the Women's Project of New York's "Women in Theatre: Mapping the Sources of Power" conference, seven playwrights—Maria Irene Fornes, Wendy MacLeod, Emily Mann, Suzan-Lori Parks, Wendy Wasserstein, Susan Yankowitz and Mary Zimmerman—took the stage of the New School for Social Research's Tishman Auditorium to speak about their backgrounds, their individual muses, and the trials and tribulations of writing for the theatre. Here are excerpts from their remarks.

Maria Irene Fornes

What generally inspires me to write is some mysterious obsession. The nature of the obsession is a little bit like the obsession one feels sometimes about a dream: You wake up and feel haunted by persons, presence, a life, an event or a feeling. For me the process of writing a play is somewhat like an investigation—finding out why this thing interests me and, ultimately, an audience. The process is similar to that activity very common in children—daydreaming. It happens to adults, too, but they are more interested in doing things that are useful. And daydreaming is not.

You sometimes see children with a peculiar look in their eyes, and you may feel they are a little bit in another world. You might say, "Wake up!" They're not asleep but they *are* in another world. To a creative person, that state of being is the most valuable, productive state of mind, because you come to understand why these characters and this world presented themselves to you. In the end, you have the real life rather than some kind of construction of the logical, intellectual, rational part of your mind.

Wendy MacLeod

A life in the theatre is a search for community, even for a family—the family we wish we'd grown up in. Thinking back on my own search for community, I realize the Yale School of Drama had its own sense of family. A little dysfunctional, but never mind.

At Yale I was told by Leon Katz that when I write I should always take the white gloves off. That piece of advice would never have been given to a man. But maybe it wouldn't need to be given to a man because a male writer wouldn't wait for that kind of permission. I was writing nice little plays, and after I got this sense of permission, that changed. Reading through my work, I realize how often my career has been fostered by men—teachers, literary managers, agents, critics and directors. This is undoubtedly because there are more men in a position to foster careers. Yet when I think of who has inspired me, I think of women. I think of my mother, who spent years of her life taking us to the ballet, the theatre, and the library. I think of my college professor who cast me in strong female roles before I believed they were right for me. And of course I think of women playwrights.

Emily Mann

I guess my work can be best labeled documentary theatre—or as the late Barney Simon from South Africa once called it, a theatre of testimony. The first play I wrote was called *Annulla, Autobiography of a Survivor*. When I was in college I thought I wanted to direct plays and I couldn't find a new play to direct. I was sitting at my father's desk over Christmas vacation and he had a huge pile of transcripts on his desk from the American Jewish Committee's oral history project on survivors of the Holocaust. I picked up one of these transcripts and it was of a young girl who had done an oral history of her mother who had survived Treblinka. She said, "I want to ask you a question—something I've never been able to ask you: Why did you survive?" And the mother, with tears in her eyes, said, "I had been the head ballerina at the National Ballet in Prague, and while I lay on the bunk knowing that everyone around me was dying and that my entire family had died, I thought of a moment of perfect beauty and tried to perfect that." She thought of herself in her tutu, in a spot of light, with a wonderful male dancer holding her. She was trying to perfect a turn on point and she said, "By thinking of perfect beauty, I lived."

I was amazed by this transcript and I said to my father, "This is so beautiful, this should be a play." And he said, "No, this belongs to the daughter who made the transcript and it is going into the archives. If you're interested in such work, make your own transcripts." So I went to my best friend's aunt, Annulla, who had survived the war and sat in her kitchen and asked her: Why did you survive? The result was a huge transcript that I turned into a play. And every subsequent play has followed from that play.

Suzan-Lori Parks

It would probably have taken me forever to start playwriting if someone hadn't told me to. I had been a novelist since third grade. I'd hang out underneath the grand piano with my notebook, scribbling. My mother would pass—only shoes and stockings visible. "What are you doing?" she'd say. "Writing," I'd say. And for the next Valentine's Day, she and Dad gave me a book: James Baldwin and Nikki Giovanni's *A Dialogue*.

Ten years later Mr. Baldwin was teaching creative writing at a college down the road from Mt. Holyoke, where I was enrolled. I would read my short stories animatedly, standing instead of sitting, with lots of gestures and funny voices. "Try playwriting," he suggested one day. And fifteen years later, here I am.

People ask me when I decided to become a playwright, and I tell them I decide to do it every day. Most days it's very hard because I'm frightened—not frightened of writing a bad play, although that happens often with me. I'm frightened of encountering the wilderness of my own spirit, which is always, no matter how many plays I write, a new and uncharted place. Every day when I sit down to write, I can't remember how it's done.

Wendy Wasserstein

How did I become a playwright? My parents, my nice middle-class Jewish parents in Brooklyn, never said to me, "Wendy, darling, please, please grow up to be a not-for-profit theatre writer."

I went to the Yale School of Drama. I remember reading Jacobean drama and to me—very roughly—it seemed that someone was kissing the skulls of women and dropping dead from the poison. I thought, This is not familiar to my experience. Often as I write plays I am trying to go toward an image, and the image that I wanted to go to was an all-female curtain call in the basement at the Yale School of Drama. *Deliverance* was playing in New Haven at the time, and I kept passing these posters of Burt Reynolds and a canoe. And I thought, I want to write the flip side of *Deliverance*.

Uncommon Women and Others was my thesis at Yale. I'll never forget this—there was an after-play discussion. Someone got up and said, "I can't get into this. It's about girls." I thought to myself, well, I've spent my life getting into *Lawrence of Arabia* and *Hamlet*, so why don't you try that?

I very much write from characters. Those people start speaking, and then I have them in the house with me and I live with them. Then at some point, it's time to get them out of the house. You can only live with someone like Dr. Gorgeous Teitelbaum from *The Sisters Rosensweig* for so long, and then it's time for her to go. But it is very like having the company of these people and trying to craft them in some way into a story.

Susan Yankowitz

I have a good story and a bad story about how I came into theatre. The good story is that my first professional experience was with the Open Theater, working with Joe Chaikin and a community of actors. The bad news is that I started by working with the Open Theater, Joe Chaikin and a community of actors. The good part is that was a wonderful way to enter the theatre. I was working with people whose entire lives were dedicated to what we all thought of as a work of art: theatre was an art form, not entertainment. I learned right away what it was to be part of a community, which was not simply a theatrical community, but a kind of paradigm of what all the '60s movements were striving for.

The bad news is that although some of the techniques have been absorbed into the present theatrical vocabulary, the movement itself virtually died. There was an international and national dialogue going on about what the theatre might be when you removed it from naturalism, when you removed it from psychology and when you removed it from character. What was the essence of theatre? That's what we were trying to find.

It's very sad, actually, to have had an initial experience which is wonderful, and for subsequent experiences to be at best mixed. That is partially because to some degree being a playwright is being a prostitute—you write something out of your most private part and you sell it. I find it a very sad time in the American theatre. And I still don't know whether on balance this is a happy story or sad a story. So we'll see if someone can help me figure that out. Let's call it a continuing story.

Mary Zimmerman

My primal scene with theatre happened when I was five years old. I was living in London with my pointy-headed academic parents. There were woods behind our house where I used to play all the time. Unbeknownst to me, every summer in these woods there was a performance of *A Midsummer Night's Dream*. I was in the woods one day and there was a rehearsal going on with grown men and women in winged costumes and long banners trailing behind them. As they rehearsed a scene, Oberon turned away from Titania and started running in this circle with an entourage of fairies running after him—they ran in a circle three or four times. Then suddenly, the actor playing Oberon collapsed on the grass laughing and said, "How many times do we run? How many times do we go around?" Everyone collapsed in hysterical laughter like I'd never seen in my life. I think that the combination of the playfulness of these grown-ups and the really clear-cut fun they were having was a hook to me that I haven't gotten over.

I'm drawn to very large texts that are mammothly popular in different parts of the world but are almost unknown here. They're safe bets; if they've been around for two thousand years, there's a reason. It's often a title or just a phrase within the text that will compel me to adapt it. My own process is a little different because I don't turn in any scripts beforehand. They're designed and cast and I start writing on the first day of rehearsal based on whom I've cast. I write in the hours between rehearsal. There are many reasons for that, but one of the main is my absolute fear of dramaturgy. I don't have any unproduced plays, to tell the truth, because I don't write them unless they have a performance date. I'm very fortunate that I'm associated with a couple of institutions that'll let me do that. The longest time I've ever spent writing a play was four weeks in rehearsal. But I'm not really writing them—I'm cribbing them, basically, from these great, great works and just figuring out how to stage them.

WHITE GLOVES OR BARE HANDS

Tina Howe

When my friend, Honor Moore—the poet, biographer and feminist—produced my first play, *The Nest*, in 1970, she used to ask me, "Which are you first, a woman or a writer?"

"A writer!" I answered without thinking twice.

"Are you sure?" she pressed.

"Absolutely! I grew up in a family of writers."

And growing up, I didn't particularly like women. In fact, I was terrified of them. My mother towered over my father, who was only five foot six.

Years later, in 1972, I actually joined a women's group where we were living in upstate New York.

I can't tell you how uncomfortable I felt. The room was filled with young mothers like me. One by one, they revealed how overwhelmed and isolated they felt. When it was my turn to identify myself, I told them I was a playwright. The minute they heard "writer" their eyes narrowed with suspicion.

"I get it," one of them said. "You're here to appropriate our pain for your plays. You don't care about sharing, you're just here to use us."

I was stung to the quick. I was not welcome. So, I left after two sessions and started a writing group closer to home, and this time men were invited. We met every two weeks to read our work. This was clearly where I belonged.

Now that I've lived through ten productions of my plays, I finally understand Honor's question. I'm most definitely a woman first. My gender defines my work *and* its reception. I'm always identified as a woman playwright. But one never makes such a distinction with the fellas—Shepard and Mamet are simply playwrights. But not us.

I remember all those lethal "Women's Playwright" panels of the '80s, how all the Wendys and I would be asked, "Can you write if you have your period?" "Can you write and nurse at the same time?" As if we are mere leaking sacks of milk and blood, ruled by the phases of the moon—Macbeth's three witches incanting over vats of newts and frogs. I'd like to see a panel of male playwrights questioned about their work in terms of their sperm counts or enlarged prostate glands.

The question I'm asked most frequently is, "Can you have a family and write for the theatre?" the answer is "Yes." You just have to be made of steel and have a partner who's behind you a hundred and fifty percent. Making a living as a playwright is almost impossible, regardless of your gender.

Let me tell you about *The Nest*. It had its first production at the Act IV Theatre in Provincetown in the summer of 1969. It was about three women friends competing for husbands.

The New York critics were appalled. When the play moved to Manhattan's Mercury Theatre, Clive Barnes said of the ten worst plays he'd seen in his life, *The Nest* was at the top of the list. He was sure we'd never hear from Tina Howe again.

My first review. Thank God I wasn't around to read it. I gave birth to my second child the week it appeared. What I found so puzzling about the experience, given the critics' dismay, was how much the audience loved it—they were rapturous.

Needless to say, we closed the following day.

So, what did I do for my second play? I whipped up even more maybe, and write *Birth and After Birth*, a piece about how women compete over fertility.

If *The Nest* was a shocker, *Birth and After Birth* left audiences speechless. It was about Sandy and Bill Apple celebrating the birthday of their four-year-old son, Nicky—played by a large, hairy man.

How was it received? The audience loved it and the critics were appalled. "What is this self-indulgent throwback to Absurdism?" they complained. It's one thing for men to take on questions of power and identity, but for a woman to approach the sacred cows of courtship and motherhood is just not done. We can write "issue" plays, but the moment we try to penetrate the mystery of the bedroom or nursery, the critics run screaming. The fellas get to work with their bare hands, but we have to don white gloves.

Theatre is a conservative art form by its very nature—a play needs immediate acceptance in order to run. It's all about money: Because we're so dependent on a healthy box office, we can't go too far ahead of the audience or the critics.

All playwrights suffer from the economics of the business. Very few of us can make a living at it, but women have it twice as hard because the theatre is still largely a male bastion. You can count the number of important female critics on one hand. This has a tremendous impact on what and how we're allowed to write.

I didn't get my first good review until *Painting Churches*—a white-glove play if ever there was one. Not that it didn't contain a few primal screams, but the setting was elegant and non-threatening. Everyone heaved a huge sigh of relief because finally I could be pigeon-holed, just as all women writers are pigeon-holed. Some of us write comedies, others write political plays. Some of us write about gender and others about race. We all have our niche. But what if we want to expand? Or, God forbid, change?

Every time I see a play by a woman that's been commercially produced, I'm painfully aware of the subterfuge she's had to adopt—the artful structure, the cautious handling of dangerous themes. The reason I'm so sensitive to these ploys is because I use them myself.

Take my new play, *Pride's Crossing*. I wanted to write about the passion of old ladies. When men age, they just get old, but when we age, we become very powerful. The membranes between what we *should* do and what we *want* to do get thinner and thinner. There's no rage like old-lady rage, just as there's no tenderness like old-lady tenderness.

As the century comes to a close, I wanted to celebrate the lives of women who lived through most of it, and who better than the thwarted women from my mother's background and generation? They came from a stultified stratum of Boston society that was all about exclusivity, fear and privilege. I wanted to articulate the howl they could never muster, but I had to be careful. I didn't want everyone bolting for the nearest exit. So I decided to open it out of town. Premiering a play in New York has just gotten too risky—for women as well as men.

The white-gloves-or-bare-hands dilemma exists on two levels. We wear gloves to protect our hands, but we also wear them to protect what we handle—food, photographs, rare manuscripts. So when I ask whether we should wear gloves to do our work, I'm not just talking about appearances. I'm also trying to figure out what we have to wear to protect our work. Because the percentage of women who have their plays produced is so low, our plays by their very nature are rare. It's not because we're less creative than men—look at the literary output of Emily Dickinson, Virginia Woolf, Doris Lessing, and the other long-ball hitters. We're just as prolific as the fellas. Just not in the theatre, for the reasons already mentioned.

We have to wear gloves to protect ourselves and our work. What I'm *really* railing against is that we're not allowed more of a selection—boxing gloves, surgical gloves, riding gloves, welding gloves, the list goes on and on. So I thought I'd add another pair to your wardrobe. They're double duty, inexpensive and mold right to the hand. They'll allow you to handle comedy, tragedy and everything in between.

(At which point Ms. Howe flings 150 pairs of latex gloves into the audience.)

POLITICALLY INCORRECT: PAULA VOGEL

An Interview with Arthur Holmberg

David Savran, in "Loose Screws," his Introduction to Vogel's The Baltimore Waltz and Other Plays, *New York, TCG, p. xii, writes that she has said "that feminism means being politically incorrect. It means avoiding the easy answer— that isn't really an answer at all—in favor of posing the question in the right way. It means refusing to construct an exemplary feminist hero. It means writing speculative rather than polemical plays."*

AH: How do you see *How I Learned to Drive* as political?

PV: A lot of people are trying to turn this into a drama about an individual family. To me it is not. It is a way of looking on a microcosmic level at how this culture sexualizes children. How we are taught at an extremely early age to look at female bodies. One of the taglines I had in my head when I was writing this play was, it takes a whole village to molest a child. JonBenet Ramsey was not a fluke. When we Americans saw the video tape of her at the beauty contest when she was five, a chill went up our collective spines. At what age are we sexualizing our children in a consumer culture to sell blue jeans and underwear? So children's bodies are sexualized all the way down from Madison Avenue to the wealthy suburb of Denver where the Ramseys lived. I would call that political and not specifically the psychopathology of an individual family. I would say that's cultural. And now we are starting to see a sexualized gaze toward young boys. Leonardo DiCaprio enjoys cult status because he looks prepubescent. Wherever there is confusion or double, triple, and quadruple standards, that is the realm of theatre. Drama lives in paradoxes and contradictions. If you look at the structure of my play, all I'm doing is asking, How do you feel about this? We see a girl of seventeen and an older man in a car seat. You think you know how you feel about this relationship? Alright, fine. Now let's go back a year earlier. Do you still think you know what you feel about this situation? Great. Now let's change the situation a little bit more. He's married to her aunt. How do you feel about that? The play allows me this kind of slippage because we have these contradictory feelings about the sexuality of boys and girls. So I tease out those contradictions. The play is a reverse syllogism. It constantly pulls the rug out from under our emotional responses by going back earlier and earlier in time. The play moves in reverse.

AH: *Drive* dramatizes in a disturbing way how we receive great harm from the people who love us.

PV: I would reverse that. I would say that we can receive great love from the people who harm us.

AH: Why is it significant to reverse it?

PV: We are now living in a culture of victimization, and great harm can be inflicted by well-intentioned therapists, social workers, and talk show hosts who encourage people to dwell in their identity as victim. Without denying or forgetting the original pain, I wanted to write about the great gifts that can also be inside that box of abuse. My play dramatizes the gifts we receive from those who hurt us.

AH: So what does Li'l Bit receive?

PV: She received the gift of how to survive.

AH: From her Uncle?

PV: Absolutely. I am going to teach you to drive like a man, he says. He becomes her mentor and shows her a way of thinking ahead ten steps down the road before anyone else to figure out what the other guy is going to do before he does it. That not only enables her to survive but actually enables her, I think, to reject him and destroy him.

AH: And she does destroy him.

PV: He gives her the gifts to do that. He gives her the training. He gives her the ego formation. You, he says, you've got a fire in the head. He gives her gifts in just about every scene. He teaches her the importance of herself as an individual and the ability to strategize to protect that. It's all there in the driving lessons. It's abuse simultaneously with a kind of affirmation and reassurance.

AH: In *Drive*, Li'l Bit looks at her painful memories, processes the experiences and then moves on. Why is it important to forgive the harm?

PV: Many people stay rooted in anger against transgressions that occurred in childhood, and this rage will be directed to other people in their adult lives and toward themselves. Whether we call it forgiveness or understanding, there comes a moment when the past has to be processed, and we have to find some control. There are two forgivenesses in the play. One forgiveness for Peck, but the most critical forgiveness would be Li'l Bit forgiving Li'l Bit as an adult looking at and understanding her complicity . . .

AH: Her destructiveness. You once said it was important to give the audience a catharsis.

PV: Catharsis purges the pity and the terror and enables the audience to transcend them. So you have her memories of the final confrontation with Peck in the hotel room and afterwards the flashback to the first driving lesson. And then the last scene, which brings us up to the present. This is a movement forward. For me, purgation means a forward movement.

AH: In *Drive*, as in many of your plays, music is a crucial element.

PV: Music contains a subliminal message that I will never be able to accomplish with words because words always involve the cognitive. Music speaks directly to the emotions. So for me as a playwright, music is an important ally. It is also important as a way of saying this was gender in 1960.

AH: Gender? You gender music?

PV: Yes. It has a message about being a man and being a woman. When you listen to the Beach Boys, what comes back is a code of the 1960s. Just like disco music brings back the entire culture of the 70s. So I used music to get to the culture of the 60s. Music is a time capsule.

AH: You're a feminist, but some critics have called your plays misogynistic.

PV: In the 70s, a lot of the people at the Women's Project [a prominent theatre company in N.Y.] thought I was misogynistic. And Julia Miles always commented that my work was so negative about women, that it was so dark and distressing. For me, being a feminist does not mean showing a positive image of women. For me being a feminist means looking at things that disturb me, looking at things that hurt me as a woman. We live in a misogynist world, and I want to see why. And I want to look and see why not just men are the enemy but how I as a woman participate in the system. To say that men are the enemy is patronizing. It makes me a victim, and I am not comfortable as a victim. It's a mistake to attribute goodness, pure abstract goodness, to either sex. I don't recognize that, so perhaps I'm not extremely feminist. To me, a play doesn't need to make me feel good. It can be a view of the world that is so upsetting that when I leave the theatre I want to say no to that play, I will not allow that to happen in my life.

AH: *Desdemona* [a play in which Vogel explores the secret lives of the women in Shakespeare's tragedy] may not have positive female role models, but it most certainly is a feminist play.

PV: *Desdemona* shows how women participate in a social system that does not allow them to bond. We bond with our husbands and our class structure rather than with each other. I don't know how you can get more feminist than that. Does it make me feel good? No. Does it worry me? Yes. Does it call on me to act? Absolutely. At the moment, we women are colluding with the patriarchal system and with the class structure. You can't deport the enemy, the enemy is inside us. The really dangerous enemy is that we have internalized misogyny and homophobia. There were a lot of headlines, "Lesbian wins Pulitzer . . . blah, blah, blah . . . " I am the first person to say, hey wait, I'm not here to make everyone else feel homophobic,

I'm homophobic. I was brought up in this country. I was taught to hate gays. I was taught to hate women. What we are taught to hate unifies us as a society. Our communal bond is that we are all racist, not just whites. Blacks are racist, Latinos are racist. We're taught racism the way we're taught homophobia and misogyny, It's all internalized. So it's not clear-cut to me, here is the good guy and here is the bad guy.

MARGARET EDSON: KINDERGARTEN IS WHERE IT HAPPENS

Gail Cameron

Margaret Edson, who was graduated from Smith College Phi Beta Kappa and *magna cum laude*, had used her Smith Scholar independent-study program on the Italian Renaissance to translate a play by a fifteenth-century woman writer. Instead of taking the obvious next step into graduate school, she worked at odd jobs and worked and lived for a year in a French convent in Rome. When she returned to her home town of Washington, she took a job as a unit clerk in the AIDS and Oncology unit of a research hospital. "The unit clerk is sort of the stage manager, the person who keep things flowing—like Radar on *M*A*S*H*. You know, all knowledge and no power. I had such a low-level job that I saw a lot of things first hand and I was too insignificant for other people to notice," she told Gail Cameron, who explored how this experience "would continue to haunt her and would eventually become the basis of *Wit*."

She dutifully enrolled in the graduate program in English at Georgetown University. First, however, she wanted to write the play about dying that she had been thinking about ever since leaving the cancer unit . . . Edson took a job in a bike shop and wrote in her spare time. "It was the perfect mix, working on the play in the mornings and hanging with the high school boys in the afternoons and evening."

Wit, says Edson, emerged as a play about kindness. It is about a person of great accomplishment who suddenly finds herself in a situation where all the skills she's built up in her life no longer serve her, and this forces her to disarm. "I wanted the main character to be someone very powerful who was also very skilled with words," Edson said. She came up with Dr. Vivian Bearing, a celebrated professor of seventeenth-century literature who knows everything there is to know about metaphysical poetry and specializes in the Holy Sonnets of John Donne. Edson based the professor's personality on tales Ruth Mortimer had told her about "the great three-named, square-rigged professors of her day"— Esther Cloudman Dunn and Mary Ellen Chase. To understand Donne's poetry, Edson spent hours in the library, poring over his work and trying to decipher the meaning behind his words. It wasn't an easy task, but she found that "if you know how to study something, you can study anything."

When Edson wrote Ruth Mortimer about the play that year, she casually inquired at the bottom of the letter "What's new with you?" expecting to hear about some new scholarly adventure. Instead, Mortimer replied that she had breast cancer. I thought "Well, she's not going to be very interested in this play," Edson says. "As it turned out, she was very interested in it. We spoke about it all the time. I came up in August with what I thought was the perfect, complete, finished draft for her to take me out to lunch over. She blocked out the whole day and went over every word—partly as a person going through cancer treatment, partly as a person who knows everything there is to know about metaphysical poetry, and partly as a person with an incredible sense of plays and theatre and what happens. Every suggestion she made was based on her vision of the play as something that was going to be produced onstage with an audience, which is something there was no guarantee of even, in my heart."

The first reading of *Wit* took place around the dining room table in the house where Edson had grown up. Edson received her degree but decided not to pursue a Ph.D. "During that year," she explains. "I tutored a student through our church in English as a Second Language, and I discovered that the thing I love most is teaching reading."

Meanwhile, *Wit* was being rejected by theatres all over the country. "The general drift was 'thanks but no thanks,'" says Edson. "Too much talk, too academic, too medical, too much illness. The first rejection was very painful, but by the third or fifth, less so. Then it became routine. I just got out a file and labeled it REJECTION—and that file got very full."

Then, in 1993, the South Coast Repertory Company in Costa Mesa, California, expressed interest in doing a reading. In the end, they decided to produce it.

In January 1994, Edson returned to Northampton to consult Ruth Mortimer. "The theatre company had a series of five questions. She was waiting for me on the couch by the fire to answer those questions. On the first, she said, 'Just leave it the way it is.' On the second, she moved one character over to the other side of the stage and had him exchange one line and had the other character give another line. That fixed every problem the other three questions addressed. Then we had dinner—rack of lamb—and it went on for hours. Ten days later, Ruth died."

Wit was a huge success in California. It ran six weeks and was then held over for another. It subsequently swept the Los Angeles Drama Critics Awards for Best World Premiere, Best Writing and Best Direction. It then lapsed back into seeming oblivion. However, Edson's old school friend, Derek Anson Jones, who, since the original dining table reading, had graduated from the Yale Drama School, continued to carry it everywhere in his backpack. While working as an assistant director for *Henry IV* in Central Park, he showed the play to Doug Hughes, who was directing, and actress Kathleen Chalfant, who originated the role of Vivian Bearing. When Hughes was named artistic director of the Long Wharf Theatre in New Haven, he selected *Wit* as the first production of the Second Stage with Derek directing. It opened in New Haven in September 1997 and in New York almost exactly a year later.

On the day the Pulitzer Prize was announced, Edson was busy leading her students in counting by twos to James Brown's "I Feel Good." When bouquets began arriving in the classroom, she connected it to the class's insect project called "Six Legs Over Georgia." "I took the opportunity to teach about the bee dance and how bees communicate with each other," she told Jim Lehrer on PBS.

The Pulitzer lunch in May was, she admits, pretty spectacular. Held in the dome of the library at Columbia University, "it was a celebration of the working person. No glamour, no polish." Edson says. "The seriousness of it made it somehow even more exciting."

Perhaps to the dismay of her legion of new fans, Edson says she has no plans to write another play. "If there is something I want to say, then I'll do it." Meanwhile, she is busy moving into a newly purchased house and is consulting on the translation of *Wit* into, so far, German, French, Portuguese and Finnish. In the fall, Edson will move to the John Hope Elementary School, near the Martin Luther King Center in Atlanta. While *New York* magazine critic John Simon declared in his review of *Wit* that Edson "should be handed the Harvard English department," her commitment to five-year-olds has only deepened. "I've learned that kindergarten is where it happens," she says. "Reading and writing is power—the thing that gives you the most power in your whole life. I like being part of students acquiring that power. I like handing that power over."

WE ARE NOT ONLY OURSELVES: NAOMI WALLACE

In Conversation with Tony Kushner

NW: What fascinates me is how much the body and politics are connected. From the day we're born, our body is pulled and stretched in different directions through the political values of our society. I'm interested in the fact that the body that labors is also the body that loves. If you live in a society where what you do for a living destroys the body, breaks the body down through labor, then that affects how you love sexually. Simply on the physical level, if you get carpal tunnel syndrome, that affects how you touch someone. And on the level of power, this comes right into love . . . can a love be possible between people from two different classes? In *One Flea Spare*, you have a sailor from the lower class and a woman from the upper class—there's a power structure they have to live with every day, and it doesn't disappear in their intimate moments.

TK: Your work is very unsparing. I've noticed many more people are in a deep state of despair in the early '90s, so I'm thinking . . .

NW: About hope? Well, I see my work as irresponsibly hopeful in a lot of ways. There are moments of possibility and transformation in my plays where structures of power suddenly become visible and we see them and we think, Aha . . . here is a place, a moment where something can change. *One Flea Spare* is a dark little play but at the end here is this little girl who has survived all this, who say, Yes, I am damaged, but I love these people. I hope the audience would see in moments like this that there is the possibility for change.

TK: Do you think that art has the power to do that? As a person with an engaged viewpoint, does art matter?

NW: Yes, it does. I've been transformed in small and large ways by certain poetry or novels or theatre . . . to me it's that moment when you're watching something and you feel like we can be bigger than we are. The best work does make us yearn toward that, toward change—not only political change, but changing ourselves.

TK: Something I really like about your work is that you dare to imagine the other in a fictional context. Not simply writing what you know but actually feeling that it is your responsibility to emphatically imagine important situations in which there are class positions and gender positions different from yours. Do you ever worry about doing that?

NW: No. I remember being in a poetry workshop in the University of Iowa and I wrote this poem about Contras killing a Nicaraguan soldier, a peasant, and I remember the person running the workshop saying, You know, I think we should just write about what we know. Years later, I thought about how absurd and reactionary and simplistic that idea is, because we should not only concern ourselves with ourselves. We are not only ourselves—we are who we interact with. It may sound simplistic, but if someone else is damaged, I am too. Saying we should only write about what we know is saying an individual is only what they experience themselves.

I think I did a relatively decent job in my play *Slaughter City* in depicting people from experiences other than mine—and I could also step back and think about when I was starting to play into stereotypes. I think that's what we don't do enough of—self-critique, stepping back and figuring out what stereotypes we might be playing into.

Both of us are white writers who have written roles for African Americans, and you have to question what you're feeling—if you feel like you're being generous or if it's some kind of charity writing roles for people of color. I feel like it's an education, an honor to be able to write them; it's not a guilt trip as a white playwright. If anything, it's a selfish thing, because I need to learn more. It's a way to challenge my own assumptions. There are pitfalls and I've fallen into a lot of them. But that's the exciting thing too—there's moments when it works. You bring in that spirituality and look for something common to all of us—get rid of all those things that have oppressed and destroyed us and search for the connection.

TK: What about writing British?

NW: I think perhaps because I read some Shakespeare and a lot of British writers, the language isn't difficult for me. *One Flea Spare* isn't written in the language of London in 1665, but it has enough of that edge that it certainly wouldn't bother you.

Placing it in a distant historical period was important to me as well. I think there are certain issues that are so locked in rhetoric or dismissed as over-determined for the stage that putting them back in time makes the visible but different enough that we aren't shut down or knee-jerked by them. In writing *One Flea Spare*, I thought, If I could put this in contemporary times, there is just so much rhetorical junk around the issues that I'll never be able to wade through them. I chose to place it in a period in which I have never lived so that I could create this world that is not bogged down by political rhetoric—I could make things strange.

TK: This is your first play set in another time period. To what extent do you feel committed to historical accuracy or historical fidelity; how much research was done?

NW: I worked six months, off and on, consulting about ten texts for help with the small details. I love to be historically accurate because the most fascinating things are the facts. There's a character who preaches in *One Flea Spare* with charcoal on his head—this is documented. The facts of history are so much more imaginative than my own imagination. I love history in that way, because its so fantastical. It's magical in a strange way.

The more history I read, the more hopeful I become. Reading history, you find out about times wherein there was more resistance and hope than you believed possible, and you discover communities where true equality existed between members—and other things like that are covered up.

TK: Let me ask you about poetry. It's unimaginable to me, the compression of idea and sound and form.

NW: I know that when I write poetry it's more scary. The space is so small in poetry and there is something in plays—I feel bigger and less lonely. When I write plays I often write a few poems about the thing first, and initially I'll incorporate part of the poem into the play but usually I'll end up cutting it out.

TK: Why do you think that is?

NW: It's almost like I need the poem to jump-start the play. I needed the emotion that was in the poem to stretch it out through the play, but to do that I need a different language.

I was thinking—this is going to sound so horrible and essentialistic and it's that awful giving birth metaphor which I hate—but I remember feeling, after the birth of my second child, that same kind of emptiness as when I write a poem. You had something new out there, taken from you, but now there were two things, yourself and it, as opposed to only one before, an element of loneliness.

TK: It's so hard to avoid those metaphors. I actually always wanted to ask you to explain a line you wrote—"to go insane or stay in the world is a choice between metaphors."

NW: That's where the hope and possibility come in for me. Sometimes things look so bleak and dark and the safety of insanity or just retiring to your bed for the rest of your life is very seductive. Sometimes I think, Wouldn't it be great to believe everything was supposed to be the way it is, that this is the natural order and we could all relax; but then I feel like I don't know who I would be to ever believe that. There's a line about being diminished by creating something that says "We live and by living we disappear." But there's something really regenerative about that—that we diminish but something else is being created through that.

TK: So, two more simple questions: Do you think there will be any life left on the planet in one hundred years?

NW: Yes, I do.

TK: Do you think it will be any fun?

NW: I guess one could say it's idealistic to be hopeful, considering the way things are going, but, would one want to live now if the answer was no? It matters what we do now, because those who live in the next hundred years could have a decent life. I have a choice over my vision and I want to believe that what we're working toward is that we will save ourselves and there may be terrible periods of darkness, but . . . why work this hour if we don't believe in some possibility that we can get together and make this change?

WHY I WRITE FOR TELEVISION

Theresa Rebeck

I'm heading west. Hollywood has crooked its finger at me, again, and even though I almost had a nervous breakdown out there a couple years ago, I'm going back to do a season in television. I'm one of those playwrights everyone worries about "losing" to Hollywood. And although I don't feel particularly lost, I do think it's about time someone explained why we go.

1. **It's not the money.** Frankly, they pay you so much out there, if you can get a minimum of work for TV or the movies you can subsidize a career in the theatre. I contend that for all its evils, Hollywood has other attractions, the principal one of which is:

2. **There's work.** I am one of those people who somewhere along the line psychologically prostrated herself on the altar of theatre. I think it is the most magical of art forms, a holy communion. I believe the world would be a better place if more people went to the theatre and what I ask of life is to never have to leave a rehearsal hall. Life, and the theatre, cannot offer me that.

There's not enough work, and I need to work. Whether or not there's money involved, I can't psychologically survive on one production a year, or a workshop, or a couple of readings. I need to write, and then get together with a bunch of actors and see how what I've written works. That's what playwrights do. And right now, the place I can do that is Los Angeles.

3. **The playwright is no longer king; she may not even be court jester.** Often, cheery outsiders inform me that "Writing for film and television must be hard because your work isn't your own. But in the theatre, the writer is king." This makes me want to laugh. With the rise of "The Development Process" has come the decline of the playwright's authority, and anyone who tells you otherwise is deluded. People who have heard one reading feel qualified to tell you how to rewrite something you may have been working on for a year. And if you don't appreciate nutcase off-the-top-of-someone's-head "feedback" it's because you're "defensive" about your work. Directors and producers ask in hushed tones, "Is she willing to rewrite?" as if playwrights are all recalcitrant children who don't inherently understand how theatre works.

Of course no one can force you to rewrite something you don't think needs to be written. But the battles can get pretty long and protracted and bloody. One director and I argued for weeks about a scene he wanted me to rewrite; he finally refused to stage it the way it was written. Another director once drove me to observe, "I am under the impression that what I wanted for the play—a play that has *my* name on it—is not even of secondary importance to you." "You're right," she told me, "It's not." At the same time, these directors are slavishly attentive to the needs of the actors. I did ask one to at least treat me with the same respect he gave them. He looked at me like I was insane.

With all due respect, I can get paid a lot of money to be treated like this in Hollywood. It does seem to me that if the theatre wants to hang onto its writers, everybody can just learn to be a little nicer to us.

4. **The theatre is getting too elite.** I never wanted to write only for the rich, and I certainly never wanted to write only for other theatre artists. Increasingly, those are the only people going to the theatre. We all know this is a problem, but nobody seems to have any idea about what to do about it.

Not only that, many theatre artists seem to like this state of affairs. If I read one more article about how we'll all have to steer ourselves away from narrative and realism because TV and film do that, and our job is to "push the envelope," I'm just going to throw up. This elitism is driving the audiences away just as surely as high ticket prices. Most people tell me they don't go to the theatre not because it's too expensive, but because it's too weird or incomprehensible and boring. They don't understand it. They don't want to come back. So we may be pushing the envelope, but if no one gets it, what's the point?

5. **Give the girl a break.** Also—and many people are not going to want to hear this one—there's not enough theatre out there for women. Every single time I have a play produced, anywhere, women hunt me down and *thank* me because they're so starved for theatre they can relate to. A lot of women I know won't go to the theatre anymore because, they tell me, they are finally tired of only being offered plays about men. There are many female artists out there, and a huge female audience, and the system is denying us access to each other.

   This is an absurd situation. The situation is, frankly, better in Hollywood, and I'm here to tell you, that place is not exactly a bastion of sexual equality.

6. **The critics have too much power, and we're all collaborators in their totalitarian state.** So, you finally jump through all your hoops, you work on a play for years, you get a production, the critics come, they kill it, and you're dead. Other theatres won't pick your work up if you got bad reviews and if you get good reviews, everyone wants to do your next play. You get asked to be on panels; you start to get grants. Producers and grant writers and artistic directors are absolute in their devotion to the critics; we all are, and as far as I can tell, these guys often don't understand what they're seeing anywhere near as well as the audience does.

   Okay, playwrights have always hated critics, and vice versa. But the critics have not always controlled our world, and it's not a good thing that they do now. If a novel gets bad press you still get into the stores, onto the library shelves; you know you're reaching somebody. Same thing with a movie. In the theatre, you get bad reviews and that's it.

7. **The money.** Okay, I admit it. It's nice to make money. Plus, I just had a son. So my thinking is not quite as reckless as it used to be.

   Still, if I sound defensive, it's because I am. I write for the best show on TV. This spring I'm directing a feature based on my one-acts, and I spend half my time worrying about getting someone to produce my new play. I told this to a friend of mine, and he said, "What are you, a schmuck?" To which I can only respond, no, I'm a playwright.

DIRECTING AND MANAGING

Women directors appear in many sections of *Women in American Theatre*. They have a long but little-known history going back to leading actresses and playwrights who guided their plays through the production process. Misha Berson picks up the story of "Women at the Helm" in the late 1980s, when a "changing of the guard" restored women to the leadership of regional theatres (which were part of a movement spearheaded by women in the 1940s and 1950s).[1] She documents the magnitude of the change that put women again at the helm, but goes on to ask a crucial question: "What does this gradual yet pronounced gender shift really signify, if anything?" She put questions to her respondents that are not often addressed because they are "considered too emotionally loaded, politically divisive or just plain rude."

Her small sampling of "new women at the helm"—Carey Perloff, Emily Mann, Mame Hunt and JoAnne Akalaitis—reveals that these women brought to their work a different style of leadership, one that, on the whole, is less hierarchical, more questioning, more collaborative and more open; one that provides a home for its artists and a "magnet" for the community.[2] Some of them attribute these characteristics to gender; others are not sure. These women have not felt "any special obligation to produce women writers," although some have often lent a helping hand. It is in dealing with boards of directors, subscribers and the press that gender stereotypes, those embedded in their upbringing and those inherent in social power structures, cause them the greatest difficulties. Despite their excellent preparation, their ability to run a large organization, manage big budgets and generally "take the heat" is questioned, while, at the same time, they feel they must "censor" themselves not to "sound shrill," "angry" or "threatening to anybody." Yet by 1997, increasing numbers of women were artistic directors and even larger numbers were managing directors, like the "Top Girls" who discuss their progress here. The majority of development directors, who do what women have historically done as volunteers for the arts, were also women.

Coming from very different kinds of theatres, playwright-director Maria Irene Fornes, avant-garde performer Elizabeth LeCompte of the Wooster Group, and Julie Taymor, creator of *The Lion King* for the Disney Corporation and winner of the first Tony ever awarded an American woman director, share with us their views of women directors and their directing process. They, too, confront the gender issues that Berson explores. Fornes sees women as well equipped to be directors by "training or nature."[3] Elizabeth LeCompte considers the Wooster Group's organization to be feminist: "The reason a company like this survived and made such enduring work is that a woman runs it. If I were a man I'd have more recognition, but then the company wouldn't be able to work the way it does."[4] Julie Taymor is very "up-front" about how women directors have to operate in order to make their way. "I think the veneration for the powerful male doesn't carry over to a powerful woman . . . So women have had to develop the ability to conduct what needs to be conducted without head-on collisions." As the woman who managed to crash the "glass proscenium," her ruminations on her career are instructive. "It's hard to know if my career would be any different if I were a man . . . there is an excitement about the twenty-year-old male director, and women have not been part of that club. A woman who's that young and doing that much is still 'risky,' rather than the next bandwagon everyone wants to hop on. When it was JoAnne Akalaitis and Anne Bogart or whoever, they never got that kind of attention. Neither did I until I got *Lion King*. And look at what I've done."[5] I'd like to echo Julie Taymor's words, saying, "Look at what women have done." Calling attention to women's accomplishments has been the objective of the several editions of this book.

HKC

WOMEN AT THE HELM

Misha Berson

A changing of the guard has begun in the American regional theatre movement.

Women artists are, at last, breaking through the glass rafters, and taking charge of some of the country's largest nonprofit theatre establishments.

Tremors of change stirred in the late 1980s, when a generation of entrenched male founder-artistic directors began to retire or move on to new pursuits. And surprise, surprise: waiting in the wings was a platoon of well-schooled, dynamic and (in some cases) controversial female theatre artists who had risen up through the regional ranks and were ready, willing and able to take over.

From 1989 to 1994 Emily Mann succeeded Nagle Jackson as the leader of Princeton's McCarter Theatre Center for the Performing Arts. JoAnne Akalaitis inherited founding producer Joseph Papp's mantle at the New York Shakespeare Festival. Anne Bogart was chosen as Adrian Hall's replacement at the Trinity Repertory Company in Providence, R.I., and Irene Lewis assumed Stan Wojewodski's top post at Center Stage in Baltimore.

Each one was the first woman to be granted the chief artistic job at those theatres. The same can be said of Sharon Ott at Berkeley Repertory Theatre; Carey Perloff at San Francisco's American Conservatory Theatre; Libby Appel at Indiana Repertory Theatre; Margaret Booker at Florida's Asolo Theatre Company; Josephine Abady at the Cleveland Play House; Tanya Berezin at Circle Repertory Company in New York; Timothy Near at San Jose Repertory Theatre; and Mame Hunt at San Francisco's Magic Theatre—all of whom took the wheel within the period.

But numbers tell only a fraction of the story. What does this gradual yet pronounced gender shift really signify, if anything?

There are provocative unspoken questions hovering over this entire break-through generation of theatrical women, questions that their male peers do not routinely face. Questions like: What impact does gender have on one's executive successes and failures? Have anti-female bias and gender tokenism really been vanquished, or do they continue to pop up in subtle and subversive ways?

And there is no shortage of women artistic directors willing to discuss the topic. For this article, I spoke with many women directors, but focused on an informal sampling: Carey Perloff at ACT and Emily Mann at the McCarter, both in the midst of their second seasons running those companies, Mame Hunt, who moved into the A.D. role at the Magic Theatre, and JoAnne Akalaitis, whose controversial dismissal from the New York Shakespeare Festival in 1993 made national headlines. These women candidly addressed a many-tentacled subject which they say often goes undiscussed at their theatres because it is considered too emotionally loaded, politically divisive or just plain rude.

Assumption #1: Women Are New at This Game.

Anyone with a thorough grasp of American theatre history can easily disprove the idea that women are newcomers to leadership posts—but can we take historical awareness for granted in these post-literate times?

As the landmark 1981 sourcebook *Women in American Theatre* (edited by Helen Krich Chinoy and Linda Walsh Jenkins and reissued by TCG in 1987 and 2006) and many other recent works of feminist scholarship have made abundantly clear, several key women directors were institutional visionaries and creative "matriarchs" in the earliest stages of the nation's regional theatre movement.

Yet something shifted in our culture after World War II, the same shift responsible for a retro-realignment in other professions: Women receded into the background, or made important contributions from the fringes, while men clustered at the top echelons.

Whatever the matrix of causes, male artists mostly commandeered the regional theatre frontlines, where the real money was raised and the large audiences congregated. And though women were instrumental in founding the anti-commercial, renegade troupes that sprang to prominence in the 1960s and '70s like a vast field of wildflowers—such dauntless women as Judith Malina, Ellen Stewart, Megan Terry, Joan Holden, Olympia Dukakis, Lyn Austin, Julia Miles, Susan Loewenberg, Margaret Booker, Vinnette Carroll and Lynne Meadow, to name a few—it took another dozen years for the directorships to open at those multimillion-dollar, multi-facility, community-entrenched anchor theatres, and for women to be deemed qualified enough to run them.

Assumption #2: Women Artistic Directors Largely Owe Their Jobs to Affirmative Action Policies and Tokenism.

Ask the McCarter's Emily Mann about this persistent (if largely unspoken) notion, and she gets adamant. "I was in training for this job for years," Mann declares. "Everything I've done has been preparation for me to do this job."

Her resume backs her up: It lists a degree from Harvard University, a Bush Fellowship at the Guthrie Theatre, a stage manager post at the Guthrie and the distinction of being the first woman to direct on the theatre's main stage, and a resident directorship at the BAM Theatre Company at the Brooklyn Academy of Music, not to mention her many achievements as a playwright.

Mann's background is typical of her female colleagues at other, comparable theatres—not in the particulars, but in the thorough apprenticeships most have served before snagging a status job. Sharon Ott spent years as a resident director at Milwaukee Repertory Theatre, and freelanced at theatres around the country. JoAnne Akalaitis was a founder and crucial member of the experimental troupe Mabou Mines for more than a decade, then a freelancer with major credits at the Guthrie Theatre, the Mark Taper Forum and other high-profile establishments. Before taking her post at the smaller-budget Magic Theatre (which nonetheless has a big reputation for generating new plays), Mame Hunt served as a proactive dramaturg and literary manager for numerous companies associated with new play production, including the Los Angeles Theatre Center and Berkeley Repertory Theatre.

"We've paid our dues, all of us," declares Hunt. "There are no miracle stories here, no shortcuts. We all worked shit jobs, apprenticed ourselves, watched the guys do it and learned from them."

And it's the same raw ambition men rely on, she suggests, that finally catapults women into these jobs: "Look at the type of women who have been promoted to positions of authority and you'll see that most are seasoned, driven and extremely ambitious people, who've gotten where they are by putting themselves out there very forcefully. I think that's what boards of directors identify and see when they're looking to hire. That's the turn-on, not gender."

Assumption #3: Women Are Running Regional Theatres Because a Lot of Highly Qualified Men Don't Want to Anymore.

An artistic director who shall remain nameless sardonically suggested to me recently that there are more top-level theatre openings for women now because "the guys" are bailing out of the business. Her offhand comment struck a loud chord.

The new wave of women (and men) replacing the old guard often walk into landmine situations. Carey Perloff, for instance, assumed control at ACT soon after an earthquake critically wounded its longtime venue, the Geary Theatre. She's still struggling to find the $24 million to repair the place. Josephine Abady, as head of the Cleveland Play House, inherited a crippling deficit along with her spiffy title. And by the time JoAnne Akalaitis stepped into Joseph Papp's enormous shoes, the New York Shakespeare Festival was unfocused and in financial disarray.

"Women are picking up the pieces," contends Akalaitis. "I knew what the deficit was, and what I was getting into. But I believed in the theatre, and felt this was an opportunity to help out. I was innocent in the best sense, but I often said, 'No one but a woman would be dumb enough to do this.'"

"Men are jumping ship," asserts Akalaitis, "not because they're unfeeling idiots, but because they want a car, a house, the money to take care of their families better. There's also a kind of fatigue, brought on both by spiritual and financial institutional crisis, that just isn't part of being an independent artist.

"But women are coming aboard in the hope that there's some possibility for renewal," she continues. "We have the energy and desire to pursue that."

Assumption #4: Women Run the Show Differently.

The question of the differences in power styles between women and men should be raised gingerly, and considered without the romanticism or denial that often clouds our perceptions about gender. Women who have achieved some authority tend to be understandably reluctant to make blanket generalizations vis-à-vis female behavior. Yet the differences, they will assure you, exist—and they matter.

"I do think there's a contrast in the ways women wield authority," Hunt says. "I see it in the different work cultures of myself and my male managing director. I like lots of people to be involved in my decision-making, lots of group brainstorming. He prefers to solicit information one-on-one. Sometimes our styles are so different it drives the rest of the staff a little crazy."

Couldn't we just chalk that up to disparate personalities? Yes—if Hunt's peers didn't offer strikingly similar observations about their own work habits. Many say they are (at least theoretically) more interested in collaborative, cooperative management structures and lateral decision-making processes instead of the top-down, trickle-down authority structure that's standard in American businesses of all kinds.

"I found ACT very hierarchical when I arrived," Perloff reflects. "It was very much an organization that had been run for a long time by a brilliant, autocratic man, and power was invested in the withholding of information. I was interested in a new structure, with much more communication. We have a policy team now, and the seven of us meet weekly."

Akalaitis goes a step further in her assessment: "I can't imagine it isn't a different institution with a woman at the top. I do think women are more open, more playful, more responsive to change, more emotionally expressive. I know that sounds like reverse sexism. But those were my assets as an artistic director. And I didn't have to bear the burden of Western civilization on my back, like all those guys do. I could say, 'I don't know.'"

Saying "I don't know" and being constantly open to change does not always inspire confidence in others, Perloff quickly learned. "One of the things that is associated with weakness is changing your mind. To say I've rethought it, let's do it differently—that's considered a terrible thing."

A place where ideas flow freely, where uncertainty and change can exist without panic—yet also a comfort zone where an extended family of artists are welcomed, appreciated and trusted. That's a common ideal for women artistic directors, even if it's frustratingly difficult to achieve. Mann isn't the only one who speaks of turning her theatre into an "artistic home" for colleagues, an image that connects to female conditioning and responsibilities through the ages. "One of the best compliments I get is when someone who comes to work here tells me, 'I love the feeling in your theatre and that must be due to you,'" she reports. "I wanted to make the kind of place for artists to work in that I wished I'd had when I was a freelancer on the road."

In the writings of earlier women artistic directors, as well as in casual conversation with contemporary ones, the notion of making the theatre a magnet, a haven, a focal point for the surrounding community also arises again and again. It's in Flanagan's dream of a nationwide network of theatres responsive to their times and constituents, in Fichandler's bold idea that young, working class, and ethnic-minority patrons were a vital part of her potential audience. "During my two years at the Public, I think the theatre became a community center, a place where a lot of things were possible," observes Akalaitis about the New York Shakespeare Festival's theatre building in lower Manhattan. "It's something I miss now that I'm on the road again. What I always wanted to do was create a social, political, artistic community in a great theatre."

Assumption #5: Women Artistic Directors Favor Plays Written by Women.

While women are still statistically underrepresented as artistic directors of the larger playhouses, consider the status of female playwrights. In the mainstage lineups especially, it is still very common to find six-play seasons in major regional companies that do not include a single work by a woman. And of those that do produce works by women, a startling few feature two or more within a given year.

Progress is being made toward greater inclusion of women writers, as well as ethnic minority authors of both sexes—but for a bevy of aesthetic, cultural and economic reasons, the change is not happening at the speed of light. And those expecting the new female theatre heads to redress the gender balance of the repertoire, and change it pronto, are barking up the wrong tree: A glance at the 1993–94 rosters for a group of the larger women-run theatres reveals no greater number of women's scripts scheduled on those main stages than in male-driven institutions.

That's due largely, perhaps, to the general nature of repertoire at the majority of resident houses—the familiar "balanced" formula of revived modern and older classics (mostly by men), local premieres of recent Broadway and Off-Broadway successes (try to name New York commercial hits by women, not counting anything by Wendy Wasserstein or Anna Deavere Smith) and, maybe, a world premiere or two of a new work. The women I canvassed declared without apology that they feel no special obligation to produce women writers. "When you do a new play you're more likely to find women writers on the short list," Emily Mann comments. "But if you present as much classical work as we do at McCarter, you won't see as many women on the list. So many, many factors go into planning a season. Ultimately all you can do is follow your gut, and look for the pieces that are most exciting to you."

Though you'd be hard-pressed to forge a common aesthetic among women artistic directors at the larger theatres, all of them have displayed a fairly eclectic taste in stage literature. And none has devoted herself primarily to the works of other women.

Observes Perloff—who made her mark staging works by Strindberg and other venerable writers at New York's Classic Stage Company—"It takes generations to compile the body of work that white men have developed for the theatre. Men have had two thousand years to develop as playwrights and women have had, what—fifty, a hundred years? They're making progress, but it's not going to happen overnight."

Yet Perloff did tap female playwright Timberlake Wertenbaker to translate and adapt the version of *Hecuba* she mounted at ACT, with Olympia Dukakis in the title role. And the first grants from ACT's new commissioning program went to Elizabeth Egloff and other women dramatists.

Even though, as Mame Hunt bluntly puts it, women A.D.s "don't feel a responsibility to produce plays by women," they are commissioning a record number of them, and presenting them more often in second stage and workshop settings than most of their male counterparts. Hunt has also cultivated a cluster of up-and-coming women writers (Claire Chafee and Marlane Meyer, among others) at the Magic Theatre—a company which has specialized in new plays for three decades, but primarily plays by men.

As for the day when mainstage subscribers at LORT companies will see as many women's names under the title as men's—it probably won't occur within our lifetime. But with more women in charge, we're probably steaming toward that destination faster.

Assumption #6: The Expectations of Women Artistic Directors— by Boards of Directors, Subscribers, the Press—Are No Different from Those That Men Face.

"One of the things we women do is rush to be liked, to do the right things, say the right things, wear the right things," Akalaitis contends. "You can't often respond honestly in the work situation and the public arena if you're female. You have to think two or three times before you react, and use a more manipulative mechanism to deal with things. I mean, Hillary had to come up with that chocolate chip cookie recipe during the presidential race. That cookie— it's a code for our standards of social behavior for women. You have to come up with that cookie, or you're damned."

In the view of Akalaitis, one of the things that lost her the directorship of the Shakespeare Festival was her failure to deliver something equivalent to Hillary's cookie—some kind of primal assurance to those who considered her unsuitable for the job from the outset, and those who were responding to her media image, which Akalaitis considered false and misleading.

"The elements of that picture were: here's this downtown, avant-garde woman who wears black, has short red spiky hair, who is smart, outspoken, honest and cold," Akalaitis recalls mordantly. "What was missing from the portrait was the visionary, intuitive artist, open to new challenges. I think my experience at the Public was disturbing and demoralizing to the theatre community in general. It sent a signal about what happens to women who assume too much power."

One can regard the Akalaitis affair as an isolated occurrence triggered by a nexus of explosive factors—the replacement of a legendary producer with a Broadway outsider, the wrath of a powerful critic, the inheritance of an overwhelming debt and a nervous board. Or one can see it strictly as a bad match of institutional personality and individual artistic temperament. But much of what Akalaitis says about the social images forced on women executives also resonates with her colleagues. And similar vibrations were stirred by the abrupt dismissals of Josephine Abady after six seasons at the helm of the Cleveland Play House, and Margaret Booker after four at Florida's Asolo Theatre Company.

"I've gotten a lot of sexist stuff since I came here," says ACT's Perloff. "People wonder: 'Is she in control of this organization? Can she cope with the heat? Does she really know what she's doing?' The perception is that women have no ability to deal with money, so the minute you're running a large organization there's this terror that you won't be able to keep things together financially. I don't think there's that same level of anxiety with a man."

Mann believes women still have to walk a very thin emotional tightrope in public in order to succeed: "We have to make sure we don't sound shrill, or overly expressive, or angry, so that we aren't too threatening to anybody. We have to learn how to censor ourselves."

The tension stems partly from the fact that this group of ground-breaking women are part of a demographic "swing shift." As baby boomers, they (and their male peers) grew up with the rules of the 1950s ringing in their young minds—"don't overshadow or threaten men, be feminine, don't reach too far or too high professionally." But theirs was a restless girlhood in a time of great cultural upheaval, and these same women began challenging and rewriting the gender rules in the late 1960s. Still, as Akalaitis puts it, "sexism is deeply rooted in this culture, and it keeps on reappearing in all kinds of forms."

An example: Akalaitis (who has two grown children) recalls going head-to-head with her board over retaining maternity leave for NYSE employees. Perloff—the mother of an infant and a toddler—has pressed her own board unsuccessfully for day-care facilities. Are these battles men would have chosen?

Perloff remains impassioned about her crusade. "One of the reasons for the theatre's failures is that we're the only profession in this country that never deals with childcare. You can't go to a political meeting, or an American Bar Association convention, or an academic meeting anymore without finding some provision for childcare. Yet how many theatres offer it to their employees or audiences?"

While there can be such lobbying on occasion without effecting the balance of power, Hunt believes that "women have had to learn and speak the language of men to get hired and to survive in this very competitive profession." And Perloff complains of it being "lonelier at the top than it is at the starting gate. When I go to meetings of artistic directors from the 'big seven' arts institutions in San Francisco, I'm the only women in the room. In many ways, I feel very, very alone in this job."

While acknowledging the special pressures on women, Mann prefers to put a positive spin on their struggles: "If you're a woman in this job you'll have a harder transition to power, have to prove yourself more, and you can't make as many mistakes. Given that, I think it's an extraordinary accomplishment that we've all done this, and it's a very, very good sign for the theatre.

"Women started this movement, then they sort of disappeared for a generation and a half. Now we're back. We're rediscovering the reasons these theatres exist, and revivifying this movement. We're part of the change that has to happen."

"If nothing else," Akalaitis sums up, "it's a matter of justice to have more women in power. I happen to believe in women's sense and sensibility, our spirit of adventure, our openness, but it's also about balance. Our theatres need the real picture—which means we need everyone involved."

MARIA IRENE FORNES: THE PLAYWRIGHT AS DIRECTOR

An Interview with Rod Wooden

MF: The very first time that a play of mine was worked on was in a workshop reading at the Actors Studio for a directors class. It was the first time that I saw a rehearsal of any play, not just a play of mine. My impulse was, from day one, to put my hands on it. I didn't think I wanted to direct then. I didn't know what directing entailed. I just thought it would be good if some things were done in a certain way, which is in a way what directing is. Writing a play is very hard work, and it is very hard after you do all that work to hand it to someone else and to set it at a distance and be gagged.

RW: You told me once that Lanford Wilson has described the playwright as the female of the theatre, and the director as the male. What did he mean by that?

MF: We were riding on a train to New Haven and he said, "When I have a play produced I feel that I understand what women mean in relation to men. As a playwright I am in the same position. The director behaves like a guy taking a woman out on a date. He's going to show her a great time. He's going to do wonderful things to your play. He's going to take her to a great restaurant, and she's going to love it. If she says, "I don't like this," she's been rude. As a playwright I have to be like a nice woman who says, "Oh, it was wonderful. Thank you very much, that was very nice." Playwrights can be banned from rehearsals.

That is the law.

RW: You've also directed other writers' plays: Chekhov, Ibsen and other classical plays. What do you think you can bring to those plays as a writer that perhaps other people don't bring?

MF: I think I understand the text as emerging from the character's head and from the writer's head. When what you practice, your craft, deals with words as they emerge from the character's mind, you can reverse it and understand the character's mind. You can understand the character's state of mind; therefore, the tone and therefore, the meaning. Because in tone there is more meaning than in all the emotional conflicts in the world.

RW: And as a painter what can you bring to your writing and directing?

MF: I started as a painter and developed a strong visual sense. In painting you make a drawing and you practice perspective; you make a drawing of two people and how, because of their position, they relate to each other. This is something you do when you are taking pictures also . . . you see how the perspectives change and you see how the picture can become a lot more interesting, more beautiful, more powerful. That kind of eye is very important for theatre, to make it a lot more beautiful or a lot more mysterious.

RW: Do you think all writers should train themselves as directors?

MF: Completely. And all directors should write, but not necessarily professionally; just to develop their craft further.

AUDIENCE QUESTION: You were talking about the playwright as female and the director as male; don't you think that's a sad indictment of theatre today?

MF: Oh yes. I don't see any reason for it. I do think that the function of the director is one of a delicate sensitivity and guidance; and of taking pleasure in seeing something flourish: the play, the performances, the set, lights. Women are by training or nature quite equipped to do this. So why suddenly should they be left out of this profession?

When I write a play, I have no idea how I'm going to stage it. Because my approach to writing is visualizing the characters in the real world not on a stage. When I edit the play, when I structure it, it's when I start imagining it in a single space. I feel if a playwright starts writing for the stage (from the very beginning) the dialogue becomes rigid and the characters stiff. It is good to get to know the characters in the real world. Then you can switch to the stage when you rewrite: How are you going to do all this that you want to do in one set? That's hard to do, but it's worth it for the sake of the liveliness of the characters.

When I watched Lee Strasberg working at the Actors Studio I thought that everything that he said about acting was very interesting, complex and delicate. But when he came to teaching directing he always asked the student giving the presentation, "What did you contribute to this?" And I felt that it was a strange term, "to contribute," for the director should not impose something to the play but make sure that what is in the play has come out in the production. The director has a lot of work to do. It isn't like the director should just sit there and watch it grow. A director should only agree to stage a play if the play has not started to grow in her mind or his mind. The director should not manufacture something around the play. The word "contribute" seemed dangerous to me.

Basically, what I am concerned about when I write is something that has to do with humanity; and that has to do with a kind of tenderness that I feel for the characters; no matter how cruel or terrible they may be. However bad things get, I still want to feel for them. As a writer I want to feel for them. As a director I want to feel for them. And as a member of the audience I want to feel for them even when they're terrible and bitchy and do horrendous things. I think it's boring unless you feel something for the characters.

ELIZABETH LECOMPTE

Alisa Solomon

Women in the avant-garde are doubly marginalized: just as women are written out of history, the avant-garde rarely makes it into official accounts of theatre. Those women theatre artists who finally do achieve wide recognition, even if their subjects are radically female, generally work in dramatic styles that play by conventional rules. But those who challenge traditional theatrical forms often remain unnoticed by all but a faithful following; when the avant-garde finds broader acceptance, it is usually its men who get touted first.

Elizabeth LeCompte was a visual artist in the 60s, "alienated," she says, "by the very male-oriented painting world." Hooking up with actor Spalding Gray, she moved to New York City in the late 60s and "gravitated toward the theatre which was so active at the time. Richard Schechner [with whom Gray was already working] needed an assistant and offered me a job: I got into theatre for the money." When Schechner decided to leave his Performance Group for a while, LeCompte inherited *Commune*, a piece he was developing from company improvisation. "I didn't know what acting or staging were supposed to be, so I made things up," LeCompte recalls. "I could tell people trusted me." Indeed, in the ensuing years, making things up in an atmosphere of trust has characterized LeCompte's work with the seven core actors of the Wooster Group.

What LeCompte calls "a little constellation next to the Performance Group" emerged as an independent company in 1975 (taking its name from the street where its theatre is located) with its first production, *Sakonnet Point*. This playful pastorale built of improvisations based on Gray's childhood bears little tonal resemblance to the feverish, even brutal intensity of more recent works. But the relative unimportance of language, the absence of any representational meaning, and the basic mechanism whereby the audience must project its own associations onto the nonlinear juxtaposition of seemingly unrelated events and objects have all remained traits of the Group's subsequent work.

LeCompte has never tried to integrate the various elements that make these juxtapositions, but "just puts them next to each other." "The choice of elements can be arbitrary," she explains. "Material can be anything. Not just written text. Something comes in the mail, or a record I hear at a party, or a performer does something that gives me pleasure."

In *Rumstick Road* (1977), LeCompte mixed autobiographical material (the suicide of Gray's mother), documentary material (slides of Gray's family snapshots, letters, recorded conversations with Gray's mother's psychiatrist) and imaginative, nondiscursive material (a silly sequence, for instance, in which a man demonstrated a method of massaging a woman's midriff with his mouth while she writhed and giggled hysterically). *Nayatt School* (1978) added an element that would become part of the Wooster Group aesthetics— the referential, irreverent use of an established dramatic text. (Here, a group of children, parodying adult behavior, performed parts of Eliot's *The Cocktail Party*.)

While the Wooster Group made differing sensibilities collide onstage, it has had to fight offstage battles, too. Some people objected to what they deemed an invasion of privacy in the use of the secretly recorded phone conversations in *Rumstick Road*. More volatile, though, have been the issues surrounding *Route 1 & 9* (1981) and *L.S.D.* (1984). In *Route 1 & 9*, videotaped scenes from Thornton Wilder's *Our Town* played in soap opera close-up rub against five white actors in blackface who make party preparations below the video monitors, and then play out Pigmeat Markham vaudeville routines. Sudden spurts of loud music well up for frenzied dances, then subside. Finally the overhead screens show a hitchhiking couple getting picked up by a truck, while an onstage TV monitor projects the Group's homemade porn movie.

The Wilder estate made some noises about the Group's scrambled use of the *Our Town* text, and some feminists objected to the pornography, but the larger debate centered on the use of blackface. Some critics condemned the production as racist, while others defended it, saying it criticized racial stereotypes. LeCompte found such judgments absurd, arguing that the use of blackface was a choice involving the quotation of theatrical material, not one made out of a political point of view.

The brouhaha around *L.S.D.* was less open to subjective interpretation; here Arthur Miller denounced the Group's cutting and pasting of *The Crucible* text, which LeCompte juxtaposed against diaries and debates of Timothy Leary and G. Gordon Liddy (with some quasi-flamenco dance routines interspersed), offering a vision of history as hallucination. Miller refused rights, and then threatened court action, so the *Crucible* excerpts were finally replaced by a text by Michael Kirby.

Such controversy surprises LeCompte. "I wanted to interpret *The Crucible*, like a director does," she says, "but I can't stick to the play even when I want to; I can't settle on one meaning." Instead, she sees language as one unprivileged element among many. Some critics have suggested that such postmodern dramaturgy is inherently feminist, but LeCompte isn't so sure: "I couldn't really say whether deconstruction is feminist, but there is something from a feminine side, a denial of certain kinds of playwriting and form. Somewhere, I just don't relate to a lot of plays."

If LeCompte is reluctant to ascribe her style to some vague notion of a female aesthetic, she does consider the Group's organization feminist. "The reason a company like this survived and made such enduring work is that a woman runs it. If I were a man, I'd have more recognition, but then the company wouldn't be able to work the way it does. And working with the company is the supreme pleasure. Remembering that is how I survive."

JULIE TAYMOR: A WOMAN IN CHARGE

Sylvianne Gold

She is low-key and unfailingly pleasant, but no detail is too small for her attention, no disturbance large enough to distract her. And, of course, two weeks later at the Tony ceremonies, Taymor would reap the rewards of that single-minded care: a Tony and a standing ovation for her direction of *The Lion King*, another Tony for designing its costumes, and the thanks of all the other *Lion King* recipients for her vision, the vision that made the Disney production the Tony-winner for best musical as well as a runaway box-office success.

She is up-front—she is always up-front—about her belief that for women directors, honey catches more flies. "I think the veneration for the powerful male doesn't carry over to a powerful woman," she says as we talk in the spacious kitchen of her lower Broadway apartment, where turn-of-the-century woodwork is a clue to the room's previous identity as an office. "So women have had to develop the ability to conduct what needs to be conducted without head-on collisions. You can hear horror stories about powerful women who, if they were men, would be considered powerhouse genius mavericks. But it's just not acceptable, in American culture, for a woman to come on that way. I think that closes doors for them. There is a way to be strong without being a pit bull."

Moreover, Taymor says, women directors have never won the kind of instant acclaim that greeted, say, Peter Sellars at the start of his career. "It's hard to know if my career would be any different if I were a man," she says. But "there is an excitement about the twenty-year-old male director, and women directors have not really been part of that club. A woman who's that young and doing that much is still 'risky,' rather than the next bandwagon everyone wants to hop on. When it was JoAnne Akalaitis or Anne Bogart or whoever, they never got that kind of attention. Neither did I until I got *Lion King*. And yet look at what I've done."

When she thanked her parents in her Tony acceptance speech for allowing her to "play, play, play," she wasn't just being cute. "I was given enormous freedom as a child," she says. "My parents allowed me to indulge my imagination and my desire to be theatrical and to create—they allowed it and supported it and never questioned my choices about going into Boston every day after school or going to Paris for a year. These are things most parents would be terrified to do with a young girl. But I knew it was the right way for me."

In Paris, she got her first exposure to masks, which would play a dominant role in her work from then on. Taymor followed that up with a work-study arrangement at Oberlin College in Ohio that allowed her to take acting classes in New York and to apprentice with the Bread and Puppet Theatre, where Peter Schumann encouraged her talents as a sculptor. At Oberlin, she majored in folklore and mythology. "I wasn't interested in studying theatre," she says. "I was always kind of moving toward being an anthropologist. I loved to study the culture of other people, and that included religion and theatre, and the origins of theatre in shamanism. That provided a very good basis for the kind of work that I've done since."

Back full time at Oberlin, she found herself working seven hours a day with Kraken, the company Herbert Blau created at the school in 1972. "That was probably the most formidable, exciting, creative time for me," she says. "Seven incredible people [one of them was Bill Irwin] locked in a gymnasium in Ohio, where you could really concentrate. It was a very idealistic period, and it couldn't have happened in New York. There would have been too many distractions. And the work was exceptional, though probably more interesting as process than as product."

New York theatregoers got a chance to judge for themselves when Kraken's *The Donner Party* and *The Seeds of Atreus* were done at the Performing Garage.

She could have continued with Blau after graduation. Instead, "excited by Indonesian shadow puppetry and masked dance and a lot of Asian forms of the theatre," she accepted a Watson Fellowship to study visual theatre in Eastern Europe, Indonesia and Japan. "So twenty years ago, I went to Indonesia for three months and stayed for four years." When the multi-ethnic troupe she put together there presented her first play, *Way of Snow*, she says, "It wasn't like I was just starting. It was sort of seminal work that put together ten years of theatre experience." (And it was the first in a long line of pieces that would combine theatre techniques from disparate cultures into a unique tapestry.)

Running her company, Teatr Loh, taught her how to walk the very fine line between exercising control and maintaining the refined posture expected of women in Indonesia's tradition-bound, essentially Islamic culture. "It was very hard to do," she says. "So it was extraordinary, to come into my own as an artist in a place like that. It was a total contradiction."

But contradiction is par for the course for Taymor, who manages to reconcile opposites in all facets of her personality. As a theatre artist, she balances her passion for masks and elaborate costuming with a thorough devotion to actors and acting. She is a vocal and willing poster child for the not-for-profit theatre, while simultaneously pursuing commercial work with what could be seen in some quarters as unseemly zeal. And her openness about her life in the theatre coexists with a surprising reticence about her private life.

"Theatre," says Taymor, "is my skin."

Taymor scoffs at the idea that in some way she sold out her artistic integrity by teaming up with Disney and creating the huge money-making machine that is *The Lion King*. Deep down, she sees it occupying a place in American culture analagous to the place the *Mahabharata* occupies in a Balinese village; Disney has allowed her to create a piece of theatre that can be embraced by the entire American village, that can work as high art and low, comedy and epic drama, for adults and children. And now that it has made her something of a marquee attraction, she is hoping that productions like *Juan Darién: A Carnival Mass* and *The Green Bird*, originally presented in limited runs by institutional theatres, will be brought to Broadway.

"What appeals to me as an artist about commercial producers," she says, "is that you know they want it to run. Therefore, they're going to support it to make sure it works, so that it *does* run—they're not interested in closing after three weeks or nine weeks. After two years of work on *Oedipus Rex*, I had two performances. Thank God there's a movie of it, or I'd be slitting my throat. It's *hard* to work on something so long and have it be a limited thing."

Although Taymor will announce to anyone who will listen that *The Lion King* could not exist if not for the not-for-profit theatre and the NEA, she doesn't accept the notion that not-for-profit theatre is by definition not commercial. "The word commercial is such a silly word," she says, "because it's all perception. No one absolutely knows what's going to be commercial and what isn't." She points out that *Juan Darién*, her dark, poetic adaptation of a short story by Horacio Quirogá, did very good box office in France and Israel, Edinburgh and San Francisco, although an unenthusiastic *New York Times* review killed its commercial potential when it was presented in New York last year at Lincoln Center Theater.

"I like the idea of reaching a wide audience with this kind of work," she says. "Any artist would probably like that. There might be *some* who like being only in little teeny places and just having their neighborhood see their work. But I find it extremely satisfying that little children and very sophisticated adults who hate Broadway and hate musicals like *The Lion King*."

TOP GIRLS

Jennifer L. Dineen

JD: I recently took a very quick, very unscientific look at a list of more than three hundred not-for-profit theatres to see how they identified their leaders and it revealed the somewhat startling statistic that women represent a slight majority of managing directors and general managers. Does that seem right?

VICKI NOLAN [Managing Director, Yale Repertory Theatre]: It may indeed be accurate, but it does not mean that all of those women are truly at the top of their organizations. I think if you were to go back to that list and select only those women who don't report to men, those who're either in equal partnerships with an artistic director or are executive directors, you'd get a very different figure. But is there a *growing* precentage of women managers who are at the top? It's my perception that there is.

JD: That same unscientific glance suggested that there are more women in management positions than artistic ones. Is this true?

VN: I think so. There appears to be more fluidity and upward growth in the management field.

LAURA PENN [Managing Director, Intiman Theatre]: Or attrition, depending on how you look at it.

JD: Why is that?

SUE FROST [Associate Producer, Goodspeed Opera House]: Managers probably burn out faster, so there's more room for movement. I also think it might be a little less threatening to have a woman in a management position as opposed to an artistic position. And it's not just in terms of people at the head of an organization. I also see that with women directors and writers. They have a much harder road to travel than women who manage.

LP: On the other hand, it *is* true that the greater number of development directors are women. In fact, the work has become so demanding and so stressful that anybody in their right mind is doing something else.

JD: Do you think that men don't seek those jobs?

LP: They have other opportunities available to them.

VN: I don't know if I agree with that. There's a long history of development being a place for women. I remember being told by a senior manager that development was a great place for a woman coming back into the market after she'd had her babies.

JD: Is this because development can trace its history in the tradition of society wives volunteering for cultural institutions?

VN: Volunteerism—absolutely. Interestingly, it used to be that the managing directors came up through the development path. We don't see that as much anymore. Now we see managing directors coming out of marketing, because our organizations have become so dependent on earned income that there is more interest in people with marketing prowess.

JD: Do you think that the presence of female leadership in not-for-profit theatres has had an impact on the kinds of corporate cultures found in those organizations?

VN: A resounding yes! I think that my management style tends to be less hierarchical—a flatter, broader style, with an expectation of shared leadership.

LP: I've noticed that people from outside theatre are constantly knocked out by how progressive we are. And I suppose part of the conflict of being a woman in a leadership role is that I'm able to be supportive of the women who work for me—yet I hesitate to give that same flexibility to myself.

SF: I would say a lot of the difference in styles has to do with being less confrontational. And I think some of that is because we have to balance so much in our lives.

VN: You know, a man said to me the other day that the reason why women are good at multitasking is that women have been required by society to multitask with their five or six or eight children in a way that men haven't.

DESIGNING

A study done in the early 1980s documented that the "Broadway barrier" excluding most women directors also worked effectively against women scenic artists. Women costume and lighting designers, on the other hand, felt few inequities, since they often shared the field with men, and, indeed, sometimes outnumbered them. The explanation is obvious: costume design involves knowledge of sewing and fashion, skills available to many women, while lighting design, which was still a new and underpaid field at the time of the survey, found most takers among women. Scenic design differs sharply because it is identified with male skills—carpentry, physical prowess, technical know-how—and male power—money, position and old-boy networks. The study concluded with the hope that "changing times will increase opportunities for women in scenic design," and that soon "there will not be male designers or female designers, but simply people who happen to love designing scenery."[1]

Although the hoped-for gender neutrality has probably not happened, much has changed on Broadway and Off- (and in women's lives). We can get some sense of what women designers are thinking and feeling a decade later from a unique, two-day gathering of leading artists at Mount Holyoke College that took place in April 1994. Organized by Vanessa James, a distinguished set and costume designer who has chaired the Mt. Holyoke theatre department, the event attracted eighteen leading designers. The objective was to "call attention to the extraordinary achievement of women in theatre, opera, ballet and film design."[2]

"When Designers Gather" is a modest sampler from the two days of public talks, roundtable discussions and informal exchanges with the audience, as well as late-night chatting among the designers themselves, all of it informative, questioning, lively and personal.[3] Marjorie Kellogg, who had been a spokesperson for the League of Professional Women's 1983 study of designers, leads off here. Her outstanding career included extensive work on Broadway, something she attributed to the "change in producing habits" in the late 1980s that brought "proven" shows from the regionals or Off-Broadway to the big theatres. These came with designers like herself, who were thus "given a chance to prove themselves." Her concern for women's work and her dedication to theatre as a collaborative process have continued to make her an inspirational spokeswoman. Patricia Zipprodt was an accomplished, energetic, creative and colorful costume designer, who, it is said, took costume design "beyond the realm of real clothes to what her fellow artists consider art." Her brief, lively remarks hit on many crucial issues—what it means to be in the Theatre Hall of Fame; how images come not only to talented visualists like herself, but are in each person's reservoir; what is the future for women in the postmodern era; and how to advise students. Her death from cancer in 1999 is a loss we mourn.[4] Patrizia von Brandenstein shares with us, very informally, that important moment when a young artist moves from stage design to film, a step few women had been able to take.

A feminist analysis by Mary Callahan Boone explores the "way gender expectations and ideas about the role of light in theatre production intersect" in the work of the much-revered Jean Rosenthal. She suggests that gender governed not only the way Rosenthal dealt with male crews, but also how she accommodated the function of light to the demands of directors and the realism of the contemporary theatre. Delores Ringer, in turn, describes some of the "feminist scenographic strategies" she developed in designing a production of Marsha Norman's *Getting Out*. Every aspect of design, from the handling of spatial arrangements to the fabric of the character's undergarments, is used to communicate the fragmented life that Norman's Arlene is trying to patch together by the end of the play.

HKC

WHEN DESIGNERS GATHER

The weekend of April 9 and 10, 1994, eighteen leading women theatre designers gathered at Mt. Holyoke College, South Hadley, Massachusetts, for a symposium conceived and organized by Vanessa James, a well-known set and costume designer, who had joined the Theatre Department. It was an inspired idea to "call attention to the extraordinary achievement of women in theatre, opera, ballet and film design" and to provide an opportunity for students, faculty and local artists to hear from these remarkable women. It turned out that the gathering was an unprecedented experience for the distinguished participants as well; they had never come together as women artists to share with one another as well as with the audience their thoughts and feelings about their art, their careers, innovations, economic constraints and personal needs. In thanking them, Vanessa James said: "You have spoken to us about passion and the love for the work and the love for the Art. You have told us about the need and desire for real collaboration and you have told us about the changing nature of the business due to technological changes and economic stress. You have allowed us, generously, to enter the world of your lives as artists and as people with feelings and emotions." Here is a modest sampler from the two days of discussions that were "full of content, controversial, instructive, often touching, often poetic and many times both frightening and inspiring."

Marjorie Kellogg: Collaboration

The subject that is on my mind a lot lately is collaboration. I think this is one of the most overused and most disrespected words in our business. We all think of ourselves as collaborators. We're in theatre; it's a collaborative business; of course we all work together. It's accepted that a good designer must be is a good collaborator. But I think that we've come to take it very much for granted. I feel that a flag should be raised when something as basic to the process of theatre becomes something that people are not really paying attention to.

One of reasons for this is the fractured nature of our careers. The typical profile of a working designer is as a freelancer living in one urban center or another. That person probably makes his or her living in many other cities in addition to the one they live in. And they're working with other people who also live in other cities and work in other cities. A large proportion of us used to live around or near New York at least. But that's really no longer the case. Of the shows I have on my schedule for next year, I'll be working with directors and designers from San Diego, Seattle, Indianapolis, Pittsburgh, Atlanta, Boston, Medford, Oregon and New York as well. I think it's also partly an economic issue; travel budgets are shrinking; to bring designers in for the requisite amount of meetings is becoming harder. Creative teams are not really assembled to have time to develop a really good collaborative relationship.

If you use people who have worked together before, there is already a kind of established knowledge that doesn't require small talk; people can get right down to work. These people usually share to some extent a common aesthetic. The tension is gone when you have a shared outlook, a shared aesthetic, a broad one, I hope.

Once you get to actually working, the first thing is that all of the people get together in one place at the very beginning. There will be no adding sound and lights at the last minute and if there is a playwright, he won't be put off in a hotel room somewhere. Everybody will be in the same room before any commitment to an idea is formed. Collaboration requires that you all start on an equal footing and feel that you can speak your mind about the play, what it meant to you, how it struck you, what you think you can do with it without any hierarchy controlling the discussion.

Scheduling sometimes keeps this from happening. A few of the regional theatres understand the importance of getting people together at the beginning of a production even if only for a few hours. It's considered a luxury. Sometimes it happens a little too late and the process has begun before they all get together, creating an imbalance. The ideas have already started to form without all the people together.

Sometimes due to time constraints the meeting doesn't happen at all and you end up talking on the telephone or faxing things. Producers have to resist the temptation to be expedient and cut to the chase because we need that moment when the relationship that will carry the creative team through the whole process is established. That says to each member, each one of you is just as necessary as all the others, that we can't really start this process without all the parts. It sets up a possibility for trust and without trust there really is no collaboration in the sense that I am using the word. There is just people doing a show together. You can do a show very successfully without collaborating. I don't find it as interesting. If collaborating isn't the only way to do a show then why bother? We bother with it and should because it is fun and stimulating and it's enriching. An open and equal creative relationship with a group of people keeps your mind really active. It's a constant source of new ideas, new information and influences that you can only get from getting close enough to somebody to understand where they're really coming from.

After you get so far in a career, what do you do to keep yourself fresh? One of the answers I have is collaboration. There's research to be shared, someone has gotten into something interesting. Dramaturgs are very good these days for coming up with interesting ideas, sketches and plans to be shared. One of the advantages of a good collaboration is that you can call somebody up late at night and say, "What are we doing here?" That will help you through; each of these little conversations shapes the production to a unified shape. The conversation is the check and balance. When time comes to put it on the stage, there are no surprises. You know where you're going, you've talked it out. If there's a problem, no scapegoat, or finger pointing, you've talked it out. You sit down and fix it. Once I looked forward to seeing my own work realized onstage. What I look forward to now is the collaborative dynamic with my colleagues, to that sense of community, that can only happen by all of us working together.

Pat Zipprodt: Visualize

I'll start with an anecdote about being in the Theatre Hall of Fame. You still "schlep." The subway still takes your tokens, and no limos are waiting for you. The real joy of it comes from seeing your name carved in stone—not in appliqué. Plays go away, costumes fade. This is one point of permanence of a life in the temporary art of theatre.

Here are some things I've been thinking about. I'm a visualist; that is my gift I found myself thinking about two moments my gift gave me. There was Molière's *Don Juan* with Richard Foreman directing. I asked him what the society in the play was like. He said it was like dirty laundry, damp, smelly. This is designer's food! Images came up on my home screen. Years ago when I was ten or eleven years old in northern Wisconsin, walking along a forest floor I saw a little white flower, an Indian Pipe, that didn't need light; it is chlorophylless. This memory kicked off my creative thinking for the costumes of the show. Another show, *Scratch* by Archibald MacLeish, was directed by Peter Hunt. It is about the Devil bringing up American historical figures from Hell. (It opened and closed in twenty-four hours.) The director talked about the character, but I had to worry about what these figures would be wearing on their feet. Then my mind went back to a trip to Mexico where I saw mummies laid in lime and preserved in a catacomb open to tourists. The bodies were sitting in chairs; their flesh shriveled to bone in their faded, wispy clothes. Suddenly, I knew how to dress my historical figures. I could see the fleshless leg bones in the old shoes. What if I hadn't gone to Mexico? No matter. Each of us has a reservoir where we find the answers when we are put in the proper atmosphere. They would come out in collaboration with others on a show.

I've been teaching. I tell them you have forgotten the most important thing in your work. Trust yourself as a human being.

Another thought. What is the future for women generally and in theatre in the twentieth-century world? I read that women are going back to their 1930s role because they don't like the conflict between home and career—all this backed up with statistical surveys. Does this trend affect women in theatre or does it exclude us? Do we march to our own drummer?

What does postmodern really mean? Willa Kim, Tharon Musser, Jane Greenwood, and I are modern; Adrienne Lobel and Marjorie Kellogg are postmodern. Generational differences? What does our art have to do with the other arts—music, literature, dance? Are we aside from the main developments? Do we have to go to Europe to find the postmodern? Or do we have to have the British come here to shows us how to stage *Carousel*? I don't know.

Awful questions—I have students and young assistants. What would I do with the gifts I was given if I were twenty-five today? What do you tell your students? Most designers spend their life on an airplane flying from job to job. We've all done it. We do more work than we want to do creatively in order to float financially. It was pointed out to me how strange our situation is. The artists can't afford to work in the theatre and the younger generation can't afford to see it.

Patrizia von Brandenstein: Film

When I finally felt that I knew enough to start working, I came up against the idea which had really never occurred to me that there were no women. I hadn't heard about Aline Bernstein or the handful of women who had become set designers of note in the theatre and I can truly say until my late twenties, I had no idea what a production designer was. I had never been on a film set and I was thirty before I ever went on one. I had developed a career in regional theatre and Off-Broadway and I kept learning and kept growing but I don't think that I was particularly suited to the work. I don't feel that I had the training and probably not the native ability but I did have something that needed artistic expression and I think I had a very powerful grounding in story, in plays. The images were never as important to me as the story, the story line, and the resulting image. I think I was looking for movies, I didn't know anything about them but I was working in Cincinnati on a production of *Hamlet* at the Playhouse in the Park and a man who had given me my first Off-Broadway job called me up and said, I'm going to San Francisco and I'm going to work on a film and I need a guide there. I need someone. Can you recommend anyone? Could I ever? And I put myself as a candidate and brazenly went out and got the job. To my knowledge there were not any women at all who did that, who worked in the production design department mostly known then as Art Direction. I think there were probably some scene designers toiling away, but I was from New York and a true neophyte in films. Along the way people vanished from that first production that I worked on. There was a certain retribution, the temperamental director and people did fall by the wayside, and as they fell I inherited their jobs, and by the end of this film which was *Play It Again, Sam*, I was the set decorator, the art director, the budget analyst. It had a spectacularly good New York crew—they had gone to San Francisco because there was a union dispute in New York—and I always say now that in every production there is one person who signs on and sort of runs away to join the gypsies and I was that person. The very first time I went to the film set, which was the first day of filming, I felt a sense of place that was right. And I think, unconsciously to be sure, because I was too scared to make it consciously but unconsciously I think I made a decision on that very day. I think I found my place in life, no one else knew or cared and I didn't have enough courage to confide this revelation to anyone and it was a good thing.

The week when we worked out my contract, the studio, which was Warner Brothers, said, well can she be controlled, as if I were some beast in a cage. Controlled? Of course, of course. For many years there just weren't any women. I was the first woman on a crew, I was the only woman on a crew for really quite a few years. I can remember being on the paint crew on *The Godfather* on the Lower East Side in New York. People had never seen a woman on a movie crew, let alone one in paint overalls. They would come out and see this young woman: their idea of a career was to marry a guy with a job. It's an interesting thing—how far we've come.

Pat Collins: Technology

Our world of theatre is not your future. (Addressing young people in audience.) I say this because there has been a Trojan Horse that has been everywhere with us—in our bedrooms and kitchens—everywhere. It is something that has consumed theatre, film, literature and made a profound change in all our lives. It is destroying all the barriers. How many of you are sitting in front of computers? How many are dealing as designers with graphics programs? Every one of us.

The community we are going to have in the future will be totally different from the past. Our brains have become accustomed to cool media—that's what postmodernism comes out of. People are watching us do our work; we have become entertainment; we are all actors. Look at the talk shows; we all have become actors in our shows. We are mixing reality with dramatization of reality. Are you surprised that we have no playwrights? Everyone is writing their own plays.

What is theatre in this context? If a DA is interviewed about corruption and being filmed, he becomes an actor. Seeing a camera makes all the difference.

If we ignore this transformation while we are puttering around in the nineteenth-century theatre, we are in trouble. It is a totally confusing and exciting time. What is the need for theatre going to be when everyone is an actor making up the play as they go along? Now I am talking serious philosophy. We have become entertainment; it is profound and diminishing.

I had a wonderful time in the nineteenth century. That's my time. This is your time. Are you prepared? We are sitting on a gigantic animal that will let you ride or it will eat you alive.

JEAN ROSENTHAL'S LIGHT: MAKING VISIBLE THE MAGICIAN

Mary Callahan Boone

As Jean Rosenthal described the narrow, formulaic conventions of lighting that dominated the theatrical stage as late as the 1930s, "Comedies were bright; dramas were uncheerful. Day was yellow; night blue. Effects were naive."[1] Rosenthal's use of light revolutionized the art of theatrical lighting, and her work (along with that of Abe Feder and Peggy Clark Kelley) established the specialized area of lighting design. In addition to specific lighting innovations, Rosenthal's ability to create an atmosphere unique to each show put her in demand as a Broadway lighting designer. Prior to her death in 1969, she had begun to explore *son et lumière* (sound and light) productions as a way to further elevate the role of light. However, the cultural, professional and artistic concerns that helped produce Rosenthal's innovations also placed limits on them. In this essay I pay particular attention to the way gender expectations and ideas about the role of light in theatre production intersect, and how Rosenthal accommodated them.[2] By exploring Rosenthal's specific contributions, I also hope to show how theatrical lighting can be read in relation to the stage meanings it helps to produce.

Rosenthal began her career as a lighting designer at a time when masculinist traditions in Western theatre were rarely challenged successfully. Indeed, she worked *within* these traditions to revolutionize theatrical lighting, shaping her notion of the function of light within certain parameters: she saw light's functioning within the mise-en-scène as most successful when it did not call attention to itself. She was firm in her insistence that although lighting must be allowed to make its unique contribution to "the happy creative whole," it must nonetheless be subservient to all other aspects of performance. While acknowledging these limits, she created lighting that was original, varied and in its day technically sophisticated. Rosenthal's belief in the necessity of the subordination of both herself and her art into a kind of domestic, wifely function within the theatre reveals an interesting intersection between the cultural expectations for women and the professional expectations for lighting designers during the period covered by her career. A 1955 article in the *Sunday Mirror Magazine* attests to this connection:

> Stage lighting, [Rosenthal] said, is an ideal occupation for a woman if she is not excessively aggressive. "That's because," she says, "in this field you must be absolutely willing to be a collaborator. Everyone else—the actors, the directors, the producers, the writers—is the star . . . And when no one in the audience knows where the light on the stage comes from, and when no one notices anything on the stage except the actors, the sets, the costumes, and the words and the music—then you know that you have done your job as it should be done."[3]

Rosenthal's quiet demeanor, her politeness, her highly tactful mode of collaboration with other artists, and her willingness to background her own contributions became her professional trademarks. In a 1950 article for *Theatre Arts*, Ellen Violett described not only Rosenthal's qualities, but also what necessitated them:

> The obstacle of a woman bossing an all-male crew had been successfully overcome. Today she is unique for her relationships with the crews: she is without temperament and the people who work with her really like her. She says she learned the hard way. "An electrician said one day that if I told him to do something just once more he'd throw a monkey wrench at me. I forget now what it was, but about half an hour later when it still wasn't done I told him just once more—you know when you're young, you're eager. Well, he threw the monkey wrench. He missed. But only because he meant to miss, and he taught me a lesson."

Rosenthal's words suggest that her accommodation to a feminized role in theatre was not merely a matter of personality. In fact, her role as lighting designer required avoiding the appearance of authority over the men working for her, something she accomplished through the curious fiction of being "without temperament." In addition to the cultural limits placed on women's emotional expressions, Rosenthal's demeanor marks the necessary illusion of invisibility that functioned in the private, offstage arena of theatre in a way that parallels Rosenthal's conception of invisibility for light itself in the public, onstage arena.[4] Rosenthal successfully negotiated expectations for both women and lighting designers in part by cultivating a professional persona that echoed traditional expectations for ladylike behavior.

Theatrical Hierarchy and Feminized Light

In contemporary Western theatre, the director still holds the power to determine the use of stage space, the interpretation of the script and the representation of a play's so-called authorial intent (at times over the articulated wishes of the playwright). Dealing with the control of public space, the position of director has been traditionally occupied by men. Even when a woman directs, the directorial position itself can still be considered masculine. In an essay written for *Upstaging Big Daddy: Directing Theatre as if Gender and Race Matter*, playwright Joan Schenkar, who directs some of her own plays, observes that traditionally the position of director is "regarded as a category for the culturally constructed male—the culturally constructed renaissance male at that—since the director, in collaborating with so many other artists and technicians, needs to control the terms and practices of several, intersecting disciplines."[5] In most conventional theatre, the contributions of all the artists involved in a production are subjugated to the director's vision of the production. Therefore, the director, who ultimately controls the use of stage space, also controls the meaning(s) being produced for the audience's consumption. Within such a hierarchy, the work of other contributing artists can all too easily be obscured, even made invisible.

Rosenthal understood the way in which lighting designers function in response to other theatre designers, and positioned herself in relation to their own placement in the theatre hierarchy: for theatre designers, lighting plays a subservient role to both set and costume design.

Traditional theatre hierarchy, combined with the subservient role of light as a medium, situates the lighting designer in a feminized role. Jean Rosenthal's career should be viewed as an attempt to work within the established cultural, professional and artistic hierarchies, which all demanded she and her art be subordinate, if not invisible. Paradoxically, she earned her well-known reputation as a lighting designer within the commercial world of New York theatre (and dance) by producing "invisible" theatrical light. It is no surprise, then, that Rosenthal's specific contributions to lighting design in mainstream theatre have themselves remained largely invisible.

Classic Realism and Light

Indeed, the classically realistic forms in which Rosenthal frequently worked when lighting Broadway productions further compounded the need for the invisible artist to produce invisible lighting. As Catherine Belsey suggests in *Critical Practice*, the conventions of classic realism position audiences to receive a "coherent, non-contradictory interpretation of the world," one that squares with dominant ideology and so appears to the audience as true.[6] In order to appear real or natural, the theatrical apparatus must itself remain invisible.

How the necessary effacement of light helps to maintain the illusion of transparency in realism can be understood by looking at the relationships that exist among light, the audience and the proscenium stage—the space that Belsey calls the "theatrical form appropriate" to realism. According to Belsey, the physical frame of the proscenium arch provides a "containment of the action"; the audience is thus presented with a "comprehensive vision of the events dramatized, which is also a comprehending, and therefore authoritative vision. In other words, in a proscenium theatre, each individual member is, literally, physically positioned to "get" what the play generally means. This physical environment reinforces the necessity for stage lighting that reaches the audience on a nondisruptive and unconscious level. Thus lighting within conventional realism emphasizes "visibility, naturalism, composition and atmosphere," while concealing its operations.[7] A production's lighting design must fit into the (re)presented fictional world in a manner that enables audiences to unselfconsciously confirm their sense of ideological truth. Such theatre requires all aspects of the lighting design to be invisible and to create an atmosphere consistent with the fictional world represented. Jean Rosenthal's talent lay in her ability to create such a naturalizing atmosphere with an artistry and finesse that few theatre artists working solely with the medium of light had ever achieved.

RE-VISIONING SCENOGRAPHY: A FEMINIST'S APPROACH TO DESIGN FOR THE THEATRE

Delores Ringer

As a feminist, theatre artist and scenographer, I have been searching for a new matrix with which to practice and to discuss designs for the theatre.[1]

My own study of feminist research had caused me to ask certain questions as a scenographer, questions which have provoked new ideas about theatrical design:

1. In the production I am currently working on, what are the explicit and implicit messages about power in gender relations?
2. How does visual language contribute to these explicit and implicit messages?
3. How do I as a woman and designer relate to the visual language and the world around me? How do I visually process information?
4. How have my relationships with other artists in the theatre and the creative and working processes I use been constructed?

Certain recurring "tendencies" in women's visual art are paralleled by what can also be called tendencies in the work of many feminist and women playwrights. These tendencies are so interrelated that it has been difficult to categorize them.

The following is intended as a patchwork of ideas, presented with the goal of provoking feminist scenographic strategies. While many of the approaches or innovations I advocate are not exclusively the province of feminist theatre and scenography, they can be adapted to serve feminist ends.

The first relevant tendency is the effort on the part of feminist play-wrights and visual artists to de-objectify female characters and visual art subjects. Rather than serving as objects surrounding and supporting the male hero, female characters, and their mental and physical struggles and growth, are at the center of feminist drama.

Another interrelated tendency in both art and drama is the assertion that women's personal experience is not trivial, that private, personal experience is at least as valuable as public experience. Perhaps more important is the suggestion by some feminist theorists that there is, or should be, no distinction between the public and the private. For that reason, the feminist stage often contains internal and external experience and internal and external images in one space. A female character's bed might be covered with the colors and textures of sexual passion; or her kitchen arranged not logically, but emotionally; or her office have dreamlike combinations of space and set dressing. Her costume and period undergarments might have her environment photocopied on them or even be constructed from the materials of her environment. I deliberately arranged the pieces of the scenery for a production of Marsha Norman's *Getting Out* in a nonlogical fashion. This was a place where Arlene was dealing with the past—a nonlogical place—a mixture of emotions, thoughts, and memories. Things with the most emotional impact were placed most prominently onstage; for example, the bed and the prison doors.

The creation of inclusive rather than exclusive community groups is another tendency of women in theatre and the visual arts. This is manifested in the process of creation as well as the resultant product; it involves transmission of shared knowledge between equals, a spiral rather than a linear flow of information. All are mutually creators and spectators, seeking a "non-subordinate affiliation."

When I designed *Getting Out*, not only did I not indicate where performance space ended on the floor plan and in the visual field, I also placed irregular shapes which cut through and obliterated conventional boundaries. Some scenic pieces extended in front of the proscenium, some behind, and no masking separated the acting area from backstage. There were only the visible theatre walls, common boundaries for everyone in the theatre.

I used patchwork as a metaphor for Arlene's life in *Getting Out*, both on the set and on the costumes. The patched nature of the costumes was fairly subtle, using similar fabrics for sides of a bodice, collar and sleeves, for example. I did not want Arlene's clothes to look like fashionable or intentional patchwork, but rather to have an uneasy, not-quite-matching, pieced-together look about them. The floor of the set was a patchwork: a piece of carpet here, a piece of linoleum, a rug, some pieces of tile. Disconnected pieces of scenery hung about and overlapped each other. Pieces of walls stood here and there and were covered with various patches of wallpaper and brown paper.

Arlene's fragmented self, which she eventually begins to pull together, was illustrated in my scenic design by various pictures of women painted on cloth. One was a traditional framed painting of a woman's torso. Another was a picture of a woman which had been cut up and distributed throughout the setting, an arrangement suggesting pieces of laundry hung out to dry. A face stared at the audience from far upstage. Nowhere was there a picture of a complete woman.

One useful strategy for the feminist designer is to envision our audience as female. The resultant, powerful inner image has a multitude of liberating and surprising ramifications for scenography which prompt questions about how women watch. At this point, a feminist re-visioning of theatrical design could include the idea of women's double-vision: as John Berger wrote, "Women watch themselves being looked at."[2] Rosemary Betterton added: "Characteristic of women's looking, then, is that it is split between surveyor and surveyed."[3] Might the tendencies discussed above in art and theatre be indicative of those who have been socialized to be the watcher and the watched at the same time? Perhaps feminist design strategies would create conditions in which we watch watchers watch.

Just as the theatre has been a forum for men's introspection, it should be a place for women's introspection, a place to ask many questions about ourselves. Designers can emphasize visually female characters' awareness of their "otherness" within a male context, their oppression, their nonownership, their double-vision, their alien-ness in the male-centered theatre space.

ORGANIZATIONS

While some women have taken the helms of extant theatres, actress Jane Alexander fought for the very existence of taxpayer support for those theatres. Journalist Marilyn Stasio chronicles Alexander's reflections on her "tough years" as chairman of the National Endowment for the Arts in the mid-1990s, when political conservatives turned both Endowments into a "political football." The Endowments were created in the late 1960s by a bipartisan coalition of legislators who recognized the importance of arts and humanities to American cultural well-being. Although they have suffered blows to funding, they still stand—thanks in part to Alexander's battles on behalf of the NEA.

Many women have focused their energies within organizations that support theatre. Not only did they create groups, such as the Women and Theatre Program in the Association for Theatre in Higher Education, but they increasingly have chaired or presided over national associations from the ATHE to the National Theatre Conference and the American Society for Theatre Research. Organizational programs focusing on women have fostered research, dialogue, camaraderie and creative collaborations. The Women and Theatre Program has played a significant role in the creation of this book from the program's beginnings in 1975.

Some feminist theatre companies serve as organizations that sponsor conferences, contests, publications, networking and other such services that benefit women theatre artists. Founded in 1986, for example, San Francisco's Brava! For Women in the Arts produces, commissions and presents original theatre, especially by women of color and lesbian playwrights, while also conducting arts education and job-training programs. In 1998, Julia Miles reviewed some of the accomplishments of the Women's Project she founded in New York, which currently is under the leadership of Loretta Greco. In addition to staging more than one hundred productions as well as more than four hundred readings and workshops, the Project has published eight anthologies of produced plays by women, fosters emerging artists and serves over three thousand predominantly at-risk New York City public school students through a curriculum-based arts education program.

LWJ

JANE ALEXANDER: SHE STOOPS TO CONQUER

Marilyn Stasio

Bloodied—but defiantly unbowed—from her four years as the embattled chairman of the National Endowment for the Arts, [actress] Jane Alexander returned to Broadway [in 1998]. "After being away from theatre for all that time, I was pretty overwhelmed by how deeply moved I was to be back onstage," she says. "It feels great to be back."

Not that she didn't apply her acting skills—at times, with desperation—to her Washington political chores. "I wasn't 'play-acting,' but in the beginning, I certainly played the role of baby politician. And it was a more conservative role than I was used to."

No stranger to the city itself, Alexander launched her career from Washington, D.C.'s Arena Stage, where she appeared in more than a dozen plays, including *The Great White Hope* with James Earl Jones. That production went on to Broadway in 1968, winning her a Tony award and propelling her into memorable stage roles in *First Monday in October*, *The Visit*, *Shadowlands* and *The Sisters Rosensweig*. Cool, classy women were her specialty, and she played them in films and on television as well as on the stage, in the process earning four Academy Award nominations, five Emmy nominations and an Emmy for the Holocaust drama *Playing for Time*. She was inducted into the Theatre Hall of Fame in 1995, two years after her NEA appointment.

To this onetime Washingtonian, the biggest shock upon her return in 1993 was how conservative the town had become, a situation that intensified with the influx of cocky Republicans who swept in with the 104th Congress. "Those were very tough years," she says of the mid-1990s, adding that the most difficult part was being separated from the creative stimulation of the life and the people she had left behind.

"In the theatre world, you get used to meeting a lot of creative people, people who are educated and sensitive and responsive to the arts," she says. Her Washington colleagues were, by contrast, "a whole new breed. They are not well educated. They are hostile and suspicious of the arts, and it was tough for me to persuade them otherwise."

Instead of holding polite discourse with legislators of the old Jacob Javits school of bipartisan civility, she found herself beating off political hit men with a mission to eliminate her agency and transfer its funding power to the states. "It was devastating on the arts," says Alexander, who watched the Endowment become "a political football." The NEA survived these attacks, but funding was cut by forty percent and individual artist grants were eliminated.

What arts organizations who depend on NEA support still have to learn, Alexander says, is that their fate is in the hands of moderate Republicans. "People forget that that's how the NEA was founded in the first place, with very strong bipartisan support. It was under Nixon, for heaven's sake, that the NEA budget increased one thousand percent."

Recalling the "naive idealist" she used to be, Alexander urges arts institutions to become aware of the political forces that determine how public monies (and more and more, private money as well) are appropriated—and to get over the notion that they, as artists, are too pure to dirty their hands with this muck. Like it or not, politics now play a part in all artistic transactions.

"I don't think the artists really understood the political situation," Alexander says. "It used to be that not-for-profit theatres had more public money from sources that did not get involved in content—there's no question that they had more individual artistic freedom." Now, she says, with the new dependency on corporate sponsors who have their own political agendas, "It just gets harder and harder to maintain that freedom."

Jane Alexander isn't afraid of a fight, but she also isn't ashamed to compromise. "They've eviscerated the major part of the agency," she admits of the unrelenting hatchet job that was done on the NEA, "but at least it's still there."

1998: YEAR OF THE WOMAN?

Julia Miles

Is this the American theatre's year of the woman? The uniquely multitalented Julie Taymor won a Tony for best director of a musical, and women were also honored for best play and best director of a play. It was, as everyone knows by now, the first time a Tony had been handed to a woman director in the fifty-two-year history of the award. Paula Vogel won the Pulitzer for *How I Learned to Drive*, and almost every major Off-Broadway theatre included a woman playwright in their season. My own company celebrated its twentieth anniversary season. Beyond the theatre, a festival of women's music, Lilith Fair, is touring the U.S. An article in the June issue of *Harper's* by Francine Prose was ironically subtitled "Are Women Writers Really Inferior?" Wherever I look, women are singled out, separated, distinguished from their male colleagues by gender. Unfortunately, whatever advances the women's movement has brought (and they have been many and important), the movement has not erased the disparity in most professional hierarchies between women and men and, thus, not eliminated the need for separate considerations, exhibitions, concerts, festivals, anthologies, theatres or magazine issues.

Last fall, an audience of primarily women—an unanticipated sell-out—at the Women's Project & Productions conference entitled "Mapping the Sources of Power" updated our conceptions of who is interested in hearing discussions about women in theatre. The impressively cross-generational group, spanning a diversity of races and cultures, had a marked activist spirit, blessedly free of laments for their proportionately small representation on the American stage. We had hoped to answer questions about the viability of same-gender theatre, but, of course, there were no definitive answers. The many students who attended cheered; they networked and took notes and exhorted each other to go out and start their own theatres.

No two of them might have the same response to *Time* magazine's recent cynical cover line—"Is Feminism Dead?"—but these young women are bene-ficiaries of 150 years of the women's movement, begun in New York by Eliza-beth Cady Stanton and Susan B. Anthony. We've been voting for seventy-eight years. Betty Friedan and Gloria Steinem, who brought the movement into our time, emphasized that we are equal to men, and the perception is that, of course women and men share the power in theatre. Most of the young women at the conference seemed unaware, or not to care particularly, about the numbers that gave the lie to that perception. Women playwrights and directors made up four percent on average of Broadway productions from 1985 to 1990; in 1995–96, the numbers scaled to a whopping six percent. Off-Broadway, where one would expect a more inclusive representation, seventeen percent of playwrights and twenty percent of directors were women (three percent and six percent, respectively, for women of color) in 1994–95, up from approximately seven percent when the Women's Project started in 1978.

That first year we received eight hundred scripts—women were obviously writing plays without the encouragement of productions. Two decades later, in October, our ninety-ninth production—Julie Herbert's *The Knee Desires the Dirt*—will open, and our hundredth will be Marlane Meyer's *The Chemistry of Change* (coproduced by Playwright's Horizons).

I'm happy about our recent success, but they must not distort our per-ceptions. We continue to occupy a small space in the theatre. It's taken time, more than most of us thought, but our talents will continue to enlarge this space. This is indeed the year of Julie Taymor, Garry Hines and Yasmina Reza, and their Broadway acclaim will pave the way for other women and other accomplishments in other years.

Women will claim their lives in the theatre, because (to quote John Guare in his afterword to Arnold Weinstein's *Red Eye of Love*, a play I produced with three other women at St. Ann's Church in Brooklyn a long time ago): "You hang in, because it still contains the possibility of the most fun anywhere."

DOCUMENTING AMERICA

The women's struggle for change, the early suffragettes told us, was "not for ourselves alone." Although women in theatre may have seemed preoccupied in recent years with their own liberation, they have by no means neglected the larger stage of public life. They have a long history of concern with the state of the nation that goes back to the 1770s, when Mercy Warren[1] propagandized for the American colonies, and in 2000 when Anna Deavere Smith explored Washington power in "The Press and the Presidency" for *House Arrest*, and beyond. The second wave of the feminist movement, which began in the 1960s, clarified how the personal is political and how gender, race, class and sexuality are social constructs rather than individual burdens. Documenting the dynamics of contemporary America from this complex perspective requires innovative performance techniques and multifaceted artists. We close with four different approaches to this important task.

Emily Mann won a directing fellowship to the Guthrie Theater in Minneapolis after graduating from Harvard University.[2] It was there that she directed her first play, *Annulla*, which was drawn from personal interviews with a Holocaust survivor and Mann's own search for her identity. Autobiographical material is used to throw light on the social and political dimensions of historical traumas, as it is in her later Broadway success, *Having Our Say*. For her other "theatre of testimony" projects, director-playwright Mann uses oral histories, interviews and research to create multiple voices that explore large public crises—violence and Vietnam vets in the triple Obie-winning *Still Life*; the murders of Mayor George Moscone and Harvey Milk in San Francisco in *Execution of Justice*; murders by the Ku Klux Klan and the American Nazi Party in *Greensboro*. These varied forms of documentary drama are her way of acting on her fundamental belief that "theatre is not only affected by the society we are in, but that theatre affects the society that we are in." In all of her plays the audience plays a vital role, as judges in some, or as guests invited to the home of the two middle-class African American teachers in *Having Our Say*. She likes to have a "mixed crowd." Her stage version of the book about the centenarian sisters was, she has explained, "built for multiracial audiences. It's built for people to come together. It's a healing piece about how we're all Americans, or we're all human beings." With the keen directorial skill that is so important to her work, she even structured two intermissions into the show, in part so that "people could talk to each other about what they were experiencing." Mann is very aware of her "responsibility" to balance her interpretation of the sources with enough objectivity to "show . . . what is out there, so that in the end you allow the audience to make its own synthesis." The critic Clive Barnes's protest that *Having Our Say* is not a play, is countered by many who believe that Emily Mann "has moved theatre in a new direction" in her theatrical explorations of the personal and the political.[3]

"I would have been dead or crazy years ago had I not become an actor," Robbie McCauley tells us, and it was as an actor that she started out in New York in the 1960s.[4] She appeared on Broadway in innovative shows like Ntozake Shange's *for colored girls . . .*, Adrienne Kennedy's *Solo Voyages* and Joe Chaikin's *Tourists and Refugees No. 2*. These liberating acting experiences "opened up voices inside me," she recalls. Much that was going on inside of her as a black woman performer "was not able to be spoken through some writer's words." Always a scribbler, she began to write her own words and "used the acting craft as vehicle to say some of the things I need to say." She created powerful solo performances about her family's survival since the nineteenth century that are searing documents of American history.[5] Using the mind and the body together, she has tried to bring about "the movement of political theatre . . . to change things." To make theatre something "for a regular audience to use . . . rather than simply having an evening in the theatre" is her aim. As a kind of "cultural worker," she had moved easily from her own remarkable performances to teaching that involves not only her students but a much larger community as well.[6] She spoke with me about a "practicum" in the theatre department of Mount Holyoke College in which the students researched the destruction of an old village to make way for the large Quabbin Reservoir. They interviewed former residents, studied local history, then performed their script and engaged the audience in a lively discussion of local issues and lore. The projects in other parts of the country McCauley discusses here are part of her "vision of having places in communities all over where art and politics, or concerns for change can happen."

Anna Deavere Smith's exploration of identity and linguistic patterns began with students in her classes, but developed as she became interested in performing solos herself based on her interviews.[7] Her unique approach and extraordinary talent for recreating the voices, the gestures and the very essence of those she interviewed brought "commissions" from many institutions going through the general American crisis of gender and racial identity.

Since 1982, she has grouped her various pieces under the rubric of "On the Road: A Search for American Character," and has performed them from San Francisco, to Princeton University, to Bellagio, Italy. Two of the most notable pieces deal with shocking public crises: *Fires in the Mirror: Crown Heights, Brooklyn and Other Identities* investigated the confrontation of races following an accident, and has been called "the most significant artistic exploration of Black-Jewish relations in our time."[8] *Twilight: Los Angeles, 1992* penetrated the many racial groups in conflict after the Rodney King tragedy. It was given a Special Achievement Award for "documenting and interpreting events of our time in a unique theatre form" by the Outer Critics Circle.

By the end of the 1990s, Smith was turning away from her highly successful monologues. "I thought my idea of going out and interviewing people and putting them on the stage was going to be a strong enough call to bring those kinds of people into the theatre . . . but it didn't."[9] Disillusioned, she turned to civic dialogue as director of the Institute on the Arts and Civic Dialogue. Funded by the Ford Foundation and based at Harvard, the Institute brought artists, scholars and other professionals together for collaborative projects that might attract "a more diverse public," and had as its "ultimate goal . . . the transformation of the identity of the artist in American society from that of a commodity to a vital and respected presence in civic life." Eva Wielgat Barnes, Smith's longtime vocal coach, takes us behind the scenes of *House Arrest*, a study of national character and the American presidency, to understand one of the many changes she explored for that production—the use of a company of actors.[10] In March of 2000, however, she performed *House Arrest* in New York as a unique solo investigation.[11]

Like so many of the multitalented women in this section, Anne Bogart is hard to pigeonhole. Is she a choreographer, writer or director for her unique productions? "I consider myself just a director. I write theoretical stuff, but I don't really write dialogue. The actors write the material . . . I'm more like a conductor." Bogart, who heads the graduate directing program at Columbia University, says, "To me teaching and directing are symbiotic. I cannot go into rehearsal unless I've been teaching, and conversely, I can't go into a classroom unless I have been in rehearsal."[12] Her students become her ensemble. She is also co-artistic director of the Saratoga International Theatre Institute, a company she founded with Japanese director Tadashi Suzuki, whose rigorous, disciplined, physical approach and Asian values have shaped SITI Company's training process. Suzuki describes Bogart's work as a fight with America in order to win America. "In a wonderfully energizing way she is caught in a paradox of shattering the very thing she loves in an attempt to discover it anew. To wake it up."[13]

Bogart's revisioning of such standard American plays as *The Women*, *The Adding Machine*, *Once in a Lifetime* and *South Pacific* is her wake-up call to an important cultural heritage. Stripping these plays of sentimentality and commercialism with her deconstructive techniques, she seeks to release for us today these "time capsules, memory capsules of who we are."[14]

Central to Bogart's struggle with American theatre is her effort to replace Lee Strasberg's "method" with the shared language of the Viewpoints, causing actors to rethink the role of emotion in their work.[15] Tina Landau, the director-playwright who has collaborated extensively with Bogart, explains that "the Viewpoints are often used to generate and then 'set' the staging . . . The text will then be 'put on' the movement. In this way, Anne chooses to set the form but allow the emotional life of the characters to remain open. The staging becomes the vessel for what goes on in the interior life."[16]

The question of emotion comes up in some reviews of her venturesome, innovative productions. In her very open way, she admits to having an "obsession visually," and that there could consequently be "something missing" in her interpretations.[17] In her "riff" on Chekhov's *The Seagull*, staged at Actors Theatre of Louisville in 1995, she seemed to have it all; the performance was praised as "formalism full of feeling, pulsating with mourning, yearning and the refusal of futility."[18] It was one of the productions Anne Bogart presented at Louisville when artistic director Jon Jory chose her to be the first director honored in their distinguished Modern Masters series. Between 1976 and 1995 she had a production record of seventy plays, which ranged from her take on the popular American canon to productions of many new American plays, a task at which playwright Paula Vogel says Bogart excels.[19] Bogart's personal credo makes a challenging close for *Women in American Theatre*.

HKC

HAVING HER SAY: EMILY MANN

An Interview with Melissa Salz Bernstein

MB: You read the book [*Having Our Say: The Delany Sisters' First 100 Years* by Sarah L. Delany and A. Elizabeth Delany with Amy Hill Hearth] and then visited the Delany sisters. Did you interview them some more?

EM: I wanted to meet them. I wanted to understand them. I wanted to have some of my own personal connections, not just through Amy and the book. And it was through meeting them that I knew how to do the play. There was a direct connection again and a growing bond that happened. At the end of the second visit Sadie said to me: "Child, I feel like I've known you all my life." That's when I knew that's where it had to go. I wanted other people to experience what I had experienced. That kind of life-expanding, heart-expanding experience. That's what happens to most people who see the play. They are transformed by meeting new people. And in some ways it's a quietly revolutionary act because there are many many white people who have never met a Sadie or a Bessie. They don't have any black friends who are peers. You know, middle-class white people with middle-class black people—they've never had the experience. And I think in some ways we have not met Bessies and Sadies in our lives, we have not heard that kind of wisdom of integration, wisdom of not allowing bitterness to eat you up, of not allowing prejudice to stand in your way, of retaining your humanity at every turn and living life happily, even knowing there's injustice. Not allowing yourself to feed on that and stop yourself. It's a great lesson for all people.

MB: I want to talk about your method. For example, with *Having Our Say*. After you read the book, how do you create a play?

EM: I have to find out what the event was. The event I decided was meeting the sisters. And then it would go from us being invited for tea, as Amy was, to "Child, I feel like I've known you all my life." That was beginning and end. And I wanted to make it even more special. I knew they couldn't just sit there and talk. I knew there had to be an event, something more specific. We were having our dress rehearsal on Papa's birthday, February 5th, and I thought, Oh, it's Papa's birthday! So they'll cook a meal onstage.

It's an amazing event that way. I thought: this would be important, that we're talking about lynchings and Jim Crow while we're potsing around making food. As I've said a number of times, I think I've learned more in the kitchens of wonderful older women that I've known as a child than I learned at Harvard, from my grandmother, my aunts and neighbors. Just sitting around the kitchen table while they're cooking and listen.

So that was the basic structure. Then when I went to see them—the key for me was they always finished each other's sentences like they thought the same thoughts. They were, as Sadie says, in some ways like one person. So though most of the stories in the book were Bessie's, I found a way to balance the play with Sadie because she knows all the stories, even though Bessie is the most voluble one, funniest and angriest. Some of them were very definitely Bessie's stories, but some of them were very definitely Sadie's. I realized where Sadie's strength is in the third act when she tells us about losing her mother—I think it is the most moving moment in the show. So I let them balance each other, finish each other's sentences, and I made it as a piece of music, you know, in rhythm.

It's very syncopated. It gives a lot of life to it. Then I said, you know we still have two old ladies talking all night, what are we going to do? So I decided to make it really quick three acts and two intermissions. Make it go by so fast that you just can't believe it, just quick snatches of conversation . . . and it flew. It took a lot of time to boil that book down to its essence, its best stuff.

MB: How much do you think is left out?

EM: Sixty percent or more. Some stuff I cut I wish I kept. Also I have actresses I had to deal with and Gloria's got a very slow rhythm so I had to cut.

MB: Did you add anything? The making of dinner is not part of the book. Did you add some fictional lines here and there?

EM: Oh sure. The whole beginning I got from what Amy had said and what I remember they said, so I wrote the beginning. Obviously I wrote the end. And then sometimes I have to write connecting lines. There's a lot that I did.

MB: Have you done that throughout all your plays?

EM: Connections probably, transition lines, yes. Sometimes I'll change word order and clarify. But I try to stay completely true to their meaning. I never change somebody's meaning, that's just a rule. I'm just constantly massaging the real language to make it come alive onstage and there's a lot of writing. Sometimes I'll take a whole paragraph that is very turgid on the page and make it into Bessie's speech or Sadie's speech.

MB: What would be your rebuttal to the article in the *New York Post*? What would you say in your defense? [Clive Barnes of the *New York Post* criticized *Having Our Say*'s Tony nomination for Best Play.]

EM: Well, you know, I didn't read the article but I hear what Clive Barnes said about it, "I loved it, but it isn't a play," basically. And my response is well,

UNIVERSITY OF WINCHESTER LIBRARY

all I know is the audience files into the theatre, the lights go down, the curtain goes up, two actresses enter, speak words to the audience and to each other, the audience laughs, they cry, then they rise to their feet every night in a standing ovation, a screaming standing ovation. If that isn't a play, I don't know what is. What's the problem here?

SHARING THE WORK

Robbie McCauley

The performance theatre work I've been doing for the last many years has involved a conscious process wherein I sought to address certain assumptions about art, history, community, the personal and the political. Those assumptions had seemed to me to be an official attitude in this society: that art about social issues and community either must be done a certain way and must say certain things in order to be relevant, or that such art is doomed to "preach to the converted" and is not good work. I wanted to do a kind of theatre that I remembered from before I was born . . . my mother's memory of the wagon shows . . . live music at the house parties . . . magnificent dresses and splendid shoes . . . good food . . . There was no talk of struggle or freedom. I thought we were already free. Memories that faded too soon.

I want to continue in the tradition of performance art which encourages people to learn from the past and to challenge the stories. I have particular obsessive urges to analyze the world I was born into. As luck would have it, with my interest in charged form and content, I arrived in New York City in 1965 at a time when experimental theatre and black theatre were present up and down the city. I would have been dead or crazy years ago had I not become an actor. A bewildered young black woman with a do-gooder attitude, I crossed into a world where I saw that one's talent helped to define one's identity, a world where I felt encouraged to follow my impulses to find beautiful ways to express hard feelings. I literally tuned in to my insides, as was the mode of the day, and seized upon the stirrings inside me as raw material. I began to create musical performance theatre pieces [these were cowritten in the 1980s with Ed Montgomery, whom she married and who is the father of her daughter, and his musical group Sedition Ensemble]. Since then, I've concentrated on engaging the audience and performers to face charged issues. Sedition Ensemble terminated. I now miss the uncompromising politics as the source of the work, but then I missed the personal stirrings. I continue to seek a way to balance both. I began to create a series about my family's survival since the nineteenth century, "Confessions of a Working Class Black Woman," and included *My Father and the Wars, Indian Blood* and *Sally's Rap*. I was revved up by the stories my family had told me. My imagination kicked in. I began to see possibilities of teaching history in a non-academic way.

"Buffalo and Other Communities" [1967 race riots]: I did this series out of the obsession for examining my feelings about survival. The work was structured like jazz music with black and white players. Having taught for several years, I was anxious to share some of the work I'd been doing with students, how one's personal biography is part of history and how that affects the actor's voice. The assignment for each actor was to interview one or more people in Buffalo about the riots. This would include a variety of people, whether or not they experienced it, including the actors themselves who either grew up in the community or had come later and heard stories, were witnesses. [Ten men and women, from age seventy to age twenty-two, black, Jewish, Italian, Protestant, Catholic, mothers, fathers.] The script would be a basis for talking about racial relations in Buffalo today. I knew that the performance would include choral passages. I like the idea of modern events having the choral voice. Thus began a way of working that became basic for subsequent projects. The actors and I declared a safe place in which to express thoughts and feelings about the subject matter, and to listen to each other. [Commenting on the relationship of her "histories" work to that of Anna Deavere Smith, she expressed her admiration, but noted her different intention.] The mirror reflecting the community back on itself and encouraging dialogue about it. The task of the actor is to identify and try to work through resistances and see how material plays from the inside out. The key is the material itself. I try to be fair. I try to be honest. The work is to get actors to be present with information and their own vulnerability in the face of it. As much work as possible must be done to play the material with one's intellect, voice, body and sense of connection to others. Here is a process by which the actors can learn and teach history.

In a Mississippi meeting two community leaders actually flinched when I described the way I work. Why work with actors rather than "real people"? I felt that the question was an insult to the work of an actor, but I understood the prejudice because of how actors are often perceived. I explained that I felt the work of artists was to connect to the community and try to interpret and reveal history. I assume that actors are everywhere, like musicians.

Acting is basic to work I create. Intelligence is a valuable element of the craft. It is an element that ought to be identified and nurtured. I believe it is an element that is, especially in the anti-intellectual culture of the United States, systematically undervalued. "Don't think," is a common admonition to the actor. This makes sense in many cases when tension and judgment are inhibiting her. The question, "What are you thinking?"—whether answered or not—may be more useful. A fiery personal analysis of ideas is raw material for work.

Becoming intellectually engaged with new details can be empowering for actors. In the Los Angeles project there was a lot of resistance from the performers, especially the men. I usually welcome resistance, especially from men. I have a talent to recognize, name, open up and explore the information inside of the resistance. Resistance is information. Perhaps bitterness too is information to be picked apart and used. Actors can rather safely explore the painful, the sad, the fearful, the so-called negative conditions and be able to perform then with energy, joy, beauty, power. Recognition of blocks and belief in the ability to penetrate them are craft elements. This work, basic to acting, is useful for audiences as well—to see examples of grappling to think clearly.

I've been fortunate to work with master directors: Lloyd Richards, Gilbert Moses, who'd trained directly with Viola Spolin; Bill Duke at the Negro Ensemble Company; Carl Weber; Joseph Chaikin. Conversational music, choruses, poetry, monologues are new and old forms at my disposal. This work is endemic to the poetry, politics and music of the 1960s black cultural movement. It requires a willingness and some technique in involving oneself personally with the content of a text. I am still experimenting with how to articulate it.

The best parts of this [L.A.] project for me happened during audience discussion. I started this work before I knew what interactive theatre was. Serious conversations happen often now in public. The more one shares the work, the more one learns, I keep telling myself. In L.A. the talkbacks often went on as long as the show, which was about an hour and twenty minutes. I feel there is a balancing act in the work between the artist/outsider and the local artists, the witnesses and the audiences. The tightrope sways also between the parameters of the personal, the aesthetic, the political, the scholarly and the hearsay. Personalizing frees the actor's voice. That is the purpose of it. It is not the same as substituting one's own personal experience for one in the performance. It is the work of exercising one's imagination and giving voice to what comes up in response to the issues of the work. This process can weed out what is irrelevant. Artists need to make unique connections with the issues. One night in the aftershow talk a black man started to speak and broke into tears. "Take your time," we echoed from the stage like folks do in church. He thanked us for showing what, he said, he no longer heard people speak of. The end of the work is often the beginning.

ANNA DEAVERE SMITH'S *HOUSE ARREST*

Eva Wielgat Barnes

House Arrest *is a performance piece in Anna Deavere Smith's extraordinary series called "On the Road: A Search for American Character." She took her theatrical investigation to the centers of power in Washington.* House Arrest *opened at The Public Theater in New York, March 2000.*

EB: Why focus on Washington?

AS: My work in the past has been about disenfranchised communities. I had never really investigated what's at the heart of things. And people talk about Washington as "inside the beltway." This idea of the inner circle. I thought it would be interesting for me—the person who's on the road searching for American character—to go there too. How could it be an authentic search for American character if I only looked in disenfranchised communities? I decided to go to the place where power is. People are there because power is there. So that's why I went to the so-called center.

EB: Why change from solo-work to a group of performers for the Washington performance?

AS: There are a lot of reasons. But first of all, I never thought of my work as a singular enterprise. I really wish I had a whole team of people to go on the road with me searching for American character, a group who studied community with me like anthropologists and archaeologists do—you know, go to the site and do the work. So I never thought of it as a singular enterprise. But even without that, I didn't go to Los Angeles and figure out what Los Angeles meant and write it in a singular voice. I shared the stage with forty-six opinions. And didn't give mine. So the point now is to see if that same thinking can go into the aesthetic which happens on the stage.

Also I was trying to answer a very big question—What is the relation of language to identity? I suppose in some way I'm also trying to contribute something to the study of acting. So it's obviously a hugely ambitious project that isn't confined to one work of art. But inasmuch as I've worked for seventeen years alone, then I think the real scientific test has to be broadened and put on more bodies and voices than mine.

The Acting Process:

Focus on the sounds you've been given. "Aaahhh" is the home base. The character lives in the pause. The character always lives in the broken sentence. I'm interested in the place where speech stops. That pause is where you feel the result of all those words. Don't worry about the logic of filling the pause. Free yourself of the why. We don't know why.

I think this is really the center of my work. If the time of Stanislavsky yielded psychological realism, the question is, what does this time yield? And the time of Stanislavsky's work had to do with the idea that Freud was also talking about, that the subconscious could speak. And it could speak, in particular, in your physical behavior, because that's what the audience saw. And what has happened is that we now have a kind of acting on television and in the movies that is mostly about that physical talking. But it used to be that actors attracted attention by their voice. In our casting process I said that I wanted an older man and they finally brought me some. These were guys who used to do radio. And they get up and this oddest energy comes forward which is all vocal energy. And I was so excited. Because in my work the whole effort is to have your vocal equipment completely alert to who this character is. In this process your psychological equipment won't be used till way down the road. My theory is to have the vocal person at the center.

Don't Look for Subtext:

What's underneath the text is your diaphragm. That's supporting the text. And we have a society where people have repressed their diaphragms. Because they're performing in a psychological, realistic tradition. Trying to look real, trying to look relaxed. Trying to look nonchalant. I'm trying to do something here that is about the alert diaphragm. The diaphragm which anticipates the true voice. Can't wait for it.

Bare Feet:

But it's part of my technique and that's what we're trying to expand on, and I really want to be in contact with the floor. You come into and go out of life with your feet bare. There's something about that, about how there needs to be a nude place of entry into the person. The foot needs to be available to that. I think Brecht has a piece about an actor in a hat. Trying to pick the right hat. So this is about making you feet available for the right shoes. 'Cause when you think of it, to walk in someone's shoes really is very hard.

Houses of Identity:

Well, I talk about being stuck in the crossroads of ambiguity. Because when you come out of your house, it's not ever that you're going to be welcomed with open arms into somebody else's house. And even if you're welcomed in at first, it would be a very peculiar situation where you were invited to stay. You know? If they already have a community or society in there. So I'm interested in just what would happen if there were some people who were willing to be outside of their houses a little bit? We could learn things from one another. But you pay a heavy price for that. Because people inside the house where you were are suspicious of you—suspicious about why you went away. So it could be hard to come back, too. And maybe this is just human nature and it'll be like this forever, but it seems like we live in a time of tribalism. So no matter how we try to do this thing about multiculturalism, we all know that the bottom line is that we're still really responsible, you know, to maintain our own houses.

EB: Why the title of *House Arrest*?

AS: That came from a conversation with these wonderful students about the idea of speaking openly—about how can we have open conversation. What inhibits us having a conversation in public about big, serious issues? What gets in the way? One thing that gets in the way is that we are protecting our houses of identity. And this one kid yelled out, "It's like we're in house arrest." Yeah! That's it! And I think that the things that are going on in Washington now give the title *House Arrest* a different kind of relevance, because of the way the presidency, or the political system, is being criminalized. The criminal justice system is creating our political game field. And I don't think many people are happy with that right now. The First Lady said in an interview that our political process is being arbitrated by the criminal justice system. It's very, very dangerous because it means that people don't want to be in political life for fear that they'll be made to look like criminals. I mean, that's what the "For Colored Girls" section of *House Arrest* is all about. You come into this space and you're treated like a common criminal. And so, this issue of being arrested, being stopped, being contained, while you're trying to speak freely or get something done, is very interesting to me right now.

VIEWPOINTS ON THEATRE NOW

Anne Bogart

I re-titled this lecture: "Six things I know for sure about working as an artist in the American theatre." One is: "treat the theatre as an art form"; the second is: "follow your interest"; three is: "we are not separate from our past"; four is: "the necessity of violence in the creative process"; five is: "you cannot hide"; six is: "choose big issues."

1. treat theatre as an art form:

I think when I was about twenty-three years old I made a decision that has formed the rest of my life and given me all the adventures I've been on. And that was never to choose to do something in the theatre, in the art form that I chose to work in, for financial reasons—in other words, it's nice to earn a lot of money for something, but never to make that choice for that reason.

Treat theatre as an art form. What does that mean? The essential impulse for one's work as an artist is a gift-giving impulse; it's not a survival one. And you get into trouble when you are working with a producer right? Who must, in all positive ways, should, and must mostly function out of the survival impulse. And that's conflict of interest. There's a struggle. But the minute you stop functioning out of the gift-giving impulse and start functioning from the survival mechanism-impulse in rehearsal, in the preparation of work, in whatever is your contribution to the theatre as an artist, the minute that happens, your work suffers and you start to die.

2. follow your interest:

Never betray your interest. What does this mean, interest? Burgeoning stock market? I don't mean that kind of interest. I mean that interest is the most important tool we have as artists if we're treating theatre as an art form. Every one of us in this room is actually interested in different things. That really personal relationship to the world is your guide as an artist.

The first big crossroad for me was when I was fifteen, seeing my first professional theatre production—that Scottish play, *Macbeth*, in Rhode Island, directed by Adrian Hall. I didn't understand a word of it, because it was Shakespeare and I was brought up on Disney. I didn't know what was happening, but my whole being pointed toward this thing, and I said, "I want to do that, I want to be a director." At fifteen! And Mr. Hall gave me the first lesson I ever had as a director—I didn't meet him till twenty-five years later—which was "Don't talk down to your audience."

After my college studies of theatre, I faced another one of those crossroads. I was seeing a film, in German, of a theatre company doing a play, *Summerfolk* by Gorky. I could read, but I didn't speak German at the time. I sat in the theatre afterwards and again, had this sensation, I didn't know what they were doing, but I knew that I had to change everything I was doing in my life and follow this thing. It did something that American productions have trouble doing. It was deep visually, intellectually, emotionally, politically. It was the best acting I had ever seen.

Later I had many invitations to direct in German-speaking countries and I accepted them all, which turned out to be a big mistake because I tried to pretend I was German and not American. I was so depressed and shut myself into a *pensione* in the north of Italy. And I had a kind of rebirth experience. I realized that I was an American. I had been embarrassed about it before because I thought, "Americans, we're superficial, we're not interesting." We have an extraordinary heritage and an amazing cultural history. To make a long story short, I embraced that and I've been happy every since. I've spent a huge amount of time and productions on what our heritage is in a trilogy of works—*American Vaudeville, Marathon Dancing* and *American Silents*. All this came about because I followed my interests.

3. we are not separate from our past:

Once I got interested in America again, after these horrific German experiences, I needed to do a little research. So I asked myself, "Self," I said, "what was the first American play that was performed?" The first play was called *Ye Bare and Ye Cubb* and it was performed in a pub in 1665. It was performed one time, and somebody came along and accused it of being blasphemous. And took it to court. This is true. The judge said, "I cannot determine whether or not this play is blasphemous because I've never seen it." The second performance of the first play—done in the colonies—was done in *court*. The judge determined that it was not blasphemous because it was entertaining. These are the roots of our theatre.

So what does that mean in terms of where we are now and how we judge plays and how we judge performances? I'm not going to really answer that question. In a conversation with Oskar Eustis, my old friend, I asked why it is that our plays don't address as many issues as plays from most other countries. Why the plays since the early fifties are mostly about you and me and our apartment and our problems. Whereas a lot of plays you saw in Europe or in Asia had to do with—yes, as should be, very personal love relationships, but always with a background of something social and political. So, I thought, well I was brought up in the Navy, with Disney, and we always said, "Art and politics don't mix." Where does that come from?

So I did a kind of root search and found out that between the years 1948 and 1952, all of those people whom I admired, and some I didn't even know about, either left the country, changed their tune (changed the way they worked) or were blacklisted. *All of them.*

Can you see how we stand on these shoulders? And that you have to investigate and internalize and understand and research and not assume that we did things this way, but that there are real reasons for them.

The other one which I think is profound and has a lot to do with who we are as theatre artists is what happened with Stanislavsky. What happened to our understanding of acting in this country? So you look at that historically. And, of course, Mr. Strasberg, who I think is the devil, I'm sorry, actually took the narrowest part of the approach, not *method*, this *approach*, and turned it into a religion. Do you see that the Americanization of the Stanislavsky system is like the air we breathe? It's so prevalent, we don't even know it's there. We don't know the difference between stage and film. We should think about this a bit.

What I want to say about assumptions is, really to look at the *context* in which our cultural movement, our theatre, is happening.

4. the necessity of violence in the creative process:

I believe in violence. I like to call it "the violence of articulation." I've come to understand that art doesn't happen improvised. It doesn't happen the first time. But there's a process of resurrection, much like Christ was resurrected. He died and is brought back through resurrection into life again. Art is created once you have killed, set it, and you find a way to repeat it. You bring life back into something you've killed.

So I started thinking, Why not start that earlier? Why not bedevil Strasberg? You have to set something onstage. You can't let everything be free. So what are your choices?

I think emotions are the most beautiful things we have as human beings. Because they change. You can't hold on to them. But you have to set something. I don't believe in setting emotions. I believe in setting the body. That if an actor agrees with another actor, that "On this word I am going to set my arm here," a deeper kind of freedom occurs. We tend to think that—we tend to have a misunderstanding of freedom—we think that freedom means "do anything." But the real freedom is when you can *be* anything. You can't be free outside and inside.

You have to commit violence in rehearsal or else you are just hanging out. You have to work, you have to work together to set something. Then you have to ask, what are you setting?

Just think about what you're setting. And think about the role of emotions. People really scare me. You know, nothing I do is original. But I've stolen and developed the Viewpoints. A month ago I was in St. Louis and someone said, "Ah, yes, the Viewpoints. That's where you don't show an emotion. And you don't have anything on your face." I thought, "Oh my God, this is so scary." The point of the Viewpoints is for you to get out of your way so that you can actually have actual experiences. And that kind of misinterpretation just terrifies me. The reason you don't focus on emotion is because you're *interested* in emotion. If I'm working here with Kate and I'm going, "Emotions! Emotions!" what's she going to feel? But I say, "This was good. Your hand here." There's a freedom.

5. you cannot hide:

You can't divorce your growth as a person from your growth as an artist. We see on the stage who you are, what your politics are, what you've read, how you treat people. It's visible. You cannot hide a bad rehearsal process from a performance. I'd love to say this isn't true. What it means is, as an artist you have to take care of those things. That it matters what you experience, what you read. You cannot hide behind your work. It's revealing, embarrassingly so. Your assumptions are visible. When I go to the theatre I see the assumptions that this group of people are working with about what theatre is. Or I see the attempt to eradicate these assumptions, to look anew.

And then the last thing under Number 5 is the importance of bringing conscience and perspective to events. That's what we do in theatre. We create events. That's our job. We create events. Not plays. Plays are part of the event. To bring perspective and conscience to events.

6. choose big issues:

You have a choice at any moment. You can choose a small one or a big one. How to always choose big issues? One way to do that is the incorporation of the other. And throughout history it's always about including the thing that has not been in there. Inclusion of "the other." I would encourage you to include things in your work that make you feel out of your element. Things that you don't understand. My colleague, Mr. Suzuki, says about international cultural exchange, which is something I'm very interested in, he says, "International cultural exchange is impossible. Therefore, we must try."

ENDNOTES

1 Female Rites

Sex Roles and Shamans

1. Knud Rasmussen, *Across Arctic America*, G. P. Putnam's Sons, 1927, pp 71–72.
2. Joseph Epes Brown, ed., *The Sacred Pipe*, Penguin reprint, 1972.
3. See for further discussion Peggy V. Beck and A. L. Walters, *The Sacred: Ways of Knowledge, Sources of Life*, Navajo Community College, Tsaile, AZ, Navajo Nation, 1977.
4. John G. Niehardt, *Black Elk Speaks*, Simon & Schuster, Pocket Books, and University of Nebraska Press, 1959, 1961.
5. Charlotte Johnson Frisbie, *Kinaaldá*, Wesleyan University Press, 1967.
6. Franz Boas, *Kwakiutl Ethnography*, Helen Codere, ed., University of Chicago Press, 1966. Reprinted by permission of the University of Chicago Press.
7. Ruth Murray Underhill, *Singing for Power*, University of California Press, 1938.
8. Mircea Eliade, *Shamanism*, Willard R. Trask, trans., Princeton University Press, 1964.
9. For more discussion of Native American shamans, see Beck and Walter.
10. R. G. Wasson et al., *María Sabina and Her Mazatec Mushroom Velada*, Harcourt Brace Jovanovich, 1974. Contemporary poet Anne Waldman's poem/chant "Fast Speaking Woman" is based on María Sabina's chant. *Fast Speaking Women & Other Chants*, City Lights, 1975.
11. Wasson et al. as quoted by Joan Halifax, ed. in *Shamanic Voices*, E. P. Dutton, 1979, 212–13.
12. See playwright Mary Austin's *The Arrow-Maker*, Houghton Mifflin, 1915. She builds the dramatic conflict around the desire of her heroine, the Chisera, to be both a shaman and a married woman with children.

Trampling Out the Vintage

1. W. C. Steel, *The Woman's Temperance Movement, A Concise History of the War on Alcohol*, Introduction by Dio Lewis, New York: National Temperance Society and Publication House, 1874, pp. 36–37.
2. Eliza Jane Trimble Thompson, Her Two Daughters, and Frances Willard, *Hillsboro Crusade Sketches and Family Records*, Cincinnati: Cranston & Curtis, 1896, pp. 57–149.
3. Mrs. Annie Wittenmyer, *History of the Woman's Temperance Crusade*, Philadelphia: Office of the Christian Woman, 1878, p. 659.
4. Steel, p. 12.
5. Jane E. Stebbins, *Fifty Years' History of the Temperance Cause, with a Full Description of the New Plan of Labor by the Women up to the Present Time*, Hartford: L. Stebbins, 1874, p. 323.
6. Wittenmyer, p. 352.
7. Reverend W. H. Daniels, ed., *The Temperance Reform and Its Great Reformers*, New York: Nelson & Phillips, 1878, p. 294.
8. Mother Stewart, *Memories of the Crusade: A Thrilling Account of the Great Uprising of the Women of Ohio in 1873, Against the Liquor Crime*, Chicago: H. J. Smith & Co., 1890, p. 194.
9. Mrs. Matilda Gilruth Carpenter, *The Crusade: Its Origin and Development at Washington Court House and Its Results*, W. G. Hubbard & Co., Publishers, 1893, p. 71.
10. J. H. Beadle, *The Women's War on Whiskey: Its History, Theory, and Prospects*, Cincinnati: Wilstach, Baldwin, & Co., 1874, pp. 47–48.
11. Steel, p. 46.
12. Wittenmyer source for this section, pp. 264, 208, 224, 176, 210–11, 450, 81, 184, 156, 685, 199.
13. Stewart, p. 188.
14. Stebbins, pp. 324–25.
15. Wittenmyer source for this section, pp. 333, 193, 265, 448, 54.
16. *Cincinnati Commercial*, March 7, 1874.
17. *Springfield Republic*, January 7, 1874.

18. Stewart, p. 336; see also *New York Daily Tribune*, March 7, 1874.
19. Steel, p. 27.
20. Carpenter, p. 104.
21. Steel, pp. 30–31.
22. Wittenmyer, p. 50.
23. Stewart, p. 220.
24. *Minutes of the First Convention of the National Woman's Christian Temperance Union*, Chicago: Woman's Temperance Publication Association, 1889, pp. 3–40.
25. *Union Signal*, December 20, 1883.
26. Wittenmyer, p. 16.

Friendship and Ritual in the WTUL

1. *Signs*, vol. I, pp. 1–29, 1975. See also Keith E. Melder, *Beginnings of Sisterhood: The American Woman's Rights Movement, 1800–1850*, Schocken Books, 1977, pp. 30–48. Nancy F. Cott, *The Bonds of Womanhood: "Woman's Sphere" in New England, 1780–1835*, Yale, 1977, pp. 160–96.
2. Rosalyn Baxandall, Linda Gordon and Susan Reverby, eds., *America's Working Women: A Documentary History—1600 to the Present*, Vintage, 1976, p. xviii.
3. Quoted in Mary E. Dreier to Margaret Dreier Robins and Raymond Robins, January 29, 1941. Margaret Dreier Robins Papers, University of Florida, Gainesville, FL.
4. Rose Schneiderman to Margaret Dreier Robins, June 4, 1936, Robins Papers; Ricki Myers Cohen: "Fannie Cohn and the International Ladies Garment Workers Union," Ph.D. thesis, University of Southern California, 1976, p. 200.
5. Anna Rudnitzky, "Time Is Passing," *Life and Labor*, vol. 2 (April 1912), p. 99.
6. Barry Schwartz, "The Social Psychology of the Gift," *The American Journal of Sociology*, vol. 73 (July 1967), p. 3.
7. In quieter factories, women workers often found diversion on the job. "To drown the monotony of work," glove-worker Agnes Nestor recalled, "we used to sing." Agnes Nestor, *Woman's Labor Leader: An Autobiography of Agnes Nestor*, Rockford, IL: Bellevue Books Publishing Co., 1954, p. 28.
8. Margaret Dreier Robins quoted in "Educational Side of Women's Trade Unionism," *New York Tribune*, October 12, 1919; *Some of the Happy Features of the Women's Trade Union League of Chicago*, WTUL of Chicago, leaflet no. 3, June 1909. See also William O'Neill, *Everyone Was Brave, A History of Feminism in America*, Quadrangle Books, 1969, pp. 104–16.
9. S. M. Franklin, "The Fifth Biennial," *Life and Labor*, vol. 5 (July 1915), p. 116.
10. For the use of birthday parties as a bonding mechanism among an age-based group, see Elizabeth Colson, "The Least Common Denominator," in *Secular Ritual*, Moore and Myerhoff, pp. 189–98.
11. Agnes Nestor to Margaret Dreier Robins, April 29, 1924, Robins Papers.
12. Margaret Dreier Robins, "The Human Side of the Industrial South," Address presented at Southern Session, Eleventh Convention of the National Women's Trade Union League, May 9, 1929, Robins Papers.
13. Schwartz, pp. 2–3.
14. *Life and Labor*, vol. 6 (April 1916), p. 59.
15. See, for example, William H. Chafe, *The American Woman, Her Changing Social, Economic and Practical Roles, 1920–1970*, Oxford University Press, 1972, pp. 73–74.
16. Leonora O'Reilly, Diary 16, March 17, 1909. Papers of Leonora O'Reilly, Schlesinger Library, Radcliffe College, Cambridge, MA.

Rites and Rights

1. Lavinia Egan, "The Seneca Falls Conference," *Equal Rights*, vol. 1, no. 25 (August 4, 1923), p. 198.
2. Hazel Mackaye, "Campaigning with Pageantry," *Equal Rights*, vol. 1, no. 39 (November 10, 1923), p. 389.
3. The Woman's Party journal, *Equal Rights*, contains a rich variety and an abundant quantity of articles on the party's pageants and its attitudes regarding their role as a vanguard of idealists. For a representative selection of citations in which both themes appear, see especially vol. 1 (1923), pp. 18, 22–24, 29–31, 35.

"Lesson I Bleed"

1. Edward Parone, ed., *Collision Course*, Random House, 1968, p. 35.
2. Janice Delaney, Mary Jane Lupton and Emily Toth, *The Curse: A Cultural History of Menstruation*, New American Library, 1976. I am indebted to Anne Harmon for calling my attention to certain culturally conditioned rites of passage, such as the practice of African genital mutilation performed on girls as young as five years of age in parts of Africa today. See also Mary Daly, *Gyn/Ecology: The Metaethics of Radical Feminism*, Beacon Press, 1978, especially ch. 5, pp. 153–77.
3. Kennedy's grotesque imagery comes from her own nightmares, which she has recorded in dream journals as described

in an interview with Lisa Lehman: "*A Rat's Mass* was based on a dream I once had when I was on a train . . . going from Paris to Rome . . . I had this dream in which I was being pursued by red, bloodied rats. It was a very powerful dream, and when I woke up the train had stopped in the Alps. It was at night. I had never felt that way. It was a crucial night in my life. So I was just haunted by that image for years, about being pursued by these big, red rats." "A Growth of Images," *The Drama Review*, vol. 21, no. 4 (1977), p. 44.

4. Adrienne Kennedy, *A Rat's Mass*, in *New Black Playwrights*, edited by William Couch, Avon Books, 1970, p. 87.

5. Robert L. Tener, "Theatre of Identity: Adrienne Kennedy's Portrait of Black Woman," *Studies in Black Literature*, vol. 6, no. 5 (1975), p. 3. To illuminate the imagery in this play, see also Merlin Stone, *When God Was a Woman*, Harcourt Brace Jovanovich, 1976, pp. 214–16.

2 The Actress

Anne Brunton Merry

1. Anne Brunton married Robert Merry in 1791. She subsequently married Thomas Wignell in 1803 and William Warren in 1806. Although most often remembered by historians as Mrs. Merry, she always performed under the name of the man to whom she was married.

2. Philadelphia, *Gazette of the United States and Philadelphia Daily Advertiser*, December 7, 1796, hereinafter cited as *Gazette of the United States*.

3. William Dunlap, *History of the American Theatre*, London, 1833, vol. I, pp. 336–37.

4. James L. Clifford, "Robert Merry—a pre-Byronic Hero," *Bulletin of the John Rylands Library*, vol. XXVII (1942), pp. 74–92.

5. Charlotte Barrett, ed., *Diary and Letters of Madam D'Arblay*, July 1791–April 1802, London, 1904–1905, pp. 39–40.

6. Dunlap, *History of the American Theatre*, vol. II, pp. 148–49.

7. William I. Warren, Journals. Channing Pollock Theatre Collection, Howard University, Washington, D.C., June 14, 1801. Hereinafter cited as Warren, Journals.

8. Charles Durang, "The Philadelphia Stage from the Year 1749 to the Year 1885," *Philadelphia Sunday Dispatch*, ch. XXXIV, December 24, 1854.

9. James Fennell, *An Apology for the Life of James Fennell*, Philadelphia, 1814, p.

366. See also Thomas Condie, "Biographical Anecdotes of Mrs. Merry of the Theatre, Philadelphia," *Philadelphia Monthly Magazine*, or *Universal Repository of Knowledge and Entertainment*, vol. I (April 1798), p. 187.

10. Durang, "The Philadelphia Stage," ch. XXXI, December 3, 1854.

11. Durang, "The Philadelphia Stage," ch. XXXII, December 10, 1854.

12. Durang, "The Philadelphia Stage."

13. *New York Evening Post*, June 25, 1805, June 27, 1805.

14. Durang, "The Philadelphia Stage," ch. XXXIX, January 28, 1855.

15. William Dunlap, *Diary of William Dunlap*, 3 vols., vol II, New York, 1930, p. 419.

16. *New York Evening Post*, March 3, 1807.

Enter the Harlot

1. Winthrop S. Hudson, *American Protestantism*, University of Chicago Press, pp. 96–110.

2. James Monroe Buckley, *Christians and the Theatre*, Nelson and Philips, 1875, pp. 10–18, 116. David Grimsted, *Melodrama Unveiled*, University of Chicago Press, 1968, p. 25.

3. Robert Hatfield, *The Theatre*, Methodist Book Depository, 1866, pp. 27, 28.

4. Thomas DeWitt Talmadge, *Sports That Kill*, Harper and Brothers, 1875, p. 17.

5. John Hodgkinson, *Narrative of His Connection with the Old America Company*, Oram, 1797, p. 22.

6. Frances Trollope, *Domestic Manners of the Americans*, Alfred A. Knopf, reprinted 1949, p. 564.

7. Albert A. Palmer, "American Theatres," *One Hundred Years of American Commerce*, Haynes Publishing Company, 1895, p. 157.

8. Daniel Frohman, *Daniel Frohman Presents*, C. Kendall and W. Sharp, 1935, p. 44.

9. Anna Cora Mowatt, *The Autobiography of an Actress*, Ticknor, Reed and Fields, 1854, pp. 214, 445.

10. Clara Morris, *Stage Confidences*, Lothrop Publishing Company, 1902, pp. 13–32.

11. William Wood, *Personal Recollections of the Stage*, H. C. Baird, 1855, p. 208.

12. Noah Ludlow, *Dramatic Life as I Found It*, G. I. Jones, 1880, p. 347. Sol Smith, *Theatrical Management in the West and South for Thirty Years*, Harper and Brothers, 1868, p. 60. Mrs. Maud Skinner, *One Man in His Time: The Adventures of H. Watkins, Strolling Player*, 1845, 1863, pp. 38, 47.

13. Hatfield, p. 24.

14. Joseph N. Ireland, *Mrs. Duff*, James R. Osgood, 1822, pp. 134–41.
15. Margaret Armstrong, *Fanny Kemble: Passionate Victorian*, Macmillan, 1938, pp. 151, 153, 184. Fanny Kemble Wister, ed., *Fanny, the American Kemble*, South Pass Press, 1972, pp. 37, 92.
16. Olive Logan, *Apropos of Women and the Theatre*, Carleton Publishers, 1869, p. 8.
17. Buckley, pp. 64, 65.
18. David Hayes Agnew, *Theatrical Amusements*, W. S. Young, 1857, pp. 6, 7.
19. Buckley, p. 65.
20. Talmadge, p. 18.
21. Robert Turnbull, *The Theatre*, Caulfield and Robins, 1837, p. 92.
22. Trollope, p. 74.
23. Buckley, pp. 50–65.
24. Samuel G. Winchester, *The Theatre*, W. S. Martien, 1840, p. 196.
25. "A Letter to Respectable Ladies Who Frequent the Theatre," *The Christian Spectator*, vol. I, no. 8 (August 1827), pp. 415, 416.
26. Winchester, p. 199.
27. Tyrone Power, *Impressions of America During the Years 1832, 1834, 1835*, Richard Bentley, 1836, vol. I, pp. 62, 172, 211, 352; vol. II, pp. 172, 191.
28. Charles Dickens, *American Notes*, Chapman and Hall, 1842, vol. 1, p. 141.
29. Meade Minnigerode, *The Fabulous Forties*, G. P. Putnam's Sons, 1924, pp. 150–56.
30. W. W. Clapp, *Record of the Boston Stage*, B. Blom, 1868, p. 298.
31. William Davidge, *The Drama Defended*, Samuel French, 1859, pp. 13, 14.
32. Mowatt, pp. 214–313.
33. Elizabeth Dexter, *Career Women of America: 1876–1940*, Marshall Jones Company, 1950, p. 87. In *American Actress: Perspectives on the Nineteenth Century* (Chicago, Nelson-Hall, 1984) Claudia Johnson points to the many advantages of a theatre career where a woman could gain "financial reward, professional status, and even a surprising equality with men." In a time when a teacher could earn $600 a year plus room and board, an ordinary actress could earn from $5,000 to $20,000 a year for what would seem to be easier and more rewarding work.

Women in Male Roles

1. All quotations in this section from George C. Odell, *Annals of the New York Stage*, Columbia University Press, 1927, vol. II, p. 560, vol. III, pp. 138, 249, 306.
2. Joseph Leach, *Bright Particular Star*, Yale University Press, 1970, p. 205.
3. Odell, vol. III, p. 575.
4. Unidentified clippings, Charlotte Cushman Scrapbook, Folger Shakespeare Library, Washington, D.C., n.d, n.p.
5. Leach, p. 241.
6. Leach, p. 65.
7. Emma Stebbins, ed., *Charlotte Cushman: Her Letters and Memories of Her Life*, Houghton, Osgood, 1972, p. 60.
8. Leach, p. 175.
9. Undated letter, Player's Club Library, New York City.
10. Eleanor Ruggles, *Prince of Players*, W. W. Norton, 1953, p. 133.
11. Lawrence Barrett, *Charlotte Cushman*, Dunlap Society, 1889, p. 21.
12. Stebbins, p. 59.
13. W. T. Price, *A Life of Charlotte Cushman*, Brentano's, 1894, p. 138.
14. William Winter, *Other Days*, Moffat, Yard, 1908, p. 154.
15. Ruggles, p. 116.
16. Leach, p. 305.
17. Leach, p. 180.
18. Leach, p. 310.
19. Leach, p. 277.
20. Ruggles, p. 61.
21. Leach, p. 209.
22. Leach, p. 310.
23. Ruggles, p. 130.
24. Leach, p. 179.

Adah Isaacs Menken

1. Paul Lewis, *Queen of the Plaza*, New York, 1964, p. 124. Confusion abounds concerning the dates of Menken's *Mazeppa* and many of the other "facts" of her life.
2. One of the first friends with whom she used the name was Augustin Daly in 1861. *Bell's Life*, London, lists this as her real name. She gave notes for a biography to Daly—he never wrote it, but published the notes in the *New York Times*, September 1868.
3. James Murdoch, *The Stage*, Philadelphia, 1880, p. 243.
4. Quote from clipping in *The Menken Portfolio, Players Connection*, Lincoln Center Library for the Performing Arts.
5. The *Albany Express* review was quoted by the *Sunday Mercury*, June 9, 1861.
6. Robert Henry Newell (alias D. C. Kerr), *My Life with Adah Isaacs Menken*, New York. No copies are extant in libraries. Lewis uses this as a source for numerous stories, though where he obtained a copy remains a mystery; perhaps from his general source, Mr. Ewing Hibbard, collector of Menken memorabilia.
7. Bernard Falk, *The Naked Lady*, London, 1934, p. 65. Quoted from a letter found in the Harvard Theatre Collection.

8. This is quoted by Charles Warren Stoddard, "La Belle Menken," *National Magazine* (February 1905), p. 479. Falk and Lewis quote it as a *New York Tribune* comment, which it is not.
9. Allan Lesser, in *Enchanting Rebel*, New York, 1947, makes this estimate; source not known.
10. Ed James, *The Life and Times of Adah Isaacs Menken*, New York, 1881. Although this book, as well as the Newell biography, is not extant, there is proof that it actually existed. It is mentioned in a clipping from *Music and Drama*, June 24, 1882, in the *Players Collection*. As for Adah's "diary," referred to by Lewis, Harvard Library disclaims all knowledge of it.
11. Lewis, pp. 6, 16, 17 for quotations in this section.
12. Falk, p. 155.
13. Lewis, pp. 139, 140.
14. *Menken Portfolio, Players Collection*, clipping.
15. *Menken Portfolio, Players Collection*, clipping.
16. Lewis, p. 124. Lewis uses this quote and following ones from undated newspapers and seems simply to attribute them to his time slot for the first New York performance in 1861, even though such reviews for that date do not exist.
17. *New York Clipper*, May 7, 1886.
18. Lewis, p. 20.
19. Falk, p. 164.
20. Lewis, p. 17.

Lydia Thompson and the "British Blondes"
1. Bernard Sobel, *A Pictorial History of Burlesque*, G. P. Putnam's Sons, 1956. Irving Zeidman, *The American Burlesque Show*, Hawthorn Books, Inc., 1967. Ann Coria and Joseph Di Mona, *This Was Burlesque*, Grosset and Dunlap, 1968.
2. Olive Logan, *Before the Footlights and Behind the Scenes*, 1870, p. 585.
3. June 5, 1869. Clipping from the Theatre Collection, New York Public Library.
4. February 17, 1895, p. 4. Clipping from the Harvard Theatre Collection.

Horrible Prettiness
Excerpted from Robert Allen, *Horrible Prettiness: Burlesque and American Culture*, University of North Carolina Press, 1991. Used by permission of the publisher.
1. Richard Grant White, "The Age of Burlesque," *Galaxy*, August 1869, pp. 256–66.
2. Howells, "The New Taste in Theatreicals," *Atlantic Monthly*, May 1869, pp. 642–45.
3. Peter Stallybrass and Allon White, *The Politics and Poetics of Trangression*, p. 5.

Henrietta Vinton Davis
1. *Washington Bee*, July 21, 1883.
2. *New York Globe*, August 4, 1883.
3. Quoted in *New York Age*, April 28, 1888.
4. Quoted in *New York Age*, May 9, 1891.
5. *New York Freeman*, March 26, 1887.
6. Quoted in *New York Age*, April 4, 1885.

Mary Shaw
1. Unmarked newspaper clipping, Theatre Collection, New York Public Library.
2. *New York Sun*, October 17, 1912.
3. Souvenir Book of Woman's Exhibition, 1902, p. 53. Theatre Collection, New York Public Library.
4. *New York Morning Telegraph*, n.d.
5. Unmarked newspaper clipping, Theatre Collection, New York Public Library.
6. Quoted in Einar Haugen, "Ibsen in America." *Norwegian-American Studies and Records*, 1959, vol. 20, p. 5.
7. Interview with Mary Shaw, February 14, 1903, Theatre Collection, New York Public Library.
8. Arthur W. Row, "Great Moments in Great Acting," *Poet Lore*, vol. 29 (1918), pp. 359–60.
9. *London Times*, July 1, 1899.
10. "Mary Shaw—A Woman of Thought and Action," *The Theatre*, vol. 2 (August 1902), p. 21.
11. William Winter, *Wallet of Time*, Moffat, Yard, and Company, 1913, vol. 2, p. 570.
12. *New York Dramatic News*, December 25, 1902.
13. Joseph P. Dannenburg, "Playing Ibsen in the Badlands," *The Theatre*, vol. 6 (August 6, 1906), pp. 219–21.
14. Untitled newspaper clipping, February 28, 1904. Theatre Collection, New York Public Library.
15. *Chicago Evening Post*, March 3, 1904.
16. *New York Magazine* program, n.d. Theatre Collection, New York Public Library.
17. "My Plays Advocate Moral Reform!" *The Theatre*, vol. 5 (December 1905), p. 298. Mary Shaw, "My Immoral Play," *McClure's*, vol. 38 (April 1912), p. 690.
18. See for details: *New York Commercial Advertiser*, October 25, 1905; *New York Times*, October 9, 1905; *New York Tribune, New York American, New York Herald* of October 31, 1905.
19. Quoted in Archibald Henderson, *George Bernard Shaw: Man of the Century*. Appleton-Century-Crofts, 1956, p. 511.
20. Rose Young, "Suffrage as Seen by Mary Shaw," *Harper's Weekly*, vol. 60 (May 8, 1915), p. 456.
21. Unmarked newspaper clipping, Theatre Collection, New York Public Library.

22. Ada Patterson, "Actresses' Clubs in America," *The Theatre*, vol. 20 (October 1914), p. 187.
23. Gamut Club pamphlet, Theatre Collection, New York Public Library.
24. Unmarked newspaper clipping, Theatre Collection, New York Public Library.
25. *Cleveland Leader*, February 2, 1913.
26. *New York Herald*, January 6, 1912.
27. For details in this section see Gamut Club pamphlet and the following: *New York Sun*, October 17, 1912; *New York Morning Telegraph*, August 8, 1914, September 8, 1914; *New York Mail*, August 27, 1914.
28. Unmarked newspaper clipping, Theatre Collection, New York Public Library.
29. *Equity* magazine, May 1930, p. 23.

Women Mimes in America

R. J. Broadbent, *A History of Pantomime*, Citadel Press, 1965 (first published 1901).
Dance Index, vol. I, no. 3 (March 1942).
Angna Enters, *Silly Girl*, Houghton Mifflin Co., 1944.
Ric Estrada, "To Be a Clown," *Dance* (August 1968).
Trudi Schoop, *Won't You Join the Dance?* National Press Books, 1974.
Marian Hannah Winter, *The Theatre of Marvels*, Benjamin Blom, Inc., 1964.
Critical reviews of Enters, Schoop and Goslar in various periodicals.

The Art of Ruth Draper

1. An interview with Ruth Draper, "Talk of the Town," *New Yorker*, March 6, 1954.
2. R. D. Skinner, "Ruth Draper, Dramatist," *Commonweal*, vol. 11 (January 8, 1930), pp. 283–284.
3. R. D. Skinner, p. 284.
4. Other useful sources: Iris Origo, "Ruth Draper and Her Company of Characters," *Cornhill Magazine*, vol. 169 (Winter 1957), pp. 383–93. Iris Origo, "Ruth Draper," *Atlantic Monthly*, vol. 202 (October 1958), pp. 56–60. M. D. Zabel, *The Art of Ruth Draper, Her Dramas and Characters, with a Memoir*, Doubleday, 1960.

Acting Female

Excerpted from Faye E. Dudden, "Introduction: Acting Female," *Women in American Theatre: Actresses and Audiences 1790–1870*, Yale University Press, 1994.

1. See Agnew, *Worlds Apart*, for his influential argument about the relationship between the emergence of the market and English Renaissance theatre. His insight about how theatre can operate as a social metaphor has been crucial to my understanding of theatre and gender.
2. Molly Haskell, *From Reverence to Rape: The Treatment of Women in the Movies*, Holt, Rinehart and Winston, 1973, p. 243. The Western philosophical tradition hostile to the theatre is traced in Jonas Barish, *Antitheatrical Prejudice*.
3. Jean-Jacques Rousseau, *Politics and the Arts: Letter to M. D'Alembert on the Theatre*, Intro. and trans. Allan Bloom, Cornell University Press, 1968, p. 47. See also p. 49: "Look through most contemporary plays; it is always a woman who knows everything, who teaches everything to men."
4. On theatre's association with a side of woman that is hidden, powerful and demonic, see Nina Auerbach, *Woman and the Demon* and *Ellen Terry*. See also her *Private Theatricals*, especially p. 80, where she cites Cary Mazer to the effect that a woman could seem a dangerous thing "by the very transgressive act of becoming someone else, of finding within herself other selves to become." See also Richard Gilman, "The Actor as Celebrity," *Humanities in Review* 1 (1982): 115–16. Gilman argues that the actor presents us "with possible selves, or more accurately with the *idea* of possible selves," and that theatre is "a release from the unitary and ordinarily inescapable self and a reminder of the possibilities of transformation." Christopher Kent provides a related assessment of the Victorian stage: "It offered striking opportunities for independence, fame and fortune, and even for those outside it the stage incarnated fantasies, providing vicarious release in the notion that here was an area of special dispensation from the normal categories, moral and social, that defined woman's role in society." Theatre has some of the same subversive potential for all socially subordinate groups: hence the importance of masking in moments of social reversal like carnival. See James C. Scott, *Domination and the Arts of Resistance*, New Haven and London: Yale University Press, 1990.
5. There is a considerable body of scholarship that documents the association between the actress and the whore. It is the subject of passing notice, for example, in Michael Booth's survey, *Theatre in the Victorian Age*, p. 113. It has received more focused attention from women scholars. See, e.g., Johnson, "Enter the Harlot," in Chinoy and Jenkins, *Women in American Theatre*, 57–65; or Johnson,

American Actress. Perhaps the most thorough and nuanced exploration of this theme is found in Tracy Davis's work on nineteenth-century British theatre. See her "Actresses and Prostitutes," "Actress in Victorian Pornography," and *Actresses As Working Women.* I found Martha Roth, "Notes Toward a Feminist Performance Aesthetic," *Women and Performance* (1983): 5–14, helpful in suggesting that this persistent association derives from the fact that a woman who acts is on display, which makes her "sexually available to any man, in fantasy and often in fact." Compare Lawrence Senelick, ed., *Gender in Performance,* xii: "To appear onstage is to display one's body to strangers: A commodity available to the gaze may, in given circumstances, be vendible in its entirety." I am also grateful to my colleague Ruth Stevensen for pointing out another connection: the acting that women do onstage may remind male audiences of the acting (i.e., dissembling) that prostitutes routinely engage in.

6. In thinking about gender and theatre, I profited greatly from excellent scholarship on the English theatre and drama, especially works by Jean E. Howard, Kristina Straub, Phyllis Rackin and Karen Newman. My ideas about the nature of public and private spheres also benefited from Mary Ryan, *Women in Public: Between Banners and Ballots, 1825–1880,* Johns Hopkins University Press, 1990, although my interests and analysis differ from Ryan's.

7. Modern feminists have made the distinction between sex and gender one of the most basic of their tenets of analysis. There are a number of conclusions to the path that gender exists only in performance or representation, but most of them wend their way across difficult theoretical terrain, including phenomenology, sociological research from the symbolic interaction school, and deconstructionist literary criticism. The best single introduction to this question is found in Laurence Senelick's introduction to Senelick, *Gender in Performance.* Senelick writes, "Like a Berkelian universe, gender exists only insofar as it is perceived" (ix). A good introduction to a phenomenological approach to theatre and identity is Bruce Wilshire, *Role Playing and Identity: The Limits of Theatre as Metaphor,* Indiana University Press, 1982. On gender as performative, see Butler, "Performative Acts and Gender Construc-

tion." I have benefited greatly from Marjorie Garber, *Vested Interests.* I have also found useful David George, "On Ambiguity: Toward a Post-Modern Performance Theory," *Theatre Research International* 14 (Spring 1989): 71–85. Of course the best-known sociologist, who has dealt with identity in terms of theatrical metaphor is Erving Goffman, in works beginning with *The Presentation of Self in Everyday Life,* Doubleday, 1959. For a specific interpretation of gender in terms derived from symbolic interaction, see Candace West and Don Zimmerman, "Doing Gender," *Gender and Society* 1 (1987): 125–51.

8. On theatrical transvestism, See Garber, *Vested Interests.* There is of course a limit to the extent to which any audience will "get it," and Garber is especially acute in noting the tendency of audiences to look "through" rather than at the cross-dressed performer, to focus on what he or she *really* is "underneath," or on the success with which he or she can "pass" for the other sex. Nevertheless, I argue, the stage is unique in presenting relatively simple access to what is otherwise a highly abstract concept, for society is deeply intolerant of individuals who reveal gender's constructedness in daily life—individuals who fail, that is, to make themselves unambiguously readable as either male or female to the casual glance of a stranger. Only onstage can we freely contemplate and even take pleasure in ambiguity and transvestism that would elsewhere be either invisible (successful "passing") or immediately censured. See Ferris, *Acting Women,* 147: "This practice of women dressing as men clearly gives the lie to the old maxim of 'we are what we look', at the same time it exposes gender as socially constructed and not innate, eternal or biologically 'natural.'" See also the very useful survey of a vast literature on cross-dressing in Vern L. Bullough and Bonnie Bullough, *Cross Dressing, Sex, and Gender,* University of Pennsylvania Press, 1993.

9. John Berger, *Ways of Seeing.* Viking Press, 1972, p. 47.

3 Here Are the Women Playwrights

Here are the Women Playwrights

1. May 1, 1983.
2. Kathleen Betsko and Rachel Koenig, *Interviews with Contemporary Women Playwrights,* Beech Tree Books, William

Morrow, 1987. Quotations from this invaluable source are identified as B/K with page reference. They are used by the generous permission of the authors and the publisher.

3. William Wright, *Lillian Hellman: The Image, the Woman*, Simon and Schuster, 1986, p. 98.
4. B/K, p. 302.
5. B/K, p. 258.
6. B/K, p. 430.
7. B/K, p. 96.
8. B/K, p. 320.
9. B/K, p. 322, 312.
10. B/K, Typescript, "The Woman Playwright," 1985, used by permission of France Burke.
11. B/K, p. 445.
12. B/K, p. xiii, Helen Keyssar, *Feminist Theatre*.
13. B/K, p. 370.
14. B/K, p. 338.
15. B/K, p. 369.
16. B/K, p. 13–14.

Mercy Warren
PLAYS

(Warren, Mercy Otis), *The Adulateur*, Boston, 1773.
(Warren, Mercy Otis), *The Adulateur* (excerpts), in *The Massachusetts Spy*, March 26 and April 23, 1772.
(Warren, Mercy Otis), *The Defeat* (excerpts), in the *Boston Gazette* May 24 and July 19, 1773.
(Warren, Mercy Otis), *The Group*, Edes and Gill, 1775.
(Warren, Mercy Otis), *The Group* (excerpts), in the *Boston Gazette,* January 23, 1775.

BOOKS

Anthony, Katharine, *First Lady of the Revolution: The Life of Mercy Otis Warren*, Doubleday and Company, Inc., 1958.
Brown, Alice, *Mercy Warren (Women of Colonial and Revolutionary Times)*, Charles Scribner's Sons, 1896.
Hosmer, James K., *The Life of Thomas Hutchinson*, Houghton Mifflin and Company, 1896.
Quinn, Arthur Hobson, *A History of American Drama from the Beginnings to the Civil War*, vol. I, 2nd ed., F. S. Crofts and Co., 1946.
Warren, Mercy Otis, *History of the Rise, Progress and Termination of the American Revolution, Interspersed with Biographical, Political and Moral Observations*, 3 vols., E. Larkin, 1805.
Warren-Adams Letters, Being chiefly a correspondence among John Adams, Samuel
Adams, and James Warren, The Massachussetts Historical Society, 1917.

ARTICLES AND UNPUBLISHED MATERIAL

Ford, Worthington Chauncey, "Mrs. Warren's *The Group,*" *Massachusetts Historical Society Proceedings*, vol. LXII (1928–1929), pp. 15–22.
Hutcheson, Maud Macdonald, "Mercy Warren, 1728–1814," *The William and Mary Quarterly*, 3rd series, vol. X, no. 3 (July 1953), pp. 378–402.
Robinson, Alice McDonnell, "The Developing Ideas of Individual Freedom and National Unity as Reflected in American Plays and the Theatre, 1772–1819," Unpublished Ph.D. dissertation, Stanford University, Stanford, CA, 1965.

Looking to Women

Unless otherwise indicated, texts used are individually published editions of Crothers's plays. Manuscripts are found in the Burnside-Frohman Collection, Theatre Collection, New York Public Library, and Rare Books, University of Pennsylvania Library.

1. Djuna Barnes, "The Tireless Rachel Crothers," *Theatre Guild*, vol. 8 (May 1931), p. 18.
2. Dates in parentheses refer to first production, usually in New York.
3. Undated clipping from an unknown Boston newspaper in Crothers Scrapbook, Special Collections, Illinois State University Library. Crothers's reference to her production of *He and She* suggests 1911 as the date of her remarks.
4. In this argument Crothers reflects the view of a woman she greatly admired, Katherine Bement Davis. Appointed New York City Commissioner of Corrections in 1914, Davis was the former supervisor of the Woman's Reformatory at Bedford, after which Crothers modeled the reform home in Act I of *Ourselves.*
5. Amy Bulley, English feminist, cited in Elaine Showalter, *A Literature of Their Own: British Women Novelists from Brontë to Lessing*, Princeton, 1977, p. 186. I am indebted to Showalter, especially in ch. 7, "Feminist Novelists," for her clear distinction between the moderate and radical positions of feminists on the subject of woman's evolution, which she demonstrates was a central concept of feminist ideology.
6. Crothers quoted in an interview with Marguerite Mooers Marshall, "What Do Women Think of Other Women?" *New York World*, 1915. Crothers Scrapbook,

Special Collections, Illinois State University Library.

7. Interview with Marguerite Mooers Marshall.

8. Rachel Crothers, "Troubles of a Playwright," *Harper's Bazaar*, vol. 45 (January 1911), p. 14.

9. *New York Sun*, January 4, 1914, in Crothers Scrapbook, vol. I, compiled by Irving Abrahamson, available on microfilm from University of Chicago Library.

10. In *Representing American Dramas National and Local*, ed. Montrose J. Moses. Boston, 1925.

11. In *Mary the Third, Old Lady 31* and *A Little Journey*, New York, 1923, p. 147. Subsequent references to this edition are in the text.

12. In *Representative Modern Plays*, ed. Richard Cordell, New York, 1930.

13. *Six One-Act Plays*, Boston, 1925.

14. No known manuscripts of the play exist. A review by Brooks Atkinson, in the *New York Times*, December 26, 1927, summarizes its plot and comments on characters. In Irving Abrahamson, "The Career of Rachel Crothers in the American Theatre," an unpublished Ph.D. dissertation, University of Chicago, 1956, p. 378.

15. Deborah S. Kolb, "The Rise and Fall of the New Woman in American Drama," *Educational Theatre Journal*, vol. 27 (May 1975), pp. 158–60.

16. Rachel Crothers, "The Construction of a Play," in *The Art of Playwriting*, Foreword by Arthur H. Quinn, 1928, reprinted New York, 1967, p. 117.

17. Eleanor Flexner, *American Playwrights: 1928–1938*, reprinted Freeport, NY, 1969.

Apropos of Women and the Folk Play

1. Frederick H. Koch, *American Folk Plays*, D. Appleton-Century Company, 1939, p. xiv.

2. Quoted in Montrose J. Moses, *The American Dramatist*, 1925, reprint, Benjamin Blom, 1964, p. 8.

3. Ruth Suckow, "The Folk Idea in American Life," *Scribner's Magazine*, September 8, 1930, p. 247.

4. Zona Gale, *The Neighbors*, in *Wisconsin Plays*, Thomas H. Dickinson, ed. B. W. Heubsch, 1914.

5. Alice Brown, *Children of the Earth*, Macmillan Company, 1915.

6. Margaret G. Mayorga, *A Short History of the American Drama: Commentaries on Plays Prior to 1920*, Dodd, Mead, and Company, 1944, p. 31.

7. Neith Boyce, *Winter's Night*, in *Fifty More Contemporary One-Act Plays*, Frank Shay, ed. D. Appleton, 1934.

8. Arthur E. Waterman, *Susan Glaspell*, Twayne Publishers, 1966, p. 69.

9. Susan Glaspell, *Trifles*, in *Literary Heritage: Drama*, Marjorie Westcott Barrows, ed. Macmillan Company, 1962.

10. Arthur Hobson Quinn, ed., *Representative American Plays: From 1767 to the Present Day*, Appleton-Century-Crofts, Inc., 1953, p. 983.

11. Burns Mantle, *American Playwrights of Today*, Dodd, Mead and Company, 1929, p. 193.

12. Lula Vollmer, *Sun-Up*, in Quinn, *Representative American Plays*.

Anne Nichols

1. "Anne Nichols Is Dead at 75; Author of *Abie's Irish Rose*," *New York Times*, September 16, 1966, p. 37.

2. Arthur Gelb, "Author of *Abie's Irish Rose* Reviews 40 Years," *New York Times*, May 21, 1962, p. 40.

3. *Encyclopedia Americana*, International Edition, 1975.

4. George Jean Nathan, *The Entertainment of a Nation or Three Sheets in the Wind*, Alfred A. Knopf, 1942, p. 34.

5. Mary Braggiotti, "Abie's Rose Grows an Olive Leaf," *New York Post*, June 26, 1943, n. pag., col. 3, Literature Collection, Lincoln Center for the Performing Arts, New York.

6. Jean Meegan, "Old Man Abie, He Just Goes Rolling," *Milwaukee Journal*, October 3, 1943, n. pag., cols. 3–4, Theatre Collection, Lincoln Center for the Performing Arts, New York.

7. Braggiotti, col. 2.

8. Gelb, p. 40.

9. Anne Nichols, "The Million Dollar Hit," *Theatre Arts* (July 1924), p. 19.

10. Braggiotti, col. 3.

11. "Anne Nichols Is Dead at 75," p. 37.

12. William B. Chase, "*Abie's Irish Rose* Funny," *New York Times*, May 24, 1922, p. 22.

13. Nichols, p. 19. See also Braggiotti, cols. 2–3.

14. "Anne Nichols Is Dead at 75," p. 37.

15. George Jean Nathan, *Material Critica*, Alfred A. Knopf, 1924, p. 229.

16. Montrose J. Moses and John Mason Brown, eds., *The American Theatre as Seen by Its Critics, 1752–1934*, W. W. Norton and Co., 1934, pp. 260–62.

17. Nathan, *Materia Critica*, pp. 229–33.

18. Robert Littell, *Read America First*, Harcourt, Brace and World, 1926, pp. 244–45.

19. Nichols, p. 19.

20. "Anne Nichols Is Dead at 75," p. 37.

21. Gelb, p. 40.

22. Nichols, p. 19.
23. Gelb, p. 40.
24. Chase, p. 22.
25. "Anne Nichols Is Dead at 75," p. 37. See also Abe Laufe. *Anatomy of a Hit.* Hawthorn Books, Inc., 1966, p. 66.
26. Gelb, p. 40.

The Comic Muse of Mary Chase

1. Lynette Carpenter, "The Stuff That Dreams Are Made of," *American Culture and Its Literature and Film, 1940–1953,* diss. Indiana University, 1979, pp. 83–92.
2. Not everyone has approved of Mrs. Chase's satire, as evidenced in Lillian Herlands Homstein, "'Though This Be Madness': Insanity in the Theatre," *College English,* vol. 7 (1945), pp. 7–9. More positive views are voiced in a rejoinder to the Hornstein article: Florence R. Scott, *"Harvey:* Or Sanity in the Theatre," *College English,* vol. 8. (1946), pp. 37–38. An excellent appreciation of *Harvey* may be found in Jordan Y. Miller, *American Dramatic Literature,* McGraw-Hill, 1961, pp. 467–69.
3. Mary Chase, *Harvey,* Oxford University Press, 1953.
4. It is ironic that in John L. Toohey, *A History of the Pulitzer Prize Plays,* Citadel Press, 1967, p. 201, Mr. Toohey says he would have awarded the Pulitzer Prize *Harvey* received to Tennessee Williams's *The Glass Menagerie,* for Williams's drama is very much a serious rendering of the themes Mary Chase handles with comic vitality.
5. Mary Chase, *Mrs. McThing,* Oxford University Press, 1952.
6. Mary Chase, *Bernardine,* Oxford University Press, 1953.

Lillian Hellman Talks About Women

The interviews on which we have drawn appear in full in *Conversations with Lillian Hellman,* edited by Jackson R. Bryer, Jackson: University Press of Mississippi, 1986.

1. Nora Ephron, "Lillian Hellman Walking, Cooking, Writing, Talking," *The New York Times Book Review,* September 23, 1973, 2, 51. Reprinted by permission of International Creative Management.
2. Bill Moyers, "Lillian Hellman: The Great Playwright Candidly Reflects on a Long, Rich Life," transcript of an interview on National Educational Television, April 1974. Used by permission of Bill Moyers, Public Affairs Television, Inc.
3. Stephanie de Pue, "Lillian Hellman: She Never Turns Down an Adventure," *Cleveland Plains Dealer,* December 28, 1975, sec. 5, 2, 8.
4. Christine Doudna, "A Still Unfinished Woman: A Conversation with Lillian Hellman," from *Rolling Stone,* no. 233 (February 24, 1977), 52–57. Reprinted by permission of Straight Arrow Publishers, Inc.
5. Marilyn Berger, "Profile of Lillian Hellman," transcript of five-part interview broadcast originally in 1981. Copyright 1979, KERA Public Communication Foundation for North Texas. Used by permission of KERA-TV Dallas/Fort Worth/Denton, Producer.
6. Sylvie Drake, "Lillian Hellman as Herself," *Los Angeles Times,* October 18, 1981, calendar, p. 1, 6. Reprinted by permission of the *Los Angeles Times.*

Lorraine Hansberry

1. Interview with Lorraine Hansberry conducted by Eleanor Fisher for Columbia Broadcasting Company, June 7, 1961.
2. Lorraine Hansberry, *To Be Young, Gifted and Black,* Prentice-Hall, 1969, pp. 11–12.
3. Interview, *op. cit.*
4. *A Raisin in the Sun/The Sign in Sidney Brustein's Window,* New American Library, 1958, p. 286.
5. *Ibid.,* p. 317.

Woman Alone, Women Together

1. Unless otherwise indicated, plays discussed have been published in *The New Woman's Theatre,* edited by Honor Moore, Vintage, 1977.
2. Gail Kriegel Mallin, *Holy Places,* Workshop production at the Women's Project, the American Place Theatre, 1979.
3. Francine Stone, *Dead Sure,* Workshop production at the Circle Repertory Theatre, 1977. Quotes are from the manuscript.
4. Myrna Lamb, *Apple Pie,* An opera, Libretto by Lamb, music by Nicholas Meyers, Workshop production at the Public Theatre, 1976, full production 1977. Quotes are from notes on production.
5. Marsha Norman, *Getting Out,* Produced at the Actors Theatre, Louisville, 1977, Mark Taper Forum, 1978; Phoenix Theatre, New York City, 1978; Theatre de Lys, 1979. Published by Dramatists Play Service, 1980. Quotes from notes on Theatre de Lys production.
6. Ntozake Shange, *for colored girls who have considered suicide/when the rainbow is enuf, A Choreopoem,* Produced by Papp at the New York Shakespeare Festival Public Theatre, 1976. Booth Theatre (Broadway), 1976. Macmillan, 1977. Shange's second

choreopoem, *Spell #7*, had a long run at the Public Theatre in 1979. In this piece the chorus included men as well as women.

7. Susan Griffin, *Voices*, Produced on California Public Television, 1974. Published by the Feminist Press, 1977. (Out of Print.) Quotes from published version.

8. Wendy Wasserstein, *Uncommon Women and Others*, Produced at the O'Neill Theatre Center, National Playwrights' Conference 1977; Phoenix Theatre, New York City, 1977. Published by Avon Books, 1979 and by the Dramatists Play Service, 1977.

9. Leigh Curran, *The Lunch Girls*, 1977. Produced at the Long Wharf Theatre, New Haven, 1977.

10. Aishah Rahman, *Unfinished Women Cry in No Man's Land While a Bird Dies in a Gilded Cage*, Produced by New York Shakespeare Festival Mobile Unit, 1977, and at the New York Shakespeare Festival Public Theatre, 1978.

11. Feminist concerns and aspirations have been dealt with in the work of women's theatre groups like Women's Experimental Theatre (New York City), the Caravan Theatre (Cambridge, MA) and At the Foot of the Mountain (Minneapolis).

12. Tina Howe, *The Art of Dining*, Produced by Joseph Papp and the Kennedy Center at the New York Shakespeare Festival Public Theatre and the Eisenhower Theatre, Kennedy Center, 1979. Quotes from the manuscript.

4 If Not an Actress, What? . . .

Women Open Augusta's First Theatre

1. Mary Julia Curtis, *The Early Charleston Stage: 1703–1798*, Ph.D. dissertation, Indiana University, 1968, pp. 122–37, 145, 167–72.

2. Thomas Cooper and David J. McCord, eds., *Statutes at Large of South Carolina*, 10 vols, A. S. Johnston, 1836–1841, vol. v, act. no. 1376, pp. 41–44.

3. David Ritchey, "The Maryland Company of Comedians," *Educational Theatre Journal*, vol. 24 (1972), pp. 355–62.

4. *Georgia State Gazette* (Augusta), August 9, August 23, September 13, September 27, 1788.

5. *Chronicle,* September 4, September 18, October 2, 6, 27, November 13, 20, 1790.

6. *Chronicle*, May 7, 1791.

7. *Chronicle*, April 16, 1791.

8. *Chronicle*, May 21, 1791.

9. Virginia E. deTreville, "The First President Visits Augusta," *Richmond County History*, vol. 4 (1972), pp. 38–53.

10. Minutes of the Trustees, April 7, 1794.

11. *City Gazette and Daily Advertiser* (Charleston), March 30, 1799.

12. City Council Minutes (Richmond County Court House, Augusta), Receipts and Expenditures from April 1805 to April 1806.

13. Monique Davis Boyce, *The First Forty Years of the Augusta, Georgia, Theatre*, M.A. thesis, University of Georgia, 1957, p. 45.

Art Theatre in Hull-House

1. Jane Addams, "The Subjective Necessity for Social Settlements," In *Philanthropy and Social Progress: Seven Essays*, by Jane Addams, Robert A. Woods, and others, 1893; reprinted McGrath Publishing Company, 1969, pp. 10, 22.

2. Jane Addams, *Twenty Years at Hull-House*, Macmillan Publishing Company, 1938, pp. 112, 385.

3. Robert A. Woods and Albert J. Kennedy, *The Settlement Horizon*, Russell Sage Foundation, 1922, p.156.

4. Addams, *Twenty Years*, pp. 383–85.

5. Woods and Kennedy, p. 157.

6. Addams, *Twenty Years*, p. 388.

7. *Hull-House Bulletin*, vol. 1, no. 2 (February 1896), p 7 Hull-House Association Papers, Jane Addams Memorial Collection, University of Illinois–Chicago Circle.

8. Walter Pietsch, Letter to Jane Addams, March 7, 1928, Jane Addams Papers, Swarthmore College Peace Collection, Swarthmore College, PA.

9. *Hull-House Bulletin*, vol. 3, no. 6 (October 1898), p. 5.

10. Addams, *Twenty Years*, p. 388.

11. *Hull-House Bulletin*, vol. 3, no. 12 (November and December 1899), p. 2.

12. Woods and Kennedy, p. 158.

13. Addams, *Twenty Years*, pp. 387–91.

14. William Dean Howells, Letter to Jane Addams, October 26, 1899, Jane Addams Papers.

15. Laura Pelham herself dated her directorship from 1901; however, programs of plays, etc., among the collections at the Jane Addams Hull-House at the University of Illinois at Chicago Circle indicate that the 1900 date is correct.

16. In published works, Jane Addams makes no mention of Walter Pietsch as the original director of drama at Hull-House. She credits Pelham as the original founder of the theatre. Pietsch's 1928 letter to Addams states that he resigned because he was about to be married.

17. *Hull-House Bulletin,* vol. 4, no. 3 (Autumn 1900), p. 6.

18. Laura Dainty Pelham, "The Story of the Hull-House Players," *The Drama,* May 22, 1916, pp. 250–51.
19. Pelham, pp. 251–61.
20. Constance D'Arcy MacKaye, *The Little Theatre in the United States,* Henry Holt, 1917, p. 115.
21. Maurice Browne, *Too Late to Lament,* Indiana University Press, 1956, p. 128.

Women Directors

1. Burns Mantle, ed., *The Best Plays of 1925–1926 and the Year Book of Drama in America,* New York: Dodd, Mead and Company, 1926, pp. 627–31.
2. These names are drawn from the listing in the Burns Mantle *Best Play* series.
3. Information about Agnes Morgan can be found in Walter Rigdon, ed. *Biographical Encyclopaedia and Who's Who of American Theatre,* James H. Heinemann, Inc., 1965; and *Notable Names in American Theatre.*
4. Much of this information is drawn from *Souvenir Program: Grand Street Follies,* 1929 Edition.
5. "Women Rush into Rivalry in Producing," *American* (New York), October 30, 1927 (page numbers cut off in clipping).
6. "Society Women Fail in Efforts to Save 'Maya,'" *New York Telegraph,* February 28, 1928 (page numbers cut off in clipping).
7. *Newport Casino Theatre Program,* August 6, 1935, p. 9.
8. Telephone interview with Wade Miller, General Manager of the Paper Mill Playhouse, Millburn, NJ, September 25, 1982.

Hallie Flanagan

1. Francis Fergusson, "The Search for New Standards in the Theatre," Address given at Barnard College, April 1955, reprint in Theatre Collection, Lincoln Center, New York Public Library.
2. Quotations from Hallie Flanagan talks and articles: "A Theatre for the People"; "Federal Theatre," speech at Civitas Club, New York; "Farewell Address to members of the Federal Theatre Summer Theatre," July 1937.
3. "What Are We Doing with Our Chance?" *Federal Theatre,* 1936.
4. "A Theatre for the People."
5. "Federal Theatre Tomorrow," May 1936.
6. "Art and Geography," *The Magazine of Art,* Washington, D.C., August 1938.
7. *Ibid.* Also, "The Tractor Invades the Theatre," *Theatre Guild Magazine,* December 1930.
8. "Federal Theatre," BBC Radio Talk, March 24, 1939.

9. *The Idea of a Theatre,* Princeton University Press, 1949, p. 14.
10. Letter to the author, April 26, 1983, from London.

Matriarchs of the Regional Theatre

1. Margo Jones, *Theatre-in-the-Round,* Rinehart, 1951, p. 92.
2. Joseph W. Zeigler, *Regional Theatre: The Revolutionary Stage,* University of Minnesota Press, 1973, p. 17.
3. Jones, pp. 40–63, 92, for her story.
4. Zeigler, p. 30.
5. Zeigler, p. 31.
6. Zeigler, p. 188.
7. Zelgler, p. 25.
8. Address, American Educational Theatre Association Convention. New York, August 1967.
9. Stuart W. Little, *Off-Broadway: The Prophetic Theatre,* Coward, McCann and Geoghegan, 1972, p. 168.
10. Zeigler, p. 194.

The Lady Is a Critic

Unless otherwise stated, quotations are from personal interviews.

1. M. F. Comtois and Lynn F. Miller, compilers, *Contemporary American Theatre Critics: A Directory and Anthology of Their Works,* Scarecrow Press, 1977, pp. 951–56.
2. Mary Pat Daly, "*Journalistic Criticism of Theatre in Eighteenth Century America,*" Ph.D. dissertation, Case Western Reserve University, 1975, pp. 4, 14, 30, for historical references.
3. James Townsend, "Mildred Aldrich," *American Women Writers: A Critical Guide from Colonial Times to the Present,* ed. Lina Mainiero, Frederick Ungar Publishing Company, 1979, vol. I, p. 37.
4. James D. Arnquist, "Amy Leslie," *Notable American Women: A Biographical Dictionary,* ed. Edward James, The Belknap Press of Harvard University, 1971, vol. II, p. 389.
5. Ishbel Ross, *Ladies of the Press,* Harper and Brothers, 1936, p. 409.
6. Brooks Atkinson, *Broadway,* Macmillan Co., 1970, pp. 258–65.
7. Eleanor Flexner, *American Playwrights 1918–38,* Simon and Schuster, Inc., 1938, p. 25.
8. Jane W. Sledman, "Claudia," *Opera News.* October 31, 1970, p. 23.
9. Lehman Engel, *The Critics,* Macmillan Co., 1976, p. 217.
10. Rosamond Gilder, "A One-Foot Shelf," *Theatre Arts* (July 1925), p. 449.

11. Caroline J. Dodge, *Rosamond Gilder and the Theatre*, Ph.D. dissertation, University of Illinois, 1974, pp. 50–53.
12. Edith Oliver, *The New Yorker*, May 15, 1978, p. 116.
13. *Time*, September 3, 1965, p. 74.
14. Claudia Cassidy in Engel, p. 229.
15. *Contemporary American Theatre Critics*, pp. 335–58. The editors asked each critic to submit two examples of his/her writing. That Ms. Holmes selected this piece is, in my opinion, indicative of her overwhelming concern in this area.
16. Clurman in Engel, p. 225.
17. Engel, p. 231.
18. Rosamond Gilder's views are drawn from the following issues of *Theatre Arts:* April 1945; February 1942; March 1944; June 1942; October 1943.
19. Engel, p. 222.
20. Basic Books, Inc., 1965, p. 56.
21. Claudia Cassidy, *Europe on-the-Aisle*, Random House, 1954, p. 224.
22. "What offsets Off-Off-Broadway's revels in amateurishness . . . is the fun of it." *Cue*, November 30, 1968, p. 10.

5 Images

The Second Face of the Idol

1. The favorable climate toward melodrama has been summarized recently by Joseph Donohue in his review of Cross's *Next Week—East Lynne*, *Theatre Survey*, vol. xx, no. 1 (May 1979), pp. 134–35.
2. David Grimsted. *Melodrama Unveiled: American Theatre and Culture*, 1800–1850, University of Chicago Press, 1968. My purpose here is only to present Professor Grimsted's conclusions as I understand them. Subsequent research may well establish that women characters in melodrama have always been more assertive than is commonly thought, even in the 1800 to 1850 period Grimsted examines. I suspect this to be, but I am only discussing the latter part of the nineteenth century here.
3. The sample plays are as follows:
   1863—L. Wallack, *Rosedale*
   1867—A. Daly, *Under the Gaslight*
   1870—I. McCloskey and O. D. Byron, *Across the Continent*
   1871—A. Daly, *Horizon*
   1874—F. Murdock, *Davy Crockett*
   1879—B. Campbell, *My Partner*
   1881—J. Miller, *Forty-Nine*
   1882—B. Campbell, *The White Slave*
   1883—I. O'Neill, *The Count of Monte Cristo*
   1886—H. C. deMille and C. Barnard, *Main Line*
   1893—D. Belasco and F. Fyles, *The Girl I Left Behind Me*
   1895—P. M. Potter, *Trilby*
   1895—E. M. Alfriend and A. C. Wheeler, *The Diamond Robbery*
   c.1898—C. Bennett, *The Royal Slave*
   1900—A. Thomas, *Arizona*
   1904—O. Wister and K. LaShelle, *The Virginian*
   1905—D. Belasco, *Girl of the Golden West*
   1905—L. Mortimer, *No Mother to Guide Her*
   1906—W. Woods, *Billy the Kid*
   1907—W. C. deMille, *The Warrens of Virginia*
4. *My Partner, The White Slave, The Diamond Robbery.*
5. *Main Line, Trilby, The Virginian.*
6. *Girl of the Golden West, The Great Divide.*
7. Tom Taylor, *The Ticket-of-Leave Man*, in *Nineteenth Century Plays*, ed. by George Rowell, Oxford University Press, 1972.
8. Augustin Daly, *Under the Gaslight*, in *Hiss the Villain*, ed. by Michael R. Booth, London: Eyre and Spottiswoode, 1964.
9. Bartley Campbell, *My Partner*, in *America's Lost Plays*, vol. 19, ed. by Napier Wilt, Indiana University Press, 1965.
10. Nellie to the "fallen" Jennie in Walter Woods' *Billy the Kid*, in *America's Lost Plays*, vol. 8, ed. by Garret H. Leverton, Indiana University Press, 1963. Reprint of 1940 edition.
11. Rosemarie K. Bank, "Melodrama as a Social Document: Social Factors in the American Frontier Play," *Theatre Studies*, vol. 22 (1975–76), pp. 42–49.
12. Grimsted appears to see the tug-of-war as typical of melodrama during the first half of the century.
13. Grimsted sees the heroine as buffer as a frequent feature of melodrama he studied.

Women in Pulitzer Prize Plays, 1918–1949

1. Montrose J. Moses, *The American Dramatist*, 1925, reprint, Benjamin Blom, 1964, p. 420. John Gassner, *Dramatic Soundings: Evaluation and Retractions Culled from Thirty Years of Dramatic Criticism*, Crown, 1968, p. 374. William Lyon Phelps, Introduction, *A New Edition of the Pulitzer Prize Plays*, ed. by Kathryn Coe and William Cordell, Random House, 1940. Gerald Weales, *American Drama Since World II*, Harcourt Brace and World, 1962, p. 154. Jane Bonin, *Prize Winning American Drama: Bibliographical and Descriptive Guide*, Scarecrow Press, 1973, p. xi. John

Toohey, *A History of the Pulitzer Prize Plays*, Citadel Press, 1967, p. 8. John Hohenberg, *The Pulitzer Prizes: A History of the Awards in Books, Drama, Music, and Journalism, Based on the Private Files Over Six Decades*, Columbia University Press, 1974, p. 354.

2. Edmond M. Gagey, *Revolution in American Drama*, Columbia University Press, 1947, pp. 1–19. Joseph Wood Krutch, *The American Drama Since 1918: An Informal History*, George Braziller (revised edition 1967), p. 11.

3. John Gassner, "Preface," *American Playwrights 1918–1938*, by Eleanor Flexner, Simon and Schuster, 1938, p. vii.

4. Hohenberg, p. 176.

5. Joanna Russ, "What Can a Heroine Do?" in *Images of Women in Fiction: Feminist Perspectives*, ed. by Susan Koppelman Cornillon, Bowling Green University Press, 1973, p. 9.

6. Simone de Beauvoir, *The Second Sex*, trans. and ed. by H. M. Parshley, Bantam Books, 1952, p. 236.

7. June B. West, "Attitudes Toward American Women as Reflected in American Literature Between the Two World Wars"; Ph.D. dissertation, University of Denver, 1954, p. 202.

8. Katherine M. Rogers, *The Troublesome Helpmate: A History of Misogyny in Literature*, University of Washington Press, 1966, p. 232.

9. Leslie Fiedler, *Love and Death in the American Novel*, Stein and Day (revised edition 1966), p. 296.

10. Judith H. Montgomery, "The American Galatea," *College English*, vol. 32 (May 1971), p. 899.

11. Mary Anne Ferguson, compiler, *Images of Women in Literature*, Houghton Mifflin, 1972, pp. 31–88.

12. Carolyn Heilbrun, "The Woman as Hero," *Texas Quarterly*, vol. 4 (Winter 1965), p. 133.

13. Hubert C. Heffner, "The Nature of Drama," in *An Introduction to Literature*, ed. by Gordon N. Ray, Houghton Mifflin, 1959, pp. 346–49. Francis Hodge, *Play Directing: Analysis, Communication and Style*, Prentice Hall, 1971, p. 41. Brander Matthews, *Dramatic Characterization, A Study of the Drama*, Houghton Mifflin, 1910, p. 152.

The Women's World of Glaspell's Trifles

1. Susan Glaspell, *Plays*, Small, Maynard, 1920.

2. Elaine Hedges, "Quilts and Women's Culture," *The Radical Teacher*, vol. 8,

(March 4, 1977). For an art critic's assessment of the aesthetics of women's quilts, see Patricia Mainardi, "Quilts: The Great American Art," *Radical America*, vol. 7, no. 1(1973), pp. 36–68.

3. Caroll Smith-Rosenberg, "The Female World of Love and Ritual: Relations Between Women in Nineteenth Century America," *Signs: Journal of Women in Culture and Society*, vol. 1, no. 1 (Autumn 1975), pp. 1–29.

Black Women in Plays by Black Playwrights

1. *The Journal of Negro Education*, vol. 2 (April 1933), pp. 179–203.

2. *The Escape: or, A Leap for Freedom*, Boston: R. F. Wallcut, 1858.

3. *Rachel*, Boston: The Cornhill Company, 1920.

4. "A Woman Playwright Speaks Her Mind," *Anthology of the American Negro in the Theatre: A Critical Approach*, ed. Lindsay Patterson, Publishers Company, Inc., 1969, pp. 75–79.

5. *Masses and Mainstream*, vol. 3 (October 1950), pp. 34–47.

6. *Black Theatre*, ed. Lindsay Patterson, Dodd, Mead, 1971, pp. 135–74.

7. *Wine in the Wilderness*, Dramatists Play Service, 1969.

8. *Wedding Band*, Samuel French, 1972.

9. *Black Theatre*, ed. Lindsay Patterson, pp. 221–76.

10. *Les Blancs: The Collected Last Plays* of Lorraine Hansberry, Vintage Books, 1973, pp. 217–13.

11. *Contemporary Black Drama*, ed. Clinton F. Oliver and Stephanie Sills, Charles Scribner's Sons, 1971, pp. 187–205.

12. *Cities in Bezique*, Samuel French, 1969, pp. 3–29.

Who Put the "Tragic" in the Tragic Mulatto?

1. Webster Smalley, ed., *Five Plays by Langston Hughes*, Indiana University Press, 1963, pp. x–xi. Copyright 1926 by Alfred A. Knopf, Inc., and renewed 1954 by Langston Hughes. Reprinted from *The Selected Poems of Langston Hughes* by Langston Hughes, by permission of Alfred A. Knopf, Inc.

2. Arthur Calhoun, *A Social History of the American Family from Colonial Times to the Present*, Arno Press and the New York Times, 1973, vol. I, p. 210. Edward Reuter, *The Mulatto in the United States*, Negro Universities Press, 1969, p. 111. George W. Williams, *History of the Negro Race in America*, Arno Press, 1968. Bernard C. Steiner, *A History of Slavery in Connecticut*, Johns Hopkins Press, 1893.

John H. Russell, *The Free Negro in Virginia*, Johns Hopkins Press, 1913. See other state histories for specific state laws. Sidney G. Fisher, *Men, Women and Manners in Colonial Times*, Lippincott and Co., 1898, vol. II, p. 118. Edward R. Turner, *The Negro in Pennsylvania: Slavery-Servitude-Freedom, 1639–1861*, American Historical Association, 1911, p. 31. Two plays of the '30s on this theme are: DeBose Heyward's *Brass Ankle* (1931), and Samuel Raphaelson's *White Man* (1936). The 1979 weekly television appearance of the Norman Lear characters Tom and Helen on "The Jeffersons" is a reminder of the continuing popularity of this theme.

3. James V. Hatch and Ted Shine, eds., *Black Theatre, USA: Forty-five Plays by Black Americans*, The Free Press, 1974, p. 184.

4. Grandma Carlson clearly reflects the attitude of the "New Negro" writers of the Harlem Renaissance. See Claude McKay's *Home to Harlem*, Harper and Brothers, 1928, and Countee Cullen's *One Way to Heaven*, Harper and Brothers, 1932, as examples of nondramatic treatment of the subject.

5. The Reverend Charles Elliott's strong admonition to the South reveals attitudes toward this illegal amalgamation. See Charles Elliott, *Sinfulness of American Slavery*, L. Swormstedt & J. H. Power, 1850, vol. I, p. 154.

6. In Hollywood, Peola, the tragic mulatto of *Imitation of Life* (1934 film of the Fannie Hurst novel), was flashing a similar brand of militancy on the screen; her whiteness, not her blackness, prompted her rebellion. By the 1949 revival *(Pinky)* not even a real-life mulatto could qualify for the role, and Jeanne Crain, white actress, appeared in the title role.

7. Adrienne Kennedy discusses her real-life mulatto aunt (the model for Clara) who "didn't belong anywhere" and herself as a writer in "A Growth of Images," *Drama Review*, vol. 21, no. 4 (December 1977), pp. 41–48.

8. There are many variations on this theme; the following ditty expresses one of the most common:

If you're white; you're right,
If you're light, you can fight,
If you're brown, stick around,
But if you're black, get back!

Creative Drama

1. Four studies with particularly strong evidence of sources related to sex are: E. C. Irwin, "The Effect of a Program of Creative Dramatics Upon Personality as Measured by the California Test of Personality, Sociograms, Teacher Ratings and Grades," Ph.D. dissertation, University of Pittsburgh, 1963; Elissa Goforth, "Fostering Creativity in Kindergarten Children Through the Use of Creative Drama," M.A. thesis, Arizona State University, 1974; Lin Sommers Wright, "The Effects of Creative Drama on Person Perception," Ph.D. dissertation, University of Minnesota, 1972; Mary E. Lunz, "Creative Dramatics and Communication Effectiveness," *Children's Theatre Review*, vol. 13, no. 3 (1974), pp. 2–3.

2. Irwin, pp. 41–44.

3. Goforth, pp. 35–36.

4. Wright, pp. 63–65A.

5. Lunz, pp. 3–5.

6. Irwin, p. 42.

7. Lunz, p. 5.

8. Alice Dalgliesh, *The Courage of Sarah Noble*, Scribner's, 1964. Madeleine L'Engle, *A Wrinkle in Time*, Ariel Books, 1962. Astrid Lindgren, *Pippi Longstocking, Pippi Goes on Board, Pippi in the South Seas, Pippi on the Run*, Viking Press. Jean Merrill, *The Pushcart War*, Scott, 1964. E. B. White, *Charlotte's Web*, Harper, 1952.

9. David Saar is the Drama Specialist for grades K–6 in the Mesa Public Schools in Mesa, Arizona.

6 Feminist Theatre

Feminist Theatre

1. Both the New Feminist Theatre (New York City) and the Los Angeles Feminist Theatre claim to be the oldest. Probably the NFT predates LAFT by only a few months. For information about the national phenomenon, I am indebted to Betty Moseley Davis, "Feminist Theatre: An Identity Crisis," paper delivered at Southeastern Theatre Conference, Norfolk, Virginia, March 1977. See also, Lillian Perinciolo, "Feminist Theatre: They're Playing in Peoria," *Ms.* (October 1975), pp. 10–4; *Ms.* (December 1977), see especially pp. 35–39, 70–75 89–90; Charlotte Rea, "Women's Theatre Groups," *Drama Review*, vol. 18, no. 4 (1974), pp. 77–87; *Theatre News*, vol. 10, no. 2 (1977).

2. Quarry, "an opera . . . pageant play . . . multimedia spectacle," revived by Women's Interart in 1976, won an Obie, as did Joyce Aaron for her work with *Acrobatics*, which she directed and coauthored, and in which she performed (produced by Interart, April 1976). Sy

Syna, mimeographed transcript of a program performed on WNYC-TV, December 21, 1976; Sy Syna, "Review," *Wisdom's Child* (New York), April 17, 1976, p. 13.

3. In 1851 the Bloomer rage hit London. Perhaps as many as a dozen Bloomer plays were on the boards during that year at the Strand, the Adelphi and the Olympic theatres. I am indebted to Richard Moody of Indiana University for alerting me to these works.

4. Many books and articles treat the political and experimental theatres of the 1960s. Among those which I found useful were Oscar G. Brockett and Robert R. Findlay, *Century of Innovation: A History of European and American Theatre and Drama Since 1870*, Prentice-Hall, 1973; Oscar G. Brockett, *Perspectives on Contemporary Theatre*, Louisiana State University Press, 1971; Margaret Croyden, *Lunatics, Lovers and Poets: The Contemporary Experimental Theatre*, New York: McGraw-Hill, 1974; James Schevill, *Break Out! In Search of New Theatrical Environments*, Chicago: Swallow Press, 1973.

5. For this information I am indebted to Betty Moseley Davis, "Women of the Open Theater," paper presented at the annual convention of the Southern Speech Communication Association, Knoxville, TN, April 1977. Davis cites as her source Joseph Chaikin, telephone interview, July 19, 1976.

6. Davis, "Feminist Theatre." See, for example, Bobbie Spalter-Roth, "WAFT Comes Out: The Franny Chicago Play," *Off Our Backs* (October 1974), p. 22; John C. Meyers, "I Want to Wake Up and Be Free," Providence (RI) *Sunday Journal Magazine*, February 29, 1976, pp. 14–17.

7. I relied most heavily on three studies: Karlyn Kohrs Campbell, "The Rhetoric of Women's Liberation: An Oxymoron," *Quarterly Journal of Speech*, vol. 58 (1972), pp. 264–71. Eva M. McMahan, "Pragmatic Paradox: The Rhetorical Challenge to Advocates of Women's Equality," paper presented at the annual convention of the Southern Speech Communication Association, Knoxville, TN, April 1977. Brenda Robinson Hancock, "Affirmation by Negation in the Women's Liberation Movement," *Quarterly Journal of Speech*, vol. 58 (1972), pp. 264–71.

8. Campbell, pp. 75, 84, 78–81, 83–84. Italics are Campbell's.

9. Many books and articles deal with promoting radical change, such as Saul D. Alinsky, *Rules for Radicals: A Practical Primer for Realistic Radicals*, New York, Random House, 1971.

10. See Delmer H. Hilyard, "Research Models and Designs for the Study of Conflict," in Fred E. Jandt, ed., *Conflict Resolution Through Communication* (Harper & Row, 1973), pp. 448–50. Campbell, p. 86. For a discussion of theatre as symbol, see Northrop Frye, *Anatomy of Criticism: Four Essays*, Princeton University Press, 1957, pp. 83–84.

11. Campbell, pp. 83–84.

12. For information about both Women's Interart Theatre and It's All Right to Be Woman Theatre I am indebted to the research efforts of Cheryl Black.

13. Survey by Action for Women in Theatre, cited by the National Commission on the Observance of International Women's Year, *The Creative Woman: A Report of the Committee on the Arts and Humanities*, Washington, D.C.: Department of State, 1976, p. 6.

14. Gretchen Cryer, "Where Are the Women Playwrights?" *New York Times*, May 20, 1973, sec. 2, p. 1.

15. National Commission on the Observance of International Women's Year, p. 6.

16. An overview of the situation against which such women's groups revolted is provided by the National Commission on the Observance of International Women's Year, pp. 6–10.

17. Margo Lewitin of Interart Theatre stresses that the theatre is "not an outpost for women's lib," but asserts that the group is "certainly political if you define politics as the need for getting women together." Margo Lewitin, telephone interview with Cheryl Black, April 8, 1977. See also Bill Marvel, "Woman's Place Is in the Center." *National Observer*, August 16, 1975, p. 26; and the Foundation Grant Application, New York State Council on the Arts, 1976.

18. Foundation Grant Application, New York State Council on the Arts, 1970–71. Also cited by Karen Malpede Taylor, *People's Theatre in Amerika*, New York: Drama Book Specialists, 1973, p. 325.

19. Ronnog Seaberg, "Womansong Theatre: Militant and Tender," *Great Speckled Bird*, April 29, 1974, p. 17.

20. "Women of Burning City," *Rat*, November 17–December 6 [1970?], p. 21. "The Cutting Edge," Jedediah Wheeler, tour manager, to Patti Gillespie, November 18, 1976 (mimeographed enclosure).

21. Georgia Dullea, "Dreams Are What a Feminist Group's Plays Are Made Of," *New York Times*, December 21, 1972, p. 42.

22. Performed by the New Feminist Theatre first as a benefit for the Redstockings Abortion Hearings in March 1969.
23. Sondra Lowell, "Art Comes to the Elevator: Women's Guerrilla Theatre," *Women*, vol. 2, no. 1 (1970), pp. 50–51.
24. Rosalyn Regelson, "Is Motherhood Holy? Not Anymore," *New York Times*, May 18, 1969, sec. 2, p. 5.
25. Application for a Foundation Grant, cited by Taylor, p. 326.
26. "The Cutting Edge" as reported by Mel Gussow, "Theatre: Women's Work: Cutting Edges 'Croon' at Performing Garage," *New York Times*, March 30, 1976, p. 39.
27. It's All Right to Be Woman Theatre, according to Rea, "Women for Women," p. 79.
28. "Women of Burning City," p. 21.
29. I have here adopted the summary of "antirhetorical" style put forth by Campbell, p. 78.
30. Mel Gussow, "Stage: Feminist Musical: *What Time of Night* Strongly Provocative," *New York Times*, June 19, 1973, p. 30, says: "The show works both as a course in consciousness raising and as a call to arms." An unidentified woman upon seeing a performance of "Women of the Burning City" remarked, "It's like three years of consciousness raising packed into one hour." See also remarks by Roberta Sklar reported by Rea, "Women for Women," p. 81.
31. See Hancock, pp. 265–67.
32. The technique is discussed in Pamela Kearon, "Power as a Function of the Group," in *Notes from the Second Year*, ed. Shulasmith Firestone, New York: Shulasmith Firestone, 1970, pp. 108–10. Sandra L. Bem and Daryl J. Bem, "Training the Woman to Know Her Place: The Power of a Nonconscious Ideology," in *Roles Women Play: Readings Toward Women's Liberation*, ed. Michele Hoffnung Garskof, Belmont, CA: Brooks/Cole, 1971, pp. 84–96.
33. Campbell, p. 86.

Omaha Magic Theatre

Compiled by Linda Jenkins from information supplied by the Omaha Magic Theatre and from published interviews with Megan Terry conducted by Dinah L. Leavitt (in the first edition of this book), and by Kathleen Betsko and Rachel Koenig (in their *Interviews with Contemporary Women Playwrights*).

Women's Interart Theatre

Written and compiled by Helen Krich Chinoy from information supplied by the staff of Women's Interart Theatre and an interview with Margot Lewitin by Arthur Sainer, "Interart Walks a Tightrope," *The Village Voice*, August 7, 1984.

At the Foot of the Mountain

Written and compiled by Linda Jenkins from personal knowledge of the company; discussions with Martha Boesing and Phyllis Jane Rose; an unpublished essay by Jeanyne Bezoier Slettom; At the Foot of the Mountain newsletters; and the introduction to *Martha Boesing: Journeys Along the Matrix*, Minneapolis, Vanilla Press, 1978.

Spiderwoman

Written and compiled by Linda Jenkins from articles by her and Diane Cartwright in *Alternative Theatre*, vol. I, no. 3, January/February 1975, p. 5; At the Foot of the Mountain's newsletter, Fall 1985, p. 3; and descriptions of the group in the Boston Women in Theatre Festival programs.

Split Britches

Written and compiled by Linda Jenkins from information on the company in the Boston Women in Theatre Festival program, an unpublished essay by Sue-Ellen Case and several unpublished interviews: Beverley Pevitts, 1982, Kentucky, with all three company members; Rhonda Blair, 1986, Massachusetts, with Lois Weaver and Peggy Shaw; and Alisa Solomon, 1986, New York, with Shaw.

A Rainbow of Voices

1. Carl G. Jung, *Two Essays on Analytical Psychology*, Meridian, 1956, p. 182.
2. Jolande Jacobi, *The Psychology of C. G. Jung*, Yale University Press, 1973, pp. 132–33.
3. Harriet Pen and Gay Abarbanell, *Guidelines to Feminist Consciousness Raising*, National Task Force on Consciousness Raising for the National Organization for Women, 1976, p. 2.
4. Honor Moore, ed., Introduction, in *The New Women's Theatre*, Vintage, 1977, p. xxxv.
5. Adrienne Rich, Introduction, in Susan Griffin, *Voices*, Old Westbury: The Feminist Press, 1975, p. 10.
6. Rich, p. 12.
7. Moore, p. xxxvi.
8. Eve Merriam, ed., *Growing Up Female in America: Ten Lives*, Dell, 1971, p. 18.
9. Moore, p. xxxv.
10. Ntozake Shange, *for colored girls who have considered suicide/when the rainbow is enuf*, Macmillan, 1977, p. xv.

11. Phyllis Funke, "Beneath the Surface of Shange," *Los Angeles Times*, "Calendar," August 7, 1977, p. 54.
12. Funke, p. 54.
13. Toni Cade Bambara, "For Colored Girls—and White Girls Too," *Ms.*, vol. 5 (September 1976), p. 38.

Feminism and Political Theatre
Written from materials provided by the theatres, reviews of their work, personal knowledge of the theatres and individuals, newspaper articles, Ruby Cohn's "Joan Holden and the San Francisco Mime Troupe" (*The Drama Review*, vol. 24, no. 2, June 1980, 41–49), and William Kleb's "The San Francisco Mime Troupe a Quarter of a Century Later" (*Theatre*, vol. 16, no. 2, Spring 1985, 58–61).

Process and Problems
Adapted from a talk at Smith College, April 18, 1986, given as part of the festivities in honor of the retirement of Helen Krich Chinoy. At the Foot of the Mountain is a professional women's theatre based in Minneapolis.

Reflections
These observations are drawn from remarks made at a panel of women in academic and professional theatre in honor of the retirement of Helen Krich Chinoy from Smith College, April 1986, as well as from a brief talk at the Women in Theatre conference, New Haven, March 1982, and recent reflections.

Making a Life in Art
Terry's comments in this section were compiled by Linda Walsh Jenkins from two interviews with Terry: Dinah L. Leavitt (DL), published in the first edition of this book; and Kathleen Betsko and Rachel Koenig (B/K), published in their *Interviews with Contemporary Women Playwrights*.

Staging Women's Experience
Excerpted from Charlotte Canning, *Feminist Theatres in the USA*, London and New York: Routledge, 1996, pp. 117–215. This study examines practices, philosophies and dilemmas as the phenomenon of specifically feminist theatres drew almost to a close in the 1990s.

1. Foundation Grant Application, New York State Council on the Arts 1970–71, cited in Karen Malpede Taylor, *People's Theatre in Amerika* (New York, Drama Book Specialists, 1973), p. 326.
2. Twila Thompson interviewed by Charlotte Canning, December 19, 1989.
3. Unidentified artist, "Comment Book," March 26, 1979, n.p.

4. RIFT, *Persephone's Return Frontiers: A Journal of Women's Studies*, vol. 3, no. 2 (1978), p. 72.
5. RIFT, *Persephone's Return*, p. 72.
6. Muriel Miguel interviewed by Charlotte Canning, April 26, 1990. Emphasis hers.

Changes and Legacies
1. Flora Davis, *Moving the Mountain: Suffrage, Equal Rights, and Beyond*, New Brunswick, NJ: Rutgers University Press, 1990, p. 472.
2. Sondra Segal interviewed by Charlotte Canning, December 21, 1989.
3. Women's Interart Center, publicity flyer, n.d., n.p.
4. Ellen Gavin interviewed by Charlotte Canning, April 9, 1990.
5. Gavin, interview.
6. This figure is computed from the dates provided for theatres in Rosemary Curb, Phyllis Mael and Beverley Byers Pevitts, "Catalog of Feminist Theatre—Parts 1 and 2," *Chrysalis*, vol. 10 (1979), pp. 67–75.

7 Feminist Theatrical Theories

Feminist Theatrical Theories
1. Anthony Storr, *Solitude: A Return to the Self*, Ballantine, 1989. Storr offers an examination of Freud and Freud's counterpart Alfred Adler, including Jung's distinctions between the two, in a manner that offers insights not always consistent with Lacan.
2. Carol Martin, ed., *A Sourcebook of Feminist Theatre and Performance*, Routledge, 1996, p. 102.
3. Yvonne Yarbro-Bejarano, as cited by Linda Walsh Jenkins in "Matrix," *Women in American Theatre*, second edition, Theatre Communications Group, 1987, p. 376.
4. Deanna Jent, Ph.D. dissertation, Northwestern University.
5. James Atlas, *The New Yorker* (March 29, 1999), pp. 60–65.
6. Ibid., 65.
7. Laura Edmondson and Jules Odendahl, interview with Sue-Ellen Case, *Theatre Insight*, no. 14, 1995.
8. Edmondson and Odendahl.
9. Lila Abu-Lughod, "Can There Be a Feminist Ethnography?" 1989.
10. Sandy Boucher, *Opening the Lotus*, Beacon Press, 1997.
11. Carlos Castaneda, *The Wheel of Time: The Shamans of Ancient Mexico. Their Thoughts about Life, Death and the Universe*, Eidolona Press, 1998.

A Feminist Theory of Theatre
Excerpted from Patti P. Gillespie, "Feminist Theory of Theatre," in *Theatre and Feminist Aesthetics*, Karen Laughlin and Catherine Schuler, eds., Madison, NJ: Fairleigh Dickinson University Press, 1995. Reprinted with permission from Associated University Presses.

1. Gerda Lerner, *The Creation of Patriarchy*, New York: Oxford University Press, 1986, p. 238.
2. Karlyn Kohrs Campbell, "What Really Distinguishes and/or Ought to Distinguish Feminist Scholarship in Communication Studies," *Women's Studies in Communication*, vol. 11, no. 2 (1988), pp. 4–5.
3. Opponents of formalism (of which New Criticism and neo-Aristotelianism were supreme examples) have often linked formalism with fascism. For one statement of this view, see Fraya Katz-Stoker, "The Other Criticism: Feminism vs. Formalism," *Images of Women in Fiction: Feminist Perspectives,* ed. Susan Koppelman Cornillon, Bowling Green University Press, 1972, pp. 313–25.
4. Cicero has been cited as the first to ask, *cui bono,* "who profits?" A useful discussion of this development appears in Lillian Robinson and Lisa Vogel, "Modernism and History," *Images of Women,* Cornillon, pp. 278–305.
5. Brecht's well-known theoretical writings are collected in *Brecht on Theatre,* trans. by John Willet, London: Methuen, 1964. Neither *Verfremdungseffekt* nor the staging techniques used to achieve it originated with Brecht. The Russian formalist Viktor Shklovsky had proposed the former as early as 1917, and Erwin Piscator regularly practiced the latter in his Piscator Theatre between 1927 and 1930. Advocates of contemporary deconstruction will, of course, see an ally in Brecht's *Verfremdungseffekt.*
6. For example, Sue-Ellen Case, "The Butch-Femme Aesthetic," in *Making a Spectacle,* ed. Lynda Hart, Ann Arbor: University of Michigan Press, 1989, pp. 282–89; Kate Davy, "Constructing the Spectator: Reception, Context, and Address in Lesbian Performance," *Performing Arts Journal,* vol. 10, no. 2 (1986), pp. 43–52; Jill Dolan, "Feminists, Lesbians, and Other Women in Theatre: Thoughts on the Politics of 'Performance,'" *Women in Theatre*, vol. 11, *Themes in Drama,* ed. James Redmond, Cambridge University Press, 1989, pp. 199–207.
7. Literary studies noted similar traits. See, for example, Elaine Showalter, "Piecing and Writing," *The Poetics of Gender*, ed. Nancy K. Miller, Columbia University Press, 1986, pp. 222–47.
8. Literary scholars made the same argument about narrative. For an extreme (and male) example applied to narrative, see Robert Scholes, *Fabulation and Metafiction*, Urbana: University of Illinois Press, 1979, pp. 26–27. Applied to theatre and from a feminist point of view, consult Martha Boesing, for many years the resident writer and director of At the Foot of the Mountain Theatre in Minneapolis, who made this suggestion first in her play *The Web, Plays in Progress,* 4.1, Theatre Communications Group, 1981, and later incorporated the idea in lectures and on mimeographed sheets distributed as a part of lectures given at several colleges and universities.
9. For example, Patti P. Gillespie, "America's Women Dramatists, 1960–1980," *Essays on Contemporary Drama*, ed. Hedwig Brock and Albert Wertheim, Munich: Max Heuber Verlag, 1981, 199; Alisa Solomon, "Doubly Marginalized: Women in the Avant-Garde," *Women in American Theatre,* ed. Helen Krich Chinoy and Linda Walsh Jenkins, New York: Crown Publishers, Inc., 1981, pp. 363–71; and Helen Krich Chinoy, "Here Are the Women Playwrights," *Women*, Chinoy and Jenkins, New York: Theatre Communications Group, 1987, pp. 341–53.
10. Sue-Ellen Case, *Feminism and Theatre*, New York: Methuen, 1988, p. 3.
11. Jill Dolan, *The Feminist Spectator as Critic*, Ann Arbor: UNI Research Press, 1988, p. 12.

Semiotics and the Gaze
Excerpted from Sue-Ellen Case, *Feminism and Theatre*, 1988. Reprinted by permission of Routledge/Taylor & Francis Books, Inc.

1. Keir Elam, *The Semiotics of Theatre and Drama*, Methuen, 1980, p. 1.
2. See Nancy Henley, *Body Politics*, Prentice-Hall, 1977.
3. Teresa de Lauretis, *Alice Doesn't: Feminism, Semiotics and Cinema*, Indiana University Press, 1984, p. 5.
4. E. Ann Kaplan, *Women and Film*, Methuen, 1981, p. 23.

The Discourse of Feminisms
Excerpted from Jill Dolan, *The Feminist Spectator as Critic*, Ann Arbor: University of

Michigan Press, 1991, ch. 1, pp. 1–18 and from "Afterword," pp. 119–121.

1. See Catherine Belsey, "Constructing the Subject: Deconstructing the Text," ed. Judith Newton and Deborah Rosenfelt, *Feminist Criticism and Social Change: Sex Class, and Race in Literature and Culture*, New York: Methuen, 1985, for a discussion of the ideal spectator's position as constructed in realism. The issue of realism and spectatorship is addressed fully in ch. 5.

2. The phrase "resistant reader" was coined with the publication of Judith Fetterley's *The Resisting Reader: A Feminist Approach to American Fiction*, Bloomington: Indiana University Press, 1978.

3. See Teresa de Lauretis, *Alice Doesn't: Feminism, Semiotics, Cinema*, Bloomington: Indiana University Press, 1984, particularly her chapter "Desire in Narrative," pp. 103–57.

4. See Alison Jaggar, *Feminist Politics and Human Nature*, Totowa, NJ: Rowman & Allanheld, 1983, for her definitions of different feminist epistemologies. See Michelene Wandor, *Carry On, Understudies*, New York: Routledge & Kegan Paul, 1986, for definitions of the feminisms in terms of British feminist theatre. In her chapter "Political Dynamics: The Feminisms," Wandor outlines radical feminism, bourgeois feminism or emancipationism, and socialist feminism as the three major tendencies "as they have emerged in the 1970s" (p. 131). See also my article "Feminists, Lesbians, and Other Women in Theatre: Thoughts on the Politics of Performance," *Themes in Drama*, vol. 11 (1989) for a longer discussion of the way in which delineating the feminisms in theatre clarifies the more obscure appellation "women in theatre." This article was originally presented as a paper at the 1987 Themes in Drama conference at the University of California, Riverside. An earlier version was published as "The Politics of Feminist Performance," *Theatre Times*, vol. 5, no. 6 (July/August 1986). Elin Diamond has expressed reservations about my use of the term "cultural" feminism, as she feels, and rightly so, that the culture is "where we all live." For now, however, I continue to maintain that "cultural" feminism is a more precise appellation than "radical" feminism.

5. See Zillah Eisenstein, *The Radical Future of Liberal Feminism*, New York: Longman, 1981, for a study of liberal feminist theory that proposes its potential for radicalism, particularly part 3, "The Contemporary Practice of Liberal Feminism," pp. 175–253.

6. See Francesca Primus, "Women's Theatres around Town: Feminist or Contemporary?" *Backstage*, December 6, 1985, for interviews with various women working in New York theatre who renounce the feminist label.

7. See my article, "Is the Postmodern Aesthetic Feminist?" *Art & Cinema*, vol. 1, no. 3 (Fall 1987), for an explication of this issue. See also Sue-Ellen Case and Jeanie Forte, "From Formalism to Feminism," *Theatre* vol. 16, no. 2 (Spring 1985), for a feminist critique of deconstructionist practice in performance.

Toward a Gestic Feminist Criticism

Excerpted from Elin Diamond, *Unmaking Mimesis: Essays on Feminism and Theater*, London and New York: Routledge, 1997, ch. 2, pp. 45–52, ch. 6, pp. 164–171.

1. See Michele Pearce, "Alien Nation: An Interview with [Suzan-Lori Parks]," *American Theatre*, vol. 11, no. 3 (March 1994), p. 26.

2. Director John Edward McGrath told me that Ruth Maleczech grabbed the video herself one day in rehearsal, and the effect was so suggestive that it became a permanent part of the show.

3. This is fully played out in Brecht's attitude toward textual authority. As is well known, he revised constantly and cared little about definitive or authoritative versions of his plays.

4. See Timothy Murray's superb discussion of *métissage* (mixed blood), mourning and colonization in McCauley's *Indian Blood* in *Discourse* (Spring 1994), pp. 29–45.

5. In *Sally's Rape*, a piece made, with Jeannie Hutchins, directly after *Indian Blood*, McCauley remembers her enslaved great-great-grandmother by stripping, climbing on an auction block and asking the audience to bid on her. After all performances, McCauley has a talkback session. At Rutgers University in 1993, the racially mixed student audience talked for over an hour about the connections the piece made available. For many, *Sally's Rape* was a history lesson.

Feminism and Psychoanalysis

Excerpted from the introduction to the chapter "Psychoanalysis" in *Critical Theory and Performance*, edited by Janelle G. Reinelt and Joseph R. Roach, Ann Arbor: University of Michigan Press, 1992, pp. 383–385.

1. For a review of Freud and subsequent treatments of psychoanalysis, see Terry Eagleton, *Literary Theory: An Introduction*, Minneapolis: University of Minnesota Press, 1983, ch. 5. Kaja Silverman is especially helpful in contrasting and comparing Freud with Lacan in *The Subject of Semiotics*, New York: Oxford University Press, 1983. See also *The Language of Psychoanalysis*, ed. J. Laplanche and J. B. Pontalis, trans. Donald Nicholson-Smith, New York: W. W. Norton, 1973. To begin reading Freud, one might start with *A General Introduction to Psychoanalysis*, trans. J. Riviere, London: Liveright Pub. Corp., 1953, or *Civilization and Its Discontents*, trans. J. Riviere, London: Hogarth Press, 1930.
2. Lacan himself is somewhat difficult to read because his major work comes in the form of a series of lectures, some of which are translated and published, although Lacan was deliberately unsystematic. *Ecrits: A Selection*, trans. Alan Sheridan, New York: W. W. Norton, 1977, is the most available text; *Feminine Sexuality*, ed. Juliet Mitchell and Jacqueline Rose, trans. Jacqueline Rose, New York: W. W. Norton, 1982, provides another source, with excellent introductions by Juliet Mitchell and Jacqueline Rose.

   Gilles Deleuze and Felix Guattari have also made an important theoretical contribution with *Anti-Oedipus*, which is their critique of Freudian categories or rather an attempt to read political, economic and social "economics" in terms of the flow of desire produced through "desire-machines." *Anti-Oedipus*, trans. Robert Hurley, Mark Seem, and Helen R. Lane, Minneapolis: University of Minnesota Press, 1983.

Women, Woman and the Subject of Feminism

Excerpted from "Women, Woman and the Subject of Feminism: Feminist Directions" in *Upstaging Big Daddy: Directing Theater as if Gender and Race Matter*, edited by Ellen Donkin and Susan Clement, Ann Arbor: University of Michigan Press, 1993.

1. Teresa de Lauretis, *Alice Doesn't: Feminism, Semiotics and Cinema*, Bloomington: Indiana University Press, 1984, p. 5.
2. Kaja Silverman, *The Subject of Semiotics*, New York: Oxford University Press, 1983, p. 183.
3. Silverman, p. 185.
4. Silverman, p. 188.
5. de Lauretis, pp. 121, 133.
6. de Lauretis, p. 134.

7. Adrienne Kennedy, *Adrienne Kennedy in One Act*, Minneapolis: University of Minnesota Press, 1988, p. 108.
8. Tina Margolis, review of *Beauty and the Beast, Women & Performance*, vol. 1, no. 1, pp. 75–78.
9. Sue-Ellen Case, "From Split Subject to Split Britches," *Feminine Focus: The New Women Playwrights*, ed. Enoch Brater, New York: Oxford University Press, 1988, p. 143.

"Not . . . but"/"Not-Not-Me"

Excerpted from "'Not . . . but'/'Not-Not-me': Musings on Cross-Gender Performance," in *Upstaging Big Daddy*, edited by Ellen Donkin and Susan Clement, Ann Arbor: University of Michigan Press, 1993, pp. 291–304.

1. Historically, cross-gender casting has kept women off the stage so that men could control theatrical representation (e.g., as with Greek, Elizabethan and Kabuki actors). In contemporary instances women have done the reverse, playing with the possibilities of Simone de Beauvoir's statement that "one is not born, but, rather, *becomes* a woman."

Focus on the Body

Excerpted from "Focus on the Body: Pain, Praxis, and Pleasure in Feminist Performance," in *Critical Theory and Performance*, edited by Janelle G. Reinelt and Joseph R. Roach, Ann Arbor: University of Michigan Press, 1992, pp. 257–258.

1. See *TDR: A Journal of Performance Studies*, vol. 32, no. 1 (1988), pp. 152–58, for a text of this piece, along with an interview of Finley.
2. See Eileen O'Neill, "(Re)presentations of Eros—Exploring Female Sexual Agency, in *"Gender/Body/Knowledge: Feminist Reconstructions of Being and Knowing*, ed. Alison M. Jaggar and Susan R. Bordo, New Brunswick, NJ: Rutgers University Press, 1989, p. 4, for a similar discussion of Cindy Sherman's self-portrait film stills, which "do not represent a particular woman but the problematics of representation itself."

Critique of Postmodern Theory, Conclusion

Excerpted from Patti P. Gillespie, "Feminist Theory of Theatre," in *Theatre and Feminist Aesthetics*, Karen Laughlin and Catherine Schuler, eds., Madison, NJ: Fairleigh Dickinson University Press, 1995.

1. Fredric Jameson, "Periodizing the 60s," in *Syntax Theory*, vol. 1, *The Ideologies of*

Theory: Essays 1971–1986, Minneapolis: University of Minnesota Press, 1988, pp. 192–93.

2. Gerda Lerner, *The Creation of Feminist Consciousness*, New York, Oxford University Press, 1993, p. vii.

3. Elin Diamond, "Brechtian Theory / Feminist Theory: Toward a Gestic Feminist Criticism," *The Drama Review*, vol. 32, no. 3 (1988), pp. 82–94; Kate Davy, "Reading Past the Heterosexual Imperative," *The Drama Review*, vol. 33, no. 3 (1989), pp. 153–70; Judith L. Stephens, "Subverting the Demon-Angel Dichotomy: Innovation and Feminist Intervention in Twentieth-Century Drama," *Text and Performance Quarterly*, vol. 9 (January 1989), pp. 53–64.

4. For two popular life-cycle theories of a social movement, see Robert Hopper, "The Revolutionary Process: A Frame of Reference for the Study of Revolutionary Movements," *Social Forces*, vol. 28 (March 1950), pp. 270–79, and Gary Schwarz, *Sect Ideologies and Social Status*, Chicago: University of Chicago Press, 1970. For a critique of such theories, see Herbert W. Simons, Elizabeth W. Mechling, and Howard N. Schreier, "The Functions of Human Communication in Mobilizing for Action from the Bottom Up: The Rhetoric of Social Movements," *Handbook of Rhetorical and Communication Theory*, ed. Carroll C. Arnold and John Waite Bowers, Boston: Allyn and Bacon, 1984, pp. 792–867.

5. Karen Offen, "Defining Feminism: A Comparative Historical Approach," *Signs*, vol. 14 (Autumn 1988), pp. 132–33. Offen identifies, in what begins to sound like Polonius' comic catalogue, "'old' and 'new' feminisms, 'social' and 'hard-core' feminisms, 'first wave' and 'second wave' feminisms, 'classical' and 'modern' feminisms, 'maximalist' and 'minimalist' feminisms, 'humanistic' and 'gynocentric' feminisms . . . 'egalitarian,' 'evangelical' and 'socialist' feminisms, 'liberal,' 'Marxist,' and 'radical' feminisms.'" A quick perusal of current literature can offer at least a dozen others: "materialist," "separatist," "bourgeois," etc.

6. Feminists like Audre Lorde urge feminists to "see difference differently"; editors of *Re-vision* urge feminists to see "the difference of women from Woman, and, that is to say as well, the *differences among women*" as liberating rather than oppressive. Both quoted by Teresa de Lauretis, "Aesthetic and Feminist Theory: Rethinking Women's Cinema," in *Female Spectators: Looking at Film and Television*, ed. E. Deirdre Pribram, New York: Verso, 1988, pp. 184, 183.

7. See, for example, Linda Alcoff, "Cultural Feminism versus Post-Structuralism," *Signs*, vol. 13 (Spring 1988), pp. 405–36; and Carolyn J. Allen, "Feminist Criticism and Postmodernism," *Tracing Literary Theory*, ed. Joseph Natoli, Urbana: University of Illinois Press, 1987, pp. 278–305.

8. Noel Carroll, *Mystifying Movies: Fads and Fallacies in Contemporary Film Theory*, New York: Columbia University Press, 1988, pp. 226, 229.

About Face

Excerpted from Dorinne Kondo, introduction to *About Face: Performing "Race" in Fashion and Theater*, 1997. Reproduced by permission of Routledge/Taylor & Francis Books, Inc.

1. For a history of the Asian American movement, see William Wei, *The Asian American Movement*, Philadelphia, Temple University Press (1993). He notes that the conventional genealogy attributing a singular origin to the Third World strike at San Francisco State in 1968 elides a far more complex history with multiple points of origin. Suchen Chan, *Asian Californians*, San Francisco, MTL/Boyd and Fraser (1991) also notes the bureaucratic usage of the term, in addition to its links to student activism. "Asian American" was taken up by the government census bureau and combined with "Pacific Islander"; consequently, the term "Asian Pacific American" or "Asian/Pacific Islander" is sometimes used in both bureaucratic and extra-bureaucratic settings.

Under the "Trickster's" Sign

Excerpted from "Under the 'Trickster's' Sign: Toward a Reading of Ntozake Shange" in *Critical Theory and Performance*, edited by Janelle G. Reinelt and Joseph R. Roach, Ann Arbor: University of Michigan Press, 1992, pp. 65–75.

1. *The Signifying Monkey* by Henry Louis Gates, Jr., New York: Oxford University Press, 1988, is perhaps the most outstanding example, but other critics such as Femi Euba and Diedre Badejo are also using Yoruba practices to inform their analyses. See, for example, Euba's *Archetypes, Imprecators, and Victims of Fate: Origins and Developments of Satire in Black Drama*, New York: Greenwood Press, 1989; and Badejo's "The Goddess Osun as a Paradigm for African Feminist Criti-

cism," *Sage: A Scholarly Journal on Black Woman*, vol. 6, no. 1 (1989), pp. 27–32.

2. Interview with Ntozake Shange by Esther Beth Sullivan, January 11, 1991.

3. Primus, like her more famous contemporary Katherine Dunham, was also a dancer-anthropologist; she had been preceded in the effort to have African dance viewed seriously by the West African Asadata Dafora, who presented dance from the Mende people of Sierra Leone during the 1920s. See for example, William Moore, "The Development of Black Modern Dance in America," *Black Tradition in American Modern Dance*, ed. Gerald E. Myers, Durham, NC: American Dance Festival, 1988, pp. 15, 17.

4. New Orleans native Luisah Teish later became a priestess of Osun in the Yoruba Lucumi tradition. She is also the author of *Jambalaya: The Natural Woman's Book of Personal Charms and Practice Rituals*, San Francisco: Harper and Row, 1985.

5. Shange reports absorbing different lessons from these three mentors: from Baraka, an appreciation of the ritual of language; from Reed, a global sense of black history and permission to change the syntax to change the mood; and, from Hurston, a demonstration that long fiction could be successfully sustained by a female character (interview with Ntozake Shange by Esther Beth Sullivan, January 11, 1991).

6. Marjorie Pryse, "Zora Neale Hurston, Alice Walker, and the 'Ancient Power' of Black Women," in *Conjuring Black Women, Fiction, and Literary Tradition*, ed. Marjorie Pryse and Hortense J. Spillers, Bloomington: Indiana University Press, 1985, p. 11.

7. Rowland Abiodun, "Woman in Yoruba Religious Images," *African Languages and Cultures*, vol. 2, no. 1 (1988), p. 3.

8. Abiodun, "Woman," p. 3.

9. Maya Deren, *Divine Horsemen: The Voodoo Gods of Haiti*, New York: Dell, 1970, p. 138.

10. Note that numerous critics such as Ogundipe and Pelton argue that the trickster designation denotes negative Christian influence and obscures Esu's divine functions. See, for example, Ayodele Ogundipe, "Esu Elegbara, the Yoruba God of Chance and Uncertainty: A Study in Yoruba Mythology," Ph.D. dissertation, Indiana University, 1978; and Robert D. Pelton, *The Trickster in West Africa: A Study in Mythic Irony and Sacred Delight*, Berkeley: University of California Press, 1980.

11. Pelton, *Trickster*, p. 133, quoting Joan Westcott, "Sculpture and Myths of Eshu-Elegba, the Yoruba Trickster," *Africa*, vol. 32 (1962), pp. 336–53.

12. Pelton, *Trickster*, 150.

13. Diedre LaPin, "Story, Medium and Masque: The Idea and Art of Yoruba Storytelling," Ph.D. dissertation, University of Wisconsin–Madison, quoted in Henry John Drewal and Margaret Thompson Drewal, *Gelede: Art and Female Power among the Yoruba*, Bloomington: Indiana University Press, 1983, p. 1.

14. Kacke Gotrick, *Apidan Theatre and Modern Drama: A Study in a Traditional Yoruba Theatre and Its Influence on Modern Drama by Yoruba Playwrights*, Göteborg, Sweden: Graphic Systems AB, 1984, pp. 115–19; LaPin, "Story, Medium and Masque," ch. 2.

15. Drewal and Drewal, *Gelede*, pp. 1–7.

16. Sandra L. Richards, "Conflicting Impulses in the Plays of Ntozake Shange," *Black American Literature Forum*, vol. 17 (1983), pp. 73–78.

17. Barbara Christian, *Black Feminist Criticism: Perspectives on Black Women Writers*, New York: Pergamon Press, 1985, pp. 31–46.

18. Ntozake Shange, *Spell #7*, in *Three Pieces*, New York: St. Martin's Press, 1981, p. 51

19. Gates, *Signifying Monkey*, p. 30.

8 Voices at the Millennium

(Quotations not endnoted are from the selection being discussed. *WAT* refers to this book.)

Voices at the Millennium

1. Summary of Findings in "Report on Status of Women Directors and Playwrights in the New York City Theatre," Prepared by Celia Braxton for Susan Jonas, New York State Council on the Arts, September 21, 1998. This major study indicates that although annual figures for "paid professional theatre" since 1975 fluctuate, there has been "virtually no increase" in women playwrights on Broadway and only a "marginal increase in use of women directors." Off-Broadway is only "marginally" better for women playwrights and directors. Off-Off-Broadway is not much more receptive to women playwrights, but women directors comprise "just over 40%," and "between 40 and 50%" of Off-Off theatres have a woman artistic director.

2. Zelda Fichandler in "The Profit in Nonprofit," *American Theatre*, Decem-

ber 2000, reminds readers that the "profit" generated by not-for-profit theatre is "of a social nature . . . a profit that is earned from the examination of reality by means of theatrical art."

STAGING DIVERSITY

1. Cherríe Moraga and Gloria Anzaldúa, eds., *This Bridge Called My Back: Writings by Radical Women of Color*, New York: Kitchen Table–Women of Color Press, 1983, p. xxiii.
2. See Sandra L. Richards, "Under the 'Trickster's' Sign: Toward a Reading of Ntozake Shange," *WAT* p. 369.
3. *This Bridge Called My Back*, p. 28–29. See also Yvonne Yarbo-Bejarano, "Cherríe Moraga's 'Shadow of a Man': Touching the Wound in Order to Heal" in *Acting Out: Feminist Performances*, Lynda Hart and Peggy Phelan, eds., Ann Arbor: University of Michigan Press, 1993, pp. 85–102. This anthology contains many challenging discussions on various aspects of lesbian identity and creativity and on the "competing identities" that have emerged from the overarching concept of "woman."
4. Jill Dolan, *The Feminist Spectator as Critic*, Ann Arbor: UMI Research Press, 1988, p. 120. See also Dolan's introduction to "Lesbian Playwrights: Diverse Interests, Identities, and Styles" in Jane T. Peterson and Suzanne Bennett, *Women Playwrights of Diversity: A Bio-Bibliographical Sourcebook*, Westport, CT: Greenwood Press, 1997, pp. 27–33. Dolan suggests the difficulties of defining "lesbian."
5. See Cherry Jones and Paula Vogel, "Theatre Role Models," *WAT* p. 424. See also Robert A. Schanke and Kimberley Bell Marra, eds., *Passing Performances: Queer Readings of Leading Players in American Theater*, Ann Arbor: University of Michigan Press, 1998.
6. See also critical reception of Pearl Cleage's *Flyin' West*, Esther Beth Sullivan, *Theatre Topics*, vol. 7, no. 1, March 1997, pp. 11–12.
7. Roberta Uno, *Unbroken Thread*, Amherst, MA: University of Massachusetts Press, 1993, p. 3.
8. Margaret Wilkerson, ed., *Nine Plays by Black Women*, American Library, 1986. Kathy A. Perkins, ed., *Black Female Playwrights*, Bloomington, IN: Indiana University Press, 1989. Perkins and Roberta Uno, eds., *Contemporary Plays by Women of Color*, London and New York: Routledge, 1996. Perkins and Judith L.

Stephens, eds., *Strange Fruit: Plays on Lynching by American Women*, Bloomington, IN: Indiana University Press, 1998.

The "colored girls Phenomenon"

Excerpted from Sydné Mahone, "The Sista Masses (1970s–1990s): African American Women Playwrights" in *Women Playwrights of Diversity: A Bio-Bibliographical Sourcebook*, by Jane T. Peterson and Suzanne Bennett, Greenwood Press, 1997. Reproduced with permission of Greenwood Publishing Group, Inc., Westport, CT.

Finding Place and Voice as a Chicana Lesbian

Excepted and edited from Cherríe Moraga, Artistic Statement in *Contemporary Plays by Women of Color*, edited by Kathy A. Perkins and Roberta Uno, London and New York: Routledge, 1996, pp. 231–232.

Fast-Talking, Quick-Thinking Black Women

Pearl Cleage, Artistic Statement, in *Contemporary Plays by Women of Color*, edited by Kathy A. Perkins and Roberta Uno, London and New York: Routledge, 1996, pp. 46–47.

The Asian American Spectator and the Politics of Realism

Excerpted from Josephine Lee, "The Asian American Spectator and the Politics of Realism" from *Performing Asian America: Race and Ethnicity on the Contemporary Stage*, Temple University Press, 1997. All rights reserved. Reprinted by permission.

1. I do not suggest "guilt by association" through the use of Eurocentric dramatic form in preference to traditional Asian staging. I am asking what difficulties can be found in the form of theatrical realism itself when considered as political or strategic theatre.

The Challenges of Diversity

Excerpted from Suzanne Bennett's Introduction to *Women Playwrights of Diversity: A Bio-Bibliographical Sourcebook* by Jane T. Peterson and Suzanne Bennett, Greenwood Press, 1997. Reproduced with permission of Greenwood Publishing Group, Inc., Westport, CT.

INTIMATE SOLOS

1. See Errol Hill, "Henrietta Vinton Davis, Shakespearean Actress," *WAT* p. 83. Muriel McKenna, "The Art of Ruth Draper," *WAT* p. 103. Jane Wagner, *The Search for Signs of Intelligent Life in the Universe*, New York: Perennial, 1991.

2. Marvin A. Carlson, *Performance: A Critical Introduction*, London and New York: Routledge, 1996, chs. 5, 7 and 8.
3. Deborah Lubar's *Blood and Stones* revealed the Israeli and Palestinian women she visited "coping with their shared historical fate," and *A Story's a Story* explored two old immigrant neighbors, a shtetl Jew and a Catholic peasant. The Bosnia project grows out of the healing skills Lubar shared with traumatized women in Bosnia.
4. See "Split Britches," *WAT* p. 298; Deb Margolin, *Of All the Nerve*, performance pieces edited by Lynda Hart, London and New York, Cassell, 1999; Dorothy Chansky, "Beyond Broadway," *Theatre Week*, September 30, 1996.
5. Mel Gussow, "The Other Life of Karen Finley," *New York Times*, September 22, 1997, The Arts, p. 4.
6. C. Carr, "'Telling the Awfullest Truth': An Interview with Karen Finley," *Acting Out: Feminist Performances*, eds. Hart and Phelan, p. 160. See also Robert J. Andreach, *Creating the Self in the Contemporary American Theatre*, Carbondale, Il · Southern Illinois University Press, pp. 1–10, and C. Carr, "On Edge," a discussion of Finley's memoir *A Different Kind of Intimacy*, in *The Village Voice*, November 14, 2000, p. 69.
7. Quotations from James Oseland, "A Goddess Unbound," *American Theatre*, March 1999, p 25.

Eve's Version

Excerpted from Deborah Lubar's *Eve's Version*, a performance piece, 1997.

I See Messiah

Excerpts from Deb Margolin, *0 Wholly Night and Other Jewish Solecisms*, a one-woman show, commissioned originally by the Jewish Museum in New York in 1996 for its "Too Jewish" exhibition and then moved to the Interart Theatre under the direction of Margot Lewitin. From author's manuscript.

Karen Finley

Excerpted from a Karen Finley interview with Richard Schechner and followed by Act II of Finley's script, *The Constant State of Desire*, in *A Sourcebook of Feminist Theatre and Performance*, edited by Carol Martin, London and New York: Routledge, 1996.

Annie Sprinkle

Excerpted from Rebecca Schneider, *The Explicit Body in Performance*, London and New York: Routledge, 1997, pp. 52, 53, 55.

ADDRESSING THE CANON

1. Helen Epstein, *The Company She Keeps: Tina Packer Builds a Theater*, Cambridge, MA: Plunkett Lake Press, 1985, p. 43.
2. Caroline Nesbitt, "Into the Woods with Shakespeare and Company," *American Theatre*, January 1999, p. 97, and p. 94 for "dropping in."
3. Epstein, p. 38ff, discusses Linklater's work with Packer. See *Freeing the Natural Voice*, Drama Book Publishers, 1976, and *Freeing Shakespeare's Voice*, Theatre Communications Group, 1992.
4. Dorothy Chansky, "In the Company of Women," *Theatre Week*, January 17, 1994. See also "Shakespeare, Feminism and Voice," Linklater and others, *New Theatre Quarterly*, February 1997, p. 48ff.
5. Alisa Solomon, *Re-dressing the Canon*, London and New York: Routledge, 1997, p. 145.
6. Ruth Maleczech, quoted in "Every Inch a King," *American Theatre*, July/August 1999, pp. 24–25.
7. See also Gay Gibson Cima, *Performing Women: Female Characters, Male Playwrights, and the Modern Stage*, Ithaca: Cornell University Press, 1996.

A Woman's Perspective on Shakespeare

Selected remarks from a discussion by Tina Packer with the audience before a performance of *The Merchant of Venice* by Shakespeare & Company at The Mount, Lenox, MA, in the summer of 1998.

In the Company of Women

Excerpted from Susan Curran Barrett, "In the Company of Women," in *Smith Alumnae Quarterly*, Spring 1995, pp 13–15.

Mabou Mines' Ruth Maleczech Plays Lear

Ruth Maleczech, quoted in "Every Inch a King," a report on a weekend-long conference on directing *King Lear* presented in New York by the Stage Directors and Choreographers Foundation, in April 1999 in *American Theatre*, July/August 1999, pp. 24–25. Excerpted from Alisa Solomon, "Three Canonical Crossings," in *Re-dressing the Canon: Essays on Theatre and Gender*, London and New York, Routledge, l997, pp. 130–141.

Strategies for Subverting the Canon

Excerpted from Gay Gibson Cima, "Strategies for Subverting the Canon," in *Upstaging Big Daddy*, edited by Ellen Donkin and Susan Clement, Ann Arbor: University of Michigan Press, 1993, pp. 91–103.

ARTISTIC PROCESS AND PROFESSIONAL POWER

ACTING

1. "The Female Actor," *Women in American Theatre*, 2nd ed., New York: TCG, 1987, p. 332ff.
2. See Linda Walsh Jenkins, "Spiderwoman" and "Split Britches," *WAT* pp. 291 and 298. Also see *Split Britches: Lesbian Practice/Feminist Performance*, edited by Sue-Ellen Case, London and New York, Routledge, 1996.
3. Text published in *Women and Performance*, vol. 6, no. 1, 1993.
4. Tina Landau lists the nine Viewpoints used by Anne Bogart as "the Four Viewpoints of Time (Tempo, Duration, Kinesthetic Response, Repetition) and Five Viewpoints of Space (Shape, Gesture, Architecture, Relationship and Topography)." Viewpoint theory is described as "a synthesis of disparate performance techniques." "The Voices of Viewpoints," *American Theatre*, January 1998, pp. 33–34. See also *Anne Bogart: Viewpoints*, edited by Michael Bigelow Dixon and Joel A. Smith, Lyme, NH: Smith & Kraus, 1995.
5. See Caroline Nesbitt, "Mother Knows Best: A Working Actress Comes to Grips with Parenthood," *American Theatre*, February 2000, pp. 59–63.

Lois Weaver on Feminist Acting

Excerpted from Elizabeth C. Stroppel, "Acting from Feminist Approaches: Lois Weaver, Anne Bogart, and Shirlene Holmes," *Theatre InSight*, no. 13, Winter 1995, pp. 15–18.

The Triune Voice

Excerpted from "Re/membering Aunt Jemima: Rescuing the Secret Voice," *Women & Performance*, vol. 6, no. 1, issue 11, 1993, pp. 77–83.

1. Sterling Brown in *Poetry of the Negro: 1746–1949*, Arna Bontemp and Langston Hughes, eds., Garden City: Doubleday, 1956, p. vii.
2. The authors wish to acknowledge the initial coinage of the term "emancipatory narratives" by Dr. Eleanor Traynor, Professor of English at Howard University. Dr. Traynor maintains that the mere act of committing a life in slavery to the printed page is an emancipatory act, an act which kills the slave and creates the free person.
3. In this paper we will use the term "bondswoman" or "bondsperson" to describe enslaved Africans and African Americans. We feel this terminology is more descriptive of the condition of the individual than the term "slave."
4. Henry Louis Gates, Jr., *The Signifying Monkey: A Theory of African American Literary Criticism*, Oxford: Oxford University Press, 1988, p. 129.
5. The term "drylongso" is used in African American vernacular to describe an individual who is regular, ordinary, average. See glossary in John Langston Gwalty, *Drylongso*, New York: Random House, 1981.

Anne Bogart—Viewpoints

Excerpted from Elizabeth C. Stroppel, *Theatre InSight*, no. 13, Winter 1995, pp. 18–21.

From Ruby Dee's Memory Book

Excerpted from Ossie Davis and Ruby Dee, *With Ossie and Ruby: In This Life Together*, HarperCollins, 1998, pp. 199, 350, 406, 423. Reprinted by permission of HarperCollins Publishers Inc. Excerpted from Ruby Dee, *My One Good Nerve*, Wiley, 1998. Reprinted with permission of John Wiley & Sons, Inc.

Joanne Woodward

Excerpted and updated from "The Female Actor," in *Women in American Theatre*, 2nd ed., New York: TCG, 1987, pp. 337–338.

1. Colette Dowling, "Joanne Woodward: With *Candida* she has again expanded the role of Woman." *Playbill*, October 1981.
2. Florence Graves and Nina Easton, "Joanne Woodward: On Women and War," *Common Cause Magazine*, November/December 1983.
3. Rex Reed, "The Three Dimensions of Joanne," Leisure Section, *New York Daily News*, October 11, 1981.
4. Graves and Easton, *Common Cause*.
5. Mark Goodman, "The Dominant Member of the Paul Newman Menage Is a Green-eyed Feminist," *People*, July 21, 1975; "National Conference to Prevent Nuclear War," *Los Angeles Times*, May 13, 1985.
6. Rachel Shteir: "Championing Odets, Unfashionable as That Is," *New York Times*, Sunday, April 27, 1997, Section 2, p. 5.

The Integrity of Estelle Parsons

Excerpted from Helen Krich Chinoy, "The Female Actor," *Women in American Theatre*, 2nd ed., TCG, 1987, pp. 338–340 and an interview with Helen Krich Chinoy, April 1998.

1. Stephen Saban, "Estelle Parsons: Oscar in the Closet," *Soho Weekly News*, January

20, 1977, AP News Features, February 14, year missing (cropped clipping).

2. Ron Cohen, "Estelle Parsons' One-Woman Marathon," Arts and People, *Women's Wear Daily*, July 21, 1983: "Guests of the Nation," Great Performances press release, January 29, 1982.

3. Teni Jentz, "Estelle Parsons: A Great Actress Stars in a Major Feminist Play," *West Side TV Shopper*, August 27–September 2, 1983; Cohen, *Women's Wear Daily*.

4. Carol Lawson, "Broadway," *New York Times*, August 6, l983; Jentz, *West Side TV Shopper*.

5. Robin Brantley, "Estelle Parsons' New Role: Director," *New York Times*, May 26, 1978.

6. Martin Burden, "Parsons Keynote Is to Open the Broadway Door to *Women*," *New York Times*, January 4, 1983.

I Love Heroines

Excerpted from Janice Paran, "Heiress Apparent: Cherry Jones Knows How to Make an Entrance," *American Theatre*, May/June 1997, pp. 11–13.

Theatre Role Models

Excerpted from "Theatre Role Models," in *The Advocate*, February 2, 1999, pp. 42–47. *The Advocate* submitted questions, which the two women answered.

Kathleen Chalfant

Excerpted from Robin Pogrebin, "The Creative Life," *New York Times*, October 20, 1998, The Arts, p. 2. Reprinted with permission from the *New York Times* Co.

PLAYWRITING

1. Julia Miles, "Greetings," *Women in Theatre: Mapping the Sources of Power* conference journal, November 1997.

2. Tina Howe, "Keynote Address," *Women in Theatre: Mapping the Sources of Power* conference journal.

3. Most of these playwrights have published collections of their plays, and have been written about in newspapers and magazines. See also Brenda Murphy, ed., *The Cambridge Companion to American Women Playwrights*, Cambridge and New York: Cambridge University Press, 1999; and Jane T. Peterson and Suzanne Bennett, *Women Playwrights of Diversity, A Bio-Bibliographical Sourcebook*, Westport, CT: Greenwood Press, 1997.

4. "A Reunion of Playwrights Shaped in One Crucible," *New York Times*, September 24, 2000, Theatre section, p. 5.

Where Do Plays Come From?

"Sources of Inspiration: Where Do Plays Come From?" *American Theatre*, vol. 15, September 1998, Women in Theatre issue, pp. 32, 33, 81–82.

White Gloves or Bare Hands

Excerpted from Tina Howe, "Women's Work: White Gloves or Bare Hands?" Keynote Speech, 20th Anniversary Women's Project, November 1, 1997, New York, *American Theatre*, vol. 15, September 1998, Women in Theatre issue, pp. 26–29.

Politically Incorrect

Arthur Holmberg, "Through the Eyes of Lolita," Interview with Paula Vogel, A.R.T. News, vol. XX, no. 1, September 1998, Cambridge, MA. *How I Learned to Drive*, which won the Pulitzer Prize for 1998, played at the A.R.T.'s Loeb Theatre that fall.

Margaret Edson

Excerpted from Gail Cameron, "Off-Broadway," *Smith Alumnae Quarterly*, Fall 1999, pp. 22–26.

We Are Not Only Ourselves

Excerpted from a conversation with Tony Kushner, Naomi Wallace's friend and fellow writer, about politics, poetry, class and change. "We Are Not Only Ourselves," published in the program for the premiere of *One Flea Spare* at The Public Theater in New York, 1997.

Why I Write for Television

Theresa Rebeck, "Why I Write for Television," Frontlines, *American Theatre*, December 1995.

DIRECTING AND MANAGING

1. See Dorothy B. Magnus, "Matriarchs of the Regional Theatre," *WAT* p. 203.

2. See also Rebecca Daniels, *Women Stage Directors Speak: Exploring the Influence of Gender on Their Work*, Jefferson, NC: McFarland & Co., 1996; excerpted in *American Theatre*, September 1993, pp. 30, 31, 80.

3. Marie Irene Fornes, known primarily for her important body of dramatic work, stages her own plays and those of others, including Ibsen and Chekhov. She is an influential teacher who had inspired a generation of Latino playwrights. See M. Robinson, *The Other American Drama*, N Y, Cambridge: Cambridge University Press, 1994.

4. See Elizabeth LeCompte in David Savran, *The Wooster Group, 1975–1985: Breaking*

the Rules, Ann Arbor, MI: UMI Research Press, 1986.

5. See Julie Taymor and Eileen Blumenthal, *Julie Taymor: Playing with Fire*, New York: Harry N. Abrams, 1999.

Women at the Helm

Excerpted and adapted from Misha Berson, "Women at the Helm," *American Theatre*, May/June 1994, pp. 14–21.

Marie Irene Fornes

Marie Irene Fornes in conversation with Rod Wooden. From *In Contact with the Gods? Directors Talk Theatre*, by Maria M. Delgado and Paul Heritage, eds., Manchester University Press, 1996. The book, from which this interview is excerpted, grew out of live conversations with international directors held as part of the City of Drama celebrations, Manchester.

Elizabeth LeCompte

Excerpted and adapted from Alisa Solomon, "Doubly Marginalized: Women in the Avant-Garde," in *Women in American Theatre*, 2nd ed., TCG, 1987, pp. 363–366.

Julie Taymor

Excerpted from Sylvianne Gold, "The Possession of Julie Taymor," *American Theatre*, September 1998, pp. 20–25. The article was written shortly after Julie Taymor won the Tony Award for best director of a musical, the first ever awarded to an American woman.

Top Girls

Excerpted from Jennifer L. Dineen, "Top Girls: Three Managers Talk About Work, Power and Prowess," *American Theatre*, Women in Theatre Issue, September 1998, pp. 64–65.

Designing

1. "Directors and Designers Report on Sex Discrimination in the Theatre," League of Professional Theatre Women, March 8, 1983; Marjorie Bradley Kellogg, "Women's Caucus Puzzles over Lack of Set Designers," *Variety*, January 12, 1983.
2. Vanessa James, "Address to the Symposium: Women in Design," April 10, 1994, sponsored by the theatre department of Mount Holyoke College, South Hadley, Massachusetts.
3. Among the many other distinguished participants were Patricia Collins, Judy Dearing, Beverley Emmons, Jane Greenwood, Willa Kim, Adrienne Lobel, Tharon Musser and Jennifer Tipton.
4. See the *New York Times* obituary for Patricia Zipprodt, July 19, 1999, for more information on her career.

When Designers Gather

Edited from transcripts of videotapes of the event made by Mt. Holyoke College, 1994.

Jean Rosenthal's Light

Excerpted from Mary Callahan Boone, "Jean Rosenthal's Light: Making Visible the Magician," *Theatre Topics*, 7:1 (1997), pp. 78–84. Reprinted with permission of the Johns Hopkins University Press.

1. Jean Rosenthal and Lael Wertenbaker, *The Magic of Light: The Craft and Career of Jean Rosenthal, Pioneer in Lighting for the Modern Stage*, Boston: Little, Brown, 1972, p. 55.
2. See Griselda Pollock, *Vision and Difference: Femininity, Feminism and Histories of Art*.
3. *Sunday Mirror Magazine*, April 10, 1955, pp. 10–11.
4. Ellen Violett, "Name in Lights," *Theatre Arts* (November 1950), pp. 24–27.
5. Joan Schenkar, "A New Way to Pay Old Debts: The Playwright Directs Her Own," in Ellen Donkin and Susan Clement, editors, *Upstaging Big Daddy: Directing Theatre as If Gender and Race Matter*, p. 254.
6. Catherine Belsey, *Critical Practice*, Methuen, 1980, pp. 68–69, 97.
7. Stanley McCandless, *A Method of Lighting the Stage*, Theatre Arts Books, 1958, p. 8.

Re-Visioning Scenography

Excerpted from Delores Ringer, "Re-Visioning Scenography," in *Theatre and Feminist Aesthetics*, edited by Karen Laughlin and Catherine Schuler, Madison, NJ: Fairleigh Dickinson University Press, 1995. Reprinted with permission from Associated University Presses.

1. See Jean Baker Miller, *Toward a New Psychology of Women*, Beacon Press, 1976.
2. John Berger, *Ways of Seeing*, Viking, 1973, p. 47.
3. Rosemary Betterton, "How do Women Look?" in *Visibly Female*, edited by Hilary Robinson, Camden Press, 1987, pp. 250–71.

Organizations

Jane Alexander

Excerpted from Marilyn Stasio, "Jane Alexander: She Stoops to Conquer," *American Theatre*, September 1998, pp. 55, 60, 82.

1998: Year of the Woman?

Julia Miles, Introduction to Women in Theatre issue of *American Theatre*, September 1998, p. 19.

DOCUMENTING AMERICA

1. See Alice McDonnell Robinson, "Mercy Warren: Satirist of the Revolution," *WAT*, p. 122.
2. Emily Mann, interviewed in Kathleen Betsko and Rachel Koenig, *Interviews with Contemporary Women Playwrights*, New York: William Morrow, 1987, pp. 258-271.
3. Sally Burke, *American Feminist Playwrights*, New York: Twayne Publishers, 1997, p. 182. See also Emily Mann in David Savran, *In Their Own Words*, New York: TCG, 1988.
4. "The Female Actor," *Women in American Theatre*, 2nd ed., New York: TCG, 1987, p. 331ff.
5. Elin Diamond, "Toward a Gestic Feminist Criticism," *WAT* p. 349.
6. Vivian Patraka Interview, "Robbie McCauley: Obsessing in Public," in *A Sourcebook of Feminist Theatre and Performance*, Carol Martin, ed., London and New York: Routledge, 1996, p. 205. On p. 233, McCauley describes her community collaborations as "part of a larger project of interviewing people in various places about historical events related to civil rights." See also Raewyn Whyte, "Robbie McCauley: Speaking History Other-Wise," in *Acting Out: Feminist Performances*, Lynda Hart and Peggy Phelan, eds., Ann Arbor: University of Michigan Press, 1993, pp. 277–294. I talked with Robbie McCauley in 1999.
7. Anna Deavere Smith, Introduction, *Fires in the Mirror*, Anchor Books, 1992.
8. Cornel West, Foreword, *Fires in the Mirror*, p. xvii.
9. Quotations from Scott T. Cummings, "Get Budged!" *American Theatre*, December 1998, p. 68. See also Carol Martin, "Anna Deavere Smith: The Word Becomes You," in Carol Martin, *A Sourcebook of Feminist Theatre and Performance*, London and New York: Routledge, pp. 125–204.
10. See Dorinne Kondo, "(Re)Visions of Race: Contemporary Race Theory and the Cultural Politics of Racial Crossover in Documentary Theater" in *Theatre Journal*, vol. 52, no. 1, March 2000, pp. 81–107.
11. See Ben Brantley's review of Anna Deavere Smith's *House Arrest* in the *New York Times*, March 27, 2000, p. E1.
12. "Anne Bogart on Directing," *Dramatics*, May 1995, theatre clipping collection, New York Public Library for the Performing Arts.
13. Tadashi Suzuki, "Creating a New/Different America" in *Anne Bogart: Viewpoints*, Michael Bigelow Dixon and Joel A. Smith, eds., Lyme, NH: Smith & Kraus, 1995, p. 85.
14. Anne Bogart quoted by Mel Gussow in *Anne Bogart: Viewpoints*, p. 146.
15. Porter Anderson, "The Meat of the Medium: Anne Bogart and the American Avant-Garde" in *Anne Bogart: Viewpoints*, p. 115.
16. Tina Landau, "Source-Work, the Viewpoints and Composition: What Are They?" in *Anne Bogart: Viewpoints*, p. 25.
17. John Istel, "Thoroughly Modest Master," *The Village Voice*, February 21, 1995, New York Public Library for the Performing Arts.
18. Alisa Solomon, "Bogart's Elegy," *The Village Voice*, p. 82, circa 1994, theatre clipping collection, New York Public Library for the Performing Arts.
19. Paula Vogel, "Anne Bogart and the New Play," in *Anne Bogart: Viewpoints*, p. 91. Bogart was awarded a 1990 Obie Award for her direction of Vogel's *The Baltimore Waltz*.

Having Her Say

Excerpted from "Emily Mann: Having Her Say," Interview by Melissa Salz Bernstein in *American Drama,* Spring 1997, vol. 6, no. 2, pp. 81–89.

Sharing the Work

Excerpted from Robbie McCauley, "Thoughts on My Career, *The Other Weapon* and Other Projects" in *Performance and Cultural Politics*, edited by Elin Diamond, Routledge, 1996, pp. 267–282.

Anna Deavere Smith's House Arrest

Excerpted from Eva Wielgat Barnes, "Anna Deavere Smith's *House Arrest*: First Edition," *TheatreForum* (www.theatreforum.org), no. 13, Summer/Fall 1998, pp. 86–92.

Viewpoints on Theatre Now

Excerpted and adapted from the typescript of Anne Bogart, "Viewpoints on Theatre Now," the Second Annual Margarita Hopkins Rand Distinguished Lecture, Theatre Department, University of Massachusetts, Amherst, April 17, 1999.

BIOGRAPHIES

DORIS ABRAMSON, professor emeritus of theatre at the University of Massachusetts, Amherst, is the author of *Negro Playwrights in American Theatre, 1925–1959*, as well as studies of early black women playwrights.

LOIS ADLER, professor of theatre, Manhattan Community College, is a former actress who coordinates a new theatre program. A longer version of this paper was read at the American Theatre Association, 1977.

ROBERT C. ALLEN is professor of American studies, history and communication studies at the University of North Carolina at Chapel Hill.

BOBBI AUSUBEL is an acting teacher, director and playwright. She was chair of the theatre division of Boston Conservatory of Arts for fifteen years, and codirector of Caravan Theater of Boston for twelve years.

ROSEMARIE K. BANK is a professor of theatre history and criticism at Kent State University, Ohio. She has published articles and reviews in *Theatre Journal, Nineteenth-Century Theatre Research, Theatre History Studies* and many others.

EVA WIELGAT BARNES teaches speech and dialects at the University of California, San Diego, and coaches in professional theatres throughout the country.

SARAH CURRAN BARRETT was formerly the coeditor of Smith College's *Alumnae Quarterly*, and is now periodicals editor for the *College Street Journal* and *Vista* at Mount Holyoke College.

SUZANNE BENNETT, a director and dramaturg, is artistic associate at the Women's Project and Productions in New York.

MARILYN BERGER is a journalist who interviewed Lillian Hellman for a PBS series in 1981.

MELISSA SALZ BERNSTEIN wrote her dissertation for the University of Colorado at Boulder on "Theatre of Testimony: The Works of Emily Mann, Anna Deavere Smith and Spalding Gray."

MISHA BERSON is a theatre critic for the *Seattle Times* and creator of the three-volume series *The San Francisco Stage*. She is also the editor of *Between Two Worlds: Contemporary Asian American Plays*.

KATHLEEN BETSKO is a playwright and the coeditor, with Rachel Koenig, of *Interviews with Contemporary Women Playwrights*.

JAMES H. BIERMAN, professor of theatre arts at the University of California at Santa Cruz, has written extensively about popular entertainment for such journals as *The Yale Review, The Drama Review* and the *SoHo News*.

RHONDA BLAIR, professor in the division of theatre at Southern Methodist University, was president of the Women in Theatre Program and was on the editorial board of *Theatre Topics*. She has been published in *Women in Performance* and *Theatre Topics* and has translated plays from Russian. She is also an actor and a director.

MARTHA BOESING, formerly the artistic director of At the Foot of the Mountain in Minneapolis, is a director and playwright with a long list of credits. She was awarded the Bush Grant for playwrights in 1984 and an NEA Fellowship for 1986–87. Members of the collective who created *The Story of a Mother* in 1977 and 1978 were Martha Boesing, Aurora Bingham, Cecilia Lee, Jan Magrane, Phyllis Jane Rose and Robyn Samuels.

ANNE BOGART, director, teacher and innovator of "Viewpoints" training, was honored in 1995 as the focus of Actors Theatre of Louisville Modern Masters series.

MARY CALLAHAN BOONE, a graduate of the doctoral program in theatre at Bowling Green State University, wrote about lighting designer Jean Rosenthal for *Theatre Topics*.

GRAYCE SUSAN BURIAN was the director of the theatre program at Schenectady Community College for many years. This paper, presented at the Popular Culture Association, 1978, is based in part on her acquaintance with Aileen Stanley, who provided a rich store of personal materials, also used in a 1986 article for *Theatre File*, London.

GAIL CAMERON, a Smith College graduate, is Atlanta correspondent for *People* magazine. She has worked for *Life* magazine and has written for *McCall's*, *New York* magazine and *Ladies' Home Journal*.

CHARLOTTE CANNING, associate professor of theatre history and criticism at the University of Texas, Austin, has published widely on feminist theory and performance in journals and anthologies; she is president of the American Society for Theatre Research, and a past president of the Women and Theatre Program of ATHE.

SUE-ELLEN CASE, professor and chair of critical studies in the theatre department, University of California, Los Angeles, is a former editor of *Theatre Journal*. Her most recent book is *The Domain-Matrix: Performing Lesbian at the End of Print Culture*. She has written many articles and also edited a number of volumes, including *Performing Feminisms: Feminist Critical Theory and Theatre*, and with Janelle Reinelt, *The Performance of Power: Theatrical Discourse and Politics*; *The Divided Home/Land*, plays by German women; and *Split Britches: Lesbian Practice/Feminist Performance*.

CLAUDETTE CHARBONNEAU was a founding member of the New York Feminist Theatre. Charbonneau has taught women's studies at SUNY Stony Brook and Brooklyn College, and as a visiting professor at University of Tampere, Finland.

GAY GIBSON CIMA is a professor in the English department of Georgetown University. She is the author of *Performing Women*, 1993, and has published articles in *Theatre Journal* and *Theatre Survey*.

BREENA CLARKE, writer, actor and journalist, has worked Off-Broadway and is the founder and artistic director of The Narratives Performing Company, as well as assistant to the deputy managing editor of *Time* magazine and associate editor of *Black Masks*.

PEARL CLEAGE is the author of the widely performed *Flyin' West* and *Blues for an Alabama Sky*, as well as essays and novels. Her work in Atlanta is discussed in this volume in Cindy Lutenbacher's study of artists in the South.

TOBY COLE is the editor of *Acting: A Handbook of the Stanislavski Method* and *Playwrights on Playwriting*, and the coeditor (with Helen Krich Chinoy) of *Actors on Acting: The Theories, Techniques and Practices of the World's Great Actors Told in Their Own Words* and *Directors on Directing: A Source Book of the Modern Theatre*.

PATRICIA COLLINS, lighting designer, has designed many major Broadway productions, including *The Sisters Rosensweig*, *The Heidi Chronicles* and *I'm Not Rappaport*, for which she received a Tony Award. She has worked in London and many regional theatres, and has designed extensively for opera.

ROSEMARY K. CURB has published widely on feminist and black theatre in *Chrysalis, Modern Drama, Melus Journal, Women's Review of Books*. With Nancy Manahan she coedited *Lesbian Nuns: Breaking Silence* (Warner, 1990).

MARY JULIA CURTIS, professor of dramatic art, University of Nebraska at Omaha, read a longer version of this paper at the American Theatre Association, 1977.

RUBY DEE was the first black woman to appear in major roles at the American Shakespeare Festival in Stratford, Connecticut. She starred on Broadway in the original production of *A Raisin in the Sun*, in 1959, and received an Obie Award for her performance in *Boesman and Lena* in 1971, and a Drama Desk award for *Wedding Band* in 1973. She and her late husband, the actor Ossie Davis, were active in the American civil rights movement for many years. In 1994, Dee and Davis were honored by the Kennedy Center for their achievements in the performing arts.

STEPHANIE DE PUE interviewed Lillian Hellman for the *Cleveland Plain Dealer* in 1975.

ELIN DIAMOND, professor of English at Rutgers University, is also the author of *Pinter's Comic Play* and editor of *Performance and Cultural Politics, 1996*. Her many articles have been published in *Modern Drama, TDR, Art and Cinema* and *Theatre Journal*.

GLENDA DICKERSON, director, writer, folklorist and educator, is professor of theatre at the University of Michigan. She has worked on and Off-Broadway, regionally and internationally, and has adapted vehicles for the stage.

JENNIFER L. DINEEN was formerly director of management programs for TCG.

JILL DOLAN holds the Z. T. Scott Family Chair at the University of Texas at Austin, was president of the Association for Theatre in Higher Education and chaired the Women and Theatre Program. She has been published in many journals, and also wrote *Presence and Desire: Essays on Gender, Sexuality, Performance.*

GRESDNA DOTY, professor emeritus of speech at Lousiana State University, is the author of *The Career of Mrs. Anne Brunton Merry in the American Theatre* and *Inside the Royal Court Theatre, 1956–1981,* coedited with Bill Harbin. She has written many articles on American and British theatre in *Theatre Survey,* the *Quarterly Journal of Speech* and other journals.

CHRISTINE DOUDNA is a journalist who interviewed Lillian Hellman for *Rolling Stone* magazine in 1977.

DAVID DOWNS, associate professor in the theatre department of Northwestern University, studied with Alvina Krause in Bloomsburg in 1972.

SYLVIE DRAKE, a former theatre critic for the *Los Angeles Times,* is the director of publications for the Denver Center for the Performing Arts and an artistic associate of the Denver Center Theatre Company. She interviewed Lillian Hellman for the *Los Angeles Times* in 1981.

FAYE E. DUDDEN is professor of history at Colgate University. Her books have won wide praise, including the 1994 George Freedley Memorial Award of the Theatre History Association.

NORA EPHRON is a screenwriter, director and producer whose films include *Silkwood, When Harry Met Sally, Sleepless in Seattle, Mixed Nuts, Michael* and *You've Got Mail.* She is also an acclaimed journalist and novelist. She interviewed Lillian Hellman for the *New York Times Book Review* in 1973.

KAREN FINLEY, performer, artist and writer, premiered her script at The Kitchen in New York City, December 1986, and performed it widely in the United States and in major European cities. She gained wide attention as one of the NEA Four whose grants from the National Endowment for the Arts were denied after congressional complaints that their work was obscene. The Supreme Court ruled against their legal challenge.

WINONA L. FLETCHER is professor emeritus of theatre/drama and of Afro-American studies at Indiana State University, where she began teaching in 1979. Prior to that, she was professor and coordinator of speech/theatre at Kentucky State University, Frankfurt, for twenty-five years. She has done important research on the Negro Units of the Federal Theatre Project.

MARIA IRENE FORNES is the author of more than forty plays, including *Fefu and Her Friends, Eyes on the Harem, The Danube, Sarita, Mud, Abingdon Square, The Conduct of Life* and *Letters from Cuba,* all of which received Obie awards. In 2003, she received the first MACHA Award for outstanding achievement in mentoring emerging Latina writers.

JEANIE FORTE, who earned her Ph.D. degree at the University of Washington, is a director and dramaturg, has taught at various colleges and universities, and is drama instructor at Jordan Middle School, Palo Alto, California. She has been published in *Theatre, Modern Drama, Theatre Journal* and *Women in Performance.*

RACHEL FRANCE, editor of *A Century of Plays by American Women,* wrote this paper as part of her larger study, *The Drama of Sex: Apropos of Women and the American Theatre.*

SUE FROST, whom Helen K. Chinoy is happy to claim as one of her own former students, is associate producer of Connecticut's Goodspeed Opera House.

PATTI P. GILLESPIE, professor emeritus of theatre, University of Maryland, College Park, has published *The Enjoyment of Theatre,* 5th edition, and *Western Theatre: Revolution and Revival,* both with Kenneth M. Cameron, as well as many essays in *American Playwrights Since 1945, Journal of Aesthetic Education* and *Text and Performance Quarterly.* An article on marriage as performed in Africa and African drama written by Anglophone women was published in *McNeese Review.*

CAROL GILLIGAN, who has spent most of her professional life studying the psychological development of girls and women, rocked the world when she discovered that none of the studies that defined "human" psychology included women. Her seminal work on the loss of self-esteem and shifts to voicelessness by girls between the ages of 11 and 14 (*In a Different Voice*) has made her one of the most respected and controversial leaders in her field.

SYLVIANNE GOLD is a New York–based writer on the arts. She wrote on Julie Taymor for *American Theatre* magazine in 1998.

LOIS C. GOTTLIEB, who teaches in the department of English, University of Guelph, is the author of *Rachel Crothers*.

PAULINE HAHN, an actress of stage, screen and television, is visiting professor of theatre at Vassar College and is writing a dissertation on Hallie Flanagan at Columbia University.

LAURILYN HARRIS, professor of theatre history and dramaturgy at Washington State University, has published articles in *Theatre Research International*, *Theatre Annual*, *Nineteenth-Century Theatre Research* and *Theatre History Studies*.

LOUISE HECK-RABI, librarian, teacher and playwright, published *Women Filmmakers: A Critical Reception* in 1984. Her Ph.D. dissertation at Wayne State University, 1976, was on Sophie Treadwell. Quotations from Treadwell's manuscripts and letters are used by permission of the Special Collections, University of Arizona Library, Tuscon.

LILLIAN HELLMAN was a playwright whose works include *Another Part of the Forest*, *The Autumn Garden*, *The Children's Hour*, *Days to Come*, *The Little Foxes*, *The Lark* (an adaptation of Jean Anouilh's *L'Alouette*), *The Searching Wind*, *Toys in the Attic* and *Watch on the Rhine*. She also worked as a journalist, screenwriter and political activist, and was well known for refusing to name names when summoned before the House Un-American Activities Committee in 1952. Hellman died in 1984.

SHIRLEE HENNIGAN, professor emeritus, drama/speech department, Lewis-Clark State College, Idaho, wrote her Ph.D. dissertation at Washington State University on women directors.

ERROL HILL was the Willard Professor of Drama and Oratory at Dartmouth College for thirty-five years. A director, playwright and scholar, he was the author of numerous publications, including *The Theatre of Black Americans* and *Shakespeare in Sable,* in which the piece excerpted here first appeared. He died in 2003.

ARTHUR HOLMBERG is the literary manager of American Repertory Theatre in Cambridge, Massachusetts.

TINA HOWE is a playwright whose works include *The Nest, Birth and After Birth, Museum, The Art of Dining, Painting Churches, Coastal Disturbances, Approaching Zanzibar, One Shoe Off* and *Pride's Crossing.* Her awards include the New York Drama Critics Circle Award for Best Play for *Pride's Crossing*, an Obie for Distinguished Playwriting, an Outer Critics Circle Award, a Rockefeller grant, two NEA fellowships, a Guggenheim fellowship, an Academy of Arts and Letters Award in Literature, and an American Theatre Wing Award. In 1987 she received a Tony Award nomination for Best Play for *Coastal Disturbances.* She has served on the council of the Dramatists Guild since 1990.

CLAUDIA D. JOHNSON, professor emeritus of the English department, University of Alabama, has published six articles and three books on American theatre, including *Shakespearean Burlesques, Memoirs of the Nineteenth Century Theatre* and *American Actress,* of which the article included here became the first chapter.

CHERRY JONES received the Tony Award for Best Actress in a Play in 2005, for her performance in *Doubt*, and in 1995, for *The Heiress.* She was also nominated for the Best Actress Tony in 1991, for her performance in *Our Country's Good*, and in 2000, for *A Moon for the Misbegotten.* Her other Broadway credits include *Stepping Out, The Night of the Iguana, Major Barbara* and *Imaginary Friends.*

PEGGY CLARK KELLEY is a distinguished lighting designer whose credits include the Broadway productions of *Brigadoon, Gentlemen Prefer Blondes, Wonderful Town, No Time for Sergeants, Auntie Mame, Mary, Mary, Bye, Bye, Birdie* and *Flower Drum Song.* In 1968 she was elected the first woman president of the United Scenic Artists. In 1977 her alma mater, Smith College, awarded her a medal, citing her "pioneering achievement in a predominately male profession." The "Reminiscences" included here were edited by Helen Krich Chinoy from an interview conducted by Jacqueline Van Voris for *Mosaic,* a study of Smith College alumnae on the occasion of the college's one-hundredth anniversary in 1975.

MARJORIE KELLOGG has designed sets for more than twenty Broadway shows, including *American Buffalo, The Best Little Whorehouse in Texas* and *Any Given Day*. She was resident designer for Tony Randall's National Actors Theatre, and designed for Circle in the Square, The Public Theater, Manhattan Theatre Club, Playwrights Horizons, Roundabout Theatre, CSC and the Talking Band. In 1995 she received the Mary L. Murphy Award for excellence in design. She has taught at Princeton University, Columbia University and Colgate University, and she is the author of four science fiction novels.

RACHEL KOENIG is a playwright and the coeditor, with Kathleen Betsko, of *Interviews with Contemporary Women Playwrights*.

DORINNE KONDO, professor of anthropology and American studies and ethnicity and director of Asian American studies, University of Southern California, is the author of *Crafting Selves: Power, Gender, and Discourses of Identity in a Japanese Workplace*, which won the 1999 J. I. Stanley Book Prize. She was the dramaturg for Anna Deavere Smith's *Twilight: Los Angeles, 1992* at Mark Taper Forum and for filming for PBS, and she was represented as a character in the Broadway version of the play.

TONY KUSHNER is a playwright whose works include *A Bright Room Called Day; Angels in America, Parts One and Two; Slavs!; Homebody/Kabul; Caroline, or Change*, a musical with composer Jeanine Tesori; and *Brundibár*, an opera with Maurice Sendak. He is the recipient of many awards, including the Pulitzer Prize for Drama, two Tony awards for best play, three Obie awards for playwriting, and an Emmy Award.

CAROLINE J. DODGE LATTA, acting teacher at Columbia College, Chicago, and artistic director of the Studio Theatre, has written entries for *Notable Women in American Theatre*, and is on the Joseph Jefferson Committee in Chicago.

DINAH L. LEAVITT, associate professor and coordinator of the theatre program at Fort Lewis College, Colorado, published *Feminist Theatre Groups* in 1980, from which her article in this collection is adapted. The former members of Lavender Cellar Theatre gathered one day in summer, 1977, and allowed the author to glimpse what their theatre had been like.

JOSEPHINE LEE, associate professor in the department of English, University of Minnesota, has served as book review editor of *Theatre Journal*.

SUSAN DYE LEE, whose Ph.D. dissertation at Northwestern University focused on the WCTU, has studied the links among temperance, suffrage and religion.

KRISTIN LINKLATER is an actress, director and teacher of widely used voice techniques, which she wrote about in *Freeing the Natural Voice*. She is the cofounder with Tina Packer of Shakespeare & Company.

DEBORAH LUBAR is a performer, writer, teacher and holistic therapist now based in Vermont. She was a tenured professor in the theatre department of Smith College and also taught at Oberlin College, Douglass College and the California Institute of Integral Studies. She has given solo performances of her original scripts, some of which are based on research and therapy with women in Israel, Palestine and Bosnia.

CINDY LUTENBACHER received her Ph.D. in theatre and drama at Northwestern University, and is assistant professor of English at Morehouse College in Atlanta. This essay is excerpted from a paper presented at the 1987 Themes in Drama conference, Riverside, California.

WENDY MACLEOD is the James E. Michael Playwright-in-Residence and an associate professor of drama at Kenyon College. Her plays include *The House of Yes, Sin, Schoolgirl Figure, The Water Children, Juvenalia* and *Things Being What They Are*.

PHYLLIS MAEL, associate professor of English, Pasadena City College, California, has published articles on contemporary drama by women in *Chrysalis, Frontiers, Kansas Quarterly* and *Dictionary of Literary Biography*.

DOROTHY B. MAGNUS was head of the speech department and theatre director at Winona State University, Minnesota. A longer version of this paper was delivered at the American Theatre Association Bicentennial Convention, August 1975, in Washington, D.C.

SYDNÉ MAHONE is a dramaturg, teacher and writer. She was director of play development at Crossroads Theatre from 1985 to 1997. She edited the joint autobiography of Ruby Dee and Ossie Davis, from which we have also drawn some excerpts for a selection on Ruby Dee in this collection.

KAREN MALPEDE, cofounder with Burl Hash of the New Cycle Theatre in 1977, has been a passionate spokesperson for feminist theatre and the peace movement. She has challenged the avant-garde theatre to emulate feminist theatre's commitment to community and regeneration, inspiring collective projects and providing leadership through her books and plays: *Three Works by the Open Theater, People's Theatre in Amerika* and *Women in Theatre: Compassion and Hope,* all volumes edited by her, and *A Monster Has Stolen the Sun and Other Plays,* a collection of her plays published in 1987 by The Marlboro Press.

EMILY MANN is a playwright and director who writes unusual plays such as *Still Life* and *Execution of Justice* that are, like *Having Our Say,* based on extensive research from which she develops her "theatre of testimony." She is artistic director of the McCarter Theatre in Princeton, New Jersey, and the recipient of many awards and honors.

DEB MARGOLIN, cofounder of the Split Britches Theatre Company, is a playwright and performance artist who has performed and taught workshops throughout the United States and Europe. Her performance pieces are published under the title *Of All the Nerve,* London and New York, Cassell Press, 1998.

BILLIE MCCANTS, a freelance writer from Michigan, interviewed Alvina Krause in Bloomsburg, Pennsylvania, in 1978 for her article "Eternal Astonishment," from which this segment is excerpted.

ROBBIE MCCAULEY is a celebrated playwright, performance artist and theatre director. Her play *Sally's Rape* received a 1992 Obie Award for Best New American Play. She is an associate professor of performing arts at Emerson College.

MURIEL MCKENNA, who was a theatre major at the University of Wisconsin, is studying solo theatre.

JULIA MILES, founding artistic director of New York's Women's Project & Productions and "trailblazer in the creation of theatre for women," is an actress, director and producer best known for her dedication to new talent. As associate director at the American Place Theatre, she became aware of the underrepresentation of women writers. With a 1978 Ford Foundation Grant she created the Women's Theatre Project, which has become one of the most important resources nurturing innumerable playwrights and directors of distinction. The company now has its own theatre, named for Miles, dedicated to women's creativity.

JEANNE-MARIE A. MILLER, professor of theatre at Howard University, published "Images of Black Women in Plays by Black Playwrights" in *College Language Association Journal,* vol. 20 (June 1977).

ELIZABETH PAYNE MOORE wrote a Ph.D. dissertation on Margaret Dreier Robins and the Women's Trade Union League at the University of Illinois-Chicago Circle.

HONOR MOORE, playwright and critic, published the anthology *The New Women's Theatre* in 1977 and a collection of poems in 1987. She published *The White Blackbird,* a biography of her grandmother, Margarett Sargent, in 1996.

CHERRÍE MORAGA was playwright-in-residence at Brava! For Women in the Arts. Her plays have been collected in *Heroes and Saints & Other Plays* and been performed widely across the country. She edited *This Bridge Called My Back: Writings by Radical Women of Color,* which won the Before Columbus Book Award in 1986.

MARLIE MOSES, professor of English, Rhode Island Junior College, read a version of this paper at the American Theatre Association, 1977, and had a paper published in *Dramatics,* 1983.

BILL MOYERS is a journalist and commentator who has received more than thirty Emmys and numerous other awards for his work in television. He served as White House Press Secretary under Lyndon Johnson, and in 1986 he formed his own company, Public Affairs Television. He conducted a television interview with Lillian Hellman in 1974.

VICKI NOLAN is managing director of the Yale Repertory Theatre in New Haven.

TINA PACKER, actress, director and teacher, is the founder and guiding spirit of Shakespeare & Company at The Mount in Lenox, Massachusetts, a major company based on the unique training developed by Packer and Kristin Linklater.

JANICE PARAN is a New Jersey–based writer and formerly resident dramaturg at Princeton's McCarter Theatre.

SUZAN-LORI PARKS is a playwright whose work includes *Topdog/Underdog*, which won the 2002 Pulitzer Prize for Drama; *In the Blood*; *Fucking A*; *Venus*; *The America Play*; *Imperceptible Mutabilities in the Third Kingdom*, among others. She is the recipient of numerous awards and grants, including several Obie awards and the 2001 MacArthur "Genius" Grant. In 2003, she published her first novel, *Getting Mother's Body* (Random House, New York).

CYNTHIA PATTERSON wrote about the National Women's Party and feminism for her Ph.D. thesis in history at Northwestern University.

SUSAN PEARSON-DAVIS, chair of the theatre and dance department, University of New Mexico, Albuquerque, wrote this essay for her critical anthology of the works of Suzan Zeder, *Wish in One Hand Spit in the Other*, published by Anchorage Press in 1990.

LAURA PENN is managing director of Seattle's Intiman Theatre.

BEVERLEY BYERS PEVITTS, president of Park University in Parkville, Missouri, was formerly professor and chair of theatre at the University of Nevada, Las Vegas, and president of the Association for Theatre in Higher Education. She edited the special "Women in Theatre" issue of *Theatre Annual* in 1986.

ROBIN POGREBIN is a culture reporter at the *New York Times*.

THERESA REBECK's plays *Spike Heels, The Family of Mann* and *Loose Knit* have all been produced in New York by Second Stage. She has written for and produced many television shows, including *NYPD Blue, L.A. Law, Law & Order* and *Brooklyn Bridge*.

JANELLE G. REINELT was a professor of theatre and dance at California State University, Davis, an editor of *Theatre Journal,* and vice president of the International Society for Theatre. Her books include *After Brecht: British Epic Theatre,* and she has edited *Crucibles of Crisis: Performing Social Change and Critical Theory and Performance* with Joseph Roach and *The Performance of Power: Theatrical Discourse and Politics, 1991.* With Sue-Ellen Case, she was editor of *Theatre Journal* and has been published in *Modern Drama, Yale Theatre, Women and Performance* and *Brecht Yearbook*.

J. DENNIS RICH taught in the department of communications and theatre, University of Illinois, Chicago Circle, and managed the Circle Theatre.

SANDRA L. RICHARDS, professor of theatre and former chair of the African American studies program at Northwestern University, has published *Ancient Songs Set Ablaze: The Theatre of Femi Osofisan* and publishes on theatre and drama in the African diaspora and Africa.

DELORES RINGER is associate professor of scenography in the department of theatre and film at the University of Kansas.

ALICE MCDONNELL ROBINSON, associate professor of theatre, University of Maryland, Baltimore, has published in *Players Magazine* and *Educational Theatre Journal* and is co-editor with Milly Barranger and Vera Mowry Roberts of *Notable Women in American Theatre,* 1987.

BARI ROLFE, a well-known teacher of mask work and commedia dell'arte, and movement for actors, was the author of *Mimes on Miming, Movement for Period Plays* and *Commedia dell' Arte*.

BETSY RYAN taught theatre at the University of Illinois and the University of Iowa and is presently managing editor of a professional journal at UCLA and an independent scholar in theatre.

ROBERT A. SCHANKE was director of theatre at Central College in Pella, Iowa. His books include *Eva Le Gallienne: A Bio-Bibliography, Shattered Applause: The Lives of Eva Le Gallienne, Ibsen in America: A Century of Change,* and *Passing Performances: Queer Readings of Leading Players in American Theatre History,* which he edited with Kim Marra.

RICHARD SCHECHNER is a professor of performance studies at New York University, and the author of several books, including *Between Theatre and Anthropology, Environmental Theater* and *Performance Studies: An Introduction*.

REBECCA SCHNEIDER has published in *The Drama Review* and *Women in Performance* and has taught at New York University, Yale University, Dartmouth College and Hampshire College.

CATHLEEN SCHURR was a founding board member of WAFT and a founding member of what is now called *Three for the Show*. She is an actress and author.

SONDRA SEGAL, actor and teacher, is co-artistic director of Women's Experimental Theatre and a creator of video documentaries.

YVONNE SHAFER, who teaches at St. John's University, has published many articles and several books, including *Approaches to Teaching Ibsen's* A Doll House, *Henrik Ibsen: Life, Work and Criticism, August Wilson: A Research and Production Sourcebook* and *American Women Playwrights, 1900–1950.*

ROBERTA SKLAR, director and teacher, was codirector of the Open Theater with Joseph Chaikin; she is co-artistic director of Women's Experimental Theatre and former Director of Public Affairs in the New York City Department of Cultural Affairs.

ANNA DEAVERE SMITH is an actress, playwright and solo artist. The Outer Critics Circle awarded her a Special Achievement Award for Documenting and Interpreting the Events of Our Time in a Unique Theatrical Form. She was awarded a MacArthur "Genius" grant in 1996 and is the director of the Institute on the Arts and Civic Dialogue at Harvard University.

ALISA SOLOMON is a journalist and theatre critic in New York and a professor of English at the City University of New York. She was the dramaturg for the Mabou Mines *Lear* production. In 1999 she won the George Jean Nathan award for criticism for *Re-dressing the Canon.*

SUSAN SPECTOR, assistant professor of speech and theatre at Baruch College, City University of New York, wrote a Ph.D. dissertation on Uta Hagen at New York University.

STARHAWK, peace activist, feminist therapist, teacher, and witch, is the author of *Dreaming the Dark* and *The Spiritual Dance: A Rebirth of the Ancient Religion of the Great Goddess,* 1979, from which her selection in this volume is taken.

MARILYN STASIO, one of the few major women theatre critics in the U.S., has written for many journals and newspapers and is also the author of *Broadway's Beautiful Losers* (1972).

KAREN STEIN, professor of English and women's studies at the University of Rhode Island, has published in *Modern Drama, Black American Literature,* and elsewhere.

JUDITH LOUISE STEPHENS, professor of humanities and theatre, Pennsylvania State University, Schuylkill campus, wrote her Ph.D. dissertation on female characters in Pulitzer Prize plays, 1918–1975, at Kent State, and has published articles in *Theatre Journal* and *Theatre Annual.*

ELIZABETH C. STROPPEL is an associate professor in the department of communication, William Paterson University, Wayne, New Jersey, where she serves as director of theatre studies. The interviews included here, originally printed in *Theatre Insight,* are excerpts from two of the one hundred women artists that she interviewed in the 1990s for her dissertation "Acting Theory, Training, and Practice from Feminist Perspectives." She received her Ph.D. from the University of Texas at Austin.

ESTHER BETH SULLIVAN is associate professor and director of undergraduate studies in the department of theatre, Ohio State University. She has been assistant editor of *Theatre Journal* and has been published in *Theatre Journal, Theatre Studies* and *Literature in Performance.* She also works in dramaturgy, direction, performance and design.

JULIET TAYLOR was interviewed by Helen Krich Chinoy, December 1979. It was especially gratifying for Professor Chinoy to explore the career of casting director with her former Smith College student.

BARBARA ANN TEER, founder and director of the National Black Theatre, was interviewed in *Women in Theatre: Compassion & Hope,* edited by Karen Malpede and published in 1983.

MEGAN TERRY, the author of more than 50 plays, was a founding member of the Open Theater and a playwright-in-residence at the Omaha Magic Theatre. In 1983 she received the Dramatists Guild's Committee for Women Annual Award in recognition of her "work as a writer of conscience and controversy and [her] many lasting contributions to the theatre."

STEPHEN URKOWITZ, associate professor of English at Hofstra University, published *Shakespeare's Revision of King Lear* in 1980.

PAULA VOGEL is a playwright whose works include *The Baltimore Waltz, Hot 'N' Throbbing, Desdemona, And Baby Makes Seven, The Oldest Profession, The Mineola Twins, The Long Christmas Ride Home* and *How I*

Learned to Drive, which received the 1998 Pulitzer Prize for Drama, an Obie, the Lortel, Drama Desk, Outer Critics Circle and New York Drama Critics Circle awards. She is a professor of creative writing at Brown University, where she directs the MFA playwriting program.

PATRIZIA VON BRANDENSTEIN, production designer, won an academy award for *Amadeus*. Her credits cover twenty major films, including *Chorus Line, Silkwood* and *Six Degrees of Separation*.

NAOMI WALLACE's play *One Flea Spare* won the Susan Smith Blackburn prize, an Obie Award, the Joseph A. Kesselring Award and was one of *Time* magazine's ten best plays of the year. In 1999 Wallace was awarded a MacArthur "genius" grant.

WENDY WASSERSTEIN is a playwright whose works include *Uncommon Women and Others, Isn't It Romantic, Old Money, The Sisters Rosensweig, An American Daughter* and *The Heidi Chronicles*, which received the 1989 Pulitzer Prize for Drama and a 1989 Tony Award for Best Play. Her plays have also received the New York Drama Critics Circle Award, the Drama Desk Award and the Outer Critics Circle Award.

BARI WATKINS earned her Ph.D. in history at Yale and served as dean or provost at various universities after teaching American history and directing the Program on Women at Northwestern University. She currently teaches at Ohio University–Lancaster.

LOIS WEAVER, along with Peggy Shaw and Deb Margolin, comprised the very influential Split Britches feminist company, was part of the Spiderwoman group and was co-artistic director of London's Gay Sweatshop theatre.

ALBERT WERTHEIM, professor of English at Indiana University, has published widely on Shakespeare, Renaissance and Restoration theatre as well as on modern British and American theatre.

MARGARET WILKERSON, associate professor in the department of Afro-American studies, University of California, edited the anthology *9 Plays by Black Women,* 1986.

MARY CATHERINE WILKINS was a founding board member of WAFT and a founding member of Back Alley Theatre. She works in the arts and humanities programming department of the Public Broadcasting Service.

LUCY WINER was a founding member of the New York Feminist Theatre. She has completed three prize-winning films, including the most recent, a documentary of male attitudes, *Rate It X*, with Paula de Koenigsberg, coproduced by Claudette Charbonneau.

ROD WOODEN is a playwright whose works include *Smoke* and *Moby Dick*.

LIN WRIGHT taught children's theatre and creative dramatics at Arizona State University for twenty-five years, and served as theatre department chair for twelve. She is a past president of the Arizona Alliance for Arts Education and the Arizona Theatre Alliance. She has written widely on her specialty.

SUSAN YANKOWITZ began her professional career as a member of Joseph Chaikin's Open Theater group. Her plays include *Terminal, Utterances, The Revenge, A Knife in the Heart, Phaedra in Delirium* and *Night Sky*. She is also an accomplished novelist and screenwriter.

MARY ZIMMERMAN is a member of the Lookingglass Theatre Company and an artistic associate of The Goodman Theatre. She has earned national and international recognition in the form of numerous awards, including the prestigious John D. and Catherine T. MacArthur Fellowship. She has won more than 20 Joseph Jefferson awards for her creative work, and in 2002 she received the Tony Award for Best Direction of a Play for *Metamorphoses*. Other acclaimed works include *Journey to the West, The Odyssey, The Arabian Nights, The Notebooks of Leonardo da Vinci* and *Eleven Rooms of Proust*. She is a professor of performance studies at Northwestern University.

PAT ZIPPRODT, costume designer, worked with the New York City Ballet, ABT, Joffrey and Metropolitan Opera. She had over fifty Broadway shows to her credit, and earned Tony awards for *Cabaret, Sweet Charity* and *Fiddler on the Roof*. Film: *The Graduate*. She was a founding member of National Theatre of the Deaf and a member of the Theatre Hall of Fame. Zipprodt died of cancer in 1999.

INDEX

Barnes, Clive, 102, 433, 478, 481
Barnes, Eva Wielgat, 479
Barnes, Peter, *The Ruling Class,* 208
Barr, Richard, 106
Barrett, Lawrence, 69
Barrett, Sarah Curran, 397
Barron, Elwyn, *A Mountain Pink,* 191
Barry, Philip, *Hotel Universe,* 155
Barrymore, Ethel, 99
Barthes, Roland, 330
Barton, Lucy, 183
Bartons, John, 398
Bates, Blanche, 88
Bates, Morgan, *A Mountain Pink,* 191
Baum, L. Frank, *Ozma of Oz,* 260
Baum, Terry, *Sacrifices,* 326
Beast's Story, A (Kennedy), 45–46
Beaty, Powhatan, 84
Beauty and the Beast, 300–301, 332, 360
Beaux Stratagem, The, 183
Becca (Kesselman), 283
Beck, Julian, 201
Beckett, Samuel, *Waiting for Godot,* 361
Before the Footlights and Behind the Scenes
    (Logan), 79
Begleiter, Marcie, 296
Belasco Theatre (New York), 421
Belitt, Ben (translator), *The Splendor and*
    Death of Joaquin Murieta, 202
Belle of Amherst, The (Harris), 51
Bellow, Saul, *The Last Analysis,* 201
Belsey, Catherine, *Critical Practice,* 470
Benchley, Robert, 145
Benjamin, Walter, 394
Bennett, James O'Donnell, 91
Bennett, Suzanne, *Women Playwrights of*
    Diversity, 378
Bentley, Eric, 202
Benton, Suzanne, 4
Berezin, Tanya, 447
Berger, John, 116, 473
Berkeley Repertory Theatre, 447, 449
Bernardine (Chase), 155, 161–62
Bernstein, Aline, 182, 193, 214
Berry, John, 416
Berson, Misha, 446
Betsko, Kathleen, *Interviews with Contempor-*
    ary Women Playwrights, 120, 121
Betterton, Rosemary, 473
Beyond the Horizon (O'Neill), 236–40
Big Knife, The (Odets), 419
Bingham, Sallie, 384
Birth and After Birth (Howe), 433–34
Bits and Pieces (Jacker), 174
Black Crook, The, xxix–xxx, 78
Black Elk, 6, 7
Black Elk Speaks (Neihardt), xxiii
Black Theatre Program, xxiv
Blackfoot Sun Dance, 9
blacks. *See* African Americans
Blair, Rhonda, 332, 361–63

Blau, Herbert, 103, 459
Blockheads, The; or the Affrighted Officers, 127
blood, in female rites of passage, 42–47
Boardman, James, 63
Boas, Franz, 8–9
body, in feminist performance art, 363–64,
    387–88, 393, 394–96
Body-Word Series, 363–64
Boesing, Martha
    Antigone Two, 291
    Caravan Theatre's influence on, 277
    at Firehouse Theatre, 313–16
    At the Foot of the Mountain, founding
        of, 290–91
    Gelding, The, 290
    Pimp, 290
    River Journal, 290, 314
    Story of a Mother, The, 291
Boesman and Lena (Fugard), 219, 416
Bogart, Anne
    American Silents, 488
    American Vaudeville, 488
    directing, approach to, 412–15
    as director and teacher, 479–80
    Marathon Dancing, 488
    at Trinity Repertory Company, 447
    Viewpoints training system, 407, 413,
        479, 489
    on work as theatre artist, 487–90
Bond, Edward, *Saved,* 201
Bonet, Wilma, 309
Bonstelle, Jessie, xxx, 96
Booker, Margaret, 447, 448, 453
Boone, Mary Callahan, 463
Booth, Edwin, 69, 70
Booth Theatre (New York), 138
Boston Remembers, 311
Boston Women in Theatre Festival, 266
Both Your Houses (Anderson), 236–40
Boucicault, Dion, *The Octoroon,* 250
Bourget, Paul, *Divorce,* 94
Bovasso, Julie, 193
Bowden, Charles, 106
Boyce, Neith, *Winter's Night,* 139–40
Boyd, Julianne, 193
Brand, Phoebe, xvi, 51
Brava! For Women in the Arts (San
    Francisco), 327, 380, 474
Bread and Puppet Theatre, 459
Breakfast Past Noon (Molinaro), 174
Brecht, Bertolt
    Caucasian Chalk Circle, The, 208
    Galileo, 206
    gestus concept, 330, 351, 352–55, 362
    Goslar, Lotte, creation of scenario for, 102
    influence on theatrical theory, 337, 339
    social and political realities, spectator
        and, 152
    Threepenny Opera, 181
    Verfremdungseffekt concept, 337, 339,
        349–50

UNIVERSITY OF WINCHESTER
LIBRARY

Odets, Clifford
  Big Knife, The, 419
  Clash by Night, 206
  Group Theatre, works for, 419
  Waiting for Lefty, 199
Oedipus Rex, 271, 460
Oenslager, Donald, 210, 211
Oesterich, James, 310
Of Thee I Sing (Kaufman and Ryskind),
  236–40
Off- and Off-Off-Broadway Theatres. *See
  also* regional theatre; *specific theatres*
  invigoration of, during 1960s, 201
  receptiveness to women playwrights and
    directors, 120, 476
  as source of creative energy, 376
Offending the Audience (Handke), 201
Oglala Sioux, 6, 7
O'Hara, Fiske, 144
Ohio State Murders, The (Kennedy), 417
Old Maid, The (Akins), xiv, 155, 236–40
Oliver, Edith, 121, 217, 218, 219
Oliver, Peter, 124, 125
Oliveros, Pauline
  Crow Two, A Ceremonial Opera, 4
  in *King Lear* production with Mabou
    Mines, 403
Olsen, Tillie, *Tell Me a Riddle,* 277
Omaha Magic Theatre, 277–79, 319
On a Porch in Maine (Draper), 106
"On the Road: A Search for American
  Character" (Smith), 478
Once in a Lifetime, 479
One Flea Spare (Wallace), 428, 440–41, 442
100,000 Horror Stories of the Plains, 278
O'Neill, Eugene
  All God's Chillun Got Wings, 251
  Anna Christie, 236–40
  Beyond the Horizon, 236–40
  Federal Theatre Project, submission of
    work for, 195
  Iceman Cometh, The, 155, 159
  plays of, directed by women, 180
  Strange Interlude, 236–40
  Touch of the Poet, A, xiv
O'Neill Theatre Center, National Critics
  Institute, 218
Open Theater
  artists working with, 277, 317, 319
  as community, 431
  experimental process and technique,
    xvii, 269, 406, 409
Opening the Bazaar (Draper), 106
Operation Sidewinder (Shepard), 201
O'Reilly, Leonora, 21
Orgasmo Adulto Escapes for the Zoo (Fo and
  Rame), 420
Orpheum Circuit, 98
Oscar award, 418
Osofisan, Femi, 369
Other Doors (Zeder), 261

Otis, James, 122–23
Ott, Sharon, 447, 449
Our Old Kentucky Home (Davis and Bruce),
  86
Our Town (Wilder), 236–40, 457
Ourselves (Crothers), 129, 130, 131
Out of Our Fathers' House (Merriam), 304,
  306–7, 308
Outer Critics Circle, 181, 424, 478
Overlie, Mary, 407
Overtones (Gerstenberg), xxxii
Owen, Rochelle, 120
Owl Answers, The (Kennedy), 46, 248, 359
Oxford Companion to the Theatre, The, 72
Ozma of Oz (Baum), 260

Packer, Tina, 396–97, 398–99
Paderewski, Jan, 104
Page, Geraldine, 50, 51
pageants
  Miss America/Miss California, 25–32
  National Woman's Party, 21–25
Painting Churches (Howe), 182, 434
Palace (New York), 98
Palmer, Alan, 426
Palmer, Albert A., 58
Palucca, 102
Pantomime Circus, 102
pantomime players, 100–103
Paper Mill Playhouse (Milburn, New
  Jersey), 194
Papp, Joseph, 178, 417, 420
Park Theatre (New York), 54
Parks, Suzan-Lori
  America Play, The, 350–51
  on playwriting, 430–31
Parris-Bailey, Linda, 384
Parrot's Cage, The (Shaw), 95
Parsons, Estelle, 51, 283, 407, 420–21
Patience and Sarah, 300
Patterson, Ada, 216
Pause that Refreshes, The, 293
Pawnee Hako, 9
Peabody, Josephine Preston, *The Piper,* xxxii
Pelham, Laura Dainty, 190–92
Penn, Laura, 461
Pentimento (Hellman), 162
People Pieces, 383
people's theatre. *See* social and political issues
performance art
  Body-Word Series (Goldberg), 363–64
  Constant State of Desire (Finley), 363,
    392–94
  Eve's Version (Lubar), 387, 388–90
  I See Messiah (Margolin), 390–92
  McCauley on, 482–84
  Post Porn Modernist (Sprinkle), 388,
    394–96
  woman's intimate self as public art, 386–88
Performance Group, 269, 395
Performing Asian America (Lee), 377–78

Weller, Michael, *Moonchildren*, 209
Werich, Jan, 102
Wertenbaker, Timberlake (translator and adapter), *Hecuba*, 452
Wesker, Arnold (adapter), *The Merchant of Venice*, 201
West, Frances, 400
West, June B., 234
West, Mae, 51
"What Can a Heroine Do?" (Russ), 234
When Ladies Meet (Crothers), 133, 134–35, 193
White, Allon, 81
White, Richard Grant, 80–81
White Fawn, The, 78
White Slave, The (Campbell), 250
White Wines (Stein), 153
Whiteman, Paul, 99
Why Marry? (Williams), 236–40
Wignell, Thomas, 53, 54–55
Wild Duck, The (Ibsen), 90, 159
Wilde, Oscar, *The Importance of Being Earnest*, 204, 207
Wilder, Thornton
    Our Town, 236–40
    Skin of Our Teeth, The, 237–40
    work for Broadway, 195
    World War II, influence of, 233
Willard, Frances, 17
Williams, Jesse Lynch, *Why Marry?*, 236–40
Williams, Tennessee
    Glass Menagerie, The, 155, 205, 207, 219
    Night of the Iguana, 219
    Streetcar Named Desire, A, 237–40
    Summer and Smoke, 205
    World War II, influence of, 233
Wilson, Lanford, 454
Wilson, Linda, 422
Winchester, Samuel, 62
Winds of the People, 311
Wine in the Wilderness (Childress), 245–46
Winer, Linda, 217, 220, 221
Winer, Lucy
    But, Something Was Wrong with the Princess, 286
    New York Feminist Theatre Troupe, founding of, 284–87
Winter, William
    as critic, 89, 90
    Vagrant Memories, 64
Winter's Night (Boyce), 139–40
Winwood, Estelle, 193
Wisdom Bridge Theatre, xxiv
Wit (Edson), 407, 426–27, 428, 438–40
Witkiewicz, Stanislaw, 202
Wittig, Monique, 332
Wolf, Rennold, 92
Wolff, Ruth, *The Abdication*, 174
Woman and Theatre Program, Association for Theatre in Higher Education, xxiv, 473

Womanrite Theatre, 317
Woman's Body and Other Natural Resources, 294, 295
Woman's Crusade, 11–17
Woman's Theatre, 180
Womansong Theatre, 273
Women, The, 479
"Women, Woman, and The Subject of Feminism: Feminist Directions" (Sullivan), 331–32
Women and Film (Kaplan), 342
Women & Performance (Jenkins), 329
Women and Theatre Program Conference (Chicago), 324
Women in American Theatre (Chinoy and Jenkins, eds.), xvii–xviii, 448
"Women in Theatre: Mapping the Sources of Power," 427–28, 429–32, 476
Women in Violence, 292–93
Women of the Burning City, 273
Women Playwrights of Diversity (Bennett), 378, 385
Women's Collage Theatre, 322
Women's Experimental Theatre, 283, 293–95, 317, 322
Women's Interart Theatre (New York), 122, 272, 274, 282–84, 327, 419
women's movement. *See also* feminist theatre
    changes and problems within, 326
    consciousness-raising groups, 173, 304, 305
    in Crothers's work, 128, 131–32, 133
    emergence of women playwrights, 119, 120, 173, 174, 476
    female theatre critics and, 220
    feminisms, differences among, 345
    feminist theatre and, 272–73, 274–75, 320
    grounding rituals, 32–34
    Hellman on, 163, 165–66, 168
    Miss America Pageant opposition, 21
    National Woman's Party, Equal Rights Pageants, 21–25
    in post-feminist era, 318
    research on and criticism of, 340
    struggle to enter public life, 116
    suffrage, 93, 136
    urban perspective of, 138
Women's One World (WOW) Cafe, 266, 298, 299
Women's One World Festival, 266
Women's Project (New York), 122, 178, 427–28, 429–32, 474, 476
"Women's Role in the Theatre" (La Gallienne), xxx
Women's Struggle Throughout History, 289
women's theatre. *See* feminist theatre
Women's Trade Union League (WTUL), 17–21
Wood, George, 76
Wood, William, 55–56, 59